MAGILL'S CINEMA ANNUAL

MAGILL'S CINEMA ANNUAL

1992

A Survey of the Films of 1991

Edited by

FRANK N. MAGILL

SALEM PRESS

Pasadena, California   Englewood Cliffs, New Jersey

LIBRARY OF CONGRESS CATALOG CARD No. 83-644357

ISBN 0-89356-411-7

ISSN 0739-2141

First Printing

PRINTED IN THE UNITED STATES OF AMERICA

PUBLISHER'S NOTE

Magill's Cinema Annual, 1992, is the eleventh annual volume in a series that developed from the twenty-one-volume core set, *Magill's Survey of Cinema*. Each annual covers the preceding year and follows a similar format in reviewing the films of the year. This format consists of four general sections: two essays of general interest, the films of 1991, lists of obituaries and awards, and the indexes.

In the first section, the first article reviews the career and accomplishments of the recipient of the Life Achievement Award, which is presented by the American Film Institute. In 1991, this award was given to the distinguished actor Kirk Douglas. Following this initial essay, the reader will find an essay that lists selected film books published in 1991. Briefly annotated, the list provides a valuable guide to the current literature about the film industry and its leaders.

The largest section of the annual, "Selected Films of 1991," is devoted to essay-reviews of one hundred significant films released in the United States in 1991. The reviews are arranged alphabetically by the title under which the film was released in the United States. Original and alternate titles are cross-referenced to the American-release title in the Title Index.

Each article begins with selected credits for the film. Credit categories include: Production, Direction, Screenplay, Cinematography, Editing, Art direction, and Music. Also included are the MPAA rating, the running time, and a list of the principal characters with the corresponding actors. This introductory information on a film not released originally in the United States also includes the country of origin and the year the film was released there. If the information for any of the standard categories was unavailable, the heading is followed by the phrase "no listing." Additional headings such as Special effects, Costume design, and Song have been included in an article's introductory top matter when appropriate. Also, the symbol (AA) in the top matter identifies those artists who have received an Academy Award for their contribution to the film from the Academy of Motion Picture Arts and Sciences.

The section of the annual labeled "More Films of 1991" supplies the reader with an alphabetical listing of an additional 196 feature films released in the United States during the year. Included are brief credits and short descriptions of the films. These films can be located, along with any cross-references, in the indexes.

Two further lists conclude the text of the volume. The first of these is the Obituaries, which provides useful information about the careers of motion-picture professionals who died in 1991. The second list is of the awards presented by ten different international associations, from the Academy of Motion Picture Arts and Sciences to the Cannes International Film Festival and the British Academy Awards.

The final section of this volume includes nine indexes that cover the films reviewed in *Magill's Cinema Annual*, 1992. Arranged in the order established in the introductory matter of the essay-reviews, the indexes are as follows: Title Index, Director Index, Screenwriter Index, Cinematographer Index, Editor Index, Art Director Index, Music Index, and Performer Index. A Subject Index is also provided. To assist the reader further, pseudonyms, foreign titles, and alternate titles are all cross-referenced. Titles of foreign films and retrospective films are followed by the year, in brackets, of their original release.

The Title Index includes all the titles of films covered in individual articles, in "More Films of 1991," and also those discussed at some length in the general essays. The next seven indexes are arranged according to artists, each of whose names is followed by a list of the films on which they worked and the titles of the essays (such as "Life Achievement Award" or "Obituaries") in which they are mentioned at length. The final listing is the Subject Index, in which any one film can be categorized under several headings. Thus, a reader can effectively use all these indexes to approach a film from any one of several directions, including not only its credits but also its subject matter.

CONTRIBUTING REVIEWERS

Michael Adams
Fairleigh Dickinson University

JoAnn Balingit
University of Delaware

Mary E. Belles
Freelance Reviewer

Brenda Berryhill
Freelance Reviewer

Cynthia K. Breckenridge
Freelance Reviewer

Beverley Bare Buehrer
Freelance Reviewer

Greg Changnon
Freelance Reviewer

Robert F. Chicatelli
Freelance Reviewer

Richard G. Cormack
Freelance Reviewer

Bill Delaney
Freelance Reviewer

Dan Georgakas
Editor, Cineaste

Douglas Gomery
University of Maryland

Sidney Gottlieb
Sacred Heart University

Roberta F. Green
Virginia Polytechnic Institute and State University

Glenn Hopp
Howard Payne University

Eleah Horwitz
Freelance Reviewer

Anahid Kassabian
Stanford University

Jim Kline
Freelance Reviewer

Patricia Kowal
Freelance Reviewer

Leon Lewis
Appalachian State University

Janet Lorenz
Freelance Reviewer

Blake Lucas
Freelance Reviewer

Marc Mancini
Loyola Marymount University

Cono Robert Marcazzo
Upsala College

Robert Mitchell
University of Arizona

Francis Poole
University of Delaware

Gaylyn Studlar
Emory University

Frederick Wasser
Temple University

James M. Welsh
Salisbury State University

CONTENTS

CONTENTS

MAGILL'S
CINEMA
ANNUAL

Life Achievement Award
Kirk Douglas

Born Issur Danielovitch in 1916 in Amsterdam, New York, Kirk Douglas did not start life within a family situation that held the promise of much success, particularly success in acting. His immigrant father, unable to read or write, was a ragman who bought the castoffs of others; he was also an alcoholic. The family, with seven children, often did not have enough money for food, much less for culture. Nevertheless, young Issur Danielovitch had his dreams, and he was willing to work to bring them to reality. Inspired by a schoolteacher, he dreamed of going to college and drama school, for he was fascinated with the legitimate theater. He proceeded to win prizes in high school for dramatic recitation, acting, and writing. Upon graduation, he hitchhiked to St. Lawrence University with a friend. He was determined to go to college, even though he only had some one hundred and fifty dollars. He obtained a loan and began a college career that would produce success at every turn: as president of the student body, as a wrestling champion, as an honor society member, and as an actor.

After graduation from college, he legally changed his name to Kirk Douglas, a change motivated as much by his encounters with anti-Semitism as with his impending need for a stage name. He was off to New York City to be an actor. There, Douglas entered the American Academy of Dramatic Arts. He was graduated in 1941 and set out to conquer Broadway. His first break came with a walk-on role as a singing telegram boy for a Katharine Cornell vehicle called *Spring Again*.

After the United States' entry into World War II, Douglas joined the Navy and served as a communications officer. Discharged in 1944, he returned to New York looking for work—radio, theater, anything. He won the male ingenue part in a Broadway comedy, *Kiss and Tell*. After a few other forgettable roles, a fellow drama school student named Betty Bacall, who had made it in Hollywood as Lauren Bacall, recommended Douglas for a role in *The Strange Love of Martha Ivers* (1946), a psychological drama being produced by Hal B. Wallis. By the time his train reached Hollywood, the role he expected, that of the hero, had been cast. Instead, after a screen test for director Lewis Milestone, Douglas was asked to play Walter O'Neill, an alcoholic district attorney whose life is marred by sins of the past: his own sins, those of his father, and those of the woman he loves. O'Neill's wife, Martha Ivers (played by Barbara Stanwyck), despises him, but they are bound together by their shared knowledge of their guilty past. In the course of the film, Martha and Walter are torn apart by the return of Martha's childhood love, Sam Masterson (played by Van Heflin), a man who shatters the respectable surface of their world.

In his first film performance, Douglas created a riveting portrayal of a man too weak to extricate himself from a destructive love. Yet, in spite of his apparently successful entry into Hollywood with *The Strange Love of Martha Ivers,* Douglas was ready to exit as promptly when no follow-up was immediately offered. He did not leave Hollywood, however, and Douglas' second motion picture, *Out of the Past* (1947), also found him cast in the second lead, this time as Whit Sterling, an elegant racketeer who hires a private detective (played by Robert Mitchum) to find his lover, Kathie Moffett (played by Jane Greer). Kathie shot Whit and ran off to Mexico with $40,000 of his money. In this film, Douglas makes the sadomasochistic triangle of Whit, Kathie, and Jeff crackle with tension. Douglas portrays Whit as both loathsome and slickly appealing, a tough guy with a sense of humor and style, but also with a self-destructive obsession for a beautiful woman he knows he cannot trust with money or with other men.

Douglas' third film, *I Walk Alone* (1948), costarred him in another *film noir* drama with Burt Lancaster, who would become a lifelong friend and frequent costar. Here, Douglas plays a duplicitous nightclub owner in yet another treacherous bad-guy role. Soon success brought the necessity for crucial career decisions: Because he refused to sign a long-term contract, Douglas was dropped by producer Wallis.

A series of rather undistinguished films such as *The Walls of Jericho* (1948) and *My Dear Secretary* (1948) followed. Douglas then played the meaty role of a straying husband in Joseph L. Mankiewicz's *A Letter to Three Wives* (1949), a star-studded production that won Academy Awards for Best Director and Best Screenplay. Douglas' performance was impressive. Nevertheless, he was still not a star, an actor around whom a film might be made. His chance at stardom came with the next film he was offered, a modestly budgeted independent production produced by Stanley Kramer, directed by former editor Mark Robson, and scripted by Carl Foreman from a Ring Lardner short story on boxing. *Champion* (1949) proved to be a film that solidly defined the Kirk Douglas screen persona that had been in the making. In the film, he plays Midge Kelly, a boxer who emerges as a kind of antihero: driven, violent, almost hysterical, but also sympathetic and fully human in his weaknesses and his strengths. The film and Douglas were both unexpected hits. For his performance, Douglas was nominated for an Academy Award as Best Actor.

Other significant roles for Douglas during this period included the lead in *Young Man with a Horn* (1950), a Michael Curtiz-directed film based on the life of jazz trumpeter Bix Beiderbecke. He then played against type as the gentleman caller in the film version of Tennessee Williams' play *The Glass Menagerie* (1950). Douglas would get solidly back to the hard-bitten type, however, with Billy Wilder's *Ace in the Hole* (1951), in which he plays a down-at-the-heels reporter who cynically exploits the situation of a man trapped in a cave-in. The reporter's machinations, aided by the trapped man's wife (played by Jan Sterling), result in death. Although the film was honored at the Venice Film Festival, it was a critical and box-office flop at home, where it was retitled *The Big Carnival.* Some reviewers accused the film of slandering American journalists with its story of the blatant media manipulation of events. It would take years for the film to be acknowledged as a classic. Perhaps *Ace in the Hole* was too *noir* even for an age of *noir* filmmaking.

In 1951, Douglas was cast in his first Western, *Along the Great Divide,* directed by veteran Hollywood director Raoul Walsh. Although Douglas has written of his awful experience in making this production, he would go on to make a number of Westerns, including a classic revisionist Western he has declared to be his favorite film: *Lonely Are the Brave* (1962), scripted by blacklisted Hollywood screenwriter Dalton Trumbo.

Yet Douglas was not through with delineating the essential postwar *noir* antihero. In *Detective Story* (1951), Douglas starred as a troubled police detective, Jim McLeod, in the film version of Sidney Kingsley's play. Despite kudos for the picture and for his performance as a man driven to suicide by his existential confrontation with crime, Warner Bros. rewarded Douglas by putting him in a forgettable Western called *The Big Trees* (1952). After fulfilling his contract with Warner, Douglas started production on *The Big Sky* (1952) with director Howard Hawks. Upon recovering from a bout of pneumonia, no doubt induced by some of the rigors of filming *The Big Sky* in Jackson Hole, Wyoming, Douglas started work on an equally big melodrama about the underside of Hollywood: Vincente Minnelli's *The Bad and the Beautiful* (1952), produced by John Houseman for the legendarily lavish studio Metro-Goldwyn-Mayer (MGM). As a ruthless Hollywood producer who will do anything to produce a successful motion picture, Douglas once again proved that his riveting screen presence did not demand a lovable part to secure audience interest. For his work in the film, he received another Academy Award nomination, but he was not among the film's five Oscar winners. Yet the film was growing evidence that perhaps no postwar leading man was defining himself in such intense, neurotic, quietly violent terms. At the same time, Douglas was establishing a pattern of working with some of the era's most talented directors: William Wyler, Wilder, Hawks, Minnelli, Elia Kazan, John Huston, and Stanley Kubrick.

Joining other stars in crossing the Atlantic for the trend in international productions, Douglas made a series of foreign-based films in the 1950's, including *Act of Love* (1953), *The Juggler* (1953), and *Ulisse* (1955; *Ulysses*, 1955), but he returned to Hollywood for films like the King Vidor-directed Western *Man Without a Star* (1955) and another successful Western, *Gunfight at the O.K. Corral* (1957). His biggest personal success of this decade, however, was Minnelli's *Lust for Life* (1956), based on Irving Stone's fictionalized biography of Vincent Van Gogh. The film was produced by Douglas' own production company, Bryna Productions, which had been named after his mother and which had offered, as its successful premier production, a rousing Western, *The Indian Fighter* (1955). Thus, Douglas was establishing himself as a savvy businessperson within a Hollywood system accustomed to using actors as paid employees. That system was adjusting, in the postwar era, to having stars become involved in all phases of production. Douglas' success in taking control of his star vehicles is not surprising considering his astute choice of material and his sometimes combative attempt to improve those earlier productions in which he was involved.

With massive talent both in front of and behind the camera, *Lust for Life* was nominated for Academy Awards in several categories. Douglas received his third nomination for Best Actor, but Yul Brynner took the award for *The King and I* (1956). Douglas' costar, Anthony Quinn, won the award for Best Supporting Actor for his portrayal of Paul Gauguin.

Most significantly during his offscreen work during these years, Douglas and his production company signed young director Stanley Kubrick to a three-picture deal that would result in the classic antiwar film *Paths of Glory* (1957). As a condemnation of the French army during World War I and a class structure that requires working-class soldiers to be willing to meet death upon the word of incompetent generals, the film was a powerful indictment of a specific war and of all wars. Not surprisingly, *Paths of Glory* was banned in France. Once again, Douglas proved himself to be a powerhouse for filmmaking, on-screen as well as off. His performance as Colonel Dax, a man who must defend three men on trial for cowardice and desertion of duty, is controlled and sympathetic. In spite of his preeminence as the film's star, Douglas lets his talented supporting players, including Ralph Meeker, Timothy Carey, and Adolphe Menjou, make equally strong impressions. Douglas' second collaboration with Kubrick, *Spartacus* (1960), became one of the most impressive spectacles in an era of cinematic spectacle-making. It was also one of the most impressively intelligent, in large measure attributable to the screenplay by Trumbo, whom Douglas dared to employ in spite of Trumbo's status as a blacklisted "communist." Recently restored, like many of Douglas' films, *Spartacus* seems even more impressive with the passage of time.

Douglas' films of the early 1960's included such melodramas as *Strangers When We Meet* (1960) and *Town Without Pity* (1961), the Oedipal horse opera *The Last Sunset* (1961), and his favorite film, *Lonely Are the Brave*. The latter received rave reviews, but Universal regarded the quiet little contemporary Western as too downbeat and too unmarketable, and the company virtually buried it. As the 1960's wore on, Douglas' career slowed down from the three-film-a-year pace he maintained in the late 1950's and early 1960's. Increasingly, he found himself in military-related roles, including a troubled officer who ends up as a rapist in Otto Preminger's *In Harm's Way* (1965) and generals in *Seven Days in May* (1964) and *Cast a Giant Shadow* (1966), the latter telling the story of Mickey Marcus, a West Point-trained American who played a role in Israel's fight for independence. These films, like many other Hollywood productions of the era, were star-laden fare, dependent as much on utilizing Douglas' marquee value as in showcasing his unique screen persona.

Through the next few years, in spite of a busy schedule, Douglas was obsessed with bringing Ken Kesey's novel *One Flew over the Cuckoo's Nest* to the screen after he bought the rights to the novel. He brought it to the Broadway stage for a short-lived run. He also wanted to play McMurphy in the film version as well, but Douglas was asked to step aside in favor of a younger actor, Jack Nicholson, and decided to give the rights to his son Michael. The film was a phenomenal box-office and critical success and earned five Academy Awards, including Nicholson's award for Best Actor. While the success of the completed film may have been bittersweet for Kirk Douglas as its "absentee" promoter, the acclaim that it received justified his long-standing enthusiasm for the project.

Moving past the age of leading-man status, Douglas attempted directing but proved himself more successful as a versatile character actor in occasional films of the 1970's and 1980's. He essayed a dual role in the popular Australian entry *The Man from Snowy*

River (1982) and took the title role as an eighty-year-old man in an impressive made-for-television film entitled *Amos* (1985) that courageously detailed nursing-home abuse. He and Burt Lancaster then teamed for an amusing takeoff on their early star images in *Tough Guys* (1986). Stricken with heart problems in 1986, Douglas began to slow down. Nevertheless, he published the autobiography *The Ragman's Son* (1988), published the best-selling novel *Dance with the Devil* (1990), and survived a near-fatal helicopter crash in 1991. Recent years have also given him reason to be proud, not only of his own career but also of that of his son Michael, who has become an Academy Award-winning producer and actor.

Without a doubt, the career of Kirk Douglas is an amazing accomplishment for anyone, especially for someone reared in economic deprivation. Although Douglas has been criticized for his flamboyant acting style, for his distinctive mannerisms, and for what some regard as a limited acting range, the broad pattern of his career reveals a number of memorably powerful portrayals. Some of these roles, such as those in *Paths of Glory* and *Lust for Life,* are well known to audiences; others, such as those in *The Juggler* and *Lonely Are the Brave*, demand reconsideration and revival. The pattern of his career, one marked by the choice of sometimes unsympathetic roles and controversial material, reveals that the determination of what constitutes filmmaking "success" may require an objective distancing: Immediate critical response may be inadequate in judging who makes a lasting contribution to cinematic history. In the long run, judged in these often unforgiving and subjective terms, Kirk Douglas is quite obviously the success he always appeared to be.

Gaylyn Studlar

SELECTED FILM BOOKS OF 1991

Acker, Ally. *Reel Women: Pioneers of the Cinema 1896 to the Present*. New York: Continuum, 1991. This is a useful compendium of biographical sketches and filmographies of women who were involved in some aspect of American filmmaking other than acting, such as producers, directors, writers, and editors.

Anderegg, Michael, ed. *Inventing Vietnam: The War in Film and Television*. Philadelphia: Temple University Press, 1991. This collection of fourteen essays examines the ways in which films have influenced postwar American opinion about the war in Vietnam.

Bakewell, William. *Hollywood Be Thy Name*. Metuchen, N.J.: Scarecrow Press, 1991. Subtitled *Random Reflections of a Movie Veteran from Silents to Talkies to TV*, this is a good-humored collection of anecdotes about actors and films from a veteran character actor.

Barranger, Milly S. *Jessica Tandy: A Bio-Bibliography*. New York: Greenwood Press, 1991. A biographical, bibliographical, and critical study of the life and career of this Academy Award-winning actress.

Berman, Judith B. *Retrofitting "Blade Runner."* Bowling Green, Ohio: Bowling Green State University Popular Press, 1991. Ridley Scott's *Blade Runner* (1982) has achieved the status of a cult film. This collection of nineteen essays analyzes the film, and the classic science-fiction short story on which it was based, in an attempt to understand the source of the film's fascination.

Bertin, Celia. *Jean Renoir: A Life in Pictures*. Baltimore: The Johns Hopkins University Press, 1991. This is the first full-length biography of the French director, whose career spanned more than four decades and who made films both in France and in Hollywood.

Blake, Richard. *Screening America: Reflections on Five Classic Films*. New York: Paulist Press, 1991. Blake is a Jesuit critic who offers straightforward analyses of five film classics of the 1930's and 1940's, in addition to thoughts on the often troubled relationship between the Catholic Church and American filmmakers.

Byars, Jackie. *All That Hollywood Allows*. Chapel Hill: University of North Carolina Press, 1991. This scholarly work offers a feminist analysis of the different varieties of Hollywood melodrama in the 1950's, including chapters on role stereotypes, race, class, and gender.

Byrge, Duane, and Robert Milton Miller. *The Screwball Comedy Films: A History and Filmography, 1934-1942*. Jefferson, N.C.: McFarland, 1991. This survey of classic screwball comedies provides information on cast and credits, as well as plot synopses, for fifty-seven films. In addition, it contains a chapter on each of the genre's important actors and directors.

Carrier, Jeffrey L. *Tallulah Bankhead: A Bio-Bibliography*. New York: Greenwood Press, 1991. A biographical, bibliographical, and critical study of the life and career of the actress, whose career spanned five decades.

Coates, Paul. *The Gorgon's Gaze: German Cinema, Expressionism, and the Image of*

Horror. New York: Cambridge University Press, 1991. A scholarly study of the sublime, the uncanny, and the monstrous—from vampires to the Holocaust— principally in German cinema, but ranging widely over eras and national borders.

Collier, Peter. *The Fondas: A Hollywood Dynasty*. New York: G. P. Putnam's Sons, 1991. The Fondas have experienced their share of controversy and turmoil; Collier (who specializes in family biographies) manages to chronicle these events without stooping to sensationalism in what is likely the most balanced look at father Henry and children Peter and Jane.

Conley, Tom. *Film Hieroglyphs: Ruptures in Classical Cinema*. Minneapolis: University of Minnesota Press, 1991. A scholarly analysis of nine films of varying types, examining the role of the viewer in determining the meaning of a film.

Cronyn, Hume. *A Terrible Liar*. New York: William Morrow, 1991. A well-written autobiography by the distinguished actor, filled with stories about people such as Alfred Hitchcock, John Gielgud, and of course Cronyn's wife, Jessica Tandy.

Cyr, Helen W. *The Third World in Film and Video, 1984-1990*. Metuchen, N.J.: Scarecrow Press, 1991. This volume updates Cyr's earlier work and lists more than a thousand titles, including both feature films and shorter works, that focus on the people and cultures of the Third World.

Denisoff, R. Serge, and William D. Romanowski. *Risky Business: Rock in Film*. New Brunswick, N.J.: Transaction, 1991. Though the authors trace the genre to its beginnings in the 1950's in their exhaustive study of the economic issues surrounding the use of rock music in film, they concentrate primarily on the films of the 1970's and 1980's.

Denzin, Norman K. *Hollywood Shot By Shot: Alcoholism in American Cinema*. New York: Aldine De Gruyter, 1991. This scholarly analysis of the figure of the alcoholic in American film between 1932 and 1989 attempts to understand how the reality and the representation of alcoholism interact with each other in American culture.

Dickerson, Gary E. *The Cinema of Baseball: Images of America, 1929-1989*. Westport, Conn.: Meckler, 1991. A scholarly analysis of baseball films produced during the sound era, noting how the dominant themes have changed over the decades.

Dixon, Wheeler Winston. *The Charm of Evil: The Life and Films of Terence Fisher*. Metuchen, N.J.: Scarecrow Press, 1991. British director Fisher resurrected the horror film genre in the late 1950's in his work at Hammer Studios with actors such as Christopher Lee and Peter Cushing. This book provides a detailed analysis of Fisher's major films, as well as an overview of his career.

_____. *The Films of Freddie Francis*. Metuchen, N.J.: Scarecrow Press, 1991. Francis is an Englishman who has a dual career as a cinematographer in many major films and as a director in a series of low-budget horror and science-fiction films. This volume, which contains two lengthy interviews with Francis, is the definitive critical summary of his career.

Ebert, Roger, and Gene Siskel. *The Future of the Movies*. Kansas City, Mo.: Andrews and McNeal, 1991. Two prominent film critics interview Martin Scorsese, Steven

Spielberg, and George Lucas regarding the state of cinema.

Edmonds, Andy. *Frame Up! The Untold Story of Roscoe "Fatty" Arbuckle*. New York: William Morrow, 1991. This biography attempts to exonerate the reputation of the silent-era comic actor who was accused of murdering a woman.

Eells, George. *Final Gig: The Man Behind the Murder*. New York: Harcourt Brace Jovanovich, 1991. Academy Award-winning actor Gig Young committed suicide after murdering his fifth wife. This biography focuses on his self-destructive private life.

Fetrow, Alan G. *Sound Films, 1927-1939*. Jefferson, N.C.: McFarland, 1991. This reference work provides filmographies for more than five thousand feature films produced in the United States during the first decade of the sound era.

Fine, Marshall. *Bloody Sam: The Life and Films of Sam Peckinpah*. New York: Donald I. Fine, 1991. This biography of the controversial director of Westerns and action films concentrates on behind-the-scenes anecdotes rather than on serious critical analysis of Peckinpah's films.

Fischer, Dennis. *Horror Film Directors, 1931-1990*. Jefferson, N.C.: McFarland, 1991. This reference work analyzes the films of one hundred directors who have worked in the horror genre, some exclusively and others as part of a more varied career. The book is divided approximately equally between prominent filmmakers and obscure or up-and-coming directors.

Friedman, Lester D. *Unspeakable Images: Ethnicity and the American Cinema*. Urbana: University of Illinois Press, 1991. A collection of scholarly essays from a variety of perspectives on the subject of ethnicity in American film. Chapters range from an extended discussion of a single film to the broad application of specific critical approaches to the subject of ethnicity.

Furmanek, Bob, and Ron Palumbo. *Abbott and Costello in Hollywood*. New York: Perigee Books, 1991. An utterly comprehensive compendium of information about the comic duo's film career, with information on cast and credits, plot synopses, summaries of reviews, and much more.

Gifford, Denis. *Books and Plays in Films, 1896-1915*. Jefferson, N.C.: McFarland, 1991. Provides the literary source for nearly three thousand films from the first two decades of cinema history.

Gledhill, Christine, ed. *Stardom: Industry of Desire*. London: Routledge, 1991. This scholarly volume contains twenty-two essays on the process by which actors are made into stars; its primary emphasis is on women.

Grenier, Richard. *Capturing the Culture: Film, Art, and Politics*. Washington, D.C.: Ethics and Public Policy Center, 1991. The politically conservative Grenier trains his wit on the liberal tendencies of contemporary cinema in this collection of essays on film in the Reagan era.

Grossman, Barbara W. *Funny Woman: The Life and Times of Fanny Brice*. Bloomington: Indiana University Press, 1991. Grossman's work stands as the definitive biography of Brice, the comic actress whose film work is less well known than her vaudeville and radio career.

Grover, Ron. *The Disney Touch*. Homewood, Ill.: Business One Irwin, 1991. This is a business-oriented look at the Disney empire, focusing on Disney chair Michael Eisner and his management team and on their resurrection of the company in the years from 1984 to 1991.

Hacker, Jonathan, and David Price. *Take Ten: Contemporary British Film Directors*. Oxford, England: Clarendon Press, 1991. This book provides chapters—containing interviews, filmographies, and bibliographies—on ten British filmmakers, including a mixture of mainstream directors as well as some who are less well known.

Hammer, Tad Bentley. *Encyclopedia of International Film Prizes*. New York: Garland, 1991. Provides a list of film awards, including Academy Awards, New York Film Critics Awards, and the Golden Palms, from forty-one film-producing countries worldwide.

Hanke, Ken. *A Critical Guide to Horror Film Series*. New York: Garland, 1991. Many horror films have been successful enough to encourage sequels. This book, arranged in chronological order, lists each such film and provides a history of the series.

Hansen, Miriam. *Babel and Babylon: Spectatorship in American Silent Film*. Cambridge, Mass.: Harvard University Press, 1991. A scholarly study of film-viewer relationships in the silent era, with particular emphasis on the role of women as spectators.

Harrison, Rex. *A Damned Serious Business*. New York: Bantam Books, 1991. Harrison died while putting the finishing touches on this autobiography. There is little gossip, as the actor concentrates on recounting his experiences on stage and in film.

Haspiel, James. *The Ultimate Marilyn: A Look at the Legend*. New York: Henry Holt, 1991. Reminiscences of a young fan who became a companion to Marilyn Monroe. Illustrated with photographs and other memorabilia and offering a perspective different from the usual Monroe volumes.

Hedges, Inez. *Breaking the Frame: Film Language and the Experience of Limits*. Bloomington: Indiana University Press, 1991. A scholarly analysis of films with unconventional narrative styles—those that break the conventions of representation, particularly with reference to gender and assumptions about male-female relationships.

Hepburn, Katharine. *Me: Stories of My Life*. New York: Alfred A. Knopf, 1991. A repetitious and rambling, but nevertheless revealing, look at a once-reclusive actress who is now telling her story. The portrait that she offers is that of an unemotional, no-nonsense woman who is very much the product of her strict New England upbringing.

Hickenlooper, George. *Reel Conversations*. New York: Citadel Press, 1991. This book contains the text of twenty-five interviews—principally with directors, but also with film critics—concerning issues in contemporary cinema.

Hoberman, J. *Bridge of Light: Yiddish Films Between Two Worlds*. New York: Museum of Modern Art, 1991. This significant scholarly work on Yiddish cinema covers films made both in Europe and in the United States, placing the works in their cultural and historical contexts.

_____. *Vulgar Modernism: Writing on Movies and Other Media*. Philadelphia: Temple University Press, 1991. This book is a collection of reviews and longer essays by the film critic of *The Village Voice*.

Horton, Andrew, ed. *Comedy/Cinema/Theory*. Berkeley: University of California Press, 1991. A collection of twelve scholarly essays on various aspects of film comedy, ranging from the Three Stooges to the more sophisticated work of Alfred Hitchcock and Woody Allen.

Howard, James. *The Complete Films of Orson Welles*. New York: Citadel Press, 1991. A typical Citadel Press effort, with plenty of still photographs illustrating information on the cast, credits, plot, and critical reception of each of the actor/director's films.

Huffhines, Kathy Schulz, ed. *Foreign Affairs*. San Francisco: Mercury House, 1991. This collection of more than two hundred brief essays on major foreign films and filmmakers was intended by the National Society of Film Critics to serve as a guide to international cinema available on videotape. The book also serves as a good introduction to the general topic of foreign film.

Jones, G. William. *Black Cinema Treasures: Lost and Found*. Denton: University of North Texas Press, 1991. An important addition to the scholarship on African-American cinema, this book focuses on sixteen films thought to have been lost that were located in a warehouse in Tyler, Texas. The work also includes a summary of the careers of four African-American film pioneers and a list of independent African-American films made from 1910 to 1957.

Kael, Pauline. *Movie Love*. New York: Dutton, 1991. Kael, who recently retired as film critic for *The New Yorker*, has long been one of the United States' most influential voices on cinema. This volume collects reviews from the period between 1988 and 1991.

Kent, Nicolas. *Naked Hollywood: Money, Power, and the Movies*. London: BBC Books, 1991. Based on the British Broadcasting Corporation television series, this volume examines Hollywood power struggles between agents, stars, producers, directors, writers, and studio bosses.

Keyssar, Helene. *Robert Altman's America*. New York: Oxford University Press, 1991. This scholarly analysis of the director's career emphasizes the role of women as agents of change in his films.

Kinnard, Roy. *The Comics Come Alive: A Guide to Comic-Strip Characters in Live-Action Productions*. Metuchen, N.J.: Scarecrow Press, 1991. An alphabetical list of comic strips that have been turned into live-action productions, either for film or television. Each entry contains information on cast and credits, as well as a brief analysis of the history of the production.

Klotman, Phyllis Rauch, ed. *Screenplays of the African American Experience*. Bloomington: Indiana University Press, 1991. This collection of six screenplays from contemporary African-American writers also contains extensive information on the cast and credits for these films, as well as biographical sketches of the filmmakers.

Kuhn, Annette, and Susannah Radstone, eds. *Women in Film: An International Guide*. New York: Fawcett Columbine, 1991. This reference work contains approximately six hundred entries on women in film. Subjects include individual actresses and directors, as well as more general topics such as the femme fatale and the Sydney Women's Film Group.

Landy, Marcia. *British Genres: Cinema and Society, 1930-1960*. Princeton, N.J.: Princeton University Press, 1991. A review of British film and its relationship to society from the beginning of the sound era through the 1950's, with chapters on major genres such as the war film, comedy, the women's film, and horror/science fiction.

——————, ed. *Imitations of Life: A Reader in Film and Television*. Detroit: Wayne State University Press, 1991. A collection of scholarly essays on the diverse aspects of melodrama in film and television. Includes a section on European and Latin American cinema.

Lax, Eric. *Woody Allen: A Biography*. New York: Alfred A. Knopf, 1991. Lax traces the development of Allen's creative impulses, from magic to standup comedy to acting in and finally directing films. This biography was written with Allen's cooperation.

Lee, David. *The Films of Spike Lee: Five for Five*. New York: Stewart, Tabori & Chang, 1991. This is an admiring review of the films of Lee, featuring photographs by his brother David and an appreciative essay by a different critic on each of his five films.

Leitch, Thomas M. *Find the Director and Other Hitchcock Games*. Athens: University of Georgia Press, 1991. Leitch argues that the various games that Alfred Hitchcock played with his audience, such as his hidden cameo appearances in each film, were methods of involving the viewer in the film.

Leonard, Maurice. *Mae West: Empress of Sex*. London: HarperCollins, 1991. Despite its title, this is a serious biography of the late actress, who has had more notoriety than appreciation.

McCann, Graham. *Rebel Males: Clift, Brando, and Dean*. London: Hamish Hamilton, 1991. A survey of the careers of Montgomery Clift, Marlon Brando, and James Dean, three actors who, in the 1950's, were self-consciously non-conformists both in their private lives and in the film roles that they chose. The book analyzes their major films, as well as their influence on contemporary actors.

McGilligan, Pat, ed. *Backstory II: Interviews with Screenwriters of the 1940s and 1950s*. Berkeley: University of California Press, 1991. The second volume in this series features fourteen more interviews with screenwriters; few are well known, although many of the subjects also directed at some point in their careers.

McGilligan, Patrick. *George Cukor: A Double Life*. New York: St. Martin's Press, 1991. Cukor was a director best known for his women's films; this is his first full-length biography. The "double life" in the title refers to the filmmaker's homosexuality, which McGilligan argues was central to his art.

MacGraw, Ali. *Moving Pictures*. New York: Bantam Books, 1991. Model-turned-actress MacGraw offers this unpretentious autobiography, in which she frankly discusses her problems with men and alcohol.

Martin, Len D. *The Columbia Checklist*. Jefferson, N.C.: McFarland, 1991. This reference work is an exhaustive checklist of the feature films, serials, cartoons, and short subjects made by Columbia Pictures between 1922 and 1988. Each entry contains information on cast and credits, as well as a brief plot synopsis.

Monaco, James. *The Encyclopedia of Film*. New York: Perigee Books, 1991. Monaco is the man behind BASELINE, "the world's leading supplier of information to the film and television industries." This volume is strictly biographical, and its primary value is its currency, with information on newly popular figures and up-to-date filmographies on veterans.

Nollen, Scott Allen. *Boris Karloff: A Critical Account of His Screen, Stage, Radio, Television, and Recording Work*. Jefferson, N.C.: McFarland, 1991. This reference volume places primary emphasis on Karloff's horror films, offering plot summaries and other information on the actor's extensive career.

Nowlan, Robert A., and Gwendolyn Wright Nowlan. *The Films of the Eighties*. Jefferson, N.C.: McFarland, 1991. This reference work contains an alphabetical list of more than 3,400 English-language feature films released from 1980 to 1989. Entries provide information on cast and credits, as well as brief plot summaries.

Parenti, Michael. *Make-Believe Media: The Politics of Entertainment*. New York: St. Martin's Press, 1991. Parenti analyzes popular American films and television programs and argues that they have intentionally promoted militarism, racism, sexism, and other undemocratic evils.

Parish, James Robert. *Prison Pictures from Hollywood*. Jefferson, N.C.: McFarland, 1991. This reference work covers 293 films, offering information on cast and credits as well as plot summaries and short critical analyses for each film.

Parish, James Robert, and Michael R. Pitts. *Hollywood Songsters: A Biographical Dictionary*. New York: Garland, 1991. Provides information on one hundred popular singers who have appeared in films, from Al Jolson to Madonna. Includes filmographies.

Parish, James Robert, and Don Stanke. *Hollywood Baby Boomers: A Biographical Dictionary*. New York: Garland, 1991. Provides career summaries for eighty-five actors who were born between 1946 and 1960. Useful for its information on individuals who are too young to appear in older reference works.

Parker, John. *The Joker's Wild: The Biography of Jack Nicholson*. London: Anaya, 1991. This breezy British biography of a quintessentially American actor focuses on behind-the-scenes stories of his film career and his complicated romantic life.

Penley, Constance, Elisabeth Lyon, Lynn Spigel, and Janet Bergstrom, eds. *Close Encounters: Film, Feminism, and Science Fiction*. Minneapolis: University of Minnesota Press, 1991. This work, an expanded version of a 1986 issue of *Camera Obscura*, is a collection of nine essays and a film script, all dealing with the issue of sexual difference in science-fiction films.

Phillips, Julia. *You'll Never Eat Lunch in This Town Again*. New York: Random House, 1991. Drugs, greed, and sex highlight this brutally frank autobiography by one of the major Hollywood producers of the 1970's. Phillips spares no one, least of all herself.

Pilkington, Ace G. *Screening Shakespeare from Richard II to Henry V*. Newark: University of Delaware Press, 1991. An analysis of the issues involved in cinematic adaptations of William Shakespeare's history plays, concentrating chiefly on British productions.

Pitts, Michael R. *Famous Movie Detectives II*. Metuchen, N.J.: Scarecrow Press, 1991. The second volume in this series examines the filmed adventures of the likes of Hercule Poirot, Perry Mason, Sherlock Holmes, and more than thirty other sleuths.

Prince, Stephen. *The Warrior's Camera*. Princeton, N.J.: Princeton University Press, 1991. A scholarly account of the career of the Japanese director Akira Kurosawa, with particular emphasis on the visual form of his films. Covers the filmmaker's entire career and not only the releases known in the West.

Rattigan, Neil. *Images of Australia*. Dallas: Southern Methodist University Press, 1991. This work provides brief analytical essays on one hundred Australian films produced from 1970 to 1991. In addition, each entry provides information on cast and credits, as well as a plot synopsis.

Raubicheck, Walter, and Walter Srebnick, eds. *Hitchcock's Rereleased Films: From "Rope" to "Vertigo."* Detroit: Wayne State University Press, 1991. Five of Hitchcock's films were rereleased in 1983 and 1984 after having been long unavailable; the sixteen essays in this book offer new insights into these films.

Rivadue, Barry. *Alice Faye: A Bio-Bibliography*. New York: Greenwood Press, 1991. A biographical, bibliographical, and critical study of this star of numerous musicals of the 1930's and 1940's.

Rogers, Ginger. *Ginger: My Story*. New York: HarperCollins, 1991. A well-written autobiography of the actress best known for her work with Fred Astaire, this book contains useful information on Rogers' life and career while avoiding any hint of mudslinging or gossip-mongering.

Rooney, Mickey. *Life Is Too Short*. New York: Random House, 1991. A breezy and uninhibited autobiography from the often-married actor, with most of the emphasis on his personal life rather than on his acting career.

Rosenberg, David. *The Movie That Changed My Life*. New York: Viking Press, 1991. Twenty-three essays by critics and literary figures, each of whom analyzes a film seen as a youth that had a major impact on his or her life. The reader learns as much about the writers as about the films in question.

Russell, Ken. *Altered States: The Autobiography of Ken Russell*. New York: Bantam Books, 1991. The controversial British filmmaker offers this take-it-or-leave-it account of his life and career.

Ruuth, Marianne. *Cruel City: The Dark Side of Hollywood's Rich and Famous*. Santa Monica, Calif.: Roundtable Publishing, 1991. Ruuth looks at famous Hollywood scandals, from Fatty Arbuckle to Natalie Wood, mostly involving stars who died under questionable circumstances.

Schickel, Richard. *Brando: A Life in Our Times*. New York: Atheneum, 1991. An insightful account of Marlon Brando's career and an intelligent analysis of his appeal make this a valuable addition to the shelf of books about this talented actor.

Schultz, Margie. *Irene Dunne: A Bio-Bibliography*. New York: Greenwood Press, 1991. A biographical, bibliographical, and critical study of this dignified star of the 1930's and 1940's.

Sharff, Stefan. *Alfred Hitchcock's High Vernacular: Theory and Practice*. New York: Columbia University Press, 1991. This scholarly analysis of the visual structure of three Hitchcock films—*Notorious* (1946), *Frenzy* (1972), and *Family Plot* (1976)— notes similarities in the two periods and argues that Hitchcock's later work retains his stamp of genius.

Smith, Gary A. *Epic Films*. Jefferson, N.C.: McFarland, 1991. This illustrated reference work offers analysis, as well as information on cast and credits, for more than 250 epic films, a term used here to refer to historical spectacle films.

Smith, R. Dixon. *Ronald Colman, Gentleman of the Cinema: A Biography and Filmography*. Jefferson, N.C.: McFarland, 1991. Though little remembered, Colman was a major star of the 1920's and 1930's. This book is a film-by-film analysis of his career.

Smith, Steven C. *A Heart at Fire's Center*. Berkeley: University of California Press, 1991. This is a biography of Bernard Herrmann, the celebrated composer of numerous film scores, including *Citizen Kane* (1941) and *The Magnificent Ambersons* (1942).

Spada, James. *Peter Lawford: The Man Who Kept the Secrets*. New York: Bantam Books, 1991. Lawford was a member of Frank Sinatra's "Rat Pack" and a relative by marriage of the Kennedys. This biography emphasizes his self-destructive private life; the "secrets" in the title refer to his involvement in John F. Kennedy's womanizing and to what he may have known about Kennedy's relationship with Marilyn Monroe.

Starr, Michael. *Peter Sellers: A Film History*. Jefferson, N.C.: McFarland, 1991. This book provides a brief chapter analyzing each of Sellers' forty-three films, from 1951 until his death in 1980. Also includes an interview with Blake Edwards, Sellers' director in the Pink Panther series and other films.

Taylor, Richard, and Ian Christie, eds. *Inside the Film Factory: New Approaches to Russian and Soviet Cinema*. London: Routledge, 1991. This work, a follow-up to the editors' *The Film Factory* (1988), continues the examination of Soviet cinema with eleven essays covering films produced from the silent era through the 1930's.

Telotte, J. P., ed. *The Cult Film Experience: Beyond All Reason*. Austin: University of Texas Press, 1991. Fourteen essays on films that have attracted a cult audience, from *Casablanca* (1942) to *The Rocky Horror Picture Show* (1975). Explores the relationship between audience and film and the response that these films evoke from their audiences.

Vineberg, Steve. *Method Actors: Three Generations of an American Acting Style*. New York: Macmillan, 1991. A historical survey of Konstantin Stanislavsky's "method" acting as practiced in the United States, studying the work of the style's principal exemplars, including Marlon Brando, James Dean, and Jack Nicholson.

Waldman, Harry. *Scenes Unseen*. Jefferson, N.C.: McFarland, 1991. A study of the unreleased and uncompleted films of sixty-four major filmmakers, from 1912 through 1990. Waldman offers a history of each production and an explanation for the film's difficulties.

Walker, Mark. *Vietnam Veteran Films*. Metuchen, N.J.: Scarecrow Press, 1991. Putting a different spin on films relating to the war in Vietnam, Walker analyzes films in which important characters are Vietnam veterans, offering a chapter on such genres as biker films, caper films, and comedies.

Weaver, Tom. *Science Fiction Stars and Horror Heroes*. Jefferson, N.C.: McFarland, 1991. Interviews with twenty-eight mostly obscure actors, directors, producers, and writers who worked in the science-fiction or horror genres between 1940 and 1970. Each chapter includes a filmography.

Williams, John A., and Dennis A. Williams. *If I Stop I'll Die: The Comedy and Tragedy of Richard Pryor*. New York: Thunder's Mouth Press, 1991. A sympathetic survey of the show business career of the star-crossed comedian.

Wilt, David. *Hardboiled in Hollywood*. Bowling Green, Ohio: Bowling Green State University Popular Press, 1991. Wilt examines the careers of five little-known writers of hard-boiled detective fiction who also worked in Hollywood as screenwriters in the 1930's and 1940's. Each chapter includes a filmography.

SELECTED
FILMS
OF
1991

THE ADDAMS FAMILY

Production: Scott Rudin; released by Paramount Pictures
Direction: Barry Sonnenfeld
Screenplay: Caroline Thompson and Larry Wilson; based on the characters created by
Charles Addams
Cinematography: Owen Roizman
Editing: Dede Allen and Jim Miller
Production design: Richard MacDonald
Art direction: Marjorie Stone McShirley
Set decoration: Cheryal Kearney
Special effects coordination: Chuck Gaspar
Visual effects supervision: Alan Munro
Makeup: Fern Buckner
Costume design: Ruth Myers
Choreography: Peter Anastos
Stunt coordination: David Ellis
Music: Marc Shaiman
Song: Hammer, "Addams Groove"
MPAA rating: PG-13
Running time: 99 minutes

Principal characters:
Morticia Addams	Anjelica Huston
Gomez Addams	Raul Julia
Fester Addams	Christopher Lloyd
Wednesday Addams	Christina Ricci
Pugsley Addams	Jimmy Workman
Granny	Judith Malina
Lurch	Carel Struycken
Abigal Craven	Elizabeth Wilson
Tully Alford	Dan Hedaya
Margaret Alford	Dana Ivey
Judge Womack	Paul Benedict
Thing	Christopher Hart

Of the crop of films in the 1980's and early 1990's inspired by other forms, *The Addams Family* is probably the most gutless. It is certainly long on glitz and texture, but that does not excuse its lack of soul and content. Consequently, this long-awaited production pales by comparison to its own advertising campaign. The filmmakers, predominantly cinematographer-turned-director Barry Sonnenfeld, stress devotion to the original source, Charles Addams' individual panel cartoons, which began appearing in *The New Yorker* magazine in 1932. To those immersed in the production, it is the unwavering loyalty to those singular images that represents the film's strength and integrity. Yet, a feature-length film for the sake of staging a handful of cherished one-line joke images is hard to justify.

The cleverly orchestrated trailers are actually better than the film in its entirety because they worked as brief, impeccably timed set pieces. Contrary to what many in the industry seem to believe, however, a narrative cannot be created by the mere stringing together of such set pieces. In such attempts, there can never be a satisfying escalation of drama. Inspired casting and baroque set design can add rich layers to a story, but when asked to be the main attraction, these secondary elements flounder. *The Addams Family* project does not even have the built-in temporal ingredients from which Warren Beatty's carefully crafted *Dick Tracy* (1990) benefited. That hawk-nosed comic-strip detective had long been engulfed in rising dramatic action. He was never without an objective—not only from one panel to the next but also from week to week. In other words, he already knew how to behave within a plot structure. Beatty, in his interpretation, was able to add a layer of cinematic character development to that expectation of linear progression already firmly in place. The resulting film was a homage to its source, but it also held together in terms of cinema conventions.

The Addams family, however, existed primarily in distilled moments of absurd commentary on society. Try to simply elongate this concept and it quickly falls apart. The very nature of the source material undermines the filmmakers' attempts at imitation. Whatever inherent wit is embodied in the static cartoon images cannot be sustained over time by texture alone. Without a commitment to developing or shaping this material to fit its new forum, the authors deliver a dull, substandard ghost of the original work. Reviews concurred that, although the characterizations are delightfully brought to life, the plot is negligible. In revisiting well-known and well-loved icons such as the Addamses, it appears to have been very difficult to give them anything to do except merely be who they are. Even with the likes of the towering Anjelica Huston and the boisterous Raul Julia, there are excruciating lags between clever moments. In addition, those plot devices that have been assembled are often insipid and uneven.

The actual tale is of what the external world does to the family, rather than anything that the family itself seeks to accomplish. Except for Gomez (Julia) harboring some guilty feelings regarding his long-lost brother Fester, the Addamses would gladly mind their own business. It is only the plan of their malicious attorney, Tully (Dan Hedaya), to steal the vast wealth stashed away behind the secret passageways of the creepy mansion that inches the action forward. By placing an imposter (Christopher Lloyd)—a nasty loan shark who bears such an uncanny resemblance to the rest of the family as to be a difficult point to swallow—into their midst, Tully manages to have the despondent Addamses evicted from their home.

If it is anyone's story, then it belongs to this imitation Fester. He begins to have real feelings of kinship for the clan, particularly the children, Wednesday (Christina Ricci) and Pugsley (Jimmy Workman), and their charming torture games. Fester eventually turns against his conniving adopted mother (Elizabeth Wilson) and Tully and sides with his newfound clan. Fester helps them to reclaim the mansion and lives happily ever after, having recovered from—yes—amnesia. He truly has been the long-lost brother all along. The film leaves the united family with the happy news from Morticia (Huston) of yet another ghoulish sibling on the way.

Ironically, the more entertaining parts of the film are not set inside the creepy mansion at all. At the children's school play, the family members play off the outside world for a refreshing change. This allows the viewer the chance to enjoy their subversive reactions and even to identify with them. The film sparks to life when Huston's Morticia registers horror at the photographs of the other children's role models—George and Barbara Bush. More devilish yet is the image of the suffering Addams family imprisoned in the auditorium while cute children dressed as cute flowers sing the terminally cute lyrics that such concerts always necessitate. The boldness of this scene is interesting, because it involves the film's audience, forcing them to identify the repressed horror in themselves. Perhaps that was what Charles Addams' vision was about. Nevertheless, the film's exploitation of such insight is rare.

Although the press releases carefully sidestepped the 1960's television show, that avenue was a much more practical one in which to undertake an adaptation of Addams' discreet and self-contained images. On a weekly television show, it is possible to tap into the same fundamentally unchanging characters and alter the situations enough to repeat the same basic theme with only a slight variation. In fact, the total effect of the film is one of loosely related sequences that might have easily been consecutive television episodes with exactly that same level of payoff.

In the sequences with Thing, the disembodied hand scutters about with a plethora of special effects and slick editing, thanks to the skills of editor Dede Allen, best known for such work as *Bonnie and Clyde* (1967) and *Little Big Man* (1970). In this venture, Allen's virtuoso techniques culminate in nothing less than a fast-paced Federal Express advertisement. While this blatant commercial insert does make logical sense in the slick world of the film, its realization is hardly most cinema enthusiasts' notion of profound achievement. Rather, this cheap textural sensationalism provides a frightening metaphor underlining where current cinema looks for inspiration.

In actuality, this film owes everything to television. Despite quite insistent denial of that show as an influence, the producers cashed in on the preexisting fans of the same-named sitcom's reruns. Furthermore, the insidious lowering of audience expectations with regard to story structure and the supplantation of a preoccupation with high-tech, formal gags stem from the fodder of network and cable programming, not to mention advertising. Providing that things happen quickly on the visual level, there is less demand made on the unfolding drama for a sense of cohesiveness. In the postmodern overlapping of media forms, this small-screen value system has bled into the realm of cinema conventions.

Most of the laughs elicited by *The Addams Family* are from children, who have had little exposure to forms other than television and similar television-informed cinema such as *Teenage Mutant Ninja Turtles* (1990). There are also those adults who call out the parade of characters ("Cousin It!") as they recognize them, enjoying a peculiarly sophomoric engagement with the film. The fact that the cartoons' placement in *The*

New Yorker once appealed to the reader on a largely intellectual level would make this seem all the more bizarre a fate for the Addams clan.

This recognition factor, however, is precisely the platform of marketing strategies employed by the commercial media, where virtually everything else matters above and before the actual quality of the film itself. The most extreme example of this ideology may be in the case of *Batman* (1989), where a once-promising script was overwhelmed by merchandizing, MTV tie-ins, and the stars' percentage points. Sadly, many who had been keeping abreast of all the prerelease struggles and misfortunes of the Addams family project wanted very much to like it when it finally arrived on the scene, as if this offscreen drama would ensure the same onscreen ingredients. *The Addams Family*, unfortunately, proves once again that the story should come first. That element alone could have enabled the dark humor of the original concept to play successfully in what should have been recognized as a completely different form. Instead, by focusing myopically on the esoteric trappings of the source work, *The Addams Family*'s creators have borne a second-rate imitation of an imitation.

Mary E. Belles

Reviews
American Film: Magazine of the Film and Television Arts. XVI, November/ December, 1991, p. 52.
Boxoffice. December, 1991, p. R-90.
Chicago Tribune. November 22, 1991, VII, p. 44.
The Christian Science Monitor. November 29, 1991, p. 16.
Cinéfantastique. XXII, February, 1992, p. 48.
Entertainment Weekly. November 29, 1991, p. 62.
The Hollywood Reporter. November 18, 1991, p. 5.
L.A. Weekly. November 22-28, 1991, XIII, p. 45.
Los Angeles Times. November 22, 1991, CC, p. F1.
The New York Times. November 22, 1991, p. B1.
Newsweek. CXVIII, November 25, 1991, p. 56.
People Weekly. XXXVI, December 2, 1991, p. 27.
Premiere. V, November, 1991, p. 106.
Theatre Crafts. October, 1991, p. 36.
Time. CXXXVIII, November 25, 1991, p. 96.
Vanity Fair. October, 1991, p. 220.
Variety. November 18, 1991, p. 2.
The Washington Post. November 22, 1991, p. B1.

AN AMERICAN TAIL
Fievel Goes West

Production: Steven Spielberg and Robert Watts for Amblimation Studios; released by Universal Pictures
Direction: Phil Nibbelink and Simon Wells
Screenplay: Flint Dille; based on a story by Charles Swenson and on characters created by David Kirschner
Editing: Nick Fletcher
Animation supervision: Nancy Beiman, Kristof Serrand, and Rob Stevenhagen
Layout supervision: Mark Marren
Background supervision: Shelley Page
Art direction: Neil Ross
Casting: Nancy Nayor and Valerie McCaffrey
Special effects supervision: Scott Santoro
Sound: Charlie Ajar, Jr., Michael C. Casper, Daniel Leahy, and Thomas Gerard
Music: James Horner
Songs: James Horner and Will Jennings, "Way Out West," "The Girl You Left Behind," and "Dreams to Dream"
MPAA rating: G
Running time: 74 minutes

Voices of principal characters:
Fievel Mousekewitz .... Phillip Glasser
Wylie Burp .... James Stewart
Tiger .... Dom DeLuise
Cat R. Waul .... John Cleese
Mama Mousekewitz .... Erica Yohn
Tanya Mousekewitz .... Cathy Cavadini
Papa Mousekewitz .... Nehemiah Persoff
Miss Kitty .... Amy Irving
T. R. Chula .... Jon Lovitz

An American Tail (1986), one of the most successful animated features of the 1980's, introduced one of the more charming original cartoon characters to grace the big screen in a while: Fievel Mousekewitz, the young Russian mouse immigrant. In the award-winning feature directed by former Disney animator Don Bluth, Fievel spent most of his time looking for his family in turn-of-the-century New York, providing the opportunity for many colorfully elaborate, episodical adventures. The film, with its beautifully detailed drawings, superb animation, and well-conceived characters, easily matched the high standards set by such Disney animated classics as *The Jungle Book* (1967), *The Rescuers* (1977), and *The Great Mouse Detective* (1986), as well as Bluth's own *The Secret of NIMH* (1982). Then, *An American Tail* received an honor shared only by Disney's *The Rescuers*: cartoon sequelitis. Unfortunately, *An American Tail: Fievel Goes West* cannot match the visual or creative excitement of its predecessor, nor is it even in the same league as its sister sequel, Disney's *The Rescuers Down Under* (1990).

The film picks up the story of Fievel and his family several years after their original adventures. Fievel (voice of Phillip Glasser) is obsessed with the American wild West and dreams of confronting a slew of desperadoes, which he subdues with the help of legendary cowboy hero Wylie Burp (voice of James Stewart). Fievel's daydream is punctured by the squalid reality of his home life in a tenement-like barrel surrounded by other equally disenchanted mouse neighbors. Their predicament is made even more despairing when the neighborhood is raided by a gang of ferocious cats led by the slick-talking English feline Cat R. Waul (voice of John Cleese).

One of the film's best animated scenes follows the destructive cat attack scene, as Fievel and his family escape from the evil cats by sailing down a sewer in a large food bowl, riding the rapidly flowing flotsam as if it were a roller coaster. Their sewer voyage ends in an underground gathering of mice, the group listening intently as the nefarious Cat R. Waul, using a puppet mouse, persuades the displaced rodents to travel to the open spaces of the West, where the cats are friendly and the opportunities for personal success are unlimited. Cleese as the voice of Cat R. Waul is hysterically amusing in this scene, attempting to feign an authentic Western cowboy twang and failing miserably as his proper British accent keeps getting in the way. Cat R. Waul's plan is to persuade the mice to travel West, where he and his feline cronies plan to use the rodents as slave labor to build a town before turning the group into mouseburgers.

Cat R. Waul's plan works, and the mice all board a train—its underbelly anyway—to head for the wild West. They are followed by Fievel's cat pal from the previous film, Tiger (voice of Dom DeLuise), whose journey West via a hilarious variety of bruising transportation methods provides some of the film's best and most colorful animated humor. Meanwhile, on the train, Fievel encounters Cat R. Waul and his gang while they are discussing their evil intentions. Cat R. Waul's cowboy tarantula stooge, T. R. Chula (voice of Jon Lovitz), chases Fievel around the train, finally knocking the mouse hero off the train and into the Western desert.

While both Fievel and Tiger struggle to survive in the desert, the rest of the mice arrive at Cat R. Waul's desolate town and, after scurrying around to find a suitable nook to call home, are put to work by the smooth-talking con cat. Tiger, meanwhile, has been captured by a tribe of comical Indian mice that first wants to eat him but later pronounces him a god when the medicine mouse has a vision. Fievel joins the group after being scooped up by a hawk and dropped in the middle of Tiger's luxurious surroundings. After trying unsuccessfully to persuade Tiger to join him, Fievel hops into a tumbleweed and—to the tune of "Rawhide"—rolls into Cat R. Waul's town, where he is reunited with his family.

When Fievel relates his desert adventures to his family and then alerts them to Cat R. Waul's evil plan, no one takes him seriously. A dejected Fievel then roams the town alone, finally meeting up with a tired old hound dog snoozing on a porch. The hound turns out to be none other than Fievel's Western hero, Wylie Burp. Unfortunately, Wylie's days as a Western good guy are long past, and he refuses to help Fievel battle the cats. He does agree, however, to train a promising apprentice, prompting Fievel to hunt down Tiger and persuade him to impersonate a heroic hound.

Tiger's transformation from a cowardly cat to a courageous canine is another one of the film's highlights, although strongly derivative of Lee Marvin's comical gunslinger training segment from *Cat Ballou* (1965). Tiger, who has had a series of uproariously comic encounters with hostile dogs throughout the film, nevertheless manages to stifle his prejudices and emerge as the film's true hero. Tiger, Wylie, and Fievel chase the cats back East and save the mice from becoming mouseburgers. Tiger is reunited with his feline sweetheart, Miss Kitty (voice of Amy Irving), who, along with Fievel's sister, Tanya (voice of Cathy Cavadini), have been providing amusing musical interludes as the town's new dance hall entertainers. In the film's sentimental conclusion, Fievel, inspired by Wylie's example, struts off into the Western horizon, his trademark Russian hat replaced by a ten-gallon model.

Several factors blunt the effectiveness of *An American Tail: Fievel Goes West*. The most serious flaw is the film's patchwork story, which not only borrows themes from the original—mice leaving their homes to seek a less hostile environment, Fievel getting lost, and cats impersonating mice—but also relies on far too many standard Western film clichés. The result is a film that is effective only in its extraneous scenes, most of them involving Tiger's character as he dodges dogs across the country, is made an Indian god, and finally becomes the true hero of the film. Fievel, who should be the film's main focus, is one of the least interesting characters, with Tiger and Cat R. Waul getting the best scenes. The animation, although lively and colorful, seems somewhat slapdash, with many scenes appearing sketchy and flat. For a film set, for the most part, in the wide-open Western spaces, the production is far from epic, a sharp contrast with the original's beautifully detailed New York cityscapes and landmarks. The musical score is also a disappointment, with all of the songs uninspired and easily forgettable. Don Bluth, the creative force behind the original, is sorely missed in the sequel. Although his animated films *The Land Before Time* (1988) and *All Dogs Go to Heaven* (1989) both suffered from an increasingly annoying amount of cuteness, his directorial savviness, emphasizing both panoramic grandeur and mouse-size inti-macy, could have brought a more fully satisfying depth to the story.

On the plus side, the film does contain several very effective extraneous bits. The character of T. R. Chula, whose part is, sadly, too brief, is a comical sight to behold, dressed as an arachnid cowpoke sporting four pairs of tiny boots on his eight spindly legs. In addition to Tiger's wild ride across the country—the film's highlight—there is a hysterically effective mini-scene involving Cat R. Waul being propelled out of his clothes and through the ceiling of his feline barroom, where he is smothered by a bosomy female before dropping back down into his clothes just in time to introduce his dance hall entertainers. Unfortunately, these brief, creative bursts fail to mask the film's overall lack of originality. Still, Fievel is such a charming and resourceful cartoon character that he is able to survive this disappointing sequel and is fully able to hold center stage in any future animated adventures, which, it is hoped, are in the planning stages.

Jim Kline

Reviews
Boston Globe. November 22, 1991, p. 33.
Cartoonist Profiles. December, 1991, p. 48.
Chicago Tribune. November 22, 1991, VII, p. 48.
The Christian Science Monitor. December 6, 1991, p. 12.
Los Angeles Times. November 22, 1991, p. F12.
Maclean's. CIV, December 9, 1991, p. 56.
The New York Times. November 22, 1991, p. B10.
USA Today. November 22, 1991, p. D6.
Variety. November 18, 1991, p. 2.
The Washington Post. November 22, 1991, p. B1.

AT PLAY IN THE FIELDS OF THE LORD

Production: Saul Zaentz; released by Universal Pictures
Direction: Hector Babenco
Screenplay: Jean-Claude Carrière and Hector Babenco; based on the novel by Peter
   Matthiessen
Cinematography: Lauro Escorel
Editing: William Anderson
Production design: Clovis Bueno
Art direction: Marlise Storchi, Antonio Vanzolini, and Roberto Mainieri
Sound: Chris Newman
Costume design: Rita Murtinho
Music: Zbigniew Preisner
MPAA rating: R
Running time: 180 minutes

> *Principal characters:*
> Lewis Moon . . . . Tom Berenger
> Martin Quarrier . . . . Aidan Quinn
> Hazel Quarrier . . . . Kathy Bates
> Leslie Huben . . . . John Lithgow
> Andy Huben . . . . Darryl Hannah
> Wolf . . . . Tom Waits
> Boronai . . . . Stenio Garcia
> Father Xantes . . . . Nelson Xavier
> Guzman . . . . José Dumont
> Billy Quarrier . . . . Niilo Kivirinta
> Aeore . . . . S. Yriwana Karaja
> Tukanu . . . . Carlos Xavante

   South America's rain forest is dying and its native inhabitants are in danger of extinction, doomed by a world that places more value on exploiting natural resources than preserving its natural wonders. Dozens of organizations have formed in an attempt to stop the destruction of the rain forest and its inhabitants. Their cause is a noble one; yet, it too is in danger of being exploited by profiteers. *At Play in the Fields of the Lord,* based on Peter Matthiessen's acclaimed 1965 novel, is a noble attempt to depict the forces intent on destroying South America's wilderness areas and its indigenous peoples in the name of God, gold, and greed. The goal of the creative artists involved in the production was to dramatize the cause, to illustrate graphically the need for the world's power-obsessed organizations to lay off this fragile and essential ecosystem. Unfortunately, a noble cause is not enough to make a film compelling and dramatically sound. *At Play in the Fields of the Lord* ultimately looks more like an exploiter than a savior.

Beautifully photographed on location in Amazonia, the film begins with the arrival of a dilapidated plane in a small outpost on the edge of the Amazonian jungle called Mae de Deus (Portuguese for "Mother of God"). The plane belongs to two expatriate Americans: the stolid, Cheyenne descendent Lewis Moon (Tom Berenger) and his scraggly, former hippie partner, Wolf (Tom Waits). Shortly after arriving, Moon's and Wolf's passports are confiscated by the local commandant, Guzman (José Dumont). Guzman promises to return their official papers if the two men agree to perform a special favor: bomb a native village located deep in the jungle. Guzman's intention is to take the tribe's land, which he believes is rich with gold.

As the two mercenaries ponder Guzman's plan, another group of Americans arrives at the small outpost. Martin Quarrier (Aidan Quinn), his wife, Hazel (Kathy Bates), and their young son, Billy (Niilo Kivirinta), are American missionaries who plan to live in a crude, abandoned mission located near the Niaruna tribe, the same tribe that Guzman wishes to destroy. Martin and his family are met by fellow missionary Leslie Huben (John Lithgow) and his wife, Andy (Darryl Hannah). Leslie is a fanatic who believes that, if the natives cannot be converted to Christianity, then they should be killed. Later, it is revealed that Leslie has made a deal with Guzman involving just such a philosophy.

Meanwhile, Moon and Wolf have agreed to Guzman's plan and take off in their plane to scout the area where the Niaruna live. When Moon spots the tribe's small village, however, located amid gorgeously thick, green vegetation, he is stunned when one of the villagers, upon seeing the plane, defiantly shoots an arrow at the craft. Later, after returning to Mae de Deus, Moon is haunted by the incident and experiences a radical spiritual transformation. After a heated confrontation with Martin—whom he ridicules as a hypocrite—Moon takes off in his plane and once again circles over the area where the Niaruna dwell. With Martin and Leslie pleading with him over the aircraft's radio to return to Mae de Deus, Moon instead tells them that he is at play in the fields of the Lord and parachutes out of the plane.

Moon lands safely and receives a hostile greeting by the Niaruna shaman, Aeore (S. Yriwana Karaja). Nevertheless, the tribe's leader, Boronai (Stenio Garcia), believes Moon to be the sky god Kisu and encourages Moon to join the tribe. Ultimately, Moon, called Kisu-Mu by the Niaruna, is inducted into the tribe, usurping Aeore's authority. Moon's intention is to save the Niaruna from the forces that wish to annihilate them.

Martin, meanwhile, has arrived at the abandoned mission and, with help from his family and from Leslie and Andy, begins to rebuild the outpost. The missionaries are later visited by some of the Niaruna who, remembering their lessons from the former missionaries, feign conversion in order to receive food and trinkets. After Leslie and Andy leave, young Billy joins a group of native boys and is soon running naked through the jungle with his new friends. Billy's conversion to the ways of the "noble savage" is short-lived when Hazel finds him and his new friends watching two teenage natives engaged in sex play. When she screams at Billy and attacks the natives, Martin reprimands her, telling her to be more tolerant. Hazel's animosity toward the natives and her primitive surroundings, however, increases to the point where she is finally driven mad and must be carted back to Mae de Deus with the help of Leslie. Her madness is reinforced by the sudden death of Billy, who succumbs after contracting a lethal jungle virus.

Before Leslie and Andy return to Mae de Deus with the deranged Hazel, the missionaries encounter the Wild Ones, the leaders of the Niaruna. Among the band of Wild Ones is Moon, who later encounters Andy while she is bathing in a river. Andy responds to Moon and, after discovering Leslie's deal with Guzman, is slowly converted to the ways of the natives. Martin, however, is outraged by Moon's meddling presence and later refuses to help Moon when he returns to the mission to beg for medicine to help save his adopted tribe from being ravaged by a strain of influenza. Moon steals the medicine and then attends to the Niaruna, who contracted the disease from Moon himself.

Martin, finally realizing that his goal to convert the natives is a futile and destructive one, runs to warn Moon and the Niaruna when he learns from a visiting Jesuit priest, Father Xantes (Nelson Xavier), about Guzman's plan to bomb the tribe. When Martin confronts Moon, Aeore becomes suspicious, believing that Moon is plotting with the white men to destroy the tribe. Moon, aware of Aeore's suspicions, tells Martin to pray to him as if he were truly the sky god Kisu. After much hesitation, Martin finally drops to his knees in front of Moon. At that moment, helicopters appear overhead and begin to massacre the tribe. Martin is killed—by a former native servant of his—while the rest of the tribe flees into the jungle.

In the film's final moments, Moon confronts Aeore while attempting to paddle to safety. In order to save himself, Moon pulls out a pistol and shoots the shaman, then paddles deep into the jungle, eventually landing on a small stretch of beach along the river, alone.

At Play in the Fields of the Lord could have been a magnificent, compassionate adventure epic along the same lines as the previous year's multi-award-winning film, *Dances with Wolves* (1990). From beginning to end, however, the film's effectiveness is sabotaged by the script's didactic dialogue and the melodramatic acting by the principal cast members. The majority of the characterizations—from Dumont's portrayal of the greasy, villainous Commandant Guzman to Lithgow's ultrarighteous Leslie Huben to Karaja's hyperactive Aeore—are all based on tired stereotypes and played with broad, foliage-chewing hamminess. Consequently, the film's overtly obvious message—preserve and protect this land and its people from all exploiters— is totally ineffective. The most unintentionally ludicrous characterization is Bates's Hazel who, at one point, is obliged to smear her body with mud and plants and then prance around naked while screaming at the top of her lungs. Bates's and Lithgow's parts are written and performed with such a ferocious theatricality that the film becomes a campy jungle potboiler rather than an ecological epic. The only actor who plays his part with a semblance of restraint is Berenger as the noble Moon. Because his approach is so sedate when compared to the others', however, the resulting clash in acting styles elicits unintentional laughter rather than heartfelt drama.

Many of the scenes are filled with an overt staginess, as if filmed in front of a live audience rather than in the South American jungles. This effect is most evident in the elaborately staged native rituals, which leave the impression that they are conducted for the benefit of visiting tourists. Several of these rituals are intercut with scenes of the missionaries conducting their own domesticated rituals in an obvious attempt at contrast. The most obvious comparison—once again made unintentionally ridiculous—occurs when Billy is shown cavorting with his native friends and then sitting bored at his birthday celebration while his party-hat-adorned parents dance to a hokey Bing Crosby tune. Such blatantly simplistic comparisons, along with the cliché-riddled characterizations, serve to insult the audience's intelligence and alienate it from the entire production, clearly not the filmmakers' intention.

In one of the film's few effective scenes, the shaman Aeore asks his tribe to paint their naked bodies with mud and colored clay, for that is the way that they are able to distinguish themselves from animals. Unfortunately, another way that human beings separate themselves from animals is by assuming a holier-than-thou attitude toward all the beasts of the forest and "unenlightened" humans. No one likes to be preached at or cajoled into accepting a new philosophy, whether that philosophy is a compassionate one or one based on greed and prejudice. Although the artists involved with *At Play in the Fields of the Lord* were motivated by compassion, their self-righteous posturings end up as exploitative rantings and are far less compassionate than the simple animal screeches and howls heard on the film's sound track.

Jim Kline

Reviews
Boxoffice. February, 1992, p. R-14.
Chicago Tribune. December 6, 1991, VII, p. 31.
The Christian Science Monitor. December 20, 1991, p. 12.
The Hollywood Reporter. December 4, 1991, p. 5.
Los Angeles. January, 1992, p. 117.
Los Angeles Times. December 6, 1991, p. F1.
The New York Times. December 6, 1991, p. B4.
The New Yorker. LXVII, December 16, 1991, p. 118.
Newsweek. December 16, 1991, p. 77.
Omni. XIV, December, 1991, p. 10.
Premiere. V, December, 1991, p. 94.
Rolling Stone. January 9, 1992, p. 95.
Time. CXXXVIII, December 30, 1991, p. 71.
Variety. December 4, 1991, p. 2.
The Washington Post. January 24, 1992, p. C7.

BACKDRAFT

Production: Richard B. Lewis, Pen Densham, and John Watson for Brian Grazer, Imagine Films Entertainment, and Trilogy Entertainment Group; released by Universal Pictures
Direction: Ron Howard
Screenplay: Gregory Widen
Cinematography: Mikael Salomon
Editing: Daniel Hanley and Michael Hill
Production design: Albert Brenner
Art direction: Carol Winstead Wood
Set decoration: Garrett Lewis
Set design: Harold Fuhrman, William B. Fosser, and Gary Baugh
Casting: Jane Jenkins, Janet Hirshenson, and Jane Alderman
Special effects and pyrotechnics: Allen Hall
Visual effects supervision: Scott Farrar
Visual effects production: Suella Kennedy
Visual effects art direction: Paul Huston
Sound: Glenn Williams
Costume design: Jodie Tillen
Stunt coordination: Walter Scott
Music: Hans Zimmer
MPAA rating: R
Running time: 136 minutes

Principal characters:
Stephen McCaffrey	Kurt Russell
Brian McCaffrey	William Baldwin
Donald Rimgale	Robert De Niro
Ronald Bartel	Donald Sutherland
Jennifer Vaitkus	Jennifer Jason Leigh
John Adcox	Scott Glenn
Helen McCaffrey	Rebecca DeMornay
Tim Krizminski	Jason Gedrick
Martin Swayzak	J. T. Walsh
Chief John Fitzgerald	Tony Mockus, Sr.
Grindle	Cedric Young
Schmidt	Jack McGee
Pengelly	Mark Wheeler
Ricco	Clint Howard

Like any son, Brian McCaffrey (William Baldwin) idealized his father, a fire fighter in the suburbs of Chicago. As a young boy, he was taken one day to a tenement fire on his father's fire truck. In order to rescue a family from the burning building, the fire fighters, including Brian's father, had to enter the blazing apartment. All seemed to go well until a secondary explosion engulfed the apartment in flames, and Brian watched helplessly from below as the fire consumed the building. While Brian stared in horror, his father's helmet, ironically, landed by the young boy's feet. As Brian held the helmet, a photographer captured the moment. The photograph became a front cover for *Life* magazine. Driven by respect for their father, Brian and his elder brother, Stephen (Kurt Russell), both become fire fighters themselves. Stephen, being the elder brother, is already a seasoned lieutenant in the famous seventieth fire district of Chicago. Stephen arranges for his younger brother, upon graduating from the academy, to train as a rookie fire fighter under his guidance.

The two brothers were never close, and working together does nothing to help that relationship. Each feels that the other is not being open enough, so instead of talking about their feelings, they argue all the time. Brian does not like the fact that Stephen has separated from his wife, Helen (Rebecca DeMornay), and chooses to live on the old family boat. During one particular fire, Stephen tells Brian to help him rescue a child who has been trapped in her room by a raging fire. Brian hesitates to go into the building until they have some help from the unit. Stephen, without any backup waterhoses for protection against the immense heat, rushes into the building and retrieves the child. Brian goes only so far into the burning inferno and then hesitates, showing his fear of the fire. When the child is saved and Stephen is the hero of the moment, Brian realizes that his brother may be right: Perhaps Brian cannot stay the course and become a committed fire fighter like his brother and father before him. The fact that he was not able to rescue the child and that he hesitated at the crucial moment makes Brian decide to accept the position of assistant to an arsonist investigator, Donald Rimgale (Robert De Niro).

Alderman Martin Swayzak (J. T. Walsh) is frustrated by Rimgale's slow progress in tracking down an arsonist. Swayzak believes that, if the fire department can find and prosecute the arsonist, his election bid for mayor will be secured. This particular arsonist appears to be a professional: At each of the three fires that Rimgale visits, the phenomenon of a backdraft has caused the death of three men. A backdraft is created when a fire has consumed all the available oxygen in an enclosed space and then burns to temperatures approaching two thousand degrees. When a small amount of oxygen is allowed into this environment, a tremendous explosion results. Eventually, through close analysis of the evidence left at the fire scenes, Rimgale discovers a little-known chemical which has been used in each of the fires.

In his investigation, Brian approaches convicted arsonist Ronald Bartel (Donald Sutherland) in the hope that, as an arsonist, Bartel may be able to help them find the culprit. The deranged Bartel suggests that the arsonist is someone who hates fires and has access to this chemical. These clues point an accusing finger toward Stephen, as Brian had seen cans that contained this chemical on Stephen's boat. The real arsonist turns out to be one of the brothers' closest friends and fellow fire fighters, John Adcox (Scott Glenn). While on the roof of a chemical factory that is on fire, Stephen accuses John of being the arsonist. John explains that there was a conspiracy directly linked with Alderman Swayzak's office. A false report, written by a number of key officials (three in all), recommended a reduction of manpower in the city's fire department, resulting in a number of fire-fighter deaths. John had created the backdrafts in order to murder those men who were involved in the corrupt report. As John, Stephen, and Brian try to exit the factory fire, the walkway that John and Stephen are using collapses and the two fire fighters fall into the fire. John dies immediately, and Stephen dies in the ambulance with Brian seated next to him. In those final moments, the fire reunited the brothers because Brian put his own life at risk to save his injured brother.

Backdraft presents fire fighters not as city municipal workers but as heroes who risk their lives each day as part of their jobs. Unlike their counterparts in the police department, where violence, murder, and lawlessness are the enemy, fire fighters must battle with the unpredictability of fire. *Backdraft* takes an exhilarating look at the power and destructive forces of fire. Traditionally, fire fighters have been taken for granted. Also, prior to *Backdraft*, the subject of fire had been used only as a safe, spectacular backdrop, such as with the burning of Atlanta in *Gone with the Wind* (1939) and with *The Towering Inferno* (1974), which romanticized fire more than any previous film. *Backdraft*, while perhaps allowing some romanticization of fire fighters, comes as close as is technically possible to portraying the almost uncontrollable force of fire. Even if the story line is predictable and the plot has enough holes to run a fire engine through, the ultimate attraction of this film is the numerous fire scenes that bind the story together to portray a believable inside account of the dangers faced by fire fighters.

Flames leap relentlessly at the camera, filling the screen with every combination of yellows and reds as the conflagration bursts and erupts around the fire fighters, who enter into the throat of the blaze in an attempt to capture "Old Man Fire." The visual experience of seeing the intensity of fire from within rather than at a safe distance is what gives *Backdraft* its uniqueness. Also, Hans Zimmer's musical score heightens the drama throughout and thereby strengthens the sensual impact of the film.

Criticism of the film was mostly directed at Gregory Widen's screenplay, despite the fact that he was a fire fighter himself and borrowed heavily from his own experiences. While the numerous blazes were perceived as wholly believable, the characters and the plot did not receive the same commendations. Many critics believe that there can only be one central hero and one villain in any film, and these roles are played respectively by the fire fighters and the seven or eight fires that they face. Despite the obvious but understandable weaknesses of the script, all the principal actors play a very definite role in the shaping of the human drama. Kurt Russell and Scott Glenn literally take on the persona of fire fighters. Many of the stunts that were required to recreate what a fire fighter must confront in a real fire were performed by the actors themselves. In fact, nearly everyone involved in the shooting of the film received some kind of minor burns. Even before shooting began, the principal actors were assigned to work with a fire station. Much of the main drama of the film falls to William Baldwin, whose performance is unexpectedly strong throughout. While perhaps not as believable a fire fighter, Baldwin nevertheless is able to give the story a focus.

Director Ron Howard was one of the principal people involved in getting *Backdraft* made into a motion picture. With Howard's teaming up with cinematographer Mikael Salomon, whose work on *The Abyss* (1989) earned for Salomon an Oscar nomination, the right elements for making a successful film about fire fighters were in place. Also, for the first time, a credit appears for the work of Allen Hall, who was responsible for the pyrotechnics that are the film's staple special effects. Such effects also extended to the making of miniature buildings by Industrial Light and Magic that would be set alight and used in composite shots with interior footage. This method was used to great effect in the scenes of the garment-factory fire. To achieve the right level of realism, special fire-resistant camera boxes were constructed to shoot some of the scenes. These boxes did not prevent Salomon from having to wear special gels and fire-retardant clothing when he hand-carried a shielded camera through the very flames through which the actors and stuntpeople had jumped only moments earlier. Professional fire fighters commented after seeing the film that the flame footage was as close to the real thing as could possibly be experienced, taking into account that there is usually a tremendous amount of smoke which could not be filmed. The budget for the fires alone was $1.25 million.

Fire fighters have an unusually dangerous job and, in order to honor their services, *Backdraft* leaves none of their risks to the imagination. When the last glowing embers are finally extinguished from a factory or house fire, the familiar red fire truck takes the weary fire fighters back to their station. The perils, thrills, heroes, and stories are concluded for another day. In the closing titles, there is a reminder that, while what has been portrayed is fiction and uses special pyrotechnic effects, there were more than 1,200,700 men and women actively employed as fire fighters in the United States in 1991. *Backdraft* is a reminder that heroes exist in every fire station in the country.

Richard G. Cormack

Reviews
American Cinematographer. LXXII, May, 1991, p. 42.
American Film: Magazine of the Film and Television Arts. XVI, May, 1991, p. 13.
Boxoffice. August, 1991, p. R-51.
Chicago Tribune. May 24, 1991, VII, p. 33.
Cinefex. November, 1991, p. 4.
Films in Review. XLII, July, 1991, p. 262.
The Hollywood Reporter. May 20, 1991, p. 5.
Los Angeles Times. May 24, 1991, p. F1.
The New Republic. June 17, 1991, p. 28.
The New York Times. May 24, 1991, p. B5.
Premiere. IV, April, 1991, p. 96.
Sight and Sound. I, August, 1991, p. 38.
Variety. May 20, 1991, p. 2.

BARTON FINK

Production: Ethan Coen for Circle Films; released by Twentieth Century-Fox
Direction: Joel Coen
Screenplay: Ethan Coen and Joel Coen
Cinematography: Roger Deakins
Editing: Roderick Jaynes
Production design: Dennis Gassner
Casting: Donna Isaacson and John Lyons
Sound: Allan Byer
Costume design: Richard Hornung
Music: Carter Burwell
MPAA rating: R
Running time: 116 minutes

Principal characters:
Barton Fink	John Turturro
Charlie Meadows	John Goodman
Audrey Taylor	Judy Davis
Jack Lipnick	Michael Lerner
W. P. Mayhew	John Mahoney
Ben Geisler	Tony Shalhoub
Lou Breeze	Jon Polito
Detective Mastrionotti	Richard Portnow
Detective Deutsch	Christopher Murney
Beauty	Isabelle Townsend

Barton Fink is a bizarre comedy about the elusive and powerful phenomenon called the creative process and its antagonistic relationship with a sloppy and unpredictable factor called life. Set primarily in a slimy, cramped, and unbearably hot Hollywood hotel room in the early 1940's, the film follows the travails of a struggling New York playwright-turned-Hollywood screenwriter, Barton Fink (John Turturro), who has dreams of exploring the simple and noble attributes of the common man. Following a critical success on Broadway, and his agent's advice, however, Barton accepts the more lucrative position of screenwriter for a major Hollywood film studio.

Arriving in Hollywood, Barton checks into the sleazy Hotel Earle. Barton's room is disturbingly dark with paper-thin walls, peeling wallpaper dripping with gooey glue, and a pesky mosquito. On one of the walls is a picture of a pretty, bathing suit-clad girl lounging on a sunny California beach, the only cheery touch to Barton's otherwise thoroughly depressing surroundings. After a fitful night's sleep, Barton, covered with mosquito bites, meets with Jack Lipnick (Michael Lerner), the head of Capital Pictures. Lipnick is a huge, boisterous, fast-talking mogul who lauds Barton's writing prowess and assigns Barton to write a wrestling picture for Wallace Beery. Back in his hotel room, Barton is gripped with a massive case of writer's block. He stares at the piece of paper in his typewriter for hours, managing to write only one sentence. Barton gazes around his room for some sort of inspiration but is greeted instead with an irritating assortment of weird sounds, the most disturbing of which is that of a man crying hysterically in the room next to his. When he calls down to the desk clerk to complain, the neighbor confronts Barton. Fortunately, he turns out to be a decent and good-natured traveling salesman, Charlie Meadows (John Goodman), who apologizes for disturbing Barton's work, and the two men strike up a friendship.

The following day, Barton meets with a studio producer, Ben Geisler (Tony Shalhoub), in the hopes that he will help him with his writing problem. Geisler, however, tells Barton to seek other screenwriters for advice. By chance, Barton runs into the famous Southern author William P. Mayhew (John Mahoney), a caricature of William Faulkner. Mayhew, drunk and dripping with syrupy cynicism, invites Barton to his office on the studio lot. When Barton arrives at Mayhew's office, he finds the famous author in an alcoholic stupor and whimpering for his secretary, Audrey (Judy Davis). Later, the three meet at a park for lunch, where Barton scolds Mayhew for wasting his talents on Hollywood and drinking his life away. Realizing that he must at least come up with an outline to his wrestling picture before his next meeting with Lipnick, Barton returns to his hotel room and panics. He calls Audrey and begs her to help him. She agrees and arrives soon afterward, then stuns Barton by confessing that she has written all of Mayhew's scripts, as well as his last two novels. Barton then begs Audrey to help him write his script. Instead, they make love.

In the morning, Barton wakes to the sound of the pesky mosquito and then screams in terror at the sight of Audrey lying dead in a pool of blood next to him. Charlie comes to Barton's aid, disposing of Audrey's body and insisting that Barton tell no one about the incident. A terrified and zombielike Barton then meets with Lipnick at the mogul's palatial mansion. When Lipnick asks Barton to describe the wrestling script to him, Barton replies that he feels uncomfortable talking about a work in progress. Lipnick's assistant, Lou Breeze (Jon Polito), insists that Barton answer Lipnick, who in turn rages at Lou, demanding that he kiss Barton's feet. When Lou refuses, Lipnick fires him and then kisses Barton's feet himself.

Barton is overwhelmed by the bizarre series of events and returns to the Hotel Earle where Charlie comforts him. Charlie then tells Barton that he is leaving town for a while on business but will return soon. Later, Barton approaches his writing desk and pages through a copy of the Bible, reading the book of Genesis, the first lines of which have metamorphosed and now read exactly like the opening sentence of his script. Wandering down to the hotel lobby, Barton encounters two detectives who question him about a mass murderer called Earl "Madman" Muntz. Barton flinches when the detectives show him a picture of Charlie. When the two men tell him that one of Madman Muntz's specialties is decapitating his victims, Barton returns to his hotel room and examines the package that Charlie gave him for safekeeping. Placing the package on his writing desk, Barton sits down and begins to write furiously, finishing the entire screenplay in one night.

To celebrate, Barton visits a United Service Organizations (USO) canteen and dances the night away. When he returns to his hotel room, he finds the two detectives reading his script, shaking Charlie's package, and eyeing the huge blood stain on his bed. After accusing Barton of being Madman Muntz's accomplice, the detectives handcuff Barton to the bed, then run out into the hallway to face Charlie as the traveling salesman suddenly returns from his trip. Charlie leaves the elevator accompanied by smoke and fire. When the detectives order Charlie to lay down his suitcase and put up his hands, Charlie puts down his case, opens it, pulls out a shotgun, and shoots one of the men. Then, as the entire hallway erupts into flames, Charlie advances on the remaining detective, screaming, "I'll show you the life of the mind!" (one of Barton's favorite phrases), and shoots the terrified man to death.

With the hotel now thoroughly charred by the fiery inferno, Charlie helps Barton escape from the handcuffs and returns to his own room, inviting Barton to visit him if he needs any help. After escaping from the hotel, his script in one hand and Charlie's package in the other, Barton gives his script to Lipnick, who, after reviewing it, tells him that it is worthless. A dejected Barton wanders down a deserted stretch of beach, still clutching Charlie's package. He meets a beautiful girl who smiles at him and asks him about the package. When Barton dodges her question, she turns and settles down on the sand in front of him, striking the same pose as the girl in the picture hanging over Barton's writing desk. With the image of the girl in front of him and the gloriously blue sea pounding in the distance, the film ends.

Stylistically, *Barton Fink* is very much a Joel and Ethan Coen film, the producing, writing, and directing team responsible for such films as *Blood Simple* (1985), *Raising Arizona* (1987), and *Miller's Crossing* (1990). As with the filmmakers' previous efforts, *Barton Fink* is liberally populated with wildly eccentric loonies struggling to understand the bizarre events that surround and envelop them. The Coens add to the confusion of the story by maintaining their usual coldly detached, deadpan point of view. This attitude, coupled with the use of unusual and surreal camera angles, emphasizes the bizarreness of the already ravingly weird plot developments. The contrast between the foreboding otherworldliness of their films and their ability to remain detached from the action creates a provocative tension which is both intriguing and confusing. It also makes the films' characters seem like hapless pawns manipulated by smug, sadistic gods who find pleasure in subjecting their creations to events and actions beyond the characters' hopelessly limited comprehension.

Although the Coens can be faulted for displaying a lack of compassion for their characters, however, they cannot be condemned for making uninteresting films. Even if the viewer feels somewhat confused by some of the strange plot developments, the stunning visual, aural, and verbal delights of their films are consistently captivating. *Barton Fink* contains examples of their best work to date. The way in which the Coens create a hellish atmosphere out of Barton's tiny, cavelike room, endowing such common objects as a buzzing insect, a whirring fan, a creaking bed, a whooshing door, and dripping wallpaper with a nightmarish yet hilarious quality is proof of their superior mastery of the cinematic medium. The sight of Barton's hotel hallway, with its slimy green carpeting lit with jaundice-yellow lamps, and the fact that it remains eerily empty except for the countless pairs of shoes set outside nearly each door are both terrifying and terrifically comic examples of their visual expertise. The most visually dazzling scene—Charlie's encounter with the detectives amid swirling, dancing hellfire—is one of the best examples of the Coens' ability to astound, delight, and awe the viewer with their mix of innovative camera work, superlative use of sound, and dynamic, surreal action.

Barton Fink contains exceptional performances, most especially John Goodman as Barton's good-natured mass murderer neighbor, Michael Lerner as the hyperkinetic studio head, and John Turturro as the title character. Turturro conveys terror, befuddlement, and a dangerously aggressive naïveté, the perfect combination of emotions given the subject matter and one that reflects the viewer's own attitude.

Although *Barton Fink*, like the Coens' previous efforts, is filmed from a highly objective point of view, it is nevertheless the filmmakers' most personal film, one that is only marginally about the travails of a serious yet naïve writer and his encounter with a fantasy world called Hollywood. It is much more a film about the creative process itself and about how creativity is shaped, and warped, by reality. It explores the difficulty of creating something meaningful and lasting when one is surrounded by chaos and indifference. Barton wants desperately to write something truly inspiring, something that celebrates the inherent goodness of the common man. Barton really knows nothing about the common man, however, preferring to rant about his artistic philosophy and how painful it is to create something meaningful. His muse finally turns out to be Charlie's mysterious package, one that might or might not contain Audrey's severed head. With the package sitting next to his typewriter, Barton finally receives the inspiration that he needs to finish his script, one that he proudly calls the finest writing he has ever done and one that is peremptorily dismissed by Lipnick. Barton carries Charlie's package with him after he leaves the hotel, yet he dares not open it. The contents remain mysterious, beguiling, inexplicable, and terrifying, like life and the creative process.

Jim Kline

Reviews
Boxoffice. August, 1991, p. R-49.
Chicago Tribune. August 23, 1991, VII, p. 29.
Film Comment. XXVII, September, 1991, p. 26.
The Hollywood Reporter. May 20, 1991, p. 6.
Los Angeles Times. August 21, 1991, p. F1.
The New York Times. August 21, 1991, p. C11.
Newsweek. CXVIII, August 26, 1991, p. 57.
Premiere. October, 1991, p. 108.
Rolling Stone. August 22, 1991, p. 71.
Time. CXXXVIII, August 26, 1991, p. 58.
Variety. May 20, 1991, p. 3.

BEAUTY AND THE BEAST

Production: Don Hahn for Walt Disney Pictures, in association with Silver Screen Partners IV; released by Buena Vista
Direction: Gary Trousdale and Kirk Wise
Screenplay: Linda Woolverton; based on the classic French fairy tale
Editing: John Carnochan
Story supervision: Roger Allers
Layout supervision: Ed Ghertner
Background supervision: Lisa Keene
Cleanup supervision: Vera Lanpher
Visual effects supervision: Randy Fullmer
Computer graphics images supervision: Jim Hillin
Animation supervision: James Baxter, Glen Keane, Andreas Deja, Nik Ranieri, Will Finn, Dave Pruiksma, Ruben A. Aquino, Chris Wahl, Russ Edmonds, Larry White, and Tony Anselmo
Animation effects supervision: Dave Bossert, Dorse Lanpher, Ted Kierscey, and Mark Myer
Art direction: Brian McEntee
Casting: Albert Tavares
Sound: Michael Farrow, John Richards, Terry Porter, Mel Metcalfe, David J. Hudson
Music: Alan Menken (AA)
Songs: Howard Ashman (lyrics) and Alan Menken (music), "Belle," "Gaston," "Be Our Guest," "Something There," "Beauty and the Beast" (AA), and "The Mob Song"
MPAA rating: G
Running time: 85 minutes

Voices of principal characters:

Belle	Paige O'Hara
Beast	Robby Benson
Lumiere	Jerry Orbach
Mrs. Potts	Angela Lansbury
Gaston	Richard White
Cogsworth/Narrator	David Ogden Stiers
Le Fou	Jesse Corti
Maurice	Rex Everhart
Chip	Bradley Michael Pierce
Wardrobe	Jo Anne Worley
Featherduster	Kimmy Robertson

In this excellent interpretation of the classic French fairy tale, Disney has again succeeded in creating an enchanting and entertaining full-length animated feature. *Beauty and the Beast* was the first full-length animated film to be nominated for an

Academy Award for Best Picture, and the film won awards from the Los Angeles Film Critics and National Board of Review, as well as a Golden Globe for Best Picture, Comedy or Musical. The musical score is rousing, composed of six memorable songs by lyricist Howard Ashman and composer Alan Menken. In fact, Menken won an Academy Award and Golden Globe Award for Best Original Score, and Menken and Ashman won Academy Awards and the Golden Globe for the title song, "Beauty and the Beast." Ashman and Menken had previously collaborated on the Disney animated feature *The Little Mermaid* (1989), for which they also won an Academy Award for the song "Under the Sea" and Menken again won for best original score. *Beauty and the Beast* also boasts a strong female lead—Belle, the Beauty of the title, who is an independent young woman enamored of books. This Disney beauty is a more mature, satisfying rendering of a fairy-tale heroine than was the more childlike Ariel of *The Little Mermaid*.

The film begins with a series of stained-glass-window-like images, as David Ogden Stiers narrates the story of the Beast's transformation from an arrogant prince to his present creature form. Once vain and conceited, this prince lived in a large and beautiful castle. One day, an old hag arrives at the door and wishes to present him with a rose in exchange for a place to stay the night. The prince, however, in an ill-fated decision, turns her from his door. The old hag is then transformed into a beautiful enchantress. Alarmed, the prince then tries to apologize, but it is too late. The enchantress turns him into the Beast, and a beast he will remain unless he earns the love of a woman before his twenty-first birthday. Should he fail, he will then remain a beast forever.

Enter Belle (voice of Paige O'Hara)—a beautiful young woman who lives in a small French village—in a moving musical sequence, entitled simply "Belle," that is reminiscent of Judy Garland's rendition of "Somewhere over the Rainbow" in the classic *The Wizard of Oz* (1939). In this song, Belle expresses her yearning to escape dull village life because the townspeople do not understand her. She wants adventure and romance. Gaston (voice of Richard White), a young man with delusions of grandeur, is also introduced in this opening sequence. Gaston is as conceited as he is handsome. He has set his sights on Belle, and nothing, he says, will prevent him from marrying her.

Belle lives with her inventor father, Maurice (voice of Rex Everhart), who is a potty but lovable white-haired gentleman. When he sets off for an inventor's congress, he and his horse Philippe go astray in the woods. Wolves chase his horse, and Maurice wanders onto the grounds of a nearby castle. Rain drives him inside. Entering the castle, he takes fright when the candelabra that he finds begins talking to him. The castle is enchanted, and Lumiere (voice of Jerry Orbach)—the candelabra—and Cogsworth (voice of David Ogden Stiers)—the stuffy mantle clock—are two of the principal inhabitants. Lumiere, with his charming Maurice Chevalier voice and demeanor, invites Maurice in, much to the chagrin of Cogsworth, the prim, head-butler type. Mrs. Potts (voice of Angela Lansbury)—the talking teapot—and Chip (voice of Bradley Michael Pierce)—her son, a teacup—arrive to serve tea. A footstool that romps around the room like a puppy dog pauses in front of the chair for Maurice to rest his feet. Then, in a terrifying moment, the Beast bounds in. This is the viewer's first glimpse of the Beast—and the animation is inspired. A mixture of animal-like and human movements, he is a fiercesome and ugly creature, with a temper to match. In a booming voice (that one would never guess was that of actor Robby Benson), he accuses Maurice of trespassing and locks him in a dungeon.

When Maurice's horse returns alone, Belle uses him to find her way to the castle, where she discovers Maurice's hat lying in the grounds. She enters the forbidding castle where she finds her father, imprisoned and ill. The Beast arrives, furious that his privacy has again been invaded. In an act of supreme self-sacrifice, Belle offers to take her father's place, forever, an offer which the Beast accepts.

Lumiere believes that Belle will be the one to break the enchantment and is delighted at her arrival. Nevertheless, the opening encounters between Belle and the Beast do not go well, as their wills and tempers clash. This Belle is a courageous yet compassionate woman. When the Beast orders her to dinner, she refuses, preferring to go hungry in her room. Later, however, she slips down to the kitchen for a snack and is treated to a rousing musical sequence, in true Busby Berkeley tradition, complete with Lumiere with top hat and cane singing "Be Our Guest" and teaspoons that dive into a punch bowl à la Esther Williams and company. It is a treat for all vintage-musical fans.

Belle and the Beast continue to butt heads, reaching a climax when Belle enters the Beast's private apartment and discovers a rose under glass—the rose that he refused to accept from the enchantress and that is losing its petals, one by one, as his twenty-first birthday approaches. He orders her to leave his room, and Belle, stricken and scared, flees the castle. Outside the grounds, on Philippe, she is attacked by wolves. The Beast saves her life and is wounded in the process, an act which brings Belle's compassion and kindness to play in their relationship, as she bandages his arm. Winter brings a delightful scene of the two playing in the snow and their first realization of their feelings for each other as they sing the ballad "Something There." They then share an elegant dinner together and dance to the beautiful musical number, and title song, "Beauty and the Beast," sung by Angela Lansbury, in an elegant gold and blue ballroom that would exceed the imaginings of any would-be Cinderella. As a gift to Belle, the Beast allows her to see her father once more, via the magic handmirror in his room. When Belle sees how ill and worried her father is, the Beast permits her to leave, thus, presumably, sealing his own fate. When Belle returns to her father and Gaston learns of her newfound affection for this Beast, he leads a group of villagers to the castle to destroy him. Belle rushes to save the Beast and, as he lays dying, returns him to his human form when she confesses her love for him.

Disney has hit a high point in the area of animation with this lovely rendering of an old fairy tale. The songwriters, the animators, and even the actors who did the voices worked closely together to bring the characters and scenes to life. The animation is superb, which is not surprising considering the separate lists of animators credited for each major character. The Beast, himself, is an intriguing mix of animal and human gestures. He is at times a snarling fierce creature and at others a gentle thing with puppy-dog eyes. His transformation during Belle's stay is both heartwarming and sincere. Lumiere and Cogsworth, a walking, talking candelabra and clock, are fantastic comic characters that relieve the inherent dreariness and gloom in the enchanted castle which would otherwise have threatened to take over under the circumstances. Fairy tales are prime candidates for animated film, as the animators of *Beauty and the Beast* have brought not only human characters and animals to life but also myriad (so-called) inanimate objects, in a "tale as old as time," with the most up-to-date innovations in computer animation.

Complementing the superb animation and story line is the musical score by lyricist Ashman and composer Menken. Unfortunately, Ashman's death the same year, March, 1991, may bring to a close this brief bout of good family entertainment. He did, however, write a few songs for another Disney film, *Aladdin*, scheduled to be released in 1992. His songs are an entertaining blend of the dramatic and the comic, as aptly demonstrated in "Gaston," a waltz sung in a local bar by Gaston's sidekick, Le Fou (voice of Jesse Corti). This song provides comic insight into one of the lead characters, Gaston, the conceited hunk who is so enamored with Belle. In this excellent expositional sequence, the viewer learns all one wants to know about Gaston and his *raison d'être*, as well as his more sinister tendencies.

In fact, the one criticism of this film might be the death of Gaston at the climax. Gaston, curiously, would appear to be the Beast's kindred spirit. He, too, is conceited and vain, as was the prince before being rendered a beast by the enchantress. Yet, the Beast is granted an opportunity for redemption that Gaston is not. At the finale, when the Beast is standing atop the castle tower in the pouring rain, about to kill Gaston, the sight of Belle reminds him of his newfound compassion, and he relents and tells Gaston to go. As the Beast turns to Belle, however, Gaston stabs him in the back and falls from the tower to his death. This final act is as pointless as it is needlessly violent. Notwithstanding, *Beauty and the Beast* is a charming musical that is entertaining for adults and children alike.

Cynthia K. Breckenridge

Reviews
Boxoffice. January, 1992, p. R-3.
Chicago Tribune. November 22, 1991, VII, p. 45.
The Christian Science Monitor. December 6, 1991, p. 12.
Cinéfantastique. XXII, February, 1992, p. 42.
The Hollywood Reporter. November 11, 1991, p. 9.
Los Angeles Times. November 15, 1991, p. F1.
The New York Times. November 13, 1991, p. B1.
Time. CXXXVIII, November 25, 1991, p. 96.
Variety. November 11, 1991, p. 2.
The Wall Street Journal. November 27, 1991, p. A7.
The Washington Post. November 22, 1991, p. B1.

LA BELLE NOISEUSE

Origin: France
Released: 1990
Released in U.S.: 1991
Production: Pierre Grise for FR3 Films Production and George Reinhart Productions; released by MK2 Productions USA
Direction: Jacques Rivette
Screenplay: Pascal Bonitzer, Christine Laurent, and Jacques Rivette; based on the novel *Le Chef-d' oeuvre inconnu* (*The Unknown Masterpiece*), by Honoré de Balzac
Cinematography: William Lubtchansky
Editing: Nicole Lubtchansky
Production design: Manu de Chauvigny
Sound: Florion Eidenbenz
Makeup: Susan Robertson
Costume design: Laurence Struz
MPAA rating: no listing
Running time: 240 minutes

> *Principal characters:*
> Édouard Frenhofer .... Michel Piccoli
> Liz .... Jane Birkin
> Marianne .... Émmanuelle Béart
> Nicolas .... David Bursztein
> Julienne .... Marianne Denicourt
> Porbus .... Gilles Arbona
> The painter's hand .... Bernard Dufour

What are the elements in the film *La Belle Noiseuse* that make its extraordinary running time of 240 minutes go by so easily, even gratifyingly? To be truthful, one must not underestimate the delight in beholding the physical beauty of Marianne (Émmanuelle Béart), who spends a large percentage of the four hours unclothed posing for artist Édouard Frenhofer (Michel Piccoli). The viewer shares the artist's perspective as he scrutinizes his subject, perusing her surface in his search for the soul that resides within.

The film's rewards, however, go far beyond the perusal of mere surfaces. Being privy to the creative process of a presumably great artist as he painstakingly proceeds from numerous exploratory sketches to the almost indiscernible realization of his subject's inner truth is as much drama as one might wish. Much footage is spent on closeups of the painter's hand (Bernard Dufour's) as it works, traveling its course of discovery—first with pen-and-ink sketches scratched in a pad, then with charcoal on large sheets of white paper, and finally with paint on canvas. The viewer never sees more than Dufour's hands and parts of his arms as he draws—as it is Piccoli who is playing Frenhofer—but his contribution to the film's success is inestimable. Perhaps more than twenty percent of the running time is spent with the artist at work; the viewer is allowed to see much of the actual process. For example, during the first ink sketches, a strict unity of time is employed: Every moment that it takes the artist to produce those three drawings is there on the screen. The privilege of watching the artist at work is itself worth the price of admission.

Yet, the film offers still much more: A complex human drama unfolds in conjunction with the artist's attempt to achieve his creative objective. Marianne at first complains because her lover, the young artist Nicolas (David Bursztein), has volunteered her services as a model without consulting her. Soon, however, she is involved in the task, and she eventually encourages Frenhofer to persist when he gets discouraged. It is interesting to consider her possible motives for posing, especially because the job involves sustaining uncomfortable, sometimes torturous, postures for long periods of time. Frenhofer contorts her body, twisting her limbs this way and that, telling her that he is going to break her, to crumble her, and then to see what is left. He says that he wants to see the inside of her body. Does she put up with all of this because she wants to be immortalized in a masterpiece? Is her patience attributable to her recognition that she is part of something important? Is she posing primarily to spite Nicolas, who she suspects is jealous?

Nicolas admires the early work of Frenhofer, who has been inactive for a decade; his desire to see the older man working again is what motivated his offer of Marianne. As she becomes increasingly involved, however, he experiences some anxiety and twinges of jealousy; he waits around hoping for the early completion or abandonment of the work. Frenhofer's wife, Liz (Jane Birkin), experiences a comparable jealousy. She is grateful that Frenhofer is at work, but her feelings are mixed because Marianne is, in effect, replacing her as the model for *La Belle Noiseuse*, a painting he abandoned ten years earlier. She is deeply hurt when he takes one of the old canvases with her likeness and paints over it the naked form of Marianne. The story's quietly startling conclusion is perfect but is better left to the discovery of those who view the film.

Director Jacques Rivette utilizes a realistic style, often with a minimum of editing. Although, at times, it is necessary to cut frequently between the painter's hand (Dufour's) and head shots of Frenhofer (Piccoli) as he observes his subject, more often there are lingering shots of the artist's hand at work (with only the sounds of the pen scratching paper and the breathing of the artist as accompaniment) or Marianne as she moves around the studio looking at the recent drawings. In one instance, the entire screen is filled with the large canvas containing the old drawing that Frenhofer is almost obliterating; the shot is held for a long duration while he brushes fresh paint over much of the area.

Numerous realistic details contribute to the impression that nothing is contrived. The viewer is witnessing a portion of these characters' lives however they happen to unfold; the camera is running and will record all. The camera follows Frenhofer and Liz down corridors as they move from one room to another in their large abbey of a home. Frenhofer's pants are wrinkled, and interior walls flaky with old paint. The bland maid serves food so unobtrusively that one hardly notices her presence. When

Frenhofer has his first session with Marianne, a seemingly interminable amount of time is spent on the artist's preparatory ritual: He must clean old inkpots, clear away unneeded objects, and put his tools in their precisely proper places.

It is Piccoli among the actors who contributes most to this sense of reality. He is always driven by the character's intentions, which are many and continually shifting. Frenhofer moves in one direction—to get a blank canvas, perhaps—but then remembers something else and moves in another direction. He is unwrapping a package, the tea arrives, and he abandons the package half-wrapped. His head is filled with so many details that one never knows which will suddenly take precedence.

Béart is almost as good, and certain scenes between Marianne and Frenhofer could serve as acting lessons on interaction. Their first session together is awkward; it is difficult to know which of them is more ill at ease. The studio must be made fit for work. Although she says nothing, her eyes seem to rebuke him for being unprepared. Finally, work commences and it is clear that she must eventually undress, but neither mentions the subject. The tension causes him to pour too much ink over the face of the first sketch, obliterating all of its detail. Turning the page of the drawing pad, he starts a second sketch. Her stare disturbs him, he says. Finally, he tells her where there is a dressing gown. When they are ready to begin work again, she drops the gown to the floor without being asked, but one can see in her eyes how vulnerable she feels. The day ends without much sense of accomplishment on either part. This scene contrasts strikingly with a much later one in which both have learned to relax with each other. They laugh and talk together as she moves around the room smoking a cigarette during a break without having bothered to cover her nakedness.

Cinematographer William Lubtchansky serves Rivette's style with a camera always unobtrusively present through a range of shots from a variety of angles and distances, making prominent whatever the viewer should be effortlessly watching. Lubtchansky has worked extensively with Rivette and with another director of the French New Wave, Jean-Luc Godard; he has also shot two documentaries for Claude Lanzmann, including the monumental *Shoah* (1985). His previous experience seems to have been a perfect preparation for the task of shooting this prodigious work.

The screenplay is based on the novel *Le Chef-d' oeuvre inconnu* (1831; *The Unknown Masterpiece*) by Honoré de Balzac that has had significant meaning for many artists. Pablo Picasso once illustrated a special edition of it, and Paul Cézanne declared that his favorite character in all literature was Frenhofer. Perhaps artists recognize the genuineness of Frenhofer the artist and empathize as he stumbles and struggles through the creative process. Rivette's *La Belle Noiseuse* may be one of a handful of films that is capable of speaking intimately to artists—of whatever medium. Yet, the film also has the directness, the uncluttered simplicity and psychological complexity, the honesty and universality, to speak powerfully to others as well. *La Belle Noiseuse* was awarded the Grand Prix at the 1991 Cannes Film Festival, earning for Rivette, one of the least internationally recognized of the directors of the French New Wave, well-earned acclaim.

Cono Robert Marcazzo

Reviews

Art in America. LXXX, January, 1992, p. 61.
Boxoffice. January, 1992, p. R-4.
Chicago Tribune. May 16, 1991, I, p. 28.
The Christian Science Monitor. October 23, 1991, p. 14.
Film Comment. XXVII, November, 1991, p. 46.
Los Angeles Times. November 8, 1991, p. F1.
The New Republic. CCV, November 4, 1991, p. 26.
New York Magazine. XXIV, November 18, 1991, p. 92.
The New York Times. October 2, 1991, p. B2.
Rolling Stone. October 31, 1991, p. 99.
Sight and Sound. I, July, 1991, p. 6.
Time. CXXXVIII, October 28, 1991, p. 101.
Variety. May 14, 1991, p. 2.
The Village Voice. XXXVI, October 2, 1991, p. 75.

BILLY BATHGATE

Production: Arlene Donovan and Robert F. Colesberry for Touchstone Pictures, in association with Touchwood Pacific Partners I; released by Buena Vista
Direction: Robert Benton
Screenplay: Tom Stoppard; based on the book by E. L. Doctorow
Cinematography: Nestor Almendros
Editing: Alan Heim, Robert Reitano, and David Ray
Production design: Patrizia von Brandenstein
Art direction: Tim Galvin, Dennis Bradford, and John Willett
Set decoration: George DeTitta, Sr., and Hilton Rosemarin
Casting: Howard Feuer
Sound: Danny Michael
Costume design: Joseph G. Aulisi
Choreography: Pat Birch
Music: Mark Isham
MPAA rating: R
Running time: 106 minutes

Principal characters:
Dutch Schultz . . . . Dustin Hoffman
Drew Preston . . . . Nicole Kidman
Billy Bathgate . . . . Loren Dean
Bo Weinberg . . . . Bruce Willis
Otto Berman . . . . Steven Hill
Irving . . . . Steve Buscemi
Mickey . . . . Billy Jaye
Lulu . . . . John Costelloe
Dixie Davis . . . . Tim Jerome
Lucky Luciano . . . . Stanley Tucci
Julie Martin . . . . Mike Starr
Jack Kelly . . . . Robert F. Colesberry

Based on an acclaimed 1989 novel by E. L. Doctorow, one of the most highly regarded of contemporary American novelists, *Billy Bathgate* is an appropriate vehicle for director Robert Benton and star Dustin Hoffman, who have dealt with similar material before. Benton and Hoffman have also worked together successfully, winning Academy Awards for *Kramer vs. Kramer* (1979). This collaboration is an evocative, often compelling portrait of innocence in conflict with evil.

Billy (Loren Dean), a teenager in the 1930's, grows up in the Bronx admiring the local gangsters. When the most famous of them all, the legendary Dutch Schultz (Dustin Hoffman), sees Billy juggling on a railroad trestle, he gives the boy ten dollars, which Billy immediately spends on a gun. Desperate to be part of the Schultz mob, Billy cons his way into Dutch's headquarters by pretending to be a numbers runner. Dutch—born Arthur Flegenheimer and referred to by his real name for most of the film—is impressed by the boy's audacity and hires him to sweep up and run errands. Billy, who adopts his last name from a street in his neighborhood, gradually becomes the gangsters' mascot and good-luck charm.

Dutch sometimes likes having the boy around; at other times, however, Billy's watching his every move irritates him. Billy witnesses Dutch having the feet of the disloyal Bo Weinberg (Bruce Willis) placed in a tub of cement preparatory to drowning the traitor. Dutch commits the murder in front of Bo's married mistress, Drew Preston (Nicole Kidman), and immediately appropriates her as his own. Only momentarily flustered, the socialite is attracted to dangerous men, and Dutch is obviously even more dangerous than Bo. Soon, she is calling him "my gangster."

Although puzzled by how Drew can switch allegiances so casually and by her relationship with her homosexual husband, Billy is drawn to the sophisticated, elegant woman whose world is even more foreign to him than that of the gangster. When the pressures of an ongoing investigation into his activities and upcoming tax evasion trial force Dutch into temporary exile in the sleepy upstate New York village of Onondaga, Billy is given the extra duty of escorting Drew when her gangster is otherwise occupied. Drew is drawn to Billy's innocence almost as much as he is to her sophistication, and they become lovers. When Dutch turns against her and has one of his henchmen follow her to Saratoga to shoot her at the racetrack, Billy saves her through complicated maneuverings and luck.

Back in New York, Dutch sees his shaky empire about to topple through the efforts of the government and rival gangs. Time is passing him by, just as it did the outlaws in the old West. As crime becomes more organized and corporate, Dutch refuses to recognize that he is a living anachronism. Growing more and more paranoid, Dutch is finally assassinated, along with his henchmen, by the mob of Lucky Luciano (Stanley Tucci), a gangster on the rise. Only Billy is spared.

Benton has dealt with this type of material on several occasions. With David Newman, he cowrote the classic *Bonnie and Clyde* (1967), which depicts the danger, the violence, and the romance of being outlaws during the Depression. Young innocents discovering the world of crime—with its attendant sense of freedom accompanied by death—is the subject of *Bad Company* (1972), Benton's first film as a director. He also treated murder in *Still of the Night* (1982), the Depression in *Places in the Heart* (1984), and small-time criminals in *Nadine* (1987) and *The Late Show* (1977), his most fully realized film. *Billy Bathgate* thus deals with typical Benton concerns, and he was clearly drawn to the film by its contrasting themes of innocence and corruption. Billy admires gangsters out of naïveté, and the film depicts his education in violence and vileness. Billy not only witnesses Bo's murder but also sees Dutch impulsively kill a police officer on the take by beating his head into the floor and shoot an uncooperative union official in the mouth at close range. The sudden, unexpected violence of these scenes makes them the most memorable, if disturbing, in the film—especially the latter, with the huge union official drowning slowly as his blood pours into his lungs. Benton forces the audience to see such events through

Billy's eyes, and he is attracted by the glamour of gangsters yet repelled by their paranoia and violence.

The contrast between glamour and violence is best seen in the racetrack episode. As the colorfully dressed socialites gather in the grandstand to watch the races, only Billy knows that one of them is in danger. Spotting Dutch's gunman, he succeeds in placing obstacles between the would-be killer and his intended victim until her husband arrives to take her to safety, to all of which Drew is blithely unaware. The cutting back and forth between Drew, Billy, the gunman, and the surrounding scene of normalcy is handled expertly by editor Alan Heim, who has worked on such films as Bob Fosse's *Lenny* (1974) and *All That Jazz* (1979).

The most impressive technical achievement is that of production designer Patrizia von Brandenstein, whose credits include *Ragtime* (1981), also based on a Doctorow novel, and *The Untouchables* (1987). The period detail throughout the film is strongly evocative of the 1930's. Von Brandenstein has expertly converted Hamlet, North Carolina, where part of the film was made, into a small upstate New York town during the Depression. The most disappointing technical aspect of *Billy Bathgate* is the cinematography of Nestor Almendros. Best known for his work with François Truffaut and Eric Rohmer, Almendros is one of the great cinematographers of the 1970's and 1980's. His Academy Award-winning work on *Days of Heaven* (1978) resulted in one of the most visually striking films of all time. He collaborated brilliantly with Benton on *Kramer vs. Kramer*, *Still of the Night*, and *Places in the Heart*, but here his colors are too dark, too muted, making the film muddy. Somber lighting is appropriate for the subject, for deglamorizing gangsters, but the result is ugly, making the film seem unnecessarily depressing at times.

The performances in *Billy Bathgate* are also uneven. Dustin Hoffman has played criminals before: the brutal thief of *Straight Time* (1978) and the reluctant crook of *Family Business* (1989). He has also presented characters with both sympathetic and unsympathetic sides, as with the profane comedian in *Lenny* and the work-obsessed father in *Kramer vs. Kramer*. In *Billy Bathgate*, Hoffman attempts to create a character who is self-assured, gentlemanly, and quick-witted, much like his newspaper columnist in *Agatha* (1979), but who is also a vicious, ruthless animal capable of anything to protect his power. Portraying a gangster who knows he should look at every side of an issue before acting yet who cannot keep himself from responding impulsively, Hoffman dominates the screen. He is full of pent-up energy, longing to burst out of the tuxedos and three-piece suits that mask Dutch's true nature. The problem with such a commanding performance is that the central character is Billy, with Hoffman reduced for the most part to a supporting role.

Impressive in even smaller parts are Stanley Tucci, whose Lucky Luciano is a subtler version of the mobster whom he played in the television series *Wiseguy*, and the much-maligned Bruce Willis, playing Bo Weinberg with a subdued humor and self-assurance instead of his trademark smirk. Even better is the veteran character actor Steven Hill as Otto "Abbadabba" Berman, Dutch's accountant and strategist and Billy's mentor. Otto becomes the film's moral center, as he is fond of his boss and eager to save him yet realistic enough to know that he will fail. Hill's deliveries provide Otto with calmness, confidence, dignity, and reason to contrast with the chaos raging around him.

The weakest performances are those of Nicole Kidman and Loren Dean. Kidman, impressive in *Dead Calm* (1989), her debut film, makes little impression here, perhaps because she is too much a modern woman trapped in a period straitjacket. Attempting to exude an air of mystery, she generates only blandness, like an adolescent dressed up in her mother's clothes. Resembling Melanie Griffith in one shot, Sigourney Weaver in another, and Penelope Ann Miller in another, Kidman fails to establish any distinctive qualities for Drew. Loren Dean seems too old and physically mature for Billy, who is fifteen in the novel. He conveys a certain presence and intelligence when he speaks or has something to do. Unfortunately, the nature of the film calls on him to be an observer much of the time, and as an observer, Dean is as blank as a wall, not yet having learned to act without dialogue or some physical business. That Dean is unable to convey Doctorow's conception of Billy as a mixture of romantic and realist whose moral growth is the point of the novel is as much the failing of Benton and screenwriter Tom Stoppard as it is the actor's.

Despite such drawbacks, *Billy Bathgate* is reasonably successful as drama, engaging the intellect in its portrayal of the corruption inherent in power and the blindness created by the ruthless quest for success. The film received mostly lukewarm reviews because it had the bad luck to appear during a period when several other gangster films had been released. Several reviewers even admitted boredom with the genre. *Billy Bathgate* lacks the operatic sweep of Francis Ford Coppola's *The Godfather, Part III* (1990) and the frenetic energy of Martin Scorsese's *GoodFellas* (1990). Benton, directing the first film that he has not written, takes perhaps too objective an approach for viewers expecting something visceral or larger than life.

Michael Adams

Reviews
Boxoffice. December, 1991, p. R-91.
Chicago Tribune. November 1, 1991, VII, p. C39.
The Christian Science Monitor. November 19, 1991, p. 11.
The Hollywood Reporter. October 28, 1991, p. 7.
Los Angeles Times. November 1, 1991, p. F1.
The Nation. XXV, December 2, 1991, p. 717.
The New Republic. CCV, November 25, 1991, p. 30.
The New York Times. November 1, 1991, p. B1.
Newsweek. CXVIII, November 4, 1991, p. 79.
Time. CXXXVIII, November 4, 1991, p. 95.
Variety. October 29, 1991, p. 3.
The Wall Street Journal. October 31, 1991, p. A20.
The Washington Post. November 1, 1991, p. B1.

BLACK ROBE

Origin: Canada and Australia
Released: 1991
Released in U.S.: 1991
Production: Robert Lantos, Stephane Reichel, and Sue Milliken for Alliance Communications and Samson Productions; released by the Samuel Goldwyn Company
Direction: Bruce Beresford
Screenplay: Brian Moore; based on his novel
Cinematography: Peter James
Editing: Tim Wellburn
Production design: Herbert Pinter
Casting: Clare Walker
Sound: Gary Wilkins
Costume design: Renee April and John Hay
Cree dialogue consultation: Helen Bobbish Atkinson
Mohawk dialogue consultation: Billy Two Rivers
Music: Georges Delerue
MPAA rating: R
Running time: 100 minutes

Principal characters:
Father Laforgue	Lothaire Bluteau
Daniel	Aden Young
Annuka	Sandrine Holt
Chomina	August Schellenberg
Chomina's wife	Tantoo Cardinal
Father Jerome	Frank Wilson
Ougebemat	Billy Two Rivers
Neehatin	Lawrence Bayne
Awandoie	Harrison Liu
Mestigoit	Yvan Labelle

Black Robe is based on the best-selling 1985 novel of the same title by the popular Canadian author Brian Moore. The protagonist, Father Laforgue (Lothaire Bluteau), is intended to represent all the courageous Jesuit priests who came to the Canadian wilderness in the seventeenth century hoping to convert the Native Americans to Christianity. Bluteau is a rather frail and ascetic-looking man who once played Jesus Christ in *Jesus of Montreal* (1989). He is a competent actor, but he has a difficult task because the story turns on what takes place inside his character's mind as a result of his exposure to the perils and temptations of this cruel and beautiful new land.

Whereas the Spanish friars seemed to have had a relatively easy job of converting the inhabitants of Central and South America to Christianity, *Black Robe* shows that the French Jesuits were facing an almost insurmountable task in the north. The natives, whom they referred to as "savages," regarded the "blackrobes" as sorcerers and believed that the baptism that the Jesuits offered was a means of destroying the native population. There was an element of truth to this belief, because the white people were bringing previously unknown diseases, such as smallpox, that were devastating to the native inhabitants. Because Moore wrote the screenplay himself, he was able to retain his novel's prevailing mood of uncanniness, which is evoked by the contrast between primitive Native Americans and seventeenth century Europeans just emerging from the barbarity and superstition of the Dark Ages.

With winter coming on, the idealistic young Father Laforgue must travel fifteen hundred miles by canoe in order to reach a remote mission in the Huron territory where two Jesuits may or may not still be alive. He is to be guided by a group of Algonquins and assisted by a young translator named Daniel (Aden Young), whose earthiness and lustiness stand in sharp contrast to the asceticism of the Jesuit priest. The cinematography features extreme long shots of canoes that seem lost on the sparkling expanses of water and dwarfed by the jagged mountains cloaked with silent evergreens.

Daniel complicates matters by falling in love with Annuka (Sandrine Holt), the daughter of the Algonquin chief, Chomina (August Schellenberg), who is leading the expedition. Annuka, like the other Indian women, has an uninhibited attitude toward sex. The film contains several very graphic scenes of sexual intercourse in which the man enters the woman from the rear. (These scenes, which are faithful to the text of the novel, were responsible for getting the film an R rating.) Father Laforgue, who has taken a vow of chastity, is tormented by the display of such sexual abandon. At the same time, the Algonquins cannot understand how a man who preaches about love and paradise can envision a heaven without the natural pleasures to be derived by carnal relations between men and women. They all regard him as a sorcerer. Laforgue obviously cannot fit in with them in any way. He is repelled by their manners, their smells, and their habit of all sleeping together in a heap and openly engaging in animal-like sexual intercourse. Even Daniel turns against Laforgue when the priest tries to separate the two lovers. Eventually, the Algonquins abandon Laforgue and paddle away, taking Annuka with them. Daniel has made a solemn vow to remain with the priest, but in the end he cannot bear to be torn from Annuka and desperately paddles after her in a canoe.

Laforgue is left in an impossible situation. He is a scholar and an urbanite. He is so dependent on his native guides that he easily gets lost in the forest when he wanders away from camp, and he has no knowledge of how to live off the land. His faith is rewarded, however, when Chomina has a change of heart and decides to honor his vow to protect the "blackrobe" entrusted to his care by the formidable representative of French power in America, Samuel de Champlain. When the Algonquins and Daniel return to where they had left Laforgue, they encounter a hunting party of hostile Iroquois who murder Chomina's wife (Tantoo Cardinal). The Iroquois carry the survivors by canoe back to their own grim, fortress-like village, where the most horrifying scenes in the film occur.

Laforgue, Daniel, Annuka, and Chomina are turned over to the chief, who forces them to strip naked and subjects them to fiendish tortures. Finally, he cuts off one of Laforgue's fingers with a razor-sharp clam shell. In these harrowing scenes, the viewer is made to understand why the French referred to the Native Americans as savages. The only film comparable to *Black Robe* in its depiction of the cruelty of Native Americans is *A Man Called Horse* (1970).

Laforgue's religious faith is sorely tested by this encounter: He wonders whether it is possible or even desirable to bring Christianity to such vicious people. The captives are tightly bound and left in the custody of one of the Iroquois braves while the chief and some of his subordinates discuss what to do with them. It seems evident that Chomina and his daughter will be killed and that the Iroquois will try to obtain ransom for the two Frenchmen in the form of muskets, gunpowder, and ammunition.

Late at night, Annuka painfully crawls over to the Indian guard and begs for a drink of water. She intentionally arouses the guard, who cuts the thongs binding her arms and legs in order to have sexual intercourse with her from behind. The viewer is further horrified to see Annuka submitting to the guard's lust while her father, her lover Daniel, and the priest lie there listening to the grunting and moaning of the bestial encounter. Annuka takes advantage of the guard's distraction to pick up a heavy club and bring it down on his head with all the strength in both her arms. She releases the other captives, and they slink out of the village in the mist of dawn.

Instead of retreating back the way they had come, Laforgue persuades the others to continue the journey toward the Huron country. Eventually, Chomina dies of the injuries that he had sustained at the hands of the Iroquois, and Daniel and Annuka leave to live with her people. The dedicated priest continues paddling upriver until he reaches the Jesuit mission in a fortified Huron village. One of the priests is dead, the other is dying. Laforgue finds that the white people's diseases have decimated the Hurons. He convinces them that their salvation lies in the baptism that he has to offer, and eventually he succeeds in his mission to baptize the entire tribe.

The film ends with a printed statement that, after accepting Christianity, the Hurons were eventually wiped out by their enemies, the Iroquois. This depressing conclusion leaves the audience with a feeling similar to that of another spectacular but disappointing film, *The Mission* (1986). It is difficult to empathize with the white protagonists when it is so obvious that, no matter how dedicated and well intentioned they might be, they can bring nothing with their culture or science but death and destruction.

Some novels are easily adapted to cinematic drama, and others suffer by the transition. The biggest problem with *Black Robe* as a film is that it is impossible to understand the protagonist Father Laforgue, and consequently, it is impossible to identify with him. In the novel, there was no such problem: The author simply told the reader what was going on inside his hero's mind. In the film, however, the viewer can only observe Laforgue from the outside, and no actor is skillful enough to convey all the turmoil that was going on inside novelist Brian Moore's character.

Normally, in a cinematic adaptation of a novel, the protagonist's subjective state is conveyed to the audience either by means of dialogue spoken to a confidant or else with the rather clumsy device of a filtered voice-over monologue representing the protagonist's stream of consciousness. In *Black Robe*, the Jesuit missionary has no one in whom to confide. The screenwriter and director rely on close-ups of Bluteau's face, and the viewer is supposed to deduce what Laforgue is thinking. There are a few brief flashbacks to Laforgue's earlier life in France; these, however, only attempt to establish his strong motivation and do nothing to explain his inner conflicts in the New World. The lonely heroes of *Man in the Wilderness* (1971) and *Jeremiah Johnson* (1972) had no one to confide in either, but they were only faced with the practical matter of staying alive. Father Laforgue's practical concerns include sheer survival, traveling fifteen hundred miles in winter with undependable guides, and converting hostile Native Americans to Christianity. His spiritual concerns include clinging to his religious faith, fighting his sexual urges, and learning to love a people that he instinctively detests.

Black Robe has a seriousness that commands respect. Audiences watch with awe but are puzzled and ultimately disappointed. The characters in this beautifully photographed film seem dwarfed by nature. The film ends up being more informative than emotionally satisfying and seeming more like a documentary than a drama.

Bill Delaney

Reviews
America. CLXVI, January 18, 1992, p. 38.
American Cinematographer. LXXIII, January, 1992, p. 26.
Boxoffice. December, 1991, p. R-93.
Chicago Tribune. November 1, 1991, VII, p. 45.
The Christian Science Monitor. November 19, 1991, p. 10.
Commonweal. CXIX, January 17, 1992, p. 17.
The Hollywood Reporter. September 9, 1991, p. 5.
Los Angeles Times. November 6, 1991, p. F1.
The New York Times. October 30, 1991, p. C15.
The New York Times. November 3, 1991, p. B21.
Time. CXXXVIII, December 30, 1991, p. 71.
Variety. September 6, 1991, p. 3.
The Washington Post. November 8, 1991, p. B7.

BOYZ 'N THE HOOD

Production: Steve Nicolaides for New Deal; released by Columbia Pictures
Direction: John Singleton
Screenplay: John Singleton
Cinematography: Charles Mills
Editing: Bruce Cannon
Art direction: Bruce Bellamy
Set decoration: Kathryn Peters
Casting: Jaki Brown
Sound: Veda Campbell
Costume design: Darryle Johnson and Shirlene Williams
Music: Stanley Clarke
MPAA rating: R
Running time: 111 minutes

Principal characters:
Tre Styles .... Cuba Gooding, Jr.
Ricky Baker .... Morris Chestnut
Doughboy .... Ice Cube
Furious Styles .... Larry Fishburne
Brandi .... Nia Long
Mrs. Baker .... Tyra Ferrell
Reva Styles .... Angela Bassett
Brandi's mother .... Meta King
The old man .... Whitman Mayo
Tre (ten years old) .... Desi Arnez Hines II
Doughboy (ten years old) .... Baha Jackson
Ricky (ten years old) .... Donovan McCrary

John Singleton's advice for young African-American filmmakers trying to break into the industry is "know your history, know where you're from." The twenty-three-year-old writer/director's first feature film follows this recommendation. *Boyz 'n the Hood* is an autobiographical, keen, and unapologetic look at the world in which Singleton grew up, his old " 'hood," the predominantly African-American community of South-Central Los Angeles. His focus, not surprisingly, is on the young African-American males who live—or try to live—in that world, where physical and psychological violence threatens constantly.

Boyz 'n the Hood spans seven years in the lives of three boys whose friendship binds them despite their disparate goals or their very different views of what opportunity the world has afforded them. When the story opens, the boys are ten years old, and Tre Styles (Desi Arnez Hines II), the main character, has just been handed over by his divorced mom, Reva Styles (Angela Bassett), to her former husband, Furious Styles (Larry Fishburne). Reva believes that Furious can teach his son to be a man. She will not be disappointed. Self-assured, even-tempered, and filled with a calm authority, Furious proves to be a wise father. He plays ball with his son, takes him for long walks, loves him, talks to him, and drills into him lessons for living. He is authoritarian in manner but is nevertheless understanding and warm. In an intimate scene as father and son stroll along the beach, young Tre recites the three rules of leadership. One rule, for example, is never respect anyone who does not respect you back.

Furious also tries to teach his son about sex and taking responsibility for its consequences. He says to Tre as they walk that "any fool . . . can make a baby, but only a real man can raise children." Furious asks why African-American brothers are slaughtering one another and even proposes the idea that whites might want it that way. The film suggests that considering radical ideas such as this one, whether true or false, may keep young African-American men from falling into violence and waste by galvanizing their sense of community responsibility. The film also insists on the necessity of a male authority, a father figure, to teach and reinforce responsible behavior in young men.

The way in which Furious rears his son is contrasted with the way Mrs. Baker (Tyra Ferrell) rears Ricky Baker (Donovan McCrary) and his half brother, Doughboy (Baha Jackson), who are Tre's best friends. Ricky and Doughboy have different fathers, and Mrs. Baker's treatment of her sons reflects her different feelings for these absent men. She dotes on and pampers Ricky, whom she hopes will go to college (she relentlessly encourages him to pursue football). Doughboy, however, she constantly chastises and belittles: "You ain't shit, just like your daddy." Ricky, given too much easy love, grows babyish and lazy. Doughboy, as expected, falls into a life of crime.

The ten-year-olds face a battery of neighborhood hazards: intimidation by a gang of older boys and the fear, fascination, and guilt aroused by the discovery of a decomposing body during one of their football games. Meanwhile, airplanes flying in low over the cheap tract houses toward Los Angeles International Airport drone constantly, and the police helicopters patrolling the neighborhood beat the air with their incessant jarring noise, a reminder that there is a war going on. This first section includes a scene of a heated confrontation between Furious and a cynical African-American police officer who is dispatched to the neighborhood on a routine call. It contrasts two common responses to the problems of African-American youth: try to teach and understand them or beat them down to silence them. Part 1 ends as Doughboy is driven away in a patrol car after his mother has turned him in for some petty crime.

Seven years later, the boys are high school seniors—Ricky (now played by Morris Chestnut) and Tre (Cuba Gooding, Jr.) are preparing to graduate, while Doughboy (Ice Cube) and his shiftless friends lounge perpetually, drinking cheap beer on Mrs. Baker's front porch. Singleton's writing shines in this group's well-honed dialogue, which is both comic and poignantly sad because it reveals their street smarts and sense of humor as well as their yearnings and illusions. "Nice boy" Tre is reintroduced as the shining star of the neighborhood; he is a good student and holds a steady job at the mall. He and his beautiful girlfriend, devout Catholic and very studious Brandi (Nia

Long), talk about sex but abstain. Meanwhile, it is revealed that Ricky—still unashamedly pampered by his mother—has fathered a child at the age of sixteen. His one-year-old son and girl-wife live with the Baker family.

Yet, the most interesting character at this point is Doughboy, who, despite his intelligence and his loving nature (he is aptly named), is becoming more self-destructive and violent to others. He has given up trying to prove his worth to his mother, who still rejects him. Instead, Doughboy loves his hot rod and his tough image, packs a pistol, and hoots at the man in a suit who comes to interview Ricky for a football scholarship. He talks disparagingly to women and is happy to answer petty insults from other boys on the strip at night by a display of gun power. Yet, thanks to rap musician Ice Cube's inspired performance, Doughboy's gentle if broken heart still glows through all of his dead-end snarling bravado. In addition, he views his suffering matter-of-factly. Doughboy represents both surly acceptance of the tragic conditions of ghetto life and, paradoxically, the grim determination that Singleton suggests is necessary for these youths' survival.

The story works toward its climax during a turbulent night which begins on the strip. Ricky inadvertently insults a gang member by tripping over him and withholding apology; Doughboy offers to uphold his brother's honor by getting out his gun. The rival gang responds with machine-gun fire from their car, which sends Ricky, Tre, and dozens of other cruising kids running for cover. Before the boys can get home, however, they are pulled over by the cynical African-American police officer introduced earlier. He is a frustrated man who uses his power to demean and abuse Tre so cruelly that the teenager is pushed beyond the point of emotional tolerance. This dark, harrowing scene and the scene that follows, in which a terrified and anguished Tre seeks Brandi's comfort, lead to the film's conclusion.

In a chance encounter, Ricky is gunned down by the gang from the strip, and Doughboy and his gang resolve to take revenge. Tre is torn between his desire to avenge Ricky's death, his need to follow his father's advice, and his own realization that violence cannot be answered with violence. He steals Furious' gun and joins the manhunt, but he soon asks Doughboy to let him out of the car. As in a parable, good triumphs over evil. Tre's inner strength guides him away from a lethal encounter, and the bad boys pursuing revenge will not, of course, have long to survive.

But perhaps the film's message is not so blunt; the story toys with existential complexities. Given the tough conditions that these young men face, one has to wonder how Tre can manage to escape the vacuum of drugs and violence for the haven of faraway Atlanta University, where he will live in a dormitory across from Brandi's. He has a smart, caring father and mother. He is self-disciplined. He makes a great effort to turn all the right corners. Yet, Ricky's absurd and tragic death makes Tre's success, ironically, seem more like a miracle of fortune than a reward for studiousness and determination. Ricky happened to be on the wrong street at the wrong time. That was why he died, not really because he was irresponsible and lazy. In fact, only Doughboy seems to have any control over his fate—another ironic twist. Doughboy knows with all certainty that avenging his brother's death will guarantee his own murder. Yet, he embraces his fate, as tragic figures must, and murders the three terrified punks in a savagely brutal scene which leaves the viewer feeling as shattered as Doughboy looks the next morning when he greets Tre at dawn to talk quietly about death and what is left of life.

Singleton's coming-of-age film won critics over, despite some complaints about its violence creating more violence (opening night riots left two dead), its didacticism, and what one critic considered its too-typically Hollywood conventions for filming the street fighting scenes. The main character, added some critics, is too good, and Doughboy is too predictably bad. Singleton is a gifted screenwriter and director, however, and most critics agreed that he successfully translated the strife of the streets and the energy of the hard-core rap culture into uniquely committed cinematic language. The violence, although wrenching, is not gratuitous, and its message about the desperation of young African-American men—and women, less directly—is candid and urgent. It is a moving film. In a year during which nineteen films by African-American directors were scheduled for release, Singleton's debut effort was one of the most impressive, and most critics agreed that it deserved attention.

Boyz 'n the Hood turned out to be, in fact, the highest grossing black-themed film ever released as well as the single most profitable new film of 1991. And when newcomer Singleton was nominated for a Best Director Academy Award, he became not only the youngest filmmaker ever to enjoy that honor but the first African-American director to be nominated for the award. This achievement was extraordinary for a person fresh out of film school at age twenty-four, without extensive experience in film, television, or theater.

Singleton maintains that the main purpose of his film is to inform, and he openly acknowledges his debt to veteran director Spike Lee, who made *Do the Right Thing* (1989), *Mo' Better Blues* (1990), and *Jungle Fever* (1991; reviewed in this volume). Singleton points out that he paved the way for other African-American directors to tell stories about their own experiences and about African-American communities. Without the proof of Lee's success, Singleton's own demand to direct his script, he believes, would have been rejected at Columbia Pictures.

Singleton also acknowledges receiving inspiration for *Boyz 'n the Hood* from Hector Babenco's *Pixote* (1981), the sobering account of disenfranchised children negotiating a bleak survival in the hostile streets of Rio de Janeiro. The two films share themes. The ability of the boys to navigate their lives through an indifferent and violent world is compromised fatally for those who do not have strong family support.

Singleton admits to having a message and probably is not bothered by those who have called the film—justly so—somewhat preachy and didactic. He is passionate and vocal about his belief in the direct correlation between African-American self-annihilation and the disintegration of the African-American family unit. He has said the film's underlying message is "Take care of your children," and he has maintained that "brothers have got to have more responsibility raising their children"—especially their sons.

JoAnn Balingit

Reviews
Boxoffice. September, 1991, p. R-61.
Chicago Tribune. July 12, 1991, VII, p. 33.
The Christian Science Monitor. July 12, 1991, p. 12.
Entertainment Weekly. March 13, 1992, p. 56.
Film Review. November, 1991, p. 35.
The Hollywood Reporter. May 15, 1991, p. 12.
Los Angeles Times. July 12, 1991, p. F1.
New York Magazine. July 22, 1991, p. 40.
The New York Times. July 12, 1991, p. B1.
The New York Times Magazine. July 14, 1991, p. 15.
Newsweek. July 15, 1991, p. 56.
Newsweek. July 22, 1991, p. 57.
People Weekly. July 22, 1991, p. 12.
Rolling Stone. September 5, 1991, p. 73.
Sight and Sound. August, 1991, p. 10.
Time. CXXXVIII, July 22, 1991, p. 12.
Variety. May 14, 1991, p. 2.
The Wall Street Journal. July 18, 1991, p. A9.
The Washington Post. July 12, 1991, p. F1.

BUGSY

Production: Mark Johnson, Barry Levinson, and Warren Beatty for Mulholland
   Productions and Baltimore Pictures; released by TriStar Pictures
Direction: Barry Levinson
Screenplay: James Toback
Cinematography: Allen Daviau
Editing: Stu Linder
Production design: Dennis Gassner (AA)
Art direction: Leslie McDonald
Set decoration: Nancy Haigh (AA)
Set design: Lawrence A. Hubbs
Casting: Ellen Chenoweth
Sound: Willie D. Burton
Sound design: Richard Beggs
Special makeup effects: Rob Bottin
Costume design: Albert Wolsky (AA)
Music: Ennio Morricone
MPAA rating: R
Running time: 135 minutes

> *Principal characters:*
> Bugsy Siegel . . . . Warren Beatty
> Virginia Hill . . . . Annette Bening
> Mickey Cohen . . . . Harvey Keitel
> Meyer Lansky . . . . Ben Kingsley
> Harry Greenberg . . . . Elliott Gould
> George Raft . . . . Joe Mantegna
> Countess di Frasso . . . . Bebe Neuwirth
> Count di Frasso . . . . Gian-Carlo Scandiuzzi
> Esta Siegel . . . . Wendy Phillips
> Jack Dragna . . . . Richard Sarafian
> Joey Adonis . . . . Lewis Van Bergen
> Charlie Luciano . . . . Bill Graham
> Gus Greenbaum . . . . James Toback

If ever there was a film begging to be directed by Warren Beatty, then *Bugsy* was it. Beatty succeeded brilliantly in combining provocative political saga with a highly charged romance in *Reds* (1981), his ambitious film about American journalist John Reed's involvement with communism. *Bugsy*—with its big-time vision, old-fashioned glamour, and captivating main character—should have been the same sort of classic filmmaking, one of those films that ages well and intensifies over repeated viewings. As conceived by director Barry Levinson, however, *Bugsy* is for the most part forgettable. Shot with dreamy, romanticized camera work and highly stylized framing, the film is lethargic and fails to build to any emotional catharsis.

Mercurial New York gangster and womanizer Benjamin "don't call me Bugsy" Siegel (Beatty) is sent by fellow crime lords Meyer Lansky (Ben Kingsley) and Charlie "Lucky" Luciano (Bill Graham) to Los Angeles to gain control of the West Coast rackets from Jack Dragna (Richard Sarafian). Soon after his arrival, Siegel, a man determined to get what he wants, visits the film set of his good friend George Raft (Joe Mantegna) and there meets and is immediately smitten with a feisty bit player named Virginia Hill (Annette Bening). Hill is already involved with one of Siegel's mob associates, Joey Adonis (Lewis Van Bergen), but Bugsy will not be deterred by her fast talk and bitter edge. Soon Siegel, with the aid of the equally unstable Mickey Cohen (Harvey Keitel), plunges ahead in both his business and his love pursuits with a ferocity that frightens and excites Hill.

Much to the dismay of Lansky and Luciano, Siegel pursues a high-profile existence in Hollywood, appearing on more than a few society pages. When he meets an Italian count (Gian-Carlo Scandiuzzi), Siegel hatches a lunatic plot to kill Benito Mussolini. At the same time, he continues to pursue the ever-elusive Hill. As suspected, the relationship between Siegel and Hill is a volatile one. They come together, they tear apart. She taunts him with her other lovers and nags him to leave his wife. He wants her desperately yet never fully trusts her, and rightfully so. Despite its actual outcome, Siegel's vision of a luxury gambling resort in the desert proves to be his final downfall, costing six times what his partners had agreed to and costing Siegel his life.

Siegel is a captivating subject for a film, but *Bugsy* fails to combine effectively the violence and the romanticism that were obviously a part of the man's life. He was charming and dangerous, a man who had vision and yet was psychotically out of control. He was obsessive and possessive, yet caring and sensitive, particularly when it came to his wife, Esta (Wendy Phillips), and his two daughters. Perhaps Siegel was too elusive a character to grasp fully. Whatever the cause, the film has a start-and-stop feel to it. While the character may be schizophrenic, the filmmakers need to keep a clear vision in order for the film to be successful; in this case, they do not. The filmmakers strive to create a mythic legend, often ignoring fact in order to create a grand visionary out of a man who made "good copy": Siegel was not the first man to envision Las Vegas, and the Flamingo was apparently the brainchild of Los Angeles entrepreneur Billy Wilkerson.

Beatty realizes one of his most explosive performances, silencing those critics who have accused him of sleepwalking through some of his past roles. Beatty proves that he still possesses old-fashioned star magnetism by infusing Siegel with charm, wit, and temper. Prior to *Bugsy*, Beatty had been nominated for eleven Academy Awards as actor, producer, director, and writer, while the films that he had produced earned forty-four nominations. *Heaven Can Wait* (1978) and *Reds* were both nominated in all four major categories, an honor that Beatty shared only with the great Orson Welles.

Barry Levinson made his directorial debut with the semiautobiographical *Diner* (1982), an exploration of growing up that examined a group of friends who frequented a Baltimore diner in the 1950's. Levinson's fragmentation of the characters was succinctly mirrored by the style and form of the film. *Bugsy*, however, proved more complicated, forcing the director to deal with a single, self-contained (although somewhat schizophrenic) character through which the story was told. Levinson's meandering and predictable technique does not lend a cohesive structure to the film, resulting in interesting moments that miss their mark by failing to provide any emotional build. Levinson's other work includes *Tin Men* (1987), *Rain Man* (1988), and *Avalon* (1990), two of which are set in the director's hometown of Baltimore.

It took writer James Toback more than six years to complete his screenplay, which originally covered Siegel's entire life but was later trimmed to focus on the period of the gangster's arrival in Hollywood through the creation of the Flamingo in Las Vegas. *Bugsy* contains some tense, incisive, yet witty writing that tends to lose its edge under the more romanticized direction of Levinson, whose penchant for visually clever shot setups (such as the corny use of the obscuring projector screen when Siegel and Hill first connect) runs counter to the material. Beatty's decision not to direct *Bugsy* himself might be traced to his conflicts with Disney Studios over *Dick Tracy* (1990).

Without a doubt, one of the film's biggest flaws is the character of Virginia Hill, as well as actress Annette Bening's interpretation of the role. The character is alarmingly one-note, and once the film reaches its midway point there is nothing left to discover about Hill. Bening's performance is more annoying than interesting, and it is a relief when she leaves the audience alone with Bugsy to be charmed, seduced, and unnerved. Bening came into high profile with her Academy Award-nominated performance as the sexually beguiling con artist in Stephen Frears's *The Grifters* (1990) after gaining critical notice as the Marquise de Merteuil in *Valmont* (1989). In *Bugsy*, however, Bening fails to imbue her character with any depth, seemingly unable to make Virginia Hill both understandable and sympathetic, qualities that are necessary if the audience is to empathize with Siegel's infatuation. The hard-edged, opinionated character practically disappears on-screen as soon as the idea to build the Flamingo germinates, despite the fact that Hill provides one of the story's major plot devices.

Despite an extensive publicity campaign that helped to produce ten Academy Award nominations, including Best Picture, Director, and Actor, *Bugsy* garnered only two awards. These were both well deserved in the visual areas of Costume Design— Albert Wolsky—and Art Direction—for production designer Dennis Gassner and set decorator Nancy Haigh. Gassner and Haigh were also nominated for *Barton Fink* (1991; reviewed in this volume).

The press found the film's real-life context to be far more interesting than the film itself. Beatty has always been a man who has known how to manipulate the press and his offscreen romances to his advantage. (One need look no further for proof of his willingness to hype a current project than Beatty's involvement with *Dick Tracy* costar Madonna.) Many reporters were more intrigued by the romance between Beatty and Bening (and their newborn daughter) than with any discussion of *Bugsy* itself.

Patricia Kowal

Reviews

America. CLXVI, February 22, 1992, p. 146.
Boxoffice. February, 1992, p. R-11.
The Christian Science Monitor. December 24, 1991, p. 13.
Commonweal. CXIX, February 14, 1992, p. 17.
Film Comment. XXVIII, January, 1992, p. 28.
The Hollywood Reporter. CCCXX, December 5, 1991, p. 5.
Interview. XXI, December, 1991, p. 72.
Los Angeles Times. December 13, 1991, CXI, p. F1.
The New York Times. December 13, 1991, CXLI, p. B1.
The New Yorker. LXVII, December 30, 1991, p. 82.
Newsweek. CXVIII, December 16, 1991, p. 75.
Rolling Stone. January 9, 1992, p. 56.
Time. CXXXVIII, December 9, 1991, p. 90.
Variety. CCXXXIII, December 5, 1991, p. 2.
The Village Voice. December 17, 1991, XXXVI, p. 65.
The Washington Post. December 20, 1991, p. D1.

THE BUTCHER'S WIFE

Production: Wallis Nicita and Lauren Lloyd; released by Paramount Pictures
Direction: Terry Hughes
Screenplay: Ezra Litwak and Marjorie Schwartz
Cinematography: Frank Tidy
Editing: Donn Cambern
Production design: Charles Rosen
Art direction: Diane Yates
Set decoration: Donald J. Remacle
Casting: Gail Levin
Sound: Art Rochester
Costume design: Theadora Van Runkle
Psychic consultation: Maria Papapetros and Laura Day
Music: Michael Gore
MPAA rating: PG-13
Running time: 104 minutes

Principal characters:
Marina	Demi Moore
Alex Tremor	Jeff Daniels
Leo Lemke	George Dzundza
Stella Kefauver	Mary Steenburgen
Grace	Frances McDormand
Robyn Graves	Margaret Colin
Eugene	Max Perlich
Gina	Miriam Margolyes
Molly	Helen Hanft
Mr. Liddle	Christopher Durang

When Leo Lemke (George Dzundza), a confirmed bachelor, takes a fishing trip to the North Carolina coast, little does he realize that he will bring home a wife. *The Butcher's Wife* takes a somewhat whimsical look at how a middle-aged Lower Manhattan butcher copes with married life after he discovers that his new bride is clairvoyant.

A few days prior to Leo's arrival on Ocracoke Island, North Carolina, Marina (Demi Moore), possessing unusual gifts of clairvoyance, witnesses signs which suggest that her husband-to-be will soon arrive. Strange cloud formations and peculiar shapes in the sand are her evidence. A few days after stepping onto the shore of Ocracoke Island, Leo returns to his neighborhood and his shop with his beautiful young bride, Marina. Because this is such a close neighborhood, everyone knows of Leo's unusual and unexpected catch.

The moment that Marina arrives, Dr. Alex Tremor (Jeff Daniels), the local psychiatrist, notices something different about her. Little does he realize that Marina's naïveté and simplicity about her clairvoyant gift would upset not only him but also the majority of the patients that he is presently treating. One of the first people to speak with Marina is Alex's girlfriend, Robyn (Margaret Colin). After only the briefest of introductions, Marina explains to Robyn that she should make the first move if she wants to be with the one she loves. Robyn immediately asks Alex to marry her, but he is confounded by this sudden unexpected marriage proposal and is not able to respond. Robyn's explanation that it was Marina who had suggested that she make the first move upsets and annoys Alex.

Marina's clairvoyant talents also begin to upset Leo, who asks that Marina not speak to his customers about their personal lives. Leo decides to speak to Alex about the way in which his wife is acting. Equally, Alex wants to find out from Marina why she is causing such distress to his patients, particularly to Stella (Mary Steenburgen), the choir mistress, and a young delinquent named Eugene (Max Perlich) who is working in Leo's store. Marina agrees to see Alex only as a concession to Leo. Little seems to be achieved from this meeting other than the fact that Alex's equilibrium is further upset by Marina's unorthodox and unscientific ways of helping people who have problems. What does become clear is that Marina and Alex are attracted to each other. Marina suggests that, if Alex wants to get to know her better, he should come skating with her. Even though such an arrangement between doctor and patient is unorthodox and perhaps unprofessional, Alex agrees. This unusual therapy session only forges the couple's feelings toward each other.

Leo, who is confused, distraught, and a little angry at the way Marina is behaving, takes some solace at the local bar. Singing cabaret that evening is Stella. Earlier in the week, while shopping at a clothing store belonging to Grace (Frances McDormand), Marina had suggested to Stella that she follow her heart and sing the blues. Leo's despondency leaves him when Stella sings a rendition by the famous Bessie Smith—Leo's favorite blues singer. Stella is sensational and receives rapturous applause from the admiring Leo. Impulsively, Leo walks Stella home and confides in her the problems that he is having with his wife. Stella listens sympathetically, not realizing that the wife that Leo is speaking about is Marina.

Through clandestine meetings, Marina continues to see Alex and Leo furthers his relationship with Stella. Marina realizes that her marriage is over and decides to return to North Carolina. The once highly professional psychiatrist Dr. Tremor has become a bumbling neurotic wreck who seeks help from Grace, a friend and former patient. To his dismay, Alex finds that Grace and Robyn, his girlfriend, are dating each other. This unexpected revelation is the turning point for Alex, who finally realizes that Marina is the one he really loves. Alex sets off for Ocracoke Island. On his arrival, Alex finds Marina waiting patiently for him in the lookout tower. Clairvoyance in the hands of Marina was a blessing and a curse, but for now, all those who chanced to cross her mystical path are in happy, worthwhile relationships—including Alex.

The Butcher's Wife explores the story of what happens when a country girl with clairvoyant gifts offers her advice to city people who believe her words implicitly.

Certainly, the concept of exploring the mystical side of clairvoyancy seems appealing. In order to place Marina into the situation where she can work her "magic," a rather clumsy wedding is arranged between Marina and Leo. The device becomes even more clumsy when it becomes apparent that the writers, Ezra Litwak and Marjorie Schwartz, intend for Marina to fall in love with Alex. While the two come from different worlds, that difference becomes inconsequential when they do actually fall in love with each other. In fact, each of the relationships in *The Butcher's Wife* is suitably distanced from one another so that Marina can speak her mind and miraculously change people's lives.

Instead of the main story focusing on Alex and Marina and their bond, the most satisfactory relationship occurs between Leo and Stella. This transference of focal point from the main characters to secondary characters is undoubtedly the main weakness of the film. Instead of Marina becoming stronger, she becomes a weaker, more confused person. In fact, what began as an affirmative action—marrying Leo— later becomes a full-blown mistake. Rather than showing the powers of clairvoyance, the story reduces Marina's advice to chance and speculation. Any statement about the world of the supernatural is quickly buried in the contrived plot. Even if the psychiatric world of Alex has been invaded and challenged by the simple gifts of Marina, both he and Marina become confused and disoriented people—such confusion being more attributable to the piercing arrows of Cupid than any other phenomenon. While the main characters of Alex and Marina become babbling idiots, Leo and Stella become stronger, more believable people. Leo, who has no notions of clairvoyance, finds Stella a worthy person, and she in turn recognizes his strengths. Subplot characters are unwittingly transposed to main plot roles and actually carry the true meaning of the film, as very little happens between Marina and Alex that is of a worthwhile nature.

The Butcher's Wife tries to achieve too much in a short space of time. Like Dorothy in *The Wizard of Oz* (1939), Marina is also taken on a mythic journey, but this particular journey is of her own design. Marina is transported into a world where people go about their daily tasks with little concern for what the future holds. What is portrayed in this film is a small community, the members of which all-too-easily ascribe their own meanings to what Marina has said. While Marina may be able to divine the future in much the same way as an Indian holy man, soothsayer, or seer might, the setting in which these clairvoyant utterances are given always seems contrived and manipulated. In fact, it falls to Leo to keep speculation in place.

The fatal flaw in *The Butcher's Wife* is that it wants to explore the supernatural—the world of the crystal ball and parapsychology—but it does not have the strength or the courage to transcend its genre. This lack of courage is evident when Marina acknowledges that she has married the wrong man and then has a dream which says that she should marry Alex. What is left is a simple love story that makes little sense of the world of the clairvoyant. Unlike her performances in *Ghost* (1990) or in *Mortal Thoughts* (1991), which dealt with psychic phenomena, Demi Moore is not convincing as a psychic.

The Butcher's Wife tries to draw together broad meanings about life by focusing on a typical neighborhood in Manhattan. Unfortunately, life is more complex and varied than what is portrayed in this limited slice-of-life story. Stereotyping can, in some settings, give greater and clearer focus to the main character, while at the same time introducing other ideas that may complement the story. When all the characters represent certain members of society rather than unique individuals, however, there is a certain amount of contrivance. Any meaning in Alex and Marina's relationship is completely lost in the resulting mayhem and confusion caused by Marina's faulty reading of her life and of who she should have married. There seems very little substance to the film, despite the fact that the potential for real exploration is present. Certainly, more could have been achieved between the meeting of a clairvoyant and a Freudian analyst. Despite good, strong acting from the four principal players— Moore, Jeff Daniels, Mary Steenburgen, and George Dzundza—*The Butcher's Wife* falls into unnecessary stereotypes in a setting that is less than believable in order to explore a subject that is, at best, ill-defined and ethereal.

Richard G. Cormack

Reviews
The American Spectator. XXV, January, 1992, p. 62.
Boston Globe. October 25, 1991, p. 47.
Boxoffice. December, 1991, p. R-90.
Chicago Tribune. October 25, 1991, VII, p. 26.
The Hollywood Reporter. October 25, 1991, p. 7.
Interview. XXI, September, 1991, p. 24.
Los Angeles Times. October 25, 1991, p. F8.
The New York Times. October 25, 1991, p. B7.
Premiere. IV, June, 1991, p. 65.
Reader. November 1, 1991, p. 2.
USA Today. October 25, 1991, p. D4.
Variety. October 25, 1991, p. 3.
The Village Voice. November 5, 1991, p. 2.
The Washington Post. October 25, 1991, p. B1.

CAPE FEAR

Production: Barbara De Fina for Amblin Entertainment, in association with Cappa
   Films and Tribeca Productions; released by Universal Pictures
Direction: Martin Scorsese
Screenplay: Wesley Strick; based on a screenplay by James R. Webb and on the novel
   The Executioners, by John D. MacDonald
Cinematography: Freddie Francis
Editing: Thelma Schoonmaker
Production design: Henry Bumstead
Art direction: Jack G. Taylor, Jr.
Set decoration: Alan Hicks
Casting: Ellen Lewis
Miniature special effects supervision: Derek Meddings
Sound: Tod Maitland
Costume design: Rita Ryack
Music: Elmer Bernstein
Score adaptation: Bernard Herrmann
MPAA rating: R
Running time: 128 minutes

> *Principal characters:*
> Max Cady .... Robert De Niro
> Sam Bowden .... Nick Nolte
> Leigh Bowden .... Jessica Lange
> Danielle Bowden .... Juliette Lewis
> Claude Kersek .... Joe Don Baker
> Lieutenant Elgart .... Robert Mitchum
> Lee Heller .... Gregory Peck
> Judge .... Martin Balsam
> Lori Davis .... Illeana Douglas

   Few directors have a visual style that so closely matches their filmic content as does
Martin Scorsese. His technique is raw, brutal, and relentlessly visceral. Often, this
style works, but sometimes it does not. Yet, one can never accuse Scorsese of being a
man without a definite vision, a need to explore the boundaries of human behavior and
motivation constantly. He seems to be driven by fear, religious guilt, and perhaps even
personal redemption. With this offering, a remake of J. Lee Thompson's 1962 pulp
thriller of the same name, *Cape Fear*, director Scorsese attempts to graft religious
concerns onto an effective-yet-banal story of revenge and retribution.
   After serving fourteen years in prison, Max Cady (Robert De Niro) is out for
revenge on Sam Bowden (Nick Nolte), the defense attorney who knowingly sup-
pressed a report on the sexual promiscuity of Cady's victim. The evidence could

possibly have won Cady an acquittal in the rape trial, but Bowden was so certain of Cady's guilt that he chose to breach legal ethics by burying the report. Instead, the charges against Cady were reduced from rape to assault and battery, and Cady received a lengthy prison sentence.

While imprisoned, the illiterate Cady taught himself to read, advancing to legal briefs and the study of law. Eventually, he was able to decipher deftly the legalities that implicate Bowden in his failure to fulfill his obligations to his client. Persuaded that it is his mission to help Bowden redeem himself by teaching him about loss, Cady sets out to terrorize Sam, his wife, Leigh (Jessica Lange), and their fifteen-year-old daughter, Danielle (Juliette Lewis). Unlike the family in the original film, these Bowdens are less than perfect; they are fraught with frailties, ranging from infidelity on Sam's part, a seething resentment in Leigh, and in Danielle, an increasing alienation from her parents, coupled with a burgeoning sexuality.

One of the difficulties in critiquing *Cape Fear* stems from the issue of expectations. Specifically, there are at least two different sets of criteria that can be employed when judging this film. One deals with the critical expectations inherent in a Martin Scorsese film: a relentless camera style (such as swooping crane shots and jump-cut editing), moral ambiguities (handled so successfully in 1990's *GoodFellas*), issues of guilt and redemption, and religious obsessions. Scorsese is a master at melding an eye for irony (particularly concerning American life) with a reverence for films and filmmaking. In *Cape Fear*, Scorsese successfully uses the unyielding camera to hammer away at the audience, to engulf the viewer in the same sort of incessant terror that Cady inflicts on the Bowdens. The disappointment in *Cape Fear*, however, is Scorsese's choice of subject matter. Despite its good intentions, the story somehow seems beneath the director's talent, and the result is distant and unemotional. Scorsese is a self-confessed perfectionist, which makes this film all the more puzzling, with its incomplete character sketches, uncomfortable plot contrivances, and accompanying quantum leaps in believability. Particularly irksome is the character of Lori (Illeana Douglas), the law clerk who is brutalized by Cady. If the audience is to understand that Sam has committed adultery in the past and that he is to feel guilt and a sense of responsibility for what happens to this innocent bystander, then why is Scorsese so quick to send Lori out of town and conveniently out of Sam's life? Sam's revelation that Cady had picked Lori because he knew that she would never testify in a sexual assault case because she knows how the system works requires a major suspension of belief on the audience's part.

If, on the other hand, the film is viewed in the more superficial, but generously forgiving light of commercial acceptability, then *Cape Fear* fares better, much in the same way as such flawed but audience-pleasing thrillers as *Jagged Edge* (1985) and *Fatal Attraction* (1987). The brutally graphic depiction of violence in *Cape Fear* has a gratuitous feel to it, in total contrast to the more ironic juxtaposition of visuals and narration that worked so effectively in *GoodFellas*.

Cape Fear is an addition to Scorsese's lengthy filmography, which began in 1973 with the release of his semiautobiographical *Mean Streets* (a film that also marked the beginning of repeated collaborations with actor Robert De Niro, who was nominated for an Academy Award for his performance in *Cape Fear*). In retrospect, the characters that De Niro has portrayed through Scorsese's work—from *Taxi Driver* (1976) to *Raging Bull* (1980) to *The King of Comedy* (1983) to the brilliant *GoodFellas*—have become increasingly alienated, men who stretch the boundaries of the audience's ability to sympathize with and understand their inner motivations. Generally speaking, writers try to sketch central protagonists that the viewer may not always like but, through an examination of their internal motivations and external circumstances, with which he or she will be able to empathize. With Scorsese (and particularly the Max Cady character in *Cape Fear*), however, one is presented with loathsome fringe-dwellers of society who still force the audience to understand what drives them to the depths of their despair. In *Cape Fear*, neither Scorsese nor De Niro is entirely successful. This, in itself, is one of the film's most glaring faults, as there is never a moment of doubt as to the true nature of Cady's character. Unlike Dr. Hannibal Lecter in Jonathan Demme's *The Silence of the Lambs* (1991; reviewed in this volume)—a man who was able to explain his contempt for certain segments of humanity and who displayed a respect and admiration for Clarice Starling—De Niro's Cady is merely the embodiment of evil, with no redeeming qualities.

Cady is, and most likely has always been, a brutal and sadistic man. Sam Bowden's breach of legal ethics pales in comparison to Cady's actions, thus making it extremely difficult for the audience not to side with the lawyer. There should have been some ambiguity, some question as to whether Cady deserved to be betrayed by his own attorney; yet, that side of the story never succeeds. The audience sees what Cady is capable of; his monstrous side is explicitly drawn out before one's very eyes. Unlike the similarly envisioned character of Hannibal "the cannibal," through whom actor Anthony Hopkins succeeded in painting a more sympathetic portrait of an equally brutal man, De Niro fails to imbue Cady with an imposing sensuality that is crucial to establishing the bond between character and audience. Few actors can be as convincing as the alienated stranger as De Niro, but in *Cape Fear*, his work is more annoying than it is terrifying. This is in contrast to the more sexually threatening, yet strangely evocative presence brought to the character by Robert Mitchum in the earlier version.

Unlike Scorsese's other works, *Cape Fear* has a distressing emotional shallowness that is more reminiscent of director Oliver Stone's self-indulgent films, mixed with the predictability of the surprising box-office draw *Fatal Attraction*. Scorsese openly acknowledged that his goal when making *Cape Fear* was twofold: first, to make a commercial crowd pleaser that was more "mainstream," and second, to address the issue of conventions of the thriller genre, such as an antagonist who refuses to die, thus exploring that fine line between convention and cliché. Both aims are understandable for a man who found films to be his salvation during a sickly childhood and who, for years, won critical acclaim and yet failed to capture the ever-important box-office dollar, the mark of success in Hollywood terms. *Raging Bull* was considered to be the best film of the 1980's by most critics, and *GoodFellas* won major critical awards; yet, Scorsese has never won an Academy Award for Best Director, and none of his films has ever been named Best Picture.

Given its pandering to petty pseudointellectualism and bourgeois sensibilities, Scorsese's *Cape Fear* was doomed from the start. It seems to be the antithesis of the B-film, which sought the indictment of the American Dream. In contrast, the far more effective *Miami Blues* (1990) succeeds in allowing its simplicity to underscore the cynicism inherent in pulp filmmaking conventions. By attempting to graft forcefully a higher morality onto a film that did not germinate from within his own tortured psyche, Scorsese failed to make a cohesive filmic statement.

Patricia Kowal

Reviews

American Cinematographer. LXXII, October, 1991, p. 34.
Boxoffice. December, 1991, p. R-87.
Chicago Tribune. November 13, 1991, V, p. 1.
The Christian Science Monitor. November 29, 1991, p. 10.
Entertainment Weekly. I, November 22, 1991, p. 56.
The Hollywood Reporter. CCCXX, November 11, 1991, p. 5.
Los Angeles Times. November 13, 1991, CX, p. F1.
The Nation. CCLIII, December 23, 1991, p. 826.
The New Republic. CCX, December 9, 1991, p. 28.
New York. XXIV, November 25, 1991, p. 88.
The New York Times. November 13, 1991, p. B1.
The New Yorker. LXVII, December 2, 1991, p. 156.
Newsweek. CXVIII, November 25, 1991, p. 56.
People Weekly. XXXVI, November 25, 1991, p. 19.
Rolling Stone. November 28, 1991, p. 101.
Variety. November 11, 1991, p. 2.
The Village Voice. November 19, 1991, XXXVI, p. 57.
The Wall Street Journal. November 21, 1991, p. A12.
The Washington Post. November 15, 1991, p. F1.

CITY OF HOPE

Production: Sarah Green and Maggie Renzi for Esperanza; released by the Samuel
   Goldwyn Company
Direction: John Sayles
Screenplay: John Sayles
Cinematography: Robert Richardson
Editing: John Sayles
Production design: Dan Bishop and Dianna Freas
Art direction: Chas. B. Plummer
Set decoration: Carolyn Cartwright
Casting: Barbara Hewson Shapiro and Eve Battaglia
Sound: Scott Breindel
Costume design: John Dunn
Music: Mason Daring
MPAA rating: R
Running time: 129 minutes

> *Principal characters:*
> Nick .... Vincent Spano
> Wynn .... Joe Morton
> Joe .... Tony LoBianco
> Rizzo .... Anthony John Denison
> Angela .... Barbara Williams
> Carl .... John Sayles
> Les .... Bill Raymond
> Reesha .... Angela Bassett
> Mad Anthony .... Josh Mostel
> Bobby .... Jace Alexander
> Zip .... Todd Graff
> Asteroid .... David Strathairn
> O'Brien .... Kevin Tighe
> Franklin .... Daryl Edwards
> Former mayor .... Ray Aranha

   One of the deepest and most provocative ironies of John Sayles's *City of Hope* is that,
ultimately, the title is not as ironic as one might expect. His previous films tend to
revolve around a common vision of basically sympathetic, playful, hardworking
innocents in one way or another overwhelmed by ingrained and inescapable social and
economic corruption. *Matewan* (1987), for example, portrays the labor struggles of
the oppressed miners of an early twentieth century West Virginia coal town as noble
and heroic, but the film moves inevitably to a concluding massacre. *Eight Men Out*
(1988) proposes that American culture can be understood by analyzing the national
pastime, but in Sayles's view baseball turns out to be not a delightful pastoral game but

yet another part of life circumscribed by greed and dishonesty—in short, "business as usual." Sayles's unflinching awareness, in all of his films, that "business as usual" is a perpetual threat to innocence, fairness, and happiness makes his work both profound and somber.

City of Hope does not lack darkness, literally and metaphorically—in fact, many of the scenes, particularly near the end, are set at nighttime—and there is enough in the film to confirm that the title is at least partially ironic: Hope is all that one has when one has nothing else, like so many of the poor souls depicted here. Yet, for all its concentration on the corruption of Hudson City, the fictional but recognizably realistic setting of the film, *City of Hope* is remarkably buoyant, as if Sayles wants to balance his relentless dramatization of "business as usual" with an affirmation of the resiliency of the human spirit.

On the surface, the film's structure seems to be epic, but it should be described more properly as panoramic. The plot is broad and complex, involving the intertwined lives of more than a dozen key characters and an even greater number of incidental, though not unimportant, figures. Sayles seems to conceive of the city as one large composite organism, and the stories that constitute the life of the city are never separate, never inconsequential. Without denying the fact of individuality—people do indeed have personal goals and private desires—Sayles nevertheless insists that the primary reality of life, for better and for worse, is social. For all its panoramic range, *City of Hope* is ultimately claustrophobic, even incestuous, because it shows that everyone is connected, people always touch one another somehow, and every kiss or punch, whisper or shout, ripples and reverberates through the streets.

Each of the main characters finds that there is no escape from responsibilities or personal entanglements. The film begins (and ends) by focusing on Nick (Vincent Spano), a young working-class man whose good looks and good fortune are not enough to make him happy. He is the son of a prosperous builder, Joe (Tony LoBianco), and Nick's do-nothing job on a construction site pays him well, but not well enough to erase his gambling and drug debts. He and his buddies Bobby (Jace Alexander) and Zip (Todd Graff) are part of a new lost generation, and their only avenues of expression—heavy-metal music and petty crime—are dead ends. While Bobby and Zip are basically mindless Bowery Boys, however, Nick consciously struggles with some serious dilemmas. He may not be particularly troubled by the fact that his father's success is based on Mafia support—everyone takes for granted that all success is based on some kind of shady dealing—but Nick does hold him responsible for the death of his older brother and desperately wants to step out of his father's shadow.

The camera pans seamlessly from Nick to Joe at the beginning, a cinematic technique that Sayles uses repeatedly to underscore the interconnectedness of all the characters. Joe's problems are in some respects not so different from Nick's. Joe is beholden not to a real but to a symbolic father, a mob boss who has bankrolled Joe's construction business but who now wants him to set fire to one of his tenement buildings to allow for a new and more profitable high rise. Joe's resulting moral crisis is admirable but ineffective: The building is burned, uprooting many poor families and killing a few squatters. One of the most disturbing themes of the film, exemplified in this episode and elsewhere, is the grim fact that knowing the right thing does not lead to doing the right thing. Even if the will to do good is not paralyzed, the force of circumstances almost always works against positive actions.

That the city of hope is a city of coercion and compromise is dramatized even in the actions of the most idealistic character of the film. Young African-American council member Wynn (Joe Morton) is indeed trying to "win" over his constituents, who are rightly skeptical of the value of working within a system that is so obviously unbalanced and corrupt. His father figure, a retired mayor (Ray Aranha), also an African American, cheerfully advises him that it is much more important to be a power broker than a moralizer. Wynn clings to his belief that perseverance, goodwill, and integrity can be the basis of social and political progress, but he ultimately learns to be a player in a game where truth and integrity are secondary, if not inconsequential. The citizens of his district rally around him, but only after he becomes something of a rhetorical rabble-rouser. Although he leads a successful march to confront the mayor with their demands, something has been lost as well as gained.

Sayles tends to diffuse the action by constantly shifting from one character's story to another, and this technique adds not only depth and richness to the film but also a kind of offbeat humor. The seriousness of the film is constantly punctuated by comical vignettes and crazy characters: Mad Anthony (Josh Mostel), the manic owner of the electronics store that displays the new staples of postmodern life that no one can be without—compact disc players and video cassette recorders; Franklin (Daryl Edwards), Wynn's brother-in-law, who stops the robbery at the electronics store with a toy gun; and Asteroid (David Strathairn), a homeless man who provides a running commentary on much of the film by mindlessly echoing what is said around him.

There are also lyrical interludes which show that the rhythm of city life is a fascinating and unpredictable blend of tension and release, romance and realism. It is no surprise to see Nick become romantically involved with Angela (Barbara Williams), an attractive young waitress, but it is indicative of the gritty realism of the film that the scenes of their lovemaking never efface the humdrum domesticity that is the substance of their lives. Angela has a sick child to care for, and it is less important to her that the earth move when she is making love than that her baby sleep through the night uninterrupted. The people of the city of hope do not have the luxury of romantic illusions of love, but this does not keep them from one another. In perhaps the most charming and exuberant scene of the entire film, Wynn and his wife (Angela Bassett) make love, and oddly enough this scene is political and educational as well as private and romantic. Such intimate scenes can play a role in breaking down the racial divisiveness that is one of the major problems in modern times.

Sayles thus fragments and interrupts the film, sacrificing narrow focus and dramatic urgency for breadth and variety, but he concludes with a series of interrelated climaxes and temporary resolutions to problems that have all along seemed insoluble. At the end of *City of Hope*, the private and political dimensions of the various stories converge. Wynn overcomes his personal reservations about using "down and dirty" techniques to realize his high ideals and, as a result, becomes an accepted leader in his community. Les (Bill Raymond), a college professor who has been mugged by two African-American teenagers and humiliated by their subsequent accusation that they attacked him only after he propositioned them, accidentally meets one of the muggers, who apologizes. The community has been polarized by the charges and counter-charges, but the involved parties at last have an honest confrontation and jog off together down the road to reconciliation.

Nick and Joe also reconcile. Nick is shot by Rizzo (Anthony John Denison), a police officer and Angela's former husband, who chases Nick, a suspect in a robbery, out of jealousy as well as out of duty. As Nick lies bleeding and perhaps dying, Joe holds him in his arms and confesses and explains his guilt in business and in family matters. The camera pulls back to a long shot, and the last moments of the film belong to Asteroid's hysterical calls for help, a cry in the dark perhaps not only for Nick but for the entire city as well. This is not a shattering conclusion, however, but a bittersweet, tragicomic coda that reinforces the poignancy and urgency of Nick and Joe's final reconciliation.

City of Hope is a carefully crafted film, and its visual style nicely supports its overall themes. By using long shots, long takes, and a mobile camera, Sayles establishes that his primary subject is the interconnected ensemble of lives that constitute the city. This panoramic approach calls to mind Robert Altman's *Nashville* (1975) but may owe as much to the long-running television series *Hill Street Blues*, which even within the confines of a small screen created a stunning vision of a city of despair and hope akin to that of Sayles.

The models for *City of Hope* are not only visual and cinematic. Sayles seems to have forged the style of this film simultaneously while working on his novel *Los Gusanos* (1991), a complex, thickly layered narrative disclosing the many lives that lie beneath any event, any story. Both *Los Gusanos* and *City of Hope* show Sayles struggling with the problem of making a work of art that is dramatic and compassionate as well as analytical and politically progressive, accurately capturing not only the hearts and minds of men and women but also the dispiriting structures and circumstances within which they are apparently trapped. Sayles is inevitably compared to Charles Dickens because of his vast scope and many characters, his portrayal of a culture half in celebration and half in flames, his emphasis on systemic rather than personal evil or corruption, and his sentimentality. Sayles's sentimentality, however, clearly evident in *City of Hope*, is much more cautious and radical than that of Dickens and does not lead to a betrayal of his deep criticisms of contemporary society. For Sayles, the modern city is one of racism, corruption, unequal opportunity, confusion, and greed, and he gives concrete expression to each of these qualities in various characters and incidents in the film. Yet, the positive message of the film is that, if many private and individual acts of selfishness go into the making of a city of corruption, then the accumulated private acts of reconciliation, compassion, honesty, and love may yet make a city of hope.

Sidney Gottlieb

Reviews

American Film: Magazine of the Film and Television Arts. XVI, June, 1991, p. 18.
Boxoffice. August, 1991, p. R-57.
Chicago Tribune. October 25, 1991, VII, p. 30.
The Christian Science Monitor. November 19, 1991, p. 10.
Film Comment. XXVII, July, 1991, p. 79.
The Hollywood Reporter. January 25, 1991, p. 10.
Los Angeles Times. October 25, 1991, p. F1.
The New York Times. October 11, 1991, p. B4.
Rolling Stone. October 31, 1991, p. 97.
Time. CXXXVIII, October 21, 1991, p. 101.
Variety. January 25, 1991, p. 2.

CITY SLICKERS

Production: Irby Smith for Castle Rock Entertainment, in association with Nelson
Entertainment and Face; released by Columbia Pictures
Direction: Ron Underwood
Screenplay: Lowell Ganz and Babaloo Mandel
Cinematography: Dean Semler
Editing: O. Nicholas Brown
Production design: Lawrence G. Paull
Art direction: Mark Mansbridge
Set decoration: Rick Simpson
Casting: Pam Dixon
Sound: Louis L. Edemann and Charles L. Campbell
Costume design: Judy Ruskin
Music: Marc Shaiman
MPAA rating: PG-13
Running time: 110 minutes

Principal characters:
Mitch Robbins	Billy Crystal
Phil Berquist	Daniel Stern
Ed Furillo	Bruno Kirby
Curly	Jack Palance (AA)
Barbara Robbins	Patricia Wettig
Bonnie Rayburn	Helen Slater
Clay Stone	Noble Willingham
Cookie	Tracey Walter
Barry Shalowitz	Josh Mostel
Ira Shalowitz	David Paymer
Ben Jessup	Bill Henderson
Lou	Jeffrey Tambor
Steve Jessup	Phill Lewis
Jeff	Kyle Secor
T. R.	Dean Hallo

City Slickers is a lively comedy adventure about three middle-aged city dwellers
coming to terms with their individual mid-life crises while playing cowboy during a
Western cattle drive. The film is rich in verbal and visual gags that emphasize the main
characters' hilarious attempts to adapt to their new wild and rugged surroundings.

The film gets off to a lively start with a frenetic scene set in Pamplona, Spain,
during the traditional running of the bulls. Mitch Robbins (Billy Crystal), Phil
Berquist (Daniel Stern), and Ed Furillo (Bruno Kirby) are American tourists who
periodically indulge in risk-taking vacations. They get their money's worth by running

through the streets of Pamplona along with thousands of other men attempting to dodge a herd of infuriated bulls. After Mitch is gored in the rear and sent flying by one of the beasts, he swears that he will never accompany his buddies again on recklessly daring adventures that he calls "desperate attempts to cling to (our) youth."

One year later, Mitch's thirty-ninth birthday sends him into an angst-filled funk, much to the dismay of his wife, Barbara (Patricia Wettig), who has planned an elaborate party for him. Before the evening's festivities, he visits his son's grammar school to participate in a special class featuring fathers and their jobs. Mitch ends up giving a hilariously gloomy soliloquy about the futility of life. During the birthday party, Mitch tries to feign having a good time. This goal proves difficult when Phil and Ed present him with their birthday present: a trip to a New Mexico dude ranch where the three of them will participate in a cattle drive. Mitch hardly has time to object to the venture when the party is interrupted by the sudden appearance of one of Phil's supermarket employees, who informs him that she is pregnant with his child. This revelation sends Phil's domineering wife into a frenzy and ends in a huge, hilarious row with Phil shouting at his wife, "If hate were people, I would be China!" After the party, Mitch confesses to Barbara how miserable he feels about his life. She agrees and tells him that his angst is threatening their marriage. She encourages Mitch to go on the cattle drive with Phil and Ed and try to recapture some of his waning happiness. Mitch finally agrees with her and begins to prepare for the dude ranch excursion.

When the three friends arrive at the ranch, they are informed by the owner that the cattle drive in which they will participate is a two-hundred-mile trek from New Mexico to Colorado and that it will be no picnic. "You come here as city slickers," he says, "but you're going home cowboys." The other urban cowboys participating in the cattle drive are brothers Ira and Barry Shalowitz (David Paymer and Josh Mostel), successful businessmen modeled after real-life ice cream entrepreneurs Ben and Jerry; father and son dentists Ben and Steve Jessup (Bill Henderson and Phill Lewis); and attractive Bonnie Rayburn (Helen Slater), the only woman participant.

Also along for the ride are two cowhands, Jeff (Kyle Secor) and T. R. (Dean Hallo). Before the drive begins, they make crude advances toward Bonnie. When Mitch tries to defuse their licentious attack by telling jokes, the two turn their wrath on him. Mitch is saved from a beating by the sudden appearance of the sadistic head cowpoke, Curly (Jack Palance), who nearly castrates one of the attackers with an adept flick of his knife.

When the time comes to begin the cattle drive, Ben Jessup encourages the others to recreate the famous "yee-hah!" scene from *Red River* (1948), after which the two-hundred-mile journey begins. The rest of the film consists of humorous "fish out of water" gags, playing up the ineptness of the city slickers as they attempt to adapt to their rugged and unfamiliar surroundings. Along the way, the three friends discuss their past lives and future goals, each man revealing deeply troubling secrets about himself. Ed's confessions are nasty, involving hate-filled attitudes toward his father and women. Ed antagonizes his friends until the three begin throwing punches at one another. All admit to being frustrated and unfulfilled and having no clue as to how to remedy their mid-life crises.

At one point, Mitch pulls out his battery-operated coffee grinder, starts it up, and immediately triggers a stampede. As punishment for his deed, Mitch is forced to ride with the evil Curly and search for strays. The two men spend the night together in the wilderness, and Mitch confronts Curly about his sadistic reputation. Instead of using Mitch as a human whittling peg, Curly reveals his tender side and the two men become friends. Curly also tells Mitch that he can overcome his depression by centering his life on the one thing that he values more than anything else. Of course, Curly says, only Mitch knows what that one thing is, and only Mitch can find out what it is. Before returning to the main group, the two men come across a cow in the process of giving birth. After the men assist the cow, which must be put to death after its painful labor, Mitch adopts the newly born calf and names it Norman.

A series of disasters follows in rapid succession: Curly suffers a heart attack and dies; the cook (Tracey Walter) gets drunk and runs his chuck wagon off a cliff and breaks his legs; and Jeff and T. R. become belligerent and threaten the city slickers, and eventually desert them. Realizing their chances of successfully completing the drive are now remote, the green cowhands decide to abandon the herd and ride to the Colorado ranch for help. Nevertheless, Ed and Phil, and finally Mitch, decide to continue driving the herd.

After the others ride off, the three friends face many difficult challenges en route to their Colorado destination. Their most vexing hazard is a raging river that proves to be a near fatal obstacle for Mitch and Norman, as both man and animal are swept away in the river's strong current. Phil and Ed are able to save the two from a watery grave by staging a daring rescue. Finally, the men reach their destination and receive an enthusiastic welcome. By that time, the three friends have come to terms with their mid-life crises and are ready to return to civilization with new, life-affirming vigor.

At its best, *City Slickers* is an uproariously funny "fish out of water" comedy, a successful mix of sight gags and one-liners, the best jokes poking fun at how crazed and desperate some people become over the thought of leading unfulfilled lives. The first scene in Pamplona, Spain, is extremely well staged, with Billy Crystal wide-eyed and frantic as he attempts to escape from the horns of a bull that seems to carry a personal grudge. The early scenes establishing each of the principal characters' personal problems are all filled with very clever lines, the standout being Mitch's monologue on the hopelessness of life delivered to his son's grammar-school class. This speech leaves his young audience depressed and the film audience howling with laughter.

The film's funny bone begins to show signs of numbness once the three principals begin their cattle drive. Jack Palance, who won the Academy Award for Best Supporting Actor by parodying his sadistic gunslinger character from *Shane* (1953), manages to keep the comedy tension between the greenhorns and the cowpokes lively. Once his character suffers his heart attack along the trail, however, the playful kidding between the slickers and the Western veterans dissolves into too many male-bonding monologues, most of which seem out of place and out of character. The plot twists at this point also play as manipulative contrivances, springing out of screenwriters Lowell Ganz and Babaloo Mandel's "damn the logic" desire to eliminate the seasoned cowhands in order to force the three principals into life-threatening—and ultimately life-affirming—challenges. The result is a film that cannot make up its mind whether to be comic or significant, a problem that plagued the screenplay for *Parenthood* (1989), also written by Ganz and Mandel.

Luckily, Crystal's charisma is strong enough to carry the film through its unconvincing scenes of mid-life angst. Crystal's eternally wide-eyed, innocent expression and deadpan delivery of both humorous and meaty lines give the film its focus and continuity. Ironically, his frisky and loving relationship with Norman the calf turns out to be a much more convincing—and much more entertaining—affair than the love/hate relationship that he has with his human friends. This playful relationship is strongly reminiscent of the hilarious man-heifer tryst that developed between Buster Keaton and his bovine leading lady in *Go West* (1925). In fact, the Keaton film seems to have been a major inspiration for *City Slickers*, as both films present a hopelessly inept city dweller struggling to adapt to the wild West, becoming romantically involved with a cow during a cattle drive, and ultimately triumphing over insurmountable challenges. Unlike *City Slickers*, however, *Go West* never lost sight of the fact that it was first and foremost a comedy, a lesson that should be branded into the hides of writers Mandel and Ganz for future reference.

Jim Kline

Reviews
American Film: Magazine of the Film and Television Arts. XVI, July, 1991, p. 50.
Boxoffice. June, 1991, p. R-33.
Chicago Tribune. June 7, 1991, VII, p. 38.
Films in Review. XLII, July, 1991, p. 253.
The Hollywood Reporter. May 30, 1991, p. 5.
Los Angeles Times. June 7, 1991, p. F1.
Maclean's. June 24, 1991, p. 48.
The New York Times. June 7, 1991, p. B6.
The New Yorker. June 17, 1991, p. 100.
Newsweek. CXVII, June 24, 1991, p. 60.
Rolling Stone. June 27, 1991, p. 77.
Sight and Sound. I, November, 1991, p. 38.
Time. CXXXVII, June 10, 1991, p. 66.
Variety. May 30, 1991, p. 2.

CLASS ACTION

Production: Ted Field, Scott Kroopf, and Robert W. Cort for Interscope Communications; released by Twentieth Century-Fox
Direction: Michael Apted
Screenplay: Carolyn Shelby, Christopher Ames, and Samantha Shad
Cinematography: Conrad L. Hall
Editing: Ian Crafford
Art direction: Mark Billerman
Set decoration: Dan May
Set design: Barbara Mesney
Sound: Michael Evje
Costume design: Rita Ryack
Music: James Horner
MPAA rating: R
Running time: 109 minutes

> *Principal characters:*
> Jedediah Tucker Ward . . . . Gene Hackman
> Maggie Ward . . . . Mary Elizabeth Mastrantonio
> Michael Grazier . . . . Colin Friels
> Estelle Ward . . . . Joanna Merlin
> Nick Holbrook . . . . Larry Fishburne
> Quinn . . . . Donald Moffat
> Pavel . . . . Jan Rubes
> Dr. Getchell . . . . Fred Dalton Thompson
> Brian . . . . Jonathan Silverman
> Judge Symes . . . . Matt Clark

David-and-Goliath lawsuits have always appealed to Jedediah Tucker Ward (Gene Hackman), a famous civil liberties attorney. His daughter, Maggie (Mary Elizabeth Mastrantonio), who is a rising young lawyer in a prestigious San Francisco corporate firm, has always sided with the establishment. Everything about the opening scene of *Class Action* is calculated to define their opposing values and temperaments. In court, Maggie, nicely tailored in a conservative suit, sums up for the jury: "Appeals . . . based on emotion have no place in a court of law. . . . The law, not charity, must decide our course here today." In an adjoining courtroom, Jed, a bit rumpled in an old blazer, begins his summation by telling the jury that they are sitting not in a court of law but at the Mad Hatter's tea party. The filmmakers smoothly crosscut between the two trials during the opening credits and contrast Maggie's modulated tones to her jury with her father's passionate plea for action to his. Jed brings cheers from the spectators at his trial, and the muffled echo of that celebration disrupts the solemnity of Maggie's remarks.

Their chief point of contention soon involves a company called Argo Motors. Jed represents a client who has been seriously maimed when his Argo car, the Meridian, ignited in a collision. Other Meridians have also caught fire on impact. As he prepares the class-action suit against Argo, Jed rails against the corporate arrogance that can market an unsafe product to unsuspecting consumers. Across town, Maggie's firm happens to represent Argo—she efficiently reminds her boss that 26 percent of their business last year came from Argo—and she is eager to defend their rights against litigious customers. Maggie complains about what she calls "the new American way: Find the guy who busted his hump to build it and rob him blind." The organization of the entire film is as carefully planned and patterned as these opening scenes.

The confrontation between parent and child uncovers long-standing animosities. In the early scenes, Estelle Ward (Joanna Merlin), Maggie's mother, figures importantly as a sounding board for both parties. Father and daughter make telling points about each other. Jed has no respect for either the leaders ("the vilest sort of corporate vermin") or the newer talent ("young Nazis") at Maggie's firm. The upcoming trial represents to Maggie a way of gaining control: "The first time I have him in a place where he doesn't make the rules." When Maggie and Jed present opening arguments, director Michael Apted effectively uses reaction shots of Estelle sitting with the spectators to make her an emotional gauge for the audience. Jed grandstands before the judge by requesting the names and addresses of all the designers who worked on the Meridian. In reply to Maggie's complaint about the difficulty of tracing all these people, Jed announces that he was given the information over the telephone from the pension department at Argo when he inquired about a former worker. He even smugly produces a complimentary newsletter that Argo mailed him. As the spectators in the courtroom laugh, Apted inserts a reaction of Estelle's discomfort over Maggie's embarrassment. Such cutting allows this scene to work on two emotional planes at once.

The first surprise comes when the film turns away from this alternation of opposing values to explore a character study of both protagonists. Apted has said that the film functions both on a personal level—an adult child and her parent settling their differences—and on a public level—the contrasting moralities of big business versus the individual. In its careful design, the first half of the motion picture emphasizes these contrasting moralities, while the second half divides its attention between the courtroom drama and Jed and Maggie's need to reconcile. Both characters face and acknowledge their flaws. For Maggie, such self-scrutiny involves accepting the judgment of Jed's assistant, Nick (Larry Fishburne): "Your biggest aspiration is to be his mirror image." She admits the way that she has made her father into a scapegoat, though she is stubborn enough to tell Jed that hers was a "constructive anger." For Jed, the realization touches on how his commitment to causes has crippled his ability to care about individuals. He tells Maggie that he always thought he was doing the right thing but that he may have been wrong, words she has never before heard him say.

As heroic, egotistical Jed Ward, Hackman excels. Few actors are more pleasurable to watch than Hackman. He has always been skilled at handling larger-than-life roles, a gift that Orson Welles called being a "king actor." The real strength of Hackman's performance, however, is his ability to bring out the private, as well as the public, side of his character. Debating the long-shot Argo case, Jed must remind even his closest assistant that he is not simply hungry for headlines. In a scene set at a funeral, he delivers a poignant eulogy that shows his frailty. This proud liberal is beginning to see himself as an anachronism in an era of Republican values. With a picture of George McGovern hanging in his office, Jed tiredly says at one point, "I should have died the day Nixon resigned."

Part of what compensates for the diminished clash of values between father and daughter as the film develops is the audience's growing fascination with the gallery of villains. For a time, it begins to seem that, the more expensive the office, the more corrupt the executive. Dehumanization describes them all. Dr. Getchell (Fred Dalton Thompson) of Argo Motors is the executive who perpetuates wrongdoing by routinely following long-established procedures and then using jargon to justify his decision by calling it a "simple actuarial analysis." Flashing a reptilian sneer, Michael Grazier (Colin Friels) ponders how to bury an incriminating piece of evidence. Quinn (Donald Moffat), the head of Maggie's firm, is nearly robotic in his adherence to form. Even as he mentions the loss of his mother, he seems nonhuman. Though none of these stereotyped characters has a trace of the depth of Maggie or Jed, they do sustain the tension in the second half of the film.

The tension, however, is based more on the simpler motives of exposing the villains than on the development of ideas. This second surprise indicates a new emphasis of the film's second half. The genre of the courtroom thriller requires that the action build to a showdown before judge and jury. By the time of the final trial scene, however, the audience knows the degree of wrongdoing in the Argo case. What makes the climactic moments compelling is not so much the obligatory trial setting as much as another staple of any good courtroom drama—the appeal of seeing very bright, highly educated people trying deftly to outwit one another. The behind-the-scenes finesse of litigators, the legal one-upmanship of anticipation and preparedness, and the uncertainty (because of information withheld from the audience in order to set up a surprise ending) about which side Maggie finally supports give *Class Action* its suspense in its later scenes.

The ending is clearly designed to respond more to the demands of the box office than those of the logic that is required by the developing drama. Some viewers may rightly question whether the artistic decision of the filmmakers to emphasize mystery and surprise in the last third of the film constitutes a refusal to explore the issues that the earlier scenes raised. The first half succeeds so well at objectively presenting the values of the characters that an audience may feel its sympathies and identification repeatedly switch from Jed to Maggie. This complexity diminishes in the second half, however, as the theme of disillusionment emerges, and also toward the end, as the emphasis falls on the clever rather than on the intelligent. This is not to deny the suspense of the ending but simply to indicate the degree to which it differs from much of the preceding film. Other courtroom dramas naturally invite comparison. *The*

Verdict (1982) makes the personal drama of the rehabilitation of Paul Newman's character and the case that he tries inseparable, and the battle-of-the-sexes comedy *Adam's Rib* (1949) presents with unsparing objectivity the values of its husband-and-wife antagonists, Spencer Tracy and Katharine Hepburn. By simplifying its resolution with melodrama, *Class Action* may not ultimately be as memorable as these classic courtroom dramas, but it remains a compelling and satisfying film.

Glenn Hopp

Reviews
Boxoffice. March, 1991, p. R-12.
Chicago Tribune. March 15, 1991, VII, p. 40.
Cineaste. XVIII, Number 3, 1991, p. 48.
Films in Review. XLII, July, 1991, p. 268.
The Hollywood Reporter. March 4, 1991, p. 8.
Los Angeles Times. March 15, 1991, p. F4.
New Statesman and Society. IV, June 21, 1991, p. 40.
The New York Times. March 15, 1991, p. B3.
People Weekly. March 25, 1991, p. 11.
Rolling Stone. March 21, 1991, p. 86.
Sight and Sound. I, July, 1991, p. 40.
USA Today. March 15, 1991, p. 4D.
Variety. March 4, 1991, p. 2.
The Wall Street Journal. March 14, 1991, p. A16.
The Washington Post. March 15, 1991, p. C1.

THE COMFORT OF STRANGERS

Origin: Italy and United States
Released: 1990
Released in U.S.: 1991
Production: Angelo Rizzoli for ERRE Produzioni, Sovereign Pictures, and Reteitalia;
   released by Skouras Pictures
Direction: Paul Schrader
Screenplay: Harold Pinter; based on the novel by Ian McEwan
Cinematography: Dante Spinotti
Editing: Bill Pankow
Production design: Gianni Quaranta
Set decoration: Stefano Paltrinieri
Sound: Drew Kunin
Costume design: Mariolina Bono and Giorgio Armani
Music: Angelo Badalamenti
MPAA rating: R
Running time: 107 minutes

> *Principal characters:*
> Robert . . . . Christopher Walken
> Mary . . . . Natasha Richardson
> Colin . . . . Rupert Everett
> Caroline . . . . Helen Mirren

The Comfort of Strangers is an unusual, absorbing film that explores the sometimes dangerous terrain of love, sexuality, and violence as they are played out within the framework of male/female relationships. Directed by Paul Schrader, whose films include *American Gigolo* (1980), *Cat People* (1982), and *Patty Hearst* (1988), and based on a novel by Ian McEwan, the film's script was written by Harold Pinter, the noted British playwright whose works for the screen include *The Servant* (1963), *The Go-Between* (1971), and *The French Lieutenant's Woman* (1981).

   The film's story is set in Venice, where a young English couple, Colin (Rupert Everett) and Mary (Natasha Richardson), have gone for a holiday in an attempt to rekindle their fading romance. As the two roam the streets of Venice or bicker in their hotel room, it becomes clear that theirs is a relationship nearing a crisis. Venice was to be the catalyst that renewed their love; instead, the holiday is deepening the rift between them. Adding a menacing twist to Colin and Mary's otherwise unremarkable problems, however, is the fact that someone is secretly watching and photographing them as they wander through the city.

   When the pair fall asleep one afternoon and wake up well past the usual closing time for local restaurants, they set off without a map to find a restaurant and quickly lose their way in the narrow, winding streets. They are rescued by Robert (Christopher Walken), an elegant man in a white suit who guides them to a gay bar where they share a bottle of wine as he tells them stories about his childhood. The stories—and Robert himself—are oddly disturbing, and Colin and Mary leave the bar half-drunk and unsettled by the experience. Too exhausted to return to their hotel, they spend the night sleeping in the streets.

The following day, they are again spotted by Robert, who insists that they accompany him to the elegant apartment that he shares with his wife, Caroline (Helen Mirren). They awaken refreshed after a long nap to discover that Robert is out and their clothes are missing—hidden by Caroline at Robert's request until they agree to stay for dinner. Caroline also confesses that she watched the pair as they slept. Later, after Robert has returned, the two women leave the room, and Robert suddenly punches Colin, an event that Colin does not mention to Mary. As they are preparing to leave after dinner, Mary notices a snapshot of Colin among several that Robert is holding.

In the days that follow their strange evening with the couple, Colin and Mary's relationship regains its passion and romance. After a trip to the beach, they find themselves walking near Robert and Caroline's home and are spotted by Caroline, who invites them in. The apartment is in disarray; Caroline and Robert are leaving for Canada. Colin accompanies Robert to his bar, where Robert tells him that he has allowed the men there to believe that Colin is his lover. Mary has remained with Caroline, who confides that the back injury from which she suffers was caused by Robert, who enjoys hurting her while they make love. She, in turn, enjoys his cruelty but says that they both realized the night of her injury that the next step in their dangerous game would be fatal. As she listens, Mary begins to grow dizzy and gradually realizes that she has been drugged. Caroline leads her into the bedroom, where the walls are covered with snapshots of Colin.

Colin and Robert return and, as Mary watches helplessly from a chair, Robert stabs Colin with a knife, then embraces Caroline and leads her from the room. The scene shifts to the police station, where Mary is being questioned about Colin's death and what the nature of their relationship with Robert and Caroline had been. Both Robert and Caroline are in custody, and when the police interrogate Robert, he begins to tell them the same childhood story that he had earlier related to Colin and Mary.

The Comfort of Strangers is a film that seems at first glance to offer an odd pairing of talents: those of writer Pinter and director Schrader. One of the theater's leading playwrights, Pinter is known for his spare dialogue and enigmatic story lines, and his career as a screenwriter has been closely associated with that of director Joseph Losey. Schrader, on the other hand, is the author of the script for *Taxi Driver* (1976), and his best-known works as a director often explore hard-hitting or violent subjects. Yet, the clash of styles to which Schrader's direction of a Pinter script might have given rise never occurs, and the film is, from its start, primarily "Pinteresque" in tone.

The film's haunting story remains a complex puzzle, and many questions are left deliberately unanswered. Why does Colin wait until much later to tell Mary that Robert has hit him? Why does Mary not mention the photograph that she has seen? Why do they return to the apartment a second time? The film's central question—and one that Mary is unable to answer—is asked by the investigating police officer near the close of the film: What did they want from Robert and Caroline? Because, despite their expressed dislike of Robert and the general air of menace accompanying their first visit, Colin and Mary are clearly fascinated by their new acquaintances.

That their own affair undergoes a dramatic renewal after the encounter is certainly a key to the mystery. Colin and Mary are two people who are very near the brink of falling out of love with each other. Their relationship seems, at the film's beginning, to exist out of habit rather than any deep sense of love or passion. Mary has two children from a previous marriage; Colin is uncertain whether he likes children at all. Yet, their meeting with Robert and Caroline touches an inner chord that evokes all the romantic ardor of the early days of their affair. In some strange, unacknowledged way, the sexual energy that is driving the older couple's lethal plans for Colin has permeated their own relationship and reawakened feelings that had begun to atrophy.

Robert and Caroline themselves fall so far outside the boundaries of conventional love that their relationship defies easy classification. The two have known each other since adolescence, and the sadistic madness in Robert's character finds an answering desire in Caroline, who confides to Mary that she believes love means a willingness to do anything for the other person. She has found, she says, great fulfillment in her utter helplessness in Robert's hands. Yet, the two have reached an impasse in their dangerous relationship; the injury to Caroline's back served as a warning that the next step would take them too far. Rather than sacrifice Caroline's life to their sado-masochistic passion, the two decide, with perverse logic, to substitute Colin as the victim of Robert's fatal cruelty. Both are clearly aroused by his murder, and they leave the room in each other's arms.

The Venetian setting of *The Comfort of Strangers* makes it a visually appealing film, with the canals and winding streets of the city playing their own part in the unfolding action. Indeed, physical beauty is one of the story's themes: Colin, with his brooding, Byronic good looks, and Mary, with her slender figure and mass of reddish-gold curls, make a stunningly attractive pair. In one amusing scene set in a restaurant, Mary teases Colin about the stares and glances that he is attracting from their fellow diners. It is Colin's beauty that first caught the older couple's attention, and Caroline describes to Mary the elation that she and her husband felt when Robert first spotted the pair and began secretly photographing Colin. The quartet of actors is uniformly good. Everett has an air of bored self-absorption that is ideal for Colin, while Richardson, who also starred in Schrader's *Patty Hearst*, brings intelligence and humor to her role. Walken, oddly but successfully cast as the Venetian-born Robert, evokes a quality of perversity and danger that sets the tone for much of the motion picture. In perhaps the most difficult of the film's roles, Mirren as Caroline creates a chilling portrait of a woman whose surface vulnerability masks a giddy form of madness.

The Comfort of Strangers is not a film to everyone's taste, and critical reaction to the motion picture was mixed. For those who respond to its particular blend of drama, suspense, and sexual menace, however, it will prove to be an absorbing and disturbing experience.

Janet Lorenz

Reviews

Boxoffice. May, 1991, p. R-30.
Chicago Tribune. April 12, 1991, V, p. 4.
Film Comment. XXVI, July, 1990, p. 52.
The Hollywood Reporter. March 26, 1991, p. 10.
Los Angeles Times. March 29, 1991, p. F13.
National Review. XLIII, May 27, 1991, p. 54.
The New Republic. CCIV, April 29, 1991, p. 26.
The New York Times. March 29, 1991, p. B1.
The New Yorker. LXVII, April 8, 1991, p. 82.
Rolling Stone. April 18, 1991, p. 98.
Time. CXXXVII, April 22, 1991, p. 84.
Variety. May 22, 1990, p. 3.
The Village Voice. April 2, 1991, p. 49.
The Washington Post. April 12, 1991, p. B7.

THE COMMITMENTS

Production: Roger Randall-Cutler and Lynda Myles for First Film, Dirty Hands, and Beacon; released by Twentieth Century-Fox
Direction: Alan Parker
Screenplay: Dick Clement, Ian La Frenais, and Roddy Doyle; based on the novel by Doyle
Cinematography: Gale Tattersall
Editing: Gerry Hambling
Production design: Brian Morris
Art direction: Mark Geraghty and Arden Gantly
Set decoration: Karen Brookes
Casting: John Hubbard and Ros Hubbard
Sound: Clive Winter
Costume design: Penny Rose
Music supervision: G. Mark Roswell
Musical arrangement: Paul Bushnell
Musical coordination: John Hughes
MPAA rating: R
Running time: 117 minutes

Principal characters:
Jimmy Rabbitte . . . . Robert Arkins
Steven Clifford . . . . Michael Aherne
Imelda Quirke . . . . Angeline Ball
Natalie Murphy . . . . Maria Doyle
Mickah Wallace . . . . Dave Finnegan
Bernie McGloughlin . . . . Bronagh Gallagher
Dean Fay . . . . Félim Gormley
Outspan Foster . . . . Glen Hansard
Joey "the Lips" Fagan . . . . Johnny Murphy
Derek Scully . . . . Kenneth McCluskey
Deco Cuffe . . . . Andrew Strong
Mr. Rabbitte . . . . Colm Meaney
Billy Mooney . . . . Dick Massey

Dublin, Ireland, may not be the most obvious place to find soul music performed, yet the city, immortalized in James Joyce's novel *Ulysses* (1922), is home to no less than forty such bands playing Blues Brothers-type music. Perhaps partly because of the successful careers of Sinéad O'Connor, U2, Van Morrison, and Bob Geldof, Ireland came to be considered part of the modern music scene. Taking Roddy Doyle's book *The Commitments* as his starting point, renowned director Alan Parker saw the possibility of turning the book about how a soul band was formed in Dublin into a film.

On a cloudy Saturday afternoon, Jimmy Rabbitte (Robert Arkins) tries to peddle sundry pieces of merchandise at the local open-air market, with little success. Jimmy stops at a wedding on his way home and is approached by his friends, Derek (Kenneth McCluskey) and Outspan (Glen Hansard), to manage their band. Because Jimmy is out of work, he accepts the offer. For Jimmy, this presents an unexpected chance to form a special band that will play soul—Dublin soul. After placing an advertisement in the local newspaper for musicians interested in soul, Jimmy—after days of auditioning people in his front room—eventually chooses the musicians who will make his vision come true.

Dean (Félim Gormley) plays a saxophone which he inherited from an uncle who had suffered a collapsed lung. Joey "the Lips" Fagan (Johnny Murphy) appears one dank Sunday morning on his Suzuki motorcycle at the back gate of Jimmy's house and declares that he has played with all the great musicians—especially those who play soul. Joey becomes the self-appointed spiritual leader of the group and Dean's mentor. Deco (Andrew Strong) is a bus conductor known for singing selections from the Motown label to his passengers. Jimmy sees Deco as the ideal lead singer with his deep, rasping voice and his commitment to the more physical demands of singing soul properly. Before Billy (Dick Massey) can become a part of the "world's hardest working band," Jimmy has him audition on a drum kit in a pawnbroker's window. Before buying the drum set, Jimmy, being a canny as well as a penniless band manager, makes sure that Billy actually can play the instruments before pawning a family ornament. For keyboard, Jimmy decides on Steven Clifford (Michael Aherne), a medical student and a church organist. Steven is a fine player, although an unlikely choice for a soul band. This being Dublin, however, the mix works. Steven borrows his "granny's" piano on the pretext that she never uses the front room. To round out the singing talent in the newly formed band, Jimmy asks Bernie (Bronagh Gallagher) to bring her friends Imelda (Angeline Ball) and Natalie (Maria Doyle) to the first meeting at Joey's mother's house.

To become successful, they need to practice. Jimmy rents a large attic above a pool hall which is both cheap and filled to capacity with junk—the owner is serving a short prison sentence. Raw talent and vision may be one thing, but sounding professional is quite another. The group requires plenty of practice, and eventually, they are good enough to be offered their first "gig" at the local community hall. From there, they get a number of bookings at local pubs and nightclubs. Jimmy is pleased that they now begin to look and sound like an authentic soul band. Their success is short-lived, however, as internal fighting and personality clashes predict the eventual breakup of the band. On the very evening that the famous Wilson Pickett is supposed to come and hear them play, Jimmy loses patience with the band members and turns his back on them. He walks away from their constant bickering offstage with the same ease with which he had put The Commitments together. Jimmy once again joins the ranks of the unemployed, glad to be free of the responsibility and hassles of managing a band.

The Commitments is much more than a film about music, even if music does seem to play an inordinately large part in the film. Director Parker imbues his films with as much as he can, in terms of both social commentary and political statement. Broad statements about the Irish people are made when Jimmy describes the Irish as the blacks of Europe, Dubliners as the blacks of Ireland, and Northsiders as the blacks of Dublin. Parker uses current issues and a background of soul music to convey something of his view of life and his political persuasion. Parker admits that *The Commitments* is a political film. *Come See the Paradise* (1990) was an attempt by Parker to convey the feelings of Japanese Americans who faced internment during World War II. *Mississippi Burning* (1989), another film by Parker, concerns itself with the investigation of the murder of three young civil rights workers in the United States in 1964. *Pink Floyd the Wall* (1981), based loosely on the band Pink Floyd's successful rock album, looks at the life of an out-of-control rock singer, Pink (Bob Geldof). *The Commitments* follows in a tradition of films dealing with interpersonal themes that have a broader base in society.

A certain feeling of hopelessness and resignation is evoked by seeing the seedier and derelict side of Dublin all but ignoring the fact that Dublin is one of the finest cities in Northern Europe. Parker strives for film realism and, admirably, achieves his aim, even if it is at the expense of an Ireland which has more to offer than tenements, washing hanging on clotheslines in run-down backyards, and derelict factories where children play amid the rubble and general decay of postindustrial Ireland. Unintentionally, Parker links the formation of The Commitments from a background of poverty with the rise of soul music from the ghettos of the American South. These images are simple, austere, and very telling in the way that they convey the hopelessness of the lives of the musicians that come to constitute the band. In fact, the success of the film rests almost entirely on having a cast which comes from this very background and thus is able to identify with the struggle of forming a group from scratch. Most of the cast of *The Commitments* had little or no acting experience prior to the film. This homespun quality, of actors playing themselves, is a continual delight throughout.

The strength, wit, and insight of the film does not come from the overall story but from the various cinematic moments that encapsulate and enliven what these musicians face in forming a band. An authenticity prevails from beginning to end; at no point is there a feeling of manipulation or contrivance. With such sincere acting, the members of the band convey a real sense of what the Irish are like in their own backyard. *The Commitments* is a film which is influenced greatly by Parker himself. As it grows organically from the dilapidated tenements of the depressed Northside of Dublin, Parker chooses each step very carefully as he tries to stay true to Doyle's original novel.

The Commitments meets all of its own expectations but manages somehow to remain an incomplete film. Even though the characters are fascinating, not much is made of their relationships with one another. Once the band has been formed and they are getting bookings to sing, Parker decides to let the music and the singing tell the story, and the rich array of characters that have been introduced simply become an amalgamation of singers and musicians. What could have been an extraordinary film of its kind dissolves into the predictable, and at times repetitive, medley of songs from the great albums of soul. This lack of cohesion on the part of Parker, whose influence is evident throughout the film, limits the appeal and durability of the film dramatically. When theme takes over from the main story and the characters become secondary to the music, a film becomes less interesting and appealing. Parker had all the right elements to make a film which went beyond the mere simple story about the formation of a band. Yet, his insistence on playing as much soul music as possible weakened an otherwise unique and enthralling film.

Richard G. Cormack

Reviews
American Film: Magazine of the Film and Television Arts. XVI, September/ October, 1991, p. 51.
Boxoffice. September, 1991, p. R-63.
Chicago Tribune. August 16, 1991, VII, p. 29.
Film Review. October, 1991, p. 32.
The Hollywood Reporter. July 19, 1991, p. 12.
L.A. Weekly. August 19, 1991, p. 55.
Los Angeles Times. August 11, 1991, p. 3.
Los Angeles Times. August 14, 1991, p. F1.
The New York Times. August 14, 1991, p. B1.
The New Yorker. LXVII, August 26, 1991, p. 68.
Newsweek. August 19, 1991, p. 55.
Time. CXXXVIII, August 26, 1991, p. 63.
Variety. July 19, 1991, p. 2.
Variety. August 12, 1991, p. 43.
The Village Voice. August 20, 1991, p. 55.
The Washington Post. September 13, 1991, p. C1.

DADDY NOSTALGIA
(DADDY NOSTALGIE)

Origin: France
Released: 1990
Released in U.S.: 1991
Production: Adolphe Viezzi for Clea Productions, Little Bear, Solyfic, and Eurisma;
  released by Avenue Pictures
Direction: Bertrand Tavernier
Screenplay: Colo Tavernier O'Hagan; dialogue by O'Hagan and Bertrand Tavernier
Cinematography: Denis Lenoir
Editing: Ariane Boeglin
Art direction: Jean-Louis Poveda
Set design: Robert Le Corre
Sound: Michel Desvois
Costume design: Christian Gasc
Music: Antoine Duhamel
MPAA rating: PG
Running time: 106 minutes

    Principal characters:
        Daddy .... Dirk Bogarde
        Caroline .... Jane Birkin
        Miche .... Odette Laure
        Juliette .... Emmanuelle Bataille
        Barbara .... Charlotte Kady
        Caroline (as a child) .... Michele Minns

The first sensory information to be relayed in the film *Daddy Nostalgia* is not visual, but auditory. A masculine (French) narrator speaks knowingly of a young girl's dream. The first image is the form of a grown woman. The adult Caroline (Jane Birkin) is seen smoking thoughtfully over her typewriter, as the omniscient voice tells how "little Caro" happily pushed her Daddy in a wheelbarrow on a magical journey. Establishing the tone of the character's somewhat fantastical relationship with her parents, the whimsical story hints at the sad longing that obviously informs her work as a writer and also metaphorically foreshadows Caroline's driving role in events to come.

A divorcée with a young son of her own, Caroline drops everything to rush to the bedside of her father (Dirk Bogarde), an aging British businessman whose most vivid memories are of traveling and socializing, not rearing his daughter. He is debonair, charming, and painfully unaware of Caroline, her likes and dislikes, or even the year of her birth. He has never read a word she has written.

Admirably taking charge of her worried French mother (Odette Laure), Caroline attempts to use this period to become closer to her father while avoiding the reality that he is dying. At first, Daddy and Caroline find a heightened childish glee in each other's mischievous company, while Miche, the withdrawn and frightened mother, portrays the majority of the resentment. The mother-daughter scenes are detailed with rich past and present tension, arousing sympathy for Caroline by showing her efforts to be nice and then her mother's hints of disapproval that cause Caroline to bristle into defensiveness. To Caroline's religious mother, a divorced writer is just short of being a heretic.

It is precisely Caroline's writing, however, that embodies the act of trying to come to terms with such issues. The superior screenplay exploits Caroline as a character who is professionally and personally justified in asking difficult, probing questions in a believable way. Director Bertrand Tavernier comments delightedly on the impressionistic script by his former wife, Colo Tavernier O'Hagan, which chooses "story but not plot." The progression is structured around Caroline's denial of the seriousness of Daddy's condition and her embracing of the new role of a "grown-up child" who is finally able to seize the attention that Daddy was too self-involved to give her years ago.

Daddy and Caroline take supreme delight in a likeness of each other's impatient disdain for the dreariness of the rest of humanity. They discover that they are bonded by his aloofness and her artistic perceptiveness. In the midst of speaking of the past, however, the evidence of Daddy's neglect sparks Caroline's painful flashback sequences.

These are gracefully carried out, in keeping with the opening mood. Caroline, as a child (Michele Minns), is quite alone amid the disembodied dancing, partying adult arms and sleeves after her father's hurtful dismissal of the poem that she has written for him. These glimpses are brief, dimly lit, and carefully stylized to be memory-like in their presentation, revolving around the lonely staircase that serves as the separating point of their two worlds. The camera visits this defining period as the eye of the adult looking back at the feelings that have stayed with Caroline. "Lucky you," is the closest she can come to confronting him with this long-ago pain at this point in the drama.

Caroline's own dissolved marriage and strained relationship with her son surface in her exchanges with Daddy. Caroline is learning to recognize the same kind of tendencies in her own life, and it disturbs her. She is also growing in the awareness that she and her mother have irreversibly switched roles. One flashback in particular manipulates time to show the aged Miche in the nursery as the child Caroline climbs the stairs, enters the room, and shuts the door.

When Caroline is pressed into seeing the whole truth by the nurse, it is a turning point which enables her to take the initiative to resolve what is possible. With Miche withdrawn and unwilling to even communicate to her husband in his native language, Caroline generously takes Daddy on a trip to the location of his long-ago youth. On the trip, they achieve the closest understanding that they could hope for. The narrator returns to tell of Daddy's weariness this time, instead of speaking for Caroline. Caroline finally lets the tears of her resentment fall, but she also allows herself to hear about the pain with which her father has been living. In this touching moment, Daddy tentatively asks to read something that she has written. These personal scenes benefit from the natural lighting and the Cinemascope format, which lends background to the moments of revelation in such a natural way as to support them. Afterward, events wind down as Caroline prepares to return to Paris and her adult life. There is a kind of poignantly underplayed "goodbye" which rings true as the family decides to share one last glass of Coca-Cola with one another while waiting for Caroline's cab, only to have the driver arrive early. There is never enough time.

It is upon entering her apartment and listening to her telephone answering machine that Caroline at last hears words of love in Daddy's own voice. Subsequently, the filmmaker returns to the distancing device of the male narrator, explaining that the next call was from her mother to tell her that her father had just died. The choice of third-person narrator existing outside of the film world raises issues slightly incongruent with the kind of clear-eyed, character-driven film that *Daddy Nostalgia* is in its most powerful moments.

Tavernier, the director of *Round Midnight* (1986) who is considered to be perhaps the most significant director of the second New Wave, is closer to the novelistic sensibilities of Jean Renoir and François Truffaut than the more brutally modernist Jean-Luc Goddard. Consequently, his style is accessible to American viewers. This moving, intimate film also does not alienate audiences with harsh political attempts to expose dramatic constructs. The majority of the film works marvelously, capturing the frustration of the old patterns that define children when they confront their pasts as returning adults.

A troublesome aspect of the film is its third-person voice-over, which undercuts the strength of the main character's efforts to make sense of her own experiences. While the narration is obviously an attempt to extend the metaphor of childhood dreams, it ultimately seems paternalistic and reactionary that Caroline does not possess the telling of her own story. It goes against modernist, or even post-modernist, sensibilities but, more to the point, it works directly against the way in which the most powerful scenes in the minimalist script influence the viewer. While locating the voice-over during the first moments of Caroline at her typewriter reveals the intention to speak to the creative act of writing, why then is the speaking voice not Caroline's? If it is a fatherly male perspective, then why is it in French rather than her father's native English? Even if she were struggling as a writer to detach herself to a third-person distance, would she be able to? The force of the story within other dimensions suggests strongly that she would not. In actuality, the director admits to putting his own real-life voice on the soundtrack because the material stirred him to remember his own father. Yet, the narration plays as if the sentimentality—kept so painstakingly at bay in the script—has crept insidiously into the execution.

Aside from stylistic issues such as these, however, the film is pure gold. Reviewers agreed unanimously that the film marks a triumphant return to the screen for Bogarde's talents. Several found it to be one of Tavernier's finest works, as well as the epitome of the "intimate" film.

Mary E. Belles

Reviews

American Film: Magazine of the Film and Television Arts. XVI, February, 1991, p. 50.

Boston Globe. May 10, 1991, CCXXXIX, p. 30.

Boxoffice. December, 1990, p. R-96.

Chicago Tribune. May 10, 1991, VII, p. 44.

The Christian Science Monitor. April 19, 1991, LXXXIII, p. 10.

The Hollywood Reporter. May 15, 1990, p. 8.

Los Angeles Times. April 19, 1991, CX, p. F4.

The New Republic. CCIV, March 4, 1991, p. 28.

The New York Times. April 12, 1991, p. B10.

Newsweek. CXVII, April 15, 1991, p. 70.

Premiere. IV, January, 1991, p. 12.

Variety. May 15, 1990, p. 3.

The Village Voice. April 16, 1991, p. 58.

The Washington Post. May 31, 1991, p. C6.

DEAD AGAIN

Production: Lindsay Doran and Charles H. Maguire for Sydney Pollack and Mirage; released by Paramount Pictures
Direction: Kenneth Branagh
Screenplay: Scott Frank
Cinematography: Matthew F. Leonetti
Editing: Peter E. Berger
Production design: Tim Harvey
Costume design: Phyllis Dalton
Makeup: Tom Burman and Bari Dreiband-Burnman
Music: Patrick Doyle
MPAA rating: R
Running time: 107 minutes

> *Principal characters:*
> Mike Church/Roman Strauss . . . . Kenneth Branagh
> Grace/Margaret Strauss . . . . Emma Thompson
> Franklyn Madson . . . . Derek Jacobi
> Gray Baker . . . . Andy Garcia
> Inga . . . . Hanna Schygulla
> Pete . . . . Wayne Knight
> Doug . . . . Campbell Scott
> Dr. Cozy Carlisle . . . . Robin Williams

When an unknown woman with amnesia and no voice (Emma Thompson) arrives inexplicably at St. Audrey's School for Boys, the head priest asks one of its old students, Mike Church (Kenneth Branagh), to discover who she is. Mike is a Los Angeles private investigator who specializes in finding lost heirs and missing people. Through a friend at the newspaper, he places an article about the woman in the hopes that someone will recognize and claim her. Because the priest will not allow the woman to stay at the school, she stays with Mike in his apartment.

Soon, an antique dealer named Franklyn Madson (Derek Jacobi) arrives at Mike's door. Madson claims that he can hypnotize the woman into remembering who she is and the traumatic event that has caused her amnesia. As proof that he is not a charlatan, he proceeds to put her into a trance in which she yells out for help. Still skeptical, Mike seeks advice from defrocked psychiatrist Cozy Carlisle (an unbilled Robin Williams), who tells him to try it.

The next day, at Madson's shop, The Laughing Duke, the antiquarian begins to elicit, under hypnosis, a part of the woman's story. Oddly, though, she begins with events in 1948, long before she was born. She tells of the meeting between a famous conductor/composer, Roman Strauss, and a pianist, Margaret. Later, after she has returned to the present, she has regained her voice but still has no idea of her current identity. Madson knows of the people about whom she has spoken, however, and he tells how Margaret had been stabbed to death brutally with a pair of scissors and how her husband had been found guilty of her murder and sentenced to death. Amazingly, the woman (who has been named Grace by Mike) looks very much like pictures of Margaret, while Roman strongly resembles Mike. The School for Boys, into which Grace had tried to gain entry, had been the old Strauss estate, where Roman and Margaret lived along with his housemaid, Inga (Hanna Schygulla, in a rare appearance in an American film), and her small son, Frankie.

Mike searches for Gray Baker (Andy Garcia), the newspaper reporter who had covered the trial and who had been interested romantically in Margaret. Meanwhile, he again consults Carlisle, who warns him that Roman and Margaret have been reincarnated as Mike and Grace. Perhaps this time, he suggests, it will be Margaret's turn to murder Mike in order to restore the balance in the cosmic ledger.

Grace's wallet is found, containing her address. Still not remembering anything but what she tells while under hypnosis, she returns to her apartment and finds that she is an artist haunted by visions of scissors, which permeate her work.

Although Grace and Mike have fallen in love, under Madson's suggestions, Grace has become obsessed with the idea that Mike/Roman will murder her again. Mike then undergoes hypnosis in order to prove that he was not Roman. Instead, the plot is given a startling new twist, and through journalist Baker, he discovers the truth about the death of Margaret Strauss. When Mike tries to contact Grace in order to tell her of his revelation, she assumes that he wants to kill her again, and she shoots and wounds him. When Madson arrives, a terrible struggle takes place, resulting in a death and a resolution to the mystery.

Dead Again is a romantic thriller with obvious supernatural overtones. The convoluted plot is relayed through multileveled narration and through the use of color footage to indicate the present and black-and-white footage to represent the past. It is the kind of plot that requires much attention on the part of the audience but that rewards them in ways that modern motion pictures rarely do. Written by relative newcomer Scott Frank, whose script for *Little Man Tate* (1991; reviewed in this volume) was filmed by actor/director Jodie Foster, it is a polished and well-crafted story which tells of the power of love, the importance of identity, and the role of fate.

While being a very contemporary film, *Dead Again* has obvious roots in the 1940's. The first background information provided in the film about the Strausses is through newspaper headlines and articles written by Gray Baker that appear under the credits. This technique recalls Orson Welles's use of headlines in *Citizen Kane* (1941). Also like Welles, conjuring up such films as *Journey into Fear* (1942) and *The Stranger* (1946), *Dead Again* uses oblique camera angles and protracted montages.

Dead Again was directed by Branagh who, also like Welles, starred in and directed a critically acclaimed film—*Henry V* (1989)—at a very young age—he was thirty. For his work on the film, Branagh was nominated for Best Actor and Best Director Academy Awards. On this, his second film, he used the same core of contributors with whom he had worked on *Henry V*: production designer Tim Harvey, composer Patrick

Doyle, and costume designer Phyllis Dalton, who won an Academy Award for her work on *Henry V.*

On the whole, Branagh has produced a highly entertaining and extremely charged film. His depiction of Los Angeles is neither the typically grubby one that is associated with detective films nor the chrome and glass high-tech one that is associated with most contemporary films. The buildings on which he chose to focus his cameras are as interesting as the characters. They are usually tall and often shot from low angles. In daylight, they can seem handsome, but by night they display another, more sinister, side. Mike's apartment, like his last name, evokes religious inclinations, with its stained glass windows and spirelike turrets, an inclination also seen in the name that he gives Grace. Grace's apartment, on the other hand, is in the famous Hightower House. Situated near the Hollywood Bowl, it is a freestanding tower inaccessible to vehicles and can be approached only by traveling through an elevator in an adjacent tower and walking across a bridge. The building has a sense of isolation which builds Grace's sense of helplessness when approached by Mike at the end of the film.

While Branagh and Thompson, who are married in real life, give outstanding performances in their dual roles, it is perhaps Jacobi in a very meaty supporting role who dominates much of the picture. As the antiquarian Madson, he hams his way through insinuating himself in Grace and Mike's lives. When he is first seen, he begins immediately to appraise Mike's furniture—undervaluing it in case he can purchase it. Later, he derives information on Teddy Roosevelt's desk from a woman whom he has regressed in hypnosis in order to cure her chocolate addiction. He is an opportunist who, oddly enough, seems to want to help. When, by the end of the film, he is reduced to the *Masterpiece Theatre* stutter that he used in the series *I Claudius*, it is entirely forgivable and makes for an amusing in-joke.

There are a few problems with the film, however. The overabundance of scissors in the film does begin to wear thin and becomes totally overdone in Grace's apartment. By the time that the villain receives poetic justice by being impaled on giant scissors, audiences are groaning. In fact, the entire ending seems strained and excessive, with more violence than was needed and the fighting going on longer than seemed logical, especially for a wounded man. Yet, if there are problems with the film, its entertainment value outweighs them.

Beverley Bare Buehrer

Reviews
American Cinematographer. LXXII, September, 1991, p. 50.
American Film: Magazine of the Film and Television Arts. XVI, September, 1991, p. 22.
Boxoffice. October, 1991, p. R-67.
Chicago Tribune. August 23, 1991, p. 7B.
The Christian Science Monitor. August 29, 1991, p. 12.

The Hollywood Reporter. August 19, 1991, p. 7.
Los Angeles Times. August 23, 1991, p. F1.
The New York Times. August 23, 1991, p. B1.
The New Yorker. LXVII, September 9, 1991, p. 76.
Newsweek. September 9, 1991, p. 67.
People Weekly. September 2, 1991, p. 15.
Rolling Stone. September 19, 1991, p. 81.
Time. CXXXVIII, September 23, 1991, p. 73.
USA Today. August 23, 1991, p. 4D.
Variety. August 26, 1991, p. 87.
The Wall Street Journal. August 29, 1991, p. A5.

DEFENDING YOUR LIFE

Production: Michael Grillo for Geffen Pictures; released by Warner Bros.
Direction: Albert Brooks
Screenplay: Albert Brooks
Cinematography: Allen Daviau
Editing: David Finfer
Production design: Ida Random
Art direction: Richard Reynolds
Set decoration: Linda DeScenna
Set design: Martha Johnston
Costume design: Deborah L. Scott
Music: Michael Gore
MPAA rating: PG-13
Running time: 111 minutes

> *Principal characters:*
> Daniel Miller .... Albert Brooks
> Julia .... Meryl Streep
> Bob Diamond .... Rip Torn
> Lena Foster .... Lee Grant
> Daniel's judge .... George D. Wallace
> Daniel's judge .... Lillian Lehman
> Dick Stanley .... Buck Henry
> Shirley Maclaine .... Shirley Maclaine

Defending Your Life is a comedy written and directed by Albert Brooks. Brooks also plays the part of the anxiety-ridden main character, Daniel Miller, who is similar to the character that Brooks played in *Broadcast News* (1987) but seems less of a type as parts of his life are reviewed, and he becomes more dynamic.

The film begins with a few glimpses of the last day of Daniel's life and quickly establishes that it is far less than ideal, a situation of which he is well aware. His stressful career as an advertising executive accentuates his anxiety. He is shown receiving a birthday present from his colleagues, giving a thank-you speech resembling a stand-up comedy routine in which the comedian makes jokes about his problems. Daniel jokes about his former wife and about wanting a higher income. Brooks calls on his past as a stand-up comic to deftly present Daniel as sympathetic and humorous, not letting his dissatisfaction with his life seem pathetic.

The film continues in this vein as Daniel claims that his plan to spend his birthday alone is desirable. He then tragicomically admits that it is a pitiful theory. He enthusiastically picks up his brand-new BMW convertible, but even this experience becomes a disappointment when the salesman draws his attention to a more elegant model just before showing him his. Daniel, extremely sensitive to and obsessed with even the most subtle distinctions of status, especially as they regard his measure of success, complains about this sales tactic but is nevertheless compelled to inquire hopefully about the price difference in the two vehicles.

In one of many humorous slices of the Los Angeles life-style lampooned in *Defending Your Life*, Daniel gets into his new car and enters his own private world, singing along to a Barbra Streisand compact disc at a high volume and completely ignoring that, with the top down, he is in full view. Paying little attention to shouted protests and less to his driving, he runs head-on into a bus. (This light comedy does not allow time to wonder about the people on the bus, although Daniel later asks another recently deceased person who claimed to recognize him if she was on the bus that he hit.)

The next scene is Judgment City, where the recently deceased are processed swiftly and efficiently in this otherworldly bureaucracy through a wheelchair assembly line and a fleet of trams. Judgment City, the tram guide informs the zombielike passengers, has been designed to appear "pleasing and very familiar," which includes billboard advertisements for the Tropicana and Sid's Steakhouse, three championship golf courses, and typical resort hotel accommodations.

The next morning, Daniel is summoned to see his defender, Bob Diamond (Rip Torn), who explains that Daniel is there to defend his life, the idea being that, if he can successfully prove that he has overcome his fears, then he will advance to become a citizen of the universe. In this original view of the afterlife, which is certain to offend any believer in one of the traditional religions who makes the mistake of taking this film literally, the usual measurements of worthiness such as faith, charity, and good deeds are disregarded in favor of having overcome fear, an achievement seen as the necessary precursor to using one's intelligence fully. Diamond explains that, on Earth, people use only 3 to 5 percent of their brains, that fear fogs one's brain and must be removed to allow for the development of intelligence and advancement in the system. Diamond also explains that when people use more than 5 percent, they don't want to be on Earth anymore. He states that there is no heaven and "actually there is no hell, though I hear L.A. is getting pretty close," a failure to move forward means another life on Earth. Daniel is embarrassed to hear that he has been sent back twenty times already and that he and those who have not yet moved forward are referred to as "little brains." He exclaims, "I'm the dunce of the universe" and desperately tries to find out from Diamond how to interpret this information in order to determine his status.

From this point, events continue to increase Daniel's anxiety about how he will be judged. He chooses from the many entertainments that are offered to go to The Bomb Shelter, a painfully stale comedy club, at which he meets a kindred spirit in witty humor in Julia (Meryl Streep) and falls in love. Daniel now has a new fear—losing Julia; he realizes that, with her admirable life (of which she only needs to look at four days instead of Daniel's nine), she will probably move forward and out of his reach if he is sent back. The evidence stacks up against him quickly: His able prosecutor, Lena Foster (Lee Grant), who is feuding with his defender (Diamond), finds many instances of fear and bad judgments in his life, while every moment spent with Julia increases his certainty that she is a prime candidate for citizenship in the universe. He is staying at the Continental, a typical low-budget hotel; she, at the Majestic, a luxury hotel with all the frills. When they visit the Past Lives Pavilion to see who they were in previous lives (the introduction is made by Shirley Maclaine as herself, a believer in reincarnation who is obviously delighted to do this cameo after all the criticism that she has received for her beliefs), Julia has been Prince Valiant, and Daniel has been a terrified native running for his life from some wild animal. Daniel becomes more certain that he will lose his trial when Diamond is unexpectedly absent one day and Dick Stanley (Buck Henry), who substitutes, says almost nothing in Daniel's defense although Stanley is purported to use an impressive 51 percent of his brain (as compared to Diamond's 48 percent).

Sure enough, Daniel is judged as needing to be sent back to Earth, the final incriminating scene coming not from his life but from the previous night in Judgment City when he decided against sleeping with Julia for reasons such as "this is already better than any sex I've ever had" (the possibility of disappointment), "by the looks of things, we aren't going to the same place" (the likelihood of loss), and "I've been defending myself so hard and I just don't want to be judged any more" (worry about his performance). He recognizes that what these reasons boil down to is "I'm af———," and his prosecutor forces him to say the word in court. The requisite happy ending occurs at the dramatic eleventh hour when Daniel, in a spirit of *carpe diem*, finally becomes courageous.

Defending Your Life succeeds as the witty comedy that it is intended to be largely because the natural and perfectly timed comic performances by Brooks and Streep keep its pace cruising along as smoothly and accurately as a Judgment City tram. There is no philosophizing about any such weighty subjects as the meaning of life and death, yet as Daniel reveals his most personal feelings through his jokes, *Defending Your Life* has bite behind some of its satire.

Brenda Berryhill

Reviews
Boxoffice. May, 1991, p. R-26.
Chicago Tribune. April 5, 1991, VII, p. 35.
The Christian Science Monitor. April 5, 1991, p. 14.
Los Angeles Times. March 22, 1991, p. F6.
The Nation. CCLII, April 22, 1991, p. 534.
The New York Times. March 22, 1991, p. C12.
The New Yorker. LXVII, April 22, 1991, p. 93.
Rolling Stone. April 4, 1991, p. 59.
Time. CXXXVII, March 25, 1991, p. 62.
Variety. CCCXLII, March 18, 1991, p. 83.
The Washington Post. April 5, 1991, p. B1.

DELIRIOUS

Production: Lawrence J. Cohen, Fred Freeman, and Doug Claybourne for Richard Donner and Star Partners III; released by Metro-Goldwyn-Mayer
Direction: Tom Mankiewicz
Screenplay: Lawrence J. Cohen and Fred Freeman
Cinematography: Robert Stevens
Editing: William Gordean and Tina Hirsch
Production design: Angelo Graham
Art direction: James J. Murakami
Set decoration: Richard Fernandez, Robert C. Goldstein, Peter J. Kelly, Lauren Polizzi, and Dianne Wager
Casting: David Rubin
Costume design: Molly Maginnis
Music: Cliff Eidelman
MPAA rating: PG
Running time: 96 minutes

Principal characters:
Jack Gable	John Candy
Louise/Janet Dubois	Mariel Hemingway
Laura/Rachel Hedison	Emma Samms
Carter Hedison	Raymond Burr
Blake Hedison	Dylan Baker
Ty Hedison	Charles Rocket
Dennis/Dr. Paul Kirkland	David Rasche
Nurse Helen Caldwell	Andrea Thompson
Mickey	Zach Grenier
Lou Sherwood	Jerry Orbach
Arlene Sherwood	Renee Taylor
Fetterman	Milt Oberman
Cable Man	Mark Boone, Jr.

Jack Gable (John Candy) is the producer/writer of the television soap opera *Beyond Our Dreams*. He is a large, self-conscious, bumbling man who has an unrequited crush on the show's leading lady, Laura (Emma Samms). Laura, who plays character Rachel Hedison, is a manipulative, scheming, and egotistical woman, both in real life and on the show. She has been involved romantically with the show's leading man, Dennis (David Rasche), but after a spat with him, she decides that she wants to accompany Jack on a weekend in Vermont. As he packs her numerous suitcases, he is hit in the chin by the car's trunk door. Upon recovering, he sees that Laura and Dennis, who plays Dr. Paul Kirkland on the soap opera, have reconciled.
Jack drives to Vermont by himself. On the way there, however, he hits a truck on a

dangerous curve. When he regains consciousness, he is in the Ashford Falls Hospital, attended by his soap-opera characters. Thinking it is some kind of elaborate joke, Jack fights the reality that he sees around him. He takes a hotel room in the fictional town and is approached by Janet Dubois (Mariel Hemingway). She says that Jack is really Jack Gates, the "Wolf of Wall Street," who has come to town to buy her father's formula. He tries to explain to her that everything is a figment of his writer's imagination. Janet is a character that he had dropped from the soap's scripts, which the show's bosses, Lou and Arlene Sherwood (Jerry Orbach and Renee Taylor), were thinking of reviving. Janet is actually an aspiring actress named Louise. When Jack demands to leave town, Janet, exasperated by his denials, tells him to write his way out.

A desperate Jack acts on this idea and sits down at his old electric Smith Corona typewriter to write a "script" in which his car is repaired immediately. As he is about to leave town, he sees the beautiful Rachel Hedison and wonders if he can win her love by writing it into the script of his present reality. Through a series of calculated and dangerous adventures, Jack does begin to attract Rachel, but the woman who is truly attracted to him is Janet. The fantasy plot revolves around the attempts made by the Hedison Pharmaceutical Company—headed by patriarch Carter Hedison (Raymond Burr) and his two sons, favorite Blake (Dylan Baker) and outcast Ty (Charles Rocket)—to buy or to steal Janet's father's formula. He has invented a metapill which allows people to eat anything that they want and never gain weight.

Every now and then, Jack's script seems to go haywire, a fact that he attributes to Arnie Fetterman (Milt Oberman), a writer whom the Sherwoods wanted to hire as a replacement because Jack refused to write out the ever-more-demanding Rachel. Just as the fantasy hits a dramatic turn, Jack awakens in the hospital set of *Beyond Our Dreams*. He thinks that his fantasy is about to start all over again, but he learns that, when he was hit on the head by the car's trunk door, he had been knocked out and had dreamed everything. The newly reborn Jack, however, realizes that it is Janet (or Louise) whom he really loves, and recognizes Laura for what she really is. He wanders the offices looking for Louise, always just missing her. Then one day, in the same New York delicatessen that he wrote into his fantasy, he hears an order for lox and cream cheese on cinnamon toast and finally finds her.

The plot for *Delirious* would seem to indicate that it is a Walter Mitty fable for the 1990's. An ineffectual man overcomes his handicaps and his dull life through the power of his own imagination, thus winning the fair maiden's hand. It might also be compared to *It's a Wonderful Life* (1946), in which the main character realizes the worth of his life and discovers what is truly of value after experiencing a fantasy adventure. Even the town names, Bedford Falls and Ashford Falls, are similar. Also appealing is the idea of a writer trapped within his own writing. It is a deliciously malicious concept that would appeal to most people who have watched brainless television programs. In fact, when Jack first realizes that this is exactly what has happened to him, he thinks that he has died and that being trapped for eternity on his own show is his personal hell.

Unfortunately, as intriguing as the plot might sound, it is handled in a rather mundane way. Part of the problem may derive from the fact that the film's major creative people are heavily steeped in a television background. Director Tom Mankiewicz was a cowriter on the ABC television series *Hart to Hart*, directing twelve of its initial episodes. His feature film debut came with the comedy *Dragnet* (1987). Also bringing with them years of television experience are the film's writers, Lawrence J. Cohen and Fred Freeman. Their credits include episodes of such television shows as *The Dick Van Dyke Show*, *The Andy Griffith Show*, *Bewitched*, and *Gilligan's Island*. Their feature film credits are less well known—*S*P*Y*S* (1974) and *The Big Bus* (1976).

This background is revealed in the film's rather pedestrian approach to the topic. The actors seem to do their best, with Raymond Burr, best known as television's Perry Mason, playing the Hedison patriarch with gusto and *Dynasty*'s Emma Samms good-humoredly parodying her own soap opera by displaying more bitchiness than Joan Collins on a bad day. Mariel Hemingway is good as the overlooked "girl next door" and Charles Rocket, from *Saturday Night Live*, and also known as private detective David Addison's eccentric brother on *Moonlighting*, plays the outcast son, Ty, with enthusiastic sleaziness and silliness. Even John Candy manages his role as the innocent caught in extraordinary situations with his usual aplomb. (Although the stunt doubles for the large Candy are very obvious and distracting.) The best thing about the film may be a surprise guest visit by Robert Wagner.

Delirious is innocuous enough, but hardly worth the high cost of theater tickets. This lightweight and slightly amusing film will probably be better accepted as a video rental, when the cost is less.

Beverley Bare Buehrer

Reviews

American Cinematographer. LXXII, February, 1991, p. 38.
Boston Globe. August 9, 1991, p. 39.
Boxoffice. October, 1991, p. R-68.
Chicago Tribune. August 13, 1991, V, p. 2.
Film Review. October, 1991, p. 28.
The Hollywood Reporter. July 17, 1991, p. 10.
Los Angeles Times. August 9, 1991, p. F8.
The New York Times. August 9, 1991, p. B7.
People Weekly. August 19, 1991, p. 11.
Premiere. IV, August, 1991, p. 12.
San Francisco Chronicle. August 10, 1991, p. C3.
USA Today. August 9, 1991, p. 5D.
Variety. August 5, 1991, p. 93.
The Washington Post. August 9, 1991, p. D6.

DOC HOLLYWOOD

Production: Susan Solt and Deborah D. Johnson; released by Warner Bros.
Direction: Michael Caton-Jones
Screenplay: Jeffrey Price, Peter S. Seaman, and Daniel Pyne; based on the book
  What? . . . Dead Again?, by Neil B. Shulman, and adapted by Laurian Leggett
Cinematography: Michael Chapman
Editing: Priscilla Nedd-Friendly
Production design: Lawrence Miller
Art direction: Eva Anna Bohn and Dale Allen Pelton
Set decoration: Cloudia Rebar
Casting: Marion Dougherty and Owens Hill
Sound: Ken King
Costume design: Richard Hornung
Music: Carter Burwell
MPAA rating: PG-13
Running time: 103 minutes

Principal characters:

Ben Stone	Michael J. Fox
Lou	Julie Warner
Dr. Hogue	Barnard Hughes
Hank	Woody Harrelson
Nick Nicholson	David Ogden Stiers
Lillian	Frances Sternhagen
Dr. Halberstrom	George Hamilton
Nancy Lee	Bridget Fonda
Melvin	Mel Winkler
Maddie	Helen Martin
Judge Evans	Roberts Blossom
Cotton	Tom Lacy
Aubrey Draper	Macon McCalman
Simon Tidwell	Raye Birk
Nurse Packer	Eyde Byrde

Doc Hollywood manipulates the viewer effectively into caring whether a young doctor stays in a small town in South Carolina with the woman he loves or leaves to find riches and fame as a cosmetic surgeon in Los Angeles. While the plot's formula is much too apparent and its outcome is predictable, the film succeeds eventually on the strength of several performances and certain values that the screenplay endorses, which are delivered irresistibly in the film's conclusion.

Under opening titles, Dr. Ben Stone (Michael J. Fox) is at work in a terribly busy hospital in Washington, D.C.—the hectic character of the place brings to mind scenes in *M*A*S*H* (1970) after a major battle. Stone, a good doctor but a callous man, ignores the emotional needs of patients but performs his other critical duties, diagnosis and physical treatment, with consummate skill. Hoping to be hired to do cosmetic surgery at a posh clinic that caters to film stars, Stone leaves Washington for Los Angeles. If he gets the job, and he most likely will because of an influential contact, he will be rich, famous in his field, and free from the distress that accompanies work at D.C. General. One of his acquaintances—he seems to have no friends—suggests, however, that doing cosmetic surgery might be a waste of his gifts, which can better serve humankind.

En route through the South, he drives his Porsche off the road in order to avoid hitting two women and their pigs blocking the way. As a result, his car collides with and destroys the newly built fence of Judge Evans (Roberts Blossom), who sentences the doctor to a period of community service; it seems that the town of Grady, South Carolina, is in need of medical practitioners. The doctor is resentful and angry at this turn of events and is condescending to the people in town who try to welcome him and convince him to stay. The only person who wins his interest is the ambulance driver, Lou (Julie Warner), whom he first sees emerging naked from a swim in the lake. Even more impressive than her beauty is the fact that she is thoroughly unperturbed at being so discovered; he is the one who grows uncomfortable as she takes some time before putting on her robe.

At this point in the narrative, every viewer, even those of elementary school age, can predict the outcome. Yet, many necessary steps in the formulaic story have still to be represented; moreover, the filmmakers have obstacles of their own making to overcome. In depicting the peculiarities of the people of fictional Grady, director Michael Caton-Jones and screenwriters Jeffrey Price, Peter S. Seaman, and Daniel Pyne have made this community disagreeable. It seems incredible at first that any stranger would choose to remain there. The pestering invasion of privacy, the injustice of the judge's sentence, the overkill in trying to keep the doctor there by taking the Porsche's engine apart tend to make one root for Stone's successful departure.

Caton-Jones has imposed a broad anything-for-a-laugh style, particularly on his supporting players. Peripheral characters, such as Lillian (Frances Sternhagen), one of three women who welcome the doctor to Grady, are used to establish background for this caricature of a town. It is sad to see such a brilliant actress as Sternhagen relegated to speaking in monotone in order to represent a small-town type. Later, in Los Angeles, Dr. Halberstrom (George Hamilton) is given similarly broad representation, except that Halberstrom represents the superficiality of big-city types. His braided ponytail is his main mark of characterization.

While the exaggeration used in parodying both small-town and big-city life can be rationalized as the way of satiric comedy, it is often of the most uninventive kind in *Doc Hollywood*. The mere idea that the Porsche engine has been dismantled, for example, is supposed to amuse. Yet, the laughter needs to be earned by imaginative development of the incongruous idea. It is much more amusing when Charlie Chaplin dissects a clock in *The Pawnshop* (1916).

Two of the supporting players manage to rise above the film's level of television situation comedy. Grady's only physician, the often cantankerous Dr. Hogue (Barnard Hughes), who will soon need a successor, has amusing and convincing early clashes with his young colleague. Hughes, an immensely skilled actor, gives his character sufficient complexity so that one cares about what he thinks. Therefore, the viewer receives some satisfaction when mutual respect develops between Hogue and Stone.

The most hilarious confrontations are between Stone and the adamant Nurse Packer (Eyde Byrde), who punches his time card each time that he arrives for or departs from work to be certain that he completes all the hours stipulated by his sentence. Shortly after he insists that this indignity stop, a grateful patient brings him a gift of a pig. The stone-faced nurse insists that the doctor remove his newly acquired animal from the premises and then punches the clock as he departs obediently.

Miraculously and gradually, despite many petty annoyances, the doctor becomes involved in the town. He goes through an evolution from the unfeeling, ambitious man who is ready to prostitute his invaluable talents to serve shallow ends to one who cares about the people whom he serves. The screenplay reveals eventually that Stone was originally a small-town boy from Indiana, as if this fact could make the transformation more convincing.

Ultimately, what does convince is the intensity of the relationship between Stone and Lou provided by the strong performances of Fox and Warner. During a dance, they discover their mutual love and move around the floor in each other's arms as if in their own magnetic field. Yet, they resist the almost overwhelming impulse to kiss. She has experienced life in New York City and knows that she must remain in Grady; he will soon depart for Los Angeles. Neither one is willing to use the other as a temporary sexual partner. Wanting them to unite makes one wish that the doctor would forgo his aspirations to leave. If the film is to satisfy, however, Grady must seem a desirable place for Stone to remain. Therefore, the screenplay works hard to juxtapose its humorous satire of small-town life with revelations of that life's worth. The screenplay also works hard to be morally correct—neither prudish nor indecent. Total frontal nudity is offered in one scene, while Stone refuses to take advantage of a vulnerable Lou in another. The juggling act to espouse homely values and, at the same time, to titillate seems apparent.

In spite of these objections, a splendidly edited climactic sequence involving the birth of a baby, the destruction of Ben's Porsche, and the ripping of his Armani shirts to provide rags for the baby's delivery demonstrates effectively the dramatic collision of opposing values. Just when Stone finds himself free to escape his rustic bondage, circumstances of such a symbolic character that they seem fated conspire to keep him there. Stone, torn between his desire for a voluptuous freedom and his feelings for Lou, is driving out of town when one of his Grady patients hails the Porsche; the man's wife is in labor in their station wagon and there is no time to transport her to a hospital. The doctor tends to her, leaving his car across the road. A sequence of shots shows a truck moving fast, its driver close to falling asleep at the wheel, the expectant father standing by the Porsche and waving frantically as the truck approaches ominously, and the doctor urging the mother on toward delivery. The predictable collision occurs a second after the baby's birth.

The filmmakers pose a question: What is the value of a Porsche and some Armani shirts compared to a new human life? How can one disagree with the implied answer?

Cono Robert Marcazzo

Reviews

Atlanta Constitution. August 2, 1991, p. C1.
Boxoffice. September, 1991, p. R-59.
Chicago Tribune. August 2, 1991, VII, p. 33.
Film Review. October, 1991, p. 29.
The Hollywood Reporter. July 29, 1991, p. 8.
Los Angeles Times. August 2, 1991, p. F1.
The New York Times. August 2, 1991, p. B1.
Newsweek. CXVIII, August 19, 1991, p. 55.
Sight and Sound. I, November, 1991, p. 39.
Time. CXXXVIII, September 9, 1991, p. 69.
Variety. July 29, 1991, p. 3.
The Washington Post. August 2, 1991, p. B1.

THE DOCTOR

Production: Laura Ziskin for Touchstone Pictures, in association with Silver Screen
 Partners IV; released by Buena Vista
Direction: Randa Haines
Screenplay: Robert Caswell; based on the book *A Taste of My Own Medicine*, by Ed
 Rosenbaum
Cinematography: John Seale
Editing: Bruce Green and Lisa Fruchtman
Production design: Ken Adam
Art direction: William J. Durrell, Jr.
Set decoration: Gary Fettis
Casting: Lynn Stalmaster
Sound: Jim Tanenbaum
Costume design: Joe I. Tompkins
Music: Michael Convertino
MPAA rating: PG-13
Running time: 125 minutes

> *Principal characters:*
> Jack MacKee . . . . William Hurt
> Anne MacKee . . . . Christine Lahti
> June Ellis . . . . Elizabeth Perkins
> Murray Caplan . . . . Mandy Patinkin
> Eli Blumfield . . . . Adam Arkin
> Nicky MacKee . . . . Charlie Korsmo
> Leslie Abbott . . . . Wendy Crewson
> Al Cade . . . . Bill Macy

The Doctor cleverly turns the standard doctor-patient relationship on its head by
dramatizing the plight of an efficient but coldly impersonal surgeon who, after
developing cancer of the larynx, becomes a common patient in the same hospital in
which he practices. Based on the book *A Taste of My Own Medicine* (1988) by Oregon
physician Ed Rosenbaum, the film chronicles the surgeon's personal encounter with
the possibility of death, showing how such an experience can teach even the most
compassionless person how to become a more empathetic human being.

Jack MacKee (William Hurt) is an accomplished and respected heart surgeon at a
large San Francisco hospital. He first appears in the hospital operating room
performing delicate open-heart surgery while listening to pop songs and encouraging
his staff to sing along to the music during the operation. Jack's partner, Dr. Murray
Caplan (Mandy Patinkin), echoes Jack's less-than-empathetic attitude toward his
patients by mimicking Jack's flippant behavior enthusiastically during the surgery.
Both men hold the same opinion of another surgeon, Eli "The Rabbi" Blumfield
(Adam Arkin), believing that Eli is much too emotionally involved with his patients to

maintain a proper professional detachment. Jack's cavalier attitude toward his patients is further demonstrated when he meets with a female patient who has recently undergone an operation which has left a massive scar on her chest. When she tells Jack that she is worried about her husband's reaction to the scar, he tells her that she resembles a Playboy centerfold. "You even have the staple marks to prove it," he chuckles as the woman grimaces. Later, on rounds with a group of interns, he tells them his professional philosophy: "A surgeon's job is to cut. Get in, fix it, and get out." He argues that it is dangerous to become too emotionally involved with a patient, that a surgeon should be more preoccupied with cutting than caring.

To appease the concerns about his health of his wife, Anne (Christine Lahti), Jack visits with a general practitioner friend, Dr. Al Cade (Bill Macy), about a bothersome "tickle" in his throat. Cade can detect nothing wrong with Jack but advises him to see a specialist. Jack chooses throat specialist Leslie Abbott (Wendy Crewson), whose bedside manner is even more impersonal than his own. After subjecting him to a less-than-gentle examination, she informs him that he has a growth on his larynx. Stunned by the news, Jack drives home to inform his family. Upon arriving home, both Jack's wife and young son, Nicky (Charlie Korsmo), are surprised to see him home so early in the day. Jack balks at telling Anne the reason until late in the evening after he has become drunk. She promises that she will help him fight the illness, but he reacts bitterly, saying that "it's not a team thing."

The next day, Anne accompanies Jack to the hospital, where he is scheduled for a biopsy. He becomes upset over the fact that he must fill out a stack of forms like a common patient, then later is infuriated when he finds out that there are no private hospital rooms available and that he must share a room with someone else. When Jack returns from his biopsy operation, he is humiliated even further when he is given a barium enema which was meant for his roommate.

The biopsy proves that Jack has a malignant tumor on his larynx, and Dr. Abbott recommends that he receive radiation therapy. Once again, Jack is treated like a common patient, filling out more forms and receiving a series of humiliating and impersonal examinations, after which he is kept in doubt about the status of his condition. He becomes drained and demeaned by the experience, to the point where he finds it hard to continue his practice. His partner, Murray, recommends that Jack stay home and rest until his treatment is over, a suggestion which Jack rejects flatly.

During his radiation therapy sessions, Jack meets other cancer patients, one of whom is June (Elizabeth Perkins), a young woman suffering from a brain tumor. When he complains to her about the humiliating treatment that he is receiving, she tells him that it took three months of extensive tests before doctors diagnosed her condition, and even then the tumor was discovered by accident. June remains calm about her condition yet gradually reveals to Jack her fears and her disappointment that she will not be able to achieve many of the goals that she had hoped to accomplish before dying. She also admits, however, that her illness has given her liberties that she has never had before.

After weeks of radiation therapy, Jack learns that his tumor has grown even larger than before. The news sends him into a panic. On an impulse, he persuades June to accompany him to Reno, Nevada, where a theater troupe that June has been wanting to see is performing. On their way to Reno, June suddenly tells Jack to stop the car so that she can get out and savor the journey rather than rush through it. They miss the performance, choosing instead to enjoy the serenity of the Nevada desert and to dance together in the moonlight. On their way home, Jack stops to call Anne to tell her where he is. She first reacts sympathetically when he tells her about the condition of his tumor. When he tells her that he is in the middle of the desert with a strange woman, however, she hangs up the telephone. Jack confesses to June that he has kept Anne at a distance for so long that he cannot let his guard down and become more intimate.

Back at the hospital, Jack begins to display a more sympathetic attitude toward his patients, a professional approach which surprises both his fellow doctors and his interns. He also decides to dismiss Dr. Abbott as his personal physician and instead seeks out Eli Blumfield, saying that he wants "The Rabbi" to perform the surgery on his larynx. Jack also apologizes to Eli for ridiculing him in the past for his sympathetic bedside manner. Just before the operation, Jack learns that June has collapsed and is in intensive care. Jack stays at her bedside late into the evening until, finally, she dies. When he returns home and tells Anne what has happened, she comforts him, although she still remains upset over the fact that he chose June over her as a confidante.

The following day, Eli performs the throat surgery on Jack. The operation is successful; however, there is a chance that Jack might never speak again. While he is recovering from the operation at home, he provokes an argument with Anne, blowing a whistle at her and writing phrases on a portable slate that ask her to forgive him and tell her that he needs her. Finally, Anne breaks down and the two embrace, Jack finally croaking, "I love you," which sends the couple into a celebratory dance. After Jack recovers from his operation, he returns to his practice as a loving, caring physician. While on his rounds, he receives a letter from June written the day before she died. In the letter, she tells Jack how to let down his guard in order to become more intimate with the people in his life. The film ends with a triumphant Jack visiting one of June's favorite retreats—the hospital roof—where he looks over the city and smiles.

The message of *The Doctor* is a noble one, preaching the need for professionals to treat their clients as human beings rather than faceless inferiors. Its premise is clever, a twist on Charles Dickens' *A Christmas Carol* which shows how a modern medical Scrooge gets a taste of his own bitter medicine, ultimately learning how crucial it is for a heart surgeon to display more heartfelt sympathy toward his patients and loved ones. The problem with *The Doctor* is that its compassionate message is delivered with a calculated, streamlined efficiency which drains much of the film of its drama. Too much is made of the ironic "tables are turned" premise and of the invincible surgeon being treated as a common patient in his own hospital. The irony becomes far too obvious and belabored, overriding the seriousness of Jack's condition. There is never the feeling that Jack is in a life-and-death situation, only that he is being treated unfairly and that his inability to feel empathy for others is destroying his marriage. Even when June's character is introduced and one learns that her condition is even more critical than that of Jack, there is still no urgency to the drama. The fact that she is close to death is secondary to the audience's concern over whether she and Jack will have an affair. When June finally dies, her death is a surprise because she seemed so blasé about her condition, never complaining about her disease except to profess a sadness over not having had the chance to accomplish as many things in her life as she had hoped. For a film about doctors, hospitals, and terminally ill patients, none of the characters adequately conveys a sense of vulnerability and no one seems to take death all that seriously. Because Jack's transformation from impersonal joker to compassionate humanitarian occurs in a universe in which the specter of imminent death is less frightening than receiving an unnecessary enema or filling out hospital forms, it is hard to accept Jack's speedy and near-painless character upheaval. The audience sees his transformation but cannot feel the pain or the urgency of the situation.

The film's inability to create a life-and-death imperativeness to the drama is a fault of the screenplay, which is far too eager to explain Jack's transformation rather than embody it. Although Hurt's performance is excellent, very low key, and filled with charming physical nuances, he cannot overcome the script's preachiness. His total character transformation, therefore, occurs on paper, not on the screen. The script's bloodlessness also affects the other performances, which, for the most part, are extremely well acted but also lack a gut-level intensity. The entire film suffers from a clinical approach to its subject matter, a critical flaw for a film preaching compassion. Director Randa Haines adds to this clinical approach by bathing most of the action in impersonal blue and antiseptic white tones. While it is obvious that she believes in the message of the film, she cannot overcome the simplistic preachiness of the script and is unable to inject some much-needed unpredictability to the action. Although the filmmakers' hearts are in the right place, they fail to infuse enough heartfelt sincerity into their endeavor, resulting in a professionally executed yet coldly impersonal film about the need for more compassion in the world.

Jim Kline

Reviews

Boxoffice. September, 1991, p. R-59.
Chicago Tribune. July 24, 1991, V, p. 1.
Films in Review. XLII, November, 1991, p. 408.
The Hollywood Reporter. July 23, 1991, p. 11.
Los Angeles Times. July 24, 1991, p. F1.
The New York Times. July 25, 1991, p. B2.
Newsweek. CXVIII, August 5, 1991, p. 54.
Rolling Stone. September 5, 1991, p. 102.
Time. CXXXVIII, September 9, 1991, p. 69.
Variety. July 23, 1991, p. 2.
The Wall Street Journal. August 8, 1991, p. A10.
The Washington Post. August 2, 1991, p. B7.

THE DOORS

Production: Bill Graham, Sasha Harari, and A. Kitman Ho for Mario Kassar and
Imagine Entertainment; released by TriStar Pictures
Direction: Oliver Stone
Screenplay: J. Randal Johnson and Oliver Stone
Cinematography: Robert Richardson
Editing: David Brenner and Joe Hutshing
Production design: Barbara Ling
Art direction: Larry Fulton
Set design: Steve Arnold and Lisette Thomas
Set decoration: Cricket Rowland
Special visual effects: Michael Owens
Sound: Tod A. Maitland
Costume design: Marlene Stewart
Executive music production: Budd Carr
Music production: Paul Rothchild
Music: The Doors
MPAA rating: R
Running time: 141 minutes

> *Principal characters:*
> Jim Morrison . . . . Val Kilmer
> Pamela Courson . . . . Meg Ryan
> John Densmore . . . . Kevin Dillon
> Ray Manzarek . . . . Kyle MacLachlan
> Robby Krieger . . . . Frank Whaley
> Patricia Kennealy . . . . Kathleen Quinlan
> Andy Warhol . . . . Crispin Glover

The Doors is director Oliver Stone's third film set during one of America's most
turbulent and colorful decades, the 1960's. As in his two previous films about that
explosive period, Stone attempts to examine the age by playing out the action from the
point of view of one strong, central character. This time, instead of chronicling a
young recruit's apocalyptic tour of duty during the height of the Vietnam War in
Platoon (1986) or examining life on the home front through the eyes of Vietnam-
veteran-turned-anti-war-activist Ron Kovic in *Born on the Fourth of July* (1989),
Stone looks at the 1960's from the point of view of one of the premier rock-and-roll
bands of the era, The Doors, and, most specifically, their charismatic lead singer, Jim
Morrison.

The film begins near the end of the short, excessive life of Morrison (Val Kilmer) as
he sits alone in a recording booth in Paris. Scraggly, with long hair and a thick beard,
overweight, and swigging whiskey from a bottle in between poetic ramblings about his

life, Morrison chants, "Is everybody in? The ceremony is about to begin." Then, to the tune of one of the band's darkest, moodiest songs, "Riders on the Storm," the scene changes to a stark, desolate desert landscape. A very young Morrison rides in a car with his parents, his brother, and his sister and witnesses the aftermath of a tragic car accident involving a truck-load of Navajos, an image that will haunt him for the rest of his life.

The scene shifts to Southern California in the mid-1960's, where Morrison is a film student at the University of California at Los Angeles (UCLA). During a showing of one of his experimental films, he is hooted out of class by his fellow students. One student, however, Ray Manzarek (Kyle MacLachlan), is transfixed by the bold images and tells Morrison that he is brilliant. Later, the two meet on the beach at Venice, and Morrison shows Manzarek some of his poetry and song lyrics. Manzarek, a keyboardist in a fledgling rock-and-roll band, is impressed and encourages Morrison to join the group. Morrison also sees a young, attractive flower child on the beach, Pam Courson (Meg Ryan), whom he later woos with his moody poetry and talk about Native American shamans who take peyote and see images "from the other side." He also talks about confronting death and pain and how these confrontations make him feel most alive.

When Morrison meets with Manzarek and the other members of Manzarek's band, friction results over Morrison's dark, obscure lyrics. The group's guitarist, Robby Krieger (Frank Whaley), finally hands Morrison the words and music to a song that he has written, "Light My Fire," and after Morrison changes the song's lighter emphasis to a more mysterious tone, the scene shifts to a tiny Los Angeles nightclub where the band performs the song in front of a small, enthusiastic crowd. After the concert, a slick, sleazy recording executive takes Morrison aside and tells him to leave the group and become a solo artist because he has a charismatic power that the others lack. While Morrison is rejecting the executive's advice, the other band members, especially the group's drummer, John Densmore (Kevin Dillon), complain about Morrison's disruptive, improvisational approach to the music.

In a scene that comes closest to explaining the group's creative influences, Morrison persuades Pam and the group to follow him to the desert and take peyote with him. Amid wild chantings and rambling confessionals, the scene explodes in a series of swirling images of swiftly moving clouds, an ancient Navajo wandering through a dark cave, and a naked, bald giant riding a white horse through the desert. The camera then dives into Morrison's eyeball and the scene, reflected in his eye, dissolves into a performance by the band at the famed Los Angeles nightclub, Whiskey A Go Go, where Morrison leads the group in one of its most infamous songs, "The End." The song is filled with references to the images that were glimpsed during the peyote desert trip and includes a Freudian passage about a man killing his father and raping his mother that causes the club's owner to ban the group from the club. Two recording executives from a new record company are in the audience that evening, however, and they sign the group to a recording contract.

A rush of colorfully corny, nostalgic images follows, detailing a 1967 San Francisco "love-in" before shifting to the band's New York television appearance on Ed Sullivan's popular variety show. Later, Morrison and the group attend a decadent New York party given by a limp, pretentious Andy Warhol (Crispin Glover). After a pompous press conference during which Morrison answers crass questions with obscure references to his fascination with death and shamans, he becomes involved with Patricia Kennealy (Kathleen Quinlan), an attractive journalist from the press meeting who exposes him to the practices of ancient witchcraft rituals involving drinking one's own blood. Afterward, Morrison is impotent with Pam, who tells him that he is becoming corrupted by fame and glory. Morrison tells her that he enjoys the fame and hangs out of their hotel window until Pam is forced to tell Morrison that she would die for him.

Three excellent, uproarious concert scenes follow, each capturing a facet of the band's strong appeal. In the first, Morrison interrupts a song, "When the Music's Over," to inform the crowd of an incident that occurred prior to the concert in which he was attacked backstage by a hostile police officer. The police officers who line the stage, protecting Morrison from his adoring fans, suddenly break up the concert and arrest Morrison for disturbing the peace. In the second—and best—concert re-creation, Morrison leads an enthusiastic San Francisco audience in a shamanistic dance amid images of bonfires, dancing Indians, and naked crowd members. Interspliced with these feverish images, performed to the band's wild, scream-infested song, "Not to Touch the Earth," Morrison confronts Pam in a dimly lit bedroom and screams at her for injecting heroin. In the darkest, most decadent concert re-creation, a horribly out-of-control Morrison again interrupts a song after confront-ing the image of the ancient Navajo, who seems to wave farewell to him. Morrison then badgers his Miami Beach audience, encouraging them to become naked and cavort. After pretending to expose his genitals to the audience, Morrison jumps into the crowd and leads them in a thundering version of "Break on Through," after which he passes out while surrounded by the screaming hordes.

The other band members are outraged by Morrison's overindulgent excesses, which result in him being indicted for indecent exposure. During recording sessions, Morrison shows up drunk. When the members accuse him of recklessness, he accuses them of distorting the original intent of the band, which was to explore the magic and mystery of "the other side." At a party given by Pam and Morrison, Pam becomes hysterical over Morrison's self-destructiveness and attacks him with a butcher knife. Morrison encourages her to stab him, but then later, dazed and overwhelmed by the recent events of his life, mumbles, "I think I'm having a nervous breakdown." After recording their album, "L.A. Woman," which the band members agree is one of their best efforts, Morrison tells them that he and Pam are leaving for Paris.

The scene returns to Morrison alone in the Paris recording studio, wrapping up his long, confessional session. Clutching an Indian ceremonial feather, he sees the ancient Navajo for the last time. Pam and Morrison settle into a small Paris apartment where, one night, Pam awakes from a restless sleep and sees the image of the naked, bald giant walking down the apartment's hallway. When she searches for Morrison, she finds him dead in the bathtub, his eyes open, an expression of peaceful contentment on his face.

At its best, *The Doors* re-creates the energetic fervor of the 1960's through the use of the band's music and the overwhelmingly raucous and celebrative concert scenes. As never before, Stone captures the essence of the 1960's appeal—its energy, excitement, and hedonistic indulgences—and Morrison himself is the perfect symbol for these ritualistic celebrations of hedonistic excesses. Stone compares Morrison to Dionysus, the orgiastic, wine-loving Greek god who was ultimately torn apart by his frenzied followers after inspiring them with his example of divine overindulgence. The comparison is a fitting one and sets up the conflict that rages within Morrison over his overindulgent tendencies and his beliefs in shamanism, of being a tribal healer encouraging deathlike confrontations in order to bring back healing messages from "the other side" to his followers. Stone's images of dancing Indians, masses of screaming fans prancing naked around a bonfire, and the earlier images of starkly beautiful, surreal desert scenes serve to bathe the film in an intense, inspiring aura of otherworldly magic.

Unfortunately, these celebrative moments of divine excess are surrounded by a hackneyed, music biography format that relies on too many stale variations of scenes from previous biographical films about struggling artists who finally achieve success only to be destroyed by fame and drugs. These clichéd docudrama scenes are hampered further by Stone's overly simplistic depiction of the 1960's as a colorful, psychedelic hippie heaven. Another serious problem inhibiting the film's success springs directly from the core subjects of the film, Morrison and the music of The Doors. Morrison, who was twenty-seven when he died in 1971, has since become a legend. Throughout his life, he attempted to convey the image of a mysterious, troubled poet. The music of The Doors, full of moody, obscure references to death, rebirth, and orgiastic, drug-induced pleasures, embodied the spirit of Morrison's own self-image more profoundly than the uninspiring facts of his self-destructive life. Morrison's self-perpetuated, poetic image and the music of The Doors are what ultimately survive and dominate the facts. When Stone tries to tell Morrison's story, concentrating on the biographical details, he destroys what is the true essence of Morrison: his legend.

Stone tries to match the band's music with his own visual interpretations of the songs. Sometimes, his interpretations do justice to the songs' distinctively moody rhythms and obscure lyrics. The early flashback segment, done to "Riders on the Storm," the colorfully cartoonish depiction of Venice Beach life, done to "Love Street," and especially the surreal desert images that interpret the lyrics of "The End" complement the music perfectly. Many of the images are too specific, however, and war against the music's hypnotic, ethereal qualities. Stone, who has admitted that Morrison was a huge influence on him as a young man growing up in the turbulent 1960's, obviously loves his subject matter.

Yet, the film, although riddled with docudrama clichés and stereotypical depictions of 1960's hippie life, ultimately triumphs over these serious detractions because of

Stone's wise usage of all the best music that was created by The Doors and by an electrifying performance by Kilmer as Morrison. As the film progresses, Kilmer begins to take on more and more of Morrison's well-documented mannerisms, voice inflections, and looks, until Kilmer, the actor, disappears and Morrison, in all of his divine, self-destructive excesses, is resurrected on screen. It is a thoroughly convincing portrayal of a legendary figure, made even more impressive by Kilmer's singing, which blends so well with the actual recordings that they are nearly indistinguishable from the original vocals.

Jim Kline

Reviews
Chicago Tribune. March 1, 1991, VII, p. 33.
The Christian Science Monitor. March 19, 1991, p. 11.
Films in Review. XLII, May, 1991, p. 193.
The Hollywood Reporter. March 1, 1991, p. 9.
Los Angeles Times. March 1, 1991, p. F1.
The New York Times. March 1, 1991, p. B1.
The New Yorker. LXVII, March 11, 1991, p. 64.
Newsweek. March 18, 1991, p. 56.
Rolling Stone. March 21, 1991, p. 83.
Time. CXXXVII, March 11, 1991, p. 73.
Variety. March 1, 1991, p. 2.
The Village Voice. March 12, 1991, p. 51.

THE DOUBLE LIFE OF VÉRONIQUE
(LA DOUBLE VIE DE VÉRONIQUE)

Origin: France and Poland
Released: 1991
Released in U.S.: 1991
Production: Leonardo de la Fuente for Sideral Productions, Tor Productions, and Le Studio Canal Plus, in association with Norsk Film; released by Miramax Films
Direction: Krzysztof Kieslowski
Screenplay: Krzysztof Kieslowski and Krzysztof Piesiewicz
Cinematography: Slawomir Idziak
Editing: Jacques Witta
Production design: Patrice Mercier
Music: Zbigniew Preisner
MPAA rating: no listing
Running time: 90 minutes

> *Principal characters:*
> Veronika/Véronique .... Irène Jacob
> Alexandre Fabbri .... Philippe Volter
> Véronique's father .... Claude Duneton
> Veronika's father .... Wladyslaw Kowalski
> Antek .... Jerzy Gudejko
> Catherine .... Sandrine Dumas
> Professor .... Louis Ducreux
> Aunt .... Halina Gryglaszewska

The Double Life of Véronique is the kind of film that American critics love. Although, by Hollywood standards, it is possessed of an incoherent plot line unmotivated by cause and effect, it has a quality of purposeful enigma, as well as enough aestheticized sexuality and European ambiance to hark back to the kind of films that entranced critics and filled art-house cinemas in the 1960's. Fueling the positive critical reception of these films was the belief of many that American films were inferior to those being made on the Continent. With 1990's Hollywood films' often simplistic action fare targeted for a teenage audience, the qualities that make The Double Life of Véronique so distinctively European also form the basis of its appeal to audiences, like those of the early 1960's, that may be hungry for something different. Those qualities make it a virtual parody of all the established stereotypes of Continental filmmaking associated with an earlier generation of filmmakers, such as Ingmar Bergman and Alain Resnais, yet the film ultimately achieves a unique identity of its own, in large measure because of the tour de force performance of Irène Jacob. Jacob plays two women, one Polish and one French, who do not know each other but who are bound together by several uncanny ties of resemblance. These ties form the basis of the film's narrative.

Directed by acclaimed Polish filmmaker Krzysztof Kieslowski, *The Double Life of Véronique* begins with the curious sight of what appears to be the upside-down horizon of a city at night. It is revealed that a Polish child, Veronika, is gazing not at a cityscape but at stars and fog. The next scene takes place in France, where a young girl named Véronique stares at leaves. The film immediately returns to Poland, a number of years later, where the grown Veronika (Jacob) sings in a chorus. Her fellow chorus members scurry for cover as it begins to rain, but Veronika is oblivious to the weather—she continues to sing in a pure, clear voice. In almost inexplicable terms, this scene sets the tone of the film's mystical atmosphere even as it establishes the central focus of Veronika's life: her devotion to her music.

After the concert, Veronika's meeting with her boyfriend leads to sex, but also a strange admission on Veronika's part. She tells Antek (Jerzy Gudejko) that she believes that she is not alone, that she has a link to someone beyond the familial and emotional connections that she can articulate. Veronika suddenly decides to go to Krakow to stay with an aunt (Halina Gryglaszewska). The mood of strangeness created in the first scenes continues as the dwarfish lawyer of Veronika's aunt arrives at the house. The lawyer may be there to discuss the terms of the aunt's will, as she and Veronika have been discussing a disturbing family pattern: Family members, such as Veronika's mother, tend to die in the midst of what appears to be perfect health.

In Krakow, Veronika succeeds in impressing a choral director with her amazing voice, but immediately after, she is struck by heart pains. As she hurriedly crosses the city square, she is caught in the middle of a political demonstration. Amid the chaos, she glimpses a woman on a tourist bus who looks exactly like her, but she does not realize she has seen the French Véronique (Jacob). That night, Veronika sings once again and collapses with heart pains. As she sits on a bench to recover, a man exposes himself to her. The next day, Veronika wins an important music competition and the opportunity to participate as a soloist in a choral performance. Antek arrives, but Veronika appears ambivalent about continuing their relationship. As Veronika performs in the concert, her voice begins to lose the pitch. Suddenly, she collapses to the floor and a man declares that she is dead. In yet another unsettling and surreal moment, the camera then looks up from inside her grave as mourners throw dirt on Veronika's coffin.

The film has rather shockingly killed off one of its protagonists after only thirty minutes, and the story then shifts to the life of Véronique. On the same day as Veronika's funeral, as Véronique is making love to her boyfriend, she feels an inexplicable grief. Without any explanation, she tells her vocal teacher that she is giving up singing. It is as if she intuitively knows that she must stop singing in order to save herself from Veronika's fate, since she too has a heart condition.

At the school where she teaches music, Véronique sees a puppet show in which a beautiful ballerina dies and is reborn as a butterfly. She is also very interested in the puppeteer, Alexandre Fabbri (Philippe Volter). Although she knows nothing of him, Véronique tells a friend that she thinks she is in love. Curious things begin to happen.

Someone from another apartment building appears to be shining a light into her room. Véronique goes to the garbage can to retrieve a string that has been sent to her in an envelope, a string that closely resembles one that held together some of Veronika's music. The film begins to take on a sinister mood as Véronique is seen walking by cemeteries. She becomes peripherally involved in a friend's court case, and suddenly a strange man demands to know why she is lying for her friend. This enigmatic episode, like so many other incidents in the film, is resolved but never fully explained.

Véronique discovers the identity of the puppeteer and reads the books that he has written for children. At the country house of her father (Claude Duneton), she receives a package, apparently from the puppeteer, and she is able to guess what is in the package before she opens it. She then receives a tape of noises. During all these events, the song that Veronika sung at her death remains a part of the film's score.

While visiting with her father (who bears an amazing resemblance to Veronika's aunt), Véronique discerns the location from which the last anonymous package that she received was mailed by examining the canceled stamp: the St. Lazare train station. In a curious coincidence, at the station sits one of the judges involved in adjudicating the musical competition in which Veronika participated. Véronique uses the sounds on the tape to guide her to a restaurant. In one corner is a table laden with open books and reading glasses that belong to the puppeteer. He reveals that he has waited forty-eight hours for her to appear and that she has been a part of a psychological test to see if a woman would respond to a call from an unknown man. He is testing his theory for a novel that he is writing.

Having fallen in love with Alexandre, Véronique is devastated by this revelation. She runs into the street and checks into a hotel. He finds her there, asks her forgiveness, and declares his love. She reveals her feeling of being in two places. In her purse, Alexandre discovers a contact sheet for photographs. He admires a photo of her taken in the Krakow square, but she explains that the person in the photograph is not her. She begins to cry and crumbles the photograph, which appears as a tangible confirmation of what she has long sensed. Later, she visits the puppeteer at his apartment. He shows her two identical puppets he has made of her and says that he is writing a story about two women born in two different cities on the same day. One of them has experiences that hurt her, but the other somehow learns from the experiences of the first and is prevented from repeating her double's mistakes. In response to Alexandre's explanation, Véronique looks crestfallen: Her life, and the almost sacred experience of her double, is becoming fodder for the puppeteer's storytelling impulse—the same impulse, ironically, that has governed *The Double Life of Véronique*.

Elliptical in construction, with the kind of narrative structure and slow pace uncharacteristic of a Hollywood film, *The Double Life of Véronique* holds its audience through the mystery at its core, a mystery in large part sustained by the acting of Irène Jacob in the roles of both Veronika and Véronique. With her ability to establish the two women as distinctively different, Jacob's acting skill is undeniable, which her 1991 prize for best actress at the Cannes Film Festival confirmed. Yet, her beauty and sensual appeal—reminiscent, said some critics, of a younger Isabella Rossellini—are also unashamedly emphasized by the film. A haunting soundtrack and glowing, evocative photography also help sustain interest in a suspenseful situation that ultimately has no resolution. Veronika's/Véronique's mystery remains exactly that—a mystery—and the women's various life experiences serve to reinforce, through their own mystery, the ultimate mystery of the women's similarities and of their fates.

While Hollywood films have often played with this theme of doubleness in more obvious and causally linked ways, rarely has a film so elusive and implausible found the aesthetic means for succeeding in the difficult task of suggesting the ineffable. Director Kieslowski, whose 1988 feature *A Short Film About Killing* took the Jury Prize at the 1988 Cannes Film Festival, shows a talent for indirection that allows *The Double Life of Véronique* to suggest something about the shared quality of all human experience and the fundamental mystery in that experience.

Gaylyn Studlar

Reviews
Chicago Tribune. January 5, 1992, XIII, p. 6.
The Christian Century. CIX, February 19, 1992, p. 196.
The Christian Science Monitor. December 17, 1991, p. 11.
The Hollywood Reporter. May 16, 1991, p. 7.
Los Angeles Times. December 13, 1991, p. F17.
The Nation. CCLIII, October 28, 1991, p. 528.
The New York Times. September 20, 1991, p. B6.
Premiere. V, November, 1991, p. 84.
San Francisco Chronicle. January 31, 1992, p. F1.
Variety. May 16, 1991, p. 10.
The Washington Post. December 13, 1991, p. C6.

124

DYING YOUNG

Production: Sally Field and Kevin McCormick for Fogwood Films; released by
Twentieth Century-Fox
Direction: Joel Schumacher
Screenplay: Richard Friedenberg; based on the novel by Marti Leimbach
Cinematography: Juan Ruiz Anchia
Editing: Robert Brown
Production design: Guy J. Comtois
Art direction: Richard Johnson
Set decoration: Cricket Rowland
Casting: Mary Goldberg
Visual consulting: Neil Spisak
Sound: David MacMillan
Costume design: Susan Becker
Music: James Newton Howard
MPAA rating: R
Running time: 105 minutes

   Principal characters:
   Hilary O'Neil .... Julia Roberts
   Victor Geddes .... Campbell Scott
   Gordon .... Vincent D'Onofrio
   Estelle Whittier .... Colleen Dewhurst
   Richard Geddes .... David Selby
   Mrs. O'Neil .... Ellen Burstyn
   Cappy .... Dion Anderson
   Malachi .... George Martin

When Twentieth Century-Fox's *Dying Young* opened in June, 1991, most Hollywood
insiders predicted a huge opening weekend at the box office for the romantic drama.
After all, the film boasted a lead performance from actress Julia Roberts, who, at the
time, was fast becoming America's premier female entertainer. In 1990, Roberts,
playing a sweet hooker, helped Garry Marshall's *Pretty Woman* become that year's
third-highest-grossing film. Roberts' subsequent effort, Joseph Ruben's *Sleeping with
the Enemy* (1991; reviewed in this volume), despite overwhelmingly negative reviews,
opened with a $13.78 million weekend gross. All signs looked positive for another
great success for Roberts. After four weeks of release during the year's busiest season,
however, *Dying Young* grossed a sad $26 million and was fast becoming one of the
summer's biggest box-office failures. If *Dying Young*'s disappointing performance
proves anything, it is the fact that even the considerable charm of Roberts cannot save
an insipid, unappealing soap bubble of a film.
   Based on Marti Leimbach's critically respected 1990 novel of the same name, the

film *Dying Young* was designed from the beginning to be a vehicle for Roberts. Producer/actress Sally Field had been so impressed with her costar in Herbert Ross's *Steel Magnolias* (1989) that, when she bought the rights to the Leimbach novel, she immediately envisioned Roberts as the book's leading character. While the novel described its heroine, Hilary O'Neil, as an intelligent, young WASP with the desire to become a veterinarian, Field and fellow producer Kevin McCormick's vision was to make the Hilary character a working-class girl with little ambition save the dream of becoming someone different. In other words, Field and McCormick, with the help of screenwriter Richard Friedenberg, were eager to stamp the Cinderella story onto the basic structure of Leimbach's narrative.

Because it appeals to the mass audience, representing the fantasy of many female filmgoers of marrying rich and being forever happy, the Cinderella story has become ʌn essential part in the blueprint for the archetypal Julia Roberts film. This framework, snatched from the Pygmalion myth, usually calls for a poor-but-pretty young woman who is given the chance to reinvent her life with the guidance of an often-older-but-always-wealthier man. This patron of the gentler sex gives the helpless girl what is missing in her life, forms her into something new, then promptly falls madly in love with her.

Pretty Woman, in which Roberts plays a prostitute who says quite seriously, "I want the fairy tale," is certainly the epitome of this tired formula. In one of Roberts' early films, Donald Petrie's *Mystic Pizza* (1988), the actress plays a working-class Connecticut waitress whose summertime relationship with a rich young preppy on vacation teaches her some of life's big lessons. In an interesting twist on the formula, *Sleeping with the Enemy* begins with the Roberts character having already discarded her meager past and become locked into a marriage with an abusive businessman. Here again, however, Roberts is given the chance to reinvent herself by throwing away her rich husband and starting a modest new life with little money in a country town. Only a couple of days pass, however, before she meets another man, a university professor with a big empty house, who shows her how happy life can be.

Staying true to the Cinderella structure, the film version of *Dying Young* strips Leimbach's heroine of her goals of pursuing animal medicine, plucks her out of her Boston home, and drops her into the blue-collar environment of downtown Oakland. After she finds her boyfriend in bed with another woman, Hilary moves back home with her mother (Ellen Burstyn), who collects dolls, watches the Home Shopping Club, and bemoans what a flop Hilary has turned out to be. Answering an ad which offers room and board for nursing work, Hilary is interrogated by wealthy patrician Richard Geddes (David Selby), whose snobbish reaction to her short skirt, high heels, and bawdy behavior leads her to storm off in disgust. Geddes' son, Victor (Campbell Scott), suffering from leukemia, spots Hilary before she leaves and dispatches butler Malachi (George Martin) to retrieve her. Victor, despite his father's advice to the contrary, gives Hilary the job. After a night of Victor vomiting because of chemotherapy, the poor girl, depressed over the pathetic life of cancer victims, quickly plans to quit.

Recognizing that her own sorry existence is one big dead end, Hilary reverses her decision and devotes her life to helping Victor. She quits smoking, stops dressing in tight, trashy clothes, and takes a liking to macrobiotic cooking. Victor begins to teach Hilary not only about German expressionism, the subject of his dissertation, but also how to act with class. Once his bout with chemotherapy is over, Victor, now in remission, suggests that the two of them rent a house in Northern California without telling Victor's domineering father. Once ensconced in their new cliffside manor, Victor and Hilary fall in love. Between sessions of making love, Hilary and Victor start friendships with Gordon (Vincent D'Onofrio), the handyman, and Estelle (Colleen Dewhurst, Campbell Scott's real-life mother), a wise old widow who reads tea leaves and gives advice.

On Christmas Eve, Victor and Hilary entertain Gordon, but the evening goes awry when Victor becomes verbally abusive. Hilary is shocked and, after discovering a used hypodermic needle, searchs for and finds Victor's plentiful morphine supply. She confronts Victor, who admits that his chemotherapy was never completed. All he wanted to do was get away from his father and die in the arms of the woman he loves. Hilary is devastated; she curses Victor's selfishness and leaves him. Her first stop is a phone booth, where she calls Victor's father and tells him where he can find his dying son.

Before his father can take Victor back to San Francisco, Estelle hosts a holiday ball, where, in true soap-opera fashion, all the characters mingle and the plot is resolved. Estelle tells Hilary to fight for the man she loves, and when Hilary runs into the departing Victor, she decides to follow him. She finds him at their rented home, where he is packing his things in order to run away again from chemotherapy. She convinces him of her great desire to help him fight cancer, and after tears, kisses, and professions of love, the two reunite to face an uncertain future.

Dying Young illustrates once again, like all the Julia Roberts vehicles before it, how filmmakers objectify the image of the beautiful star, not only visually but within the narrative as well. The film contains a major subplot in which Victor instructs Hilary on intellectual subjects of which she has never been privy, one of which is the art of German expressionist Gustav Klimt. Victor, falling for the vibrant Hilary, seems to equate her image with the red-haired woman whom Klimt seemed to paint over and over again. To make the point as obvious as possible, director Joel Schumacher includes a scene in which Hilary stands while watching a slide show of Klimt's art and the faces of the two women—Victor's love and inspiration and Klimt's muse and model—merge into one. By film's end, Hilary is remade by Victor into a perfectly suitable mate: her clothes are different, her hairdo more tame, and her language more refined and meaningful.

Throughout the film, Schumacher's camera lingers on Roberts' famous mile-wide smile, her notorious full lips, her shapely long legs, and her luscious mane of auburn hair. It is as if Roberts becomes merely another prop used in the film; she is as much a part of the set dressing as the elegant oceanside cottage that Victor rents or the large pink cadillac that Hilary drives. Schumacher's early career as a production designer clearly influences his style as a director, as the emphasis is on the look of the film. Schumacher is less concerned with the emotional developments of his characters than with how they appear when emoting.

The creative team behind *Dying Young* recognizes Roberts' great appeal and has fashioned a film that showcases rather than challenges her. Consequently, her performance as Hilary merely reflects her own glamorous persona. The character of Hilary is designed to be so likable that the dramatic potential of her relationship with a dying man is never fully explored. Roberts never connects emotionally with Campbell Scott, who was so good in Norman René's *Longtime Companion* (1990) but is underused here. *Dying Young* fails to achieve any hint of significance and becomes a simple presentation of why America loves Julia Roberts. Perhaps its dismal box-office returns and its harsh critical reception suggest that it may indeed be time for Hollywood to give Roberts something new to do.

Greg Changnon

Reviews
American Cinematographer. LXXII, August, 1991, p. 28.
Boxoffice. August, 1991, p. R-53.
Chicago Tribune. June 21, 1991, VII, p. 35.
Entertainment Weekly. LXXIV, July 12, 1991, p. 38.
Film Review. September, 1991, p. 28.
The Hollywood Reporter. June 18, 1991, p. 9.
Los Angeles Times. June 21, 1991, p. F1.
The New York Times. June 21, 1991, p. B4.
Newsweek. CXVIII, July 1, 1991, p. 62.
Rolling Stone. August 8, 1991, p. 78.
Sight and Sound. I, September, 1991, p. 38.
Time. CXXXVII, July 1, 1991, p. 76.
Variety. June 18, 1991, p. 2.
The Washington Post. June 21, 1991, p. B1.

EUROPA, EUROPA

Origin: France and Germany
Released: 1990
Released in U.S.: 1991
Production: Margaret Menegoz for Les Films Du Losange and Arthur Brauner for CCC Filmkunst GMBH; released by Orion Classics
Direction: Agnieszka Holland
Screenplay: Agnieszka Holland; based on the autobiography of Solomon Perel
Cinematography: Jacek Petrycki
Editing: Ewa Smal and Isabelle Lorente
Art direction: Allan Starski
Sound: Elisabeth Mondi
Costume design: Wieslawa Starska and Malgorzata Stefaniak
Music: Zbigniew Preisner
MPAA rating: R
Running time: 115 minutes

> *Principal characters:*
> Solomon Perel (as a young man) .... Marco Hofschneider
> Leni .... Julie Delpy
> Robert Kellerman .... André Wilms
> Leni's mother .... Halina Labonarska
> Zenek .... Andrzej Mastalerz
> Gerd .... Ashley Wanninger
> Captain von Lerenau .... Hanns Zischler
> David Perel .... Piotr Kozlowski
> Isaak Perel .... Rene Hofschneider
> Azriel Perel .... Klaus Abramowsky
> Rebecca Perel .... Michele Gleizer
> Bertha Perel .... Marta Sandrowicz
> Solomon Perel (as an old man) .... Himself

World War II continues to provide a rich source of true life stories. *Europa, Europa* is one such incredible event. It is the story of Solomon Perel (Solly), a young German Jew who witnessed the atrocities of the war, ironically, by fighting for the Germans against the Soviets on the front line. As a circumcised Jew, he walked a knife's edge of being discovered and shot by the fervently anti-Semitic German army throughout the seven years of the war. For more than forty years, Perel's story remained a darkly held secret until, as an old man living in Israel, holding onto those traumatic events became too painful.

According to Jewish tradition, Solly (Marco Hofschneider) had been circumcised as a baby. This singular event was to play an incredible role in his life when the German war machine started rolling through Europe. By the time that Solly was thirteen, Hitler had limited Jewish involvement in German life and culture. On the night of Solly's Bar Mitzvah, his apartment is attacked by Hitler's supporters. The Hitler Youth, who had been parading the streets constantly drumming up anti-Semitic feeling, attack the Jews with tremendous force and brutality. At the time of the attack, Solly is taking a bath, and he flees naked into the yard behind the apartment building. When the rioting is quelled, Solly returns to his apartment to find all its contents destroyed and his beloved sister, Bertha (Marta Sandrowicz), lying dead on the dining room table. She is the first family casualty of what will become the largest attempt at eliminating the Jewish race in Europe through genocide. The family has little alternative but to leave Peine, Germany, and return to the father's birthplace of Lodz, Poland. No sooner do they arrive in Lodz than war is declared. Solly's father, Azriel (Klaus Abramowsky), fears for the safety of his youngest sons, and Solly and Isaak (Rene Hofschneider) are instructed by their parents to go as far east as possible. While crossing a river by night, along with hordes of other fleeing Poles, Solly is separated from Isaak. Solly must swim to the other side of the river, where he is found by some Soviet soldiers and transported to an orphanage. At the orphanage, he is indoctrinated into the thinking of the communist regime, becoming a very good student.

After two years of relative peace and quiet at the orphanage, where Solly continues to receive mail from his parents, Adolf Hitler's planes attack the defenseless school. The pact with Joseph Stalin, which was meant to last ten years, is broken, and a war which will cause the deaths of millions of Soviet soldiers begins. Some of the students are helped onto a truck, and the rest, including Solly, must march farther east in the hope of reaching safety. Inevitably, they meet the advancing German army, who quickly separate Jews from non-Jews. Solly convinces the German soldiers that he is actually a German who was forced to join the orphanage. During the conversation with his captors, it is also discovered that he can speak Russian, which pleases the Germans. Stalin's son has been captured at the front, and Solly can translate for the Soviets the circumstances under which this prestigious prisoner was caught.

As a boy soldier, Solly becomes part of the German offensive against the Soviet army. Fighting in the trenches is a miserable experience for Solly which is brightened by his friendship with Robert Kellerman (André Wilms). Unfortunately for Solly, Robert is homosexual and is attracted to Solly. While Solly is bathing one night, Robert surprises the young man. Thinking that his true identity will be discovered, Solly is amazed to find that Robert is as intent on keeping his secret as is Solly. As the fierce fighting continues, Solly becomes the only survivor, having lost his only true friend, Robert. Communicating with the Soviets through a radio link, he tells them that he is really a Jew and that he wants to cross over that night to their side. Just as the Soviets are coming to meet him, a group of German soldiers mows them down. Solly becomes a hero for setting up such an elaborate trap.

As a war hero, Solly is sent to the most famous school for the training of Hitler Youth. While at the school, he becomes enamored with Leni (Julie Delpy), a young woman who serves meals there. She wants Solly to make her pregnant so that she can give her child to Hitler, as all women of her age have been called to do. Solly refuses her proposition, which makes Leni so angry that she never speaks to him again. With his training completed, Solly becomes a soldier once again. During an attack by Soviet soldiers, the building in which Solly and his fellow troops are hiding is completely surrounded. Solly makes a mad dash for the Soviet side. Instead of Solly being accepted as a Soviet, however, the camp commander gives the nearest liberated Jew a gun and tells him he can do whatever he wants with the captured German. A moment before the trigger is pulled, Solly's name is shouted out by another Jew. Yet another incredible coincidence saves Solly's life: Here, in the middle of the Soviet Union, is his brother, Isaak, only recently liberated. Solly is told that his entire family died in the ghettos of Poland.

What makes *Europa, Europa* a unique film is the fact that the story of Solomon Perel's life during the seven years that Europe was at war (1938-1945) almost remained a secret. A portrayal of Perel's life seems more related to fiction than to fact, and the life-saving coincidences read like a well-crafted novel. Yet, these events took place. The very fact that a Jew could be quietly and eagerly accepted into the top school for Hitler Youth only affirms how ludicrous the Nazi system was under the Hitler regime. Regardless of whether Perel was being indoctrinated by communists, as he was when living in the Soviet orphanage, or whether his German teachers were preaching to him about how the Jewish people were to be destroyed, Perel held onto only one idea: self-preservation. In fact, the experiences to which the teenage Perel was subjected are probably beyond the understanding of most people. Yet, Perel's tenacity and strong personality make him a true hero.

As long as there exists a Jewish nation and a Jewish religion, the Holocaust will be remembered and spoken about for generations to come. Telling this sad, yet inspiring, story so many years after the war does raise the question as to its relevance. *Europa, Europa*, however, acquaints a new generation with the incredible hatred and resentment that the Third Reich promoted during the years prior to the invasion of Poland on September 1, 1938. Ironically, and in keeping with the incredible story of Perel's life, it was individual Germans who showed the bewildered and frightened Perel genuine concern and friendship. When the Germans captured Perel in the Soviet Union, they were delighted to find "a jewel amongst so much filth." Perel convinced his captors that he was German because he spoke the language with a perfect accent. When Perel tried to desert the German army, he inadvertently led the Soviets, whom he is hoping to join, into a German ambush and became a hero in the process. Hearing of Solly's daring exploits on the battlefield, Captain von Lerenau (Hanns Zischler) wishes to adopt him as his son after the war. A fellow soldier discovered that Solly was Jewish but chose to keep it a secret from the authorities. The fact that Perel seemed to be happiest when he was at the school for Hitler Youth is an irony in itself. The tremendous strain and fear that Perel is under, however, is most evident when he speaks with Leni's mother (Halina Labonarska), who suspects that he is a Jew. Understandably, Perel breaks down and cries when he is finally able to tell someone whom he trusts about his closely held secret.

Europa, Europa deals with the inconsistencies of war. Enormous hatred was shown to a specific minority. Entire towns were stripped of their Semitic identity. Yet, throughout the turmoil of Europe at this time, created by the ever-advancing armies of Hitler, personal friendships and hope were Perel's constant companions as he endured a living nightmare. Director Agnieszka Holland deserves much of the credit for conveying a sense of the feelings and emotions that Perel experienced during those tumultuous years. By using historically appropriate and authentic settings, a real sense of the period is achieved throughout the story. The most memorable scene is when Solly takes a tram trip through the ghetto in Litzmannstadt, which is off-limits even to Germans, in the hope of discovering the whereabouts of his parents from their last known address. Riding the tram through the ghetto only further emphasizes his loneliness in his alien culture. The selection of Marco Hofschneider to play the part of Solly was well made, as he brings the right feeling of teenage aloofness yet manages at all times to convey the emotional feelings that Solly experienced during the odyssey of his traumatic youth. *Europa, Europa* won numerous awards, including a Golden Globe Award, Best Foreign-Language Film from both the New York Film Critics and the National Board of Review, and the Jury Prize at Cannes.

Richard G. Cormack

Reviews
Boxoffice. August, 1991, p. R-55.
Chicago Tribune. November 8, 1991, VII, p. 41.
The Christian Science Monitor. August 2, 1991, p. 13.
Films in Review. XLII, September, 1991, p. 340.
The Hollywood Reporter. July 10, 1991, p. 7.
Los Angeles Times. July 12, 1991, p. F10.
National Review. XLIII, September 9, 1991, p. 45.
The New Republic. July 8, 1991, p. 26.
The New York Times. June 28, 1991, p. B6.
The New Yorker. LXVII, July 1, 1991, p. 81.
Variety. CCCXLII, March 11, 1991, p. 63.
The Village Voice. July 2, 1991, p. 57.
Vogue. June, 1991, p. 70.
The Wall Street Journal. July 25, 1991, p. A6.
The Washington Post. August 9, 1991, p. D1.

FATHER OF THE BRIDE

Production: Nancy Meyers, Carol Baum, and Howard Rosenman for Touchstone
Pictures, in association with Touchwood Pacific Partners I, Sandy Gallin, and
Sandollar Productions; released by Buena Vista
Direction: Charles Shyer
Screenplay: Frances Goodrich, Albert Hackett, Nancy Meyers, and Charles Shyer;
based on the novel by Edward Streeter
Cinematography: John Lindley
Editing: Richard Marks
Production design: Sandy Veneziano
Art direction: Erin Cummins
Set decoration: Cynthia McCormac
Casting: Donna Isaacson
Sound: C. Darin Knight
Costume design: Susan Becker
Music: Alan Silvestri
MPAA rating: PG
Running time: 114 minutes

> *Principal characters:*
> George Banks .... Steve Martin
> Nina Banks .... Diane Keaton
> Annie Banks .... Kimberly Williams
> Franck Eggelhoffer .... Martin Short
> Matty Banks .... Kieran Culkin
> Bryan MacKenzie .... George Newbern
> Howard Weinstein .... B. D. Wong
> John MacKenzie .... Peter Michael Goetz
> Joanna MacKenzie .... Kate McGregor Stewart

Remaking popular films of the past is always risky: Comparisons will always be
made to the original script, the original presentation, and the original actors. The 1991
version of *Father of the Bride* is no exception. In 1950, director Vincente Minnelli
made his version starring Spencer Tracy in the title role and Elizabeth Taylor as his
daughter. Director Charles Shyer cast Steve Martin to fill Tracy's shoes and an
unknown actress, Kimberly Williams, to fill Taylor's. While Shyer's attempts at
comedy are often successful and the film is certainly updated, it still seems to fall short
of the goal established by such a successful earlier film.

Much of the original script is still present in this remake. In fact, so much of the
earlier dialogue is used that the screenwriters from the first film, Frances Goodrich
and Albert Hackett, are given cowriting credit. (Another carryover from the first film
is that Tom Irish—who played Ben Banks, the bride's younger brother, in the 1950

film—has a cameo as great-uncle Ben.) This is not to say that the newer version has not been modernized or had its tone altered. For one thing, the bride and her mother have changed. They have become independent women: Mother Nina Banks (Diane Keaton) has her own business and daughter Annie (Williams) her own career goals. Unfortunately, their newfound strength is still not turned upon the industry that preys on its customers' dreams, high expectations, and egos. *Father of the Bride* never really lampoons the wedding industry, as did Robert Altman's *A Wedding* (1978). *Father of the Bride* is meant to be a much gentler film.

As in the first version, the film begins with the father, George Banks (Martin), addressing the camera directly. His monologue from amid the ruins of his home—where the wedding recently ended—acts as the frame from within which the story is told. When his daughter, Annie, arrived home from studying abroad, she had some important news: She was engaged to a young man she met in Rome, Bryan MacKenzie (George Newbern). Mother is excited; Father is upset. All the predictable events follow: meeting the young man in question, meeting the future in-laws, picking a wedding coordinator, and planning the wedding. None of this goes well for George. He agonizes over everything, especially the costs involved. Yet, all of his distress is really covering up the most upsetting fact of all—he will be losing his daughter.

The film follows the Banks family members through their matrimonial adventure in a series of anecdotes. Because this is a Steve Martin film, the emphasis is placed on the humorous, but sometimes the jokes defy reason or are painted too broadly. Why does George not simply put down his future in-laws' savings passbook when he makes his escape from the family's dogs? In addition, who has not heard the jokes about hot dogs coming in packages of eight while buns come in packages of twelve? Seeing Martin's character lash out at that tired old tirade makes it seem like obvious filler material between the wedding planning vignettes. There is also a preponderance of voice-overs, as if the audience could not understand the jokes if they were not explained. Martin manages, however, not only to be amusing in most of the film but also to show a deep tenderness under his wedding angst. Diane Keaton as the mother of the bride (originally played by Joan Bennett in the 1950 version) is very restrained. In fact, she is so restrained that she often seems to disappear. Keaton's comic flair has been substantially wasted in this supporting role.

There are some nice touches in the updated version: the one-on-one basketball game between father and daughter (as she wears a classic black dress, pearls, and gym shoes), the lace-covered athletic shoes that the bride wears under her dress, and the times that George sees his daughter not as a grown woman but as the little girl he has nurtured. The best touch—and certainly the most humorous—is that provided by Martin Short as Franck, the wedding coordinator (played in 1950 by Leo G. Carroll). His European accent defies description and often deciphering. What Short does with this small role is unrelentingly comic. He creates a character who runs the gamut from being a wimpy snob to a competent professional—and makes it all believable.

Unlike the first film, in which Spencer Tracy undergoes a genuine nightmare of a wedding (a scene absent from this version), it is difficult to feel sorry for the 1991 family which seems to have so much going for it, even at this hectic time in its existence. Perhaps this is the reason that Short's Franck is so hilarious. He comes in and entirely disrupts the perfect home of this likable, staid, and perfect family, exactly as the audience would like to shake them up.

This version of *Father of the Bride* is fluffier than the original. It may be a well-meaning film, as it tries to provide some family entertainment, but it is a bit like the father's checkbook: full going into the wedding ceremony but empty of all but a few pleasant memories coming out.

Beverley Bare Buehrer

Reviews

American Cinematographer. LXXIII, February, 1992, p. 54.
Boxoffice. February, 1992, p. R-12.
The Christian Science Monitor. December 20, 1991, p. 12.
The Hollywood Reporter. December 9, 1991, p. 6.
Los Angeles Times. December 20, 1991, p. F16.
The New York Times. December 20, 1991, p. B6.
Newsweek. CXIX, January 6, 1992, p. 53.
People Weekly. December 23, 1991, p. 18.
Premiere. V, January, 1992, p. 26.
Time. CXXXVIII, December 30, 1991, p. 71.
Variety. December 9, 1991, p. 19.
The Wall Street Journal. December 19, 1991, p. A12.
The Washington Post. December 20, 1991, p. D1.

LA FEMME NIKITA

Origin: France and Italy
Released: 1990
Released in U.S.: 1991
Production: Gaumont and Cecchi Gori Group Tiger Cinematografica; released by the
   Samuel Goldwyn Company
Direction: Luc Besson
Screenplay: Luc Besson
Cinematography: Thierry Arbogast
Editing: Olivier Mauffroy
Production design: Dan Weil
Sound: Pierre Befve and Gérard Lamps
Costume design: Anne Angelini
Music: Eric Serra
MPAA rating: R
Running time: 117 minutes

> *Principal characters:*
> Nikita .... Anne Parillaud
> Bob .... Tcheky Karyo
> Marco .... Jean-Hugues Anglade
> Amande .... Jeanne Moreau
> Victor .... Jean Reno
> Chief of Intelligence .... Jean Bouise
> Ambassador .... Philippe du Anerand
> Interrogating Officer .... Roland Blanche
> Chief Grossman .... Philippe Leroy-Beaulieu
> Rico .... Marc Duret
> Pharmacist .... Jacques Boudet

Luc Besson may be the most popular and successful filmmaker in France. His *Le Grand Bleu* (1988; *The Big Blue*) was France's highest grossing film of the 1980's, and *La Femme Nikita* was France's biggest French-made box-office hit of 1990, as well as the top-grossing foreign-language film in the United States in 1991. Besson conceived of *La Femme Nikita* while listening to the Elton John tune, "Nikita," at a time when he was trying to create a film to suit actress Anne Parillaud. Unlike the sentimental *Le Grand Bleu*, this film returns to the sleek stylized format of Besson's earlier works, such as *L'Avant Dernier* (1981) and *Subway* (1985).

Nikita is a member of a gang of junkies. Barely conscious and begging for a fix, Nikita watches her companions rob a pharmacy. The pharmacist (Jacques Boudet) bursts in brandishing a rifle, and is stunned to find one of the intruding gang members to be his own son. The others take advantage of the man's confusion and shoot him, deriving an eerie joy from the kill. They seem to take equal pleasure in firing on the surrounding police officers as in being fired on themselves. When one of the officers finds Nikita under the counter, he mistakes her drug-induced daze for docility and attempts to talk her into surrendering. Nikita puts her gun to the officer's throat and pleads for the narcotics that she so desperately wants. When he replies that they are all gone, Nikita shoots him without emotion and before he can change his answer.

After brutalizing every member of the police and court with whom she comes in contact, Nikita is sentenced to life in prison. She shows vulnerability for the first time when she believes she is about to be executed by lethal injection. While crying for her mother, Nikita loses consciousness. She awakens in a room that is painted white, ceiling to floor, including the furniture. Nikita is puzzled when Bob (Tcheky Karyo) enters, introduces himself, and asks her if she would like to work for the government. It is all too overwhelming for Nikita who, having believed herself to be in heaven, is disappointed to find she is merely in another sort of prison. Bob allows her to sleep a while longer, then returns to explain, gently but firmly, Nikita's situation.

Nikita is in an underground operations center of a French intelligence agency. As far as the police, her family, and any official records go, Nikita died in prison. What Bob proposes is that Nikita agree to be trained as an agency employee, be given a new identity, and spend her life working for the country that could have taken her life but did not. If she refuses this offer, the agency will see to it that Nikita is executed, as was previously scheduled. Reluctantly, Nikita agrees.

The sequences covering Nikita's "training" are fascinating and humorous. Her classes range from marksmanship—in which she needs no training—to computer science—during which she frightens the teacher who would show her how to use a "mouse" by showing him a real mouse. She also learns ballet and martial arts—two subjects that Nikita tends to confuse. The instruction that is initially most foreign and ultimately most enjoyable to Nikita is given by Amande (Jeanne Moreau). Amande supervises Nikita's daily lessons in how to dress, apply makeup, sit, walk, and speak like a lady. In other words, how to take full advantage of her femininity, a quality that has been buried very deep within Nikita for a long time.

All the while, it is Bob who scolds, encourages, inspires, and rewards Nikita's progress. He fights for her when the agency fears that she will never complete her education to their satisfaction. He exchanges her graffiti-covered walls and iron cot for prints of Edgar Degas paintings and tasteful antique furniture. He remembers her birthdays with cakes and candles.

On Nikita's twenty-third birthday, which is also the anniversary of her third year in the agency, Bob takes Nikita out for dinner. It is the first time that Nikita has stepped outside since she was imprisoned for murder. Then a drug-crazed fiend, Nikita is now a beautiful young woman, thrilled by the Paris night, the elegant restaurant, and the gift-wrapped package that Bob presents to her. What Nikita mistakes for a short vacation from work, however, is the beginning of the work for which she has been training. Bob's gift is a gun. As she stares panic stricken at him and at the gun, Bob instructs Nikita to assassinate an enemy of the agency who is dining at another table with his family, then escape through a window in the ladies rest room. Nikita follows her orders, the act of murder as unnatural to her now as it was natural three years before, but when she gets to the window that was described for her escape, she finds it bricked shut. When Nikita finally returns to the agency, frightened, bruised, but having escaped the victim's bodyguards and made her way back unaided, Bob explains that this evening's events were a test of her skills and, having passed, Nikita graduates. Torn between striking and embracing Bob, Nikita does both, then vows never to let her feelings for him emerge again.

Looking much like a baby bird being pushed out of its nest, Nikita leaves the agency to begin her new life. She is now known as Marie, a nurse in a nearby hospital. Nikita rents an apartment that appears to be decrepit and filthy, and transforms it into a charming and inviting home in a similar way to the transformation that was worked on herself. Nikita's first excursion into the world is a trip to the grocery store, the freedom to shop being more freedom than she has had for years. There she meets the shy, sweet cashier, Marco (Jean-Hugues Anglade).

Inviting Marco to her apartment for dinner, Nikita pounces on him even as he tries to explain that he is not used to being pursued by a woman. While it may seem that Nikita is merely trying to make up for lost time, she really does grow to care for Marco, and he for her. Yet, Marco has no idea where Nikita has come from or what she does for a living. Nikita herself has almost forgotten her immediate past, until one day the telephone rings and a voice asks for "Josephine," the code name that always precedes instructions for an assignment. As Marco becomes more inquisitive about Nikita's past, Bob intervenes, pretending to be Nikita's uncle, filled with reminiscences about her childhood. As Marco reveals that he and Nikita are engaged to be married, Nikita gazes at Bob with a mixture of pride over how far she has come and longing to explore the feelings that they might have for each other but that their work must prevent them from exploring.

Nikita is delighted to accept a vacation for herself and Marco, supposedly an engagement present from Bob. To Nikita's dismay, however, a voice on the phone in their Venice hotel room asks for Josephine. As Marco calls for his fiancée to hurry with her bath because room service has arrived, Nikita follows the instructions that are given to her over a headset found in the medicine chest. She assembles a rifle that is hidden in various spots around the bathroom and shoots through the bathroom window at a woman stepping into a gondola below. Nikita cries the whole time, then frantically hides the rifle under the soapsuds in her bath just before Marco breaks in to see if she is all right.

As the strain of her new profession becomes greater with every assignment, Nikita finds herself just as trapped in her new life as she was in her old. No longer a slave to drugs, Nikita is now a slave to the state, still forced to murder for her own survival. As Bob and Marco meet to confess their love for Nikita and figure out what she may be planning to do, Nikita is forced to decide whether to keep the promise that she made to Bob three years ago, keep the love that she has with Marco, or abandon them both and take her chances on yet another life—one of her own making.

Besson's impressive cast works well together. Perhaps this is because Besson wrote each part to fit the actor, especially the challenging title role for Parillaud, whom he wished to rescue from the mindless starlet roles for which she was becoming known. When he began to write the part of Amande, Besson claims to have heard Moreau's voice in his head saying the lines. Besson delights in casting against type, having Karyo, seen in *L'Ours* (1988; *The Bear*, 1989), play the reserved and intense government agent, and Anglade, known in France for more serious roles, as the playful and devoted lover. All the elements combine to make a thriller that is comic and touching, as well as exceptionally thrilling.

Eleah Horwitz

Reviews
Boxoffice. April, 1991, p. R-23.
Chicago Tribune. April 3, 1991, V, p. 3.
Commonweal. CXVIII, June 1, 1991, p. 372.
The Hollywood Reporter. March 14, 1991, p. 11.
Los Angeles Times. CC, March 15, 1991, p. F16.
The New Republic. CCIV, May 6, 1991, p. 26.
New Woman. XXI, April, 1991, p. 30.
The New York Times. March 15, 1991, p. B9.
Rolling Stone. March 21, 1991, p. 86.
Variety. April 5, 1991, p. 10.
Video Review. XII, October, 1991, p. 104.
The Village Voice. March 12, 1991, p. 52.
The Wall Street Journal. March 14, 1991, p. A16.
The Washington Post. April 4, 1991, p. D9.

THE FISHER KING

Production: Debra Hill and Lynda Obst; released by TriStar Pictures
Direction: Terry Gilliam
Screenplay: Richard LaGravenese
Cinematography: Roger Pratt
Editing: Lesley Walker
Production design: Mel Bourne
Art direction: P. Michael Johnston
Set decoration: Cindy Carr, Kevin McCarthy, and Joseph L. Bird
Set design: Jason R. Weil and Rick Heinrichs
Casting: Howard Feuer
Sound: Thomas Causey and Dennis Maitland II
Costume design: Beatrix Pasztor
Music: George Fenton
MPAA rating: R
Running time: 137 minutes

Principal characters:
Parry .... Robin Williams
Jack Lucas .... Jeff Bridges
Lydia .... Amanda Plummer
Anne Napolitano .... Mercedes Ruehl (AA)
Homeless cabaret singer .... Michael Jeter

Jack Lucas (Jeff Bridges) is New York City's top radio "shock jock." One day, however, his derisive retorts to a caller bring his career to an abrupt halt. Cynically attacking the "Yuppie scum" who frequent bistros such as the one at which the caller has had trouble with women, Jack flippantly tells the man to wipe them out before they have a chance to multiply. The caller enters the bar with a shotgun, murders seven innocent people, and then commits suicide. Jack's sense of guilt sends him immediately into a deep emotional abyss.

Three years later, Jack's burden has been dulled by constant doses of alcohol. His own slick, high-rise life-style has given way to a seedy apartment over a video store owned by his girlfriend, Anne (Mercedes Ruehl). Believing he is being punished for his sins, Jack attempts to escape through suicide. Yet, just before jumping, weighted, into the river, Jack is attacked by thugs. He is doused with gasoline but at the last minute is saved by a pixilated homeless man, Parry (Robin Williams).

Parry believes himself to be a knight on a mission—to retrieve the Holy Grail from its resting place in a billionaire's mansion on Fifth Avenue. Although Parry has saved Jack's life, there is a stronger bond between the two. Parry used to be a university professor of medieval history until he was broken emotionally by the death of his wife. She was shot to death right in front of him by Jack's deranged caller. Parry escapes his painful memories by escaping reality.

Parry attempts to enlist Jack in his quest for the Grail, but instead Jack helps Parry to win a date with Parry's fair damsel in distress, the shy and lonely Lydia (Amanda Plummer). With Jack's coaching and Anne's assistance, the foursome go out to dinner, and it would seem that Parry has won the woman of his dreams. Fate is not that kind to the pure-hearted Parry, however, and Jack's guilt is not shed that easily. On his way home from the date, Parry is pursued by the Red Knight, a horrifying vision that symbolizes the tragedy in Parry's past. While running from it, Parry is attacked by the same thugs who beat Jack. Seriously injured, Parry is sent to a mental hospital, where he lapses into a coma which resembles the one he was in after the death of his wife. In one last attempt to alleviate his guilt and to help Parry, Jack breaks into the billionaire's mansion and retrieves the "Holy Grail" for his friend. This act restores Parry, who is as unbalanced as before but who now has Jack's friendship and the love of Lydia.

In medieval mythology, the Fisher King is the guardian of the Holy Grail, the cup from which Jesus drank at the Last Supper and that was used to collect drops of his blood at the Crucifixion. After the Fisher King loses the Grail, the king and his kingdom begin to die. With the help of an unaffected fool, however, the king regains his ability to see and experience the Grail, and he and his lands are restored. In director Terry Gilliam's film (and in the script by Richard LaGravenese, which was nominated for an Academy Award for Best Original Screenplay), Parry and Jack are both fools and kings. They have both lost their way, and both are in need of redemption: Jack from his guilt and Parry from his tragedy. Yet, Gilliam has made Jack the Fisher King who is dying and Parry the fool who shows him the way, although on the surface it would seem that it is Jack who is trying to save Parry.

The Fisher King is a drama and a comedy fused by two love stories. It revolves around the intertwining lives of four people: Jack, Parry, Anne, and Lydia. The result, which in the hands of a less-inspired director might have been flatly confusing, is a heartwarming and beguiling mix of fantasy and reality, madness and sanity. It is a parable of human redemption that the talented Gilliam tells with an artist's skill.

Gilliam is noted for lavishly produced films that usually are not successful commercially. The myth of the Fisher King is particularly well suited to Gilliam, who broke away from being the cartoonist member of the Monty Python comedy group when he directed *Monty Python and the Holy Grail* (1974) with fellow Python member Terry Jones. Gilliam's films became more and more opulent and fantastic with *Jabberwocky* (1977), *Time Bandits* (1980), and *Brazil* (1985). The legendary battles between Gilliam and Universal Studios boss Sidney Sheinberg over the final cut and distribution of *Brazil* resulted in the director being labeled a maverick who was as loose with his film's budget as he was with the realities of filmmaking in Hollywood. When *The Adventures of Baron Munchausen* (1989) turned into a financial fiasco, losing millions, it seemed as if his career might have gone entirely off track. (In his own defense, Gilliam said that *The Adventures of Baron Munchausen* was grossly underbudgeted and that the fault was not his. *The Fisher King* was completed on schedule and on budget.)

The one thing that can be said about *The Fisher King* in relation to other Gilliam epics is that it is a decidedly more commercial venture. It is much more accessible than his other films, with more mainstream stars and a more contemporary story. While the traditional Gilliam trademarks are present—especially an extravagant, almost baroque, visual style—they do not dwarf the story, as they have in the past. Nevertheless, in presenting his highly visual style, Gilliam may have overused his dizzying camerawork; the camera dips and circles over Jack's claustrophobic radio room (where shadows like prison bars are cast on the room's walls) and looks at the world from a skewed angle when representing the world as seen through Parry's eyes.

The Fisher King, however, really belongs to the actors. Jeff Bridges, while using his comic abilities effectively in the film, is the film's anchor. His solid performance allows Gilliam and Robin Williams, both of whom are known for pushing things to their extremes, to be expansive in their work while never overwhelming the film. Williams plays Parry for more than merely the laughs provided by a fool and was nominated for a Best Actor Academy Award and won a Golden Globe Award for his effort. Through his character, the film can make its points without ever losing its humor or beating the audience over the head with platitudes.

Amanda Plummer, who had appeared with Williams previously in *The World According to Garp* (1982), and Mercedes Ruehl, who gave an entertaining performance as the mafioso wife in *Married to the Mob* (1988), give compelling and convincing performances that easily hold their own against those of Bridges and Williams. In fact, Ruehl won an Academy Award as well as a Golden Globe Award for Best Supporting Actress for her portrayal of Anne. One special standout is Michael Jeter as a homeless cabaret singer who steals every scene in which he appears.

All combined, Gilliam has made a compelling and entertaining film. At the September, 1991, Toronto Film Festival, it was the most popular film, winning the top prize. The film's box-office receipts indicate that Gilliam finally has redeemed his own reputation and has crossed over into mainstream filmmaking.

Beverley Bare Buehrer

Reviews
Boxoffice. November, 1991, p. R-78.
Chicago Tribune. September 20, 1991, p. 7C.
The Christian Science Monitor. September 20, 1991, p. 12.
Films in Review. January/February, 1992, p. 44.
The Hollywood Reporter. September 10, 1991, p. 9.
Los Angeles Times. September 20, 1991, p. F1.
The New York Times. September 20, 1991, p. B4.
Newsweek. September 23, 1991, p. 57.
Time. CXXXVIII, September 23, 1991, p. 68.
Variety. September 10, 1991, p. 2.
The Wall Street Journal. September 19, 1991, p. A12.
The Washington Post. September 20, 1991, p. B1.

THE FIVE HEARTBEATS

Production: Loretha C. Jones; released by Twentieth Century-Fox
Direction: Robert Townsend
Screenplay: Robert Townsend and Keenan Ivory Wayans
Cinematography: Bill Dill
Editing: John Carter
Production design: Wynn Thomas
Art direction: Don Diers
Set decoration: Samara Schaffer
Sound: David Brownlow
Costume design: Ruthe Carter
Choreography: Michael Peters
Music: Stanley Clarke
Music production supervision: Steve Tyrell and George Duke
MPAA rating: R
Running time: 122 minutes

Principal characters:
Duck Matthews	Robert Townsend
Eddie King, Jr.	Michael Wright
J. T. Matthews	Leon
Dresser	Harry J. Lennix
Choirboy	Tico Wells
Jimmy Potter	Chuck Patterson
Eleanor Potter	Diahann Carroll
Big Red	Hawthorne James
Sarge	Harold Nicholas
Michael "Flash" Turner	John Canada Terrell
Duck's baby sister	Tressa Thomas

Robert Townsend gained international prominence in 1987 when he wrote, produced, directed, and starred in the successful comedy *Hollywood Shuffle*. The inspiration for *The Five Heartbeats* was drawn from Townsend's memories of listening to The Temptations, The Spinners, and The Four Tops.

Amateur Night at the local club is the setting for introducing The Five Heartbeats, an African-American singing group. The five singers are all close friends and each has a unique personality: Donald "Duck" Matthews (Townsend) is the main composer; Eddie King, Jr. (Michael Wright) is the egotistical lead singer; James Thomas "J. T." Matthews (Leon) is purely a ladies' man; Terrance "Dresser" Williams (Harry J. Lennix) is the dancer and self-appointed choreographer; and Anthony "Choirboy" Stone (Tico Wells) wants to sing R&B (rhythm and blues) outside his father's church.

As a singing group, their act is acceptable but by no means polished. In fact, much of their time is wasted trying to persuade all the members to arrive on time at their various evening engagements. Eddie, who has a gambling problem, is by far the most unpredictable member of the group. Eddie arrives one evening just in time to sing the opening bars of their first number. The group sings in contests with the hope that they might be discovered. This particular evening, they are in luck. Jimmy Potter (Chuck Patterson) approaches the group and offers them his services. Naturally, they accept his offer. Jimmy's wife, Eleanor (Diahann Carroll), is not as optimistic as her husband—she has seen him lose too many groups in the past to bigger managers and record companies. Jimmy believes that he has discovered a potentially successful group and that this time he will hold the purse strings himself.

The first change that Jimmy makes with the group is to introduce a well-known choreographer. Sarge (Harold Nicholas) is first met with disdain by the group, especially by Dresser, who considers his own dancing talents to be considerable. Before the men have any more time to argue, however, Sarge does a routine that leaves the neophyte singers speechless. By the time they enter their next contest, the group has a much more professional act and a stage routine that makes their original act moribund. The organizers of this contest, however, change the rules to suit themselves: Instead of allowing the group's accompanist to play, they say that the resident pianist must accompany the five singers, which is a ploy to discredit The Five Heartbeats. When the crowd becomes restless, the group takes over the playing and gives their song its true pace and beat. The change is dramatic, and the audience loves their singing.

More success follows as an old acquaintance of Jimmy, Big Red (Hawthorne James), offers the group a record contract. With the release of their first single, The Five Heartbeats go on a tour to promote their songs. As with most aspiring groups, they are booked into small, dimly lit clubs where music is only secondary to drinking and having a good time. One bright spot during this less-than-successful tour is the arrival of the cover to their latest album. Big Red's production man explains that a photograph of a white family sitting on a beach was used for the cover because it will give the record a cross-over audience, making it appeal to both the white and black communities. Without a second thought, the record sleeve is thrown high into the air of a dusty mid-Western town.

No sooner does the group reach a level of success and wealth than the relationship among the members begins to break down. Eddie signs a new contract with Big Red, and when Jimmy threatens to reveal Big Red's crooked operation, Jimmy is struck by a garbage truck on leaving his apartment block. Big Red is charged with the murder and sentenced to a long prison term. After this incident, Eddie leaves the group and continues using drugs. His replacement, Michael "Flash" Turner (John Canada Terrell), only joins the group to serve his own selfish goals of recording a solo album, and he leaves at the first opportunity. For Duck, the greatest tragedy for The Five Heartbeats is that his brother, J. T., marries the only woman that Duck has ever loved. After many years, the group reunites one afternoon for a barbecue lunch, and all the old sores and regrets are forgotten and forgiven.

There is much to commend in this film, but there is also much that does not make sense. Townsend's script was inspired by his experiences traveling with singing group The Dells, a group which has been together for thirty-eight years. Townsend's original conception of the film was changed by his time with this group, which had faced hard times over the years. His intention now was to tell the story of a fictional group of African-American singers who make it to the top of their profession and then find the trappings of success too much to handle. Creating a story out of the kind of life that was lived by many of the groups during the 1960's is a story worth telling. In order for that same union of events and happenings to be interesting, however, a certain amount of fictionalization was necessary in producing *The Five Heartbeats*. Therefore, while the core idea is commendable, the actual manipulation of the story does not serve the original purpose.

Another film that attempts to present those behind the music world is *Listen Up: The Lives of Quincy Jones* (1990), a documentary of the renowned music producer and composer Quincy Jones. This documentary tries to show the struggles that performers must endure in order to meet the demands of the concert circuit and the struggle in producing their art. Both films (despite the fact that *Listen Up* is a documentary), however, ignore the many long hours that a group must spend in creating an act and that a songwriter must spend to write a song. In *The Five Heartbeats*, the only time that anything remotely similar to creating a song is shown is a musical interlude in which Duck's sister (Tressa Thomas) helps Duck to finish his song by uncrumpling the pieces of paper on which he has been writing and singing the song herself. Apart from this stylized treatment of songwriting, which is essential to most singing groups, there is no sense of the struggle that these men go through to create music.

Criticism of this approach to storytelling comes easily because Townsend's version of how an R&B group makes it to the top incorporates recognizable figures. The choreographer, Sarge, is in real life Harold Nicholas, who with his brother Fayard became the legendary Nicholas Brothers, one of the most acclaimed teams in the history of dance. The incorporation of such known personalities, along with the use of actual footage from the performances of The Four Tops, only creates a pseudo backdrop to make The Five Heartbeats appear more authentic.

Merely showing the negative side of *The Five Heartbeats*, however, would not do justice to the obvious craft that went into the making of the film. All the major and minor acting parts are delivered with authenticity and feeling. Even if it is difficult to get a sense of the comradeship that exists between the principal singers, each manages to leave his particular mark on the film. The music is particularly well chosen and complements the action throughout. While the pacing is extremely disjointed—the conclusion of the film happens in a matter of a few scenes—there is always enough happening to keep the story moving.

While *The Five Heartbeats* is not the definitive study of African-American singers of the 1960's, Townsend has created a film with high production values, even if the subject matter seems clichéd.

Richard G. Cormack

Reviews

American Film: Magazine of the Film and Television Arts. XVI, April, 1991, p. 49.
Black Film Review. VI, Number 4, 1991, p. 20.
Boxoffice. June, 1991, p. R-36.
Chicago Tribune. March 29, 1991, VII, p. 31.
The Detroit News. March 29, 1991, p. C3.
The Hollywood Reporter. March 25, 1991, p. 6.
L.A. Weekly. April 5, 1991, p. 25.
Los Angeles Times. March 29, 1991, p. Fl.
The New York Times. March 29, 1991, p. B4.
Rolling Stone. April 18, 1991, p. 101.
USA Today. March 29, 1991, p. D5.
Variety. March 25, 1991, p. 2.
The Village Voice. XXXVI, April 2, 1991, p. 49.
The Washington Post. March 29, 1991, p. B1.

FOR THE BOYS

Production: Bette Midler, Bonnie Bruckheimer, and Margaret South for All Girl Productions and Mark Rydell; released by Twentieth Century-Fox
Direction: Mark Rydell
Screenplay: Marshall Brickman, Neal Jimenez, and Lindy Laub; based on a story by Jimenez and Laub
Cinematography: Stephen Goldblatt
Editing: Jerry Greenberg and Jere Huggins
Production design: Assheton Gorton
Art direction: Dianne Wager and Don Woodruff
Set decoration: Marvin March
Casting: Lynn Stalmaster
Sound: Jim Webb
Makeup: Jill Rockow and Michelle Burke
Costume design: Wayne Finkelman
Choreography: Joe Layton
Music: Dave Grusin
MPAA rating: R
Running time: 145 minutes

Principal characters:
Dixie Leonard .... Bette Midler
Eddie Sparks .... James Caan
Art Silver .... George Segal
Shephard .... Patrick O'Neal
Danny .... Christopher Rydell
Jeff Brooks .... Arye Gross
Sam Schiff .... Norman Fell
Margaret Sparks .... Shannon Wilcox
Michael Leonard .... Arliss Howard

Conventional wisdom has it that "they don't make movies the way they used to," but director Mark Rydell tries hard in *For the Boys*, an expensive musical production from Twentieth Century-Fox. The film attempts to capture a sense of the 1940's, the 1950's, and the 1960's, while telling the story of a song-and-dance team that soared to popularity after apparently being mismatched for a United Service Organizations (USO) performance in England during World War II. Federico Fellini took a similar approach in *Ginger e Fred* (1985; *Ginger and Fred*, 1986), which starred Marcello Mastroianni and Giulietta Masina as two second-rate hoofers who had become famous in Italy imitating Fred Astaire and Ginger Rogers and who are reunited as oldsters thirty years later for an Italian television special. Whereas Fellini went for satire in *Ginger and Fred*, however, Rydell is aiming for sentiment in *For the Boys*, and he hits the mark.

Instead of Ginger and Fred, Rydell presents Dixie and Eddie, with James Caan as Eddie Sparks and Bette Midler as Dixie Leonard (who appears to be a Bette Midler who is thirty years before her time). Midler's performance earned for her a Golden Globe Award as well as an Academy Award nomination. Controversy developed later, however, over the source of the story when Mark Harris, Martha Raye's seventh husband, threatened to sue the producer, contending that Dixie's career followed a twenty-page treatment that Raye had submitted to Bette Midler, based upon Raye's own involvement with the USO during World War II, Korea, and Vietnam.

For the Boys is an old-fashioned film—heavy on entertainment and lubricated with schmaltz. Indeed, some reviewers may have been too embarrassed to admit that they liked it. The film centers on nostalgia: Big Band nostalgia, World War II nostalgia (beginning with clones of the Andrews Sisters before jumping abroad to entertain the troops), early television nostalgia, darkside-of-the-1950's nostalgia (a television writer and gagman is blacklisted after insulting a politically powerful gossip columnist), and even Vietnam nostalgia. The danger of indulging in nostalgia is that the film also edges toward sentimentality. *For the Boys* also succeeds in effectively re-creating the gritty mood of the Korean and Vietnam wars, but it threatens to become a bit smug and preachy.

The film is designed, of course, to showcase the talents of Bette Midler. In *For the Boys*, the Rose is in bloom again, and some reviewers seemed overly eager to prune it. On the other hand, *For the Boys* had powerful mass-market support from several national magazines and network television news shows. The film will have special appeal to the fans of the saucy Midler, as it highlights her talents for 1940's camp nostalgia, but there is far more to this film. Midler is overwhelming, however, and costar Caan must scramble to keep up with her (although he is not miscast).

The story begins in 1991, and the plot borrows a few pages from Fellini's *Ginger and Fred*. A television special is being organized for old Eddie Sparks, who is about to be given a presidential award for a lifetime of service to his country. The producers want his wartime partner Dixie Leonard to participate in the award ceremony, but Dixie, now an old woman, has not spoken to Eddie for twenty-five years. A functionary (played by Arye Gross) is sent to persuade her to attend. He finds a tough and embittered old woman who tells him the story of her career to explain her reluctance.

Dixie first met Eddie Sparks fifty years before in 1942, when she was summoned by her uncle, Art Silver (George Segal), to England to perform with Eddie for the troops. She is supposed to be shy and unsure of herself (a tall order for Bette Midler), but she is a natural performer and upstages Eddie both by her energetic singing and by her deadpan wit. Eddie cannot stand her, but they are a hit together. Art, who is Eddie's writer, predicts they will be "as big as Burns and Allen or Hope and Crosby" (although, at times, they sound more like Abbott and Costello and seem to get along about as well as that comedy team did). The film is about "the birth of a singing and comedy team," Rydell claimed in a publicity statement, "like George Burns finding Gracie Allen, or Sid Caesar finding Imogene Coca." Although they are a "perfect team," Rydell added, "they're both married to other people and have children and families independent of one another, but they have a perfect marriage on stage—a perfect show-business marriage."

Eddie is an egoist, married to a drunken spouse (effectively played by Shannon Wilcox as chilly and aloof). He and his wife have a family of three children, which the script quickly tucks away. Dixie is married to a pilot who is able to hear her sing once with the USO unit before the script kills him off. She also has a son, Danny (Christopher Rydell), who later graduates from the Citadel in South Carolina only to be killed, eventually, in Vietnam. His tragic fate cannot occur, however, until the script brings Eddie and Dixie to Vietnam to perform on the very day that an enemy attack results in Danny's demise, so that Dixie can witness his death. After this event, Dixie has nothing further to do with Eddie.

Eddie always puts his career first, ahead of friends, family, and personal loyalties. Dixie has other, more human priorities. She is the long-suffering wife and mother who will leave a successful television series if the sponsor attempts to give her any political grief. When Art, Dixie's uncle and Eddie's writer and longtime friend, is branded a Communist in the 1950's, Eddie lets him go to save his own career and to keep his coffee sponsor happy. Dixie has much more integrity and moxie, however, and she resigns from the series out of protest. Eddie is a flag-waving moral coward. Without Dixie, his television show fails.

Eddie is also slow to understand the way in which the world changes around him: He takes the same patriotic enthusiasm to Korea and Vietnam that he had taken into World War II. Yet, Korea is awful. Art notices the difference, speaks his mind about Korea, is overheard by the right-wing columnist, and is blacklisted. The difference in Vietnam is that the soldiers have no stomach for the war they are fighting, especially after the Tet Offensive. Vietnam and Danny's death drive a wedge between Eddie and Dixie that causes their twenty-five-year separation. Will Dixie stand by Eddie at the television award ceremony? The film takes its time to answer that question, and the audience cannot be sure until the very end. The answer is worth waiting for.

For the Boys drew some critical flak for its casting of James Caan as Eddie Sparks, who seems to be a relatively dull second banana to Dixie Leonard, both as a singer and as a comedian. The talent spread is in keeping with the characters, however, and *For the Boys* was regarded as another important comeback picture for Caan, who was praised on the television show *20/20* as one of the best of a generation of actors that was showcased in 1991, including Robert De Niro (*Cape Fear*; reviewed in this volume), Al Pacino (*Frankie and Johnny*; reviewed in this volume), Dustin Hoffman (*Billy Bathgate*; reviewed in this volume), and Robert Duvall (*Rambling Rose*; reviewed in this volume). Certainly, *For the Boys* could be considered Caan's most important comeback role after his portrayal of Stephen King's tormented writer in *Misery* (1990), in which he was eclipsed by Kathy Bates, although not to the extent that he is eclipsed by Bette Midler in *For the Boys*. The actor's career had slumped during the late 1970's and 1980's after peaking when Caan played Sonny Corleone in Francis Ford Coppola's *Godfather* series. Caan won an Emmy Award for his portrayal of

Chicago Bears running back Brian Piccolo in the made-for-television film *Brian's Song* (1970), and he was nominated for an Academy Award for *The Godfather* (1972). Thereafter, Caan developed a reputation for being temperamental and difficult, but he was fortunate to have powerful friends who believed in his talent, notably Coppola, Rob Reiner, and Rydell, who considered Caan "one of the four or five best actors in America." Commenting on the Eddie Sparks character for *The New York Times*, Rydell claimed: "There are very few actors who could have played this part—a megalomaniacal, entertaining, charming and complicated character. I needed someone to carry their weight against as giant a talent as Bette Midler."

The fact that *For the Boys* opened to mixed reviews might have created the misleading impression that it was seriously flawed, when in fact it received some strong endorsements from the very day it opened. David Denby of *New York Magazine* called it "the best movie about show business since *The Rose*" (1979), which was also directed by Rydell for Midler. Richard Schickel of *Time* described it as "an ambitious film" that "wears its ambitions lightly and lovably." Bob Thomas of the Associated Press considered it "the best slam-bang entertainment of the year." The *Variety* survey of critics indicated a trend in the film's favor. The film did not fare so well, however, with other critics. For example, Stephen Hunter of the *Baltimore Sun* praised it backhandedly for its "seven or so minutes of dynamite music," but at the same time criticized it as a "tear-jerker that never nudges when it can pound and never pounds when it can smash." The film costs ran to about $50 million, but by January, 1992, had grossed less than $20 million.

For the Boys is a musical wrapped in a melodrama that succeeds brilliantly when graced with Dave Grusin's music and Midler's flamboyant singing talents. Its melodramatic story is protracted and falls a bit short of supporting its epic scope, but overall the film is quite remarkable and entertaining.

James M. Welsh

Reviews
Boxoffice. December, 1991, p. R-87.
Chicago Tribune. November 27, 1991, V, p. 3.
Films in Review. XLII, January/February, 1992, p. 47.
The Hollywood Reporter. November 18, 1991, p. 5.
Los Angeles Times. November 22, 1991, p. F1.
New York Magazine. December 2, 1991, p. 138.
The New York Times. November 22, 1991, p. B3.
The New Yorker. LXVII, December 16, 1991, p. 117.
Newsweek. CXVIII, November 25, 1991, p. 54.
People Weekly. December 2, 1991, p. 30.
Time. CXXXVIII, December 2, 1991, p. 86.
Variety. November 18, 1991, p. 2.
The Washington Post. November 27, 1991, p. B1.

FRANKIE AND JOHNNY

Production: Garry Marshall; released by Paramount Pictures
Direction: Garry Marshall
Screenplay: Terrence McNally; based on his play *Frankie and Johnny in the Clair de Lune*
Cinematography: Dante Spinotti
Editing: Battle Davis and Jacqueline Cambas
Production design: Albert Brenner
Art direction: Carol W. Wood
Set decoration: Kathe Klopp and Kathleen Dolan
Set design: Harold L. Fuhrman
Costume design: Rosanna Norton
Music: Marvin Hamlisch
MPAA rating: R
Running time: 118 minutes

Principal characters:
Johnny .... Al Pacino
Frankie .... Michelle Pfeiffer
Nick .... Hector Elizondo
Tim .... Nathan Lane
Cora .... Kate Nelligan
Nedda .... Jane Morris
Tino .... Greg Lewis
Luther .... Al Fann
Jorge .... Fernando Lopez
Peter .... Glenn Plummer

Frankie and Johnny is bittersweet. It is a mix of charming and endearing, yet it is infuriating in its superficiality and flippancy. The project had all the potential to be a compelling examination of the human emotions of fear and the need to love (and be loved), yet the droll execution turns the film into an extended farcical episode of a television situational comedy. Director Garry Marshall once again reaches for fairy-tale material that is similar to *Pretty Woman* (1990), this time reversing the roles inhabited by Richard Gere and Julia Roberts.

Frankie and Johnny is the story of two working-class people who find love, hope, and each other in a New York City coffee shop. Johnny (Al Pacino) is a former convict who, during a two-year stint in prison for forgery, discovered the joy of cooking. On his first day at work, he is immediately smitten with Frankie (Michelle Pfeiffer), a thirty-six-year-old waitress who has given up on love, let alone the notion of a Prince Charming arriving on a white steed. Johnny is convinced that the two are destined to be lovers, just like the song, but Frankie is quick to remind him that the pair had a less-than-fortuitous outcome to their relationship. Johnny tells her that she shot him, so Frankie has the definite upper hand. Because Frankie refuses to succumb to Johnny's relentless advances, Johnny desperately searches for love in all the wrong places, including with Cora (Kate Nelligan), a promiscuous, aging waitress who would be more than willing to trade in her two boyfriends for one Mr. Right. Frankie slowly warms up to Johnny and finally has sex with him, but Johnny's overbearing insistence that they immediately have a relationship scares her. Persistence wins out, however, in this classic story of boy-meets-girl, boy-loses-girl, boy-gets-girl-back.

For the adaptation of his acclaimed stage play *Frankie and Johnny in the Clair de Lune* (1988) to the screen, writer Terrence McNally decided that it was necessary to open up the feel of the piece, which originally explored the search for love and intimacy by two middle-aged characters as they spend their first night together. The entire play took place in Frankie's dreary Manhattan apartment and featured only two characters, acted on stage by Academy Award winners Kathy Bates and F. Murray Abraham. In fact, McNally wrote the role of Frankie for Bates, and she was awarded an Obie for the New York production of the play.

In the never-ending search for big box-office dollars, however, studio executives decided that, in order for the film to have wider audience appeal, the respected stage actors should be replaced with more enticing Hollywood superstars. The beautiful, frail-looking Michelle Pfeiffer aggressively pursued—and won—the role of Frankie, much to the dismay of critics who believed that the sleek blonde actress was far too glamorous to be believable as a woman who was a loser at love. Critics were quickly silenced, however, by Pfeiffer's interpretation of the character. Obviously, references made in the play to Frankie's lumpy appearance had to be eliminated, and the focus shifted to the woman's fear of getting hurt once again in a relationship. Pfeiffer plays the character as a woman of obvious good looks who has chosen to ignore her potential for fear of attracting attention.

Pfeiffer made a far-from-auspicious film debut in the disastrous *Grease II* (1982), followed by an equally embarrassing performance opposite Al Pacino in director Brian DePalma's remake of *Scarface* (1983), an update of the 1932 Howard Hawks gangster classic that starred Paul Muni. The actress' early work seemed destined to categorize her in the "pretty but not very talented" class of Hollywood actresses that constantly revolves through studio doors. To Pfeiffer's credit, however, she worked at her craft, was able to survive the fickleness that pervades the industry, and began to turn in consistently stellar performances. She received an Academy Award nomination for Best Actress for her work as the cynical singer Susie Diamond in *The Fabulous Baker Boys* (1989), as well as winning honors from the New York Film Critics, the National Society of Film Critics, and the Los Angeles Film Critics. (Her sultry rendition of "Makin' Whoopee" atop a piano in the film shows signs of becoming a classic cinema moment.) Pfeiffer's portrayal of Madame de Tourvel in *Dangerous Liaisons* (1988) earned for her a Best Supporting Actress Academy Award nomination. Her other work includes *Tequila Sunrise* (1988), Jonathan Demme's *Married to the Mob* (1988), and *The Russia House* (1990).

A former joke writer and stand-up comedian, director Garry Marshall earned fame for his work on such groundbreaking television shows as *Happy Days* and *Laverne and Shirley*. He proved his adeptness at executing the clockwork one-liners that have characterized his work, and *Frankie and Johnny* is no exception. Yet, Marshall's work has been marred consistently by his willingness to sacrifice a scene's emotional momentum in favor of a clever punch line. Despite the film's puzzling success, Marshall's *Pretty Woman*, the Cinderella tale of a Hollywood hooker who finds happiness with a rich, but emotionally crippled businessman, failed to move beyond the kind of predictability that has dominated the director's work. Consistently, throughout a body of flawed and maudlin work that includes his directorial debut *Young Doctors in Love* (1982), *The Flamingo Kid* (1984), *Nothing in Common* (1986), *Overboard* (1987), and *Beaches* (1988), Marshall displays a penchant for standard but amusing plot devices to move along the story. In addition, he seldom chooses a surprising camera move or editing pattern. To his credit, however, the director has shown a predilection for emotionally appealing subject matter that often strives to offer insight into both upper-class and working-class people.

One of the things that Terrence McNally did to adapt his play to film was populate the coffee shop with an array of eccentric secondary characters and give Frankie the requisite sympathetic gay neighbor, perhaps with the hope that the audience will understand that Frankie truly is a woman to care about despite her hardened, seemingly impenetrable exterior. The problem, however, is that the writer—or is it the director?—has created clichéd types, not characters. McNally does not breathe life into them as he has with Frankie; the author's obvious love for her is evident in the way in which he understands her fear and her pain. Not even Johnny is sketched with such beautifully precise strokes of sympathy. Perhaps it is Pacino's interpretation of Johnny's single-minded pursuit of love, happiness, and the American Dream that fails to imbue the character with much depth or complexity. It is never a question of whether Johnny will win over Frankie; it is merely a matter of time. With such a limited plot structure, execution becomes crucial. When only one character is fully conceived, it is easy to become enamored with that character and to rely on that person to pull the story through to its predetermined conclusion. In many ways, this is the same problem encountered in *Batman* (1989). Michael Keaton as Batman possessed a depth of pain and complexity that was unmatched by any of the other characters within the story and certainly not by the overblown performance of Jack Nicholson as the Joker. As a result, it was easy to sense a dichotomy, to feel as though one were watching two different films simultaneously.

In *Frankie and Johnny*, Pacino offers little nuance and shading to Johnny. There was a time when he was one of the most powerful actors on the screen. A student of "The Method," Pacino showed promise of replacing Marlon Brando as the king of intensity, much as Michael Corleone inherited the "family" in Francis Ford Coppola's *The Godfather* (1972). Pacino left Hollywood for awhile to work on the stage, winning critical acclaim for his work in *American Buffalo*, and when he returned to film, he chose a role perfectly suited for him: the alcoholic cop going through a mid-life crisis in *Sea of Love* (1989). After his over-the-top performance as a villain in Warren Beatty's *Dick Tracy* (1990), however, Pacino seemed determined to seize his roles as if each were a grand star turn designed to grab the public's eye with its importance.

Frankie and Johnny proved a disappointment at the box office despite some positive critical reviews that applauded the film's comic vision. It is more likely to capture an audience on home video, however, because of its strong television sitcom structure. Director Marshall relies on his ace-in-the-hole—the power of Pfeiffer's acting ability—to salvage his otherwise weak story. The film seems a fitting metaphor, however, for life in a time in which the most emotionally vulnerable thing a person can reveal is one's age.

Patricia Kowal

Reviews
Chicago Tribune. October 11, 1991, VII, p. 43.
The Christian Science Monitor. LXXXIII, October 15, 1991, p. 10.
The Hollywood Reporter. CCCXIX, October 7, 1991, p. 5.
L.A. Weekly. October 18-24, 1991, XIII, p. 35.
Los Angeles Times. October 11, 1991, p. F1.
Maclean's. CIV, October 21, 1991, p. 98.
The New York Times. October 11, 1991, CXLI, p. B1.
The New Yorker. LXVII, October 21, 1991, p. 125.
Newsweek. CXVIII, October 14, 1991, p. 68.
Rolling Stone. October 31, 1991, p. 95.
Time. CXXXVIII, October 21, 1991, p. 101.
Variety. October 7, 1991, p. 3.
The Village Voice. XXXVI, October 22, 1991, p. 64.
The Washington Post. October 11, 1991, p. D7.

FRIED GREEN TOMATOES

Production: Jon Avnet and Jordan Kerner for Universal Pictures and Act III Communi-
cations, in association with Electric Shadow Productions; released by Universal
Pictures
Direction: Jon Avnet
Screenplay: Fannie Flagg and Carol Sobieski; based on the novel *Fried Green
Tomatoes at the Whistle Stop Cafe*, by Flagg
Cinematography: Geoffrey Simpson
Editing: Debra Neil
Production design: Barbara Ling
Art direction: Larry Fulton
Set decoration: Deborah Schutt
Casting: David Rubin
Sound: Mary Ellis
Costume design: Elizabeth McBride
Music: Thomas Newman
MPAA rating: PG-13
Running time: 130 minutes

Principal characters:

Evelyn Couch	Kathy Bates
Ninny Threadgoode	Jessica Tandy
Idgie Threadgoode	Mary Stuart Masterson
Ruth Jamison	Mary-Louise Parker
Ed Couch	Gailard Sartain
Big George	Stan Shaw
Sipsey	Cicely Tyson
Grady	Gary Basarba
Frank Bennett	Nick Searcy
Smokey Lonesome	Tim Scott
Buddy Threadgoode	Chris O'Donnell
Mrs. Threadgoode	Lois Smith
Reverend Scroggins	Richard Riehle

Evelyn Couch (Kathy Bates) visits her husband's aunt in a nursing home and, while
there, happens to start a conversation with one of the residents, Ninny Threadgoode
(Jessica Tandy). Thus, *Fried Green Tomatoes* uses the age-old storytelling device of a
present-day raconteur telling a younger person what happened during her life. With
nothing better to do, Evelyn—who never could get along with her husband's aunt—
settles down and listens to Ninny's tale of life in Whistle Stop, Alabama.

Ninny begins her tale with the day that an old rusted truck was pulled out of the
river. This truck belonged to the husband of Ruth Jamison (Mary-Louise Parker),

Frank Bennett (Nick Searcy), who years earlier had disappeared without a trace. Ninny, a coy storyteller, uses this mystery to introduce Evelyn to the Threadgoode family and the relationship between Ruth and Idgie Threadgoode (Mary Stuart Masterson). The story really begins years earlier during the wedding dinner of one of the Threadgoodes. Buddy Threadgoode (Chris O'Donnell), Idgie's older brother, gets his foot caught in a railway track while trying to retrieve Ruth's bonnet and is killed by a passing train. This horrible death, witnessed by both Idgie and Ruth, causes Idgie, the youngest daughter of the Threadgoodes, to become quite wild and wayward. By the time that she is an adolescent, her parents have no control over her, and she eventually spends most of her time gambling and drinking at a riverside saloon.

Mrs. Threadgoode (Lois Smith), in an effort to reform her wayward daughter, invites Ruth for the summer in the hope that Ruth might be able to talk some sense into Idgie. Ruth and Idgie become good friends. Ninny enjoys telling Evelyn these old stories, but Evelyn is going through a personal crisis in her own life: She believes that she is worthless and that her marriage is falling apart. While Ninny does not have any real advice to give Evelyn, the two women become close friends through the recounting of the story about Whistle Stop.

Ruth marries Frank Bennett, who soon becomes an abusive husband; a visit by Idgie reveals that Bennett is beating his wife. When Ruth's mother dies, a pregnant and frightened Ruth sends a letter to Idgie telling her to come and take her back to Whistle Stop, where they open the Whistle Stop Cafe. Bennett comes one night to the café and tries to abduct their baby son. Before he can put the child in his truck, however, he is killed by a blow to the head. Within a few weeks, a detective from Georgia comes to the café and asks about Bennett's whereabouts. Because Idgie had been heard making a threat to Bennett years before that she would kill him if he ever harmed Ruth again, Idgie becomes the prime suspect.

Evelyn is now totally gripped by the story of the Whistle Stop Cafe, and she begins to identify with the strong character of Idgie. Despite making her husband, Ed Couch (Gailard Sartain), delicious meals, Evelyn cannot rekindle the romance in her marriage. During another meeting, Ninny explains to Evelyn that there was a trial but that the Reverend Scroggins (Richard Riehle) vouched that Idgie was on a three-day revival meeting and that she could not possibly have killed Bennett. By this time, Evelyn wants to take control of her own life in the same way that Idgie seems to be taking control of hers. When two young women drive into a parking space that Evelyn has been waiting for, she decides to crash into their car. Pleased with her continuing self-discovery, Evelyn returns to the nursing home one day to find that Ninny has been discharged. Unfortunately, during her stay, Ninny's house in Whistle Stop has been condemned and razed to the ground, so Evelyn offers to take her into their home.

There is still the final question, however, of who killed Frank Bennett. Ninny explains that, as Bennett was leaving the café with Ruth's baby, Sipsey (Cicely Tyson), the black housekeeper, hit Bennett over the head with an iron frying pan and killed him. Idgie and Sipsey's son, Big George (Stan Shaw), then disposed of the body by making it into barbecue sauce. Evelyn, knowing that Ruth had died of cancer, inquires about Idgie's fate. Ninny shows a note on Ruth's grave to Evelyn. In the note is a reference to a bee charmer—a nickname given to Idgie by Ruth—and the fact that Ruth is still remembered. Evelyn finally realizes that Ninny is Idgie and that she was describing her life with Ruth throughout the many hours that they had talked at the nursing home.

Telling a story through the use of long flashbacks can be dangerous: Very often, flashbacks hold up the action and the forward movement of the story line. In *Fried Green Tomatoes*, however, this danger is avoided, partly because of the already well-rounded story of Fannie Flagg, on whose novel the film is based, and who was nominated along with Carol Sobieski for an Academy Award for Best Adapted Screenplay.

Many stories set in the South, particularly those set in the 1930's, prove fascinating and insightful. In *Fried Green Tomatoes*, the issue of race is dealt with quite strongly and overtly. Although the African-American characters of the story—Big George and Sipsey—act as background figures, their presence is felt throughout the film. The Ku Klux Klan comes one evening to the Whistle Stop Cafe to remind Idgie and Ruth that African Americans must not be allowed to eat with whites, heightening the racial tension. As her "colored man," Big George is arrested with Idgie after Bennett's truck is pulled from the river. In fact, if Idgie had not been willing to go on trial, then Big George would have been found guilty by less-honest means. While never a dominant theme, racism is nevertheless addressed and not simply ignored as irrelevant to the main story.

In *Fried Green Tomatoes*, director Jon Avnet generally uses the typical modern approach, using a stedicam to create a continuous shot from one room to the next or a shot that starts from above and then pans down onto the subject. This approach, however, was not Avnet's most effective one. Perhaps the most visually powerful scene in the film occurs when Ruth is on her deathbed and Idgie tells her a familiar tall tale for the last time. The scene is set in a large room, and the camera remains fixed while Idgie walks to the far end. By the time that she returns to the bed, Ruth has died. There are few scenes that can evoke such sadness yet depict the warm friendship that they have shared over the years. This instance acts as a reminder of how powerful the stationary camera can be, without continually cutting from close-up to master scene.

Like *Driving Miss Daisy* (1989), this film focuses on friendship, using the South as its background. The continual movement back and forth through the retelling of Ninny's story creates a window through which the viewer is able to experience on a firsthand basis what happened at Whistle Stop. By using an evocative, nostalgic small-town setting, another dimension is added to the film. In addition, close friendship, while certainly not particular to the South, somehow has its best expression in the language and ways of Southerners. These factors, coupled with the strong need of many people to hear and tell stories, make *Fried Green Tomatoes* a delight for filmgoers.

For her role as Ninny, Jessica Tandy was nominated for an Academy Award for Best Supporting Actress. While Tandy and Kathy Bates both give fine performances, much of the credit for the motion picture's continuity belongs to the relationship that Mary Stuart Masterson and Mary-Louise Parker bring to the film. There is a definite sense that, as the character of Idgie grows in maturity, so does Masterson's performance. The early scenes in which Idgie plays the young tomboy are not as believable as when she plays the café owner or when she is tried for murder. Equally, Parker, as the often confused and downtrodden Ruth, manages to bring to her role a sense of strength, while at the same time maintaining an underlying fragility. Parker's strength is revealed in her reactions to what is happening around her, not in what she says. This nonverbal approach complements Masterson's performance, as she generally puts all of her reactions and feelings into the dialogue and very little into body language or subtle nuances.

There is no one feature that can account for the homogeneous feeling that *Fried Green Tomatoes* manages to create. Storytelling is, by definition, primal, and Flagg's well-rounded novel, *Fried Green Tomatoes at the Whistle Stop Cafe* (1987), undoubtedly adds to this sense of wholeness and solidity. The use of Ninny as the raconteur, in addition to the interchange between past and present, provides the viewer with perhaps the most satisfying way of being told a story. Whistle Stop, Alabama, and *Fried Green Tomatoes* are reminders of the past and of the fact that real friendship is still the most valuable human commodity.

Richard G. Cormack

Reviews
Boston Globe. January 10, 1992, p. 73.
Boxoffice. February, 1992, p. R-13.
Chicago Tribune. January 10, 1992, VII, p. 30.
The Hollywood Reporter. December 23, 1991, p. 5.
The Houston Post. January 10, 1992, p. E4.
Los Angeles Times. December 27, 1991, p. F1.
The New Republic. CCVI, February 3, 1992, p. 28.
The New York Times. December 27, 1991, p. B3.
Time. CXXXIX, January 27, 1992, p. 67.
Variety. December 23, 1991, p. 2.
The Wall Street Journal. January 9, 1992, p. A10.
The Washington Post. January 10, 1992, p. D6.

158

GRAND CANYON

Production: Lawrence Kasdan, Charles Okun, and Michael Grillo; released by
   Twentieth Century-Fox
Direction: Lawrence Kasdan
Screenplay: Lawrence Kasdan and Meg Kasdan
Cinematography: Owen Roizman
Editing: Carol Littleton
Production design: Bo Welch
Art direction: Tom Duffield
Set decoration: Cheryl Carasik
Casting: Jennifer Shull
Special visual effects: Dream Quest Images
Sound: David MacMillan, Kevin O'Connell, and Rick Kline
Costume design: Aggie Guerard Rodgers
Music: James Newton Howard
MPAA rating: R
Running time: 134 minutes

   Principal characters:
   Simon .... Danny Glover
   Mack .... Kevin Kline
   Davis .... Steve Martin
   Claire .... Mary McDonnell
   Dee .... Mary-Louise Parker
   Jane .... Alfre Woodard
   Roberto .... Jeremy Sisto
   Otis .... Patrick Malone
   Deborah .... Tina Lifford

   Lawrence Kasdan's *The Big Chill* (1983) was the original film anthem of the baby-
boomers. Many who loved the film believed that it portrayed, with both fresh humor
and seriousness, that generation's confused transition from the 1960's into the 1980's
and the painful search for life's truest values. In *Grand Canyon*, producer-director-
writer Kasdan attempts to reveal the baby-boomers ten years later—more mature and
economically stable, but hounded by the ghosts of spiritual longings they cannot
satisfy. Set in 1990's Los Angeles, the film also takes a look at crime, racial and class
tensions, and urban anxiety. The film opens with scenes from a city basketball court.
The players are young African Americans, and the neighborhood is certainly not
affluent. A helicopter overhead makes the first of many appearances—its probing
searchlight and the propeller's rhythmic concussions are sinister. One suspects that
there is reason, even in the midst of fun, to be afraid. The opening scenes prepare the
viewer for an exploration of cultural differences.
   Meanwhile, Mack (Kevin Kline) and his close friend, Davis (Steve Martin), watch

the Los Angeles Lakers at the Coliseum. As they are leaving, Davis, a successful producer of gory, brutal films about big-city violence, plies his friend Mack with well-meaning yet gloomy and darkly mischievous pronouncements on life. Because Mack has become obsessed with the fragility of life, Davis' well-meaning but bleak encouragement does little to reassure him. Impetuously taking a side street to escape a bad traffic jam outside the Coliseum, Mack becomes lost in a dangerous neighborhood. To make matters worse, his car breaks down and it is getting dark. Threatened by a gang, he is saved by the arrival of a tow-truck driver, Simon (Danny Glover), who is able to convince the gang's leader that he should leave them both alone without committing a crime that he will later regret. At the station, Mack and Simon talk while Mack waits for his car. Their experience has bonded them, and they seem to have become instant, if tentative, friends. Simon talks about seeing the Grand Canyon recently. Gazing out over the sublime expanse of the canyon, he recalls, assured him that life must somehow be positive and made his problems seem much less important.

This early scene establishes Simon as the character whose stability and warmth will provide an anchor for the others, whose uncertainties more easily disarm them. It also suggests the central conflict that each character will face: how to protect his or her own frail sensibilities from the chaos of contemporary urban life without becoming crushed by the world. Each of the six major characters in the story is forced, at some point, to deal with the harsh realities of city life. A speech by Mack's wife, Claire (Mary McDonnell), late in the film about small miracles reinforces one of Kasdan's themes—a contemporary version of carpe diem—that people need to pause and be thankful for simple pleasures. Gazing out over the Grand Canyon, holding a baby, enjoying the company of a relative or friend, or exchanging good wishes with a stranger on the street are miraculous pleasures for the soul.

Appropriately, the film cuts to Davis in his screening room, where he and his executives are watching a bloody scene from one of Davis' ultraviolent films. In it, a crazed man hijacks a bus and shoots the driver. Davis is outraged because "the brains shot" has been edited out. He demands to have it back in the film, explaining that gore is what his audience wants. Meanwhile, Mack and Claire are going through a summer ritual: Their fifteen-year-old son Roberto (Jeremy Sisto) is heading off to camp. His departure is particularly painful for Claire, as it reminds her that Roberto is growing up and will soon leave home.

The next few scenes in the film illustrate Kasdan's efforts to tie six urban lives together by illustrating their sudden involvements in similar conflicts. Scenes from the characters' daily lives are skillfully interspliced, and ordinary yet extraordinary things happen to all six in the space of a few hours. Davis is accosted and shot by a man who wanted his Rolex watch. The same morning, during her jog, Claire finds an abandoned baby girl hidden in the bushes, whom she takes home with her. At the office, Mack finds himself holding hands with his secretary, Dee (Mary-Louise Parker), a lonely woman who would like to have an affair with him. Simon, meanwhile, has arrived home from the grocery store and immediately calls his daughter, a deaf student at Gallaudet University in Washington, D.C., on a telephone/

teletype machine; this tender scene again underscores Simon's good-heartedness and stoicism. The film moves back to Mack's workplace, where Dee and her friend Jane (Alfre Woodard) are having coffee and discussing men, in particular Dee's infatuation with Mack. In his office, Mack is having a disturbing telephone conversation with his wife: She tells him about the child that she has found and hints that she wants to adopt her. Mack, however, is not enthusiastic.

The story shifts to the other side of town, where Simon is having dinner with his sister, Deborah (Tina Lifford), and her children. Simon's nephew, Otis (Patrick Malone), has joined a gang. Simon encourages him to get out of it. Overhead, a police helicopter pounds the air. The helicopter is a recurring motif, signaling violence and even despair, and is an image that this film shares with *Boyz 'n the Hood* (1991; reviewed in this volume), a film about the bitter reality of life for young African Americans in South Central Los Angeles. The helicopter, once a symbol of the Vietnam War, has become a symbol of the urban wars waged in the United States. The helicopter had portent: The following day, Deborah's house is sprayed with machine-gun fire in a lengthy attack—the most harrowing scene in the film—while she and her young daughter cower on the floor. Next, the helicopter motif transports the audience to Dee's apartment; she is lonely, yearning, and sad. Davis, on the other hand, surveying the Los Angeles skyline at dawn from his high-rise hospital room, is inspired by a new muse: He will forsake films of violence and urban pestilence for films that celebrate "the life force" instead, he later tells Claire. His close encounter with death has apparently given him new vision.

As the story weaves in and out of these six people's lives, only their fear of chaos and instability remains constant. They love one another and smile often, but under it all tremors are brewing. An actual earthquake does arrive, chasing Mack and Claire from their beautiful home. Next door, their elderly neighbor dies from a heart attack. That night, Mack and Claire dream their anxiety. Mack's dream, a flying sequence, reveals that he is troubled over his secretary Dee and their one-night affair. Claire dreams a slow-motion train chase that divulges her primordial fear of the breakup of her family. Mack and Claire are still at odds over her plan to adopt the orphan.

The film goes on to explore Mack's relationship with Simon and the inescapable caution with which each enters this friendship. Much of their initial discomfort, beautifully conveyed by the actors, is attributable to the men's overawareness of the obstacles of race. Mack is especially concerned that he will offend Simon and confesses he does not wish to be seen as a guilty white liberal do-gooder when he offers to help Simon's sister find a safer place to rear her family. A friend of Mack owns a complex in a good neighborhood, but Simon mentions that it is also all-white. Nevertheless, Simon appreciates Mack's effort to reach out and is moved to reminisce about his father and about how habit drove him to face life's odds. This breakfast scene between the two men is warm, leisurely paced, and intuitively played. The dialogue for once manages to transcend the banalities and didacticism that mar other scenes in *Grand Canyon*, in which the conversation treads over philosophical questions about contemporary life with little originality and less grace.

Mack's most important gift to Simon turns out to be not his help with Deborah's housing or even his offer of friendship but his impetuous decision to introduce Simon to Jane, Dee's friend at work. Jane and Simon quickly decide that they are made for each other. This blossoming romance is compared to that of Roberto and his girlfriend from camp. Kasdan's sensitivity to adolescent feelings of first love is clear. Less clear is why Dee, pacing Mack's office as she delivers a strident attack on her boss for spurning her, should feel so wronged by an episode that she helped to create. She lectures him on why she should be allowed to hate him. Dee seems at this point to be an unattractive brat on the verge of a 1990's-woman breakdown. On the other hand, the scene does effectively show how a lovesick person can make a perfect fool of herself. Unfortunately, the character of Dee is not as strongly developed as those of Mack, Claire, or Simon, and viewers may find her childish angst and reaction to loneliness more annoying than deserving of empathy. The character of Claire has much more depth. Although the idea of finding a baby in the bushes and wanting to adopt it is much more farfetched than the possibility of a love-struck secretary, Claire's speech about daily miracles is convincing. It persuades the audience as well as Mack that, by taking this child in, she is doing the only responsible, logical, and loving thing possible. Mack finally relents, and Claire's adoption plans forge ahead.

Mack's acceptance of his wife's need for and commitment to the foundling girl puts into motion the complex machinery of closure that Kasdan manufactures in order to draw many related but separate plot threads to a somewhat satisfying end. Davis decides that he was a "moron" for thinking that he would stop making films of violence, as he must keep telling the truth that Americans want to see. Simon and Jane fall more deeply in love. Otis, chastened after witnessing a street murder, decides to quit his old neighborhood gang. Mack and Simon share a basketball game that is free of their former nervousness over race. In the final scene, Mack with baby, Claire, Simon, Jane, Roberto, and Otis arrive at the Grand Canyon. It was Simon's idea to take them all there. Gazing out over this spiritual paradise, Mack can finally agree with his new friend that life is not that bad.

Despite the unwieldy number of major characters, the plot's loose threads, and the self-consciousness revealed in the film's deadly earnest (and too often banal) mystical monologues, *Grand Canyon* garnered the respect of most reviewers. They appreciated the plot's surprises and the intelligence with which Meg and Lawrence Kasdan constructed the screenplay and forged the characters. For their effort, the Kasdans were nominated for an Academy Award for Best Original Screenplay. Kasdan's film was often compared to the satirical *L.A. Story* (1991; reviewed in this volume) and called a darker, more intense version of that film. Yet many positive reviews especially noted *Grand Canyon*'s offbeat humor and its final hopefulness—an affirmation of life in the city at fortysomething and of contemporary life in general. The performances throughout are sure and sensitive, especially Danny Glover's as Simon, easily the fullest and most interesting character in the film.

JoAnn Balingit

Reviews
Boxoffice. February, 1992, p. R-12.
Chicago Tribune. January 10, 1992, VII, p. 31.
The Christian Science Monitor. January 3, 1992, p. 12.
Entertainment Weekly. January 10, 1992, p. 52.
The Hollywood Reporter. December 16, 1991, p. 7.
Los Angeles Times. December 25, 1991, p. F1.
The New Republic. CCV, January 20, 1992, p. 28.
The New York Times. December 25, 1991, The Living Arts, p. 13.
Time. CXXXVIII, December 30, 1991, p. 70.
Variety. December 16, 1991, p. 2.
The Wall Street Journal. December 26, 1991, p. A5.
The Washington Post. January 10, 1992, p. D1.

GUILTY BY SUSPICION

Production: Arnon Milchan; released by Warner Bros.
Direction: Irwin Winkler
Screenplay: Irwin Winkler
Cinematography: Michael Ballhaus
Editing: Priscilla Nedd
Production design: Leslie Dilley
Art direction: Leslie McDonald
Set decoration: Nancy Haigh
Sound: Richard Lightstone
Costume design: Richard Bruno
Music: James Newton Howard
MPAA rating: PG-13
Running time: 105 minutes

Principal characters:
David Merrill .... Robert De Niro
Ruth Merrill .... Annette Bening
Bunny Baxter .... George Wendt
Dorothy Nolan .... Patricia Wettig
Felix Graff .... Sam Wanamaker
Paulie Merrill .... Luke Edwards
Larry Nolan .... Chris Cooper
Darryl Zanuck .... Ben Piazza
Joe Lesser .... Martin Scorsese

During the troubling era of the Hollywood witch hunts, "golden boy" film director David Merrill (Robert De Niro) returns from Paris in 1951 to find an eerily paranoic chill has come over the film capital. Twentieth Century-Fox boss Darryl Zanuck (Ben Piazza) dangles a plum assignment if only David will "cooperate" with the House Committee on Un-American Activities' witch hunt by naming the names of friends and colleagues whose only crime had been to attend a pro-Soviet Union rally or a Communist meeting during the period of World War II when the Soviet Union was an ally of the United States. At first, Merrill refuses and his career crashes to a halt. After struggling with his problem, Merrill confronts the committee, sticks to his principles, and dramatically does not capitulate.

This is not so much the story of a single person, but a composite, synthesizing portrait of the painful paths of dozens of blacklisted men and women. The glue that holds the film together, however, is the subtle performance of De Niro. There is little of the expected De Niro bravura, but in a gripping final sequence as Merrill, he denounces the House Committee on Un-American Activities, knowing that his career as a Hollywood filmmaker is over and that his life will be forever transformed.

Longtime producer Irwin Winkler made his directorial debut with *Guilty by Suspicion* and also wrote the screenplay. Winkler's inspiration came from his days at the beginning of his career in the mail room at the William Morris Talent Agency. There he was able, from the bottom up, to observe careers being destroyed. Winkler had produced thirty-five major films prior to *Guilty by Suspicion*, including *They Shoot Horses Don't They?* (1969), *Rocky* (1976), *Raging Bull* (1980), *The Right Stuff* (1983), and the award-winning *GoodFellas* (1990). After his separation from longtime partner Robert Chartoff, Winkler embarked on a period of self-examination and concluded that he wished to be more immediately involved in the filmmaking process. This commitment led him to write and direct *Guilty by Suspicion*.

The conservative ambiance of 1950's Hollywood was captured in *Guilty by Suspicion* for $13 million, half the usual cost of a Hollywood feature of the early 1990's. Despite shooting on the run, the cinematic details in *Guilty by Suspicion* are fascinating. In particular, the brown-suited, cigar-smoking backwater of the halls of power in Washington, D.C., during the Eisenhower Administration seems eerie. Leslie Dilley's production design is superb. Cinematographer Michael Ballhaus' rich gloom is stunning.

The music in the film is ironic and poignant. Throughout this tale of power and paranoia, one hears Nat King Cole sing "Straighten Up and Fly Right," Billie Holliday belt out "They Can't Take That Away From Me," and Dianne Reeves perform "Easy Come, Easy Go." Merrill refuses to "fly right," the powers-that-be do "take it away" from him, and the former golden boy finds it is not "easy come, easy go."

The casting is, at times, self-reflexive. For example, the lawyer, Felix Graff, is played by classy veteran actor Sam Wanamaker, who had spent a decade acting in London rather than capitulate to the House Committee on Un-American Activities. In small parts appear Joan Scott, the widow of the Hollywood Ten's Adrian Scott, and Ileana Douglas, granddaughter of Helen Gahagan Douglas and Melvyn Douglas, both of whom were blacklisted.

Award-winning film director Martin Scorsese appears as director Joe Lesser. At one point, the audience sees Lesser's uncompleted film on a Moviola in the background. It is director Joseph Losey's *The Boy with Green Hair* (1948). Losey was blacklisted, and like his fictional counterpart Lesser, fled to Great Britain in order to wait out the intolerance.

The Lesser/Losey connection is not the only historical one in the film. Twentieth Century-Fox boss, Zanuck, is named directly and vividly portrayed by a much too tall, but otherwise perfect, Ben Piazza. Many others are hinted at. In the opening of *Guilty by Suspicion*, Larry Nolan (Chris Cooper) confesses to members of the House Committee on Un-American Activities. Larry Parks, the real actor, was one of the first to inform. The last name "Nolan" probably comes from Gypo Nolan, the lead character in director John Ford's award-winning tale *The Informer* (1935).

Merrill is based on Metro-Goldwyn-Mayer director John Berry, whose career was cut short in 1951. Indeed, prior to production, Winkler met with Berry and learned how the blacklisted man had made a sixteen-millimeter film, *The Hollywood Ten*

(1951), worked in France and Great Britain, and then, two decades later, was able to return to the United States to reenter the Hollywood industry for such efforts as *The Bad News Bears Go to Japan* (1978).

There are two delicious sequences in which the audience sees 1950's filmmaking in action. For director Howard Hawks's *Gentlemen Prefer Blondes* (1953), Zanuck deals with the rushes of the film, deciding which take to keep. Part of a production number is also shown before the camera. Later, when Merrill has sunk to accepting any job, he directs a "seven-day wonder" at the Monogram studio. The film seems to be *High Noon* (1952), however, in which a sheriff (Gary Cooper) is abandoned by his friends when the "bad guys" come looking for him. That film was produced by Stanley Kramer (and written by blacklisted screenwriter Carl Foreman) for United Artists on the same location ranch.

The story is told with admirable simplicity and a lack of sensationalism. By making Merrill devoted solely to his art, however, *Guilty by Suspicion* skirts thorny political issues of commitment and progressive action. At times Merrill comes across as a bemused naïf. By 1951, however, the despicable purges of the House Committee on Un-American Activities had created headlines around the world. By then, the famed Hollywood Ten had stood up to the committee, refused to talk, and gone to jail.

Douglas Gomery

Reviews
America. CLXIV, April 20, 1991, p. 448.
American Cinematographer. LXXII, March, 1991, p. 26.
Boston Globe. March 15, 1991, p. 41.
Chicago Tribune. March 15, 1991, p. C7.
Films in Review. XLII, July, 1991, p. 267.
The Hollywood Reporter. March 6, 1991, p. 9.
Los Angeles Times. March 15, 1991, p. F1.
National Review. XLIII, April 15, 1991, p. 45.
The New York Times. March 15, 1991, p. B1.
Rolling Stone. April 4, 1991, p. 60.
USA Today. March 15, 1991, p. 4D.
Variety. CCCXLII, March 6, 1991, p. 2.
The Village Voice. March 26, 1991, p. 52.
The Wall Street Journal. March 28, 1991, p. A12.
The Washington Post. March 16, 1991, p. 1D.

HE SAID, SHE SAID

Production: Frank Mancuso, Jr.; released by Paramount Pictures
Direction: Ken Kwapis (*He Said*) and Marisa Silver (*She Said*)
Screenplay: Brian Hohlfeld
Cinematography: Stephen H. Burum
Editing: Sidney Levin
Production design: Michael Corenblith
Art direction: David James Bomba
Set design: Siobhan C. Roome and Bruton Jones
Set decoration: Merideth Boswell
Sound: Richard Bryce Goodman
Costume design: Deena Appel
Music: Miles Goodman
MPAA rating: PG-13
Running time: 115 minutes

Principal characters:
Dan Hanson .... Kevin Bacon
Lorie Bryer .... Elizabeth Perkins
Wally Thurman .... Nathan Lane
Mark .... Anthony LaPaglia
Linda .... Sharon Stone
Bill Weller .... Stanley Anderson
Cindy .... Charlayne Woodard
Eric .... Danton Stone
Mr. Spepk .... Phil Leeds
Mrs. Spepk .... Rita Karin

Greek morality plays would seem to have little in common with the film *He Said, She Said*, but it would appear that a modern society needs to review its moral and ethical code from time to time as the Greeks once did. Courting couples are faced with an unusual dilemma that did not present itself to their parents' generation: Should they get married or merely live together? Dan Hanson (Kevin Bacon) is a young available man-about-town who thinks that he has the pick of any girl who comes his way. Lorie Bryer (Elizabeth Perkins) is a young, upwardly mobile woman who enjoys the company of men but who is looking for something more than dating and partying. *He Said, She Said* allows both Lorie and Dan to give their respective views of how they see their relationship develop.

A local television station creates a program around Lorie and Dan, who originally start out together as rivals writing a joint newspaper column. The particular issue presented to them on this show is about whether a piece of road should be built in a historic part of the city. He is for the project, she is against such a development. Then, without warning, Lorie throws her coffee cup at Dan and storms off the set. This is seen live by the television audience. Dan does not know what has happened to Lorie and, on returning to their apartment, finds all of his belongings thrown out into the hallway. Mr. and Mrs. Spepk (Phil Leeds and Rita Karin), his neighbors, invite Dan into their apartment, and they talk about life, especially Dan's relationship with Lorie. A flashback shows Dan's meeting with Lorie when she first came to work on the same newspaper. Before they have time to introduce themselves, an old flame of Dan's storms into his office. Once she leaves, Lorie tells Dan that he can come out from underneath the desk. Lorie has come to work at the newspaper, and they eventually write a joint column and star on a television program together. From this rather rocky beginning, they come to like each other enough to start living together. Because this story has two sides, Lorie then gives her version of how she sees her relationship with Dan. Through the use of another major flashback, this time from the point of view of Lorie, the story that led up to the coffee cup-throwing saga is told again. Apparently, Dan was always complaining that Lorie never cleaned her cup properly, and he seemed to care more about those kinds of trivial matters than expressing his true feelings to her.

Boy-meets-girl stories remain the staple of Hollywood and will continue to act as an inspiration for as long as films are made. The difficulty, however, is to approach this timeless subject and present a new and interesting dimension. Two directors, Ken Kwapis and Marisa Silver, a couple in real life, teamed up to direct half a film each. This approach may seem a little artificial, as it assumes that only a woman director can give the female version and that only a male director can give the viewpoint of his gender. Therefore, from the beginning, the motion picture becomes stereotyped. Initially, the two directors' approaches do not add or detract from the actual drama that occurs between Dan and Lorie. What does become somewhat obvious is when the same essential story, first stated by Dan, is then repeated by Lorie. The second time around, there are really only minor changes, which effectually means that the story is being repeated for its own sake. This, at first appearances, seems a recipe for disaster, but somehow the integrity of the film survives. Very often, by completely breaking the accepted rules of storytelling, of never repeating what has already been stated, a better understanding of that story is achieved. By seeing the same story repeated, in this case that of Dan and Lorie, the viewer can understand better the motives that people bring to a relationship.

Very often, flashbacks will do one of two things: They will either slow the whole picture down or will send it off on a tangent, taking away from the real flow of the film. Unfortunately, after Dan has given what is supposed to be his version, the kernel of the story is almost fully explained. The idea is to play the story from his perspective and then from hers, which is where the possibility of success lies. The material becomes too unwieldy, however, and what might have had significance in modern society, in which living together has become common practice, turns into a convoluted story concerning misunderstanding, petty jealousies, suspicion, defensiveness, and rivalry.

These same elements make for enjoyable dramatic situations, but they do not add up in *He Said, She Said*.

At first, to repeat almost exactly the same story, line for line, with only a slight change of perspective could be conceived as risky and confusing in the best of circumstances. Thankfully, the actual story is not that complicated and the thread of it is not easily lost. The real trouble about giving his version and then giving her version is that neither one seems to be entirely their own. In fact, there is the overall sense that there is also another story being told—that of the director. Because this film has two directors sharing the story at different times, this other story comes across just as strongly as "his version" and "her version."

The main conflict of the story is that Dan maintains that he is not ready to settle down while Lorie is ready for some commitment in their relationship. Once again, a grand theme is touched on but the real reasons that Dan cannot make any commitment are not explored; like much of the earlier part of the film, they must be taken at face value. This lapse is the result of the fact that it takes considerable time to find out exactly what is happening with this couple. Once this has been discovered, the rest is clear sailing. Lorie is certainly not the perfect woman, and she does not have all the answers. It would seem that she is somewhat bigoted in her view about men and is very much a feminist, considering herself the underdog from the moment she joins the newspaper. Even though Dan and Lorie have much to understand about themselves, as well as each other, these self-revelatory facts are not where the film derives its strength. Nor does moving back and forth between the different versions of the story give this film any kind of endearing quality.

What does make it appealing are the performances of Bacon and Perkins. In spite of its obvious weaknesses, *He Said, She Said* maintains an air of believability that mostly comes from these two talented performers. Through all the arguments and bad feelings that this relationship seems to cause, there is a feeling of hope and love. These same themes are explored in the films *When Harry Met Sally* (1989) and *Stanley and Iris* (1990). Each of these three films, in its own way, explores the relationship of men and women who are unable to express their true feelings to their partners. Each film also shows that there is the necessity for change, and this has to occur before any real relationship can happen. By using an unmarried couple as its starting point, *He Said, She Said* tackles the delicate and sometimes confusing feelings that arise as to whether marriage is the only option available to the present generation.

Humor certainly provides an important ingredient to the telling of this story. Much of the anxiety that is created between Dan and Lorie is attributable to the fact that they are living together but cannot quite relate to each other as a married couple. When they visit Lorie's parents, the conversation immediately turns to Dan being asked the most intimate details about his love life. Lorie concludes the conversation by telling the family gathering exactly what type and color of prophylactics that they use. One of the most amusing scenes in the film is when Dan seeks the help of a counselor. The counselor sees that Dan is unable to allow himself to become intimate with other people. In order to overcome his inhibitions, the counselor suggests that he tell a glove puppet how much he loves it. Thus, in its own way, *He Said, She Said* takes a lighthearted look at one of the most perplexing relationships set before humanity and manages to present it with humor and good taste.

Richard G. Cormack

Reviews

American Cinematographer. LXXII, April, 1991, p. 44.

American Film: Magazine of the Film and Television Arts. XVI, March, 1991, p. 56.

Boston Globe. February 22, 1991, p. 27.

Chicago Tribune. February 25, 1991, V, p. 7.

The Hollywood Reporter. February 22, 1991, p. 10.

Los Angeles Times. February 22, 1991, p. F4.

The New York Times. February 22, 1991, p. C17.

USA Today. February 22, 1991, p. D6.

Variety. February 22, 1991, p. 2.

The Village Voice. XXXVI, February 26, 1991, p. 56.

The Washington Post. February 22, 1991, p. B7.

HIGH HEELS
(TACONES LEJANOS)

Origin: Spain
Released: 1991
Released in U.S.: 1991
Production: Agustín Almodóvar for El Deseo S.A. and CIBY 2000; released by Miramax Films
Direction: Pedro Almodóvar
Screenplay: Pedro Almodóvar
Cinematography: Alfredo Mayo
Editing: José Salcedo
Production design: Esther García
Set decoration: Carlos G. Cambero
Set design: Pierre-Louis Thevenet
Sound: Jean Paul Mugel
Costume design: José María Cossio
Music: Ryuichi Sakamoto
Songs: Luz Casal
MPAA rating: R
Running time: 115 minutes

> *Principal characters:*
> Rebecca .... Victoria Abril
> Becky del Paramo .... Marisa Paredes
> Femme Lethal/Judge Dominguez .... Miguel Bosé
> Manuel .... Feodor Atkine
> Chon .... Bibi Andersen
> Rebecca (as a child) .... Rocío Muñoz

Pedro Almodóvar's previous films have all made parodic references to melodramatic conventions, but in *High Heels*, his ninth film, he takes on the genre of melodrama squarely. The plot has all the necessary features and then some: a love triangle, a mother-daughter reunion, an unhappy marriage, a mystery character, and affairs galore. It is to the melodrama what *Dallas* was to the soap opera: so excessive that it is at once a camp send-up and a perfect example.

The story begins with a mother and a daughter. Becky del Paramo (Marisa Paredes) is a pop star who believes that stardom and motherhood are incompatible. Her young daughter, Rebecca (Rocío Muñoz), is devoted to her in spite of the fact that Becky is constantly cutting records and touring, leaving Rebecca behind. After several scenes from Rebecca's childhood, the film cuts to the present day, where the adult Rebecca (Victoria Abril) meets Becky at the airport on her return to Madrid after a fifteen-year absence. Becky is in Madrid for a concert engagement, but she hopes to reunite with

Rebecca, who married and became a nightly news anchor. It turns out, however, that Rebecca has married one of Becky's former lovers, Manuel (Feodor Atkine), and that he wants to divorce Rebecca and would like to rekindle his relationship with Becky. Manuel owns the television station for which Rebecca serves as news anchor.

Rebecca takes Manuel and Becky to a drag club to see her friend Femme Lethal (played by Spanish pop star Miguel Bosé) deliver his impersonation of the young Becky del Paramo. Lethal joins them at their table after his performance and asks Becky for a keepsake. She gives him an earring and asks for something in exchange. Lethal gives her one of his foam falsies. He asks Rebecca to help him change out of his costume, and he does something to and with her that is neither rape nor seduction, but both. After they have sex, Rebecca flees in confusion.

Manuel suddenly is found dead, and Judge Dominguez, who is assigned to the case, begins his investigation by questioning Rebecca and Becky. He discovers that Manuel saw three women on the night of his murder: He had sex with one, one ended their affair, and one found his body. These were respectively, the woman who delivered the news in sign language (and to whom Manuel had promised Rebecca's job), Becky, and Rebecca.

Rebecca goes to a shop to pick up her photographs, which are switched with another woman's. As she is realizing that the photographs are not hers, she notices one of Lethal. The woman tells her that he is her boyfriend, a drug dealer, and she has not seen him in several months. Rebecca is infuriated that her friend and lover is such a scoundrel.

On the day that Manuel is buried, Rebecca insists on doing her nightly newscast as usual. In the middle of reporting Manuel's death, however, she falls apart, confessing that she killed him. She explains that she still loves him, that his death did not accomplish the relief of suffering that she had hoped. She shows the photographs that she had picked up earlier, of their home and possessions, and explains that now these objects are only memories. Rebecca is taken to prison, along with a woman who is a prostitute and wanted to be arrested in order to be with her lover. Becky, unable to cope with the fact that her daughter is a murderer, refuses to talk to Rebecca.

Judge Dominguez becomes increasingly mysterious, seeming to suspect and even wanting to believe that Rebecca is covering for someone, possibly Becky. He begins to reveal things that he should not know—about Rebecca's marriage to Manuel, Becky's recent and past relationships with Manuel, and Rebecca's marital fidelity. He persuades them that he is trying to help, but his reasons remain hidden. He brings mother and daughter together by convincing Becky that Rebecca needs her, and Rebecca unleashes her feelings on Becky. She talks about her childhood feelings of rejection and abandonment, explaining that she killed Becky's second husband—by switching his uppers and downers—so that she and Becky could be together and Becky could follow her career plans. Becky realizes that Rebecca needs her and loves her, and when her concert engagement begins, she breaks down in tears on stage. Becky suffers a heart attack, and decides that, because she is dying anyway, she should take responsibility for the murder. She does so on her deathbed, releasing Rebecca so that she and the judge, who is the man who plays Femme Lethal, can marry.

High Heels overflows with genre references. In addition to Becky's final grand gesture of maternal suffering (a favorite of film melodrama), the plot has enough twists and turns to do any drawing-room comedy or parlor mystery proud. Perhaps most important, it contains enough oedipal urges to send shivers of ecstasy down any psychoanalyst's spine. Rebecca kills her mother's husband in order to keep her mother to herself. She marries her mother's former lover. She takes as a lover—and eventually marries—a man who impersonates her mother and whose own mother is obsessed with Rebecca's. Interestingly, the Oedipus complex gets a few twists here, not least because the genders of the players shift quite fluidly. Rebecca continues to compete with her "fathers" for her mother well past the age when she ought to have switched over to her father as an object of desire. Nevertheless, she is resolutely heterosexual in a film world in which other sexualities are regularly and calmly displayed. The man · she marries, whom the film clearly marks as the correct object choice for her, exhibits inconsistent gender identifications. *High Heels* shows no commitment to rigid definitions of sexuality.

The film does, however, have a surprisingly traditional view of masculinity and femininity. Femininity concerns itself with romance and sex, and ownership and power are consistently attributed to men. While Becky and Rebecca are performers, professionally on display and personally preoccupied with their lovers and each other, Manuel owns a television station and Dominguez is a judge. The men represent not only ownership and authority but also powers of particular kinds. The media are among the most powerful institutions in the economic sphere, and the law is part of the state. Manuel has the power to replace Rebecca, a possibility that was actually a real threat, and Dominguez holds Rebecca's fate in his hands. Manuel and Dominguez participate not in display and romance but in the exercise of financial and state authority.

Nevertheless, *High Heels* gives this authority very little attention. The world of the film centers on the women, never extending beyond the relationships of the main characters. Character development is strangely circumscribed: On the one hand, the film is entirely devoted to working out relationships, particularly the one between Becky and Rebecca, but on the other hand, they exist only in relation to each other and the men that they circulate between them. In this way, the film creates—quite literally—a fantasy world in which nothing but sexuality complicates sexuality and gender identities.

The direction displays these boundaries in unusual ways. The film takes place almost entirely in one plane; rarely do characters move toward or away from the camera, but only across its field of vision. The moments of movement in "depth" signal psychological "depth," as in the scene when Becky first meets with Rebecca after her imprisonment. Rebecca tells Becky decades of feelings, after which she walks away from Becky (and the camera). This use of space reflects and marks how tightly Almodóvar controls the world that he creates. This control is just one among several features of Almodóvar's style. Flouting many of the conventions of cinematic realism, his films seem in many ways more like paintings. Not only are they visually two-dimensional, but he also splashes color all over them. The palette of Almodóvar films comes from a hyper-real, bordering on garish, realm. Part of his trademark camp comes from this technique: He parodies not only plot and genre conventions but also the usually stable register of color.

The enclosure of the film world, the flatness of movement, and the creation of a fantasy world have a peculiar parallel in the relationship between time and plot. Much of the plot becomes at least confusing and often completely implausible if one considers how time might have unfolded between cuts. For example, how and why fifteen years had elapsed since Becky and Rebecca had last seen each other is never explained. Even more uncertain is time in the judge's life. In order for him to maintain all of his various and secret identities, his days would have to be substantially longer—or his need for sleep substantially less—than the norm. The boundaries defining the film's plot prevent the treatment of certain issues and avoid questions of real time altogether by simply never raising them.

As in his previous widely released films, *Women on the Verge of a Nervous Breakdown* (1988) and *Tie Me Up! Tie Me Down!* (1990), in *High Heels* Almodóvar displays a highly idiosyncratic vision of sexuality and human relationships. Camp and color, parody and performance, motherhood and movement are all reoriented to show each from unusual angles. As always, Almodóvar has exceeded the bounds of cinematic reality and convention, and as always the result is comic, absorbing, and troubling.

Anahid Kassabian

Reviews

American Film: Magazine of the Film and Television Arts. XVII, January, 1992, p. 38.
Boxoffice. January, 1992, p. R-6.
The Christian Science Monitor. December 20, 1991, p. 12.
The Hollywood Reporter. December 20, 1991, p. 8.
Los Angeles Times. December 20, 1991, p. F12.
The New Republic. CCVI, February 3, 1992, p. 28.
The New York Times. December 20, 1991, p. B3.
The New Yorker. LXVII, February 10, 1992, p. 81.
Newsweek. CXIX, January 6, 1992, p. 52.
People Weekly. January 20, 1992, p. 13.
Rolling Stone. January 9, 1992, p. 56.
Time. CXXXIX, February 10, 1992, p. 76.
Variety. October 17, 1991, p. 2.
Vogue. January, 1992, p. 61.
The Washington Post. December 20, 1991, p. D7.

HOMICIDE

Production: Michael Hausman and Edward R. Pressman for Cinehaus; released by
Triumph
Direction: David Mamet
Screenplay: David Mamet
Cinematography: Roger Deakins
Editing: Barbara Tulliver
Production design: Michael Merritt
Art direction: Susan Kaufman
Sound: John Pritchett
Costume design: Nan Cibula
Music: Aleric Jans
MPAA rating: R
Running time: 102 minutes

Principal characters:
Bobby Gold	Joe Mantegna
Tim Sullivan	William H. Macy
Chava	Natalija Nogulich
Randolph	Ving Rhames
Miss Klein	Rebecca Pidgeon
Senna	Vincent Guastaferro
Olcott	Lionel Mark Smith
Frank	Jack Wallace

David Mamet, the Pulitzer Prize-winning playwright turned filmmaker who
received praise from critics for two earlier films, *House of Games* (1987) with Joe
Mantegna and *Things Change* (1988), an offbeat comedy that featured Mantegna and
Don Ameche, here turns his attention to the world of big-city crime and the police. As
writer and director, Mamet has added a new twist to the typical detective story. Rather
than simply showing hard-nosed cops in action, chasing criminals and living out the
drama of "good guys versus bad guys," he instead explores the emotional struggle of
a detective who must face and confront his Jewishness.

The film opens with a raid by Federal Bureau of Investigation (FBI) agents as they
attempt to capture an African-American drug dealer in a run-down, inner-city
tenement building. As they mount their assault, the suspect escapes by climbing
through a false closet, leaving the FBI empty-handed. City leaders, believing that the
FBI bungled the raid, want the local police to step in and get the dealer off the streets.
The fact that the dealer is still at large has left a politically sensitive police
administration frustrated. Streetwise detectives and close friends Bobby Gold (Joe
Mantegna) and Tim Sullivan (William H. Macy) are assigned to the case.

Following a tip, Gold and Sullivan are on their way to track down a lead when they
come upon a crime scene in a low-income African-American neighborhood. Two

uniformed patrol officers have just responded to a report of a murder at a candy store. Gold examines the victim, an elderly white woman who has been shot. He notices that she is wearing a Star of David necklace, but he finds nothing to indicate that this is anything more than a routine killing. Meanwhile, several other units arrive on the scene. Gold explains that he and Sullivan were on their way to track down the drug dealer and that they do not want to become involved in the murder investigation. At this point, the victim's family arrives to discuss the situation with Gold's superior. The family believes that the woman's murder was somehow related to anti-Semitism. The commander decides on the spot to put Gold on the case. After expressing his displeasure at this change of assignment, Gold questions some local kids, who tell him that the woman was murdered for her money. Apparently, everyone in the predominately black neighborhood believed that the victim kept a large amount of cash hidden in her basement. Even so, Gold has trouble believing that robbery was the motive.

Later at the police station, while Gold is trying to piece together some facts in the case, he receives a call from a member of the woman's family who reports that a shot has been fired at his apartment. After thoroughly examining the apartment, however, Gold is skeptical that any shot was fired, believing that the family is paranoid. The family makes an emotional appeal to Gold's sense of his own Jewish heritage. Up until this moment, Gold has resisted any involvement of his ethnic or religious feelings in the case. He is a cop and a Jew, but his duties to his job and his religion have never been in conflict. Gold reassures them that he wants to solve the case wherever the facts may lead. When he checks the adjacent rooftops for evidence, he finds a piece of paper with the word "grofazt" written on it.

Later that night, Gold goes back to the candy store to look for clues. Searching the basement, he finds an empty ammunition crate that contains a packing list for twenty Thompson submachine guns. The invoice is dated 1946, and the crate also contains a list of names. Gold checks with the Bureau of Alcohol, Tobacco, and Firearms and learns that the guns were stolen. He turns the list of names over to police investigators. Meanwhile, his partner Sullivan is curious and a bit bewildered by Gold's sudden zealousness in trying to solve the murder. Gold himself seems confused by his deepening personal involvement in the case.

Gold goes to a shoe repair shop run by an elderly Jewish man who had been a victim of Nazi persecution during World War II in an attempt to discover what the word "grofazt" means. The man tells him that it was an acronym used at the end of the war by a special Nazi group to mean Adolf Hitler's "final solution." Translated, the acronym stood for "greatest strategist of all time." Gold is intrigued enough by the emerging overtones of anti-Semitism in the case to visit a Jewish library to find an authoritative definition of "grofazt." At the library he suspects that the staff members, although seemingly interested in helping him, are withholding information. On a hunch, he tracks down another lead, which takes him to an abandoned building in the inner city. As he approaches the building, he is accosted by several armed youths who take him inside. What appeared to be an abandoned building is in fact being used as the communications nerve center for a Jewish terrorist organization. The leader questions him about his loyalty to Judaism and asks that he supply them with the list of names that he had found in the candy store. Gold refuses on the grounds that he cannot deliver evidence that is being held by the police in a murder case. Once more, Gold is confronted with the conflict between his duties as a cop and as a Jew. The group leader finally releases Gold but warns him not to pry into the group's affairs.

Out on the streets again, Gold runs into a young woman who is a member of the group. She is on her way to investigate a print shop whose owner is suspected of printing anti-Semitic literature. Gold pressures the woman into allowing him to accompany her. Because it is late at night and the shop is closed, they must break into the building. In a back room, Gold finds proof that the shop is being used to print anti-Semitic posters, handbills, and other propaganda. As he and the woman leave the building, an explosive device detonates that sets the shop on fire. In a café later that same night, he is confronted by members of the Jewish militant group, who again press him for the list of names. When Gold continues to refuse, they threaten to blackmail him with photographs that show him breaking into the print shop. Gold, however, continues to refuse.

Suddenly, the film cuts to a raid on another suspected hideout of the black drug dealer. Gold's partner, Sullivan, is pinned down in the tenement. Gold joins the police outside the building. When Sullivan radios that he has been hit, Gold makes a dramatic attempt to reach his fallen partner. Unable to get medical help because of the intense firefight, Gold watches helplessly as Sullivan dies in his arms. Gold then pursues the suspect, and they finally confront each other in the basement. Gold is wounded in the leg just before reinforcements arrive and kill the suspect.

Some months later, Gold visits the police station where he worked. Because he has been recovering from his injuries, he has been left out of the continued investigation into the woman's murder. In a surprising turn, several of the African-American children that he had questioned earlier are now suspects in the crime. The motive is robbery. As Gold tries to absorb this development, he is handed a note by a fellow officer. On it is written a definition of the word "grofazt." Apparently, it is the name of a pigeon feed.

It appears that Mamet wanted to do two things in *Homicide*: first, to make an action cop film, and second, to explore what it means to be a Jewish member of a big-city police force in the contemporary United States. The screenplay was adapted by Mamet from *Suspects* (1986), a novel by William J. Caunitz. When the major studios read the script, however, there was a feeling among them that the film would lack commercial appeal. Eventually, independent producer Edward R. Pressman assisted Michael Hausman and Mamet in getting the project off the ground. *Homicide* is not a typical Hollywood police story. There is more going on than the usual formula for such films. For example, there are overtones of racism and anti-Semitism surrounding the murder investigation which trouble the main character. These concerns, which gradually emerge and finally become the film's main focus, are of such emotional and social complexity and volatility that they compete with the action-adventure aspect of the drama. In fact, there is little real action, except during the opening and closing scenes when police attempt to capture the elusive drug dealer. None of the action in *Homicide* is of the intensity that is found in films such as *Bullitt* (1968) or *The French Connection* (1971).

It could be argued that the emphasis on acting and not action is what sets this film apart from others in the genre. There is a very theatrical quality to Mantegna's portrayal of Gold that is probably attributable in part to the fact that Mamet had worked with Mantegna in his plays since the early 1970's, when they met at Goddard College in Plainfield, Vermont. The dialogue in *Homicide* also sounds realistic. Gold and Sullivan develop as characters not so much because of what they do but because of what they say. Although extremely explicit at times, the language works in defining the personalities of these hard-nosed, cynical police officers.

Homicide was shot in the kind of locations that one finds in the decaying neighborhoods of cities such as Boston or Philadelphia. The lighting is mostly low-key, which is suited to the rather moody tone of this drama. There are no innovative special effects here, and the camera angles are unremarkable. Overall, the style is what might be called straight or minimalist.

Homicide, like Mamet's two other films, did not do well at the box office, which may be because its ambition exceeded its execution. Ideally, the plot, character development, and theme would have been more in balance. In this film, however, there seems to have been too much to tell and too little time to tell it. The audience never learns who killed the woman, why the Jewish terrorist group wants the list of names that Gold found, and even whether Gold in the end has undergone any personal transformation as a result of his confrontation with his Jewishness. It is almost like watching two different films strangely edited together. The juxtapositions, although often interesting, still call for a stronger commitment to blend one story with the other. Perhaps Mamet's experiment will ultimately lead to the kind of film that he seems to have wanted to make in *Homicide*.

Francis Poole

Reviews

Boxoffice. October, 1991, p. R-73.
Chicago Tribune. October 18, 1991, VII, p. 42.
The Christian Science Monitor. October 29, 1991, p. 11.
Film Review. November, 1991, p. 34.
The Hollywood Reporter. May 10, 1991, p. 8.
Los Angeles Times. September 16, 1991, p. F1.
The New York Times. October 6, 1991, p. 22.
Newsweek. CXVI, October 14, 1991, p. 70.
Rolling Stone. October 31, 1991, p. 99.
Time. CXXXVIII, October 21, 1991, p. 101.
Variety. May 10, 1991, p. 2.

HOOK

Production: Kathleen Kennedy, Frank Marshall, and Gerald R. Molen for Amblin Entertainment; released by TriStar Pictures
Direction: Steven Spielberg
Screenplay: Jim V. Hart and Malia Scotch Marmo; based on a story by Hart and Nick Castle and on the original stage play and books by J. M. Barrie
Cinematography: Dean Cundey
Editing: Michael Kahn
Production design: Norman Garwood
Art direction: Andrew Precht and Thomas E. Sanders
Set decoration: Garrett Lewis
Set design: Henry Alberti, Thomas Betts, Joseph Hodges, Peter J. Kelly, Joseph G. Pacelli, Jr., and Jacques Valin
Casting: Janet Hirshenson, Jane Jenkins, and Michael Hirshenson
Visual consultation: John Napier
Visual effects supervision: Eric Brevig
Special effects supervision: Michael Lantieri
Sound: Ron Judkins
Costume design: Anthony Powell
Choreography: Vince Paterson
Stunt coordination: Gary Hymes
Music: John Williams
Song: John Williams (music) and Leslie Bricusse (lyrics), "When You're Alone"
MPAA rating: PG
Running time: 135 minutes

Principal characters:

Captain Hook	Dustin Hoffman
Peter Pan/Peter Banning	Robin Williams
Tinkerbell	Julia Roberts
Smee	Bob Hoskins
Granny Wendy	Maggie Smith
Moira	Caroline Goodall
Jack	Charlie Korsmo
Maggie	Amber Scott
Liza	Laurel Cronin
Inspector Good	Phil Collins
Tootles	Arthur Malet
Pockets	Isaiah Robinson
Ace	Jasen Fisher
Rufio	Dante Basco
Thudbutt	Raushan Hammond

Don't Ask .... James Madio
Too Small .... Thomas Tulak
Latchboy .... Alex Zuckerman
No Nap .... Ahmad Stoner
Gutless .... Glenn Close

In this sequel to *Peter Pan* (1904), Peter Banning (Robin Williams) is a busy, middle-aged corporate executive in charge of acquisitions and mergers who discovers that his grown-up life is not as wonderful as it seems. His wife, Moira (Caroline Goodall), and his two children, Jack (Charlie Korsmo) and Maggie (Amber Scott), are unhappy because they rarely see him. Banning even sends his assistant to videotape Jack's important baseball game, thus further alienating his son. When the family flies to London to visit Granny Wendy (Maggie Smith), who is Moira's grandmother and who claims to be the "real" Wendy from the classic children's story, the aging woman cannot believe the change in Banning, who was reared by Wendy as an orphaned teenager. It is not until Banning's children are kidnapped, however, that Wendy reveals his true history: Peter Banning was once Peter Pan.

Jack and Maggie have been dragged away to the fantastic Neverland by Peter's ancient nemesis, Captain Hook (Dustin Hoffman). Banning's old companion, the pixie Tinkerbell (Julia Roberts), leads him to Hook's pirate ship, where the captain discovers that his former adversary is no longer worth fighting. Banning agrees to ready himself for a battle for his children in three days. Still not believing himself that he is Peter Pan, Banning joins the Lost Boys at their hideout. Their leader, Rufio (Dante Basco), challenges Tinkerbell's assertion that Banning is truly "the Pan," but Too Small (Thomas Tulak) persuades some of them to believe in him. The Lost Boys try to remind Banning of his former self and to prepare him for his upcoming duel.

Meanwhile, Hook and his first mate, Smee (Bob Hoskins), have their own plan. Hook decides to win the affections of Banning's children in order to savor his victory more fully. Maggie will not listen, but Hook plays upon Jack's anger and disappointment. Hook even arranges an elaborate baseball game so that he can root for his newfound "son." Banning witnesses the event and fears that he is a bad father. These thoughts trigger other memories, and soon his childhood identity comes back to him. He momentarily forgets his adult life and even kisses Tinkerbell when she suddenly (but temporarily) grows to human size and confesses her love for him. He soon remembers his wife and children, however, and leads the Lost Boys to the final battle with the pirates. Rufio is killed by Hook, but Banning emerges victorious when the gigantic crocodile that Hook had defeated and stuffed comes back to life and eats the villainous pirate. Banning returns with his children to London and vows to spend more time with his family. He has rediscovered the child within himself.

Hook was adapted from J. M. Barrie's *Peter Pan*, a children's book made famous as a hit stage play. The most successful Hollywood fantasy maker of the 1980's, Steven Spielberg, sought to fashion a pure blockbuster for the 1990's. Spielberg hired Dustin Hoffman, Robin Williams, Julia Roberts, Bob Hoskins, and Maggie Smith to film his particular take on the theme of never growing up. In the process, Spielberg created a massive amusement park ride. The money spent can only be labeled staggering. No film came to symbolize the excesses of the Hollywood film industry of the 1990's more than *Hook*. Still, critics across the nation tended to like *Hook*, but with reservations. For example, those reviewers surveyed by *Variety* offered no consensus: Some liked it, some hated it, and most were indifferent. All conceded that *Hook* was pure Spielberg, only not as fun and fascinating as *E. T.: The Extraterrestrial* (1982).

The stars of *Hook* represent among the most famous in the Hollywood film business. Oscar winners Williams and Hoffman headed the all-star cast. With Roberts as the seven-inch feisty flying pixie, Tinkerbell, Spielberg added the hottest actress of the late 1980's. Also on board were Hoskins and Smith, respected British players, adding a touch of class. Possibly the greatest star of *Hook* is George Lucas' Industrial Light and Magic's wondrous special effects. For example, Lucas' magicians were able to reconstruct Roberts into a lovable seven-inch Tinkerbell using blue screens, optical printing, special matting, and digital compression. Yet, it was not the actors' performances or even the special effects that seemed to draw the most commentary. There was unprecedented profit participation. Spielberg and his stars had inked contracts that tied their compensation to the millions garnered at the box office. It was estimated that *Hook* might have to make in excess of three hundred million dollars before it began to make money for its studio, Sony's TriStar Pictures.

Thematically, Spielberg brings typical concerns to *Hook*. In this epic fantasy, innocents are imperiled, "Lost Boys" refuse to grow up, and quirky cartoon-like pirates show no mercy. The core of *Hook* is its marvelous special world, a magical setting for the typical Spielbergian concern of struggling with adulthood. The inspiration for the sets that created this world came from visual consultant John Napier, the celebrated theatrical designer of *Cats*, *Les Miserables*, and *Miss Saigon*. Never-land was created on Sony Pictures' Stage 30, where snow fell in one quadrant, autumn leaves drifted to earth in another, flowers bloomed in yet another, and summer glory emerged in yet another. Tons of fresh topsoil and hundreds of exotic plants were rotated daily. Live beavers, storks, and flamingos populated the environs. A complex system of wires and pulleys—combined with a "flying camera" mechanism called Cablecam—made it possible to fly.

Yet, there was more. On Stage 27, the ultimate Spielberg play toy, a full-sized pirate ship Jolly Roger and the surrounding pirate wharf, was anchored where two generations before Metro-Goldwyn-Mayer (MGM) had mounted 1939's *The Wizard of Oz*. The ship was thirty-five feet wide, one hundred seventy feet long, and seventy feet high. It rested in three feet of water, and several of its cannons actually fired. Flying around this pirate ship set were hundreds of the most talented stuntpeople that Spielberg's assistants could find, all trying to make viewers believe that they were back in a classic Warner Bros. adventure, such as *The Sea Hawk* (1940) or *Captain Blood* (1935).

Hook represented the first gamble by a Japanese owner of a Hollywood film studio. TriStar, a division of Sony Pictures, banked on backing the newest blockbuster.

Indeed, the massive *Hook* sets could be found at the Sony Pictures Studios, the former MGM studios, in Culver City, California. This historic complex had been ceded to Sony as part of its takeover of Columbia Pictures. *Hook*, which began production midway through February, 1991, functioned as the talk of the Hollywood film business for nearly a year. The film was also the talk of the 1991 Christmas season. Although *Hook* received Academy Award nominations in the categories of Art Direction, Costume Design, Makeup, and Visual Effects, and "When You're Alone" was nominated for Original Song, the film failed to garner a single award.

In the end, *Hook* offered a conventional gamble—spectacle for spectacle's sake. By production designer Norman Garwood's estimation, the sets alone required more than one million board feet of lumber, twenty-five thousand gallons of paint, two hundred tons of plaster, ten miles of rope, and six hundred thousand gallons of water. To interviewer after interviewer, "proud papa" Spielberg boasted of his excess; nothing like it had been seen in Hollywood since the heady days of the studio system of the late 1930's, in the very classics that Spielberg so much admires. On that level alone, Spielberg succeeded.

Douglas Gomery

Reviews
American Cinematographer. LXXII, December, 1991, p. 26.
Boston Globe. December 11, 1991, p. 53.
Boxoffice. January, 1992, p. R-1.
Chicago Tribune. December 11, 1991, p. C1.
Cinéfantastique. XXII, December, 1991, p. 28.
The Hollywood Reporter. December 9, 1991, p. 9.
Los Angeles Times. December 11, 1991, p. F1.
The New York Times. December 11, 1991, p. B1.
The New Yorker. LXVII, December 30, 1991, p. 80.
Newsweek. December 16, 1991, p. 75.
Premiere. V, December, 1991, p. 62.
Rolling Stone. January 9, 1992, p. 54.
Time. CXXXVIII, December 16, 1991, p. 74.
Variety. December 9, 1991, p. 2.
The Village Voice. December 17, 1991, p. 68.
The Washington Post. December 11, 1991, p. C1.

HOT SHOTS!

Production: Bill Badalato for PAP; released by Twentieth Century-Fox
Direction: Jim Abrahams
Screenplay: Jim Abrahams and Pat Proft
Cinematography: Bill Butler
Editing: Jane Kurson and Eric Sears
Production design: William A. Elliott
Costume design: Mary Malin
Music: Sylvester Levay
MPAA rating: PG-13
Running time: 85 minutes

Principal characters:
Topper Harley .... Charlie Sheen
Kent Gregory .... Cary Elwes
Ramada Thompson .... Valeria Golino
Admiral Benson .... Lloyd Bridges
Lieutenant Commander Block .... Kevin Dunn
Jim "Wash Out" Pfaffenbach .... Jon Cryer
Pete "Dead Meat" Thompson .... William O'Leary
Kowalski .... Kristy Swanson
Wilson .... Efrem Zimbalist, Jr.
Buzz Harley .... Bill Irwin
Mrs. "Dead Meat" Thompson .... Heidi Swedberg

Topper Harley (Charlie Sheen), a maverick jet pilot, is haunted by the disgraceful actions of his aviator father. Although temporarily dismissed from duty for insubordination (he lost his jet but is paying it off at ten dollars a month) and living with Indians under the alias of "Fluffy Bunny Feet," Harley is called back to action for operation Sleepy Weasel.

At the air base, Harley runs into a variety of fellow pilots. There is the self-assured, narcissistic ace, Kent Gregory (Cary Elwes); the eager Jim "Wash Out" Pfaffenbach (Jon Cryer), whose career is hampered by a severe case of walleye vision; and the sincere Pete "Dead Meat" Thompson (William O'Leary), whose nickname indicates his future. Directly running the Sleepy Weasel outfit is Lieutenant Commander Block (Kevin Dunn), who is in league with an unscrupulous industrialist (Efrem Zimbalist, Jr.) who wants the Navy's jets to fail so that the Navy will buy his. The job of running the entire mission, however, belongs to Admiral Benson (Lloyd Bridges), who, during his distinguished career, has had almost every body part wounded in war and replaced. He now seems to have much trouble concentrating on even the simplest of tasks.

To make sure that Harley really is "fit" to fly his missions, he is sent for psychological evaluation at the office of the base psychologist, the beautiful Ramada Thompson (Valeria Golino). A definite romantic attraction develops between Ramada and Harley, only to become a triangle when she runs into her past love, Kent Gregory. Ramada discovers that Harley is suffering from "paternal conflict syndrome," and to complicate matters even more, Harley's father is blamed for the death of Gregory's father. Because of Harley Sr., Gregory Sr. was killed in a freak hunting accident.

In spite of these conflicts, the flying unit must unite to execute their mission: bomb the nuclear plants off Falafel Heights in Iraq, with a secondary target of a mime school. Block has chosen Harley because, at the mention of his father's name, Harley chokes. In this way, the mission will be sabotaged. At the last minute, however, Block sees the error of his ways and confesses to Harley that he had been in love with Harley's mother. He was an eyewitness to his father's legendary "disgrace" and had lied about it. Harley's father was actually a hero. Now, it is Harley's turn to be a hero. He saves the mission and returns to the ship in triumph. Back at the base, however, he sees Ramada in Gregory's arms and assumes the worst. He returns to the reservation only to find Ramada, or "Little Sizzling Belly" as she is now known, waiting for him.

Hot Shots! is one of those zany comedies in which no action occurs without a curved reaction and no cliché is heard without a response from left field. The first mainstream film to truly exploit this type of send-up parody was *Airplane!* (1980). It was written and directed by David and Jerry Zucker and Jim Abrahams, or the ZAZ team, as they came to be known. They followed their spoof of all the airport films with a spoof of spy films and musicals. The result was the underrated *Top Secret* (1984). The trio then worked on a television parody of police shows, *Police Squad!*, which developed into *The Naked Gun* (1988) and its sequel, *The Naked Gun 2½* (1991).

Abrahams then worked independently as a director, making such films as *Big Business* (1988) and *Welcome Home, Roxy Carmichael* (1990). After having made his reputation as part of the team known for its deflation of film pretension, he directed this parody of the megahit *Top Gun* (1986) without the Zucker brothers, but with the help of cowriter Pat Proft. Proft, who was the executive producer of the film, and Abrahams had worked together on the *Police Squad!* television series and *The Naked Gun*.

There is no mistaking the fact that this is a spoof of *Top Gun*. The music is the same, the setting is the same, and even the aerial work was overseen by the same man who created the flying sequences for the original, Richard T. Stevens. Yet, Abrahams and Proft do not stop with parodying only one film. Twenty-six films are listed officially as being "researched" for *Hot Shots!*, and the sharp-eyed and the not-so-sharp-eyed will recognize tributes to *Gone with the Wind* (1939), *Rocky* (1976), and *Superman* (1978) in the film's slowest section, a romantic musical interlude. Of special amusement, however, is the takeoff on the food seduction scene from *Nine and a Half Weeks* (1986). Beginning with a simple grape and strawberry, Ramada and Harley soon escalate to pizza and olives. When an ice cube sizzles on her stomach, Harley is soon frying an order of eggs, bacon, and hashbrowns. In addition, for the cinematically astute, when Wilson is punished in a dentist's chair at the end of the film, he is about to be drilled by a man who cryptically asks "Is it safe?" The allusion to *Marathon Man* (1976) is rewarding and conjures up images of tortures befitting the unprincipled and mercenary.

Another "stolen" scene is that of the ship's crew waiting for Harley's return (in a wingless plane that drops onto the deck) taken right from *Memphis Belle* (1990). Also, Valeria Golino, best known as Tom Cruise's girlfriend in *Rain Man* (1988), sings "The Man I Love" à la Michelle Pfeiffer in *The Fabulous Baker Boys* (1989) while perched atop a grand piano, but Golino sacrifices Pfeiffer's sultriness for slapstick. The scene in which Harley is found living with Indians is right out of *Dances with Wolves* (1990). The wolf who lives there looks familiar, as it was trained by the same people who worked on Kevin Costner's film.

Other animals make an amusing addition to the film. The Welsh corgi chasing a jet's tires was Bud the Wonder Dog, last seen in *The Accidental Tourist* (1988). One running gag centers on a Chihuahua which seems to belong to no one but which always is about to be sat upon—in places ranging from an Indian tepee to a jet cockpit. According to the studio, two matching Chihuahuas were used, Jake for acting and Elwood for stunts.

It is doubtful that the *Hot Shots!* script received Navy approval, as is usual for films about the armed forces. It is more likely that it was never even submitted to them. Therefore, a problem arose regarding how to shoot aircraft carrier scenes without actually being on one. To solve this problem, a land jetty was used at the deserted Marineland facility in Palos Verdes, California. There, an L-shaped wooden deck was constructed, and the jetty's height combined with advanced planning allowed the cameras to capture the feel of a ship at sea. On this aircraft carrier, however, planes parallel park, use parking meters, and have handicapped spots and valet parking.

As with the previous spoofs with which Abrahams has been connected, the casting was well done, with serious actors lending an additional charm to comic characters. Charlie Sheen, often considered a pretentious "brat packer," does a good job of playing his character straight and producing laughs—just as Leslie Nielsen has done since he first appeared in *Airplane!* Similarly, Lloyd Bridges lends an unexpected note of humor as Admiral Benson, who has flown 194 missions but was shot down every time and therefore never landed a plane. Solid performances by Cryer, Elwes, and Golino reinforce and complement Sheen's character while providing their own humorous situations. After Sheen's Harley and Elwes' Gregory reconcile at the end of the film, what do they discuss? The battle? Flying? Past differences? The woman whom they both love? No, they discuss the subtle distinctions between chafing dishes and Crockpots until a voice-over asks Harley what he is going to do now that he has completed his mission successfully. Harley answers, in best commercial and parody fashion, "I'm going to Disney World!" and is handed a stack of money.

Such unexpected punch lines and curves are well-conceived and well-delivered in *Hot Shots!* With the exception of the short musical interlude, they also come at the viewer continuously, at full speed, and are often hidden in the background. As with all of their previous films, Abrahams keeps up the ZAZ team's tradition of filling the film's end credits with unusual trivia. Who would have thought that a delicious brownie topping recipe could be found in those ever-lengthening film credits?

Beverley Bare Buehrer

Reviews
Boston Globe. July 31, 1991, p. 25.
Boxoffice. October, 1991, p. R-67.
Chicago Tribune. July 31, 1991, V, p. 1.
The Christian Science Monitor. September 13, 1991, p. 12.
The Hollywood Reporter. July 26, 1991, p. 8.
Los Angeles Times. July 31, 1991, p. F1.
New York. August 19, 1991, p. 51.
The New York Times. July 31, 1991, p. B11.
People Weekly. August 12, 1991, p. 12.
Premiere. IV, June, 1991, p. 70.
San Francisco Chronicle. July 31, 1991, p. E1.
Time. August 19, 1991, p. 65.
Variety. August 5, 1991, p. 93.
Video. XV, March, 1992, p. 52.
The Washington Post. July 31, 1991, p. B6.

JFK

Production: A. Kitman Ho and Oliver Stone for Ixtlan Corporation, in association with Le Studio Canal Plus, Regency Enterprises, and Alcor Films; released by Warner Bros.

Direction: Oliver Stone

Screenplay: Oliver Stone and Zachary Sklar; based on the books *On the Trail of the Assassins*, by Jim Garrison, and *Crossfire: The Plot That Killed Kennedy*, by Jim Marrs

Cinematography: Robert Richardson (AA)

Editing: Joe Hutshing (AA) and Pietro Scalia (AA)

Production design: Victor Kempster

Art direction: Derek R. Hill and Alan R. Tomkins

Set decoration: Crispian Sallis

Set design: Mary Finn

Casting: Risa Bramon Garcia, Billy Hopkins, and Heidi Levitt

Sound: Tod A. Maitland

Costume design: Marlene Stewart

Music: John Williams

MPAA rating: R

Running time: 189 minutes

Principal characters:
Jim Garrison	Kevin Costner
Liz Garrison	Sissy Spacek
David Ferrie	Joe Pesci
Clay Shaw	Tommy Lee Jones
Lee Harvey Oswald	Gary Oldman
Dean Andrews	John Candy
Jack Martin	Jack Lemmon
Senator Russell Long	Walter Matthau
Guy Bannister	Ed Asner
X	Donald Sutherland
Willie O'Keefe	Kevin Bacon
Jack Ruby	Brian Doyle-Murray
Bill Newman	Vincent D'Onofrio
Earl Warren	Jim Garrison

Oliver Stone, the Academy Award-winning director of *Platoon* (1986), *Born on the Fourth of July* (1989), and *The Doors* (1991; reviewed in this volume), returns with *JFK* to the tumultuous 1960's for his themes and inspiration. In making a film based on the continuing questions surrounding the assassination of President John F. Kennedy, Stone revived many of the lingering doubts that Americans have about the conclusions of the Warren Commission investigation.

In September, 1964, members of the Warren Commission reached a narrow consensus in finding that the murder of Kennedy in Dallas on November 22, 1963, was most probably the act of one disturbed man, Lee Harvey Oswald. Questions about that conclusion, however, continued to haunt the American public. In 1976, Congress created the House Select Committee on Assassinations to conduct a full and complete investigation into the deaths of President Kennedy and Martin Luther King, Jr. The committee stated in its summary of findings that Kennedy "was probably assassinated as a result of a conspiracy."

What Stone offers in *JFK* is a dramatic interweaving of a number of different assassination theories proposed by independent investigators and researchers in the years after the Warren Commission issued its report. Among the sources that he used are Jim Garrison's book *On the Trail of the Assassins* (1988), *Crossfire: The Plot That Killed Kennedy* (1989), by Jim Marrs, and investigations conducted by the House Select Committee on Assassinations. The framework of *JFK* is based in part on former New Orleans District Attorney Jim Garrison's account of his attempt to uncover a possible conspiracy in Kennedy's assassination. Garrison (Kevin Costner) is the main character, and his investigation into the assassination serves as the dramatic structure upon which Stone hangs various conspiracy theories.

The film opens with a segment from President Dwight D. Eisenhower's farewell address, in which he warns the nation about the growth of the "military-industrial complex." News clips of Kennedy during the years of his presidency follow, leading into the fatal motorcade in Dallas and the assassination itself. Archival footage of President and Mrs. Kennedy arriving in Dallas and riding in the motorcade is edited together with carefully staged reenactments of the shootings in Dealey Plaza, to chilling effect. At times, it is not clear whether actual news film or Stone's re-creations are being shown. These powerful opening sequences set the tone and mood for what is to follow and establish one of *JFK*'s most interesting cinematic devices, that is, the use of documentary footage intercut with dramatic restagings. Other scenes that occur later in the film, however, such as the pressing of the dead Oswald's palm to the barrel of the murder rifle, are pure fabrications based on Garrison's suppositions about what might have happened. This docudrama approach to history, while providing a spellbinding re-creation of events, also runs the risk of distorting history.

While most of the crowd that is gathered to watch the television news coverage of the assassination in a neighborhood bar is subdued and saddened, there are those who express a hatred of Kennedy, among them former Federal Bureau of Investigation (FBI) agent and right-wing militant Guy Bannister (Ed Asner). Bannister, who is a private investigator, and his part-time assistant, Jack Martin (Jack Lemmon), discover that certain files have been tampered with in Bannister's office. Bannister, in a drunken rage, accuses Martin of going through his papers and pistol-whips him. The report of that pistol-whipping will later lead Garrison to question Martin about Bannister's possible involvement in the assassination.

Meanwhile, Oswald (Gary Oldman) has been arrested in Dallas and charged with the murders of President Kennedy and Dallas police officer J. D. Tippit. When Garrison learns that Oswald had been in New Orleans during the summer of 1963 passing out pro-Castro leaflets, he launches an investigation to determine Oswald's New Orleans connections. He has hardly begun looking into Oswald's past when Oswald is shot and killed in the basement of Dallas police headquarters by Jack Ruby (Brian Doyle-Murray), a Dallas strip-joint owner. Garrison's assistants discover, however, that the eccentric David Ferrie (Joe Pesci), an expert pilot and right-wing militant, made a suspicious trip to Texas that coincided with the assassination. Garrison smells a rat but is unable to convince the FBI to join in his investigation of Ferrie.

Three years later, Senator Russell Long (Walter Matthau) confides to Garrison his doubts that Oswald was the triggerman. Long believes that Oswald was what he said he was: a patsy. Nagging suspicions about the assassination lead Garrison to the twenty-six-volume Warren Commission report, which he carefully studies. Certain puzzling inconsistencies in the report reinforce his skepticism. Backtracking, Garrison questions Jack Martin about reports that Guy Bannister was running an anticommunist league out of his office in the summer of 1963, an office that was conveniently across the street from FBI headquarters. Stone's reenactment of Martin's testimony places both Ferrie and Oswald in Bannister's office that summer.

Garrison has lunch with New Orleans attorney Dean Andrews (John Candy), who allegedly was asked by a man named Clay Bertrand to go to Dallas the day after the assassination to represent Oswald. When Garrison begins to probe him about his involvement with Clay Bertrand, Andrews becomes evasive and defensive and implies that, if he talks about Clay Bertrand's involvement in an alleged conspiracy, then he and others could become targets of retaliation themselves. This meeting fuels Garrison's suspicions that a possible conspiracy existed in the assassination. Later, Willie O'Keefe (Kevin Bacon), a convicted male prostitute serving time in the state penitentiary at Angola, Louisiana, tells Garrison that he and Bertrand attended a party at which Ferrie discussed killing Kennedy. Again, Stone uses artistic license in dramatizing O'Keefe's description of the party. O'Keefe's account of his relationship with Bertrand and Ferrie portrayed them as members of a group involved in right-wing politics and kinky sex. At this point, Garrison is persuaded that his investigation is leading in the direction of the discovery of a conspiracy.

Garrison and a member of his staff travel to Dallas to examine the site of the assassination. Standing in the sixth-floor window of the school book depository, they try to visualize how one gunman could have shot Kennedy. Looking down on Elm Street through the scope of a rifle as they try to reenact the shooting, they realize not only that Oswald was probably incapable of firing all the shots but also that Dealey Plaza was an ideal location for a team of assassins to set up a crossfire.

Back in New Orleans, Garrison's team discovers that Clay Bertrand is actually Clay Shaw (Tommy Lee Jones), a well-to-do businessman with possible Central Intelligence Agency (CIA) connections. Garrison calls Shaw in for questioning and asks him about Ferrie, O'Keefe, and Oswald. Although Shaw denies knowing them or anything about the assassination, Garrison believes that he has enough evidence in the testimony of O'Keefe and Ferrie to charge Shaw with conspiracy. Suddenly, however, everything begins to unravel for Garrison. His investigation is leaked to the news media, he finds that his office has been bugged, members of his staff are harrassed by the FBI, and Ferrie, who was to be a key witness for the prosecution, is found dead of an apparent suicide.

Garrison goes to Washington, D.C., where he meets with "X" (Donald Sutherland), a former member of a secret Pentagon military-intelligence unit. Stone based the character of X on retired Air Force Colonel L. Fletcher Prouty, a former aide to the Joint Chiefs of Staff and a consultant on the film. X suggests to Garrison that Kennedy was killed by a conspiracy involving the CIA, the military, and others in government who wanted Kennedy out of the way because of his refusal to support the Bay of Pigs invasion, his desire to defuse the Cold War, and his plans to pull military advisers out of Vietnam as the prelude to a total withdrawal from Southeast Asia. This meeting profoundly affects Garrison and renews his commitment to press forward with his prosecution of Clay Shaw. When Garrison returns to New Orleans, he has Shaw arrested and charged with conspiracy in the assassination of Kennedy. The national news media become caught up in the sensational nature of the case, and soon reporters and journalists flock to New Orleans to cover Garrison and the trial. A network television special intending to discredit Garrison and his investigation is aired.

At the trial, Garrison first must prove that there was a conspiracy in the assassination of President Kennedy. Using charts, maps, autopsy photos, and the testimony of ballistics and firearm experts, he lays the groundwork in support of the argument that more than one assassin was responsible for the murder of Kennedy. In perhaps the most dramatic moment in *JFK*, Garrison shows the jury the Zapruder film, the 8mm film shot with a home movie camera that recorded the actual assassination. By analyzing the film frame by frame, he effectively casts doubt on the single-bullet theory that became the cornerstone of the Warren Commission conclusion that Oswald was the lone assassin. Garrison proposes an alternative explanation involving two and perhaps three assassins. In his highly emotional closing speech to the jury, he implicates high officials in the FBI, the CIA, the military, and big business in an elaborate coup d'état. In the only trial of an individual charged in connection with the assassination, the jury takes less than an hour to find Shaw not guilty.

Stone's intentions remain unclear, and he never answers the major question that he raises in blending the various assassination theories that are woven together in this film: Who was really behind Kennedy's murder? The warning by Eisenhower to beware of the military-industrial complex and the clues offered by X suggesting there was a secret government plot to kill Kennedy do not constitute proof of a conspiracy. Nevertheless, the evidence uncovered by independent researchers and presented in *JFK* does raise serious doubts about the lone-assassin theory. Stone has resurrected one of the darkest episodes and most perplexing mysteries in American history. If, as he has said, the Warren Commission report was a mythical document, then it is apparently the aim of this film to encourage those who see it, especially the young, to replace the mythology of the official explanation with the mythology of *JFK*. Obviously Stone is hoping that future generations will continue to probe the assassination for answers and thereby gain an understanding of how the tragedy has shaped the United States.

Stone won a Golden Globe Award for best director and was nominated for a Director's Guild of America Award. *JFK* received eight Academy Award nominations including one for best director, best adapted screenplay, and best picture. In a year in which the darkly terrifying thriller *The Silence of the Lambs* (reviewed in this volume) swept up five Academy Awards, including best picture and best director, *JFK* managed to win for film editing and cinematography. Ultimately, audiences will decide whether the film raises legitimate questions about what really happened that day in Dallas or whether it is simply a good whodunit.

Francis Poole

Reviews
American Cinematographer. LXXIII, February, 1992, p. 42.
Boxoffice. February, 1992, p. R-10.
The Hollywood Reporter. December 16, 1991, p. 7.
Los Angeles Times. December 20, 1991, p. F1.
New Statesman and Society. October 4, 1991, p. 10.
The New York Times. December 20, 1991, p. B1.
The New Yorker. LXVII, January 13, 1992, p. 73.
Newsweek. CXVIII, December 23, 1991, p. 46.
Rolling Stone. January 23, 1992, p. 48.
Variety. December 16, 1991, p. 2.
The Wall Street Journal. December 19, 1991, p. A12.
The Washington Post. CXIV, June 2, 1991, p. D3.

JU DOU

Origin: China
Released: 1990
Released in U.S.: 1991
Production: Zhang Wen-ze, Yasuyoshi Tokuma, and Hu Ji-an for China Film, China Film Export and Import, Tokuma Shoten Publishing, and Tokuma Communications; released by Miramax Films
Direction: Zhang Yi-mou and Yang Feng-liang
Screenplay: Liu Heng
Cinematography: Gu Chang-wei
Editing: Du Yuan
Art direction: Cao Jiu-ping and Xia Ru-jin
Production management: Fen Yi-tian and Michio Yokoo
Sound: Li Lan-hua
Costume design: Zhang Zhi-an
Music: Zhao Ji-pin
MPAA rating: no listing
Running time: 94 minutes
Also known as: Secret Love, Hidden Faces

    Principal characters:
        Ju Dou .... Gong Li
        Yang Tian-qing .... Li Bao-tian
        Yang Jin-shan .... Li Wei
        Yang Tian-bai (as an infant) .... Zhang Yi
        Yang Tian-bai (as a youth) .... Zheng Ji-an

    Village life in China has often been presented in Hollywood films as less than idyllic. The emphasis has usually been on poverty and cruel warlords, but older people have generally been projected as kindly and wise. In *Ju Dou*, made in modern China, the brutality of village life is depicted as a fundamental aspect of Confucian values. Particularly strong emphasis is placed on the plight of women and the baneful power of the ruling gerontocracy.

    The film's exhibition history has been almost as torturous as the lives of its fictional characters. *Ju Dou* was nominated for an Academy Award as Best Foreign Language Film in 1990, the first Chinese film ever so honored. The Chinese government initially was pleased with the recognition, especially because the film had been funded by a Japanese company in a joint venture. Second thoughts soon led the government to reconsider its views. The government asked for the film to be withdrawn from competition, banned the director from attending the ceremonies, and forbade distribution of the film in China. Given the $2 million in production costs, a large sum by Chinese standards, these decisions may have enormous consequences. Other foreign companies are not likely to invest in films that are not allowed to be shown to their national audience and might be kept from entering international festivals and international distribution.

Ironically, the film that has generated so much political backlash does not have an overtly political theme. Set in Northwest China in the 1920's, *Ju Dou* is a sexual tragedy. Yang Jin-shan (Li Wei), an old man who owns a dye factory, has just purchased his third wife, Ju Dou (Gong Li), a beautiful young woman. Jin-shan has sought this marriage in order to produce an heir. When Ju Dou does not immediately become pregnant, Jin-shan begins to beat and torture her as a punishment.

Observing the couple is Yang Tian-qing (Li Bao-tian), an adopted "son" who is actually a poor nephew in the Yang clan and Jin-shan's only employee. Tian-qing knows that Jin-shan has beaten his other two wives to death. While he is appalled by the treatment given Ju Dou, he cannot summon the courage to intervene. One night, he grasps a weapon and begins to ascend the stairs to the room where Jin-shan is torturing her. After taking a few steps, he loses courage, tosses his weapon away, and flees to his room.

In the morning, through a hole in a stable wall, Tian-qing is able to spy on Ju Dou bathing. When she becomes aware of the peep hole, she is embarrassed and angered. Slowly, however, she realizes that Tian-qing might be able to save her life. Knowing that she is being secretly viewed, she exposes herself to his gaze and makes certain that he sees all of her bruises. One day, when Jin-shan is away on a chore, Ju Dou tells Tian-qing that her husband is impotent. Unless she can conceive a child with Tian-qing, she is doomed. Tian-qing is emotionally and sexually seduced. Their illicit union soon produces the desired pregnancy.

The entire Yang clan celebrates the birth of Yang Tian-bai (played as an infant by Zhang Yi). Tian-qing dares not reveal the truth—the consequences for him would be exile or perhaps death. Jin-shan now treats his wife better and Tian-qing has the limited joy of being near his son. The only period of happiness that the lovers will ever know comes unexpectedly when Jin-shan suffers an accident which leaves him paralyzed from the waist down. He spends his days seated in a bucket on wheels that becomes a virtual prison. The lovers now flaunt their relationship, sometimes hoisting Jin-shan on a rig so that his bucket is suspended in midair. This family drama is played out entirely within the dye factory. Jin-shan's pride does not allow him to appeal to the clan for help by admitting that his wife has been unfaithful and that Tian-bai is not his son.

The dye factory is symbolic of the feudalistic relationships being played out. From the outside, the house looks magnificent. It is a mansion built in the Ming Dynasty that is now a national cultural monument. Other homes from the Ming and Qing Dynasties surround it and give the film a majestic ambiance. Yet, the dye factory is hopelessly outdated. The machinery is made of wood with primitive levers and hoists. Power for grinding comes from animals. Boards creak and sag. The animals and their feed are found directly adjacent to where the humans live. In contrast to this grim world, the outside world sees long banners of cloth hanging in the courtyard. These have been dyed twelve different colors in different vats and hoisted to dry on rigs reaching high over the adjoining rooftops. Hanging from these rafters, the brightly colored strips, in various shades of red and yellow, look like glorious banners that aesthetically enrich each of the seasons.

Tian-bai proves to be a mysterious child. As a baby, he is placed in a confining crib and clothed in tight robes. He is slow to learn speech and comes to dislike Tian-qing, unaware that Tian-qing is his father. To his parents' horror, he forms an attachment to Jin-shan and often pulls the old man's cart, giving Jin-shan added mobility. The old man attempts various revenges on Ju Dou and Tian-qing, including arson, but he is always foiled. His plotting ends abruptly when Tian-bai accidentally overturns the cart into a vat of red dye and Jin-shan drowns.

Rather than liberating the lovers, however, Jin-shan's death brings new sorrow. The Yang clan decrees that Tian-qing may continue to work in the dye factory but that he must lodge elsewhere. Seven hard years pass. The child, still unaware of his origin, comes to hate Tian-qing for what he perceives as liberties with his mother. When Ju Dou again becomes pregnant, she performs a self-abortion that leaves her sterile; a new baby would have meant her death. It is also impossible for her and Tian-qing to flee; no other village would take them, and the Yang clan would seek them out for punishment.

The lovers realize that their lives are ruined. They retreat to a deep cave where they make love for the last time and then lie side by side as they suffocate in what will be a double suicide. Their plan is undone by Tian-bai (played by Zheng Ji-an as a youth). Alarmed by his mother's long absence, Tian-bai discovers the lovers' hiding place. After carrying his mother back to their home, Tian-bai drags the half-dead Tian-qing to the dye vats and drowns him in the same red dye in which Jin-shan perished. Ju Dou, too weak to walk, crawls down the staircase in a futile effort to stop the murder. Overwhelmed by what has become of her life, she finally rebels. Taking a torch, she sets the factory ablaze, killing herself and her son.

Some eight thousand yards of cloth were used throughout the film, and all are burned in the climactic scene, which, of course, could have only one take. As the flames climb up the hanging cloth, the unspoken reference to the coming revolutionary changes is self-evident. The scene is also a stylistic coup. Until these moments, the film has been shot in naturalistic detail. Now the cameras come closer and closer to the flames until they become a blazing abstraction. The final freeze frame could be a canvas from the school of abstract expressionism.

The Chinese government might easily have embraced *Ju Dou*: The attack on Confucian values and feudalism fits government policy, and the right of women to rebel is also a cornerstone of revolutionary thought. The problem that overwhelmed *Ju Dou* was that it was completed at the time of the Tiananmen Square massacre in Peking. The film's ideological assault on outdated male elders suddenly took on an unacceptable contemporary bite.

The high artistic quality of *Ju Dou* comes as no surprise to those who have followed Chinese cinema. Director Zhang Yi-mou already has an international reputation and is associated with what is called The Fifth Generation. These filmmakers have moved Chinese film away from its traditional sentimentalism, its stylized acting, and the legacy of socialist realism. Their work is strongly visual, and Zhang has himself worked as a cinematographer. This film was shot by Gu Chang-wei, who has been involved in nearly every breakthrough film in China. He has also done some commercial work in the West and won the Eastman-Kodak Award at the 1989 Hawaii Film Festival.

In terms of acting, Gong Li carries the film with her exquisite portrayal of Ju Dou. Her artistic high point comes in the scenes when she overcomes her modesty to show herself to Tian-qing. The sequences are tame by Western standards but are bold for China and are extremely fine cinema. Zheng Ji-an as the demonic youth Tian-bai would be credible in the best devil-in-human-shape films that have been so popular. Li Bao-tian as Tian-qing occasionally slips into wooden poses and grimacing, as does Li Wei as the sinister Jin-shan, but they are generally effective.

Foreign films often require specific knowledge of their society to be accessible to foreign audiences, but that is not the case with *Ju Dou*. While knowledge of Chinese culture is helpful, the story can be appreciated independent of such knowledge. When the director was asked about how foreign audiences might perceive his film, he replied that they might not understand all the metaphysical issues, but they would easily comprehend the existential ones. All audiences can understand the tragedy of a woman who must commit adultery to stay alive, must keep the identity of his father from her only child, must conclude that a double suicide is her only escape from unhappiness, and must finally cause the death of a son who has murdered his unknown father after being consumed by a rage whose source he cannot comprehend.

Dan Georgakas

Reviews
Boxoffice. January, 1991, p. R-8.
Chicago Tribune. April 12, 1991, VII, p. 37.
The Christian Science Monitor. October 4, 1990, p. 14.
Films in Review. XLII, July, 1991, p. 264.
The Hollywood Reporter. October 25, 1990, p. 21.
Los Angeles Times. March 6, 1991, p. F7.
The New York Times. February 25, 1991, p. B1.
Newsweek. CXVII, April 15, 1991, p. 70.
Time. CXXXVII, March 18, 1991, p. 78.
Variety. CCCXXXIX, May 30, 1990, p. 27.
The Wall Street Journal. April 4, 1991, p. A12.
The Washington Post. March 22, 1991, p. F7.

JUNGLE FEVER

Production: Spike Lee for 40 Acres and a Mule Filmworks; released by Universal
 Pictures
Direction: Spike Lee
Screenplay: Spike Lee
Cinematography: Ernest Dickerson
Editing: Sam Pollard
Production design: Wynn Thomas
Set decoration: Ted Glass
Casting: Robi Reed
Sound: Russell Williams II
Sound design: Skip Lievsay
Costume design: Ruth E. Carter
Music: Terence Blanchard
Songs: Stevie Wonder, "Livin' for the City," "Feeding Off the Love of the Land," and
 "Jungle Fever"
MPAA rating: R
Running time: 132 minutes

 Principal characters:
 Flipper Purify .... Wesley Snipes
 Angie Tucci .... Annabella Sciorra
 Cyrus .... Spike Lee
 The Good Reverend Doctor Purify .... Ossie Davis
 Lucinda Purify .... Ruby Dee
 Gator Purify .... Samuel L. Jackson
 Drew Purify .... Lonette McKee
 Paulie Carbone .... John Turturro
 Mike Tucci .... Frank Vincent
 Lou Carbone .... Anthony Quinn
 Orin Goode .... Tyra Ferrell
 Ming .... Veronica Timbers
 Charlie Tucci .... David Dundara
 James Tucci .... Michael Imperioli
 Jerry .... Tim Robbins
 Sonny .... Brad Dourif

 Jungle Fever is producer/director/writer Spike Lee's updated version of Stanley
Kramer's *Guess Who's Coming to Dinner?* (1967), both films examining society's
difficulty in accepting interracial love affairs. Although Lee presents his film from a
much more explicit and volatile perspective than Kramer's, he ultimately repeats the
same mistake. Lee preaches tolerance and develops a more liberal point of view rather

than concentrating on developing believable and sympathetic characters.

Beautifully and vibrantly photographed with energetic and fluidly moving camerawork by Lee's favorite cinematographer, Ernest Dickerson, the film begins with an elaborate tracking shot through a block of New York's Harlem district before diving into the bedroom window of Flipper and Drew Purify (Wesley Snipes and Lonette McKee), catching them in a passionate session of lovemaking. Their precocious young daughter, Ming (Veronica Timbers), giggles in her bedroom at the sounds emanating from her parents' room, then later walks with her father through the colorfully quirky Harlem neighborhood on her way to school. With this loving, close-knit family relationship firmly and concisely established, Lee then presents Flipper's less-than-harmonious professional environment. Flipper is the only African-American employee of an architectural designing firm, one he believes that he has helped become successful with his innovative art/design contributions.

This particular morning, Flipper is upset with his bosses Jerry (Tim Robbins) and Sonny (Brad Dourif), who have gone against his request for an African-American secretary and have instead hired an Italian-American woman, Angie Tucci (Annabella Sciorra). After a heated conversation with his bosses, Flipper reluctantly decides to give Angie a try. Angie's home life is presented in stark contrast to Flipper's. She lives in the Bensonhurst district with her fiery father (Frank Vincent) and two loudmouth brothers (Michael Imperioli and David Dundara), acting as their surrogate mother. When Angie's longtime boyfriend, Paulie (John Turturro), arrives to pick her up, her brothers harass him and threaten him with death if he tries to become too intimate with their sister.

One evening, both Flipper and Angie work late at the office. With foreboding music playing in the background, the couple chat about their personal aspirations and end up talking late into the night. When their talk turns to racial attitudes and infidelity, Flipper confesses that he has never cheated on his wife and then impulsively initiates sex with Angie, and the two make love on Flipper's desk. The following day, Ming notices that her father is extremely subdued as he walks her to school, and she asks him if something is wrong. Flipper remains quiet. Later, when he confronts his bosses about becoming a partner, they react coolly and Flipper erupts into a rage, ultimately handing in his resignation. Afterward, he meets with his best friend, Cyrus (Spike Lee), and tells him about the disastrous meeting. He also confesses his sexual encounter with Angie, to which Cyrus reacts calmly until Flipper tells him that she is white. Then Cyrus mutters "nuclear holocaust" and tells Flipper that he is a victim of jungle fever. The scene with Flipper and Cyrus is intercut with a parallel scene involving Angie confessing to her girlfriends her encounter with Flipper. Like Cyrus, Angie's friends react with shock and outrage, one friend confessing that the idea of a black man and a white woman having sex is disgusting. The conversation between Flipper and Cyrus is finally interrupted by the sudden appearance of Flipper's crack cocaine-addicted brother, Gator (Samuel L. Jackson), who asks Flipper for money.

Flipper continues his affair with Angie, and soon their clandestine relationship becomes the talk of both their neighborhoods. When Flipper returns home one evening, he finds his belongings scattered over the street and Drew screaming at him from their bedroom window, telling him that their marriage is finished. A more brutal scene erupts at Angie's household, with her father attacking and beating her nearly to death until her brothers step in and hold him back. Drew finds some comfort talking with her girlfriends about the situation, the women throwing out conflicting attitudes about interracial relationships with Drew finally admitting, "It don't matter what color she is. My man is gone."

Angie, meanwhile, meets with Paulie at his place of business, a candy store/ newsstand which he owns with his stay-at-home widower father (Anthony Quinn). When she tells him that their relationship is over, Paulie goes home, locks himself in the bathroom, and cries in despair. His father reacts by breaking down the door, beating him for acting weak, calling Angie names, and praising his own martyred dead wife. Later, Paulie meets with some of his friends, who use Paulie's store as a local hangout/meeting place. One of Paulie's magazine suppliers is Orin Goode (Tyra Ferrell), an attractive African-American woman who is openly friendly with him, much to the amusement of Paulie's bigoted friends, who get into a heated discussion about how nonwhite races are "taking over" their neighborhood.

Flipper and Angie eventually move into an apartment together. Soon afterward, the couple has dinner with Flipper's parents. Flipper's father, the Good Reverend Doctor Purify (Ossie Davis), gives a hate-filled dinner-table sermon on the history of sexual relations between blacks and whites during pre-Civil War times. Later, Flipper's mother (Ruby Dee) asks him to find Gator, who has stolen the reverend's television set in order to buy drugs. Flipper ends up searching through a two-story warehouse called the Taj Mahal, a favorite hangout for crack addicts, and he is appalled at the sight of hundreds upon hundreds of dazed junkies staggering around the building in a drug-induced stupor. Flipper finds Gator, who is nearly comatose from ingesting drugs, and tells him that he is no longer considered part of the family.

With Frank Sinatra crooning "Hello Young Lovers" on the soundtrack, Flipper tells Angie that their relationship is over, that it was doomed to fail because it was based on curiosity rather than love. Paulie, meanwhile, is beaten up by his candy-store friends on his way to see Orin. When Gator once again invades his mother and father's home in search of money, the reverend shoots him to death. The film's final moments echo its first: Flipper and Drew make love in their upstairs bedroom, Drew this time crying tears of sorrow while Ming giggles with joy in her room at the sound of her parents' lovemaking.

Jungle Fever is very similar in structure and thematic content to *Do the Right Thing* (1989), Lee's other explosive examination of racial tensions set in a tightly knit, predominantly African-American New York community. In both films, Lee presents an assortment of racially mixed characters interacting and espousing conflicting viewpoints on the possibility of racial harmony. Lee is a master at capturing the look, smell, and rhythmically rich atmosphere of his gritty, urban environments. Once he has expertly established this vibrant urban setting, however, he has difficulty populating it with characters who do more than merely shout, cajole, and pontificate.

The audience needs to know more about Flipper and Angie, about why they dared to break through cultural barriers and risk alienating themselves from family and friends in order to indulge in a love affair which goes against their racist upbringings. Lee's character, Cyrus, glibly explains the attraction between the couple as a case of jungle fever—a combination of curiosity and lust. If that is the case, then why would these characters continue their relationship to the point of moving in with each other? Surely it would take more than curiosity and lust to keep them together. Yet, Lee refuses to offer any further explanation for his main characters' mutual attraction. The result is a feeling of gross manipulation, that Lee has set up the relationship merely as an excuse to create a forum of opinions on the question of love between the races. The result is a film that plays like an Oprah Winfrey-style television talk show on the subject of interracial love affairs rather than a film populated with three-dimensional characters.

Lee also has problems sticking to the main focus of the story, as he introduces an even more volatile subplot: the ghetto drug problem. Lee's portrayal of the degrading life of crack addicts is so frighteningly vivid that the film's main subject pales in comparison. The film's most effective scene is Flipper's horrific visit to the Taj Mahal, played out to the tune of Stevie Wonder's explosively chilling song about urban street life, "Livin' for the City." The scene is so gripping, and so well played by Samuel L. Jackson as the hopelessly addicted yet still slyly humorous and beguiling Gator, that it further undermines the already underdeveloped love affair between Flipper and Angie.

Lee's use of music as an ironic comment to the film's action, for the most part, seems to evidence a lack of respect for his characters. Although the use of Wonder's excellent original song score is well woven into the film's action, Lee's use of Frank Sinatra ballads during heated debates between Paulie's bigoted friends and violent confrontations between couples, as well as the use of Mahalia Jackson spirituals during the scene in which the reverend shoots his son to death, is so obviously ironic that it demeans the action and the characters. Even Wonder's final compassionate song, "Feeding Off the Love of the Land," played over the credits, is cheapened by Lee's use of sing-along printed lyrics.

Aside from Jackson's performance as Gator, the only other actor who manages to rise above the film's heated rhetoric to create a truly effective character is John Turturro as the liberal-minded and intelligently outspoken Paulie. Although Paulie has the dubious distinction of embodying Lee's own personal viewpoint, preaching tolerance and compassion between the races, Turturro is able to project a heartfelt sincerity onto his lines. Paulie finally convinces the audience with his actions that interracial affairs can grow and mature if they are grounded in mutual respect and genuine affection, rather than being merely the result of a dangerously scorching infection of jungle fever.

At one point during the film, Flipper makes a derogatory comment about Walt Disney, saying, "This 'love will overcome everything' is like a Disney film. I've always hated Disney films." Lee's films have always been the antithesis of the traditional, lighthearted, and eternally optimistic Disney-type fantasy. Yet, when Lee insists on grappling with life's more explosive and complex questions by preaching to his viewers rather than involving them with the drama inherent in the subject matter, he comes very close to creating a variation of the simplistic, two-dimensional Disney film. Instead of approaching his subject matter from the liberal-yet-cardboard-character viewpoint of a Stanley Kramer, whose *Guess Who's Coming to Dinner?* was a major influence on Lee, he might do better to understand why such cartoon creatures as Bambi and Pinocchio can seem more vibrantly alive and empathetic than some of his volatile, real-world speechmakers.

Jim Kline

Reviews

Boxoffice. August, 1991, p. R-52.
Chicago Tribune. June 7, 1991, VII, p. 37.
The Christian Science Monitor. June 13, 1991, p. 12.
Film Comment. XXVII, September, 1991, p. 13.
Films in Review. XLII, July, 1991, p. 258.
The Hollywood Reporter. May 17, 1991, p. 14.
Los Angeles Times. June 7, 1991, p. F1.
The New York Times. June 7, 1991, p. B1.
The New Yorker. June 17, 1991, p. 99.
Newsweek. June 10, 1991, p. 44.
Time. June 17, 1991, p. 64.
Variety. May 17, 1991, p. 2.

KAFKA

Production: Stuart Cornfeld and Harry Benn for Price1 and Baltimore Pictures; released by Miramax Films
Direction: Steven Soderbergh
Screenplay: Lem Dobbs
Cinematography: Walt Lloyd
Editing: Steven Soderbergh
Production design: Gavin Bocquet and Tony Woollard
Art direction: Les Tomkins, Jiri Matolin, and Philip Elton
Set decoration: Joanne Woollard
Casting: Susie Figgis
Sound: Paul Ledford
Sound design: Mark Mangini
Costume design: Michael Jeffery
Music: Cliff Martinez
MPAA rating: PG-13
Running time: 98 minutes

> *Principal characters:*
> Kafka . . . . Jeremy Irons
> Gabriela . . . . Theresa Russell
> Burgel . . . . Joel Grey
> Dr. Murnau . . . . Ian Holm
> Bizzlebek . . . . Jeroen Krabbé
> Inspector Grubach . . . . Armin Mueller-Stahl
> Chief Clerk . . . . Alec Guinness
> Castle Henchman . . . . Brian Glover
> Assistant Ludwig . . . . Keith Allen
> Assistant Oscar . . . . Simon McBurney
> Keeper of the Files . . . . Robert Flemyng

With *sex, lies and videotape* (1989), writer-director Steven Soderbergh made one of the most heralded debuts in American film history. An original, personal, moving, and comic look at loneliness and infidelity in contemporary Louisiana, *sex, lies and videotape* seems to have little in common with Soderbergh's follow-up film, *Kafka*, a coolly intellectual murder mystery set in 1919 Prague.

Kafka does not focus on the biographical facts of Franz Kafka's life but uses the writer as the central figure in a Kafkaesque plot similar to those in his stories and novels. Kafka (Jeremy Irons) is a mild-mannered insurance clerk performing depressingly dull duties in an enormous office crammed with workers monotonously pounding their typewriters while watched by the tyrannical Burgel (Joel Grey). Kafka works on his fiction at night, but when a fellow clerk disappears and later turns up dead, he devotes most of his energies to solving the mystery. Kafka is attracted to another office worker, Gabriela (Theresa Russell) and discovers that she and the dead man belong to a group of anarchists who set off bombs to kill their enemies. After Gabriela fails to enlist Kafka in their cause as a propagandist, she also disappears.

Kafka's assistants, Ludwig (Keith Allen) and Oscar (Simon McBurney), attempt to abduct him only to be foiled by Bizzlebek (Jeroen Krabbé), a gravestone cutter and sculptor who admires such Kafka stories as "The Penal Colony." Kafka knows that the answer to the mystery lies inside the castle in the center of Prague, and Bizzlebek shows him a secret entrance to its interior. Inside the castle, Kafka discovers that the supposedly dead Dr. Murnau (Ian Holm) is conducting bizarre medical experiments on the brains of abductees. These experiments are meant to suggest the horrors that await Europe in the coming decades. Kafka is immediately in danger but is saved because he has brought with him an anarchist's bomb concealed in a briefcase. When the bomb goes off, chaos erupts and Dr. Murnau is killed. Kafka escapes to return to the tedium of his everyday life.

Lem Dobbs completed the screenplay for *Kafka* in 1980 and spent a decade trying to get it produced. In addition to wanting to do something unlike his first film, Soderbergh may have been attracted to *Kafka* for its similarities to the themes of *sex, lies and videotape*. Both films are concerned with the alienation and anguish that result from loneliness. While the protagonists of the earlier film retreat from their despair into sex, Kafka attempts to turn the emotional numbness of his life and the lives of everyone he encounters into art. His writing, as he explains to Gabriela, serves his private needs; no readers are necessary.

Soderbergh and Dobbs intend *Kafka* to be a meditation upon Kafka's themes, but their approach is too dispassionate, too objective to be emotionally or even intellectually engaging. With this impersonal tone, their film resembles the hero of *sex, lies and videotape*, with his videotapes of women discussing sex. This similarity is appropriate because the main subject of *Kafka* is not writers, anarchists, or Nazi prototypes but film itself. *Kafka* succeeds best as an exercise in cinematic style. The black-and-white cinematography of Walt Lloyd and the production design of Gavin Bocquet and Tony Woollard create an atmosphere similar to that in such masterpieces of German expressionism as Robert Wiene's *Das Cabinett des Dr. Caligari* (1920; *The Cabinet of Dr. Caligari*). Dr. Murnau's experiments result in pathetic creatures much like the somnambulist of Wiene's film. Dr. Murnau is named for F. W. Murnau, the director of *Nosferatu* (1922).

Kafka borrows from German expressionism its lighting evocative of evil and danger; its sets suggestive of claustrophobia, impersonality, and sterility; and its symbols, such as the typewriters, that represent the cold, mechanical qualities of modern life. These stylistic elements also recall Orson Welles's flawed Kafka adaptation *Le Procès* (1962; *The Trial*). More important, *Kafka* resembles another Wellesian film in which the filmmaker serves only as actor: Carol Reed's *The Third Man* (1949). With a naïve, ineffectual hero falling into a labyrinth of evil and deceit to emerge wiser but lonelier, *Kafka* is a self-conscious tribute to *The Third Man*. In addition, Cliff Martinez's score, employing the cimbalon, an instrument used in

Eastern European gypsy music, echoes Anton Karas' zither music in *The Third Man*. Soderbergh abandons such heady influences when Kafka breaks into the castle and enters a world of garish color. The director said that he switched to color for this sequence to give Dr. Murnau's milieu an otherworldly quality. Because Dr. Murnau's laboratory resembles that of Dr. Frankenstein, with a victim/potential monster suspended vertically beneath some fantastic instrument, the scene, with its lurid color and magnified image of an exposed brain, seems a homage to such Hammer Films classics as *The Curse of Frankenstein* (1957). Such a tribute is fitting for a film combining the pulp with the arty.

The performances in *Kafka* are uneven. Russell has presence when playing a seductress in films such as *Black Widow* (1987) but is unconvincing as a political activist. Grey is too animated as the nosy Burgel. The great Alec Guinness has little to do as Kafka's boss. Holm is sufficiently menacing as Dr. Murnau. Armin Mueller-Stahl, as a sympathetic police inspector, and Krabbé bring needed touches of subtlety and humanity to their roles. McBurney and Allen nearly steal the film, however, by doing a music-hall routine as the very unidentical twins who turn on Kafka. Their office antics—including a typewriting race—emphasize the absurdity of Kafka's world.

Irons's Academy Award-winning role as the self-assured Claus von Bülow in *Reversal of Fortune* (1990) was a departure for the actor. Irons has made a career of portraying tentative, insecure characters in the television series *Brideshead Revisited* (1981) and in the films *Betrayal* (1983) and *Dead Ringers* (1988), especially as the weaker brother. Playing Kafka as an inquisitive yet uncertain man in need of love and commitment, Irons creates a needed moral center for *Kafka*.

Michael Adams

Reviews
Boxoffice. January, 1992, p. R-5.
Chicago Tribune. February 7, 1992, VII, p. 29.
The Christian Science Monitor. LXXXIV, December 9, 1991, p. 10.
The Hollywood Reporter. December 3, 1991, p. 8.
Los Angeles Times. December 4, 1991, p. F1.
The New Republic. CCV, January 6, 1992, p. 28.
The New York Times. December 4, 1991, p. B1.
Newsweek. CXIX, February 3, 1992, p. 63.
Playboy. XXXIX, March, 1992, p. 20.
Rolling Stone. February 6, 1992, p. 88.
San Francisco Chronicle. January 17, 1992, p. D1.
USA Today. December 4, 1991, p. D5.
Variety. CCCXLV, December 3, 1991, p. 2.
The Wall Street Journal. January 23, 1992, p. A14.
The Washington Post. February 7, 1992, p. B7.

L.A. STORY

Production: Daniel Melnick and Michael Rachmil; and Mario Kassar and Steve
  Martin (executive producers) for Carolco and Daniel Melnick/IndieProd/L.A.
  Films; released by TriStar Pictures
Direction: Mick Jackson
Screenplay: Steve Martin
Cinematography: Andrew Dunn
Editing: Richard A. Harris
Production design: Lawrence Miller
Art direction: Charles Breen
Set decoration: Chris Butler
Sound: Jim Webb
Costume design: Rudy Dillon
Music: Peter Melnick
MPAA rating: PG-13
Running time: 95 minutes

Principal characters:

Harris K. Telemacher	Steve Martin
Sara McDowel	Victoria Tennant
Roland Mackey	Richard E. Grant
Trudi	Marilu Henner
SanDeE*	Sarah Jessica Parker
Ariel	Susan Forristal
Frank Swan	Kevin Pollak
Morris Frost	Sam McMurray
Maitre D' at L'Idiot	Patrick Stewart

L.A. Story is a sprightly, satirical love story in which the city of Los Angeles is
featured as one of the main characters of the film. Steve Martin, who wrote and stars in
the film, fills the screen with joke after joke based on every cliché about the City of
Angels. In between the barrage of sight gags lampooning earthquakes, L.A.'s
predictable weather, health fads, swimming pools, beach nymphets, eccentric architecture, dining rituals, freeway traffic, freeway shootings, and freeway signs that
reveal the meaning of life in between traffic reports, the film manages to tell an
effective story about true love found amid blinding sunshine, eternal blue skies, and
chainsaw jugglers.

The film opens with a wonderful parody of Frederico Fellini's famous opening
segment from *La Dolce Vita* (1960): Instead of having a giant statue of Christ fly over
the city via helicopter, a giant plaster hot dog zooms over a swimming pool filled with
beautiful bikini-clad women. Harris K. Telemacher (Martin) is then glimpsed
sweating in a massive traffic jam from which he escapes by taking his regular shortcut

through backyards, down alleys, across front lawns, and down public stairways, until he arrives at his place of employment, a local television station where he is the news program's wacky weatherman.

After his ridiculously comical broadcast—which the program director still thinks has too many intellectual jokes—Harris ponders his mental state: He cannot understand why he is unfulfilled while, at the same time, feeling perpetually happy. He seems to have everything going for him—a pretty, but superficial girlfriend, Trudi (Marilu Henner); a good-paying, vacuous job; a trendy car; and designer pants—and he has just sold a condo during a time when the real-estate market is sluggish. Nevertheless, Harris believes that his happy, flashy exterior is actually covering up a frustrated, shabby interior.

During a Sunday brunch with friends, Harris is introduced to an English journalist, Sara (Victoria Tennant), who is in town to write an article on Los Angeles for the *London Times*. Harris feels an immediate attraction for Sara but tries to repress his desires, especially after Trudi slaps him with her purse for gazing too longingly at Sara at the brunch table.

Later, when Harris and Trudi are driving home, Harris' car stalls on the freeway in front of an electric freeway traffic indicator sign. When the sign flashes, "Hiya," at Harris and he answers back, suddenly man and machine strike up a conversation. At first, Harris thinks that he has been caught in an elaborate practical joke and looks around for a hidden camera. When the sign gives him personal advice, however, and tells him to expect the weather to affect his life on two separate occasions, Harris thanks the sign for the information and drives off.

Soon afterward, Harris is fired from his job for having taped his weekend weather forecast in advance, thus fulfilling half of the sign's prophecy. Instead of feeling depressed about losing his job, however, Harris is relieved. He is even more relieved when he finds out from Trudi that she has been having an affair with his agent, thus freeing him to pursue Sara. He meets Sara again when she calls him for an interview, then later crashes into her when he roller-skates through a museum while his friend, Ariel (Susan Forristal), films his "performance art" stunt. Harris, Sara, and Sara's former husband Roland (Richard E. Grant) have dinner together, after which Harris and Sara end up in front of the magical freeway sign when it "drives" the two to its location. When the sign prints, "KISS HER, YOU FOOL!" Harris obliges, much to Sara's surprise. Harris confesses to Sara that he is falling in love with her. Sara, not wanting to get involved with anyone at the moment, especially when she is not sure about her feelings for Roland, who wants her to reconcile with him, finally tells Harris to give her time to think about the situation.

The following evening, Harris takes Sara to a dinner party and they make love in the garden outside the restaurant. Later, they stroll down trendy Melrose Avenue and share a magical moment in a gardenlike setting where flowers bloom all around them, grass grows in front of their footsteps, statues bow as they stroll by, and they finally transform into children. Harris and Sara know that they are falling in love, but Sara tells him that she has promised to meet with her former husband over the weekend at a

Santa Barbara hotel—El Pollo del Mar—and talk over the possibility of reconciliation.

Feeling frustrated and angry, Harris turns to a young woman that he met in a clothing store, SanDeE* (Sarah Jessica Parker). He and SanDeE* drive to Santa Barbara for their own romantic interlude and book a room at the same hotel in which Sara and Roland are staying. In fact, they are given the room right next door. The couples delight in hearing each other make love through the walls of their adjoining rooms, each unaware of the other couple's identity. When Harris and Sara meet in the hall outside their rooms, both feel betrayed by the other's actions.

After the weekend in Santa Barbara, Sara decides to return to England, forsaking both Roland and Harris. Harris tries to persuade Sara not to leave, telling her that, if it were in his power, he would arrange for a tremendous storm to keep her plane from taking off. Strangely enough, when Sara boards her plane for England, a sudden, violent storm erupts and her flight is canceled. Thus, the second half of the sign's weather prophecy is fulfilled. Sara returns to Harris and finds him standing in his front yard in the pouring rain waiting for her to arrive. As the two embrace in a long, loving kiss, the storm passes, the sun shines once again, and the sign reveals its final message: "What I really want to do is direct."

L.A. Story is saturated with whimsy, magic, absurd jokes, and impossible encounters. Most of the jokes are visual representations of old clichés about life in L.A. Because they are based on these hackneyed clichés, most of the jokes fall flat. For example, when Harris and Trudi are driving down the freeway and hear on the radio that it is the first day of spring, Harris panics, screams that it is the start of freeway shooting season, pulls out a handgun, and starts firing at other motorists. The joke is labored, appearing out of the blue, and the "freeway shooting season" idea is never referred to again even though many more scenes take place on the freeway. In the worst example of an absurd, overused joke about Los Angeles involving how difficult it is to make a reservation at trendy restaurants, Harris meets at his bank with the owner of an exclusive, French restaurant—called L'Idiot—so that the restaurateur can study Harris' credit history in order to determine whether Harris is financially stable enough to qualify for a reservation. The entire scene is far too elaborate and squashes the tired joke with overkill. Other jokes about earthquakes, the weather, and the fact that everyone drives everywhere in Los Angeles are all equally flat and obvious.

What saves the film from being merely a series of absurdist jokes about the City of Angels is the element of fairy-tale magic that pervades the action, and the idea that true love exists in a world of flash and fashion. Martin, whose earlier starring/writing effort, *Roxanne* (1987), was an updated version of one of the most beautifully romantic love stories ever written, Edmond Rostand's play *Cyrano de Bergerac* (1897), returns to the theme of romantic love, this time frequently referring to passages from William Shakespeare's plays in order to underscore his message. There is a wonderful scene in the film that takes place in a graveyard in which Harris, walking with Sara, points out the headstone of Shakespeare who, according to Harris, was writing *Hamlet Part II: The Revenge* when he passed away in Los Angeles. As they stroll along, they encounter a gravedigger played by Rick Moranis in an effective cameo. The three of them then act out the famous graveyard scene from *Hamlet* after the gravedigger finds the skull of an old magician and Harris remarks, "I knew him well." Martin also has his character paraphrase passages from *Macbeth* to comment on life in Los Angeles, which, to him, is filled with much flash and excitement that really does not mean anything. The Shakespearean reference that is the most relevant to the story flashes on the traffic sign near the end of the film: "There are more things in heaven and earth . . . than are dreamt of in your philosophy." It is appropriate that this quote appears at the end of the film, as much of the previous action is endowed with magical qualities.

In a scene near the end of the film in which Harris and Sara kiss in front of the traffic sign, Harris, in a voice-over comment, says that a kiss may not be the truth, but it is something that everyone wishes were the truth. Martin, who majored in philosophy in college while working as a magician at Disneyland, is obviously presenting a philosophy in which he believes, or at least wishes were true. Throughout the film, he mixes magic, whimsy, and absurdity with comments on the power of love, the belief in something beyond surface reality, beyond superficial, artificial happiness.

Martin is a wonderful actor. In the scene in which he discovers that his girlfriend has been cheating on him for three years, Harris first stands dejected in front of her, then slowly shuffles away out of her house and down the stairs leading to his car. He is filmed from behind, and the audience sees his sagging body and shuffling footsteps suddenly transform into an exaggerated, goofy dance of delight as he realizes that he is now free to pursue his true love. The brief scene is one small example of Martin's ability to shift the mood of the film from one wacky moment to the next and still keep in character. Martin—his philosophy and his character—dominates the film and overshadows the rest of the characters, who, at times, struggle to adapt to his style of comedy, although Parker, as SanDeE*, is very effective as she perpetually spins and twirls while babbling on about the benefits of enemas and her dream of becoming a "spokesmodel." The comedy itself, although very much in the romantic style of *Roxanne*, also reflects the type of wild, cartoonish jokes that dominated such earlier films of Martin's as *The Jerk* (1979), *Dead Men Don't Wear Plaid* (1982), and *The Man With Two Brains* (1983). Unfortunately, many of these cartoonish antics are annoying and distract from his central theme of the magical powers of love.

At first glance, one might think that Martin is attempting to create a West Coast homage to Woody Allen, whose films *Annie Hall* (1977) and *Manhattan* (1979) celebrate romantic love while celebrating the benefits of living in Allen's own favorite city, New York. Nevertheless, Allen's films never ridicule his surroundings in the way in which Martin's does. Although Martin is never nasty with his jokes about living in Los Angeles, the jokes are too wildly absurd and do nothing to define the real essence of what it is really like to live in Los Angeles. A much more honest feel for the city is reflected in the many colorful locations that are used in the film, all of which are presented in bright, vibrant colors, accentuating the film's fairy-tale theme. Like Allen, Martin believes in the power of love, how it makes living in any environment a much more exciting, magical experience. His theme is universal, one that transcends time and place.

Jim Kline

Reviews
Chicago Tribune. February 8, 1991, VII, p. 18.
Commonweal. CXVIII, April 19, 1991, p. 259.
Films in Review. XLII, May, 1991, p. 189.
The Hollywood Reporter. February 7, 1991, p. 6.
Los Angeles Times. February 8, 1991, p. F1.
The New Republic. CCIV, March 11, 1991, p. 28.
The New York Times. February 8, 1991, p. B9.
The New Yorker. LXVI, February 11, 1991, p. 70.
Newsweek. February 11, 1991, p. 58.
Rolling Stone. February 21, 1991, p. 47.
Variety. February 7, 1991, p. 2.
The Wall Street Journal. February 7, 1991, p. A12.
The Washington Post. February 8, 1991, p. B1.

LIFE IS SWEET

Origin: Great Britain
Released: 1991
Released in U.S.: 1991
Production: Simon Channing-Williams for Film Four International, British Screen, and Thin Man Films; released by October Films
Direction: Mike Leigh
Screenplay: Mike Leigh
Cinematography: Dick Pope
Editing: Jon Gregory
Production design: Alison Chitty
Art direction: Sophie Becher
Music: Rachel Portman
MPAA rating: no listing
Running time: 102 minutes

> *Principal characters:*
> Wendy .... Alison Steadman
> Andy .... Jim Broadbent
> Natalie .... Claire Skinner
> Nicola .... Jane Horrocks
> Aubrey .... Timothy Spall
> Patsy .... Stephen Rea
> Nicola's lover .... David Thewlis

Director-screenwriter Mike Leigh's focus may at first seem to be narrow to the point of monotony: Since he began making films for television in 1971, he has concentrated on the English working class, utilizing a style that on the surface seems resolutely, even insistently, naturalistic. Yet, in cinema, stylistic appearances do not always fully signal deeper intentions. Leigh seems as interested as any contemporary filmmaker in addressing the complex nature of cinematic language. Filmmakers who have done so often gravitate to a deceptive simplicity of presentation while incorporating semi-improvisational methods into their manner of working, as Leigh does. This does not mean, however, that considerable sophistication is not brought to bear on both the visual and dramatic momentum of their works. The open and exploratory filmmaker is often the one who may be looked to when searching for answers to cinema's ambiguities—specifically regarding the central issue of the relationship between perceived reality and dramatic organization.

That issue is a guiding light in *Life Is Sweet*, Leigh's third theatrical feature. The film's four principal characters, members of a family, tend to hold themselves as riddles to one another—opaque and bland in three instances, asserting a scattered and wild energy filled with seemingly impenetrable contradictions in the fourth. In doing so, they seem to conform to a view of life as unordered and only intermittently interesting. Nevertheless, on closer examination, all four individuals consciously seek to present their lives with a dramatic purposefulness that, by film's end, both they and the viewer might grasp. They carefully choose moments of self-revelation, with the seeming inconsistency of the vagrant moments that make up their lives throughout the film contributing to the crystallizations of character that finally materialize.

Set in a London suburb, *Life Is Sweet* quickly establishes the ambiance and rhythms of the essentially conventional life of a contemporary family, consisting of a husband and wife and twin adult daughters who still live at home. The father, Andy (Jim Broadbent), supervises a big industrial kitchen while dreaming of being more independent. The mother, Wendy (Alison Steadman), sells baby clothes and holds down a second job teaching a dance class for little girls. Although Wendy savors memories of her daughters' childhood—when each learned ballet and seemed to epitomize appealingly feminine girlhood—the two strawberry-haired young women have each matured into something far out of their mother's sense of archetypal experience. Natalie (Claire Skinner) could pass for a boy with her quiet poise and even nature, her short hair, her job as a plumber, and her habit of playing pool for leisure. By contrast, her sister, Nicola (Jane Horrocks), flies in the face of the family's customarily cheerful placidity. She is its resident rebel without a cause—long hair askew, cigarette always flaunted in a hostile hand, her voice a grating chirp. It is one of the film's immediate charms that the three other family members accept her ways with good-natured (if covertly melancholy) resignation. Her sense of her own identity seems to allow for no sense of daily purpose other than to seethe with neurotic rancor, and she wears her lack of life's direction like a badge of honor.

Nicola is not the film's only tortured soul. Wendy's friend Aubrey (Timothy Spall), who takes center stage in an elaborate, somewhat torturous subplot, is a pathetic child-man bent on opening a French restaurant, Le Regret Rien, with dishes such as tongues in rhubarb hollandaise sauce and quails on a bed of spinach and tripe. He enlists the indefatigable Wendy as a waitress, but on opening night no customers arrive to brave the bill of fare. The unhappy chef-proprietor, in a state of mounting anxiety and despair, becomes completely drunk and smashes much of the restaurant's interior, while also making an ill-considered pass at Wendy. Naturally, the good-hearted woman manages to take it all in stride. Interestingly, Aubrey's ambitions are mirrored in Andy's more modest intention of fixing up a humble catering wagon into an impressive fast-food business of his own. It is a dream that seems almost stillborn by film's end, as he recuperates from a foot injury.

Obsessions with food are one of the film's most prominent motifs, lightly and comically enough in Aubrey's and Andy's plans, more darkly in Nicola's anorexia/bulimia. Her condition is reflected even in her surreptitious, quirky sexual relationship with a young man (David Thewlis) who is not the callously detached user that he at first appears to be. The boyfriend's final refusal to carry on with a purely sexual relationship—he wants to experience a feeling of love or at least joyful companionship with the unhappy girl—sets in motion a climax that finds Nicola in unexpected confrontations with her mother and sister. Nicola learns from Wendy that she almost died during a stay in the hospital brought about by an earlier stage of anorexia and that the family she treats with such scorn has loved her through all of her problems. In a final, memorable scene of shared self-insight and communion, the two sisters enjoy a moment of rapport that suggests an emotional evolution for the family. Natalie has known of her sister's nightly binging and purging for a long time and has had the grace and maturity to let Nicola work out her own problem and come to terms with her own life.

The viewer may ask whether this family is as ordinary as even Leigh himself might suggest. To answer that question, the film's naturalistic surface must be seen as a surface, cleverly disguising a spiritual nobility that enables these characters to transcend the apparent limitations that circumscribe them. The problem of people who are related—and of all those who love each other—is to allow individual identity to the one they care about, rather than projecting onto the other person an identity that they could better understand. A character who understands this conflict especially well is Nicola's boyfriend (although his attitude is also mirrored in different ways by Nicola's father, mother, and sister). In an especially unexpected and pleasurable scene, his sexual rejection of her is accompanied by an impassioned plea to her to throw aside the pretensions of a stance built on books and feminist manifestos that she does not understand and to come to terms with who she really is. He makes no judgments and holds no presumptions about what that identity might be. This treatment of a character who could be portrayed derisively and contemptuously is underscored by Leigh's impassive camera and subtle dramatic emphases.

Leigh's approach might profitably be compared to that of Henry Jaglom in *Eating* (1990), a similarly designed work in its preoccupation with food and also a film within the free-flowing, naturalistic narrative tradition that nurtured Leigh. Jaglom also tries to give his film over to character insight, but it is only held together by an obsession with his own ideas. The "slice of life" aesthetic has many traps to set aside that kind of self-indulgence: The deception of thinking of oneself as an observer of life can leave too much space to diminish the stature of the figures and landscapes in a work of art. Leigh is like the great experimenters within naturalism in his implicit grasp of the fact that these figures and landscapes, while carved from reality, must have a very specific power. He realizes that cinematic art must allow the world it evokes to transcend its time and place and have a tragicomic appeal—*Life Is Sweet* surely boasts this duality—while its characters must be vessels for insight, so that the viewer's awareness is sharpened rather than made more complacent.

Intensely engaged with actors, who are extraordinary in this film, and his sense of the formal contours of the work, Leigh's work resembles that of John Cassavetes among contemporary filmmakers, except for that director's sentimentality. Leigh has more native discretion, and if his independent, unorthodox way of making cinema vibrant is much less obvious than that of Cassavetes—who always seemed bold in his challenges to mainstream style—it arguably goes further in transforming the texture of ordinary life so that it becomes extraordinary. Leigh's framing has a natural elegance and is never ragged, while his use of close-ups is sparing and effective. The steady, sometimes wry, and often philosophical gaze of Leigh's camera most resembles that of the great naturalistic classicist Yasujiro Ozu, famed for the precision of his compositions and editing. The final scene between the sisters in *Life Is Sweet* even resonates with affinities with the most memorable scene—also between two young women—in Ozu's *Tokyo Monogatari* (1953; *Tokyo Story*, 1967). In Ozu's scene, one character observed with cheerful profundity that "life is disappointing" but the veteran Japanese director's treatment suggests that he knew as surely as Leigh that this was not the whole truth. He would not find the title of Leigh's film ironic.

Blake Lucas

Reviews

Boxoffice. March, 1992, p. R-25.
Chicago Tribune. December 27, 1991, VII, p. 29.
The Christian Science Monitor. November 19, 1991, p. 10.
Film Comment. XXVII, September, 1991, p. 18.
The Hollywood Reporter. October 14, 1991, p. 9.
Los Angeles Times. November 13, 1991, p. F1.
The Nation. CCLIII, December 2, 1991, p. 717.
The New York Times. October 25, 1991, p. C10.
The New Yorker. LXVII, November 4, 1991, p. 101.
Newsweek. January 6, 1992, p. 52.
The Times Literary Supplement. March 29, 1991, p. 15.
The Village Voice. October 29, 1991, p. 59.
The Wall Street Journal. November 7, 1991, p. A12.
The Washington Post. December 27, 1991, p. C1.

LITTLE MAN TATE

Production: Scott Rudin and Peggy Rajski; released by Orion Pictures
Direction: Jodie Foster
Screenplay: Scott Frank
Cinematography: Mike Southon
Editing: Lynzee Klingman
Production design: Jon Hutman
Art direction: Adam Lustig
Set decoration: Sam Schaffer
Casting: Avy Kaufman and Lina Todd
Sound: Douglas Axtell
Costume design: Susan Lyall
Music: Mark Isham
MPAA rating: PG
Running time: 99 minutes

Principal characters:
Dede Tate .... Jodie Foster
Jane Grierson .... Dianne Wiest
Fred Tate .... Adam Hann-Byrd
Eddie .... Harry Connick, Jr.
Garth .... David Pierce
Damon Wells .... P. J. Ochlan
Gina .... Debi Mazar
Miss Nimvel .... Celia Weston
Winston F. Buckner .... George Plimpton

Seldom is a debut awaited with more fanfare and anticipation than was *Little Man Tate*. Twenty-eight-year-old director Jodie Foster graced the cover of *Time* magazine and the film was pronounced an "audacious winner" before anyone else was given the chance to vote. It seemed only logical that this gifted veteran of twenty-five years in the entertainment business would prove herself as masterful behind the camera as in front of it. After all, Foster literally grew up on the set and screen before the nation's very eyes, but not in the manner in which Elizabeth Taylor or Judy Garland did in the cloister of the MGM back lot. Steered by her mother, Foster's career choices had always been bold and controversial. The characters that she played seemed consistently wise beyond her years and the films frequently fell out of the realm of ordinary mainstream cinema. If that were not enough, her reactions to the unfortunate John Hinckley incident (in which Hinckley shot President Ronald Reagan in order to impress Foster) further informed her public of her maturity and competence.

As a Yale graduate and confessed control-freak, Foster should have been a sure bet for the outstanding first-time director. Yet, somehow, this triumph did not occur. Why was there such disappointment, and was it fair to have expected so much of this film? Such questions are worth pondering because they speak to where society's highest aspirations for modern cinema lie.

It should have been a "nice little film." Young Fred Tate (Adam Hann-Byrd) is a genius but also alienated from his peers, worrying too much for the world at large. He is drawn from his stifled existence with his low-brow single mother, Dede (Jodie Foster), to the pursuit of knowledge and achievement with Jane Grierson (Dianne Wiest), who heads a school for not-so-sensitive gifted children. Without the strong nurturing force of Dede, however, Fred's spirit withers. Not until the two women join forces and give him all that he needs can he finally be a well-adjusted and happy little boy.

At first, it might seem that many things in the film succeed dramatically. Unlike some filmmakers, young and old alike, Foster is able to articulate small moments with precision. She establishes some impressive rhythms at the outset and demonstrates that she knows how to turn a scene and how to underline tension. The style is about contrast and is supported well by the set design and, at first, by the cutting patterns.

After several scenes, however, there is a failure to establish any clear linear progression. The unfolding events seem scattered over too broad a range and yet are still not enough. The articulation of who is developing and how remains undramatized. Scott Frank's screenplay appears to have turning points, but they do not fall into the right places. Furthermore, certain moments that might have worked well are spoiled by an overbearing musical score. The young director should have had more faith in what she does right: establishing believable communication between actors.

Fundamentally, *Little Man Tate* fails miserably by trying to tell too many stories and mastering none. Fred is unhappy, but he is too cosmic, too attuned. He has no real dilemma other than wanting to have more stimulation and acceptance. Consequently, he does not serve as a main character that the audience can watch develop. Rather, people and events continue to be arbitrarily cruel to him until, one day, they simply stop doing so. It seems that Fred is merely a catalyst for the incomplete women to become whole. Yet, here again, there is no clarity of vision.

Dede at first does not want her son to go with Jane, then allows him to do so when she sees that he needs stimulation. She is portrayed as making the right decision but is punished with an absurd drowning episode involving a friend's child that does not even qualify as good melodrama. The nuances of her shift toward understanding with Jane remain an offscreen mystery. Scenes are cut short that seem effective at first, a practice that becomes annoying because it continuously sidetracks the film's dramatic build. The fledgling director is astute at giving individual scenes an internal pulse, but together they go nowhere. The character of Jane, the one closest to having the appropriate beats of a story, is abruptly dropped just as she becomes more interesting. Hence, the film's intended climactic moments are externally forced and disconnected, and the final party scene smacks of a *deus ex machina*.

The telling irony is that Foster's fans are mostly intelligent film students or connoisseurs, not cult-type fans who will sit through virtually anything to see their beloved icon on-screen. It appears that the novice director succumbed to a vulnerability toward the subject matter that fostered a blind spot in her perspective large enough to obscure the flaws in the script.

It is understandable that Fred Tate's poignant isolation would ring true to Foster. Her own life had been informed by the diverse forces of her own independent mother, those mentors surrounding her at the French school for gifted children, and such intense and creative artists as Martin Scorsese. Nevertheless, basic identification with subject matter is no substitute for focus.

The case is problematic because no one expected Foster to mistake running gags—such as a recurring motif of a magician's long cape stuck in a car door—for theme. Yet, in all fairness, maybe more film goers should have. There are certainly variables in how one understands what it is to be a good director. When looking from the outside in, it is obvious to most that a great director has a vision, a command of the themes and forms that she or he wants to explore. A protégé in the interactive process of filmmaking, however, would have a less academic perspective. A sense of control over the immediate surroundings—along with the awe at the sheer act of getting the all-but-impossible job done—would be incorporated into the young actor's definition of "auteur."

Perhaps it was not realistic to expect Foster, educated as she was, to live up to rarefied critical standards. Looking at those films that have been important for her career offers further insight. Foster's earliest triumphs consisted of interesting fringe-dwellers of larger wholes. Her quirky adolescent in *Alice Doesn't Live Here Anymore* (1975) was a delightful foil, with much hinted at but left hanging. When Scorsese used her again the next year in *Taxi Driver* (1976), her teenage prostitute in that convoluted story could have been a heightened continuation. Few critics spend much time discussing her role in the more conventional *Freaky Friday* (1977). As an adult, she chose to act in the convoluted Mary Lambert film *Siesta* (1987), and with her performance in *The Accused* (1988)—not technically her story at all—she stole the show from Kelly McGillis and was rewarded with the Academy Award for Best Actress. In the commercially successful *The Silence of the Lambs* (1991; reviewed in this volume), which was structured clearly to focus on her character's progression, promoters and audiences alike dwelt on Anthony Hopkins' virtuoso monster, Hannibal Lecter. Even as Foster's performance in that film shone, director Jonathan Demme insidiously kept her character from "owning" the film by cutting away on the shot of her final realization of her duplicity to the image of Lecter disappearing into a crowd. It is almost a preliminary for what was to happen when Foster donned the director's hat herself. Clearly, the context of contemporary film gives little support to the classical guidelines for solid structure and linear character development.

So in the end, *Little Man Tate* falls short of its promise, mainly because of a failed script that was much too close to home for the director to recognize its shortcomings. Certainly, many of the isolated moments ring true. There are some nicely done effects that serve the wonder of childhood instead of death and destruction. In addition, most of the style is thought out yet not pretentious. The camera is placed knowingly, but the angles do not give the viewer a headache. General audiences did not experience the deep letdown that her admirers might have. Foster will be absolved and allowed to try again because other directors have sinned much more and, more important, because she will not be seeking forgiveness. One admires that in a director.

Mary E. Belles

Reviews
American Cinematographer. LXXII, September, 1991, p. 45.
American Film: Magazine of the Film and Television Arts. XVI, November, 1991, p. 44.
Boxoffice. December, 1991, p. R-89.
Chicago Tribune. October 18, 1991, VII, p. 43.
The Christian Science Monitor. October 15, 1991, LXXXIII, p. 10.
Film Comment. XXVII, January, 1992, p. 38.
The Hollywood Reporter. September 3, 1991, p. 10.
L.A. Weekly. October 11-17, 1991, XIII, p. 35.
Los Angeles Times. October 9, 1991, p. F1.
The New York Times. October 9, 1991, CXLI, p. B1.
Newsweek. CXVIII, October 21, 1991, p. 65.
Rolling Stone. October 31, 1991, p. 97.
Time. CXXXVIII, October 14, 1991, p. 68.
Variety. September 3, 1991, p. 2.
The Village Voice. October 15, 1991, XXXVI, p. 66.
The Wall Street Journal. October 17, 1991, p. A20.
The Washington Post. October 18, 1991, p. D7.

MADAME BOVARY

Origin: France
Released: 1991
Released in U.S.: 1991
Production: Marin Karmitz for MK2 Productions; released by the Samuel Goldwyn
   Company
Direction: Claude Chabrol
Screenplay: Claude Chabrol; based on the novel by Gustave Flaubert
Cinematography: Jean Rabier
Editing: Monique Fardoulis
Set design: Michele Abbe
Sound: Jean-Bernard Thomasson
Costume design: Corinne Jorry
Music: Matthieu Chabrol
MPAA rating: no listing
Running time: 130 minutes

> *Principal characters:*
> Emma Bovary .... Isabelle Huppert
> Charles Bovary .... Jean-François Balmer
> Rodolphe Boulanger .... Christophe Malavoy
> Monsieur Homais .... Jean Yanne
> Léon Dupuis .... Lucas Belvaux
> Abbot Bournisien .... Jacques Dynam
> Justin .... Yves Verhoeven

This ninth film version of Gustave Flaubert's classic novel *Madame Bovary* came to the screen primarily through the efforts of veteran French director Claude Chabrol. Chabrol asserted that he had a longstanding desire to film the novel and that this version is "a film of absolute and unprecedented fidelity" with regard to Flaubert's work. Yet it is that fidelity which both impressed and dismayed critics. Some faulted the film for overwhelming its story with impressive period detail that tempts the viewer's attention away from the plight of Flaubert's controversial protagonist, Emma Bovary. In contrast, the film also received enthusiastic praise for its re-creation of nineteenth century life in France and for its subtle interpretation of what critics of Flaubert's time regarded as an unsubtle (if not obscene) heroine.

In a letter, Flaubert once stated that he thought Emma Bovary resembled many women of his time, the "poor obscure souls" whose sorrows were "as humid with repressed melancholy as the mossy walls" on the "hidden provincial courtyards" that surrounded them. It has come to light that Flaubert's 1857 novel was partially based on a real-life incident brought to his attention by friends in 1848. Rouen newspapers carried the story of a woman named Delphine Delamare, the wife of a country physician who committed suicide, supposedly after shaming herself with massive indebtedness and flagrant adultery. From this event, Flaubert shaped his own fictional story of Emma Bovary, whose pursuit of personal fulfillment leads her into direct confrontation with the conventions of provincial bourgeois society.

In Chabrol's adaptation of the novel, the audience first glimpses Emma (Isabelle Huppert) when, in a drunken stupor, her father breaks his leg and a doctor must be called to their farm. The doctor, Charles Bovary (Jean-François Balmer), is a middle-aged widower, shy and awkward even in the presence of a self-possessed adolescent such as Emma. Invited to return to the farm by Emma's father, Charles is left speechless by Emma's silent but effective flirtations. In the next scene, Charles asks for Emma's hand in marriage, followed by one of the many ellipses in the film that condense time (and occasionally leave the viewer confused). The next scene opens with their wedding procession across the farm's open fields. Typical of a film that is beautifully photographed throughout, the wedding procession paints a picture of undeniable pastoral beauty, but already Emma reveals the dissatisfaction that will help drive her to destruction: She comments that a night wedding would have been better.

Emma takes up residence with her husband in the small town of Yonville-l'Abbaye. She performs the tasks of a dutiful wife and occupies her time with sewing, music, and other activities appropriate to her new station in life. It quickly becomes clear, however, that the life of the bourgeois housewife is too confining for Emma. The voice-over narration (spoken by François Perier) comments that Emma becomes increasingly detached from her husband. She and Charles are invited to a ball at the Marquis d'Andervillers' mansion. Emma is ecstatic; Charles is ill at ease at the dance, but Emma's beauty and charm are rewarded by attention from the aristocratic men in attendance. Nevertheless, the ball must end. In the days that follow, Emma grows increasingly despondent to the point that she can no longer function. Her husband is frantic with worry, but he is at a loss to help her. Finally, in desperation, he decides that they will move to a larger town in the hopes that the change will do Emma good.

Once they become established in a larger town, Emma improves and gives birth to a daughter, Berthe. Emma has a brief flirtation with Léon (Lucas Belvaux), a young man working as a law clerk. Although she knows that their interest in each other threatens to compromise her situation as the wife of a respectable man, Emma is flattered by Léon's infatuation with her. She is also intrigued by his ability to discuss music and culture. At Sunday gatherings, Charles plays chess with the chemist Homais (Jean Yanne) while Emma listens to Léon read poetry.

Emma's temptations are not only sexual ones, as she must also reject a greedy merchant's offer to extend her credit for new dresses. Emma is moved to tears, but a visit to her priest, Abbot Bournisien (Jacques Dynam), is of no help in reconciling her feelings: He offers clichés to warn her against the material world. His advice is of little use to Emma because she is tempted by more than sex and consumer goods; she is tempted by her own imagination and her dreams of a romantically charged life of excitement and pleasure.

Léon leaves for Paris, and Emma offers him a restrained goodbye. Her sexual temptation is removed, but only temporarily. A local aristocrat, Rodolphe Boulanger (Christophe Malavoy), arrives at the Bovary house with a servant who requires treatment. Boulanger looks at Emma with obvious sexual interest. Time passes, and the audience sees Boulanger spiriting Emma into an empty room at the town hall. Outside, the citizens are gathered for the town fair and agricultural prizes are being announced. Inside, Rodolphe proceeds to seduce Emma, not with kisses but with words that play to her imagination with whispered musings on love and destiny. The contrast between the mundane reality of Emma's life—evidenced by the town fair— and her inner desires—given voice by Boulanger for the purpose of seduction— effectively reveals the impossibility of Emma's situation in one of the film's most impressive uses of editing.

Rodolphe waits several weeks to see Emma merely to increase her desire. Playing into the hands of Emma's would-be lover, Charles suggests that Emma and Rodolphe go horseback riding to improve his wife's mood. Emma and Rodolphe ride through the woods and become lovers, an idea that appeals to Emma perhaps more than its actuality. Ironically, her cuckolded husband buys her a horse as a surprise gift. Charles's kindnesses are not enough for Emma, who steals away from her bed at night to meet Rodolphe. The lovers begin to tire of each other, however, and Emma repents. Yet her renewed attempt to live the life of a devoted wife and mother is interrupted by an incident that leaves her disillusioned.

Homais wants Charles to perform an experimental operation on a clubfooted patient in order to gain fame (and more patients). Charles is reluctant, but Emma and Homais persuade him to perform the surgery. Charles operates on the man, but something goes terribly wrong; the patient's foot and leg turn into a repulsive mass of swollen, festering flesh. Ultimately, another doctor must be called in to amputate the leg in order to save the young man's life. Charles's reputation as a doctor suffers, and Emma rejects him. Her love for Rodolphe finds renewal in her disappointment, causing her to repent of her previous repentance. Emma frequents the draper's shop and begins to go into heavy debt in order to secure fashionable clothes.

As common as her pretensions may appear, Emma is more than a poseur. She has the courage of her romantic convictions. She wants to run away with Rodolphe. When he sends a letter telling her that he will not leave his life, his land, and his holdings for her, Emma collapses into a fever. To contribute to her recovery, Charlès takes her to the theater in Rouen. There, she sees Léon. Charles starts for home but leaves Emma alone to attend to business. Léon calls on her and reveals his continuing obsession. She rejects him—"forget me," she says—but nevertheless agrees to see him the next day. Meeting at a nearby cathedral, they climb into a carriage—where their affair begins.

At home, Emma secures a proxy from her husband in order to obtain more credit without his knowledge. She also continues her affair with Léon. Finally, a summons is issued against her for eight thousand francs, which she owes to merchants. Failing to seduce the moneylender into relenting to her pleas, she goes to her friends to raise the money. With a bailiff coming to the house in anticipation of confiscating their property, Emma knows that she will no longer be able to hide her profligate ways from her husband. She goes to Rouen, where she pleads with Léon to embezzle from his law firm for her, but he refuses. She goes to the local judge to stop the summons. He openly declares his sexual attraction to her, but she rejects him.

In desperation, Emma runs to Rodolphe's mansion. She assumes a masquerade of love until she admits that she needs money before they can become lovers again. His refusal is met by her rage—which appears, as interpreted by actress Isabelle Huppert, as less a spectacle of hysteria than a demonstration of the pent-up power of Emma that has been straitjacketed by the social conventions of her gender.

Emma's fury spent, she returns to town. She enters the chemist's shop and, to the horror of Justin (Yves Verhoeven), the chemist's assistant, she begins to eat arsenic out of a bin. She swears Justin to secrecy and returns home to die what she believes will be a quick and peaceful death. Yet, her wishes will not be fulfilled even in this: Her death will be a long and tortuous ordeal marked by unspeakable pain and the grotesque reactions of a body violated by poison. Charles begs the doctor to save his wife, but Emma says that she must die "so I won't torment you any more." After bidding her daughter goodbye, she succumbs to tormenting hallucinations and dies in Charles's arms. A postscript reveals that Charles died not long after his wife. Their orphaned daughter lived in poverty and became a mill worker.

Emma Bovary is destroyed by her refusal of a reality in which her vague ambitions can only be twisted, diverted, or thwarted. Although she victimizes others, Emma can also be seen as a victim of a society that affords women few creative options for their ambitions and imagination. In the face of what she regards as a boring, predictable bourgeois existence, Emma becomes defined by equally predictable transgressions— she becomes an adulterous, profligate wife. Yet, in spite of her rebellion, she is ultimately dependent on men and defined by them. Chabrol and his film collaborators offer Flaubert's story in such a fashion as to create the impression that Emma Bovary is a complex human being. She cannot easily be labeled a neurotic, a nymphomaniac, or an opportunist, terms that have often been applied to Flaubert's heroine. In Chabrol's film, Emma is inscribed as an individual with a penchant for melodramatic excess; she also emerges as a symbol of how society shapes and constrains women.

Having made his directorial debut in 1958, Chabrol has created a varied career which includes a number of films that have centralized women who step outside social norms. This experience, and the intensity often characteristic of Chabrol's films, is brought to bear on *Madame Bovary*'s sensitivity to its intense heroine, but the film refuses to succumb to Emma's point of view. In spite of the fact that the viewer is rarely privy to a direct verbal expression of Emma's feelings, the impressive casting of the film—with Huppert's delicately nuanced performance as Emma and Balmer's sympathetic portrayal of her bland husband—contributes to the success of Chabrol's *Madame Bovary* as a thoughtful and thought-provoking rendition of Flaubert's carefully observed novel. Perhaps that is the most that one can ask of any film adaptation, especially one that dares to bring a much-revered, yet controversial classic to the screen.

Gaylyn Studlar

Reviews
Boxoffice. February, 1992, p. R-16.
Chicago Tribune. December 25, 1991, V, p. 3.
The Christian Science Monitor. January 13, 1992, p. 11.
Film Comment. XXVII, November, 1991, p. 6.
The Hollywood Reporter. December 17, 1991, p. 10.
Los Angeles Times. December 25, 1991, p. F12.
The New Republic. CCVI, January 6, 1992, p. 28.
New Woman. XXII, January, 1992, p. 27.
The New York Times. December 25, 1991, p. A13.
Newsweek. CXIX, January 6, 1992, p. 52.
Rolling Stone. January 9, 1992, p. 56.
Variety. CCCXLIII, April 29, 1991, p. 91.
The Washington Post. December 25, 1991, p. D2.

THE MAN IN THE MOON

Production: Mark Rydell; released by Metro-Goldwyn-Mayer
Direction: Robert Mulligan
Screenplay: Jenny Wingfield
Cinematography: Freddie Francis
Editing: Trudy Ship
Production design: Gene Callahan
Sound: Peter Bentley
Costume design: Peter Saldutti and Dawni Saldutti
Music: James Newton Howard
MPAA rating: PG-13
Running time: 99 minutes

Principal characters:
Matthew Trant	Sam Waterston
Abigail Trant	Tess Harper
Marie Foster	Gail Strickland
Dani Trant	Reese Witherspoon
Court Foster	Jason London
Maureen Trant	Emily Warfield
Billy Sanders	Bentley Mitchum
Will Sanders	Ernie Lively

The Man in the Moon is a charming coming-of-age film set in the Louisiana of the 1950's. It garnered mostly favorable reviews despite some weighty events at its conclusion, which many believed mar what could have been a perfect little film. Robert Mulligan possesses expertise in the direction of adolescent themes, especially in nostalgic settings, and his sense of control seems almost a throwback to a school of articulating human experience that the mainstream cinema has largely abandoned. In addition, the good writing and believable performances save the film from falling prey to the sentimentality that the genre has inspired over the years.

Although much is going on for these characters in their small world, the pacing is efficient without ever seeming the slightest bit hurried. Dani Trant (Reese Witherspoon) is the long-legged fourteen-year-old whom her father (Sam Waterston) bemoans as "wild as a jackrabbit." Dani is infatuated with Elvis Presley and the local swimming hole, while her older, responsible sister Maureen (Emily Warfield) fends off two generations of pawing men and longs for something truer out of life. When widow Marie Foster (Gail Strickland) returns to work the neighboring homestead, there is immediate animosity between her handsome eldest son, Court (Jason London), and Dani, which quickly turns to affection and Dani's first crush. As always, Dani looks to Maureen for guidance, and Maureen is sympathetic and kind enough to demonstrate such things as the proper kissing technique. It appears that Dani is finally beginning to act more grown-up and responsible, but a nighttime swimming episode causes an unfortunate accident for her pregnant mother (Tess Harper), which angers her father and adds to Maureen's burden at home.

Court, meanwhile, is becoming more frustrated while trying to support his mother and brothers on the run-down farm. When her father insists that Dani's beau come to the house in the daytime, Dani is devastated to see how deeply Court is struck by Maureen. Maureen tries to resist, but she and Court share the similar frustrations of family burdens and a longing for escape. They fall in love. Soon after, Court is killed in a terrible accident and Dani holds Maureen responsible, vowing that she never wants to be close to her sister again. Ultimately, however, Dani discovers a deeper capability for compassion after realizing that her sister's suffering is actually greater than her own.

Perhaps it is because the early scenes are so much more real than films usually are that the final plot device seems harsh. Court's death is an unmistakably jolting point in the narrative, but it is upsetting to watch. His reckless driving style is established early in the film, and he is inexperienced in the role that has been foisted on him by his father's absence. While modern urban society has sentimentalized rural life in the 1950's, life on the farm only a few generations ago was hard and, before government agencies began to regulate safety factors, very dangerous. Ironically, it is likely that *The Village Voice* critic who berated the "punishing Puritan ethic" that lurks beneath this film's love story would not object to a similar level of fatalism in a modern-day, coming-of-age story in New York City.

The Man in the Moon might instead be reevaluated in terms of what the inclusion of the film's tragic event means to its themes. No matter how expediently Court's death serves to wrap up the plot, the question should be whether the sequence supports or undercuts the central premise. Jenny Wingfield's screenplay is so accurate throughout that it is hard to accept that she simply wrote herself into a corner and gave up without a fight. Even more telling is the body of Mulligan's work. As far back as the acclaimed adaptation of Harper Lee's novel *To Kill a Mockingbird* (1962), the director has infused mortality into the realm of childhood. Mulligan holds a decidedly fatalistic, but consistent sense that a youngster's first awareness about the complexities of life is tied to somber events. Mulligan obviously believes that death is a part of growing up and that those first brushes with it take precedence in one's formative years but only click into sharp focus in hindsight. In his sweetly humorous *Summer of '42* (1971), the story of teenage Hermie's longing for an older woman is propelled forward by the devastating news that her husband has been killed in the war. It is an indelible part of the boy's past, a factor in the loss of his virginity that also implies a loss of innocence in a world at war.

Likewise, in *The Man in the Moon*, the way in which potentially melodramatic events are integrated into the lives of the two sisters is in keeping with the overwhelming realities that people experience in their lives. Life is jumbled and unfathomable, and the "man in the moon" that the sisters discuss in the opening and closing scenes is that metaphoric pondering of fate which so often is arbitrarily cruel. If *The Man in the Moon* is compared to a film with a more exploitative use of heavy-handed plot twists, such as the tearjerker *Dominick and Eugene* (1988), then it is possible to appreciate the difference between a fine dramatic articulation of the human experience and well-intentioned sentimentality. The plot twists of *The Man in the Moon* are woven deep into its fabric, making every character deal with them in a fashion that reveals emotional truth. Mulligan's assured direction does not squander the force of the film's tragedy, pushing instead toward the reality that such tragedy effects.

At its core, the story is about sisters, and their relationship is developed through discreet moments. Mulligan's film commits itself to the competition and betrayal, and finally the newfound compassion, that Dani experiences toward Maureen. The abruptness of the young suitor's death serves as a shortcut for what might have taken months or years to resolve otherwise. In two scenes at the cemetery, the clarity of the direction transcends any qualms with the plot. First, the stunned and grieving Dani lingers behind the others and crouches behind a tree to watch the nonchalance of the grave-diggers as they lower Court's coffin. Her sullen, self-centered behavior in the scenes that follow reprises the childish gap in understanding that was at the heart of Court's deeper attraction to Maureen. Later, when Dani watches a grief-stricken Maureen weep over the grave of the boy, she is quietly struck by the magnitude of her elder sister's loss. Stepping forward for the very first time to comfort, Dani moves at last toward the threshold of mature understanding, narrowing that gap between the two young women. In a film, a clear-eyed moment such as this is rare.

Mary E. Belles

Reviews
Chicago Tribune. October 4, 1991, VII, p. 23.
Los Angeles Times. October 3, 1991, p. F1.
New Woman. XXI, November, 1991, p. 28.
The New York Times. October 4, 1991, CXLI, p. C13.
People Weekly. XXXVI, October 28, 1991, p. 16.
Playboy. XXXVIII, November, 1991, p. 32.
San Francisco Chronicle. October 4, 1991, p. D5.
Seventeen. L, September, 1991, p. 136.
Us. November, 1991, p. 83.
USA Today. October 4, 1991, p. D6.
Variety. CCCXLIV, September 23, 1991, p. 76.
The Village Voice. October 22, 1991, XXXVI, p. 70.
The Village Voice. November 29, 1991, XXXVI, p. 70.
The Washington Post. October 4, 1991, p. B7.
Washingtonian. XXVII, November, 1991, p. 34.

MEETING VENUS

Origin: Great Britain
Released: 1991
Released in U.S.: 1991
Production: David Puttnam for Enigma, in association with Fujisankei Communications Group, British Sky Broadcasting, and County Natwest Ventures; released by Warner Bros.
Direction: István Szabó
Screenplay: István Szabó and Michael Hirst
Cinematography: Lajos Koltai
Editing: Jim Clark
Production design: Attila Kovacs
Casting: Patsy Pollock
Sound: Simon Kaye
Costume design: Catherine Leterrier
Music: Richard Wagner
Music consultation: Daisy Boschan
MPAA rating: PG-13
Running time: 119 minutes

Principal characters:

Karin Anderson	Glenn Close
	(sung by Kiri Te Kanawa)
Zoltan Szanto	Niels Arestrup
Picabia	Erland Josephson
Jean Gabor	Moscu Alcalay
Miss Malikoff	Macha Meril
Monique Angelo	Johanna Ter Steege
Maria Krawiecki	Maite Nahyr
Stefano Del Sarto	Victor Poletti
Von Schneider	Marian Labuda
Taylor	Jay O. Sanders
Von Binder	Dieter Laser
Yvone	Maria de Medeiros
Jana	Ildiko Bánsági
Edith	Dorottya Udvaros
Dancer	Johara Racz
Toushkau	Etienne Chicot
Isaac Partnoi	Roberto Pollack
Delfin van Delf	Rita Scholl
Thomas	François Delaive
Etienne Tailleur	André Chaumeau

Co-written by its director, István Szabó, *Meeting Venus* goes from the sublime to the ridiculous to the sublime. The sublimity in each instance is attributable primarily to great music, which—the film demonstrates admirably in its concluding segment—has the beauty and power to elevate both superior and paltry souls. What is ridiculous is the film's middle segment, with its numerous soap opera plot complications involving both heterosexual and homosexual love affairs, infidelity, conflict between unions and management, backstage politics, and bigoted wrangling among people of different nations.

Szabó shows in a visual prologue that serious musicians are capable of mundane, childish, and even silly behavior. Under opening titles, members of the orchestra of the Opera Europa in Paris tune their instruments before rehearsal. One scratches his back with his bow, others play a European variation of the game pat-a-cake, and another prankishly throws a paper airplane at the back of an unsuspecting colleague's head.

A Hungarian conductor, Zoltan Szanto (Niels Arestrup), arrives in Paris; he is to conduct a new production of Richard Wagner's *Tannhäuser*. Although travel is now relatively uninhibited between Eastern and Western Europe, Szanto is regarded suspiciously by customs officials. The case containing his baton is opened as if it might conceal a lethal weapon. This sequence is a prelude to the bickering and mistrust on the basis of national difference that occurs later in the film.

Picabia (Erland Josephson), director of the Opera Europa, greets Szanto at the airport and then escorts him to a rehearsal room where the creative team is assembled, awaiting his arrival. The scene is utterly convincing as a meeting of an outstanding guest conductor with administrators and highly reputed, international artists of a major opera house. The screenplay in this early segment is exceptionally literate; the dialogue is civilized, witty, and intelligent. In addition, the complexity of the situation is captured in a sequence of shots that shows, despite the obedience of all to ceremony, the individuality of responses: blatant worship of the guest conductor, reserved politeness, and skepticism. The beginnings of a creative partnership are composed of delicate moments in which potentially vulnerable artists try to find the most fertile connections to one another.

Szanto gathers his singers around a piano almost immediately and accompanies them as they sing solo passages from the opera. It is moving to observe his pleasure in their voices and musicality and in the knowledge that he is at last free to work with the greatest of artists, no matter what their national origins. One cannot overestimate the contribution of the fine singers—Dame Kiri Te Kanawa, René Kollo, Hakan Hage-gard, and Waltraud Meier—whose voices are heard on the soundtrack and who make understandable the admiration and strong emotions felt by Szanto. It is clear that he loves music and is profoundly joyful that he will be able to do Wagner justice with such outstanding artistic resources at his disposal.

Disillusionment soon follows, however, as union and personal concerns intrude. Each group—orchestra, chorus, stagehands—makes what seem to Szanto petty demands compared to the objective of bringing *Tannhäuser* to triumphant realization. In the middle of a musical phrase, everyone stops for a coffee break. Rehearsal cannot begin because the stagehand whose job it is to raise the fire curtain is not present. Although he tries to adapt to these practices, Szanto is consistently frustrated by the interruptions; to his mind, nothing should take precedence over the work, which is for him a passionate commitment. He soon concludes that these people do not love music.

The film shifts its tone as focus is put on the personal lives of the characters. The great prima donna Karin Anderson (Glenn Close) arrives and puzzles the new conductor by being exceptionally warm to everyone except him, to whom she is brutally cold. During one of the many arguments among the company that disrupt rehearsals—in this instance, an American singer is chastized because he is American—Szanto, enraged, sits at the piano and starts to pound the keys and sing a parody of international hatred in which most of the politically incorrect words for various groups are used. Anderson immediately empathizes with his frustration and joins him in singing the absurd ditty, contributing some of her own improvised lyrics; together, they succeed in diffusing the tension in the group. Everyone applauds them and goes back to work.

This event leads to an affair between the conductor and the prima donna. Szanto, however, is married; his wife, Edith (Dorottya Udvaros), and daughter, Jana (Ildiko Bánsági), are in Budapest. Yet, he becomes jealously concerned when he learns that Karin Anderson has fallen in love with other conductors before him. Soon, the viewer is in a realm somewhere between soap opera and bedroom farce.

Plot complications accelerate and compound; tensions abound. A pregnant former lover of Szanto happens to be a member of the orchestra. Another singer, Monique Angelo (Johanna Ter Steege) has made it clear that she is willing to sleep with Szanto and becomes jealous when she realizes that Anderson is ruining that possibility. Anderson goes to Budapest to give a recital. Szanto also makes the trip and introduces her to his wife and daughter backstage. Edith soon suspects her husband's infidelity. Meanwhile, in one subplot, the American singer, Steve Taylor (Jay O. Sanders) is unfaithful to his lover, the opera's stage director von Binder (Dieter Laser), who responds in a histrionic fashion. Later, antagonism between Szanto and the management intensifies until the conductor makes a universally understood obscene gesture and walks out of the rehearsal.

The film has traveled the route from realistic depiction of major artists grappling with their creative work to broadly contrived situation comedy peopled with the same characters—but with their most interesting traits hidden. Consistent with the new tone are two Italian caricatures, members of the company who sing, eat, and attempt to make love at every opportunity—even in the kitchen, where they can perform more than one of the activities simultaneously.

The shifting of stylistic gears is bothersome. It is likely that Szabó's overall intention is to show that great music overcomes everything, even the destructive small-mindedness of which men and women are capable. If he had established in early frames the broad style at which he eventually arrives, however, then the viewer would be willing to accept moments that seem annoyingly incredible without such preparation.

The film rises again to sublimity on the tide of its music passionately performed. Although the fire curtain cannot be raised on opening night because of difficulties with the union (sparing the audience a view of absurd postmodernist sets and dancers' costumes that are little more than black jock straps for the males and bras and panties for the women), the principals in the cast march out in front of the fire curtain, the chorus utilizes the auditorium's aisles, and the music succeeds in spite of everything, even some still-seen traces of the intended Peter Sellars-like production.

A significant technical problem in a film about opera is the lip-synching, which here is occasionally imprecise; even when it is accurate, performers do not always seem connected to the music that they are singing. Glenn Close, however, is a masterful exception in this regard. Dame Kiri Te Kanawa is the voice of Elizabeth, and Close is her embodiment, seeming to be singing music that she knows and feels intimately. Close's free, exuberant, and elegant performance is certainly one of the film's strong points. Close and her costar are often better than their material, not including, of course, Wagner's glorious opera. Niels Arestrup is every bit the European Leonard Bernstein, a conductor impassioned at the podium, whose expressive face and gesture validates what the listener feels, enhancing the response to great music.

As the opening night performance of *Tannhäuser* soars toward its conclusion, shots of Szanto, Anderson, and others performing at the peak of their powers and loving one another through their shared accomplishment are juxtaposed with shots of others in the offstage human drama—including Szanto's wife—who are listening rapt and moved despite the quarrels that they have had with those performing. The music is everything, and the richness of those moments when it envelops listeners and performers in its magical and profound web binds them together and supersedes their previous concerns and conflicts. It even makes the viewer want to forgive the earlier digression into the realm of not-so-inventive farce.

Cono Robert Marcazzo

Reviews

Boxoffice. January, 1992, p. R-3.
Chicago Tribune. December 13, 1991, VII, p. 54.
The Christian Science Monitor. December 17, 1991, p. 11.
Film Review. October, 1991, p. 31.
The Hollywood Reporter. October 7, 1991, p. 5.
Los Angeles Times. November 15, 1991, p. F10.
The New Republic. CCV, December 16, 1991, p. 34.
The New York Times. November 15, 1991, p. B1.
Opera News. LVI, November, 1991, p. 16.
Variety. September 6, 1991, p. 3.
The Wall Street Journal. December 5, 1991, p. A12.
The Washington Post. December 13, 1991, p. C1.

MISTER JOHNSON

Production: Michael Fitzgerald; released by Avenue Pictures
Direction: Bruce Beresford
Screenplay: William Boyd; based on the novel by Joyce Cary
Cinematography: Peter James
Editing: Humphrey Dixon
Production design: Herbert Pinter
Art direction: Fabian Adibe
Set decoration: Graham Sumner
Sound: Leslie Hodgson
Costume design: Rosemary Burrows
Music: Georges Delerue
MPAA rating: PG-13
Running time: 103 minutes

Principal characters:
Mister Johnson .... Maynard Eziashi
Harry Rudbeck .... Pierce Brosnan
Sargy Gollup .... Edward Woodward
Celia Rudbeck .... Beatie Edney
Bulteen .... Denis Quilley
Tring .... Nick Reding
Bamu .... Bella Enahoro
Waziri .... Femi Fatoba

Mister Johnson presents another examination of the character of the fool. The title character (Maynard Eziashi) is a native Nigerian clerk working for district officer Harry Rudbeck (Pierce Brosnan) in the high-water year of British colonial rule in West Africa: 1923. Johnson has fully embraced the values of his colonial masters and is determined to be more English than the English. The story follows the increasingly absurd twists and turns of this man as he operates between the two cultures—of the colonized and the colonials—until he meets his final, tragic end.

All three of the prime creators of this film, the celebrated English novelist Joyce Cary, the screenwriter William Boyd, and the Australian film director Bruce Beresford, have spent a portion of their lives in West Africa. Boyd and Beresford have realized Cary's original theme, which is not so much a direct attack on imperialism as a cautionary tale of the price paid when a man has adopted an identity that is not his birthright. Beresford, following the triumph and popularity of *Driving Miss Daisy* (1989), has filmed a story with a moral that is of interest even as the politics of imperialism become moot and fade.

The film begins with Johnson stating his intentions to his future wife, Bamu (Bella Enahoro). The opening images of a black man clad in a Western suit and a pith helmet courting a black woman in her native outfit establishes the tensions of the drama. Johnson's idea of success comes from the white world, and he wears the clothes that signify his ambition to accumulate money and material possessions. Nevertheless, he is still physically a part of tribal Africa and must obey the tribal customs in order to build a family and a home. The second scene shows Johnson using his fast-talking skills in English to fend off the demands of his local creditors and his English boss, Rudbeck.

Rudbeck is a young man on the first assignment of his civil service career. He is responsible for administering a vast undeveloped region. Though he is a man of modest education, he is obviously already bored and frustrated by his daily duties of judging petty village disputes and handling the various intrigues of the local waziri (Femi Fatoba). His Westernizing instincts lead him to focus all of his creativity and sense of achievement on building a road that will link the village of Fada with the rest of Africa. The home office approves of such activities but refuses to finance them adequately. Rudbeck is about to give up when Johnson, perhaps more current with the wiles of Western financing, shows Rudbeck how to juggle the books to continue the road building.

Soon, an auditor from the home office, Tring (Nick Reding), discovers the doctored accounting books. Johnson becomes the scapegoat and is forced to seek new employment with a white trader named Sargy Gollup (Edward Woodward). Gollup soon comes to realize that Johnson is a chiseler, a cheat, and a first-class entrepreneur. Gollup is an unrepentant racist who is perplexed by Johnson's Anglophilia. His response is a drunken compliment that the African is too good for his own color. Johnson naturally loses his respect for Gollup and for the trader's possessions, and he is fired again.

Johnson must go back to the native way of supporting his wife and newborn infant, but he drifts back to Fada and returns to the road-building crew under Rudbeck. Johnson becomes indispensable again, and the road is completed through his negotiating and conniving. All seems triumphant, but the wheels of misfortune turn again when Rudbeck discovers the unauthorized road fees that Johnson has been extorting from travelers. Once again, he must fire Johnson, who finds that his family is being repossessed by his father-in-law because Johnson cannot make his bridal payments. The waziri refuses to help, and Johnson desperately realizes that he has fallen between both cultures and is now a virtual outcast.

Gollup catches Johnson stealing from his strongbox. In the ensuing struggle, Johnson kills Gollup and flees, hoping to find refuge with his wife's tribe. The authorities are alerted. In a final, gut-wrenching act, Rudbeck, as the official British officer, must judge and condemn Johnson, a man whom he genuinely likes. Rudbeck must also oblige Johnson's request to be shot by Rudbeck in order to avoid an impersonal hanging. The final moments are only bearable because Johnson refuses to engage in self-pity and freely confesses his guilt and acquiescence in his punishment.

Beresford has engaged a strong cast to enact his story. Eziashi was recruited out of the London theater scene at the age of twenty-two to return to his native Nigeria for the film. He brings an admirable energy and freshness to a role that seems based in equal measures on such figures as Herman Melville's Billy Budd and the film character Duddy Kravitz. Television actor Woodward returns to work with Beresford after having starred in the film *Breaker Morant* (1980) that began both of their careers. Another television veteran, Brosnan demonstrates an appropriate gravity and vulnerability in his supporting role, particularly in his scenes with his wife in which he tries to allay her fears about being in Africa and in his final scene, in which he is trapped by his role and must do something that is repugnant to his personal feelings.

With *Driving Miss Daisy*, Beresford scored a popular success after completing a string of such uneven films as *King David* (1985) and *Her Alibi* (1989), but he still received some criticism and was slighted by the Academy of Motion Picture Arts and Sciences when he was not nominated in the Best Director category. *Mister Johnson* avoids the sentimentality of his previous efforts and the obvious polemics of some films about Africa, such as *Cry Freedom* (1987). Though he has never shown a great affinity for landscapes, Beresford has chosen a story that is very well integrated with the land: The audience can feel its presence and how it determines the actions of both the natives and the colonials.

Frederick Wasser

Reviews
Boxoffice. January, 1991, p. R-9.
Chicago Tribune. April 19, 1991, VII, p. 36.
The Christian Science Monitor. April 24, 1991, p. 14.
The Hollywood Reporter. September 11, 1990, p. 7.
Los Angeles Times. March 29, 1991, p. F8.
National Review. XLIII, May 13, 1991, p. 56.
The New York Times. March 22, 1991, p. C13.
The New Yorker. LXVII, April 8, 1991, p. 82.
Sight and Sound. LXIX, Spring, 1990, p. 94.
The Times Literary Supplement. March 29, 1991, p. 15.
Variety. September 10, 1990, p. 3.
The Washington Post. April 26, 1991, p. B1.

MOBSTERS

Production: Steve Roth; released by Universal Pictures
Direction: Michael Karbelnikoff
Screenplay: Michael Mahern and Nicholas Kazan; based on a story by Mahern
Cinematography: Lajos Koltai
Editing: Scott Smith and Joe D'Augustine
Production design: Richard Sylbert
Art direction: Peter Lansdown Smith
Set decoration: George R. Nelson
Casting: Bonnie Timmermann and Nancy Naylor
Sound: Michael Evje
Costume design: Ellen Mirojnick
Music: Michael Small
MPAA rating: R
Running time: 104 minutes

Principal characters:
Charlie "Lucky" Luciano . . . . Christian Slater
Meyer Lansky . . . . Patrick Dempsey
Benjamin "Bugsy" Siegel . . . . Richard Grieco
Frank Costello . . . . Costas Mandylor
Arnold Rothstein . . . . F. Murray Abraham
Mara Motes . . . . Lara Flynn Boyle
Don Faranzano . . . . Michael Gambon
Tommy Reina . . . . Christopher Penn
Don Masseria . . . . Anthony Quinn
Mad Dog Coll . . . . Nicholas Sadler
Anna Lansky . . . . Leslie Bega

Arguments at the breakfast table took on new dimensions when James Cagney shoved a grapefruit into the face of Mae Clarke in *The Public Enemy* (1931). Cagney epitomized the ruthless, charming, lady-slapping heel in the gangster films of the 1930's, but film historians cite D. W. Griffith's silent *The Musketeers of Pig Alley* (1912) as the first important gangster film. Walter Miller and Lillian Gish, as the hero and heroine, were heroically embroiled in a battle between two rival gangster factions. It took some time, however, for the gangster film to come into its own in the 1920's. This film genre began to flourish with the coming of sound and the emergence of gangster bosses played by Cagney, Edward G. Robinson, Humphrey Bogart, and Paul Muni. The list of actors who enhanced their careers playing hoods and gangsters includes George Raft, Cesar Romero, Buster Crabbe, Anthony Quinn, Alan Ladd, and Kirk Douglas. More recently, Marlon Brando, Al Pacino, Robert De Niro, Robert Duvall, and James Caan have all entered the dark and dangerous world of the Mob.

Gangsters often seem dapper and seductive to audiences, who view them as sinister, exciting, and somewhat invincible. They are men on a mission who would lay down their lives for the family business or for the honor of their don. Filmgoers may not condone their behavior, but they are always fascinated by them and find them hypnotically attractive. The commercial and critical success of *The Godfather* films of Francis Ford Coppola, Martin Scorsese's *GoodFellas* (1990), and Barry Levinson's *Bugsy* (1991; reviewed in this volume) proved that, if the gangster story is portrayed in a dramatic, truthful, and believable fashion, then the fans will come back to view the tale one more time. In 1990, "mobster fever" was beginning to rise with the upcoming release of two major films by major filmmakers: *The Godfather, Part III* and *GoodFellas*. In the midst of this anticipation, Universal Pictures decided to follow the trend and make a film based on the true story of the rise of organized crime from 1917 through 1931, aptly entitled *Mobsters*.

According to the press releases, *Mobsters* was to trace "the strong bonds of friendship and loyalty that developed between four young men." These four fledgling gangsters were Charlie "Lucky" Luciano (Christian Slater), Meyer Lansky (Patrick Dempsey), Benjamin "Bugsy" Siegel (Richard Grieco), and Frank Costello (Costas Mandylor). Academy Award-winner F. Murray Abraham was brought in to play gambler Arnold Rothstein, and two-time Oscar winner Anthony Quinn portrayed crime boss Don Masseria. The new "spin" on this film was to pit the new younger hoods against the vintage older bosses.

These four gangsters came from immigrant families on New York's lower East Side, which at that time (around 1917) was steeped in poverty and oppression. To illustrate this fact, and perhaps to pay tribute to the old Warner Bros. films, the opening of *Mobsters* is shot in black and white. This technique helps to achieve a certain street grittiness and to create the look of Matt and Hester streets, where the four main characters went through their early street gang phase. The credit for this style goes to cinematographer Lajos Koltai, whose work was seen in *White Palace* (1990) and in the Oscar-winning foreign film *Mephisto* (1981), and also to production designer Richard Sylbert, a two-time Oscar winner for *Dick Tracy* (1990) and *Who's Afraid of Virginia Woolf?* (1966).

The story begins to unfold against this rather stark and impressive backdrop, and the audience is given rather quick glimpses of the events that drove these young men to become giants in the crime world. Luciano saved Lansky's life, who had been the head of a rival gang, the four youths witnessed the assassination of a relative at the feet of Don Masseria (Quinn), and Luciano stood by as his father was humiliated by Don Faranzano (Michael Gambon). Although these were significant experiences that haunted the youths, they are given only several minutes of screen time. If close attention has not been paid to these vignettes, then most people will be confused by the complicated story line.

Director Michael Karbelnikoff, who made his feature debut with *Mobsters*, gained recognition primarily for directing some memorable commercials. This background is evident in the film's next scene. Five years have gone by, and the audience sees four dashing, debonair men, eyes flashing and looking like runway models. Unfortunately, this scene is the first indication that the film is mostly style and little substance. While many well-known gangsters were well-groomed fashion plates, these real-life bosses always possessed a darkly threatening quality lurking underneath the freshly pressed suit. In *Mobsters*, the actors simply seem to be posing, and there is nothing menacing about them, nothing smoldering underneath their handsome faces.

The true story of Luciano, Lansky, Siegel, and Costello is remarkable because they were the architects of organized crime. Prohibition was originally intended to control the behavior of American society, but it created the opposite effect: Bootlegging, the foundation on which they built their empire, unleashed a frenzy of crime on the country. It turned street thugs into rich crime bosses. Such individuals are rich, complex personalities, but *Mobsters* chooses to deal with only the veneer of their story, the gloss and the cosmetics, without touching on its heart and soul.

Luciano formed an alliance with the three other men at a time when a gang war was brewing between two powerful dons: Masseria and Faranzano. Luciano was able to play the older dons, like pawns on a chessboard, by his cunning, his calculating brilliance, and his charm. He kept his vendetta against both men in check until the right moment to strike and to finish some old "family business."

This central figure of Luciano requires a presence and a power to contend with the vintage dons. The character should be a stalking panther ready to pounce on his prey with precision and accuracy, all the while being outwardly charming and amiable. It certainly is a rich subtext for an actor, but Christian Slater portrays Luciano like a college kid hanging out with his buddies. There is no finesse or skill to his character, no street savvy, no substance, and it is inconceivable that he is capable of masterminding this complicated plot. In the scene where Faranzano hangs him by his thumbs, burns him with cigarettes, and slashes his face, Slater reacts as if it were some college fraternity prank rather than an extremely serious threat.

The rest of the young gangsters seem to be more interested in their own sex appeal than in relating to one another as friends. None of them even remotely indicates that he had any history with the others. The real-life gangsters were boyhood friends who became a family and worked as a close-knit unit with precision and lethal accuracy. They had a bond that cemented them together and made them a force to be reckoned with by even the most powerful members of the mob. Yet, the audience never sees this quality in *Mobsters*. Instead, there are four young actors posing and parading through the script with no common thread between them—except perhaps, their clothes. With no real relationships propelling the story forward, the film fails to capture any sustained interest.

Robert F. Chicatelli

Reviews
American Film: Magazine of the Film and Television Arts. XVI, July, 1991, p. 51.

Boxoffice. September, 1991, p. R-60.
Chicago Tribune. July 26, 1991, VII, p. 38.
The Christian Science Monitor. August 23, 1991, p. 14.
Films in Review. XLII, September, 1991, p. 341.
The Hollywood Reporter. July 26, 1991, p. 10.
Los Angeles Times. July 26, 1991, p. F1.
The New York Times. July 26, 1991, p. B5.
Premiere. IV, August, 1991, p. 68.
USA Today. July 26, 1991, p. D1.
Variety. July 26, 1991, p. 3.
The Washington Post. July 26, 1991, p. D6.

MY FATHER'S GLORY
(LA GLOIRE DE MON PÈRE)

Origin: France
Released: 1990
Released in U.S.: 1991
Production: Alan Poiré for Gaumont, Productions de la Gueville, and TF1 Films; released by Orion Classics
Direction: Yves Robert
Screenplay: Jérôme Tonnère, Louis Nucera, and Yves Robert; based on the autobiography by Marcel Pagnol
Cinematography: Robert Alazraki
Editing: Pierre Gillette
Production design: Jacques Dugied
Art direction: Marc Goldstaub and Guy Azzi
Casting: Gérard Moulevrier
Sound: Monique Andre
Costume design: Agnès Negre
Music: Vladimir Cosma
MPAA rating: G
Running time: 110 minutes

Principal characters:
Joseph .... Philippe Caubère
Augustine .... Nathalie Roussel
Uncle Jules .... Didier Pain
Aunt Rose .... Thérèse Liotard
Marcel .... Julien Ciamaca
Paul .... Victorien Delmare
Lili .... Joris Molinas
Marcel (five years old) .... Benoit Martin

Paying homage to a happy childhood spent in turn-of-the-century southern France, *My Father's Glory* is based on the first volume of the autobiography of Marcel Pagnol, *Souvenirs d'enfance* (1957; *Memories of Childhood*). Pagnol was a French novelist, playwright, filmmaker, and one of the elite few to be inducted into the Académie Française.

Highlighting Pagnol's early life, the narrator, the adult Marcel, relates in the first person key events in the life of young Marcel (Benoit Martin), starting with his birth in Aubagne to his young and pretty seamstress mother, Augustine (Nathalie Roussel), and his schoolteacher father, Joseph (Philippe Caubère). The narrative then proceeds quickly through Marcel's early years, dwelling on his learning to read when only four years old: When Augustine would go out shopping, she would bring the toddler into

Joseph's classroom to sit quietly until her return. One day, Marcel surprises Joseph by responding to a statement written on the blackboard, after which his father proceeds to test him in an amusing scene underscoring the developing bond of pride between father and son. The two begin to spend a considerable amount of time together. In one instance, when Marcel and Joseph are at his father's school, another teacher returns from his vacation bursting with pride. He has a photograph of himself with a fish he caught on his trip. Joseph says a few condescending words and walks away, telling Marcel that vanity is the worst of sins.

As with most memories of childhood, certain events stand out, and Marcel dwells on the most memorable occasions. One such memory is of Marcel and his aunt Rose (Thérèse Liotard) going to the park every Sunday. Rose, Augustine's sister and a spinster, stays with Marcel's family, now living in Marseilles. One time, "their" bench is taken, occupied by a rather large, well-dressed gentleman. Aunt Rose wants to pass on, but Marcel stamps his foot and gets his way—the gentleman on the bench moves his things and yields a spot for Rose to sit down. When Marcel returns from playing, he finds them happily engaged in conversation. From that day forward, the bench is always occupied by this same man, Jules (Didier Pain). Marcel is told by Rose that the man is the owner of the park, and that Marcel must never tell anyone about him or he will not let them come back. Their meetings in the park become more frequent. One day, when Marcel and Rose go as usual to the park, which is completely deserted because of a pouring rain, they meet Jules, who has been waiting for them despite the downpour. In a heart-warming scene, Rose and Jules waltz in the rain to Vladimir Cosma's swelling score and are married soon afterward.

After the couple's honeymoon, Uncle Jules confesses to Marcel that he is not really the owner of the park, an extremely romantic notion to the child, but is in truth a mere deputy clerk. It is at this point that Marcel first experiences disillusionment with the adult world: Adults can lie. Jules will later go so far as to tell Marcel that adults can lie to children if it is for their own good.

Although the sisters, Rose and Augustine, get along well, Jules and Joseph have their differences. Old-world, traditionalist Jules attends mass; Joseph, the scientific and educated man, disdains any religious sentiment. Despite their differences, both families remain close, and they decide to spend a joint vacation in a rustic cabin in the Provence countryside. This excursion forms the remainder of the story. By this time, both families have grown in number. Marcel is now eleven years old (now played by Julien Ciamaca), and he has a five-year-old brother, Paul (Victorien Delmare), and a baby sister. Also, Rose and Jules have a new baby. Once they arrive, the family returns to the basics: The boys bathe nude outside with hoses, while the two men shave cheek to cheek, sharing the mirror and singing a duet. It is amid this idyllic setting that Uncle Jules proposes a hunting trip which bespectacled academician Joseph cannot refuse.

Marcel is proud of his father, but he is afraid that Jules is a better hunter and will put Joseph to shame by bringing back the most game. Marcel is humiliated when Jules stumps his father by asking him what the best game in the area is. (The answer is the bartavelle, a type of partridge.) Marcel decides that he must also go in order to help

Joseph. When his father tells him that he cannot because he is too little, he throws a temper tantrum. Jules then magnanimously tells Marcel that "of course" he may go. Satisfied, Marcel goes up to bed with his brother. Alone together, Paul tells Marcel that he saw the adults packing for the hunt, that they are going the next day (not the following one as they had told Marcel), and that they plan to slip out early before he is awake. Incensed and remembering that Jules has lied to him before, Marcel decides to follow them without their knowledge.

The trip turns into an adventure for Marcel—one that he likens to that of Robinson Crusoe, about whom he is reading—as he follows his father and uncle, surreptitiously scares out game for his father to shoot, becomes lost in the wilderness, and makes friends with a local boy, Lili (Joris Molinas). The trip proves to be a reaffirmation of his filial pride when, upon finding Joseph and Jules, he emerges from the brush brandishing two bartavelles that his father shot: "my father's glory." When Joseph and Marcel make a proud trek to the village to show off the birds, they run into the local priest, whom Joseph has been avoiding. The priest, however, is very knowledgeable about the bartavelle, impressing educated Joseph. When the priest offers to take a photograph of Joseph with his quarry, Marcel's flattered father poses with the birds in a scene reminiscent of the beginning of the film, when Joseph's colleague showed off his fish photograph. Instead of disliking his father, Marcel instead poses with him, the narrator voicing his realization that his father was not perfect, but that his actions merely pointed up how human he was.

Among other things, the film is a study in the art of growing up. Marcel admires his father for his intelligence and high ideals, yet he learns to accept Joseph's limitations, as well as the occasional contradictions between his words and his actions. The film also highlights the character's ambiguity when confronted with the vast changes of the new century: When Joseph starts his new post in Marseilles, he begins with a lecture on the marvels of the new age. It is October 1, 1900, and Joseph lauds the technological advances that will come to fruition in the coming century. He is full of hope looking forward to all the time-saving devices that will be invented, to electricity, gas, and telephones. Yet, although the characters welcome these innovations—Joseph and Augustine admire Rose and Jules's new gas stove and lights—the film ends with the happiest time of the families' lives: their return to nature to revel in a simpler and more basic way of life.

Ciamaca is enchanting in the lead as the eleven-year-old Marcel, with his sensitive good looks and fine acting. When he kisses his mother's hand or helps her change to walking shoes on a dusty country road, he conveys the devotion of a loving son for a young mother who is more like a pretty older sister. Caubère is excellent as the priggish yet sincere schoolteacher, with his wire-rimmed glasses that never leave his face and his stiff collar. Pain, with his large frame, heavy accent (rolling the letter *r* in a way which even an American can appreciate), and his pockets full of sweets, is a study in comic excess.

The scenes of Provence are sweeping, conveying the vastness of the rural country-side and replete with the almost constant chirp of the cicadas. Cinematographer

Robert Alazraki has captured the beauty and power of a summer storm and a huge, almost surreal, country moon. The men play boules in the village square, boys bring home huge loaves of unwrapped bread under their arms, and families stroll in the park on Sunday after church. The director, Yves Robert, a former colleague of Pagnol, has indeed evoked the essence of a bygone age, the France of Maurice Chevalier, but without the citified sophistication of Paris. Robert said that he wanted to make a film of Pagnol's memoirs for a long time and even approached Pagnol in the 1960's with the idea. It was not until long after Pagnol's death, however, that he was granted the rights. His care in presenting this much-coveted project is evident throughout the film—in his choice of actors and the performances that he wins from each and in his astute treatment of the subject matter.

Although American audiences may find the film a bit slow-moving, it was extremely popular in France. *My Father's Glory* is a rare film: There is no sex or violence, no nasty surprises, no Freudian interpretations. The story is a simple one of Pagnol's appreciation of and fondness for his childhood and his love for his family. He does not regret the passage of the "good old days"; instead, he realizes that any era can be magic when one is a child. Moreover, he shows that the passage from the fantasy of childhood to the reality of adulthood need not be disillusioning but can, instead, enhance one's love and understanding of the world. These memories of childhood are like his remote cabin in Provence: They offer a means of recapturing a time and place which are dear to him.

Cynthia K. Breckenridge

Reviews
Boxoffice. September, 1991, p. R-64.
Chicago Tribune. August 9, 1991, VII, p. 26.
The Christian Science Monitor. August 13, 1991, p. 11.
The Hollywood Reporter. January 14, 1991, p. 20.
Los Angeles Times. July 5, 1991, p. F6.
The New Republic. CCV, July 15, 1991, p. 28.
The New York Times. June 21, 1991, p. B4.
Sight and Sound. I, June, 1991, p. 43.
Time. CXXXVII, July 1, 1991, p. 75.
Variety. January 10, 1991, p. 14.
The Wall Street Journal. June 27, 1991, p. A12.
The Washington Post. July 19, 1991, p. B6.

MY GIRL

Production: Brian Grazer for Imagine Films Entertainment and Howard Zieff; released by Columbia Pictures
Direction: Howard Zieff
Screenplay: Laurice Elehwany
Cinematography: Paul Elliott
Editing: Wendy Greene Bricmont
Production design: Joseph T. Garrity
Art direction: Pat Tagliaferro
Set decoration: Linda Allen
Casting: Mary Colquhoun
Sound: Steve C. Aaron
Costume design: Karen Patch
Music: James Newton Howard
MPAA rating: PG
Running time: 102 minutes

Principal characters:

Harry Sultenfuss	Dan Aykroyd
Shelly DeVoto	Jamie Lee Curtis
Thomas J. Sennett	Macaulay Culkin
Vada Sultenfuss	Anna Chlumsky
Phil Sultenfuss	Richard Masur
Mr. Bixler	Griffin Dunne
Gramoo Sultenfuss	Ann Nelson
Dr. Welty	Peter Michael Goetz
Nurse Randall	Jane Hallaren
Judy	Cassi Abel
Thomas J.'s mother	Glenda Chism

Eleven-year-old Vada Sultenfuss (Anna Chlumsky) is a quirky young lady. She has been living, she tells the audience, for three years with a chicken bone stuck in her throat, and now she believes that she has breast cancer. She knows this because her left breast is growing significantly faster than her right. Her father, Harry (Dan Aykroyd), is even quirkier—when she informs him that she has breast cancer, he asks her to get the mayonnaise from the refrigerator. All this is in the first sequence of *My Girl.* In the second, Vada collects money from a group of boys to show them a corpse; in the process, one discovers not only that her father is a mortician but also that this is another dimension of family living. Vada explains to the boys that the corpses sometimes are not quite dead, and the one she promised to show them has escaped. She then "finds" it in the body of her Gramoo (Ann Nelson), sitting peacefully in the den to the terror of her granddaughter's young clients; the truth of the matter is that Gramoo lives in a virtually impenetrable fog. Like the family in George S. Kaufman and Moss Hart's *You Can't Take It with You*, the Sultenfusses say much about "normal" family life through their own eccentricities.

Her mother's death in childbirth and her father's profession combine to produce an obsession with death and dying in Vada. She is, in short, a hypochondriac who regularly visits her doctor (Peter Michael Goetz) with complaints of every illness from which her father's clients have died—including cancer of the prostate. In contrast, her best friend, Thomas J. Sennett (Macaulay Culkin), is a normal eleven-year-old kid, but he is allergic to "everything." Together, they ride bikes, fish, play cards, discuss life and adult behavior and the future, and share a first kiss. *My Girl* considers Vada's relationships to her father—who has withdrawn from emotional life since his wife's death—to Thomas J., and to the prospect of adulthood.

To add to Vada's confusion about her place in the world, a new woman enters the Sultenfuss family scene. Harry places an advertisement for a makeup artist, and Shelly DeVoto (Jamie Lee Curtis) answers it. She decides to take the job because "all of my former clients are going to die, and everyone here used to be alive, so they have something in common." She lives in a motor home, dresses like a hippie, and brings warmth into an otherwise alienated household. She tries to suggest to Harry that he talk with Vada and pay more attention to her, an idea that he rejects as unnecessary. Nevertheless, Shelly succeeds in bringing Harry out of his shell through romance: For his first date in twenty years, Harry takes her to his weekly bingo game.

Over the course of the summer, Vada registers for an adult creative writing course given by her English teacher (Griffin Dunne), with whom she is madly in love. She and Thomas J. continue their rounds of the neighborhood and eleven-year-old preoccupations, and Shelly and Harry grow closer and closer. When Vada panics because she is hemorrhaging, Shelly explains menstruation to her, an aspect of womanhood that Vada finds extremely unfair. Shelly and Harry decide to marry, and Vada worries that her father loves Shelly more than her.

One day, Vada and Thomas J. discover a beehive that they assume has been abandoned. They knock it down with rocks, and when the bees come swarming out, they run frantically down to the lake and jump into it. In the process, however, Vada has lost her mood ring in the woods. Days later, Thomas J. goes back to find it, and as he does the bees attack him. Because he is allergic to bee stings, he does not survive the attack. When Vada learns of his death, all of her worst fears and imaginings converge and come to crisis. She is certain that she causes death—both her mother's and Thomas J.'s—and that she is important to no one. She confesses her love to Mr. Bixler, her English teacher, who tries to let her down gently until Vada sees a woman leaving his house, whom he introduces as his fiancée. Vada flees, believing her nightmares confirmed: Her father prefers Shelly, Mr. Bixler prefers Suzanne, and she is unloved.

Through the process of learning to grieve for Thomas J., Vada discovers that her father does not blame her for her mother's death, that he indeed loves her very much, and that he understands her feelings about losing Thomas J. She develops a new friendship with Judy (Cassi Abel), and returns to—or perhaps finds for the first time—a "normal" eleven-year-old everyday routine.

The issues raised in *My Girl* range widely—from the philosophical questions of mortality to the psychological processes of grief, from adolescence to family relationships and structures, from friendship to sexuality. The press kit provided by Columbia Pictures contains, unusually, statements from four child development experts on the relevance of this film for young people. While there may be a range of feelings about the suitability of the film for children, the inclusion of this material makes it clear that Columbia envisions the film as a serious treatment of important emotional issues.

This "self-image" has both positive and negative consequences. On the one hand, *My Girl* treats both adolescence and grieving with unusual complexity and sensitivity. Vada's confusion over adult sexuality and marriage provokes her to explore these matters with Thomas J. As they sit in the willow tree by the side of the lake, she asks him why people get married and suggests that they try a kiss, "like they do on TV" (as Thomas J. puts it), to "see what all the fuss is about." After they kiss—the briefest lip-to-lip contact imaginable—Vada panics at the silence between them. She tells Thomas J. to say something, to which he responds by standing up, putting his hand over his heart, and reciting the "Pledge of Allegiance." Vada immediately joins in. Rarely has a film scene been more faithful to the sense of early adolescence in all its curiosity and terror.

On the other hand, *My Girl* sometimes lapses into an annoying pretension. Particularly frustrating is director Howard Zieff's telegraphing of Thomas J.'s death. At every opportunity, he drops a clue to the coming catastrophe. While Vada carries on about her various "illnesses," Thomas J. mentions his severe allergies only in passing. There is a long close-up of a dead fish in the water, and when Vada asks if it got away, Thomas J. tells her it did. During their first encounter with the beehive, they yell "Run for your life!" as the bees attack. Nurse Randall (Jane Hallaren) asks Thomas J. why Vada is so preoccupied with illness and death, and when Thomas J. replies that it is because she is trying to understand it, Nurse Randall tells him how lucky Vada is to have him as a friend. Zieff hits viewers over the head with an anvil to make sure that they are prepared for Thomas J.'s demise in exactly the ways that Vada was not. This technique infantilizes viewers, drawing them into collusion with a superiority over Vada that they may not, or may not want to, feel.

The resolution of Vada's difficulties with grieving is similarly unsatisfying. During one of the final sequences, she is eating in a restaurant with her father, and Thomas J.'s mother (Glenda Chism) walks by. They chat, and Mrs. Sennett gives Vada her mood ring, which Thomas J. was found holding. Vada promises to visit the Sennett's, and as Mrs. Sennett is walking away, Vada calls out to her: "Don't worry about Thomas J., Mrs. Sennett. My mother will take care of him." While this is surely a neat gesture of closure, signaling the fact that Vada has come to terms with both deaths, it is also clichéd. At precisely these moments, *My Girl* is reminiscent of *Terms of Endearment* (1983). It works, and it works well, but its predictability leaves a seed of resentment behind that undermines its effect.

To the credit of Zieff, director of photography Paul Elliott, production designer Joseph T. Garrity, and editor Wendy Greene Bricmont, however, *My Girl* has an uncommonly fast pace for a drama. The continuous motion of the camera and lively editing pace, juxtaposed with the peaceful, green small-town setting, make *My Girl* a visual magnet that can appeal to a wide audience. Unlike most films focused on relationships, *My Girl* provides a degree of visual activity belied by the relative quiet of the on-screen events, which means that neither fans of MTV-era quick-cutting techniques nor devotees of dialogue-based filmmaking will be disappointed.

James Newton Howard's score takes a similar tack. Howard uses twenty-three songs, including Creedence Clearwater Revival's "Bad Moon Rising," George and Ira Gershwin's "I Got Rhythm," and Ravi Shankar's "Maru-Bihag," but he chooses more traditional scoring techniques for most of the action in the film. While many contemporary films use mainly popular music—such as *The Big Chill* (1983) and *Good Morning, Vietnam* (1987)—and many others use classical orchestral scores—such as *Dead Again* (1991; reviewed in this volume) and *Terminator II: Judgment Day* (1991; reviewed in this volume)—the soundtrack for *My Girl* is peppered with popular songs connected by orchestral tissue. Moreover, Howard does not use songs only when the characters can hear them; some kinds of scenes (such as the one with Vada and Thomas J. riding bikes) are scored in some cases with songs, in others with orchestral music. This eclecticism gives the score flexibility and, as a fringe benefit, marketability as a soundtrack album. It does not, however, give the film a definitive musical image.

Actually, unevenness may well be the hallmark of *My Girl*. It promises a level of insight it cannot deliver—that families, adolescence, and grieving are all relational processes is not news. Without the psychological and philosophical pretensions of its marketing, however, it is an endearing and enjoyable film. Without the artistic pretensions of its direction, it would have been an unqualified pleasure.

Anahid Kassabian

Reviews
Boston Globe. November 27, 1991, p. 23.
Boxoffice. January, 1992, p. R-2.
Chicago Tribune. November 27, 1991, V, p. 1.
The Christian Science Monitor. December 30, 1991, p. 11.
The Hollywood Reporter. November 27, 1991, p. 11.
Los Angeles Times. November 27, 1991, p. F8.
Maclean's. CIV, December 9, 1991, p. 55.
The New York Times. November 27, 1991, p. B3.
Newsweek. CXVIII, December 9, 1991, p. 74.
San Francisco Chronicle. November 27, 1991, p. E1.
Variety. November 26, 1991, p. 2.
The Wall Street Journal. December 5, 1991, p. A12.

MY MOTHER'S CASTLE
(LE CHÂTEAU DE MA MÈRE)

Origin: France
Released: 1990
Released in U.S.: 1991
Production: Alain Poiré for Gaumont, Productions de la Gueville, and TF1 Films; released by Orion Classics
Direction: Yves Robert
Screenplay: Jérôme Tonnère, Louis Nucera, and Yves Robert; based on the autobiography by Marcel Pagnol
Cinematography: Robert Alazraki
Editing: Pierre Gillette
Production design: Jacques Dugied
Art direction: Marc Goldstaub and Guy Azzi
Casting: Gérard Moulevrier
Sound: Monique Andre
Costume design: Agnès Negre
Music: Vladimir Cosma
MPAA rating: PG
Running time: 98 minutes

Principal characters:

Marcel	Julien Ciamaca
Joseph	Philippe Caubère
Augustine	Nathalie Roussel
Uncle Jules	Didier Pain
Aunt Rose	Thérèse Liotard
Paul	Victorien Delmare
Lili	Joris Molinas
Drunken guard	Jean Carmet
Bouzigue	Philippe Uchan
Isabelle	Julie Timmerman
Marcel (forty years old)	Alain Ganas
Marcel (as narrator)	Jean-Pierre Darras

According to French novelist Marcel Pagnol, life consists of moments of joy obliterated by moments of unforgettable sorrow. Yet, two films based on his memoirs, *La Gloire de mon père* (1990; *My Father's Glory*, 1991; reviewed in this volume) and *My Mother's Castle*, shot simultaneously with the same casts, are joyous views of life in which the sorrow remains mostly unmentioned. In *My Mother's Castle*, the death of Augustine (Nathalie Roussel), the mother of Marcel (Julien Ciamaca), is given brief treatment—a voice-over coupled with a shot of Marcel's hand clasping his brother's as they follow the casket in the funeral cortege. The deaths of Marcel's brother, Paul (Victorien Delmare), and his friend Lili des Bellons (Joris Molinas) are included as part of a summary of the years between Marcel's boyhood, which is the film's focus, and his adult life as a filmmaker, which is represented briefly in the film's denouement.

My Mother's Castle is a reminiscence of richly gratifying, easy-to-ponder portions of life, not an exploration of troublesome conflicts or the disturbing tangles that occur in human relationships. It is a gentle, calming film. (Quite understandably, Air France screened it on transatlantic flights.) The most sustained and intense look at a character's discomfort—"pain" would be too strong a word—grows out of Pagnol's memory of his father, Joseph (Philippe Caubère), breaking the law. Joseph trespasses with his family in order to shorten their walk to the village of La Treille in the hills of Provence, where they have a country villa. A former student of Joseph, Bouzigue (Philippe Uchan), is employed as a canal spiker, who checks and writes reports on the canal's condition. He presents his former teacher with a key to unlock doors in the walls that separate the grounds of a series of adjacent private estates, and he encourages the family to travel the expeditious canalside route. Joseph feels great trepidation about doing something so irregular, but at the persistent urging of his family and of Bouzigue, he finally relents. What follows are amusing sequences in which the crouching family, afraid of being seen, make their way from one door to the next. Soon this becomes part of the routine itinerary to their country villa.

In a climactic sequence, as the family approaches the final leg of their illegal journey, Augustine becomes paralyzed with fear because of a premonition that they will be caught. She subdues her apprehension, and they go on. Joseph discovers that the final door, which gives them passage to legitimate roads, has been chained and padlocked. They are trapped on the property, with the imposing manor house towering over them in the distance like an ominous, living presence. An arrogantly petty, power-greedy guard (Jean Carmet), probably emboldened by drink, and his mangy, barking, but seemingly harmless dog, Masher, confront them, and the guard takes full advantage of his opportunity to humiliate them. Joseph, keenly aware of the fact that one loses one's power when one is wrong, suffers the indignity mostly in silence. Augustine finds the episode too much to bear and faints. Afterward, Joseph fears that he will be dismissed from his teaching position when the guard's report is filed and it becomes known that he broke the law. He is indeed affecting as, nearly in tears, he expresses his apprehension to Augustine. Consistent with the film's tone, this conflict is resolved happily.

In the denouement, the adult Marcel (Alain Ganas), without realizing it, has purchased for his newly founded film company the very estate that contains what had been the castle of his mother's fear. In an emotional and symbolic gesture, he picks up a boulder and smashes open the door that had been locked years earlier, prohibiting the family's escape.

The screenplay employs an episodic structure suitable for its biographical content. Mostly, pleasant incidents are included: happy exchanges between Marcel and his mother, an outdoor dinner party with friends, Marcel daydreaming about his beloved

Provençal hills instead of paying attention to his teacher, his preparation to represent his school in the scholarship exams, the family arriving at La Treille for holidays and being greeted by Marcel's boyhood friend Lili, who, Marcel realizes, probably has waited hours for their appearance. There are no wrenching family struggles; parents take gentle admonishment from their children with surprising grace and good humor. Even the poetic justice doled out to the belligerent guard is of a mild, amusing sort, nothing like the painful confrontations that occur in some of Pagnol's fiction.

There is a hilarious sequence depicting one of Marcel's rites of passage—his first infatuation with a member of the opposite sex. Isabelle (Julie Timmerman), the daughter of an alcoholic poet, lives near their vacation retreat. The boy's admiration for her becomes unbounded when she plays the piano for him; the miracle of seeing her delicate hands make such music moves him profoundly. She takes advantage of her new admirer by persuading him to play games in which he subjugates his will to hers and performs such demeaning acts as assuming the guise of a slave fanning her reclining figure, or getting down on his knees and barking like a dog. Marcel's spying brother happens to witness some of the worst indignities and reports them to their father; Joseph—to Marcel's amazement—becomes highly intolerant of having his son humiliated and forbids Marcel to see her again.

One of director Yves Robert's main accomplishments in the film is to keep this good-spirited story of a successful family from becoming saccharine. There are moments that nearly do, such as a lingering close-up shot of the young Marcel's face as he reacts to being fed cod liver oil; freeze the frame in the shot's final moment and the result would be the French equivalent of a Norman Rockwell illustration. Yet, the extremely brief dalliances with being charming are overwhelmed by the basic honesty and forthrightness of the work. Cinematographer Robert Alazraki's camera roams the Provençal hills lovingly but unostentatiously. The voice-overs of the elderly Marcel (Jean-Pierre Darras), which link the segments, make it clear that these are an old man's reminiscences of his childhood; it is easy to accept that the distance of time has put a veil over specific details to make most look pleasant.

Robert focuses on moments in which characters express their depth of feeling for one another unashamedly. In one, Joseph admits touchingly to his son that he is afraid that he will lose him after Marcel has gone to the lycée, where he will probably grow smarter than his father; Marcel rejoins that he will teach his father everything that he learns. In another sequence, Uncle Jules (Didier Pain) tells Joseph that, during Christmas Mass, he has asked God to show His presence to his brother-in-law. The family members become uneasy momentarily because Joseph is an atheist. To their relief, he replies that the prayer is evidence of his friendship and thanks Jules for that gift. The two friends embrace repeatedly as the beaming family watches.

The wholesomeness and nurturing character of family life seems part of Pagnol's faith. Even in his novels, *Jean de Florette* (1962) and *Manon des Sources* (1962), in which sorrow often obliterates joy, one can see a consistency of perspective: The good people are decent family people, and their sometimes villainous adversaries are single men living alone.

My Mother's Castle is richly supplied with moments of loving human interaction. It is a sharp contrast to many current motion pictures where a commonplace image—rather than two friends embracing—is one man or woman destroying the body of another. Art can serve by helping people to confront life's thornier questions: its unpleasantness, catastrophes, and violence. Yet, there is also a need for artistic acknowledgment and reinforcement of what is positive. *My Mother's Castle* performs the latter function admirably.

Cono Robert Marcazzo

Reviews
Boxoffice. September, 1991, p. R-64.
Chicago Tribune. September 13, 1991, VII, p. 31.
The Christian Science Monitor. August 13, 1991, p. 11.
The Hollywood Reporter. July 22, 1991, p. 10.
Los Angeles Times. August 2, 1991, p. F8.
National Review. XLIII, September 23, 1991, p. 56.
The New Republic. CCV, July 15, 1991, p. 28.
The New York Times. July 26, 1991, p. B3.
Sight and Sound. I, August, 1991, p. 40.
Time. CXXXVII, July 1, 1991, p. 75.
Variety. January 15, 1991, p. 14.
The Village Voice. XXXVI, September 3, 1991, p. 53.
The Washington Post. August 16, 1991, p. D6.

MY OWN PRIVATE IDAHO

Production: Laurie Parker for New Line Cinema; released by Fine Line Features
Direction: Gus Van Sant, Jr.
Screenplay: Gus Van Sant, Jr.
Cinematography: Eric Alan Edwards and John Campbell
Editing: Curtiss Clayton
Production design: David Brisbin
Art direction: Ken Hardy
Set decoration: Melissa Stewart
Sound: Reinhard Stergar, Robert Marts, Jan Cyr, and Jon Huck
Costume design: Beatrix Aruna Pasztor
MPAA rating: R
Running time: 102 minutes

Principal characters:
Mike Waters	River Phoenix
Scott Favor	Keanu Reeves
Richard Waters	James Russo
Bob Pigeon	William Richert
Gary	Rodney Harvey
Carmella	Chiara Caselli
Digger	Michael Parker
Denise	Jessie Thomas
Budd	Flea
Alena	Grace Zabriskie
Jack Favor	Tom Troupe
Hans	Udo Kier
Jane Lightwork	Sally Curtice
Walt	Robert Lee Pitchlynn
Daddy Carroll	Mickey Cottrell

Director/screenwriter Gus Van Sant, Jr., specializes in quirky, scruffy-looking films about down-and-out lowlifes, street hustlers, drug addicts, and destitute people barely surviving on the edge of society. He also specializes in compassion. His previous film, *Drugstore Cowboy* (1989), was a profoundly moving examination of the life of a teenage junkie as he and his muddle-headed gang of drug addicts stumble around the Pacific Northwest robbing drug stores and hospitals. Although the characters were hardly model citizens, Van Sant managed to make them wonderfully real and compassionate human beings worthy of the audience's sympathy.

With *My Own Private Idaho*, Van Sant returns to the seamy, desperately impoverished world of street hustlers, a world that he had explored previously in his first film, *Mala Noche* (1986). Mixing styles as disparate as those of William Shakespeare, cinema verité, and gay porn films, Van Sant once again infuses his film with a deeply felt compassion and a love for society's losers.

The film opens on a dictionary definition of narcolepsy—"a condition characterized by brief attacks of deep sleep." Then, a lonely stretch of highway somewhere in Idaho fills the screen. Mike Waters (River Phoenix) stands beside the road waiting for a ride and speaks to himself about having been on this road before, a road that he calls his own. Mike is suddenly gripped by a series of blurry, faded, home film-type images of himself as a child being comforted by his mother. Then, with these old memories swirling in his mind along with images of a small farmhouse alone in a gorgeous landscape with swirling clouds overhead, Mike collapses in the middle of the highway and sinks into a private, narcoleptic dream world. Other images of sun-drenched vistas and salmon spawning in a swiftly running river continue to bathe the screen, accompanied by the comical yet haunting country song "Lonesome Cattle Call," featuring yodeling expert Tex Owens. As the images slowly fade, the scene changes to a dingy Seattle hotel room where Mike, sitting and shivering in a chair, is being fellated by a scrungy, obese man. When Mike reaches orgasm, he imagines his country farmhouse falling from the sky and crashing on the deserted Idaho road.

After his hotel encounter, Mike, a gay street hustler, returns to his usual urban haunts, standing along busy street corners or in front of adult bookstores waiting to be picked up by male clients. Mike is surprised when he is picked up by a wealthy older woman, Alena (Grace Zabriskie), who takes him to her mansion for a sex session. Once there, he encounters two fellow hustlers who have also been hired by Alena. One of the young men is Mike's friend Scott Favor (Keanu Reeves), who the audience later learns is the son of the mayor of Portland and is destined to inherit a fortune on his twenty-first birthday, which is only a week away. Unlike Mike, Scott is heterosexual and only engages in homosexual relationships as a form of rebellion against his upscale father. Mike's encounter with Alena ends before it has a chance to begin when she approaches him in her bedroom and he has one of his narcoleptic fits, brought on by the fact that she reminds him of his mother. When he awakes the next morning, he is in the arms of Scott, both of them having been driven to Portland by one of Alena's friends, Hans (Udo Kier), an aggressively gay car parts salesman.

In a wonderfully comical scene, the camera swoops into an adult bookstore and pans across a wall covered with gay pornographic magazines, each of the covers of the magazines featuring photographs of some of the street hustlers. Scott is featured on a magazine entitled *Male Call*, while Mike poses on one entitled *G-String*. Suddenly, their photographs come alive, and Scott begins talking to the other young men featured on the covers of the magazines. Soon, the entire wall is alive with animated, cacophonous covers.

This playful scene segues into another radically different stylistic segment with the appearance of a chunky, middle-aged destitute man named Big Bob Pigeon (William Richert). Suddenly, the gang of rowdy hustlers begins speaking in Shakespearean-tinged dialogue, parodying the Bard's *Henry IV*. Bob is a Falstaffian father figure to the brood, and Scott is Prince Hal. Scott greets the derelict as his "psychedelic street teacher," proudly claiming Bob to be his true father, the man whom he loves more than anyone else.

The gang settles into an abandoned apartment building and reenacts several scenes from Shakespeare's famous historical play, mixing street dialogue with passages from the original. Like the original play, the gang is anxiously awaiting the day that Scott will inherit his fortune so that they can take advantage of his new wealth and escape from their desperate life-style. Scott, however, admits to Bob privately that, when he does reach his twenty-first birthday, "I don't want to have any more to do with this life. I'll change when everyone expects it the least."

When their hideout is raided by the police and Scott is forced into an unpleasant confrontation with his father (Tom Troupe), he decides to leave Portland with Mike and journey to Idaho to visit with Mike's older brother, Richard (James Russo), who lives in a decrepit trailer. The meeting with Richard is painful for Mike. He is flooded with memories of his childhood, memories of his mother abusing him and his brother and then abandoning them both. Later, when Richard tries to tell Mike who his real father is, saying that he was a Las Vegas con man who was shot to death by their mother while the family was at a drive-in theater, Mike suddenly screams that he knows the identity of his real father: Richard. Richard is stunned at the revelation and says, "You know too much." Both brothers carry deep, devastating memories of their reckless mother. Both also long for a sense of family, a sense of normalcy in their shattered, desperate lives.

When Richard shows Mike a postcard that he received from their mother when she worked as a hotel maid, Mike and Scott decide to track her down. They visit the hotel featured in the postcard and learn that she quit a year ago and traveled to Italy in search of her own family. While at the hotel, Mike and Scott encounter Hans, who invites them up to his room. Their kinky sexual encounter with the car parts salesman is filmed in a collage of expressively static poses, each pose artfully composed and bathed in warm skin tones. Afterward, the two young men sell Scott's motorcycle and use the money to journey to Italy, where they plan to continue their search for Mike's mother.

In Italy, they end up at the country farmhouse where Mike's mother was employed as a maid and an English tutor. Unfortunately, they learn from the establishment's pretty young female resident, Carmella (Chiara Caselli), that Mike's mother returned to the United States months ago. A despondent Mike rages internally while he watches Scott and Carmella become more and more intimate with each other. Finally, Scott tells Mike that he has fallen in love with Carmella and that they will be returning to the United States together.

Returning to Portland, Mike, more desperate than ever, collapses on the street while an elegantly dressed Scott is glimpsed riding by in a limousine. Later, when Mike again joins Bob and his gang, they watch as Scott and Carmella exit from their limousine and enter a posh restaurant. Realizing that Scott has come into his inheritance, the group invades the restaurant and confronts Scott. Scott, echoing Prince Hal's denouncement of his roguish association with Falstaff, tells Bob, "Now that I've changed, and until I change back, don't come near me." The dejected Bob scuttles out of the restaurant, along with the rest of Scott's hustler friends. That night, Bob has a heart attack and dies.

The next day, the hustlers hold a funeral for Bob. Nearby in the same cemetery, Scott and his new upscale associates attend a funeral for Scott's recently deceased father. The contrast in the ceremonies is strikingly apparent; the funeral for Scott's father is a sedate affair, while the ceremony for Bob is an orgiastic free-for-all.

In the final moments of the film, Mike is back on the lonely stretch of Idaho highway, a road that he again calls his own. "This road never ends," he says. "It probably goes all around the world." Mike then falls into another narcoleptic stupor, collapsing in the middle of the desolate highway. A truck suddenly pulls up and two strangers get out, steal Mike's belongings, and drive away. Then, as the camera pulls back, revealing an endless ribbon of highway, another car pulls up to the comatose Mike. The driver gathers him up in his arms and places him in his car, and the car disappears over the horizon.

My Own Private Idaho is a visually rich, stylistically eclectic odyssey detailing one man's desperate search for comfort, compassion, and a place to call home. The desire to establish family roots in a harsh environment populated by urban derelicts is a theme that Van Sant has toyed with in all of his films. In *My Own Private Idaho*, however, the theme saturates every scene. Mike is obsessed with his early memories of family life, the only pleasant memories that he has. His narcoleptic seizures are filled with dreams of his personal conception of paradise, one that includes a comforting mother and a simple farmhouse surrounded by dynamic natural beauty. Whenever harsh reality becomes too threatening or too ugly, Mike sinks into his perfect dream world and finds the life that he longs to live.

Van Sant illustrates his central theme with an amazing variety of cinematic and theatrical styles. Some of the styles, especially the scenes parodying Shakespeare's *Henry IV*, seem inappropriate for the gritty urban setting and work against the film's overall effectiveness. Yet, even these scenes are endowed with Van Sant's trademark cinema verité style and, although the *Henry IV* parody segments go on for too long, they still strongly illustrate the film's main theme, giving Mike's desire for family and home a timeless, historical resonance.

Like Van Sant's other films, the structure of *My Own Private Idaho* is very loose and episodic, appearing improvisational but in reality possessing a strong driving force that connects all the seemingly incongruous segments. The acting seems ragged and unrehearsed, yet ultimately the performances are extremely disciplined and powerfully effective. River Phoenix as the eternally befuddled Mike gives an amazing performance. His dialogue is simple, but his physical mannerisms and facial expressions strongly convey his desperate longings for family and comfort. His character's narcoleptic seizures, which happen at the most inopportune times, are both humorous and frightening, emphasizing Mike's extreme vulnerability in a world filled with brutal, manipulative con artists and borderline degenerates. Although the other cast members also give excellent performances, it is Phoenix who is truly outstanding, eliciting heartfelt sympathy from the audience.

Van Sant is a bold, innovative filmmaker. His mentor seems to be another cinematic giant, Orson Welles, to whom he pays homage in *My Own Private Idaho* by recreating key scenes from *Chimes at Midnight* (1967), Welles's own version of Shakespeare's plays featuring the rotund rogue Falstaff. Like Welles, Van Sant has created a distinct cinematic style, using it to express his own personal view of the world—a nightmarish one filled with horrors, obsessions, and above all compassion, understanding, and love for those who need it the most.

Jim Kline

Reviews

American Film: Magazine of the Film and Television Arts. XVI, September, 1991, p. 32.
Boxoffice. October, 1991, p. R-72.
Chicago Tribune. October 18, 1991, VII, p. 44.
Esquire. October, 1991, p. 52.
Film Comment. XXVII, November, 1991, p. 42.
The Hollywood Reporter. September 5, 1991, p. 5.
L.A. Weekly. October 18-24, 1991, p. 30.
Los Angeles Times. October 18, 1991, p. F1.
Maclean's. October 28, 1991, p. 101.
The New York Times. September 27, 1991, p. B1.
The New Yorker. LXVII, October 7, 1991, p. 100.
Newsweek. CXVIII, October 7, 1991, p. 66.
Variety. September 4, 1991, p. 2.
The Wall Street Journal. October 3, 1991, p. A14.
The Washington Post. October 18, 1991, p. D1.

THE NAKED GUN 2½
The Smell of Fear

Production: Robert K. Weiss for Zucker/Abrahams/Zucker; released by Paramount
   Pictures
Direction: David Zucker
Screenplay: David Zucker and Pat Proft
Cinematography: Robert Stevens
Editing: James Symons and Chris Greenbury
Production design: John J. Lloyd
Set decoration: Mickey S. Michaels
Set design: James Tocci
Casting: Mindy Marin
Sound: Richard Bryce Goodman
Costume design: Taryn Dechellis
Music: Ira Newborn
MPAA rating: PG-13
Running time: 85 minutes

> *Principal characters:*
> Lieutenant Frank Drebin . . . . Leslie Nielsen
> Jane Spencer . . . . Priscilla Presley
> Captain Ed Hocken . . . . George Kennedy
> Nordberg . . . . O. J. Simpson
> Quentin Hapsburg . . . . Robert Goulet
> Dr. Meinheimer/Earl Hacker . . . . Richard Griffiths
> Commissioner Brumford . . . . Jacqueline Brookes
> Hector Savage . . . . Anthony James
> George Bush . . . . John Roarke
> Barbara Bush . . . . Margery Ross
> John Sununu . . . . Peter Van Norden
> Ted Olsen . . . . Ed Williams
> Baggett . . . . Lloyd Bochner

   To lay out a plot summary is to mask the humor and delight of *The Naked Gun 2½:
The Smell of Fear*. The film begins as Lieutenant Frank Drebin (Leslie Nielsen), in the
nation's capitol to receive an award, makes a complete farce of a formal White House
dinner. No one misses the wrath of Drebin's misdeeds, including President George
Bush (John Roarke), First Lady Barbara Bush (Margery Ross), and White House Chief
of Staff John Sununu (Peter Van Norden). The flimsy plot then sees evil Quentin
Hapsburg (Robert Goulet) kidnap the president's wheelchair-bound energy adviser,
Dr. Meinheimer (Richard Griffiths), in an effort to favor evil oil, coal, and nuclear
energy. Drebin foils that plan and saves the nation for a progressive energy policy. In

solving the case of the kidnapped adviser, Drebin encounters and woos his lost amour, Jane Spencer (Priscilla Presley). The stage is then set for yet another sequel, to be entitled (tentatively) *The Naked Gun 33⅓: For the Record.*

The Naked Gun 2½ stands as a classic summer comedy. The humor is broad and obvious. *The Naked Gun 2½* takes direct aim at the sophomoric funny bone and hits its target. Director David Zucker, his brother, Jerry, and their longtime partner, Jim Abrahams, have made this brand of comic silliness their own. The trio created the original 1988 release, *The Naked Gun: From the Files of Police Squad!*, which had been derived from their *Police Squad!* television series of 1982. The original film proved a modest hit and, three summers later, *The Naked Gun 2½* was born.

The rules for a successful sequel have been followed strictly in *The Naked Gun 2½*. The creative trio of Zucker, Abrahams, and Zucker started by signing the four top stars from the original: Nielsen, Presley, George Kennedy, and O. J. Simpson. Their script was then dotted with variations of jokes from the original. Indeed, even the running times of the two films are the same. Yet, there is a key difference between them. Jerry Zucker and Jim Abrahams did little but bless the idea, as they were hard at work on their own careers. *The Naked Gun 2½* is David Zucker's film.

The familiar sick jokes of the original are well done here. Zucker has an eye and ear for motion pictures, television, and pop culture clichés. *The Naked Gun 2½* thus opens with a flashing red police cruiser light going everywhere, finally stopping with its driver getting out and being slapped by none other than actress Zsa Zsa Gabor. (A year earlier Gabor had made headlines around the world for slapping a Beverly Hills police officer.) For *The Naked Gun 2½*, no gag or parody seems inappropriate. Zucker's humor spans a wide range of comedic devices: from subtle parody and gentle satire to the most obvious belches, burps, and pratfalls.

The best jokes come with film references. There is a wonderful send-up of the shower sequence in Alfred Hitchcock's *Psycho* (1960) which ends with the killer and victim, here Jane Spencer, singing a duet of "The Way We Were." After Drebin and Spencer finally rendezvous in a truly blue jazz club, they go back to her place and do a wonderful rendition of entwined lovers at a potter's wheel, straight from the big hit film of the previous summer, *Ghost* (1990). (This gag was foreshadowed as the centerpiece of the film's advertising campaign.) Another joke has the consummation of Drebin and Spencer's relationship portrayed as a rocket blasting off, a train running into a tunnel, and a frankfurter lying gently in a hot dog bun. Sigmund Freud is alive and well in motion pictures.

Nielsen's Drebin is at the core of the film. He remains a curious, predictable hero, bumbling and falling to the delight of the audience. He nearly drowns and is almost decapitated by vicious dogs. This formula depends on Nielsen acting oblivious to all that is going on around him, and he is up to the task. This is hardly classic acting, but it makes for effective comedy.

Like the original, *The Naked Gun 2½* has strong political overtones. The film begins inside the White House, making fun of a popular president. The parody is biting and the portrait is hardly endearing. Roarke's Bush is nearly as effective as Dana Carvey's from the television show *Saturday Night Live*. Bush may have ranked high in popularity polls in the summer of 1991, but to Zucker, he represented the worst in ineffective leadership.

There is an overt political message, as Drebin allows Dr. Meinheimer to deliver his message for "safe and sane" energy policies. With the film's villains trying to keep the public from discovering that cleaner, safer, and less expensive fuel alternatives are available, Zucker argues that the worst elements of society reside in the oil, coal, and nuclear industries. The Safe Energy Communication Council, the Rocky Mountain Institute, and the Natural Resources Defense Council, among others, advised Zucker.

All Zucker, Abrahams, and Zucker efforts contain interesting character portraits, and *The Naked Gun 2½* is no exception. In particular, one should single out the dual role essayed by Griffiths as energy czar Dr. Meinheimer and the evil double Earl Hacker and Goulet as the evil Quentin Hapsburg. Goulet, the quintessential lounge singer, evokes a smirk which gives evil genius exactly the right look of mad foolishness.

The Naked Gun 2½ opened to a weekend take of more than $20 million in the United States and Canada, and the film made Paramount Pictures a large amount of money. The box-office attraction of *The Naked Gun 2½* was enhanced as Paramount Pictures presented a sweepstakes card, with prizes ranging from film posters to compact disk players, to anyone who purchased a ticket.

The critical response was not nearly as favorable. Most reviewers were pleased, however, as represented by two "thumbs up" from the influential Roger Ebert and Gene Siskel. *Variety* summed up typical response best by claiming that the film was "at least 2½ times less funny than its hilarious progenitor. But that still adds up to enough laughs . . . to make this a lucrative bit of silliness for hot-weather audiences."

Douglas Gomery

Reviews
Boston Globe. June 28, 1991, p. 69.
Boxoffice. September, 1991, p. R-61.
Chicago Tribune. June 28, 1991, Take 2, p. 3.
The Christian Science Monitor. July 5, 1991, p. 10.
Film Journal. July 6, 1991, p. 17.
Films in Review. XLII, September, 1991, p. 335.
The Hollywood Reporter. June 28, 1991, p. 8.
Los Angeles Times. June 28, 1991, p. F1.
The New York Times. June 28, 1991, p. B1.
The New Yorker. LXVII, July 29, 1991, p. 60.
Variety. June 28, 1991, p. 2.
The Wall Street Journal. July 11, 1991, p. A8.
The Washington Post. June 28, 1991, p. D1.

NAKED LUNCH

Origin: Canada and Great Britain
Released: 1991
Released in U.S.: 1991
Production: Jeremy Thomas; released by Twentieth Century-Fox
Direction: David Cronenberg
Screenplay: David Cronenberg; based on the book by William S. Burroughs
Cinematography: Peter Suschitzky
Editing: Ronald Sanders
Production design: Carol Spier
Art direction: James McAlteer
Set decoration: Elinor Rose Galbraith
Casting: Deidre Bowen
Sound: Bryan Day
Costume design: Denise Cronenberg
Special creatures and effects design: Chris Walas, Inc.
Music: Howard Shore
Alto saxophone solos: Ornette Coleman
MPAA rating: R
Running time: 115 minutes

Principal characters:
William Lee	Peter Weller
Joan Frost/Joan Lee	Judy Davis
Tom Frost	Ian Holm
Yves Cloquet	Julian Sands
Dr. Benway	Roy Scheider
Fadela	Monique Mercure
Hank	Nicholas Campbell
Martin	Michael Zelniker
Hans	Robert A. Silverman
Kiki	Joseph Scorsiani

David Cronenberg's film of William S. Burroughs' bizarre and highly controversial novel *Naked Lunch* (1959) is only loosely based on its source. It borrows images from the book but focuses more on Burroughs himself and the tortuous process that he endured while simultaneously battling his drug addiction and trying to write. It appears that Cronenberg constructed his film by combining elements of the novel with material from Burroughs' other writings, such as *Exterminator!* (1973), *Queer* (1985), and *Interzone* (1989). Cronenberg also uses details of Burroughs' adventures in the Beat literary movement chronicled elsewhere. The main character, William Lee (Peter

Weller), is a combination of the novel's protagonist and Burroughs, the author.

The structure of the novel was too disjointed and fragmentary to be transferred to film faithfully. The language gushes forth in hallucinatory spasms. Scenes jump unpredictably from straight narrative to frenzied vaudeville sequences in a kind of wacky montage. Characters float in and out of the action with little or no explicit comment by the author. Cronenberg, however, has made a brilliant attempt in his screenplay to depict the consciousness of Burroughs in the depths of his addiction and to show how *Naked Lunch* was vomited up from the depths of that perilous and terrifying mental state.

Cronenberg sets the film in the nightmare world of Interzone, the physical and mental region where the novel is written. In both the novel and the film, Interzone is an imaginary, metaphysical locale based on Tangier, the city where Burroughs actually wrote *Naked Lunch*. In the novel, Interzone is an obvious reference to the status of Tangier as an international zone, which it was until 1957. As a center of unregulated free enterprise, Tangier attracted drifters, schemers, and con artists from all over the world. At the same time, its reputation as a zone of permissiveness contributed to the influx, and its exotic atmosphere drew artists, poets, and writers.

Burroughs went to Tangier in 1953 to find a sanctuary, a place where he could feed his drug addiction and write without interference. He had been wandering aimlessly in the South American jungles after accidentally shooting his wife, Joan Vollmer, in Mexico City in 1951. One of the few personal possessions that Burroughs brought with him was a portable typewriter that he wanted badly to put to good use. He considered writing an account of his wife's death, but the thought of probing his subconscious on that matter frightened him. Slowly though, his plan for a novel based on his impressions of Tangier, his addiction and withdrawal began to materialize. The fragmented, unconnected quality of his work would be an actual imprint of the development of the work.

In preparing to film *Naked Lunch*, Cronenberg had planned to do much of the shooting in Tangier, but the Gulf War interfered. Cronenberg had to scramble at the last minute to relocate. In short order, a cavernous warehouse in Toronto became the setting for *Naked Lunch*. The labyrinthine passages of Interzone were constructed to simulate the Tangier Casbah as seen through the paranoid and hallucinating eyes of the main character. Cronenberg fashioned a Tangier of the imagination, a Tangier much closer to the Interzone of the novel.

The film opens in a dingy New York City apartment as Lee, an exterminator and would-be writer, runs out of bug powder while trying to spray for cockroaches. After work, he goes to a café where Hank (Nicholas Campbell) and Martin (Michael Zelniker)—two buddies based on Jack Kerouac and Allen Ginsberg, respectively—are discussing writing. Later at home, he finds his wife, Joan (Judy Davis), shooting up bug powder. She tells Lee, "It's a very literary high. A Kafka high. It makes you feel like a bug." Lee tries some himself and is soon hooked.

Shortly thereafter, Lee is picked up by some narcotics officers for questioning. At the end of the interrogation session, they leave him alone with a large, roachlike bug that identifies itself as his case officer. The bug, which speaks out of an anallike opening beneath its wings, tells Lee that his wife is an agent of Interzone Incorporated and that she may not even be human. The bug also suggests that he exterminate her. After a visit to Dr. Benway (Roy Scheider), from whom he seeks help in curing his addiction to bug powder, Lee discovers his wife at home, getting high and having "literary" sex with his friends Hank and Martin. Lee shoots Joan up with more bug powder and tells her to get ready for their "William Tell" routine. Joan places a glass on top of her head and Lee fires, missing the glass and hitting her in the forehead. (Burroughs actually killed his wife in much the same way.) Following the shooting, Lee flees to Interzone.

After arriving in Interzone, Lee buys a secondhand typewriter and begins typing up his Interzone report on Joan's death. The title of the report will be *Naked Lunch*. His contacts with homosexual patrons at an Interzone bar lead Lee to question his own sexuality. Later, while typing his report, he nods off and the typewriter meta- morphoses into a half machine/half bug, or "bugwriter." The bugwriter wants Lee to type what it dictates and casually tells Lee that "homosexuality is the best cover an agent ever had."

In one bar, Lee meets a decadent habitué who tries to sell him the black meat of a South American centipede, which is a highly potent aphrodisiac. He also encounters a mugwump, a bluish, reptilian creature with phallic tubes sprouting comblike from its head. The tubes dispense an addictive, semenlike juice. Lee also meets Tom (Ian Holm) and Joan Frost (Judy Davis again), two characters based on the expatriate writers Paul and Jane Bowles. Tom seems eccentric and fastidious, while Joan is coolly sophisticated, intelligent, and detached. She is shadowed by an Arab maid, Fadela (Monique Mercure), who practices magic in order to control her. Lee tells them that killing his wife was an accident. Tom responds that "there are no accidents." Back in Lee's room, his bugwriter tells him to seduce Joan.

Though Lee now shares his room with Kiki (Joseph Scorsiani), a male lover, he proceeds to seduce Joan Frost. Alone with her in the Frosts' apartment, Lee and Joan embrace as she types an erotic stream-of-consciousness piece on an Arabic typewriter. As Joan continues fingering the keys, the typewriter becomes sexually aroused, finally sprouting a penis. A ménage à trois ensues between it, Joan, and Lee. Following this encounter, Lee returns to his room to write. Tom Frost arrives and, waving a pistol around, attempts to steal Lee's bugwriter. Lee's reports from Interzone are piling up, and typed sheets lie scattered over the floor of his room. Lee's friends, Hank and Martin, arrive in Interzone and are greatly impressed with his work. Seeing that Lee seems depressed, they offer encouragement and help in putting his manuscript in order. Their attempts to persuade him to return to the United States are rebuffed, however, and they leave.

Yves Cloquet (Julian Sands), a wealthy and perverse Interzone expatriate, takes Lee on a drive through the countryside. Enroute Lee delivers an outrageous but comic monologue about a talking anus. (In fact, the dialogue throughout the film has the kind of witty, satirical edge found in the novel.) Cloquet, meanwhile, has designs on Lee's young lover, Kiki. In one of the most disturbing scenes in the film, Cloquet lures Kiki to his home and engages in a sex act with him that transforms both men into a creature that is half insect, half human. The creature may represent Lee's (and Burroughs') attitude both of attraction and repulsion toward homosexuality. The scene is also an example of Cronenberg's attempt to interpret an episode from Burroughs' novel literally. His genius for envisioning such creatures recalls his work in *Videodrome* (1983) and *The Fly* (1986).

Lee's bugwriter tells him that Joan is at the mugwump market with Fadela. The market itself is a kind of meat rack and torture chamber where mugwumps are bound hand and foot and hung by chains from the ceiling. These captive mugwumps are used to dispense mugwump juice to thirsty addicts. In an encounter between Lee, Joan, and Fadela, the latter reveals herself to be Dr. Benway in disguise. Lee tells Benway that he wants Joan. In the final scene, Lee and Joan drive toward the frontier of Annexia; they seem to be making their escape from the nightmare of Interzone. At the border checkpoint, guards tell Lee he must write something before he will be admitted. As if predestined to repeat the awful event that first pushed Lee to write *Naked Lunch*, he shoots Joan Frost in the head and is then welcomed to enter Annexia.

An odd assortment of creatures and mutants interacts with the humans in *Naked Lunch*. Besides the bugwriters and mugwumps, there are sex blobs (a sort of loathsome lapdog) and giant centipedes. Cronenberg, whose career was established with a string of originally conceived and successful horror films, is adept at creating a universe in which the unimaginable coexists with the mundane. All the creatures in *Naked Lunch* are the kinds of creepy-crawly things that might be conjured up by the imagination of an addict. These bizarre inhabitants of Interzone are perfect complements to the grotesque humans who reside there.

Peter Weller, best known for his role as the stoic cyborg in *Robocop* (1987) and *Robocop II* (1990), gives the character of Lee just the right blend of aloofness and controlled intensity. Judy Davis plays both Joan Lee and Joan Frost with a kind of dreamy intelligence that is almost erotic. Roy Scheider brings a playful energy to his cameo as Dr. Benway. While reviews of the film were mixed, critics were generally open-minded in assessing the film. Cronenberg's screenplay was called brash yet inspired, and one critic called the film amazingly tight and coherent. The risks that Cronenberg takes in *Naked Lunch* were probably dictated by the difficulty that he faced in bringing Burroughs' novel to the screen. In combining elements of the original *Naked Lunch* with details from Burroughs' life and by giving a more conventional structure to his story, Cronenberg has made the film more accessible than the novel. By focusing more on the writer as a lost soul submerged in the world of drugs and decadent sex, Cronenberg gives insight into not only the destructiveness of addiction but the creative process as well.

Francis Poole

Reviews

American Film: Magazine of the Film and Television Arts. XVII, January, 1992, p. 30.

Boxoffice. February, 1992, p. R-13.

Chicago Tribune. January 10, 1992, VII, p. 34.

Cinéfantastique. XXII, February, 1992, p. 12.

Film Comment. XXVIII, January/February, 1992, p. 14.

The Hollywood Reporter. December 20, 1991, p. 8.

Los Angeles Times. December 27, 1991, p. F1.

Maclean's. April 15, 1991, p. 59.

The New York Times. December 27, 1991, p. B1.

The New Yorker. LXVII, February 10, 1992, p. 81.

Newsweek. January 13, 1992, p. 67.

Rolling Stone. February 6, 1992, p. 87.

Time. CXXXVIII, December 30, 1991, p. 72.

Variety. December 20, 1991, p. 2.

The Wall Street Journal. January 16, 1992, p. A11.

The Washington Post. January 10, 1992, p. D7.

NEW JACK CITY

Production: Doug McHenry and George Jackson; released by Warner Bros.
Direction: Mario Van Peebles
Screenplay: Thomas Lee Wright and Barry Michael Cooper; based on a story by
  Wright
Cinematography: Francis Kenny
Editing: Steven Kemper
Production design: Charles C. Bennett
Art direction: Barbara Matis and Laura Brock
Sound: Frank Stetner
Costume design: Bernard Johnson
Music: Michel Colombier
MPAA rating: R
Running time: 97 minutes

> *Principal characters:*
> Nino Brown . . . . Wesley Snipes
> Scotty Appleton . . . . Ice-T
> Detective Stone . . . . Mario Van Peebles
> Nick Peretti . . . . Judd Nelson
> Gee Money . . . . Allen Payne
> Pookie . . . . Chris Rock
> Kim Park . . . . Russell Wong
> Kareem . . . . Christopher Williams
> Duh Duh Duh . . . . Bill Nunn
> Gangster . . . . Anthony DeSando

There is no question that *New Jack City* is about New York City: The film begins with a series of aerial tracking shots that take the viewer from Liberty Island across to the Battery, then up to Midtown, finally settling in Harlem. The film is tough and timely. Despite its antidrug message, however, it was also controversial.

New Jack City became controversial during its opening week because of shootings that occurred in Brooklyn, where one hundred shots were fired and one man was killed, and because of outbreaks of violence in other cities. A riot broke out at the Mann Westwood Theatre in Los Angeles when 1,500 patrons had to be turned away from the theater on opening night. Mario Van Peebles, the director, appeared on television to assure viewers that such random violence and shootings had nothing to do with the film's content, pointing out that similar outbreaks had accompanied other films as well, such as *The Godfather, Part III* (1990) and *Superman II* (1980), because of the frustration of people who could not gain admission to sold-out houses. Some theaters cancelled the film in order to avoid future problems.

Certainly, the message of *New Jack City* is not controversial. It is as conventional as the original film production code that governed gangster films of the 1930's. Its primary message is "crime does not pay." Van Peebles is angry about what crack cocaine has done to his people and angry about what Reaganomics has done to their standard of living. (The film's urban desolation looks more like the South Bronx at times than Harlem.) Rap music gives *New Jack City* its distinctive pulse, pace, and energy. Ice-T, a rap artist who is against drugs, plays one of the two detectives who try to bust a drug kingpin named Nino Brown, played by Wesley Snipes, who was also seen in Spike Lee's *Mo' Better Blues* (1990).

Brown has organized a drug consortium called the Cash Money Brothers and set up a factory in a housing project that he and his thugs have taken over. The building is fortified, and inside Brown controls a smooth operation that produces crack and then sells and dispenses it to a carefully controlled clientele. He is smart, ruthless, and arrogant. He stands up to the Mafia, and a gang war results. After the Mafia hit Brown's men, Brown sends his killer down to Little Italy and takes out a Mafia capo.

Heading up the Cash Money Brothers with Nino Brown is his childhood buddy "Gee Money" Wells (Allen Payne), who himself develops a crack habit. Determined to take Brown down is Scotty Appleton (Ice-T), assigned to the case with his sidekick Nick Peretti (Judd Nelson, the film's token white) by Detective Stone (played by Van Peebles, the film's director). They recruit a recovered crack dealer named Pookie (Chris Rock), who infiltrates Nino's organization. Pookie cannot stay away from crack, however, blows his cover, and is murdered by Nino's thugs.

At that point, Scotty goes undercover himself, while Peretti breaks into Nino's house, cracks the safe, and obtains the Cash Money Brothers' financial records— evidence that cannot be used in court because it is obtained without a search warrant. The police raid the headquarters of the Cash Money Brothers. Nino escapes, but trouble has developed within his organization. Nino steals Gee Money's woman. Demoralized, Gee Money begins using crack. Nino ruthlessly kills Gee Money, whom he can no longer trust, though not, apparently, without some regret. Meanwhile, Scotty is moving in on his prey.

At the last minute, Scotty's cover is blown, but he gets his man, beating him senseless. He hates Nino, who had murdered Scotty's mother, but Peretti stops Scotty from killing Nino. Nino is brought to court, but plea-bargains his sentence down to a year in prison. Justice is done, however, but not by the courts. An angry old man who had been brutalized by Nino shoots him down after the trial—not a very hopeful denouement.

Screenwriter Barry Michael Cooper coined the phrase "new jack" in a Village Voice essay in order to describe the mood of contemporary urban street life, and the film is mainly about black culture. The story, by Thomas Lee Wright, is rather too ambitious and rather too busy. It was partly influenced by the career of druglord Nicky Barnes, who dominated heroin dealing in Harlem in the 1970's, but the film is updated to the crack trade of the 1990's.

The film is set up like a police "buddy film" with white and black partners, but the emphasis is almost entirely on Ice-T, a charismatic presence, and little attention is given to Nelson, who is cool and cocky and not much else. The dominant contrast and dramatic interest is between Ice-T and Snipes's villain, who has a kind of brutal charisma of his own but is not glamorized. The Nino Brown character is, at times, more interesting than the Ice-T adversary, but his brutal; calculating ruthlessness is only explained in the most superficial way. The antidrug message of the film is not superficial, however, and an epilogue insists that the problem cannot be solved by slogans.

New Jack City is an important motion picture if only because it introduces a new, young, dynamic, and articulate directing talent. Van Peebles, whose father, Melvin Van Peebles, directed and produced the breakthrough film *Sweet Sweetback's Badass Song* in 1970, certainly has a more significant film agenda than Eddie Murphy, whose *Harlem Nights* (1989) seems more trivial than ever when compared to *New Jack City*. The social impact of *New Jack City* is more akin to Spike Lee's *Do the Right Thing* (1989). As a police buddy film, *New Jack City* goes beyond the genre and puts its violence within a thoughtful context. It is a very promising debut film.

James M. Welsh

Reviews

Black Film Review. VI, Number 4, 1991, p. 10.
Chicago Tribune. March 8, 1991, VII, p. 28.
Cineaste. XVIII, Number 3, 1991, p. 49.
Film Review. September, 1991, p. 28.
The Hollywood Reporter. January 28, 1991, p. 47.
Los Angeles Times. March 8, 1991, p. F14.
The New York Times. March 8, 1991, p. B6.
Newsweek. March 25, 1991, p. 52.
Rolling Stone. April 4, 1991, p. 60.
Sight and Sound. I, September, 1991, p. 41.
Variety. January 28, 1991, p. 8.
The Wall Street Journal. March 21, 1991, p. A16.
The Washington Post. March 8, 1991, p. D1.
The Washington Post Weekend. March 8, 1991, p. 37.

NOT WITHOUT MY DAUGHTER

Production: Harry J. Ufland and Mary Jane Ufland for Pathe Entertainment; released
  by Metro-Goldwyn-Mayer
Direction: Brian Gilbert
Screenplay: David W. Rintels; based on the book by Betty Mahmoody, with William
  Hoffer
Cinematography: Peter Hannan
Editing: Terry Rawlings
Production design: Anthony Pratt
Art direction: Desmond Crowe and Avi Avivi
Set decoration: Anat Avivi
Costume design: Nic Ede
Music: Jerry Goldsmith
MPAA rating: PG-13
Running time: 120 minutes

> *Principal characters:*
> Betty .... Sally Field
> Moody .... Alfred Molina
> Mahtob .... Sheila Rosenthal
> Houssein .... Roshan Seth
> Nasserine .... Soudabeh Farrokhnia

The impact of Islamic fundamentalism on the rights of women does not seem a
likely theme for an American film that is aimed at a mass audience, but such is the
theme of *Not Without My Daughter*. The time is 1984, and the place is Iran. The main
protagonist is an American woman who finds herself in house captivity, unable to have
her fundamental human rights acknowledged, much less observed. The story is all the
more gripping because it is based on the true-life experience of Betty Mahmoody.

Not Without My Daughter begins in Michigan, where an upper-middle-class family
is enjoying an afternoon by the lake. Gray-haired elders are obviously proud of their
daughter Betty (Sally Field), their six-year-old granddaughter Mahtob (Sheila Rosenthal), and their son-in-law Moody Mahmoody (Alfred Molina), an Iranian-born
doctor. Moody has lived in the United States for twenty-five years and seems to be as
assimilated as any immigrant can be. Betty is so mainstream and suburban that one
wonders how she fell in love with a non-Christian from a faraway land.

The lakeside bliss, however, proves to be deceptive. It is soon learned that the
hostage crisis with Iran has had horrible consequences for the Mahmoodys. Moody
has felt a negative impact on his career and has just lost yet another job. His nation of
origin is never given as grounds for dismissal, but he is inclined to think that is the
only reason. Two hospital colleagues are shown making malicious comments about
Islam and Iran that are unambiguously directed at Moody. Betty is certain that her
husband can find another, better job and that the discrimination, while real, is not as

endemic or deep-rooted as Moody believes. Another pressure on Moody is that he has been receiving letters from his sister Nasserine (Soudabeh Farrokhnia), asking that he come home to Tehran for a visit. Moody confides to his wife that he is extremely homesick and would like to see his family. Betty is apprehensive, but Moody swears on the holy Koran that no harm will come to her or Mahtob. The family packs for what is to be a two-week vacation.

The arrival at Tehran's airport sounds the film's central theme. Although a bit heavy-handed, the scene is not as unrealistic as it may seem to those who are unfamiliar with such homecomings. A score of relatives happily swarm around Moody as if he were a conquering prince. Betty, all but ignored, is appalled by the sight of all the family's women clad in black chadors, a shapeless body-length garment with a hood that completely covers a woman's scalp. Visitors are not required by Iranian law to wear a chador, but the women present one to Betty as a "gift" and Moody asks her to wear it as a courtesy. The first ride through Tehran and subsequent rides are handled in an expressionistic style which reflects Betty's terror at hostile sights and sounds. Pictures of Ayatollah Khomeini are everywhere, as are soldiers armed with submachine guns. Loudspeakers blare out prayers and political harangues. Women in black or gray chadors swarm about like so many worker ants.

Once in the Mahmoody home, Moody begins a personality change that is not credibly rendered on the screen, but which obviously occurred in real life. Although apparently arguing heartily with his family, he is clearly delighted to be back with them and psychologically isolates himself from his wife. One must assume that the doctor was never as thoroughly Americanized as indicated in the initial scenes, as he refutes a quarter century of his life to embrace Islamic fundamentalism and Iranian nationalism in less than two weeks. Without a word about his plans to his wife, he announces that she and Mahtob are going to remain with him permanently in Iran.

Up to this moment, Betty has been able to control her emotions only because she has believed that she will be going home soon. She now goes before a Mahmoody family council to reveal the oath that Moody had sworn to her on the Koran, but her plea has no effect. She finds that she cannot leave the house alone nor use the phone. Her husband collects all their credit cards, identification, and money. Finally, she is informed that the chador will be her standard garb. Betty now undergoes her own transformation from middle-class suburban mother to a wily woman seeking international contacts in order to gain her own freedom and that of her child. Her immediate needs are to master some of the language, obtain money for phone calls and taxis, and gain enough trust to be let on the street alone. There are failed attempts to use the phone and gain access to the street. Each of these makes her husband more suspicious and more physical in his oppression. In due course, he will strike her face and body.

Betty's first serious escape attempt leads her and her daughter to the Swiss Embassy. The American government has broken all relations with the Iranians, and the Swiss are handling American interests. A woman consul informs Betty that the Swiss cannot directly aid her: As a woman in Iran, Betty has no rights. Although she is still an American citizen, she cannot legally travel without her husband's permission. In addition, the Swiss have no housing for her and cannot grant political asylum to her. Betty is also told that there are hundreds of American women in similar situations. Her only solace is that the Swiss agree to stay in contact. Her name will be added to those for whom they are seeking diplomatic relief. At this juncture, the film becomes dependent on a flimsy set of circumstances. Through sheer accident, Betty is able to form a contact with a "friendly" shopkeeper, who puts her in touch with an underground network. The chances of Betty finding such a network through blind luck are almost nothing. One assumes that the Central Intelligence Agency (CIA) or some other U.S. agency set up the escape route and that the Swiss provided Betty with her first contact. This is the only credible explanation, but given the continuing repression in Iran, such a scenario could not be admitted openly, even in 1991.

An account is given, however, of how Betty Mahmoody lived for eighteen months, playacting at compliance while scheming to escape. She attends religious classes, and her daughter is enrolled in a public school. Betty meets another American woman in a situation like her own, but this woman, who has been severely beaten on more than one occasion, has come to accept her status. In the Mahmoody household, some of the younger women begin to show sympathy for Betty, as do some of the Iranian women at her daughter's school. These women bend the rules to accommodate Betty's needs, but they never openly or directly aid her.

The climax to Betty's trials in Tehran comes when her father dies. Moody unexpectedly announces that he will allow her to attend the funeral. For a moment, Betty thinks that he has reverted to the man that she married, but she is quickly informed that Mahtob will not accompany her. Moreover, Betty is to settle all of their financial accounts in America and return with American dollars. If she does not do as she is told, she will never see her daughter again. Betty also understands that, once in America, she may not have the courage to return. Her daughter, feeling abandoned, will soon become like the women that she has lived among for more than a year. Betty decides that she must now undertake the underground escape route, whatever the risk.

The flight of Betty and Mahtob is classic melodrama. Betty meets with the Swiss consul and together they snatch Mahtob from her school. A series of car changes through dangerous checkpoints follows, until mother and daughter arrive in the northern area of Kurdistan. There, a horseman takes them through the badlands, fends off informers, and safely delivers them to a car on the Turkish side of the border. One wonders why so many people are taking such risks. Are they being paid, and if so, by whom? In the final scene, Betty and Mahtob walk down a deserted Turkish street. They see a U.S. flag fluttering over what must be a consulate office.

Strong criticism has been leveled at the film for being xenophobic and anti-Muslim. Even such a sober critic as Vincent Canby of *The New York Times* wrote, "*Not Without My Daughter* probably didn't set out to be biased against all things Muslim, but when such a complex, loaded subject is treated so witlessly, the effect is certainly bigoted." Such criticism rules out the possibility that it is not Islam which is being criticized but a certain sect of Islam in a given time and place, just as a film about the Salem witch trials would not necessarily indict Puritanism or Christianity. The film also goes to some pain to show various Iranians sympathetically, including an imam who comes to the Mahmoody house and finds many of its practices extreme. Another criticism is that some of the film was shot in Israel, a fact that was kept out of the official credits. This filming might be interpreted as being part of the endless propaganda war about Middle East rivalries. The fact remains that, when Betty Mahmoody first told her story on American television, hundreds of other American women phoned in with similar tales involving not only Iran, but other Muslim nations. In Betty's case, one also needs to bear in mind that her treatment was all the more harsh because of the intense political struggle between Iran's leaders and the United States government.

Stripped of its political specifics, *Not Without My Daughter* may be seen as speaking directly to the question of women's rights. Betty was trapped in a feminist's nightmare. Her problem was all the more acute because she knew that she might be able to free herself if she were willing to leave her child behind. Betty is a choice role for two-time Academy Award-winner Sally Fields. The transformation from the Betty of Michigan to the Betty who arrives in Turkey is completely convincing. The same cannot be said for Alfred Molina's Moody. Although a well-respected Shakespearean actor, neither his Michigan Moody nor his Iranian Moody comes to life. This contrasts sharply with the strong supporting performance by Soudabeh Farrokhnia, who is always a convincing Nasserine whether she is plotting to keep Moody in Tehran, cooing at the sight of Ayatollah Khomeini on television, or slightly warming to a Betty who she thinks has become genuinely compliant. Her Nasserine is not a villain, but instead is a woman who completely identifies with the dominant values of her culture. Roshan Seth is equally convincing as the worldly Iranian who aids Betty. He agonizes over what has happened to his country, and he is at once sensitive to its history and supportive of Westernization. *Not Without My Daughter* is about the disastrous nature of religious fanaticism, especially when that fanaticism is codified into secular law and spiked with national chauvinism.

Dan Georgakas

Reviews
Boston Globe. January 11, 1991, p. 69.
Boxoffice. March, 1991, p. R-13.
Chatelaine. LXIV, April, 1991, p. 14.
Chicago Tribune. January 11, 1991, VII, p. 23.
The Hollywood Reporter. January 7, 1991, p. 8.
Los Angeles Times. January 11, 1991, p. F1.
New Woman. XXI, March, 1991, p. 40.
The New York Times. January 11, 1991, p. B2.
USA Today. January 11, 1991, p. D1.
Variety. January 7, 1991, p. 2.
Video Review. XII, October, 1991, p. 113.
The Washington Post. January 11, 1991, p. D1.

THE OBJECT OF BEAUTY

Production: Jon S. Denny for BBC Films; released by Avenue Pictures
Direction: Michael Lindsay-Hogg
Screenplay: Michael Lindsay-Hogg
Cinematography: David Watkin
Editing: Ruth Foster
Production design: Derek Dodd
Sound: John Pritchard
Costume design: Les Lansdown
Music: Tom Bähler
MPAA rating: R
Running time: 101 minutes

Principal characters:
Jake	John Malkovich
Tina	Andie MacDowell
Joan	Lolita Davidovich
Jenny	Rudi Davies
Mr. Mercer	Joss Ackland
Victor Swayle	Bill Paterson
Steve	Ricci Harnett
Larry	Peter Riegert
Mr. Slaughter	Jack Shepherd
Mrs. Doughty	Rosemary Martin
Frankie	Roger Lloyd Pack
Gordon	Andrew Hawkins
Art evaluator	Pip Torrens

With the supremely bogus act of blessing himself in the opening moments of *The Object of Beauty*, Jake (John Malkovich) defines the tone that propels the farcical story but also causes it to fall short.

This opening sequence, in which Jake prays that his credit card will be accepted, is the most effectively paced portion of a rather long-winded commentary on contemporary materialist values. It also serves to introduce the young, not exactly married, couple Jake and Tina (Andie MacDowell). Though all the resplendent trappings of wealth hover around them, an undercurrent of tension is currently breaking through the façade of their overextended, spoiled-brat existence. The "moment of truth" for these largely symbolic characters, in the form of financial ruin, supplies the predominant narrative trajectory of the film. Yet, by bouncing plot developments tangentially off of the "object" in question—the couple's valuable "little Henry Moore" bronze sculpture—filmmaker Michael Lindsay-Hogg widens the scope of this throwback to a comedy of manners. Subsequently, Lindsay-Hogg fosters a sense of detachment toward the protagonists which is not in keeping with the nonironic expectations of mainstream cinema.

Jake and Tina are made entertaining to watch without the burden of the standard level of audience identification. Allowing viewers to remain at a distance entices them to be significantly more attuned to social and cultural commentary than in a purely character-driven, "invisibly" structured motion picture. In simple terms, this treatment makes for a very self-conscious, frequently puzzling cinematic experience for the average viewer. For those viewers who are more sophisticated, cynical, or jaded, however, the skewed premise offers the hope of other things.

Jake, a son of wealth who is, not surprisingly, alienated from his family, has always maintained a sophisticated level of consumption through market savvy and the sheer manipulation of every situation. For several years, he and Tina have led a disgustingly comfortable existence, but because of fate, arbitrariness, or Marxist social forces active in the world, an unexpected cocoa strike threatens Jake's resources. Suddenly, all is plunged into jeopardy for these two, and they must come up with a way to remain solvent or give up their life-style, a situation for which they begin to blame each other.

Malkovich's Jake is, without a doubt, the most interesting thing on which to focus in the film. With the entertaining surprises in his delivery, he energetically rivals the expensive piece of art for center stage. His ridiculous yen for a kitchen of his own carries just the right level of shallow frustration coupled with the fleeting glimmer of potential that typifies the culture in which he lives. The same cannot be said for MacDowell's portrayal of Tina. Because the character of Tina is so helpless and untalented, it might have seemed inspired to cast a blandly beautiful former model in the role. Such intellectual reasoning does not necessarily translate into a wise choice, however, and there are some dull stretches when one is expected to concentrate on Tina. At times, however, the direction and bizarre attention to detail lift the film out of the doldrums toward black comedy, pointed perceptions about corruption, and surprising poignancy.

The bronze sculpture embodies Tina's sole security, as well as a tie to her life before Jake. For Jake, it represents potential, equity, and a resource to be exploited. The film's subplot develops around the only character for whom the statue can be seen for the work of beauty that it was created to be. Jenny (Rudi Davies), a pathetically poor, deaf, and mute chambermaid, is symbolically attuned to things which others in the world of this film cannot appreciate. She cannot resist taking the piece merely because it "spoke" to her, and she seems to deserve to have it. It is an unexpected and slightly ironic turn to cast her as a thief, as likewise it is to have her punk-rock brother turn out to be sensitive in the end and to have the insurance detective be one of the few decent, non-self-serving representatives of the establishment.

The others are all tainted, from the hotel manager to the couple to the jeweler, and they all scramble to one-up one another in their attempts to monopolize the resources of society. It does not seem to matter who among them receives the spoils—the reality is that nothing will change for Jenny or her brother. A statement about the rich always reclaiming their possessions seems as stale as one concerning the dignity of the poor, but the scenes with Jenny have a strange, almost religious aura. The whiteness of the light and the music in these sequences lend an almost otherworldly character to the parts of the whole. At its ambitious moments, the contrast comes to the foreground, as in the dinner scenes. First, Jake is shown complaining over his overpriced spaghetti to Tina, who is not especially listening or not listening, but rather trying to think of the proper response. This exchange is followed by a scene with Jenny and her brother in which they resignedly consume a frugal meal in the squalor of their lower-class London flat.

Ultimately, however, the film does not portray enough with this kind of criticism to make a clear statement. Furthermore, it does not have quite enough purely entertaining moments to be merely a farce. While it is true that one can appreciate the couple's mistrust and sparring over the disappearance of the statue, for which they suspect each other, without caring about them, it is a shock later in the film to find that these same characters are being treated in a manner suggesting that the audience take their potential for growth and change seriously.

The grace of the Hollywood high-class romantic comedy does not come through, except in the way that Malkovich's satire turns it inside out. While not a foreign film, *The Object of Beauty* has distinctively European sensibilities. Yet, the players who are chosen to be critiqued most substantially represent American materialism. This confusion of American and European approaches occurs again in the ending, in which Jake and Tina are allowed to play a rather straight line on the hard-times-bring-people-closer adage, which seems distinctively out of sync with anything continental.

Harkening back to the halfheartedly contemptuous, yet optimistically opportunistic nature of the blessing that Jake passes over himself at the outset, the final moments of this social critique are unconvincing. *The Object of Beauty* may be more akin to the old order of comedy that kept the ruling classes intact: It does not make enough of a statement. The final message seems strangely coopted by the vapidness and superficiality of the 1980's. Portraying the status quo, however elegantly or competently, is historically not enough. Perhaps the problem of the film is in the ambiguity of its ending. Leaving the two superficial characters on a potentially optimistic note—that they might change a bit for the better—has strangely little resonance; it is a bit too forgiving for critical commentary. It is postmodern in its ultimate bankruptcy regarding any form of agenda—the truest "sign of the times" of all.

Mary E. Belles

Reviews
Boston Globe. April 19, 1991, CCXXIX, p. 42.
Boxoffice. March, 1991, p. R-14.
Chicago Tribune. April 26, 1991, VII, p. 42.
The Christian Science Monitor. May 17, 1991, p. 12.
Entertainment Weekly. April 26, 1991, p. 34.

Film Journal. XCIV, April/May, 1991, p. 39.
The Hollywood Reporter. March 22, 1991, p. 9.
Los Angeles Times. April 12, 1991, p. F1.
Movieline. May, 1991, p. 26.
The Nation. CCLII, April 22, 1991, p. 534.
The New York Times. April 12, 1991, p. B3.
The New Yorker. LXVII, April 22, 1991, p. 93.
Sight and Sound. I, November, 1991, p. 50.
Time. CXXXVII, April 22, 1991, p. 84.
Variety. March 22, 1991, p. 2.
The Village Voice. April 23, 1991, XXXVI, p. 51.
The Washington Post. April 19, 1991, p. D7.

ONCE AROUND

Production: Amy Robinson and Griffin Dunne for Double Play; released by Universal Pictures
Direction: Lasse Hallström
Screenplay: Malia Scotch Marmo
Cinematography: Theo Van De Sande
Editing: Andrew Mondshein
Production design: David Gropman
Art direction: Dan Davis and Michael Foxworthy
Sound: Danny Michael
Costume design: Renee Kalfus
Music: James Horner
MPAA rating: R
Running time: 114 minutes

Principal characters:
Sam Sharpe .... Richard Dreyfuss
Renata Bella .... Holly Hunter
Joe Bella .... Danny Aiello
Jan Bella .... Laura San Giacomo
Marilyn Bella .... Gena Rowlands
Gail Bella .... Roxanne Hart
Tony Bella .... Danton Stone
Peter Hedges .... Tim Guinee
Jim Redstone .... Greg Germann
Rob .... Griffin Dunne

Renata Bella (Holly Hunter) enjoys the support and warmth of her Italian family. She cherishes her sister Jan (Laura San Giacomo), and though Renata drops the bouquet that Jan tosses her at her wedding, the assumption in the Bella family is that Renata will soon marry her longtime boyfriend Rob (Griffin Dunne). Rob, however, has no such plans. On the night of her breakup, Renata rushes to the home of her parents, Joe (Danny Aiello) and Marilyn (Gena Rowlands), tearfully describes her misery, and then crawls into bed with them.

Needing a fresh start, Renata travels to the Caribbean in order to take a quick course on selling time-shares in condominiums. She meets Sam Sharpe (Richard Dreyfuss), a rich, obnoxious businessman who immediately falls in love with her and who gradually wins her love. Their rapid courtship, wedding, and the start of their life together develops in contrast to the mixed reactions of Renata's family. As their relationship intensifies, Renata articulates perfectly the stress that she feels: "Leaving my family is like renouncing my citizenship, moving to Russia, becoming Protestant." The discord that is created by Sam's intrusion into the Bella family forms the main conflict of the film: The richness of the joys, sorrows, and passions that are generated by his intrusion becomes its main theme.

The importance of family is even built carefully into the structure of the motion picture. The plot organizes itself around the traditional milestones in a family's life— scenes are set at a wedding, engagement, birthday dinner, retirement, baptism, and memorial service—while the characters interact, quarrel, forgive, and change. These scenes, a few of them presented wordlessly in montage, gain much energy from the tension between the public settings and the private strain that is created by Sam's aggressive and domineering presence. In addition to dramatizing these formal gatherings in the life of the Bellas, however, the filmmakers also utilize everyday settings well. Joe's mild birthday depression takes the form of random complaints in the kitchen while the rest of the family bustle about preparing his dinner and cake. A number of short scenes show him in the den trying to master his retirement gift of a pottery wheel. Most important, four key conversations between Renata or Jan and their parents occur late at night at the foot of the parents' bed, an ideal spot for reviewing the day, telling troubles, clearing the air, and sharing confidences.

Aiello's performance as Joe becomes, perhaps, the most satisfying one in the film. Aiello has rightly referred to his character as "a full human being," and he succeeds at capturing this richness and humanity. When Sam and Renata arrange for a belly dancer to arrive at the front door during Joe's birthday dinner, Aiello conveys Joe's self-consciousness as well as his ability, once he is coaxed to join in the dance, of shedding his inhibitions and enjoying himself. Later, after a family dinner erupts in hostility over Sam and Renata's desire to have the others defer to them, Aiello displays Joe's firmness and sure sense of himself as patriarch. A moment that showcases the best of this ensemble of actors, this dinner scene is the highlight of the film.

Hunter, as Renata, communicates well her character's uniqueness and volatility. At the beginning of the film, Renata appears to collapse in tears after Jan's wedding, but when her boyfriend Rob tries to comfort her, he sees that she is really shaking with laughter. Though Rob is puzzled, the audience senses the emotional distance between them. When Renata later meets Sam, an older man, she tells him, "Men of my own generation don't understand me at all." Sam's company seems to loosen Renata's emotions still more. In one playful bedroom scene, Renata's mouselike giggles spill out of her, a sound that illustrates the character's zest almost as well as the dialogue. Yet, Hunter's performance also centers on bringing out the dividedness in Renata. The key moment is again the dinner scene, and this confrontation climaxes Renata's growing struggle to define herself by having her make the difficult choice between husband and family.

Just as the Bellas define themselves in relation to one another and thrive on family, Sam is a study of isolation. Renata first glimpses him standing alone on a ridge of rock overlooking a Caribbean sunset. He tells her that he is divorced and speaks often of the Lithuanian heritage of his deceased parents. The different ethnic background and lack of family ties highlight Sam's status as outsider. His money—or his garish display of his wealth—sets him apart from others as well. He seems more comfortable responding to people in groups rather than as individuals, and he naturally tries to assume control of any gathering that he attends.

His most tender moment in the film occurs when he tries to apologize to Renata for creating a scene at her grandmother's memorial service. As Renata, pregnant with their child, silently watches home movies of herself and Jan as children, Sam swings the projector's image onto Renata's swelling womb. The picture of one family in childhood now flickers on another waiting to be born. Renata lowers her gaze to watch, allowing Sam to fumble through his apology without her having to look at him. This combination of awkwardness and showmanship reflects both Sam's good intentions and his difficulty in becoming part of his new family.

These difficulties owe to his hard-sell personality. His good intentions notwithstanding, Sam is a triumph of tackiness. Renata first witnesses his rapid-fire banter before the future condominium salespeople, a performance dotted with tawdry one-liners ("Is that a rock in your pocket, or are you just glad to see me?"). A super salesman extolling the very idea of selling is the perfect image of Sam in his element. Later, he repeats the one-liner above from the bandstand at his own wedding reception while he addresses the guests and his new family. The subsequent gulp of silence does not seem to bother him, and by calling on his reluctant father-in-law for a song, Sam generates enough foot stomping and shouts of encouragement to give his wedding the echo of a high school pep rally. Dreyfuss is perfectly cast in this role, though as the part is written and played, it is often easier to recognize Sam's surface pushiness than his underlying charm. Perhaps both qualities are evident in some of Sam's greetings to his new family. Always the crack salesman, he makes an arresting first impression. His first words to his future sister-in-law and her husband are, "I hope you both have a lifetime of great sex and joy." On first meeting Renata's mother, Sam asks cryptically, "How do you explain a rose to someone who has never seen a rose before?" These are words not easily understood or forgotten, an indication of Sam's emphasis on style over substance.

Director Lasse Hallström utilizes various visual circles as a recurrent stylistic device that reflect the film's exuberant tone, add unity, and also reveal character. The opening shot of the film reveals Joe wheeling his car around and around a traffic circle in celebration of Jan's wedding. Later Sam shows off to Joe his stretch limousine by having the driver spin once around the same circle. He also takes the Bellas ice skating, leading them in comic spins and glides on a local pond while "The Emperor Waltz" plays on his chauffeur's portable stereo. The camera often observes such lyrical moments with a concluding shot from high overhead. For other, more subdued scenes, such as the many montages of family dinners and the birth of Sam and Renata's child when the entire family joins hands around Renata and the baby, the camera slowly pans around characters, describing a circle at eye level.

The bittersweet tone of *Once Around* as well as its emphasis on family and romantic relationships recalls some famous motion pictures from Hollywood's golden era, such as *Made for Each Other* (1939), with James Stewart and Carole Lombard, and *Penny Serenade* (1941), with Cary Grant and Irene Dunne. These films also traced the comic and dramatic ups and downs of couples trying to establish themselves against the backdrop of in-laws, work, and holidays. Such films probably remain memorable more for their sentiment than for their art. Watching Hollywood stars cope with the frictions of family and day-to-day life seems to be a surefire premise. If *Once Around* benefits from adapting the simple virtues of these films, then it must also partake of their vices. In the last third of all three films, for example, the necessity of covering a wide emotional range in the couples' lives leads to some episodic plotting and sudden shifts in tone. Stewart and Lombard leave a New Year's Eve party to discover that their baby has taken ill, and the remainder of that motion picture becomes a race against time and a blizzard to fly in the life-saving serum. A climactic moment in *Penny Serenade* comes when Grant and Dunne tearfully ask a judge not to take away their adopted daughter. *Once Around* also veers in the direction of soap opera, though somewhat more subtly, as the audience is rushed from one crisis to the next. Like the array of emotions of its two famous prototypes, wearing its heart on its sleeve is for *Once Around* both its main strength and its one shortcoming.

Glenn Hopp

Reviews
American Cinematographer. LXXII, March, 1991, p. 62.
Boxoffice. March, 1991, p. R-12.
Chicago Tribune. January 18, 1991, VII, p. 36.
The Christian Science Monitor. February 8, 1991, p. 10.
Film Review. September, 1991, p. 31.
The Hollywood Reporter. January 16, 1991, p. 11.
Life. XIII, December, 1990, p. 31.
Los Angeles Times. January 18, 1991, p. F18.
The New York Times. January 18, 1991, p. B6.
Newsweek. CXVII, February 11, 1991, p. 58.
Premiere. IV, December, 1990, p. 22.
Variety. January 16, 1991, p. 2.
The Wall Street Journal. January 17, 1991, p. A9.
The Washington Post. January 18, 1991, p. C7.

ONLY THE LONELY

Production: John Hughes and Hunt Lowry for Hughes Entertainment; released by
    Twentieth Century-Fox
Direction: Chris Columbus
Screenplay: Chris Columbus
Cinematography: Julio Macat
Editing: Raja Gosnell
Production design: John Muto
Art direction: Dan Webster
Set design: Bill Arnold, Gary Baugh, and Karen Fletcher-Trujillo
Set decoration: Rosemary Brandenburg
Casting: Jane Jenkins and Janet Hirshenson
Sound: Jim Alexander
Costume design: Mary E. Vogt
Music: Maurice Jarre
MPAA rating: PG-13
Running time: 102 minutes

Principal characters:
Danny Muldoon	John Candy
Rose Muldoon	Maureen O'Hara
Theresa Luna	Ally Sheedy
Patrick Muldoon	Kevin Dunn
Doyle Ryan	Milo O'Shea
Spats Shannon	Bert Remsen
Nick Acropolis	Anthony Quinn
Sal Buonarte	James Belushi
Johnny Luna	Joe V. Greco
Father Strapovic	Marvin J. McIntyre
Billy	Macaulay Culkin

This follow-up teaming of Chris Columbus and John Hughes falls as far away from the megahit *Home Alone* (1990) as imaginable. The pair responsible for the third-highest-grossing film of all time have turned out a product of much smaller proportions. Written and directed by Columbus, *Only the Lonely* is an honest, homegrown, full-fledged story—warts and all.

In an age when motion pictures have served to extend the parameters of the world so fully, this film is an effort to get back in touch with the constraints of life. The script follows the faltering development of Danny Muldoon (John Candy), a gentle, rotund, thirty-eight-year-old Irish cop living with his sharp-tongued mother, Rose Muldoon (Maureen O'Hara). There is little action-packed thrill for Danny in his work. He and partner Sal (James Belushi) transport prisoners or dead bodies in their less-than-dynamic police van with little fanfare. The challenging force in Danny's life appears in the form of Theresa (Ally Sheedy), the introverted daughter of the local mortician. Painfully shy and hesitant, this young woman seems directly evolved from Sheedy's virtuoso misfit role in producer Hughes's *The Breakfast Club* (1985). Rose loudly voices her disdain for her slender, Sicilian-American future daughter-in-law, fearing that Theresa will pry her son away.

O'Hara's casting marks a rare case of inspiration coming full circle. Her return to films after a twenty-year absence blessed writer/director Columbus with an incarnation of the very model that he had used to create the character of Rose: Mary Kate Danaher, as feistily portrayed by O'Hara in the John Ford classic *The Quiet Man* (1952). Also noteworthy is the restraint of Candy, who works hard to imbue Danny with a light comic touch that is secondary to the dramatic flow. This is no easy feat because of the expectation that, at any moment, he will launch into the exaggerated brand of humor that has burdened many comedies. Most films that are fashioned to extend the style of such late-night television programming as *SCTV* and *Saturday Night Live* often ignore historical narrative criteria in order to make use of personality performers. Anyone expecting a rip-roaring John Candy vehicle for low-brow farce or absurd situational comedy will not be instantly gratified by this film.

Only the Lonely represents a small, brave attempt at more serious filmmaking by Columbus, the "boy wonder" known for the screenplays for such films as *Gremlins* (1984), a well-orchestrated, ironic send-up of American consumer values played to the tune of *It's a Wonderful Life* (1946). Columbus admits that his virtuosity most frequently comes from scavenging cinema history. *Only the Lonely* marks his attempt to hold the glib manipulation of cinema references at arm's length long enough to fashion a story which is more indebted to real life.

Undoubtedly, *Only the Lonely* is a flawed film. The common complaint of critics was that the script is awkward and not humorous enough, that it does not extend comedic moments to the epic proportions that it could have. This assessment is not entirely inaccurate, but it ignores the fact that this story marks virtually a coming-of-age step for its author. The disjunctive awkwardness of Columbus' finding of a "grown-up" voice is mirrored in his narrative treatment. One may observe that modern cinema in general has somewhat lost its ability to tell stories with any sense of authority—particularly in relation to comedy. The majority of economically successful comic releases exhibit a hyperbole of tone and slickness that steers them far out of the realm of everyday experience. While the script often fails to soar, it would be an overstatement to say that the film does not have moments that work. The gentle, claustrophobic delineations of the neighborhood are designed to act upon the characters in a way that few films even attempt.

Unfortunately, many of the scenes in *Only the Lonely* do seem to be holding back. The director has erred in the direction of believable verisimilitude over the heightening of dramatic beats. Nevertheless, the story focuses exactly on what it is supposed to: a man's breaking away from the existence that he has known with a strong mother, in order to have a chance at a future. The arc of the plot encompasses the entire shift of

Danny Muldoon's priorities. If the laughter is more restrained and the fantasy sequences are held in check, then it is an indication that the filmmaker is struggling to rediscover the use of humor in the service of a larger drama. While Danny's imaginary scenarios depicting his mother in peril do not soar to the giddy heights of the Hitchcockian black comedy *Throw Momma from the Train* (1987), that film does not have the payoff that *Only the Lonely* does for those perceptive enough to recognize it.

The final fantasy installment specifically underlines Danny's emotional break-through. The earlier surreal episodes articulated Danny's paranoia by illustrating the tragic results of neglecting his mother, with the nonfantasy scenes that immediately follow dramatizing Danny's reaction to this guilt. The last sequence, however, shows Rose turning the tables and taking charge in yet another of her son's imaginary episodes. The progression of these fantasies reflects Danny's understanding that his mother is strong enough to look after herself. It completes the character's internal development within a structure which also intelligently places Danny's proposal of marriage in the middle of the story and not at the climax. This is in contrast to the many films that present the suggestion of marriage as the ultimate rescue, after which all problems dissolve. Columbus' script (uneven as it may be) diligently raises issues that undercut such an unrealistic ideology: He shows how the topic forces Danny's and Theresa's problems to the surface. Theresa is willing to walk away from her "big chance" at marriage and pursue her own agenda. She calls off the wedding and completes plans to move to New York for her career. Danny is the one who must earn the right to the potential fulfillment that matrimony represents by entering into it as an adult. He examines his ties with his mother and transfers to New York in order to work things out with Theresa.

One of the most poignant images is that of Theresa at work in the lonely mortuary. She applies makeup to a corpse while watching a vintage Clark Gable film on videotape. She freezes the frame and the camera pans to the profile in the coffin: It is literally a dead ringer for the former matinee idol. This is her "art." Theresa has dreams, like many others, of working in the theater in New York City, but her cosmetology skills are wasted on the dead. This is the picture's one forgivable film-history crutch. It is not a cheap exploitation of intertexuality: The image offers a very real and heartrending insight into the role that film can take in lonely lives.

The cinematography and production design conscientiously define a real-life Chicago neighborhood. The music, while a bit sappy at incidental moments, cleverly underscores Rose's heritage with Irish flavor and the developing romance of Theresa and Danny with Italian opera.

Many responsible, sensitive choices have been thought out. This film tries to address a specific set of reference points that Columbus felt deserved to be brought to life. He attempted to do so in a tone that supported the material, to make use of his storytelling skills without resorting to stunts and gimmickry at every turn. Though high-production-value films such as *Total Recall* (1990) may begin with an interesting premise, the articulation of this idea can leave one emotionally famished. There should be leeway in the cinema to accommodate smaller, more intimate attempts such as *Only the Lonely*. Perhaps only those in touch with their own loneliness can tap into the implications that this story offers.

Mary E. Belles

Reviews
Boston Globe. May 24, 1991, CCXXXIX, p. 48.
Chicago Tribune. May 24, 1991, CXLIV, p. 42.
Film Review. September, 1991, p. 32.
Films in Review. XLII, September, 1991, p. 341.
The Hollywood Reporter. May 17, 1991, p. 10.
Los Angeles Times. May 24, 1991, CX, p. F6.
National Review. XLIII, June 24, 1991, p. 49.
The New York Times. May 24, 1991, p. B7.
Rolling Stone. June 27, 1991, p. 78.
San Francisco Chronicle. May 24, 1991, CXXVII, p. E1.
USA Today. May 24, 1991, p. D7.
Variety. May 17, 1991, p. 2.
The Village Voice. June 4, 1991, XXXVI, p. 97.
The Washington Post. May 24, 1991, CXIV, p. B6.

OPEN DOORS
(PORTE APERTE)

Origin: Italy
Released: 1989
Released in U.S.: 1991
Production: Angelo Rizzoli for Erre Produzioni, Istituto Luce, and Urania Film; released by Orion Classics
Direction: Gianni Amelio
Screenplay: Gianni Amelio, Vincenzo Cerami, and Alessandro Sermoneta; based on the novel by Leonardo Sciascia
Cinematography: Tonino Nardi
Editing: Simona Paggi
Art direction: Franco Velchi and Amedeo Fago
Set decoration: Massimo Tavazzi and Lorenzo D'Ambrosio
Costume design: Gianna Gissi
Music: Franco Piersanti
MPAA rating: R
Running time: 109 minutes

Principal characters:
Vito Di Francesco	Gian Maria Volonte
Tommaso Scalia	Ennio Fantastichini
Judge Sanna	Renzo Giovampietro
Giovanni Consolo	Renato Carpentieri
Spadafora	Tuccio Musumeci
Public prosecutor	Silverio Blasi

Most legal dramas feature defendants who try to prove their innocence, or at least extenuating circumstances in their cases that merit them some degree of mercy. *Open Doors*, however, proceeds along quite different lines of development. The film begins on a March morning in 1937 in Palermo, Sicily. Tommaso Scalia (Ennio Fantastichini) is shown committing three premeditated murders: He kills the man who has recently fired him from his job at the Fascist Confederation of Professionals and Artists, he kills his replacement, and he rapes and kills his wife after driving her into the countryside. He then returns to his home to prepare a snack for his son, lies down on his bed, and awaits the police. Once arrested, he pleads guilty and requests the death sentence, a punishment that he deems proper for his actions.

The film's dramatic focus is on one of the trial judges, Vito Di Francesco (Gian Maria Volonte), a man who is personally opposed to the death penalty and not at all enamored of the Fascist regime. His function at the trial may be somewhat confusing to those who are unfamiliar with the legal system in Italy. Rather than a jury of twelve with prosecuting and defense attorneys, the Italian system uses a panel of three judges and three laypersons. The judges question the defendants and witnesses, who may have counsel, not simply to convict the accused but to uncover the details of the crime.

Di Francesco is told that, if he functions as expected on this case, then his legal future knows no limits. The murders are headline stories in the press and the courtroom is jammed with spectators. Di Francesco, however, refuses to accept the case at face value. He asks numerous probing questions, which slowly reveal the corruption of the Fascist system even when judged by its own rules and logic. The killer and his victims have been involved in financial misdoings and wife-sharing that amounts to a kind of prostitution. The Chief Magistrate (Renzo Giovampietro) originally assumes that Di Francesco's questions are a clever ploy that will make the final death verdict all the more weighty. When he realizes that Di Francesco is sincere, his demeanor changes. Di Francesco is told that, whatever doubts he may have about the nature of the legal system, it is essentially sound. The death sentence, he is told, makes it possible for people to live without fear, to live "with the doors open."

Di Francesco has a different moral perspective. He is appalled by a political system whose ethos not only drove Scalia to murder but also taught him to demand voluntarily his own execution. The death penalty is a symbol of the repression and disinformation that are used by governments in order to retain power. In this light, the death penalty does not exist to protect the average citizen but to protect those who govern.

Pressures of every kind are brought to bear on Di Francesco. What he thinks is a chance encounter with his former schoolteacher becomes a formal house call during which he is severely reprimanded for his behavior by the widow of one of the slain officials. His own family, completely at ease with the system, quietly encourages him to stay on the side of power. The defendant refuses to help in any way. The judge is also aware that, whatever happens at the trial, there can be a government appeal to a higher court, which will surely impose the death sentence.

Di Francesco is about to admit defeat when he finds an unexpected ally in one of the jurors, Giovanni Consolo (Renato Carpentieri). Consolo, the son of a peasant and now a well-to-do farmer, mounts moral arguments of which even Di Francesco had not thought. Together they persuade the other jurors to accept their point of view, but their victory proves fleeting. The government, as expected, appeals the case. A new set of jurors annuls the original verdict and, within months, Scalia is executed before a firing squad. Di Francesco, his career in ruins, is sent to an insignificant provincial court.

Beginning to question the wisdom of his actions, Di Francesco decides to visit Consolo. Accompanied by his young daughter, the widowed judge travels by cart to the Consolo farm, where he finds a wedding feast taking place in a huge barn. The judge, feeling that he is in touch with the true Sicily, wonders anew where Consolo got his values. His answer comes when Consolo takes him into the main house, which contains a room that is filled from top to bottom with books. The library had come with the house and Consolo has been reading all of his life. From these books, from authors such as Fyodor Dostoevski, Consolo came to the arguments and views that finally won over the other jurors.

Taking a stroll through the countryside, Di Francesco and Consolo consider if what they have done really mattered. Consolo thinks it did: What they attempted will be referred to long after the death sentences have been forgotten and, with the limited means available to them, they resisted injustice. He is sure that things will be better one day and that acts such as theirs contribute to that better day. Di Francesco feels an enormous bond with a man whose interest in books is far from academic. He too declares that he has faith.

Much in this film of ideas revolves around the acting of Volonte. Long Italy's premiere dramatic actor, Volonte is known to most Americans only from his role as Bartolomeo Vanzetti in *Sacco and Vanzetti* (1971). Preparations for the role of Di Francesco included losing weight to such a degree that he appears gaunt. He did this in order to "physically reconstruct the figure of this southern Italian from the 30s." Volonte also found a barber who gave him a haircut associated with that time and place. These exterior details serve him well in the film, but he reached the essence of his character by copying the entire screenplay by hand two to three times. His efforts have been rewarded by three international prizes for acting.

Director Gianni Amelio and cinematographer Tonino Nardi made important decisions regarding the rendering of Palermo and Sicily. For Americans accustomed to the stark villages and isolated villas in films such as *The Godfather* trilogy (1972, 1974, 1990), *Open Doors* offers a fuller view of Sicily. Palermo is revealed as a gracious city, full of lovely walks and vistas which a man such as Di Francesco would know well. The trip into the countryside is not into the barren mountains but along the lush coast where oranges, lemons, and grains have flourished for centuries. The long wedding table recalls the work of the School of Naples painters active in the nineteenth century. The romantic optimism of the farm scenes enhances the ideological views of Di Francesco and Consolo.

Amelio was surprised by some of the reaction to his film. When he began the project, he thought that he was reconstructing an interesting news story from a troubled time in Italy. He hoped that it would not be seen as simply a period piece and of interest only to Italians. As soon as he began to hold screenings in Italy, he was repeatedly and heatedly challenged for expressing opposition to the death penalty. He was told by more than one audience that his timing was bad. A youth in Florence asked, "Why did you make this film against the death penalty, when in this day and age the death penalty would be so useful?" Rather than being limited to a national audience, the film won four European Film Awards and was nominated for an Academy Award for Best Foreign-Language Film. In his press notes regarding the film, Amelio has written, "I, who was afraid of doing a period piece, am now asking myself a different question: 'have I instead made a film about today?'"

Dan Georgakas

Reviews
Chicago Tribune. July 19, 1991, VII, p. 34.

Commonweal. CXVIII, July 12, 1991, p. 437.
Films in Review. XLII, July, 1991, p. 268.
The Hollywood Reporter. February 12, 1991, p. 8.
Los Angeles Times. March 8, 1991, p. F6.
The Nation. CCLIV, January 20, 1992, p. 64.
National Review. XLIII, March 18, 1991, p. 63.
The New York Times. September 27, 1991, p. B2.
The New Yorker. LXVII, March 25, 1991, p. 72.
Variety. CCCXXXIX, May 9, 1990, p. 31.
The Washington Post. May 14, 1991, p. D4.

OTHER PEOPLE'S MONEY

Production: Norman Jewison and Ric Kidney for Yorktown Productions; released by
  Warner Bros.
Direction: Norman Jewison
Screenplay: Alvin Sargent; based on the play by Jerry Sterner
Cinematography: Haskell Wexler
Editing: Lou Lombardo, Michael Pacek, and Hubert de la Bouillerie
Production design: Philip Rosenberg
Art direction: Robert Guerra and Nathan Haas
Set decoration: Tom Roysden
Costume design: Theoni V. Aldredge
Music: David Newman
MPAA rating: R
Running time: 101 minutes

> *Principal characters:*
> Lawrence Garfield .... Danny DeVito
> Andrew (Jorgy) Jorgenson .... Gregory Peck
> Kate Sullivan .... Penelope Ann Miller
> Bea Sullivan .... Piper Laurie
> William J. Coles .... Dean Jones
> Ozzie .... Tom Aldredge
> Arthur .... R. D. Call

American films have been traditionally disinclined to deal directly with uncomfortable social situations. More than a decade passed after the United States withdrew
from the debacle in Vietnam before *Platoon* (1986) was produced. The grim facts of
the Great Depression were displaced until after World War II, when they emerged
obliquely in the mood of the *film noir* "B" motion pictures of the late 1940's. The
assassination of John F. Kennedy was not seriously examined until Oliver Stone's *JFK*
(1991; reviewed in this volume) was released more than a quarter-century later. In
1991, however, the rampant greed, amorality, absence of ethics, and social viciousness
that marked corporate economic strategies during the 1980's had already been placed
as prominent features of *Other People's Money*. This film uses as its central motivating
situation the attempted takeover of a paternalistic, previously productive company by
a corporate raider who has no scruples about destroying existing firms for huge profits.
    The method that Norman Jewison, the producer and director, and Alvin Sargent,
the screenwriter, have used to make a sensitive subject palatable is to project it in the
form of a dark comedy. The muted but still pointed commentary is delivered within
the familiar conventions of a contemporary love story, while the somewhat melodramatic power struggle at the core of the plot is used as a vehicle to display the latest
styles of wealth and power both for chastisement and for delectation. Jewison's
direction is typically professional, maintaining a pace and rhythm that commands

attention, and the megamodern corporate suites in New York and the authentic old factories in New England are photographed in compelling, hard-edge tableaus by Haskell Wexler. None of this style would matter much, however, without Danny DeVito's bravura performance as "Larry the Liquidator."

DeVito's character is an indication of the change in American society that began in the middle of the twentieth century. Lawrence Garfield is a summary of everything wrong with the 1980's; he is an ego-bloated, ruthless, avaricious, inconsiderate takeover artist whose insatiable appetites camouflage a void where his soul ought to be. The imaginative conceit of the film is to take an updated equivalent of the banker, Potter, played by Lionel Barrymore in Frank Capra's classic *It's a Wonderful Life* (1946)—a truly archetypal villain who represents the evil forces destroying small-town America—and actually turn him into a subject of sympathy and the audience's central point of identification. The hero of Capra's film, George Bailey (Jimmy Stewart), is here too in a sense, a marvelous vision of integrity and rectitude as portrayed definitively by Gregory Peck, but now he is an outsider, the owner of a family firm whose old-fashioned ideals seem like a memory from antiquity, a phantom from another time that has been rendered irrelevant by forces beyond almost everyone's control. Peck's rocklike Andrew "Jorgy" Jorgenson might be a fitting antagonist for Garfield, but the purpose of this film is not to arrange a contest of competing economic philosophies, as that could undercut the potential for entertainment inherent in DeVito's archly comic conception. Instead, the financial issues are essentially used as a frame for DeVito as he faces the task of making Garfield not only understandable in his various lusts for food, women, money, and perhaps love, but actually sympathetic so that the audience can feel comfortable in his presence.

From the start, Garfield seizes the stage, introducing himself in a monologue that is ostensibly a paean to the pleasures of making huge amounts of money by knowing more, thinking faster, acting tougher, and masking emotion better than other people. Yet, the speech is also a full-force demonstration of roguish charm that assures that one will not be bored in his company. Initially, his appeal is toward the fascination that most people have with someone who is very successful and powerful, and Garfield's demonstration of style and complete confidence in himself is an enduring aspect of the cinema's ability to make amoral behavior acceptable by the sheer force of its dynamic, distinctive attributes. This goal is not extraordinarily difficult to accomplish, although DeVito's variance from the general norm of debonair masculine charmers enhances his presentation. Where his performance really becomes impressive is in his ability to add additional dimensions to Garfield, such as a quick wit that cuts through social posturing and hypocrisy in an American version of classic British repartee and a wistful, hidden level of sentiment that makes him endearing. DeVito is able to make all these aspects a coherent part of his character, a testament to the range of his acting, although some of the softer features are so conventionally written—stuffed toys in bed and amateurish violin playing in sharp contrast to his perfection in everything else—that it takes all of his craft to make them plausible.

The problem that the film faces is Garfield's status as the hero: What kind of a hero could shut down a company and drive an entire town's work force onto the dole. No degree of personal charm can compensate for this kind of thoughtlessness and inhumanity, and the basic dramatic tension of the story is built around the struggle between Garfield and Jorgenson for the control of the family-founded cable manufacturing company that has been losing money (despite its debt-free, efficient operation) because of misguided economic programs on the national level. Garfield learns from his very user-friendly computer "Carmen"—which, with his chauffeur, Arthur (R. D. Call), is the closest thing to a friend that he has—that the company is a perfect target for a hostile takeover, leading to liquidation and a substantial sum for him. He begins proceedings to win a stock fight by attempting to gain control covertly of a majority of the shares and then by persuading the stockholders that they deserve a better return on their investment. Jorgenson is understandably enraged that his life's work is being measured by the bottom line on a short-term basis, and he is determined to resist what he regards as a kind of pestilence infecting the economic health of the nation. To challenge Garfield on his own ground, he is persuaded by his associate/companion Bea Sullivan, played with characteristic assurance by Piper Laurie, that Bea's daughter from a previous marriage would be the perfect representative of the company's interests. At this crucial point, the film shifts significantly toward the contrivance of the romance theme, as Kate Sullivan (Penelope Ann Miller) happens to be a young, razor-sharp corporate lawyer who becomes a fitting foil for Garfield—both in the boardroom and, by implication, in the bedroom.

Appropriately, Garfield is immediately attracted to and challenged by Sullivan. Their stormy courtship-rivalry—echoing similar duels between such strong-willed semiadversaries as Kate and Petruchio in William Shakespeare's *The Taming of the Shrew*—forms the central focus of the film. Because this romantic conflict is given more attention than the corporate contest, even as it supposedly grows naturally out of its strategies, the crucial question of acquisitive capitalism versus traditional free enterprise is somewhat submerged. Consequently, the potential for this debate's real dramatic fire is reduced to a smoldering background until the actual shareholders' meeting in which Garfield and Jorgenson both address the investors. While the two narrative patterns are clearly interlinked, the affair between Garfield and Sullivan and the fight for the company are actually separated because the legal maneuvering ultimately has no effect on the final vote. The film concentrates on the romantic relationship, and although there are many enjoyable moments on this track— especially in the coarse, crude, and sexually explicit but nonerotic badinage between Garfield and Sullivan—these two people are so interested in money, power, clothes, and other accoutrements of privilege that their possible romantic attachment does not seem that important either to them or to the audience. Garfield's professions of love notwithstanding, it is hard to see his interest in Sullivan as much more than another quest for a gaudy acquisition, another trophy to show how a poor boy from the Bronx has succeeded in conquering the exclusive world of big money and prestige. Miller, who has previously played sweet young girls in such films as *The Freshman* (1990), is adequate some of the time, but her part requires a combination of the young Katharine

Hepburn—class, spirit, elegance, and composure—and possibly Kathleen Turner at her most smoulderingly sexy. This feat may be too much to ask from anyone.

The climax of the film is the stockholders' meeting. Peck's role has demanded little to this point except the kind of qualities that have been his signature since *To Kill a Mockingbird* (1962). Yet, to see Jorgenson framed before the productive fire of his machinery, his loyal work force in action behind him, is enough to establish the kind of heartland American values that the film sets in opposition to the false glamorization of leveraged-buyout kings like Michael Milken, Ivan Boesky, and their ilk. The marvelous moment of Jorgenson's inspiring, timely argument is extended by the necessity of having Garfield try to top or counteract his plea, and the tension is palpable because the film has shifted the sympathy of the audience away from Garfield by providing another point of identification. The writing by Sargent—a veteran who has also written *Paper Moon* (1973), *Ordinary People* (1980), and *White Palace* (1990)—is extremely effective in this scene, and DeVito is able to handle the alteration in focus with ease. Garfield's reply to Jorgenson is logically and emotionally convincing, the final vote is plausible, and Garfield is able to avoid becoming a villain even while Jorgenson remains the personification of valor.

Because the film industry is ruled by cautious executives unable or unwilling to trust the audience, an unlikely happy ending is tacked onto the film when a Japanese concern arrives as a *deus ex machina* ready to provide a new market for the company, thus making its dismantling unnecessary for Garfield, who is now in control. As the film ends, he and Sullivan are apparently on track to gratify their various lusts. This union of power figures is sanctioned by the beneficent results of their "work," their reward being not only money but also the opportunity for self-admiration and self-gratification. Yet, even the calculation behind this last contrivance is somewhat submerged in Garfield's gleeful anticipation of imminent pleasure—DeVito's creation of an image of attractiveness from the raw material of narcissistic debauchery.

Leon Lewis

Reviews
Boxoffice. December, 1991, p. R-90.
Chicago Tribune. October 18, 1991, VII, p. 48.
The Christian Science Monitor. November 8, 1991, p. 13.
The Hollywood Reporter. October 16, 1991, p. 5.
Los Angeles Times. October 18, 1991, p. F1.
The New York Times. October 18, 1991, p. B1.
Newsweek. October 28, 1991, p. 66.
Time. CXXXVIII, October 28, 1991, p. 92.
Variety. October 16, 1991, p. 2.
The Village Voice. November 5, 1991, p. 72.
The Wall Street Journal. October 24, 1991, p. A14.
The Washington.Post. October 18, 1991, p. D1.

PARIS IS BURNING

Production: Jennie Livingston and Barry Swimar for Off-White Productions; released
by Prestige
Direction: Jennie Livingston
Cinematography: Paul Gibson
Editing: Jonathan Oppenheim
MPAA rating: no listing
Running time: 78 minutes

Principal characters:
Pepper Labeija .... Himself
Willi Ninja .... Himself
Kim Pendavis .... Himself
Freddie Pendavis .... Himself
Octavia Saint Laurent .... Himself
Angie Xtravaganza .... Himself
Venus Xtravaganza .... Himself
Paris Dupree .... Himself

Paris Is Burning is the name of a drag queen ball and a controversial feature-length
documentary produced and directed by Jennie Livingston. It features the infamous
"vogue" phenomenon that Madonna co-opted into a hit pop song before the theatrical
release of the film, but with a significant distinction. To the community of gay, mostly
African-American and Hispanic males who practice voguing, this acting out or
"striking a pose" is taken very seriously. Their efforts toward appearing "real" in
style, costume, and attitude are literally grounded in camouflage survival tactics. The
viewer is told again and again that the essence of this realness—looking as close as
possible to the straight world—is not a satire. It is the fulfillment of a fantasy, but not
merely one of the immediate sensual thrill of cross-dressing. Rather, the participants
view voguing and drag queen balls as efforts that they must make simply to be allowed
to exist—or as one individual puts it, "to get home with no blood on you." Lest any
viewer doubt this sense of jeopardy in the film, the fatalistic end of one of the key
characters lends sobering credence to the premise.

Shot with a low-budget, cinema verité approach, the film keeps its own stylistic
encroachment to a minimum (frequently using simple black-and-white intertitles and
talking-head interviews) and thereby allows the sometimes flamboyant subjects' style
to take precedence. The filmmakers do interact with the men, but not in a self-
congratulatory manner. In fact, the low-level light and the locations often seem to be
out of a no-frills student film recording the events at a fraternity house.

Much of the seventy-eight minutes of screen time needs to be informative, to supply
the mainstream viewer with a foundation describing the evolution of the urban gay
life-style. There is a certain amount that must be grasped in order to see the drag balls

for what they really are, beneath the spectacle. The act of voguing, for example, came from the verbal sparring called "shade" in which two individuals in the gay community would take part to insult each other. As the older queen, Pepper, points out, gay men cannot call one another by the derogatory names that someone from the straight world would use. Therefore, the need to be creative grew until it became facing off with no words at all, with the two individuals dancing out their dislike. The men use other terms such as "mopping" for stealing, which many of the men do in order to procure the finest clothing for their "ball-walks." They live primarily in "houses" named for prominent ball-walkers who fill the void of parent for many of the youths.

The aspiration to realness is part of the need for fulfillment and of the dream of escape. Therefore, there are many categories in drag contests, including Butch-Queen, Executive, and Military Man. These categories represent the socioeconomic realm of longing for these men. They dress in business suits and carry briefcases in order to fill a role that they believe is being denied them by society at large. The gay men also assume the dress and attitude of the heterosexual punk gang members who commit hate crimes against them—to be successful in this category is vital for many. The balls are thus a form of ceremonial display for the skills that constitute a necessary part of their daily existence.

The emotional hook of this largely political film comes in the singling out of some key individuals. In both fiction and nonfiction, the cinema speaks best through characters, and *Paris Is Burning* gives several of the main characters a forum to express their philosophies, hopes, and aspirations. Most are young outcasts, living in these constructed family units, seeking acceptance, and belonging with one another in lieu of the trappings of middle-class success forever out of their reach. It is hard to refuse to identify with the painful revelations of their similar stories of rejection from both society and their own families.

The film describes the structure of the community in a straightforward, public-television fashion. The low-key effectiveness of this technique pushes the viewer toward accepting a strongly positive thesis regarding the existence of these gay vogue houses: They are an alternative to gang violence. The members belong to self-described urban gay street gangs and act out their conflicts harmlessly on the fiercely competitive dance floor. When this situation is compared to the violence and neighborhood terrorism of heterosexual gangs, there is a strong statement to be made for society embracing, rather than shunning, homosexuality.

The team spirit and the sense of commitment to the ball make it seem not ridiculous when a clear-eyed and articulate young man compares the event to an Olympic sport, such as gymnastics. The front-runners simply want the same kind of validation of their excellence that American society gives to professional football or other such violent pastimes. The men in *Paris Is Burning* want their craft to be recognized.

The men who star in *Paris Is Burning* have been victimized by the larger world for some time. They are united in a life-style of brotherhood in the face of a heterosexual society that would do them harm, or at the very least keep them at an economic status that impedes their achievement of the so-called American Dream. The film is about the metamorphosizing phenomenon of this community in the interest of survival. Without being condescending, the motion picture is quite sad and touching because the men are vulnerable to the same fantasy illusions that conservative ideology and the media create.

As with most controversial films, the most frustrating thing to realize is that those viewers who would even consider seeing and learning from them are those already likely to be sympathetic to their causes. Thus, this film's positive message about the gay community's amazing alternative to gang violence, as well as the dignity and humanity of the gay subculture, will probably not reach the audiences that could most benefit from it because they are not likely to attend arthouse theaters. Unless *Paris Is Burning* is brought to television or a clip is shown at the Academy Awards ceremony, mainstream viewers will likely remain unexposed to its powerful ideas.

Mary E. Belles

Reviews
Black Film Review. VI, Number 3, 1991, p. 26.
Chicago Tribune. August 9, 1991, VII, p. 21.
Los Angeles Times. August 9, 1991, p. F1.
Mother Jones. XVI, March/April, 1991, p. 75.
The New Republic. CCIV, April 22, 1991, p. 30.
New York Magazine. XXIV, May 13, 1991, p. 96.
The New York Times. March 13, 1991, p. C13.
The New York Times Magazine. April 7, 1991, II, p. 20.
The New Yorker. LXVII, March 25, 1991, p. 72.
Newsweek. CXVIII, August 12, 1991, p. 62.
People Weekly. XXXVI, August 26, 1991, p. 13.
Rolling Stone. April 4, 1991, p. 60.
Time. CXXXVII, May 13, 1991, p. 69.
Variety. CCCXLI, October 15, 1990, p. 78.
The Wall Street Journal. August 22, 1991, p. A10.
The Washington Post. August 9, 1991, p. D6.

POISON

Production: Christine Vachon for Bronze Eye; released by Zeitgeist Films
Direction: Todd Haynes
Screenplay: Todd Haynes
Cinematography: Maryse Alberti (color) and Barry Ellsworth (black and white)
Editing: James Lyons and Todd Haynes
Production design: Sarah Stollman
Art direction: Chas Plummer
Set decoration: John Hansen
Casting: Andrew Harpending, Kim Ainouz, Laura Barnett, and John Kelly
Sound: Mary Ellen Porto
Costume design: Jessica Haston
Music: James Bennett
MPAA rating: no listing
Running time: 85 minutes

> *Principal characters:*
> **Hero**
> Felicia Beacon .... Edith Meeks
> Millie Sklar .... Millie White
> Gregory Lazar .... Buck Smith
> **Horror**
> Dr. Graves .... Larry Maxwell
> Nancy Olsen .... Susan Norman
> Deputy Hansen .... Al Quagliata
> **Homo**
> John Broom .... Scott Renderer
> Jack Bolton .... James Lyons
> Rass .... John R. Lombardi
> Young Broom .... Tony Pemberton
> Young Bolton .... Andrew Harpending

   The preface to viewing Todd Haynes's controversial first feature-length project is at least as dramatic as the work itself. Condemned by the Reverend Donald Wildmon, the head of the American Family Association, for assumed graphic and explicit homosexual pornography, *Poison* also took the Grand Prize at the 1991 Sundance Film Festival. This highly stylized film was completed in part with funds allotted by the National Endowment of the Arts, and it was supported by its chairman John E. Frohnmayer as a socially responsible work of art. Haynes had already achieved both praise and notoriety with *Superstar: The Karen Carpenter Story* (1987), which became inaccessible because of legal entanglements with the late singer's brother, Richard Carpenter. That forty-three-minute film used Barbie-type dolls and newsreel footage to depict the tragic phenomenon of anorexia nervosa that ended the life and career of a young woman who seemed to be successful.

Poison is the type of motion picture that requires the viewer to take an active role. With three separate parables on deviance and punishment crashing against one another in both form and content throughout, the pressure is on the audience first to distinguish what is going on and then to make the thematic connections that bind the work together as a consciously uneasy whole. It is a reflexive, deconstructionist exercise that calls into question the communicative and manipulative power of image and iconography. As such, it should elicit delight from frustrated scholars and connoisseurs of the film medium. For those willing to be thus engaged, the experience—disturbing as its thematics are—is extra-ordinarily entertaining on the level of camp. Two of the film's sections in particular represent a send-up in form while they make serious points.

The story entitled "Hero" is shot in the quasi-cinema verité and interview style that evolved out of the earnest documentary tradition in Western culture, but it also makes use of the reactionary trend of "dramatizations-as-truth." This mock-documentary probes what has happened to an abused seven-year-old boy who shot his father in order to protect his mother and then flew out the window. The conflicting reports from neighbors, teachers, classmates, and social workers suggest an inability to explain away behavior or individuals designated as "deviant" by society. The most eerie screen moments radiate from Richie's religiously deluded mother, Felicia Beacon (Edith Meeks). She believes that her little boy was "a gift from God" who simply flew up into the clouds after he fulfilled his mission. All the classic telltale signs of abuse are hinted at as the other interviewees speak of Richie's unlucky, accident-prone, and irrationally irritating existence.

It is hard work for the first half hour of the film to relate the differing information to the proper story, especially given that the film's opening shot shows a black-and-white impression of what must be little Richie Beacon's point of view of the patricidal event. This scene, however, is not in keeping with the color newsfilm look of the rest of the "Hero" piece; it is readily associated with the exaggerated style of the "Horror" episode. Such an unfortunate miscalculation adds unnecessary confusion for those audience members who are already generous and willing to go along with and embrace the conflictive nature of the form itself. Flaws of this nature occasionally conspire to hold back the work, but the willingness to make bold connections and assertions usually pulls the film forward.

Most recognizable and satisfying is the "Horror" segment, which follows a tortured and alienated "mad scientist" to his inevitable destruction. This gem of camp humor uses low-key black-and-white cinematography, exaggerated camera angles, and intentionally atrocious acting—iconographic staples that had their roots in German expressionism and first came through to the American consciousness in the low-budget *films noirs* of the 1940's and 1950's. In those B-pictures in the panic-stricken vein of Rudolph Mate's *D.O.A.* (1950), one finds the darker side of life explored and the unsuspecting protagonist punishable to extremes far beyond what he deserves.

The unease of that period has become predominantly denoted as symptomatic evidence of McCarthyism. In the 1990's, sexual stigmatization seemed destined to fill the gap left by the cooling down of the Cold War.

Brilliant, dedicated Dr. Graves (Larry Maxwell) is shunned by his colleagues and rendered an outcast because of his ambitious work to distill the components of the human sex drive. Enter a young medical student, Nancy Olsen (Susan Norman), who has dedicated her own career to the furtherance of Dr. Graves's research. In a distracted moment upon meeting his admirer, the good doctor mistakenly consumes the sex component and is transformed into the terrible "Leper Sex Killer." As densely populated with metaphor (particularly acquired immune deficiency syndrome) as with bad effects and bad taste, this romp is immediately accessible to almost all viewers. By being hilariously consistent within itself, the episode is able to coax audience members who are not readily inclined toward critical examination. While the most heavy-handed segment, "Horror" successfully delivers the level of expectations that it sets up. Part of its reception may be owed to the sensibilities fostered by the trend of viewing old television shows, such as *Leave It to Beaver* and *The Donna Reed Show*, in an ironic manner—the tip of the iceberg referred to as "postmodernism." One must acknowledge, however, that *Poison* is simply not that difficult a film. Contrast it to the explosive political works of Jean-Luc Goddard, and the film appears tame.

While most reviewers agreed that Haynes's work is a commendable art film that should be encouraged, some implied that the outrage and controversy surrounding it was more specifically a reflection of American culture than anything in Haynes's personality. The "Homo" section of the film—the part that is most realistic in form, openly deals with a homosexual narrative, and is drawn most explicitly from the works of imprisoned gay writer Jean Genet—is the source of both the real and imagined "offensive" material. The story line, which traces the obsession of alienated prisoner John Broom (Scott Renderer) for another male inmate, Jack Bolton (James Lyons), whom Broom finally rapes, is actually shot very discreetly with regard to sexual content.

It is a pastoral, romantic flashback sequence that offers the most repellent presentation (and prompted walkouts at the Sundance Film Festival). In a bizarre depiction of the grace and humiliation of the persecuted, the filmmaker displays reformatory boys spitting relentlessly into the face and open mouth of one who has been unluckily targeted as their scapegoat. This boy eventually grows up to be the object of his fellow inmate's desire. The remainder of "Homo" is handled in a gritty, somber manner which is almost repressed at times. The filmmakers are so earnest as to be marred by their verisimilitude, because the plot shifts are not particularly easy to follow. The tone is dark and muffled, but the viewer's interest is carried by the force of the emotion that John Broom feels. In this scenario, the convicted outcasts act out the victimization and humiliation cycle on outsiders to their own alternate microcosm of society.

Haynes seems indebted to the Soviet school of editing promoted by Sergi Eisenstein, which grounds the need for violence in formal construction as the means to articulating political conflict. The abruptness of the meshing together of the contrasting structures ensures tension in the presentation of issues about which the audience should feel dissonance. These parallels successfully reinforce the film's themes in such a way as to make the final product stand not as a neat summation but as a synthesis in which the final product is somehow a bit more than merely its parts added up. Decidedly neither a smooth and glossy product nor a perfectly honed manifesto, *Poison* is very sophisticated at times and remarkably enjoyable throughout. For distraught critics suffering the post-Reagan retrogressive political climate of the early 1990's, it may not have been a call to arms, but it may have had the right balance to begin an inroad at this juncture.

Mary E. Belles

Reviews
Chicago Tribune. July 12, 1991, VII, p. 32.
Cineaste. XVIII, Number 3, 1991, p. 42.
Entertainment Weekly. April 26, 1991, p. 38.
The Hollywood Reporter. May 17, 1991, p. 11.
The Houston Post. June 14, 1991, p. E4.
L.A. Weekly. May 17-23, 1991, XIII, p. 29.
Los Angeles. May, 1991, p. 139.
Los Angeles Times. April 3, 1991, p. F1.
The Nation. CCLII, April 22, 1991, p. 534.
The New York Times. April 5, 1991, p. B2.
The New York Times. April 14, 1991, p. 15.
Newsweek. CXVII, April 29, 1991, p. 61.
Rolling Stone. April 18, 1991, p. 99.
Sight and Sound. I, October, 1991, p. 56.
Time. CXXXVII, May 13, 1991, p. 69.
Variety. January 28, 1991, p. 3.
The Village Voice. April 9, 1991, XXXVI, p. 53.

THE PRINCE OF TIDES

Production: Barbra Streisand and Andrew Karsch for Barwood/Longfellow; released by Columbia Pictures
Direction: Barbra Streisand
Screenplay: Pat Conroy and Becky Johnston; based on the novel by Conroy
Cinematography: Stephen Goldblatt
Editing: Don Zimmerman
Production design: Paul Sylbert
Art direction: W. Steven Graham
Set decoration: Caryl Heller, Arthur Howe, Jr., and Leslie Ann Pope
Set design: Chris Shriver
Casting: Bonnie Finnegan
Sound: Kay Rose
Costume design: Ruth Morley
Music: James Newton Howard
MPAA rating: R
Running time: 132 minutes

Principal characters:

Tom Wingo	Nick Nolte
Dr. Susan Lowenstein	Barbra Streisand
Sallie Wingo	Blythe Danner
Lila Wingo Newbury	Kate Nelligan
Savannah Wingo	Melinda Dillon
Herbert Woodruff	Jeroen Krabbé
Bernard Woodruff	Jason Gould
Eddie	George Carlin

Even at this early stage in her career as a director, it is apparent that Barbra Streisand has a marked preference for making films that harken back to the heyday of the Hollywood studio system, when big stars and big production values formed the foundation for building big, glossy films. Typically, these might deal with real-life problems but ensured that their subjects had a larger-than-life emotional appeal. With her debut directorial effort, *Yentl* (1983), Streisand proved that she could make a musical as grand in scope and as cinematically virtuosic as any classic studio venture. Some, however, suggested that she lacked generosity toward other actors. Critics pointed to the fact that *Yentl* displayed her many talents to advantage but wasted Mandy Patinkin in the role of Avigdor, not even allowing the accomplished vocalist/actor to sing. While no one doubted her talent in directing, producing, and screenwriting, some wondered whether Streisand could detach her ego from any film enterprise so that the material, rather than Streisand, became the focal point.

The Prince of Tides is a step in the right direction, as Streisand proves that she can direct actors, other than herself, both to their advantage and to the advantage of the story. In response to the film, the Academy of Motion Picture Arts and Sciences nominated *The Prince of Tides* in some half-dozen major Academy Award categories, including Best Picture, Best Actor, Best Supporting Actress, Best Screenplay Adaptation, and Best Cinematography. Conspicuously absent from this list, however, was a nomination for director Streisand. Streisand's own self-conscious presence in the film in the central role of psychiatrist Susan Lowenstein may be, as some critics have suggested, the film's weakest link, even as her obvious directorial talent is one of its strongest in telling novelist Pat Conroy's tale of a troubled hero, Tom Wingo (Nick Nolte), and his struggle toward a healing that extends beyond himself to embrace his sister, wife, and mother.

As Tom, Nolte unleashes an emotional range and power that has only fitfully been utilized in an acting career that has emphasized his quirky machismo in films such as *48 Hrs.* (1982), *Under Fire* (1983), and *Extreme Prejudice* (1987). Instead, *The Prince of Tides* calls upon those qualities previously allowed to surface in such Nolte film roles as "Poot" Elliot in *North Dallas Forty* (1979) in which he portrayed a professional football player whose physical deterioration is matched only by his disillusionment with the inhumanity of the "game" he plays. In *The Prince of Tides*, Nolte is cast as Tom Wingo, a football coach whose life is falling apart because of the bitter secrets that haunt his psyche and those of his entire family, that have driven his brother to a premature death, that have motivated his sister's latest suicide attempt, and that haunt his own most intimate relationships, even those with his loving wife, Sallie (Blythe Danner), and his three young daughters.

In a drawling South Carolina accent, Tom begins the film with a voice-over that introduces the audience to his family and to the South Carolina tidewater country that he loves. He also tells of his unhappy childhood, marred most of all by a violent father from whom the three Wingo children—Tom, Luke, and Savannah—often escaped by plunging into the bay and forming an underwater circle of young humanity bound together literally by hands but also by their hearts and their fears. Tom's adult life is not as obviously problematic as his childhood, but he has lost his job and his easy humor belies a bitterness that becomes frighteningly evident whenever he comes into contact with his mother, Lila (Kate Nelligan), a woman he says he enjoys hating. She arrives at Tom's house to discuss the latest Wingo family crisis: Tom's sister, Savannah (Melinda Dillon), has tried to kill herself yet again, and Lila asks Tom to go and be with Savannah. Tom is furious with his mother's presumption that he can or will go. They argue at the top of their voices, but he finally agrees to make the trip. What does he have at home to keep him? As he tells his alienated wife, "our life's a mess."

Upon his arrival in New York, Tom meets with Savannah's therapist, Dr. Susan Lowenstein (Streisand), who says she needs Tom to be his sister's memory, to fill in all those gaps in Savannah's mind that may hold the key to why she wants to die. Tom settles into Savannah's apartment with the help of Eddie (George Carlin), a friend of his sister. After his initial hostility is directed at Dr. Lowenstein for the way in which Savannah is being treated in the psychiatric ward, Tom revises his opinion of her method of treatment and begins his sessions with her to fill in those details of their troubled childhood.

Dr. Lowenstein has already noted the curious reactions of Tom's mother and father to Savannah's illness. She asks Tom about Callanwolde, a word that the now wordless Savannah first uttered when she was found after her suicide attempt. Tom links the word to his mother's social ambitions, to the Callanwolde League to which she hoped to belong in spite of the family's humble status as shrimpers. Tom speaks of his mother's contradictory emotional messages and her fear that her children will be "disloyal" and write about their "hideous family." As Tom reveals the past to Dr. Lowenstein, he tends to Savannah, who still does not respond to her environment. At home, things are not progressing either. In a telephone conversation, Sallie tells Tom that she is seeing another man. Tom begins to feel an attraction to Susan Lowenstein. At a party hosted by Eddie, they talk, and, at his insistence, he takes her home. There he meets her surly adolescent son, Bernard (Jason Gould). Susan reveals that Bernard is a talented violinist but that he wants to play football, and she asks Tom to coach him. After a rocky beginning, he and Bernard develop a warm and respectful relationship that elicits the ire of Susan's husband, concert violinist Herbert Woodruff (Jeroen Krabbé).

Susan asks Tom to interpret his sister's dreams, those that appear in the children's books she has written. Tom shows Susan home movies taken when he was a child. He tells her of his brother Luke, who was courageous enough to stand up to their father and who served in Vietnam and returned to the island a hero. When Lila divorced their father and decided to sell much of their land for a government power plant, Luke blew up the construction site and was shot to death. In spite of these painful revelations, Tom does not cry. He has not yet broken through his defenses or brought to full consciousness the source of his and Savannah's most deeply felt pain.

Tom returns home for his youngest daughter's birthday. Sallie tells him that her lover has proposed marriage. All Tom can do is joke about it, a response to painful situations that Dr. Lowenstein has suggested is Tom's way of defending himself against emotional pain. After another flashback showing a violent fight between Tom's parents, in an unexpected twist, Tom and his family are shown visiting his father on his shrimp boat. Surprisingly, "grandpa" is, as Tom declares, good with the kids, patient and loving. With his son, he is no longer violent, but cold, silent, and defensive. Lila, remarried into the moneyed class, meets with Tom in her magnificent home to present him with articles on mental illness that she thinks Savannah's doctor should see. She asks what he is revealing about their family. To her dismay, Tom tells her that he will tell the truth about Callanwolde.

Back in New York, Tom begins another session with Dr. Lowenstein. He reveals the core, traumatic event that has shaped Savannah's troubled destiny. One evening before their father came home, three escaped criminals from Callanwolde prison broke into their home and raped Savannah and Lila. After much coaxing, Tom breaks down and reveals the truth that he has been unable to face: He too was raped. Luke entered the house and shot two of the men, while Lila stabbed the other. More horror followed, for

Lila decided that they must not tell anyone, neither the police nor their father. They buried the bodies and cleaned the house. When their father arrived home, they sat down to dinner as usual. Three days later, Savannah tried to kill herself. The event that "did not happen" was already beginning to wreak havoc on its victims.

While Tom reveals his innermost troubles, he begins to be sensitive to the reasons why Susan Lowenstein appears to him to be such a "sad" person. Her husband, obviously jealous of Tom's relationship with Bernard (and perhaps also with Susan), invites Tom to a dinner party where he attempts to humiliate Tom with a caricatured violin rendition of "Dixie." Tom successfully deflects the insult, when, in an equally caricatured Southern drawl, he praises Woodruff's performance of "Mozart." Woodruff insults Tom's profession as a coach and cruelly violates patient-doctor confidence by revealing that Tom's sister is Susan's patient. Finally, Woodruff proceeds to insult Susan by protecting his mistress at her expense; Tom elicits an apology from him by unusual means. He and Susan leave, and they become lovers.

What follows is a long sequence detailing Tom and Susan's apparently idyllic relationship. The lovers realize, however, that their relationship must end, as Tom's sister improves with the help of the information Tom has provided. Sallie wants Tom back in their marriage, a development that Susan has accurately predicted. She and Tom say goodbye. He returns home to the embraces of his family and to the land that he loves. Nevertheless, as he admits, he still thinks often of Susan Lowenstein and how much she did for him.

The Prince of Tides, as an adaptation of a popular novel, may not please those familiar with Pat Conroy's book, even though the author contributed to the writing of the screenplay. Some critics noted that large sections of Conroy's novel were sacrificed, perhaps at the expense of fattening Streisand's role to a degree unmotivated by the material. Although Streisand gets the "star treatment" in terms of flattering photography and screen time, however, there can be little argument that she gives the film to Nick Nolte, and it is his performance that carries the film and gives it its poignancy. Excellent supporting performances are offered by Blythe Danner and Kate Nelligan (the latter in an Academy Award-nominated performance accomplished under pounds of old-age makeup through much of the film). Unfortunately, male characters other than Tom are often painted in broad, one-dimensional terms and the character of Bernard appears gratuitous, inserted merely to prove Tom's masculine, fatherly virtues.

At times, the melodramatic qualities of the film (the stereotypes, the lush music, the soft-focus photography) threaten to overwhelm the feeling of psychological truth that lies at the core of *The Prince of Tides* and that Nolte's performance so effectively conveys. Also troubling is the film's casual treatment of the dubious ethics involved in Susan Lowenstein's sexual involvement with Tom. In spite of the film's multiple Oscar nominations, it failed to win a single award. Despite what was obviously Hollywood's public rejection of Streisand and of her directorial ambitions, her talent cannot be dismissed. One can only wait in anticipation to see whether the multitalented Streisand will move forward another step toward becoming a director whose romantically infused sensibility and demanding perfectionism help to make her one of the industry's best directors, rather than a woman perceived by her contemporaries as merely one of its most egotistical.

Gaylyn Studlar

Reviews

American Film: Magazine of the Film and Television Arts. XVII, January/February, 1992, p. 50.
Boxoffice. December, 1991, p. R-88.
Chicago Tribune. December 25, 1991, V, p. 1.
The Christian Science Monitor. December 27, 1991, p. 13.
The Hollywood Reporter. December 2, 1991, p. 5.
Los Angeles Times. December 25, 1991, p. F1.
The New York Times. December 25, 1991, p. B11.
The New Yorker. LXVII, January 27, 1992, p. 60.
Newsweek. CXVIII, December 30, 1991, p. 57.
Premiere. V, December, 1991, p. 86.
Rolling Stone. January 9, 1992, p. 55.
Variety. December 2, 1991, p. 2.
The Washington Post. December 25, 1991, p. D1.

PROSPERO'S BOOKS

Origin: Great Britain and France
Released: 1991
Released in U.S.: 1991
Production: Kees Kasander for Allarts-Cinea and Camera One-Penta, in association with Elsevier-Vendex, Film Four International, VPRO Television, Canal Plus, and NHK; released by Miramax Films
Direction: Peter Greenaway
Screenplay: Peter Greenaway; based on the play *The Tempest*, by William Shakespeare
Cinematography: Sacha Vierny
Editing: Marina Bodbijl
Production design: Ben Van Os and Jan Roelfs
Set decoration: Bem Zuydwijk, Rick Overberg, and Wendy Valentijn
Sound: Garth Marshall
Costume design: Dien van Straalen
Choreography: Karine Saporta and Michael Clark
Music: Michael Nyman
MPAA rating: R
Running time: 124 minutes

Principal characters:
Prospero	John Gielgud
Caliban	Michael Clark
Alonso	Michel Blanc
Gonzalo	Erland Josephson
Miranda	Isabelle Pasco
Antonio	Tom Bell
Sebastian	Kenneth Cranham
Ferdinand	Mark Rylance
Adrian	Gerard Thoolen
Francisco	Pierre Bokma
Trinculo	Jim van der Woude
Stephano	Michiel Romeyn
Ariel	Orpheo
	Paul Russell
	James Thierree
	Emil Wolk

Prospero's Books is director Peter Greenaway's freely adapted retelling of Shakespeare's *The Tempest*, and as is often true of Greenaway's works, the film generated admiration, controversy, and a fair measure of bewilderment among viewers and critics alike. With John Gielgud in the title role, the film offers a powerful performance by one of the theater's preeminent Shakespearean actors, yet *Prospero's Books* is as far from a traditional interpretation of Shakespeare as Greenaway's *The Cook, the Thief, His Wife, and Her Lover* (1990) is from Julia Child.

Using a groundbreaking combination of film and television techniques, Greenaway creates a vision of Prospero's magical world that is part dazzling cinematography and part Quantel Paintbox, a remarkable advance in video technology. The result is a blending of 35mm film and high-definition television, or HDTV, that allows the director a hitherto unattainable level of hands-on control over the picture's optical effects. For Greenaway, who began his career as a painter, this technique gives rise to myriad possibilities.

The story of *The Tempest* centers on Prospero, once the Duke of Milan and now a castaway with his daughter, Miranda (Isabelle Pasco), on an island inhabited only by spirits and the misshapen Caliban (Michael Clark). Twelve years earlier, Prospero was betrayed and sent into exile by his brother, Antonio (Tom Bell), in league with Alonso, the king of Naples (Michel Blanc). Since his arrival on the island, Prospero has vanquished Caliban's sorceress mother, freed the spirits that she had imprisoned, and employed them himself in his own study of sorcery. Now his powers have brought his enemies within his reach as he creates a tempest that causes the wreck of the king's ship on the island's shores.

The king's son, Ferdinand (Mark Rylance), separated from the others in the storm, is the first of the company to encounter Prospero and his daughter, and, as Prospero had hoped, he and Miranda fall in love. To test the young man's character and the strength of his love, Prospero pretends to mistrust him and opposes the match. With the aid of the spirit Ariel (played in the film by four actors: Orpheo, Paul Russell, James Thierree, and Emil Wolk), Prospero also oversees the movements of Alonso, who has washed ashore on another part of the island with his brother, Sebastian (Kenneth Cranham), and the treacherous Antonio. With them is Prospero's old friend and counselor, Gonzalo (Erland Josephson). When Sebastian and Antonio plot to murder the king and Gonzalo while they sleep, Prospero sends Ariel to them with a warning. (This segment of the story has been altered by Greenaway, who makes Prospero's magic the agent that drives the two conspirators.) Caliban is also embroiled in a conspiracy, plotting with two of the king's men to overthrow Prospero. They, too, are thwarted by Ariel at Prospero's behest.

When Prospero at last reveals himself to the assembled company, he reminds Alonso and Antonio of their betrayal and then forgives them. He is restored to his rightful position by the king, who is filled with remorse over his former actions and overjoyed to learn that his son is alive and betrothed to Miranda. Prospero frees Ariel and the other spirits and abandons his magical powers, begging the audience's forgiveness and approval so that he, too, can be set free.

Greenaway has based his concept for *Prospero's Books* on a brief passage from the play in which Prospero recalls how Gonzalo aided him at the time of his banishment: "Knowing I lov'd my books, he furnish'd me/ From mine own library with volumes that/ I prize above my dukedom." The books themselves, twenty-four volumes in all, provide the film with its structure as Greenaway imagines their subjects and contents and brings them to life on the screen. It is from these books that Prospero has gained his powers—he relinquishes his sorcery by throwing them into the sea—and it is in their realization that Greenaway makes the fullest use of his own technological magic. With titles such as *An Alphabetical Inventory of the Dead, a Bestiary of Past, Present and Future Animals*, and *The Ninety-Two Conceits of the Minotaur*, the volumes represent the sum total of human knowledge up to that time, much of which is lost when Prospero destroys them. Each book is given a brief description in voice-over narration as it appears, sparking a series of vivid, sometimes graphic, often mysterious visual images that capture the essence of its contents.

The books' relationship to the story lies in one of the twists that Greenaway has given to his interpretation of Shakespeare's tale; here, it is Prospero—sitting alone in his room imagining a tale of revenge on his enemies—who is the author of *The Tempest*. Until the story's final moments, all of its action takes place only in Prospero's reveries, and the shape that he gives its plot is drawn from the books he has studied in his exile. A book on water leads him to create the tempest that sets the story in motion, a book of mirrors hints that what the audience sees is merely a reflection of reality, a book on architecture served as the model for the palace in which Prospero lives, and so on throughout the story. The last two books—the only two saved from destruction— are *A Book of Thirty-Five Plays* dating from 1623, with room in it for one final entry, and *A Play Called "The Tempest."*

Yet while the play begins its life in Prospero's imagination, it takes on a life of its own as it nears its close. As Prospero's revenge fantasy reaches its peak, he realizes at last that he is abusing his powers with the pain and fear he is causing and, frightened by his own brutality, he abandons his dream and forgives his enemies. Rather than fading with their creator's fantasy, however, the characters he has manipulated are suddenly made real by his recovery of his own humanity, and the story's final reconciliation becomes possible.

Until this point, all the characters have spoken with Prospero's voice, sometimes exclusively and sometimes in tandem with their own—a dramatic conceit that results in almost the entire play being read by John Gielgud himself. For Gielgud, who made his acting debut in 1921, a film version of *The Tempest* had been a long-held ambition, and it was at his suggestion that Greenaway undertook the film. Having played Prospero several times on the stage, he brings to the role a wealth of experience and talent that makes this performance rewarding even for those discouraged by the film's visual excesses. Many critics complained, however, that the rest of the film's cast, which includes such respected performers as Erland Josephson and Michel Blanc, is largely underutilized. Only avant-garde dancer Michael Clark, whose overt sexuality and tortured physical movements make a startling impression as Caliban, escapes being overpowered by Greenaway's own directorial pyrotechnics.

Indeed, for the uninitiated, *Prospero's Books* can be an unsettling immersion in a filmmaking style that has won for its director both international acclaim and condemnation. Greenaway's films are elaborate constructions that return repeatedly to the themes of power, sex, and violence, but with an emotional distance and formal style that transform them into cinematic paintings come to life. The sheer physical beauty of the films is often stunning, and Greenaway's refusal to hold to the traditions of narrative structure and conventional social mores makes his work both challenging and controversial. In *Prospero's Books*, Greenaway fills Prospero's island palace with dozens of naked sprites and spirits, all literally dancing attendance on their master and as much a part of the decor as the elaborate Renaissance architecture and carefully decorated sets. What becomes apparent after only a few such scenes is that nudity on so grand a scale quickly loses its ability to shock. It is, as Greenaway intended, simply one of the many aspects that constitute the film's visual imagery.

That a director so absorbed by the unconventional would take a Shakespearean drama as his subject is only surprising on first consideration. For Greenaway, the challenge in filming *The Tempest* lay in finding a way to break through the barriers of traditional interpretation. He discussed his approach in an interview with *Screen International*: "There's a way here that a baroque excess of information somehow in itself is non-narrative because you are totally lost, there's no way that you can use the props of narrative in order to make things coherent. You have to try to find other systems." With *Prospero's Books*, Greenaway explores his own new creative systems even as he forces his audience to find a new approach to a once-familiar play.

Janet Lorenz

Reviews
American Film: Magazine of the Film and Television Arts. XVI, November, 1991, p. 34.
Boxoffice. January, 1992, p. R-5.
Chicago Tribune. November 27, 1991, V, p. 3.
Commonweal. CXIX, January 31, 1992, p. 25.
Film Comment. XXVII, November, 1991, p. 50.
Film Review. September, 1991, p. 29.
The Hollywood Reporter. September 26, 1991, p. 5.
L.A. Weekly. November 29-December 5, 1991, p. 35.
Los Angeles Times. November 27, 1991, p. F1.
The New York Times. September 28, 1991, p. 12.
Plays and Players. November, 1991, p. 22.
Screen International. September 13, 1991, p. 16.
Sight and Sound. I, September, 1991, p. 44.
Variety. September 3, 1991, p. 2.
The Village Voice. November 26, 1991, p. 64.

QUEENS LOGIC

Production: Stuart Oken and Russ Smith for New Visions Pictures; released by Seven Arts through New Line Cinema
Direction: Steve Rash
Screenplay: Tony Spiridakis; based on a story by Spiridakis and Joseph W. Savino
Cinematography: Amir Mokri
Editing: Patrick Kennedy
Production design: Edward Pisoni
Set decoration: Marcie Dale
Sound: Tom Brandau
Costume design: Linda Bass
Music: Joe Jackson
Music supervision: Gary Goetzman and Sharon Boyle
MPAA rating: R
Running time: 112 minutes

Principal characters:
Al	Joe Mantegna
Eliot	John Malkovich
Dennis	Kevin Bacon
Carla	Linda Fiorentino
Ray	Ken Olin
Patricia	Chloe Webb
Grace	Jamie Lee Curtis
Vinny	Tony Spiridakis
Monte	Tom Waits
Marty	Michael Zelniker
Maria	Kelly Bishop
Jeremy	Terry Kinney
Jack	Ed Marinaro

In black-and-white, a boy climbs a rope to the Hellgate Bridge, which separates Queens from Manhattan in New York City. His friends anxiously watch and wait, fearful that he might fall to the water and rocks below. The boy easily reaches the top, however, and is triumphant—king of the world, or at least of Queens. As color fades in gradually, the film introduces these children in their adult forms. The self-appointed hero, Al (Joe Mantegna), now a fish-store owner, still behaves like the king of Queens, offering praise or criticism to pedestrians from his current throne: a vintage convertible. The appreciative onlookers were Al's cousin, Ray (Ken Olin); Al's wife, Carla (Linda Fiorentino); Ray's fiancée, Patricia (Chloe Webb); and assorted pals and hangers-on Dennis (Kevin Bacon), Eliot (John Malkovich), Vinny (Tony Spiridakis), and Monte (Tom Waits).

It is twenty years later, and the clique has bigger, if less inviting, bridges to climb. Ray is supposed to be married this weekend but has a case of cold feet so contagious that even Al, whose anniversary is tonight, is having second thoughts about marriage. Throaty singer/songwriter Waits plays Monte, who buys a new Monte Carlo every year because it goes with his name. Monte is an occasional companion of the Queens regulars but looks the sort of ragged scary character that a stranger would cross the street to avoid. When Monte is not hanging out at the local bar, he is, or fancies himself to be, a jeweler. Predictably, the goods in question are of questionable origin. Nevertheless, Al goes to Monte to purchase an anniversary ring for Carla. An experienced huckster himself, Al bargains the price down from ten thousand dollars to four thousand plus tickets to a ball game. Still, Al is afraid to go home. And well he should be.

While Carla sits at home, wearing Al's favorite dress and listening to her mother berate her for marrying a fishmonger, Al sits in a bar, proudly showing off the new ring and extolling the joys of matrimony. If marriage is so wonderful, however, why is Al spending his anniversary with the guys? When he finally arrives home, Carla is waiting for him with a packed suitcase and a right hook.

Examples such as this understandably worry Ray. A talented artist, Ray dreams of painting frescoes in Italy, and he is afraid that marriage would signal the end of that dream. His fiancée, Patricia, owns and operates a successful beauty salon and has no illusions about their approaching marriage. Patricia assures Ray that she will be happy spending the rest of her life doing his laundry and being his muse, as well as his "love slave." Ray, however, cannot assure Patricia that he will show up for the wedding. When it occurs to her that Ray is contemplating leaving her at the altar, Patricia interrupts Ray in the shower to tell him that this is one decision he is going to have to make on his own. Then, for emphasis, Patricia flushes the toilet to divert the cold water from Ray's shower, leaving Ray scalded but no less confused about marriage.

Eliot, Al's associate at the fish store, lives with Patricia and Ray, has done so for years, and plans to continue to do so indefinitely. Eliot is a homophobic homosexual: He accepts that he is gay but abhors the company of other gay men. His friends encourage him to date, but Eliot insists that he is content with his friends and his life the way it is. Though it is commendable that Eliot's homosexuality is not an issue with his arrogantly macho friends, it is unclear whether this is the result of understanding or mere apathy. Bacon plays Dennis, the prodigal pal returning to Queens from Hollywood, where he has gone to find fortune and fame in the music industry. Dennis describes his life and work on the West Coast so glowingly it becomes obvious that his existence must be horrible and that he is too embarrassed to admit it.

Last, and perhaps least, is struggling actor Vinny. This role, played by the author of *Queens Logic*, epitomizes the logic of Queens. Unfortunately, it is not a flattering representation. Like his friends, Vinny claims to be struggling to get out of Queens, but deep down he has no intention of ever leaving the comfort and familiarity of his neighborhood.

Ray's bachelor party, which is heralded as a good excuse to get these friends all together for a weekend even though they already spend most weekends and weekdays together, is the event on which the story centers. While Carla and Patricia attempt to spend a night out without their mates, the men congregate at Vinny's apartment. The party consists of the above-mentioned men and any women that they could persuade, coerce, or trick into attending. Among the women that are invited to the party is Grace (Jamie Lee Curtis). In this cameo role, Curtis plays a wealthy woman who becomes attracted to Al when they meet in a grocery store. She arrives at the party and virtually kidnaps Al for an evening of celebrating the wonders of Queens. Leaning against a gravestone in a local cemetery, Grace and Al share each others' life stories, a few compliments, and some of the banal aphorisms that the film tends to substitute for actual dialogue, such as: "When you dance you have to let the other person lead once in a while" and "Throw away your anger."

Meanwhile, Carla and Patricia, ostensibly having run out of things to do in New York, arrive at the party to check up on their men. Carla weeps when she learns that Al has left the party with another woman. Patricia also receives a shock when she enters one of the bedrooms to find Ray passed out on the bed next to a partially naked woman, who had presumably taken advantage of Ray's fear of marriage, his ego as a painter, and his present drunkenness. Ray chases Patricia into the hall, where he tries to apologize and explain his feelings, but Patricia understands them all too well. In a verbose but perceptive speech, Patricia explains that, in addition to being the woman that Ray loves, she is the quintessential embodiment of Queens and that, even if Ray makes it to Italy to paint frescoes, as long as he is with her, he will always be home.

Just as the party seems almost over, Ray receives a call from Al, who, as the result of some inexplicable epiphany at the hands of Grace, feels compelled to again climb the Hellgate Bridge. Ray grabs the guys and they hurry to the bridge, unsure whether they will be able to stop Al's misguided attempt to recapture his youth or arrive only in time to retrieve his broken bones from the rocks below. An obvious question remains: If they are so frustrated with their lives in Queens, why do Al and his friends not try crossing the bridge instead of climbing it?

Clearly screenwriter Spiridakis' relationship with his hometown is of the love/hate variety. Through his characters, he glorifies the life and the place that he himself has left. They continually argue with one another and eventually with themselves, pledging their patriotism to their native burg while frantically devising methods to escape.

It is unfortunate that most of the film's impressive cast chose to portray their characters as larger and louder than life. Mannerisms and accents go beyond what is necessary to convey locale, and the characters seem to be caricatures of themselves. Ironically, the smallest roles are the ones that ring the truest: Curtis as the eccentric who is excited by Al's fear and confusion; Ed Marinaro as Jack the bartender, who would rather drown his patrons' sorrows than analyze them; Terry Kinney as the party-goer who tries to strike up a relationship with Eliot only to be insulted and rejected; and Michael Zelniker as the shy pianist who is as frightened by this peculiar fraternity as he is intrigued.

It is difficult to sympathize with the film's band of overgrown and whiny children. Except for Bacon, who finally admits to everyone—one at a time—that he is a failure in Hollywood, these men have nothing exceptional to complain about, yet they drone on and on about the most common of events and decisions that affect everyone in every city in the world. Prenuptial jitters, marital squabbles, and business responsibilities are legitimate concerns, but this script takes two hours to come to the conclusions that the audience can guess in the first ten minutes: Al and Carla will reconcile; Ray and Patricia will marry; Eliot, Dennis, and Vinny will continue in and out of relationships indefinitely; and none of them will ever leave Queens.

Eleah Horwitz

Reviews
Chicago Tribune. February 1, 1991, VII, p. 23.
Cosmopolitan. CCX, March, 1991, p. 92.
Films in Review. XLII, May, 1991, p. 192.
The Hollywood Reporter. February 1, 1991, p. 12.
Los Angeles Times. February 1, 1991, p. F8.
The New York Times. February 1, 1991, p. B10.
Premiere. III, July 1, 1990, p. 84.
San Francisco Chronicle. April 19, 1991, p. E6.
Variety. February 1, 1991, p. 2.
Video. XV, September, 1991, p. 67.
Video Review. XII, October, 1991, p. 120.
Village View. February 1-7, 1991, p. 25.

A RAGE IN HARLEM

Production: Stephen Woolley and Kerry Boyle for Palace; released by Miramax
Direction: Bill Duke
Screenplay: John Toles-Bey and Bobby Crawford; based on the novel by Chester
    Himes
Cinematography: Toyomichi Kurita
Editing: Curtiss Clayton
Production design: Steven Legler
Sound: Paul Cote
Costume design: Nile Samples
Music: Elmer Bernstein
MPAA rating: R
Running time: 108 minutes

> *Principal characters:*
> Jackson .... Forest Whitaker
> Goldy .... Gregory Hines
> Imabelle .... Robin Givens
> Big Kathy .... Zakes Mokae
> Easy Money .... Danny Glover
> Slim .... Badja Djola
> Jodie .... John Toles-Bey
> Hank .... Ron Taylor
> Coffin Ed Johnson .... Stack Pierce
> Grave Digger Jones .... George Wallace
> Claude X .... Willard E. Pugh
> Screamin' Jay Hawkins .... Himself

A deal about to go wrong opens *A Rage in Harlem.* Slim (Badja Djola) and his trusted sidekicks, Jodie (John Toles-Bey) and Hank (Ron Taylor), have met with other underworld criminals to pass over a trunk of gold ore that they recently stole. A rival gang bursts into the little shack, which is stuck in the dark and forgotten backwoods of Natchez, Mississippi. Soon to follow are the local police, who have been keeping an eye on these unsavory characters. Shots are fired within the shack, and the police fire on the various hoodlums who emerge from the fracas. Miraculously, Imabelle (Robin Givens), Slim's girlfriend, escapes with the trunk of gold ore. Imabelle drives to Harlem, where she hopes to sell the gold nuggets to Slim's contact, Easy Money (Danny Glover).

Penniless and tired of running, Imabelle wanders into the annual Undertaker's Ball, which is in full swing. While she stands at the bar, a man accidentally pours water down the front of her figure-hugging, scarlet dress. Jackson (Forest Whitaker), a gauche undertaker's accountant, tries to make amends by wiping the water from her cleavage, which does not upset the streetwise Imabelle. A little later, she returns to dance with Jackson and invites herself back to his apartment. With as much ease as a spider spins a web, she seduces the churchgoing Jackson in his room. Being a good Christian, he proposes to Imabelle. She is caught off guard, as her motives are anything but honorable.

Before their relationship can progress any further, however, Slim discovers where Imabelle is hiding and retrieves both her and his twice-stolen gold. Without realizing the dangers that might come his way, Jackson sets out to get Imabelle back. The only person who can help him discover her whereabouts is his stepbrother, Goldy (Gregory Hines). Unfortunately, they have not spoken to each other since their mother died five years previously. Jackson and Goldy share nothing in common. Goldy enjoys any kind of gambling, legal or illegal, impersonates a priest as one of his scams for getting money (he keeps a gun in his hollowed-out Bible), and seems to be more than friendly with the transvestite Big Kathy (Zakes Mokae), the owner of the bordello that Goldy frequents. Jackson is not only love-sick but desperate as well, and when he tells Goldy about the gold, his slimy stepbrother seizes the opportunity of getting rich quick. Finding Imabelle does not appear to be Goldy's first priority.

In the meantime, Slim and his boys meet with Easy Money in his office, and there is considerable tension between the two men when Easy Money makes lurid suggestions about himself and Imabelle. Finally, Easy Money crosses the line of discretion with Slim (even Slim has his limits), and a shoot-out ensues in which almost everyone is killed except Slim, who manages to escape with the briefcase of money.

As Slim is fleeing from yet another scene of bloodletting and mayhem, he crashes into Jackson and Goldy, who now seek revenge on Slim for murdering Big Kathy while they were trying to rescue Imabelle. The three men continue their fight in a ballroom located in the same building. Out of anger and desperation, Jackson challenges the villainous Slim to a duel for Imabelle. Slim takes up the challenge but also keeps his switchblade. Jackson narrowly escapes Slim's knife. Finally, Slim has Jackson on the floor and is ready to run his blade across Jackson's throat. At that very moment, Imabelle shoots Slim in the back. Imabelle decides to flee Harlem, but the enamored Jackson manages to leap onto the departing train that was taking Imabelle away from the rage in Harlem—a rage which she seems to have created.

A Rage in Harlem is the third Chester Himes novel to be adapted into a motion picture. The two previous films were *Cotton Comes to Harlem* (1970) and *Come Back, Charleston Blue* (1972), both of which starred Godfrey Cambridge as Grave Digger Jones and Raymond St. Jacques as Coffin Ed Johnson. In terms of production, direction, and overall interest, *A Rage in Harlem* is the best of the trio.

Himes began writing while serving time in the Ohio State Penitentiary but it was not until he moved to Paris, France, that he began writing novels seriously. Because Himes was fascinated with Harlem to the point of obsession, his novels were attempts to portray the black ghetto subculture, with its violence, hypocrisy, loose women, and crime. He also portrayed the extremes of evangelical religion, which aided rather than alleviated much of the crime that was rampant in Harlem during the 1950's and 1960's.

Himes did not write from the point of view of a social reformer in the way that Charles Dickens or George Eliot wrote social commentaries. His writing was not intended to be didactic or moralizing. The cast of characters that Himes created was completely fictional; there was never any sense of autobiography in these denizens of Harlem. In fact, Himes's personal knowledge of Harlem was quite limited, and he drew more from his own experiences as a convicted felon. Himes's style was influenced by his frustration and anger at the plight of African Americans. Using his vantage point as a writer, Himes observed, analyzed, and then wrote about those black communities that harbored and nurtured mobsterism, gambling, and pimping. From the Sunday morning revival meeting, to the bordello that is constantly being raided, to the streetwise children who watch the merchants flaunt their custom-made Packards, Himes observed the veritable jungle that *A Rage in Harlem* reveals remorselessly.

From this somewhat jaded perspective, Himes wrote nine novels set in Harlem, seven of which were optioned by Samuel Goldwyn, Jr., in 1967. Driven in part by the fact that the central characters were black police officers, Goldwyn optioned *For Love of Imabelle* (1957), which was the original title for *A Rage in Harlem*, as well as *The Crazy Kill* (1959), *The Real Cool Killers* (1959), *All Shot Up* (1960), *The Big Gold Dream* (1960), *Cotton Comes to Harlem* (1965), and *The Heat's On* (1966). Goldwyn hoped to follow a trend started by Universal Pictures' *In the Heat of the Night* (1967), which starred Sidney Poitier as a black Philadelphia police detective. This particular point of film history is all but lost in *A Rage in Harlem*, since the two black detectives, Coffin Ed (Stack Pierce) and Grave Digger (George Wallace), are of minor consequence to the story. Scriptwriters John Toles-Bey and Bobby Crawford reduce these roles to incidental scenes that play like Laurel and Hardy routines.

In the original novel, Himes seemed to revel in throat cutting and using acid as a form of antiseptic for open wounds. In this adaptation, these gorier points are played down. Instead, the story centers much more on Jackson, the devout Christian who is happy living in his one-room apartment with a picture of Jesus and Jackson's buxom mother hanging side by side above his bed. Into this mundane existence comes the beautiful figure of Imabelle, a woman who has tight dresses and loose morals. Imabelle is running away not only from her enraged boyfriend but also from the kind of person that she has become. While this mismatching has all the ingredients of comedy, there is an underlying feeling that Imabelle and Jackson's relationship is not real. Although Jackson is a sweet, innocuous character and Imabelle is the double-dealing scam artist, their interactions do not get beyond some simple conversations and perfunctory lovemaking. Usually, it is the woman who is cast in the role of trying to reform the wayward man; however, here the roles are reversed, surely a potential mine for all kinds of comedic possibilities. Regrettably, while the premise seems promising, the mayhem surrounding Imabelle's life detracts from any meaningful relationship. While it is obvious why the portly Jackson loves the beautiful Imabelle, the reverse is not at all clear.

While Robin Givens plays the part of Imabelle to the full extent of her sexuality, however, the performance seems overbearing and unnatural. This is Givens' first motion picture, and her approach to the part of Imabelle is similar in style to that of Kathleen Turner in *Body Heat* (1981) and not so dissimilar in style to that of Lauren Bacall in *To Have and Have Not* (1944). Givens does offer a spectacular Imabelle, which is mainly attributable to the skintight dresses that she was sewn into before each day's shooting. This sensuality alone is not enough to make *A Rage in Harlem* anything more than an imaginary story by the novelist Chester Himes about the kind of criminal element that lived in Harlem during the 1950's.

Richard G. Cormack

Reviews

American Film: Magazine of the Film and Television Arts. XVI, March, 1991, p. 58.
Black Film Review. VI, Number 4, 1991, p. 16.
Chicago Tribune. May 3, 1991, VII, p. 35.
Ebony. XLVI, January, 1991, p. 128.
Film Review. September, 1991, p. 33.
The Hollywood Reporter. May 3, 1991, p. 9.
Los Angeles Times. May 3, 1991, p. F1.
The New York Times. May 3, 1991, p. B3.
Newsweek. May 13, 1991, p. 71.
Rolling Stone. June 13, 1991, p. 108.
Sight and Sound. I, September, 1991, p. 46.
Variety. April 30, 1991, p. 2.
The Village Voice. May 7, 1991, p. 55.
The Washington Post. May 3, 1991, p. B1.

RAMBLING ROSE

Production: Renny Harlin for Mario Kassar and Edgar J. Scherick; released by Seven
    Arts through New Line Cinema
Direction: Martha Coolidge
Screenplay: Calder Willingham; based on Willingham's novel
Cinematography: Johnny E. Jensen
Editing: Steven Cohen
Production design: John Vallone
Art direction: Christiaan Wagener
Set decoration: Bob Gould
Production management: Mary E. Kane
Casting: Aleta Chappelle
Sound: Richard Van Dyke
Costume design: Jane Robinson
Music: Elmer Bernstein
MPAA rating: R
Running time: 112 minutes

Principal characters:

Rose	Laura Dern
Daddy	Robert Duvall
Mother	Diane Ladd
Buddy	Lukas Haas
Willcox Hillyer	John Heard
Dr. Martinson	Kevin Conway
Dave Wilkie	Robert Burke
Doll	Lisa Jakub
Waski	Evan Lockwood

Told by an adult in a framing story, *Rambling Rose* presents a dark tale of the effects
that the coming of a nineteen-year-old housekeeper, Rose (Laura Dern), had on a
Georgia household in the 1930's. Through the eyes of a thirteen-year-old boy, this
moody, sometimes comic reminiscence sees the unexpected changes that the sexually
permissive Rose makes in an uptight world, testing a marriage and bringing a sense of
life.

    Rambling Rose is an autobiographical tale, penned by noted author and screenwriter
Calder Willingham, who was born in Atlanta and reared in Rome, Georgia. Willingham's memories form the thirteen-year-old Buddy Hillyer. Indeed, Willingham had a
father called Daddy, (Robert Duvall), a sister nicknamed Doll, (Lisa Jakub), and a
brother called Waski (Evan Lockwood). It took eighteen years for the novel to make it
to the screen. In the early 1970's, Willingham, who wrote the scripts for *Paths of Glory*
(1957), *One-Eyed Jacks* (1961), *The Graduate* (1967), *Little Big Man* (1970), and

Thieves Like Us (1974), turned his memories into a screenplay but could get no one in Hollywood to turn it into a film. The project gained momentum in 1986 when executive producer Edgar J. Scherick sent the script to director Martha Coolidge.

Coolidge is one of a handful of successful working female directors in Hollywood. Her other credits include the cult hit *Valley Girl* (1983) and *Real Genius* (1985). To make her way, however, Coolidge has also had to labor in episodic television (*Twilight Zone* and *Sledge Hammer*), as well as preside over made-for-television films. Coolidge overlays *Rambling Rose* with a modern-day feminist sense. The film's climatic scene comes when Mother (Diane Ladd) stands up to Dr. Martinson (Kevin Conway) and her husband, demanding that they not sanction a radical hysterectomy to curb the wild ways of the socially embarrassing "Rambling" Rose.

The star of *Rambling Rose* is Ladd's real-life daughter, Laura Dern. With her angular, lanky figure and radiant face, under curls coming from everywhere, Dern's Rose comes alive. Here is an accomplished actress doing her best work, following such critical successes as *Mask* (1985), *Blue Velvet* (1986), and *Wild at Heart* (1990). Dern was nominated for an Academy Award and shared Best Actress honors at the 1991 Montreal World Film Festival for this performance. *Rambling Rose* also previewed at film festivals in Boston, Toronto, and Telluride, Colorado. Like *Driving Miss Daisy* (1989), *Rambling Rose* is properly judged a specialized Hollywood production, set up to win awards. Although the film had its national premiere on the weekend of September 20, 1991, it had its world premiere August 22, 1991, at the Montreal festival. As such, *Rambling Rose* was released in late September in selected theaters, not to thousands of screens across the nation.

Dern does not offer the sole outstanding performance. The heart of *Rambling Rose* is its distinguished cast. This is not Hollywood as mass entertainment, but Hollywood as ensemble acting. The best work comes from Duvall, remembered for *Apocalypse Now* (1979) and *Tender Mercies* (1983), and Ladd, famed for *Alice Doesn't Live Here Anymore* (1975) and *Wild at Heart*, and who was also nominated for an Academy Award for Best Supporting Actress. Behind the camera, however, many were in new roles. *Rambling Rose* was the first producer credit for Renny Harlin, straight from his directing stints on *Die Hard II: Die Harder* (1990) and *The Adventures of Ford Fairlane* (1990). This young Finnish director, best known for action films replete with wild special effects, surprised many in Hollywood by choosing as his initial production such a quintessential American tale. Yet, Harlin did draw on contacts that he had developed in the mass entertainment side of Hollywood. For example, he employed John Vallone of *Die Hard II* and *Star Trek: The Motion Picture* (1979) to help design this period piece with great effectiveness. The mise-en-scène of *Rambling Rose* equals the acting in evoking a mood of rural Georgia during the Great Depression.

Harlin and Coolidge were able to re-create small-town Georgia in loving detail. They found their "Georgia" in Wilmington, North Carolina, complete with cobblestone streets, stately historic homes, and embellished mansions. For a scene in which Rose goes to town, the filmmakers changed part of downtown Wilmington. Modern conveniences were removed, vintage cars were added, and storefronts were transformed to Great Depression shabbiness. For the home of the Hillyer family, the filmmakers found a century-old Victorian clapboard farmhouse, twenty miles outside of town.

All these details and images were lensed by a Danish-born cinematographer, Johnny E. Jensen. Jensen had worked with Coolidge on several television films, but *Rambling Rose* was his first feature film. British-born costume designer Jane Robinson also did a fine job with the garish costumes of the lead character. The credits on *Rambling Rose* are distinguished in nearly all other categories. For example, composer Elmer Bernstein is one of the great technicians of Hollywood history, with nine Academy Award nominations (one Oscar), an Emmy, two Golden Globes, and any number of other honors. His lush scores marked *The Ten Commandments* (1956), *The Magnificent Seven* (1960), *To Kill a Mockingbird* (1962), *Hud* (1963), *Hawaii* (1966), and dozens of others. In terms of its use of music, *Rambling Rose* is a throwback to 1930's sumptuous orchestration.

Yet, the whole of *Rambling Rose* is less than the sum of all these great parts. The film does not mesh as a narrative. For example, the audience is thrown off balance by a family which seems so well off during a devastating depression. One sees wonderful characters, but there is precious little story bringing them together for memorable scenes. *Rambling Rose* has a collection of great performances, but it is not a great film. The problem with the narrative surely stems from the fact that this is a novel made into a film. The novel is filled with memories of a young boy now grown. The filmmakers tried to re-create thoughts on film by having a framing story; that is, the film starts with the grown-up Buddy in 1971, some thirty-six years after the main story has taken place, returning to visit his father and learning that Rose is dead. That artificial device is maudlin at best and only serves to remind the audience that film is a medium of texture and image, not of brain waves and interiors.

In the end, *Rambling Rose* strives for distinction in a style and story reminiscent of a film made for television. To emphasize faces, one sees "shot, reaction shot, shot" in editing, so one never captures the flow of the scene. That choice of editing leaves a choppy feeling and, in the end, a disjointed narrative. It might have been better to let Laura Dern and her fellow actors display their considerable talents in long takes of drama and power.

Douglas Gomery

Reviews
American Film: Magazine of the Film and Television Arts. XVI, July, 1991, p. 26.
Boxoffice. September, 1991, p. R-63.
Chicago Tribune. September 20, 1991, VII, p. 31.
Film Comment. XXVII, November, 1991, p. 16.
Film Review. November, 1991, p. 38.
The Hollywood Reporter. August 23, 1991, p. 10.

Los Angeles Times. September 20, 1991, p. F8.
The New York Times. September 20, 1991, p. B2.
Newsweek. September 23, 1991, p. 58.
The Philadelphia Inquirer. September 27, 1991, Weekend, p. 3.
Sight and Sound. I, November, 1991, p. 51.
Variety. August 23, 1991, p. 3.
The Wall Street Journal. September 26, 1991, p. A17.
The Washington Post. September 27, 1991, p. C12.

THE RAPTURE

Production: Nick Wechsler, Nancy Tenenbaum, and Karen Koch for New Line
Cinema, in association with Wechsler/Tenenbaum/Parker; released by Fine Line
Features
Direction: Michael Tolkin
Screenplay: Michael Tolkin
Cinematography: Bojan Bazelli
Editing: Suzanne Fenn
Production design: Robin Standefer
Art direction: Kathleen M. McKernin
Set decoration: Susan Benjamin
Casting: Deborah Aquilla
Sound: David Kelson
Costume design: Michael A. Jackson
Music: Thomas Newman
MPAA rating: R
Running time: 102 minutes

Principal characters:
Sharon .... Mimi Rogers
Vic .... Patrick Bauchau
Randy .... David Duchovny
Mary .... Kimberly Cullum
Henry .... Dick Anthony Williams
Sheriff Foster .... Will Patton
The first boy .... De Vaughn Nixon
The older boy .... Christian Belnavis
Paula .... Terri Hanauer
Bartender .... Marvin Elkins
Louis .... Douglas Roberts
Angie .... Carole Davis
Tommy .... James Le Gros
First evangelist .... Scott Burkholder
Second evangelist .... Vince Grant

The Rapture is a film that dares to deal with religion, a subject rarely addressed
in American films. When issues of faith and spirituality have been approached,
Hollywood has often offered them under the guise of history, of biblical spectacle,
massaged into box-office boffo by directors such as Cecil B. De Mille with the help of
sexual sensationalism and state-of-the-art technological wizardry. To abandon this
successful formula and examine questions of contemporary faith would obviously run
the risk of insulting the beliefs of certain members of the American public. Yet, *The*

Rapture, produced by the same team that brought Steven Soderbergh's *sex, lies and videotape* (1989) to fruition, chooses to plunge headlong into the question of faith in the contemporary United States.

Depicting the spiritual in highly personalized terms reminiscent of European filmmakers such as Robert Bresson and Ingmar Bergman, fledgling writer/director Michael Tolkin shapes the first half of *The Rapture* into a startling drama centering on the joy and pain of faith as experienced by one convert, Sharon (Mimi Rogers). Yet, the issue of Sharon's personal faith ultimately assumes sensationally spectacular and tragic proportions in the latter part of the film when her life becomes enmeshed in the apocalyptic prophecies invoked by some American fundamentalist sects.

Sharon initially appears as both the most unlikely candidate for religious conversion and its most logical participant. She is a telephone information operator. The boring sameness and anonymity of her job are counterpointed, but also curiously paralleled, by the pattern of her personal life—or at least what she has of one. Her leisure hours are filled with impersonal sexual adventures played in tandem with Vic (Patrick Bauchau). Vic scours Los Angeles' bars for attractive, amicable couples to bring back to Sharon for group sex. On one such encounter, Sharon meets Randy (David Duchovny), who reveals that he has killed a man for money. They start a relationship, but Sharon realizes that her relationship with him is as meaningless as everything else in her life. She tells Randy that she feels empty, hopeless, and desperate.

At work, Sharon's interest is piqued by coworkers whose lunchroom conversations are marked by cryptic comments on prayer, musical notes, and signs of Armageddon, the final coming of Christ. Sharon attempts to listen in on their conversations; she is especially fascinated with their references to a dream containing a pearl. In yet another sexual encounter with strangers, she finds herself fascinated with a woman's tattoo, which shows a mysterious hand lifting a pearl into the sky. Sharon attempts to talk to her coworkers about this image, and she tells them that she dreams about the pearl. At once, they confront her with the fact that she is lying. She must pray, they tell her; one must have faith to dream of the pearl.

Within the confines of her virtually empty apartment, Sharon talks to a pair of door-to-door evangelists (Scott Burkholder and Vince Grant). While she scolds them for dismissing the salvation of those who believe in religions other than Christianity, she finds her attitude toward her own life changing within an alarming emotional upheaval. She confronts Randy with her need to find a new direction in her life. In spite of this declaration, her confusion increases. She ventures into new, even more dangerous sexual encounters and contemplates suicide. Finally, she achieves her faith and dreams of the pearl.

Sharon's life is transformed. Her joy in telling all of her faith, of her being reborn in Christ, threatens her job. She begins to ask her telephone customers if they have met Jesus. Her supervisor intervenes, but he too is a believer and introduces her to a sect led by the prophecy of a young African-American child (played at this point in the film by De Vaughn Nixon). Sharon meets with Randy, who is willing to have her faith carry both of them in a relationship based on love. When we next see Sharon and Randy, several years have passed. They sit in church with their daughter, Mary (Kimberly Cullum). Randy is a successful businessman and devout Christian; he, Sharon, and their daughter live in a beautiful home. Sharon is happy, but Randy senses that something is going to happen, and it soon does. A fired employee goes berserk and, on a vengeful rampage, kills Randy and several others in his office.

After her husband's death, Sharon has visions of Randy standing on desert rocks and exhorting her. The boy prophet (now Christian Belnavis) tells her that God may be calling her to the desert. She goes, taking Mary with her. She expects the Rapture, the moment in which God will take them up bodily into Heaven in anticipation of the end of the world, but after several weeks, her faith begins to waver. Mary refuses to eat and asks her mother why they cannot die and meet Daddy in Heaven. Finally, Sharon takes a gun and kills her daughter. She attempts to kill herself but cannot: To do so would mean that she could never enter Heaven. On her way home, she is stopped for speeding by a sheriff (Will Patton) who attempted to help her during her stay in the desert. She admits that she killed her daughter. In some ways, Sharon's experience in the desert parallels that of Abraham, who was asked by God to kill his only son; in the Bible, however, God stays Abraham's hand. Sharon is not so lucky, and what might be interpreted as the end of a tragic story of faith apparently gone awry becomes something else in the hands of Tolkin. Sharon is imprisoned for her crime, but Armageddon is at hand. Unfortunately, Sharon's experience in the desert has left her faith shattered. She believes that God has broken his promise to her by letting her kill her daughter.

Sharon's daughter appears to her in jail in the presence of two angels. Mary pleads with her mother to declare her love for God, but Sharon refuses to do so. The heavenly trumpets sound and the prison bars fall to the floor. Even in the face of this incontrovertible evidence that God does exist, Sharon is defiant. Life on Earth is ending; the Four Horsemen of the Apocalypse literally ride into action. Sharon sees them on the prison television set as they begin their final apocalyptic mission. As the prison collapses, Sheriff Foster appears. He and Sharon ride off on a motorcycle with the horsemen in hot pursuit behind them. In fulfillment of her religious beliefs, Sharon and the sheriff are lifted up, but not directly into Heaven. Sharon and Sheriff Foster stand in a dark space where Mary asks if they will declare their love for God. Sheriff Foster declares his and is taken into Heaven to be with God, but Sharon refuses yet again. Mary begs her mother, but Sharon refuses until it is too late. The last trumpet sounds. She is left to linger in a kind of purgatory of empty darkness, forever separated from her child, her husband, and the God that she has come to regard as cruel.

The Rapture is a disturbing film that certainly can be assumed to please virtually no one when it comes to matters of faith. The potential for controversy is obvious, especially in the uncomfortable connection of *The Rapture* to American religious thought in its most popular, media-saturated manifestations. Its view of Sharon's life after her conversion could be taken to confirm some of the notions promulgated by many fundamentalist "televangelists" who claim that those who are born-again will participate in direct material reward for their faith. Yet, the film dares to turn that

Heaven on Earth into a nightmare that Sharon (and the audience) cannot easily reconcile with belief in a loving God.

While the extremism of Sharon's experiences might tempt some viewers to dismiss her fundamental problem to be a lack of faith rather than a failure of the object of her faith, the film raises questions that are not easily answered. Unfortunately, any theological questions raised by the film become obscured by the film's heavy-handed portrayal of the final days. Utilizing special effects that are not much different from those found in Rex Ingram's 1921 film *The Four Horsemen of the Apocalypse*, *The Rapture* becomes mired in sensational and wholly unconvincing visual images that undermine the enormity of Sharon's spiritual decisions. The low-budget nature of the film's production cannot be blamed entirely for these images, but the reasoning behind them, as some critics pointed out, is not clear. Is *The Rapture's* Apocalypse so flatly conventional in its presentation because that is the way Sharon and the faithful conceive of it? Is Tolkin ironically commenting on that particular view of the most momentous of imaginable events? The ambiguity of the film's handling of this narrative episode threatens to overwhelm the spiritual matters that have informed the rest of the film's riveting personal drama.

That *The Rapture* lingers in the mind long after it is over is a tribute in large measure to Mimi Rogers' sensitive and convincing delineation of Sharon and to the power inherent in the issues that Tolkin courageously, if not completely successfully, attempts to address. With participation in organized religion on the rise in the United States, it will be interesting to see if Tolkin or other American filmmakers brave the potential controversy and dare to bring other thoughtful representations of religious experience to the screen, especially within a cultural climate marked by the troubled convergence of spiritual, moral, and political issues in the lives of many Americans.

Gaylyn Studlar

Reviews
Boxoffice. December, 1991, p. R-91.
Chicago Tribune. November 8, 1991, VII, p. 40.
The Christian Century. CVIII, October 23, 1991, p. 956.
The Christian Science Monitor. December 9, 1991, p. 11.
The Hollywood Reporter. October 1, 1991, p. 5.
The Humanist. LII, January, 1992, p. 46.
Los Angeles Times. October 4, 1991, p. F1.
National Catholic Reporter. October 18, 1991, p. 16.
The New York Times. September 30, 1991, p. B3.
The New York Times. October 13, 1991, p. H13.
Newsweek. CXVIII, October 14, 1991, p. 70.
Variety. September 5, 1991, p. 7.
The Washington Post. November 25, 1991, p. D4.

REGARDING HENRY

Production: Mike Nichols and Scott Rudin; released by Paramount Pictures
Direction: Mike Nichols
Screenplay: Jeffrey Abrams
Cinematography: Giuseppe Rotunno
Editing: Sam O'Steen
Production design: Tony Walton
Art direction: Dan Davis and William Elliott
Set decoration: Susan Bode, Amy Marshall, and Cindy Carr
Casting: Juliet Taylor and Ellen Lewis
Sound: James Sabat and Gene Cantamessa
Costume design: Ann Roth
Music: Hans Zimmer
MPAA rating: PG-13
Running time: 107 minutes

Principal characters:

Henry Turner	Harrison Ford
Sarah Turner	Annette Bening
Bradley	Bill Nunn
Rachel Turner	Mikki Allen
Charlie	Donald Moffat
Mrs. O'Brien	Nancy Marchand
Rosella	Aida Linares
Jessica	Elizabeth Wilson
Bruce	Bruce Altman
Linda	Rebecca Miller

Many moons have come and gone since director Mike Nichols gave the 1960's one of its most influential comedies with the 1967 release of *The Graduate*. By the end of the 1980's, however, after three decades of making popular and innovative films, it seemed that Nichols had misplaced his creative tools. His *Working Girl* (1988), although immensely watchable, was dismissed by most critics as an overblown fairy tale. Despite receiving six Academy Award nominations, including acting nods for its three female leads, the bittersweet comedy about a secretary on the rise was knocked for its derogatory jabs at career women. The 1990 release *Postcards from the Edge*, which garnered yet another Academy Award nomination for Meryl Streep, suffered greatly from a flaccid script and a very blunt satirical spin on the drug-addicted actress phenomenon. With the idiotic *Regarding Henry*, Nichols may have reached the nadir of his creative experience.

Regarding Henry comes only three years after Nichols, in *Working Girl*, saluted the intensely driven Manhattan businesswomen who could only find happiness on the higher rungs of the ladder of success. In those interim years, however, American society began to regret the money-hungry, selfish lives of days gone by and embraced a more sensible, generous way of living. After Ronald Reagan came George Bush, and after *Working Girl* Nichols brings to this kinder and gentler film-going public *Regarding Henry*, a contemporary fable about a corporate lawyer who is shot in the head only to recover and remember just how much a loving family and a meager income really mean. Unfortunately, it seems that Nichols finds striking a chord with American viewers more worthwhile and valuable than crafting a lucid, intelligent film.

To his coworkers, family, and friends, Henry Turner (Harrison Ford) is a man who is merely tolerable rather than lovable. He berates his daughter (Mikki Allen) for household spills, demands strict attention from his exhausted secretary (Elizabeth Wilson), and spends so little time at home that his wife (Annette Bening) is forced to find love in the arms of another man. In the courtroom, however, Turner, a relentless dynamo, can do no wrong for his corporate clients; the film opens with his brutal victory in court over a poor crippled senior citizen and his doting, sad-eyed wife. Before Turner can really savor the victory, however, he falls into a coma when he is shot in the head and chest by a convenience-store robber.

After a dismal Christmas season saved only by Henry's awakening, his wife, Sarah, is flabbergasted by his subsequent failure to recognize her, his daughter, and any kind of normal human behavior. Sarah and their daughter, Rachel, are also hurt by their ritzy New York friends' heartless comments about their bleak future in the upper class with the brain-damaged Henry. Henry's boss (Donald Moffat) and others provide words and gestures of condolence, but their sentiments are forced, artificial, and almost meaningless. Henry is moved to a clinic specializing in brain disorders, where he undergoes physical rehabilitation with the help of a cheery, angelic therapist (Bill Nunn). By the time that Henry can walk, talk, and paint huge canvases of Ritz cracker packages, Sarah and Rachel are ready to take him home. Unfortunately, he still does not know who they are, and only after Rachel teaches him to tie his shoes and sparks in him a memory of their apartment's carpeting does he agree to go with them.

Once ensconced at home, Rachel begins to reacquaint Henry with the sentimental joys of fatherhood, while Sarah worries how they can afford to continue living their high-society life. Henry, a walking, talking zombie, relearns household tasks and finds tremendous fun in knocking over glasses and playing with kitchen cleaning powders. One day, Henry ventures into the New York streets and returns home with a shaggy and helpless puppy. Henry learns to read slowly and surely, and, as more of a goodwill gesture than a practical decision, is invited back to his law firm one day a week.

As in any dramatic narrative, all is not well in Henry's world. Sarah is continually worried about the family's financial situation and wonders when a man who now knows little about human nature can begin to satisfy her in bed. Henry, rereading all his legal briefs, begins to realize the morally corrupt tricks with which he used to win cases in his previous life. In defeating the disabled elder gentleman of the film's opening minutes, Henry discovers he withheld evidence that would have proved that a hospital error caused the older man's disabilities. Meanwhile, Rachel is sent to a socially acceptable boarding school because Sarah believes that this action will not only reinforce their faltering social standing but also protect Rachel from becoming too depressed around her damaged father. The final blow comes when Sarah and Henry overhear someone call Henry an "imbecile" at a chic party and, consequently, Henry suffers a setback in his recuperative progress.

Sarah calls Bradley, Henry's former therapist, who tells the disheartened Henry to keep trying. Henry is soon able to make love to his wife and to wish for Rachel to return home. When he discovers the letters that detail his wife's love affair with a colleague, Henry flees from the safety of his home, despite Sarah's cries for forgiveness. Henry soon discovers that he also was carrying on an extramarital dalliance with another office associate (Rebecca Miller) before his accident. He ends his career as a lawyer, reprimanding all his coworkers for their immorality, and gives the revealing evidence back to the wronged victim so that he and his wife can seek long-deserved justice. Henry returns home to Sarah, who asks for another chance. He gives it to her, and the couple moves from their expensive upper East Side digs to the quaint and modest neighborhood of Greenwich Village. They are able to kiss openly in the park, to wear their hair in funky styles, and to enjoy each other's goofy company— in short, to enjoy everything that their successful upper-class lives never allowed them to do in the past. As the film ends, the couple rescues Rachel from her snooty private school, and the family is finally cemented together with love and appreciation.

What is missing from *Regarding Henry* is the biting satirical wit that distinguished a Mike Nichols comedy of years past. For example, it has none of the caustic lampooning of contemporary society that made *The Graduate* the unforgettable classic it has become. It also does not possess the carefully observed jabs at matrimony that transformed the underappreciated *Heartburn* (1986) from the dismal flop it could have been into the extremely interesting misfire it turned out to be. Furthermore, it lacks the wicked absurdities that Nichols found lurking in the world of combat in *Catch-22* (1970) or the brutal humor that he mined from the desperate couplings of foolish young lovers in *Carnal Knowledge* (1971). For *Regarding Henry*, Nichols seems to have traded in his sarcasm and keen sense of irony for hyped-up sentiment, which is shoved into every frame of the film. In scenes where he once would have poked fun or attempted a send-up, he relies shamelessly on schmaltz. At the moment when Henry and Sarah overhear the callous remarks of party goers about Henry's state of mind, the audience is treated to a ground swell of touching background music and a close-up of the couple's sad faces. Once upon a time, Nichols would not have let the offending parties off so easy.

A major factor of *Regarding Henry*'s failure to generate any real emotion is the film's irrational screenplay written by twenty-three-year-old Jeffrey Abrams. What-ever attracted Nichols to the script, which he calls in the film's production notes "surprisingly funny and very moving," remains invisible on the screen. What is apparent is the glaring impracticalities that pop up everywhere within the narrative. Who could ever believe that a man just learning to read again could tackle and even comprehend complicated legal briefs? It is also difficult to believe that a man who loses his mind and faculties through a twist of fate would not feel intense anger; he becomes a lovable fool who wears rumpled clothing and a messy hairdo. Ultimately, even the film's final message is shoddy. With the Turner family happy at last, the filmmakers seem to be saying that suffering a massive head injury is an extremely beneficial experience for the American male.

Among a slew of slightly above-average performances, Annette Bening's engaging turn as Sarah is a highlight. Nichols has always shown a brilliance in the direction of his female actors—Elizabeth Taylor in 1966's *Who's Afraid of Virginia Woolf?*, Anne Bancroft in *The Graduate*, Ann-Margret in *Carnal Knowledge*, and both Meryl Streep and Cher in 1983's *Silkwood*. Bening's performance is another example of his adept handling of women performers. The actress brings an intelligent radiance to the role; the sequence in which she softly reminds Henry of the first moment the couple met is the only one that really tugs at the heart. Bening provides the only glimmer of hope in an otherwise irredeemable film.

Greg Changnon

Reviews
Boxoffice. August, 1991, p. R-48.
Chicago Tribune. July 10, 1991, V, p. 1.
Films in Review. XLII, September, 1991, p. 335.
The Hollywood Reporter. July 8, 1991, p. 7.
Los Angeles Times. July 10, 1991, p. F1.
The New York Times. July 10, 1991, p. B1.
Newsweek. CXVIII, July 15, 1991, p. 56.
People Weekly. July 22, 1991, p. 10.
Premiere. IV, July, 1991, p. 44.
Rolling Stone. August 8, 1991, p. 78.
Sight and Sound. I, October, 1991, p. 57.
Time. CXXXVIII, July 15, 1991, p. 72.
TV Time. July 15, 1991, p. 72.
Variety. July 8, 1991, p. 2.
The Washington Post. July 10, 1991, p. F1.

RHAPSODY IN AUGUST

Origin: Japan
Released: 1991
Released in U.S.: 1991
Production: Hisao Kurosawa for Feature Film Enterprise 2; released by Orion Classics
Direction: Akira Kurosawa
Screenplay: Akira Kurosawa; based on the novel *Nabe-no-naka*, by Kiyoko Murata
Cinematography: Takao Saito and Masaharu Ueda
Art direction: Yoshiro Muraki
Sound: Kenichi Benitani
Creative consulting: Ishiro Honda
Music: Shinichiro Ikebe
MPAA rating: PG
Running time: 98 minutes

Principal characters:
```
Kane ............................. Sachiko Murase
Clark .............................. Richard Gere
Tami ........................... Tomoko Ohtakara
Shinjiro ......................... Mitsunori Isaki
Tateo .......................... Hidetaka Yoshioka
Minako ............................. Mie Suzuki
Machiko ...................... Narumi Kayashima
Yoshie ........................... Toshie Negishi
Noboru ..................... Choichiro Kawarasaki
Tadao ............................ Hisashi Igawa
```

Rhapsody in August takes a long hard look at what effect the dropping of the atomic bomb had on three generations of a Japanese family. There is no better director than Akira Kurosawa to raise this sensitive issue and to take a retrospective look at the consequences of this wartime action.

High in the hills of lush, green farmland near the city of Nagasaki, four grandchildren spend the summer with their grandmother, Kane (Sachiko Murase). Kane's brother is dying, and the parents of the children have gone to Hawaii to see him. Many years have passed since Kane and her brother have seen each other. In fact, so much time has passed that Kane is reluctant to make the trip to Hawaii. Kane comes from a family of ten brothers and sisters and she cannot remember this particular brother very well. While the children are playing, Kane writes the names of her brothers and sisters on a chalkboard.

Each evening, the grandmother recounts stories from her childhood. One such story is of a brother who, instead of becoming a tradesperson, elopes with his sweetheart. Two burnt cedar trees that resemble two people committing suicide mark the place where the brother and his new wife built their house. Kane recounts a story concerning another brother who would draw nothing but staring eyes. During the day, the four children—Tami (Tomoko Ohtakara), her sister Shinjiro (Mitsunori Isaki), Tateo (Hidetaka Yoshioka), and his sister Minako (Mie Suzuki)—play around the property. They explore the forest where the cedars were burnt and look at the lake where one of Kane's brothers used to swim.

Kane receives a telegram from Hawaii asking if she would come and visit her dying brother. This is a hard decision for Kane; something inside of her prevents her from going. Thinking about her family brings strong emotions for Kane. During the many conversations she has with her grandchildren she begins to speak about the war. To the children's horror, they find out that their grandfather was killed by the atomic bomb dropped on Nagasaki. Kane takes them out into the courtyard one day and points toward Nagasaki. From this vantage point, she tells the children how she witnessed the mushroom cloud as it rose into the air signaling death and destruction. Such memories are hard for Kane to forget and confusing for the young children. Until that moment, the children viewed the bombing of Hiroshima and Nagasaki as events of past history. Moved by what they have heard from their grandmother, the children start to speak to one another about the bomb.

When Tadao (Hisashi Igawa), Kane's son, and his wife, Machiko (Narumi Kayashima), return from Hawaii, he speaks with great excitement about the wonderful business that Kane's brother has created. Tadao's brother-in-law, Noboru (Choichiro Kawarasaki), and Kane's daughter, Yoshie (Toshie Negishi), speak over dinner one night about the possibility of both families working in the uncle's business. Yet Kane has been thinking about the destruction and loss of life caused by the bomb and becomes angry with her children, who only seem to be thinking about themselves and their careers.

Kane invites her brother's son, Clark (Richard Gere), to come and visit her in Japan. Thinking that Clark represents all that is wrong about the United States, the four children decide to leave the airport before Clark arrives. Clark and Kane relate to each other very well, and Kane enjoys having him in her house. Even the children eventually accept him. As is the village tradition, all the women meet at a Buddhist shrine on the ninth of August to remember the dropping of the atomic bomb. Clark, along with the children, comes to the shrine as one of the onlookers.

Kane receives news that her brother is dead. For most of the summer, Kane has been recounting and reliving the memories of the war. This last piece of news completely unsettles her, and during a violent thunderstorm Kane runs around the house covering the children in the belief that an atomic bomb has been dropped. Even though the children should return home, Tateo decides to stay for a few more days. While the rainstorm continues, Kane takes her umbrella and goes out into the storm, not knowing where she is going or why. Frantic with worry, the entire family rushes after the demented Kane to bring her back.

Any film made by Kurosawa garners immediate and unequivocal respect. In his eighties, Kurosawa continues to make films that not only are cinematically enchanting but also contain strong personal stories. *Rhapsody in August* stands alone in this respect when compared with his other cinematic endeavors. While Kurosawa is at home making such great epics as *Rashomon* (1950), *Shichinin no samurai* (1954; *Seven Samurai*), and his samurai epic *Kagemusha* (1980), *Rhapsody in August* reveals yet another side of the director. This time, the screen is not filled with sword-wielding samurai or death and destruction. Rather, this film is the day-to-day account of an old Japanese woman who finally tries to come to terms with the consequences of the atomic bomb. Through telling her stories to another generation, Kane (played with fine poise and intense feeling by Sachiko Murase) brings the horror and trauma into the present.

As the film is set in the rural highlands above Nagasaki, the quiet countryside offers a peaceful environment for the retelling of Kane's life. Kurosawa's film manages to tell Kane's story in one long, uninterrupted sequence; there are no sudden movements from one scene to the next. There is a clear sense that Kane actually speaks for the Japanese people, as well as for Kurosawa himself.

Rhapsody in August is not the first time that Kurosawa has tried to deal with the emotional impact of the war on the Japanese nation as well as on the individual. *Ikimono no kiroku* (1955; *I Live in Fear*) deals retrospectively with the problem facing the Japanese nation ten years after the bombing. Kurosawa tried to show that the continual manufacturing and development of the bomb carries with it a high psychological cost. This particular theme is never touched upon in *Rhapsody in August*, which suggests a shift in Kurosawa's attitude toward finally healing the psychological scars of the only country that experienced the full destructive power of the atom bomb. The issue is not the bomb but the people who were its target.

There are certain scene sequences that act as poignant reminders of the psychological impact that the bombing had on the people of Japan. One of the first places that Clark visits on his arrival in Japan is a school where, each year, those who as children survived the bombing plant flowers as a remembrance of those who were lost. Kurosawa achieves in this simple scene a point where cinema truly reflects reality. Having used the earlier stories of Kane to explain how she felt about the bombing, Kurosawa then broadens that theme to include the entire Japanese nation. Another emotional moment occurs when Kane joins the women of the village in their Buddhist chanting. This small, open-sided Buddhist meeting place, set in cultivated farmland, adds to the intensity of the day of remembrance.

Kurosawa maintained that this film was never intended as one last slight toward the United States for dropping the bomb. Rather, it is an in-depth look at how the various generations dealt with the bombing in the fifty years that followed. With this film, Kurosawa created a very profound statement about war without ascribing blame to any one nation. When the Japanese-American Clark apologizes to Kane for what happened in Nagasaki, it is not an admission of guilt or wrongdoing but a genuine sense of shared suffering between the two nations.

Rhapsody in August continues the trend in Japanese filmmaking of directors and writers trying to make sense of the atomic bomb through the experience of film. Prior to Kurosawa's *I Live in Fear*, Hideo Oba made *Nagasaki no kane* (1950; *The Bells of Nagasaki*), a film based on the autobiography of Dr. Takashi Nagai, who eventually died of leukemia caused by the high levels of radiation. After Oba's film came Kaneto Shindo's *Genbaku no ko* (1952; *Children of the Atom Bomb*) and Hodeo Sekigawa's *Hiroshima* (1953). If *Rhapsody in August* can be seen as reflecting the mood and feeling of modern Japan, then time has certainly healed many of the festering wounds that were evident in those earlier films.

Kurosawa's motion picture is a deeply moving experience that is only heightened by the effect of the final scenes. Kane has found the previous weeks too demanding. Her children seem to live in denial of the bombing, while her grandchildren seek a new understanding that is not based on some textbook account. Kurosawa leaves the viewer with the image of Kane running full flight into a rainstorm. Her umbrella is inside-out and she is soaking wet. Behind her, the entire family runs desperately, trying to catch her. The final episode of Nagasaki is behind her, and she can fight the inner storm that it has caused in the same way that she can fight the rainstorm. Through the character of Kane, Kurosawa has resolved the inner conflict of *I Live in Fear* and has transformed those same feelings to give cinema yet another masterpiece in the form of *Rhapsody in August*.

Richard G. Cormack

Reviews

Boxoffice. February, 1992, p. R-17.
Chicago Tribune. June 16, 1991, XIII, p. 12.
The Christian Science Monitor. December 20, 1991, p. 12.
The Hollywood Reporter. May 13, 1991, p. 6.
Interview. XXII, January, 1992, p. 28.
Los Angeles Times. December 23, 1991, p. F1.
New Woman. XXII, January, 1992, p. 27.
The New York Times. December 20, 1991, p. B8.
The Times Literary Supplement. October 4, 1991, p. 22.
Variety. May 13, 1991, p. 2.
The Village Voice. December 24, 1991, p. 72.
The Wall Street Journal. January 2, 1992, p. A7.
The Washington Post. February 8, 1992, p. D9.

RICOCHET

Production: Joel Silver and Michael Levy for HBO, Cinema Plus L.P., and Silver
  Pictures; released by Warner Bros.
Direction: Russell Mulcahy
Screenplay: Steven E. de Souza; based on a story by Fred Dekker and Menno Meyjes
Cinematography: Peter Levy
Editing: Peter Honess
Production design: Jaymes Hinkle
Art direction: Christiaan Wagener
Set decoration: Richard Goddard and Sam Gross
Set design: Eric Orbom
Casting: Robin Lippin and Fern Cassel
Sound: Ed Novick
Costume design: Marilyn Vance-Straker
Music: Alan Silvestri
MPAA rating: R
Running time: 105 minutes

> *Principal characters:*
> Nick Styles .... Denzel Washington
> Earl Talbot Blake .... John Lithgow
> Odessa .... Ice-T
> Larry .... Kevin Pollak
> Brimleigh .... Lindsay Wagner
> Alice .... Victoria Dillard
> Farris .... John Cothran, Jr.
> Kim .... Josh Evans

Ricochet is another in a long line of police thrillers, sometimes known as
"policiers," that often centralize fast-paced action, melodramatic polarities of good
and evil, and sufficient plot twists to prolong suspense. The box-office requirements of
such action films would appear to have been well learned by the producer of *Ricochet*,
Joel Silver—whose credits include *48 Hrs.* (1982), *Predator* (1987), *Lethal Weapon*
(1987), and *Die Hard* (1988)—but *Ricochet* cannot be ranked with either its producer's
best work or the best examples of the subgenre. Nevertheless, it is typical of such
films, and as to be expected, *Ricochet* indulges in many overly familiar conventions of
the action police film. In trying to give those conventions a new twist, *Ricochet* turns
the familiar battle between criminals and law enforcement into a very personal battle
between two men—one black and one white, one on the rise within the public world of
urban politics and one who operates within a private world of obsession in which only
revenge and retribution give life meaning.

Introduced by striking graphics reminiscent of those credit sequences designed by
Saul Bass for the suspense thrillers of Alfred Hitchcock, *Ricochet* begins in a stylish

manner that is sustained by at least one aspect of the film: its impressive casting. Denzel Washington, who won the 1990 Academy Award for Best Supporting Actor, portrays Nick Styles, a self-confident rookie police officer whose life is altered, for both good and bad, by a chance occurrence. At a street carnival, he surprises a killer, Earl Talbot Blake, played by John Lithgow. Lithgow, whose film, theatrical, and television career had earned for him two Academy Award nominations for Best Supporting Actor, Tony and Drama Desk Awards, as well as an Emmy, portrays Blake as a quietly ruthless psychopath whose physical normality is marred by his one cloudy eye, even as his ability to mimic normal behavior must always give way to his murderous impulses.

Unlike Blake, whose background remains a mystery and whose psychopathology is not given any explanation, Styles is depicted as a good kid who emerges from a potentially problematic beginning. A pastor's son, he grows up in a rough neighborhood in Los Angeles. Yet, the film does not exploit the potential interest in such a complex situation. Instead, the plot throws it away, preferring instead to use Styles's background merely to give him the neighborhood connections that will later prove useful to the film's plot. Likewise, Styles's cool confidence is presented early but given no depth of explanation. When Blake leaps out a window after a drug deal turns violent, Styles captures him with a casual authority reminiscent of Clint Eastwood's unflappable "Dirty" Harry Calahan, Hollywood's cop icon of the 1970's. "Don't you hate it," Styles jokes as he levels his gun at Blake. Unfortunately, Blake manages to grab a bystander as a hostage. Remaining calm, Styles arrests Blake in an outrageous and unexpected maneuver. Styles strips to his underwear to prove to Blake not only that he is willing to drop his revolver in exchange for the hostage's release but also that he has nothing (literally) to hide. Blake is ready to shoot Styles point-blank, but the young officer is not as dumb (or as stripped down) as he appears: Styles grabs another gun hidden in the back waist of his undershorts. He shoots Blake in the leg and successfully retrieves the hostage.

Another coincidental occurrence figures in Styles's arrest of Blake in this sequence. The entire event is captured on videotape by a bystander (an anachronism because this is supposed to be 1984). The videotape of the dramatic rescue makes Styles an immediate media sensation. With his partner, Larry (Kevin Pollak), he is promoted to the rank of detective. As Styles enjoys accolades, Blake goes to a prison hospital; his catatonic state is broken by his glimpse of the prison ward television. He sees the news coverage of Styles. At this moment, Blake acquires the obsession that he needs to live: He decides that he will destroy Styles's life in retribution for what Styles has done to him.

The film picks up the action several years later. Styles is an assistant district attorney. He is married, is the father of two children, and lives in a beautiful home. He is on a fast track to the top. Courted by the black political junta of Los Angeles, he is being groomed to run for public office. Styles is blissfully unaware of the fact that Blake, who was convicted and sent to prison, is utilizing his seven-year sentence to plot an elaborate revenge scheme. He is also unaware that Blake does not plan on waiting until he is paroled or has served his term to set his scheme into motion.

Using his psychopathic obsession with Styles as the motivational fuel for his every action, Blake quickly establishes himself as a power within the prison social structure. As an "Aryan gladiator" in prison "games" fought to the death, he proves himself to be unmatched in both physical strength and sheer brutality. Enlisting the aid of other prisoners who respect and fear him, Blake succeeds in plotting and executing an elaborate escape plan that results in the murder of the entire parole board and a number of guards. That the escape is wholly unbelievable in its particulars seems of little concern to the makers of *Ricochet*. Of more apparent concern is establishing needed details that will make Blake's return to Styles's world undetectable. Blake switches dental records with a prisoner who also escapes, promptly kills the man, and burns the body. Blake is now completely free to take his revenge against Styles because the authorities (and Styles) think that it was he who died a few miles from the prison in the fiery crash of the escape vehicle.

Everything is set into place so that Blake may exact his revenge against Styles with excruciating deliberation. It becomes apparent that Styles's vulnerability to Blake's cruel schemes is constructed by the film as a kind of punishment for the young officer-turned-lawyer's hubris, as Styles's movement to the top of his profession is not without its compromises. Although sketched with broad strokes, the film does suggest that Styles's family receives less and less of his time. His political ambitions appear to outweigh an unwavering commitment to the law. In some respects, he regards himself as above the law. Styles enters a drug factory to see an old friend, Odessa (Ice T), and to ask Odessa and his fellow drug dealers not to sell drugs at Styles's pet project: the Tower Center, a venture that may benefit his career aspirations more than the community that it is aimed at helping.

Upon his arrival in Los Angeles, Blake, with the help of henchman Kim (Josh Evans), proceeds to tape-record Styles, to make contact with his children, and to utilize numerous undetected invasions into Styles's life to incriminate him in child pornography. Finally, Blake and Kim kidnap Styles, inject him with various illegal drugs, and photograph him in compromising positions with a prostitute (who infects him with a sexually transmitted disease). When Styles is finally left at city hall in a totally incoherent state, his claims of being kidnapped by a convict who is officially dead are met with disbelief, even by his wife.

Blake is not through with Styles, however, and the former's almost superhuman ability to plant false information leads Styles into behavior that appears deranged to his bosses, the media, and his family. Styles is suspended from his job after a videotape of his semiconscious encounter with the prostitute is broadcast. His marriage is in shambles, but things become even worse. Blake kills Styles's partner and nimbly tosses the murder weapon into Styles's hands.

At this point in the plot, Styles finally regains a measure of the self-confidence that marked his first appearance in the film. At least he has the sense to realize that he can never explain his fingerprints on the weapon that killed Larry. He goes to Odessa, who takes charge of Styles's wife and children and helps to formulate a plan to exact revenge on Blake and to restore Styles's reputation. While sitting in a bar waiting to see television news confirmation of Styles's arrest for his partner's murder, Blake sees something that he did not anticipate: Styles standing on the roof of a building, apparently deranged and threatening to jump. Blake is furious at the idea that Styles may kill himself and thwart his plans for Styles's tortuous future in prison. He arrives at the ghetto apartment house in time to see Styles blow up the cocaine factory/ghetto apartment building on which he stands. Styles escapes down an air shaft as Blake is spotted by Odessa and his friends, who make sure that Blake cannot escape detection by the television cameras. Blake follows Styles up on the open spires of the Twin Towers (modeled after Los Angeles' most famous folk architecture creation, the Watts Towers). Conforming to the tendency of recent policiers and detective films to take the action vertically rather than horizontally in the traditional car chase made famous in *Bullitt* (1968) and *The French Connection* films (1971 and 1975), *Ricochet* ends with grisly hand-to-hand combat between Styles and Blake that culminates in Blake's fall to his death. Styles is rescued and reunited with his family.

Ricochet suffers from a tiresome, superficial screenplay by Steven E. de Souza that depends on incredible episodes, such as the prison breakout and a handwrestling match between Styles and Blake, to further its story line. Within a film that eschews character development, the proven talents of Washington and Lithgow seem wasted as they are forced to speak clichéd and predictable dialogue that does little more than keep them busy as the violence unfolds with predictable bloodletting. Not surprisingly within such a context, the film's most engaging performance is that of rap singer Ice-T as Odessa. Perhaps *Ricochet* inadvertently reveals that the action formula that screenwriter de Souza has apparently mastered in purely box-office terms is wearing thin. Subtlety of motivation and complexity of feeling are not the stuff of which *Ricochet* is made. Adding to the film's contrived feeling is a kind of film-school obsession with camera movement and flashy cinematography. Yet, this obsession (like Earl Talbot Blake's) does little more than uncover the fundamental hollowness at the center of all the film's gratuitously violent activity. Because of the thinness of the plot and the characterization, the camera has little to reveal and can only remain fixed on surfaces that hardly require explanation.

Nevertheless, many critics regarded the film as among the summer's more watchable action draws, even though the "silliness" of the film's screenplay was a sore point among several reviewers. Its box-office returns, while not making the film a staggering success, were quite respectable. In fact, *Ricochet* may have demonstrated that the shift to supporting actors in leading roles is the logical (and economical) way to go with action films of this nature. Yet, even if policiers can succeed in formulating their appeal to audiences around the spectacle of action rather than with the spectacle of star personalities, one can only hope that the human-centered aspects of such film dramas will receive a modicum of the attention that the makers of *Ricochet* obviously devoted to special effects and stunts.

Gaylyn Studlar

Reviews
Boston Globe. October 5, 1991, p. 10.
Boxoffice. December, 1991, p. R-93.
Chicago Tribune. October 7, 1991, V, p. 4.
The Hollywood Reporter. October 7, 1991, p. 5.
The Houston Post. October 9, 1991, p. D2.
Jet. LXXX, October 14, 1991, p. 56.
Los Angeles Times. October 7, 1991, p. F7.
The New York Times. October 7, 1991, p. B7.
San Francisco Chronicle. October 8, 1991, p. E1.
USA Today. October 7, 1991, p. D4.
Variety. October 7, 1991, p. 3.
The Washington Post. October 5, 1991, p. D7.

ROBIN HOOD
Prince of Thieves

Production: John Watson, Pen Densham, and Richard B. Lewis for James G. Robinson and Morgan Creek; released by Warner Bros.
Direction: Kevin Reynolds
Screenplay: Pen Densham and John Watson; based on a story by Densham
Cinematography: Doug Milsome
Editing: Peter Boyle
Production design: John Graysmark
Art direction: Alan Tomkins, Fred Carter, and John F. Ralph
Set decoration: Peter Young
Casting: Ilene Starger
Sound: Chris Munro
Costume design: John Bloomfield
Stunt coordination: Paul Weston
Music: Michael Kamen
Song: Bryan Adams (performer) and M. Kamen, B. Adams, and R. J. Lange (music and lyrics), "(Everything I Do) I Do It for You"
Song: Jeff Lynne (performer) and M. Kamen and J. Lynne (music and lyrics), "Wild Times"
MPAA rating: PG-13
Running time: 141 minutes

Principal characters:
Robin of Locksley	Kevin Costner
Azeem	Morgan Freeman
Marian	Mary Elizabeth Mastrantonio
Will Scarlett	Christian Slater
Sheriff of Nottingham	Alan Rickman
Mortianna	Geraldine McEwan
Friar Tuck	Micheal McShane
Lord Locksley	Brian Blessed
Guy of Gisborne	Michael Wincott
Little John	Nick Brimble
Fanny	Soo Drouet
Wulf	Daniel Newman
Bull	Daniel Peacock
Duncan	Walter Sparrow
Bishop	Harold Innocent
Much	Jack Wild

In 1990, both Warner Bros. and Twentieth Century-Fox went head to head in competition to see who would be first to bring out a film adaptation of the legend of

Robin Hood. Fox's version starred Patrick Bergin as the hero and a decidedly adolescent-looking and petulant Uma Thurman as his Maid Marian. It was the film that reached audiences first, but not in theaters. Fox beat out the touted Warner summer release by airing it on the Fox television network in early May. (There was also said to be a TriStar version in the works, but nothing came of it.) Warner was not far behind. With the bankable Kevin Costner in the lead, their version was released just one month later. On its first weekend, it grossed more than $25.5 million. Only one other film that was not a sequel had done better on its opening week, *Batman* (1989). Considering that Costner was the darling of audiences after winning seven Academy Awards for a project which no one thought he could accomplish, *Dances with Wolves* (1990), these numbers were not surprising. What was so amazing about the opening grosses is that they directly contradicted the fact that virtually every critic panned the film and especially Costner's interpretation of the legendary hero.

This version uses the standard legend of Robin Hood (minus King John) but brings a considerable amount of darkness and modern "political correctness" to the tale. Robin of Locksley (Costner) has defied his father (Brian Blessed) and followed his king on the Third Crusade. By 1194, he has been captured and held in a Jerusalem dungeon. He manages to escape along with Azeem (Morgan Freeman), a Moor also in the dungeon awaiting his death sentence. Obligated to stay with Robin until he saves his life in repayment, Azeem accompanies Robin back to England. There Robin finds that his father has been falsely convicted of devil worshipping and then murdered. His lands have been confiscated by the Sheriff of Nottingham (Alan Rickman), who is plotting to enlist the help of the barons to dethrone King Richard the Lionheart while he is out of the country fighting the Crusades.

After killing a few of the Sheriff's men to save a young boy, Robin and Azeem seek sanctuary in Sherwood Forest. There they are waylaid by outlaw peasants who have banded together. They soon accept Robin, and the former nobleman eventually leads the peasants against the tyranny that has impoverished and enslaved them. They are aided in their fight by Marian (Mary Elizabeth Mastrantonio), cousin of the King and sister of Robin's crusading companion, who is loved by Robin and lusted after by the Sheriff. On the Sheriff's side is an old witch named Mortianna (Geraldine McEwan) who divines his future and gives him advice. There is also the expected cast of characters: a nasty Guy of Gisborne (Michael Wincott), a hearty Friar Tuck (Micheal McShane), a strong Little John (Nick Brimble), and an oddly begrudging Will Scarlett (Christian Slater).

While *Robin Hood: Prince of Thieves* is often filmed in excessive close-ups accompanied by dizzying camera movement, it does have a wonderfully authentic look to it. Filmed on location in England and France, it is radiant in the greens, browns, and golds of the time. The interior of the medieval city of Nottingham was reconstructed on the back lot of Shepperton Studio, but its exterior was filmed at the eight-hundred-year-old walled city of Carcassonne in France. Many of the paving stones used in the long corridor of the Sheriff's castle were from the set of Franco Zeffirelli's production of *Hamlet* (1990), starring Mel Gibson. As for Sherwood

Forest, it was actually re-created at two locations: New Forest, a royal hunting preserve since the time of William the Conqueror, and Burnham Beeches in Buckinghamshire, where Robin battles the mercenary Celts and where action had to be halted whenever a plane took off or landed at nearby Heathrow airport.

Although it looks good, there are problems with the film. By bringing the story up to date, writer Pen Densham has kept the action (many of the film's production staff referred to it as "Raiders of the Lost Sherwood Forest") but often sacrificed the wit that has come to exemplify the legend. By making Robin Hood a politically correct, angst-ridden hero instead of the cheeky rebel, he has changed the hero from Falstaff to Hamlet. In addition, for a film whose title invokes "family entertainment," there may be too much violence and other mayhem for younger members of the audience.

For his part, Costner looks terrific as Robin Hood, but when he speaks, his slight English accent comes and goes and his sincerity totally overwhelms what little cleverness the script allows him. It was a daunting task to take on a role which most audience members would associate with an audacious Errol Flynn, but perhaps Costner is miscast in the role. Many critics said that Costner plays the role more like an earnest Gary Cooper than a charming Flynn. Freeman as the Moorish Azeem does give the film an interesting twist and a degree of wise humor, but it is Rickman's Sheriff who walks off with the show. Also seen as the Bruce Willis adversary in *Die Hard* (1988), he spews one-liners and mugs for the camera in a role which he described as a combination of Richard III and a rock star. While his portrayal of the nasty fiend is entertaining, it unfortunately takes the bite out of his villainy and makes him more campy and less threatening to the straightforward hero. Mastrantonio plays Marian more as an independent modern woman, and she looks more urban Italian than medieval English. She came to the part at the last moment after Robin Wright, who had originally been cast as Marian, dropped out of the production after becoming pregnant.

Perhaps because of the race against Fox's *Robin Hood*, Warner rushed its version. Director Kevin Reynolds was only given ten weeks for preproduction. Costner arrived, exhausted after finishing *Dances with Wolves*, three days before filming began. There was no time for rehearsals, and the shooting schedule was reduced from fifteen to thirteen weeks.

Reynolds' only feature films before *Robin Hood* were *Fandango* (1985), also with Costner, and *The Beast* (1988), a little-seen film about Soviet tanks in Afghanistan. He had helped his good friend Costner with *Dances with Wolves* (he directed the buffalo hunt scenes) and was said to be the main reason that Costner accepted the role of the legendary English outlaw. By the end of the troubled and hasty shoot, however, the two Kevins had a strained relationship, and Reynolds was fighting the studio over the final cut of the film. For example, it was said that one of the subplot points cut was the one in which the Sheriff finds out that the witch Mortianna is really his mother. So upset was Reynolds with the released version that he refused to appear at a press preview of the film in New Orleans. Costner, who was already in the city working on his next project, stayed out of the dispute.

Most scholars agree that there is a thread of truth to the legend of Robin Hood, but Reynolds had said that he did not want to make a historical drama. If the historians are right, then he has not done so. Even though Warner touted the efforts taken to ensure accuracy, historians found many fallacies in this version: gun powder appears fifty years before it was invented, wanted posters are printed two hundred years before the printing press, and it would be four hundred years before the telescope would be conceived. If Flynn's Robin Hood can have sequins on his tunic, however, then Costner's should be allowed a degree of license as well. This *Robin Hood* may not be a great film, but audiences found it to be great fun.

Beverley Bare Buehrer

Reviews

American Film: Magazine of the Film and Television Arts. XVI, June, 1991, p. 56.
Boxoffice. August, 1991, p. R-50.
Chicago Tribune. June 14, 1991, p. 7C.
The Christian Science Monitor. June 14, 1991, p. 14.
Cinéfantastique. XXI, June, 1991, p. 8.
Films in Review. XLII, July, 1991, p. 252.
The Hollywood Reporter. June 12, 1991, p. 6.
Los Angeles Times. June 14, 1991, p. F1.
New York. June 24, 1991, p. 47.
The New York Times. June 14, 1991, p. B1.
New Yorker. July 1, 1991, p. 83.
Newsweek. June 24, 1991, p. 60.
People Weekly. June 24, 1991, p. 17.
Rolling Stone. July 11, 1991, p. 11.
Time. CXXXVII, June 24, 1991, p. 58.
The Times Literary Supplement. August 2, 1991, p. 16.
USA Today. June 14, 1991, p. 1D.
Variety. June 17, 1991, p. 65.

THE ROCKETEER

Production: Lawrence Gordon, Charles Gordon, and Lloyd Levin for Walt Disney
Pictures, in association with Silver Screen Partners IV; released by Buena Vista
Direction: Joe Johnston
Screenplay: Danny Bilson and Paul De Meo; based on a story by Bilson, De Meo, and
William Dear, and on the novel by Dave Stevens
Cinematography: Hiro Narita
Editing: Arthur Schmidt
Production design: Jim Bissell
Art direction: Christopher Burian-Mohr
Set decoration: Linda DeScenna
Set design: Carl J. Stensel, Paul Sonski, and John Berger
Casting: Nancy Foy
Special visual effects: Industrial Light and Magic
Visual effects supervision: Ken Ralston
Visual effects production: Patricia Blau
Visual effects art direction: John Bell
Sound: Thomas Causey
Costume design: Marilyn Vance-Straker
Music: James Horner
MPAA rating: PG
Running time: 110 minutes

Principal characters:

Cliff Secord	Bill Campbell
Jenny Blake	Jennifer Connelly
Peevy	Alan Arkin
Neville Sinclair	Timothy Dalton
Eddie Valentine	Paul Sorvino
Howard Hughes	Terry O'Quinn
Fitch	Ed Lauter
Wooly	James Handy
Lothar	Tiny Ron
Spanish Johnny	Robert Guy Miranda
Rusty	John Lavachielli
Bigelow	Eddie Jones

The Rocketeer is a lavish homage to 1930's design, 1940's serials, and the
confidence in technology that characterized America during the post-World War II
decades. Surprisingly, the film takes its immediate source not in some old-time
cliffhanger but in a more recent work: Dave Stevens' 1981 cult comic book success of
the same name. Yet, *The Rocketeer*'s roots run far deeper. It conjures up the age-old

flying myth, which the ancient Greeks embodied in Icarus and comic books revived in the 1930's, most notably in the character of Superman. The film paints a clear-cut portrait of good and evil in conflict, an approach that marked 1940's filmmaking. It also directly alludes to a spate of grade-Z cliffhanger serials that appeared in the immediate postwar period. *King of the Rocket Men* (condensed and released in 1949 as *Lost Planet Airmen*), *Radar Men from the Moon* (1951; condensed and released in 1952 as *Retik, the Moon Menace*), and *Zombies of the Stratosphere* (1952; condensed and released in 1958 as *Satan's Satellites*) all featured helmeted characters who soared via a rocket backpack.

These latter serials reflected a postwar, "gee-whiz" confidence, one that assumed that technology would spawn all manner of marvels; it would no longer be necessary to be some otherworldly demigod to achieve personal flight. (Such a device, the Bell jet pack, was actually created but proved useless.) A similar confidence may have paved the way for *The Rocketeer* because it was in 1991 that the United States reasserted its technological hubris during the Gulf War, when the conflict with Iraq became a black-versus-white parallel to what the world experienced in the 1940's.

The specter of World War II seems deceptively distant, however, from *The Rocketeer*'s opening, set in 1938 Los Angeles. Cliff Secord (Bill Campbell) is a Jimmy Stewart-like innocent who takes a yellow, cartoonlike plane, the Gee-Bee, on a maiden flight. Secord's flight is aborted, however, when gunfire from a chase involving the Federal Bureau of Investigation (FBI) taking place on the ground strikes and damages the Gee-Bee. The reason for the pursuit is that the FBI and the criminals are trying to seize the X-3, a temperamental flying backpack designed by eccentric genius Howard Hughes (Terry O'Quinn).

A mobster hides the X-3 in a hangar, where Secord and tinkerer-mentor Peevy (Alan Arkin) discover it. The maiden flight is breathtaking if nearly out of control, with Secord scything through fields of wheat and skipping along ponds. The sequence, as with all the film's flights, is a special-effects spectacle which is made visceral by numerous point-of-view shots that hurtle viewers along with Secord.

The narrative soon slows down for a bit of exposition. The audience meets Jenny Blake (Jennifer Connelly), Secord's sweet girlfriend. (In Stevens' original comic book, the character was far less innocent. The girlfriend was instead Betty Page, a pouty pinup queen from the era. Walt Disney Pictures did not approve, and, oddly, all that remains of Page's overt sexuality is Connelly's bosomy costumes.) Also introduced is Neville Sinclair (Timothy Dalton), a matinee idol who, it is eventually learned, is a Nazi spy. (The character is based loosely on Errol Flynn, who was rumored to have been a Nazi agent.) Gangster Eddie Valentine (Paul Sorvino) colludes with Sinclair to obtain the X-3.

Every attempt is made to contrast Sinclair's hollow urbanity with Secord's sturdy sincerity. Secord and Peevy live in a casual California bungalow, while Sinclair's home is a replica of Frank Lloyd Wright's well-known, Mayan-inspired Ennis-Brown house. Secord eats at the Bull Dog Cafe, a kitschy, animal-shaped diner which actually once stood near Hollywood. Sinclair, on the other hand, dines at the South Seas Club, a lavish, cavernous Art Deco night spot which is frequented by the likes of Clark Gable and W. C. Fields. In an early scene, Sinclair swashbuckles his way across a film set while Secord awkwardly knocks down one of the set walls. (It crashes onto Sinclair, in a bit of tongue-and-cheek foreshadowing.)

The contrast between the two men turns to conflict when Sinclair asks Jenny to dinner, having met her on the set while she was working as a bit player and having overheard Secord tell her that he has the backpack. While Sinclair plays a hero, Jenny's boyfriend, Secord, becomes a more authentic hero when he dons the backpack and helmet to save a pilot from a sputtering stunt plane. Newspaper reporters call the unidentified flyer "the Rocketeer," and the label sticks.

The spectacular aerial rescue comes at an appropriate point in the narrative. Until then, *The Rocketeer* may have been moving at a somewhat slow pace for audiences accustomed to frenetic cliffhanger-like classics such as *Raiders of the Lost Ark* (1981) and *Star Wars* (1977). From here, however, the film barely pauses for a breath. Various henchmen attempt to seize the X-3, the FBI tries to beat them to it, and both Secord and Peevy manage to remain a few steps ahead. Secord flies right through the South Seas Club as Sinclair tries to catch him. Secord is, in turn, apprehended by the FBI.

Secord finally meets Hughes, the X-3's designer, who shows him and the FBI a Nazi documentary on a planned conquest of the United States by German soldiers who will fly through the skies. Secord wants only to save Jenny from the clutches of Sinclair, who has abducted her from the club. The FBI refuses, so Secord flies from Hughes's hangar to the planetarium at Griffith Park, where Sinclair, Valentine, and assorted gangsters await. They have offered to trade Jenny for the X-3.

Up to this point, director Joe Johnston and screenwriters Danny Bilson and Paul De Meo have taken great pains to ensure historical accuracy: Real or reconstructed edifices, historical celebrities, and a warm, dusty spectrum of colors help to anchor the film to prewar Hollywood. *The Rocketeer*'s climax, however, though spectacular, is preposterous. A looming dirigible appears over the planetarium, Nazi storm troopers pour out from adjacent foliage, and an all-out battle among FBI agents, German soldiers, and mobsters breaks out. In a bit of wry plot development, Valentine sides with the FBI when he discovers Sinclair's fascist leanings, claiming "I may not make an honest buck, but I'm one hundred percent American!"

Sinclair escapes to the dirigible with Jenny in tow. Secord rockets to the rescue. He battles Sinclair and assorted villains atop the now-flaming aircraft. Sinclair dons the X-3 in an attempt to escape but instead crashes into the landmark Hollywood sign. Peevy and Hughes, at the last second, rescue Secord and Jenny via aircraft. In admiration of his derring-do, Hughes gives Secord a brand-new racing plane.

Though visually spectacular and atmospherically definitive, *The Rocketeer* has problems of both tone and theme. It cannot decide whether its material should be treated as campy or earnest. (More often than not, it leans toward the latter.) In addition, it seems to toy with the notion that while Secord, its straight-arrow protagonist, is an Everyman who can rise above the mundane and achieve real-life heroics, Sinclair, mired in the make-believe theatrics of his silver-screen characters, can only achieve greatness by allying himself with the forces of darkness. Yet, this theme is half-born: It has too many inconsistencies to work (if it was ever intended to) and is undercut both by Dalton's vividly drawn villain and by the simple fact that Neville Sinclair has all the best lines.

Marc Mancini

Reviews
American Cinematographer. LXXII, June, 1991, p. 44.
Boxoffice. August, 1991, p. R-53.
Chicago Tribune. June 21, 1991, VII, p. 35.
The Christian Science Monitor. June 28, 1991, p. 12.
Cinéfantastique. XXII, August, 1991, p. 17.
Cinefex. November, 1991, p. 20.
The Hollywood Reporter. June 10, 1991, p. 7.
Los Angeles Times. June 21, 1991, p. F1.
The New York Times. June 21, 1991, p. B1.
Newsweek. CXVII, June 24, 1991, p. 61.
Sight and Sound. I, August, 1991, p. 55.
Variety. June 10, 1991, p. 2.
The Washington Post. June 21, 1991, p. B1.

ROSENCRANTZ AND GUILDENSTERN ARE DEAD

Production: Michael Brandman and Emanuel Azenberg for Thirteen WNET; released
 by Cinecom Entertainment
Direction: Tom Stoppard
Screenplay: Tom Stoppard; based on his play
Cinematography: Peter Biziou
Editing: Nicolas Gaster
Production design: Vaughan Edwards
Art direction: Ivo Husnjak
Sound: Louis Kramer
Costume design: Andreane Neofitou
Music: Stanley Myers
MPAA rating: PG
Running time: 118 minutes

> *Principal characters:*
> Rosencrantz .... Gary Oldman
> Guildenstern .... Tim Roth
> The Player .... Richard Dreyfuss
> Hamlet .... Iain Glen
> Claudius .... Donald Sumpter
> Polonius .... Ian Richardson
> Gertrude .... Joanna Miles
> Ophelia .... Joanna Roth

One of the most celebrated plays of the modern theater, *Rosencrantz and
Guildenstern Are Dead* is an entertaining and provocative comment on the absurdity
of life that is very much in the tradition of Samuel Beckett's famous absurdist play *En
attendant Godot* (1952; *Waiting for Godot*, 1954). First performed in 1966 as an
Oxford University production, the Tom Stoppard play received immediate critical
acclaim and was produced at London's Old Vic Theatre the following year before
moving to Broadway, where it won the 1968 Tony Award and New York Drama Critics
Circle Award for Best Play of the Year.

Inspired by William Shakespeare's *Hamlet* (c. 1600-1601) and built around two very
minor characters from that most famous tragedy, the play is filled with funny, absurd
observations on human existence, on how the events of a person's life are sometimes
beyond that person's control and comprehension, and on how the fate of even the most
insignificant human being is inevitably the same as that of the most well known and
celebrated historical figure. Because the play is very much a theatrical endeavor, with
minimal sets, and is filled with many playful puns and comments on how easily
language can serve to confuse rather than clarify meaning, it would seem to be a weak
choice for a cinematic adaptation. With the strong guiding hand of playwright

Stoppard, however, who wrote the screenplay and makes his directorial debut with the film, *Rosencrantz and Guildenstern Are Dead* manages to be a very lively and adept cinematic treatment of this modern theatrical classic.

The film opens on a dusty, rural road as two figures on horseback trudge silently and aimlessly along the trail. When one of the men, Rosencrantz (Gary Oldman), stops to retrieve a gold coin half buried along the side of the road, he and his companion, Guildenstern (Tim Roth), take a lunch break in a nearby forest grove and engage in a game of head-and-tails coin tossing. Guildenstern becomes somewhat alarmed when coin after coin is tossed and each turns up heads, an incredible stunt that defies logic but seems to have little impact on Rosencrantz, who methodically continues to flip the coin and tally the results. The coin tossing interlude brings with it the uneasy feeling that something is not quite right in the world, that a belief in a logical universe with set principles and natural laws may no longer apply. The two men begin to ponder their reasons for being on the road in the first place and finally remember that they were summoned by someone and are on some sort of mission. The purpose of their mission becomes even more muddled when a troupe of actors appears and the head Player (Richard Dreyfuss) attempts to persuade them to pay the troupe for a performance, one that will emphasize their special brand of drama, which inevitably includes torrid sex, windy rhetoric, and bloody death. Rosencrantz and Guildenstern indulge in another coin-tossing game with the Player, with all the coins once again coming up heads. When a coin finally turns up tails, however, the two men suddenly find themselves in the interior of a castle.

Rosencrantz and Guildenstern soon learn that it is the King and Queen of Denmark, Claudius (Donald Sumpter) and Gertrude (Joanna Miles), who have summoned them. The king and queen, who speak lines from *Hamlet* (they are, after all, exclusive creations of Shakespeare's play and exist only in that play's context), inform the two men that they have been sent for in order to learn why the queen's son, Hamlet (Iain Glen), who is also their childhood friend, is behaving so strangely. In order to prepare for their confrontation with Hamlet, the men engage in a playful game of questions, which confuses the two more than ever. When Hamlet appears and greets them, they re-create the greeting scene from Shakespeare's original play. Then, after Hamlet departs, they criticize each other for not having learned anything definite about Hamlet's strange behavior, which they can only assume to be abnormal because they cannot remember what he was like when they knew him from an earlier time.

As the two men stumble about the castle, hearing snatches of conversations from the other characters, who speak lines from the original play, they begin to participate in scenes that were not meant to include them: They watch from a balcony as Hamlet mouths the words to his famous "To be or not to be" soliloquy. They interrupt Hamlet's encounter with Ophelia (Joanna Roth) when Hamlet tells her to go to a nunnery. They eavesdrop, along with the old man Polonius (Ian Richardson), as Hamlet encounters his mother, Queen Gertrude, and then cower in horror as Hamlet overhears the old man and runs him through with a sword. They are also present when the acting troupe rehearses and watch as the troupe performs the rest of the original play in pantomime, even acting out their own deaths, which, of course, they fail to comprehend. When the actors perform for the king and queen, the king is outraged at the implications of the action, which shows him killing Hamlet's father so that he can marry Hamlet's mother and assume the throne. The king then orders Rosencrantz and Guildenstern to accompany Hamlet to England, where they are to give a special letter to the king.

Suddenly, they wake up in the hull of a ship bound for England, with Hamlet asleep in an adjoining cabin. They open Claudius' letter and read that they are to present Hamlet to the English king, who will then execute him. Stunned at this news—and not realizing that Hamlet has overheard their reading of the letter—they ponder whether to inform Hamlet of the fate that awaits him in England. As they ponder, they finally fall asleep, at which time Hamlet steals their letter and replaces it with one of his own. The two men are rudely awakened when the ship is attacked by pirates. Hamlet escapes with the pirates and Rosencrantz and Guildenstern find themselves on board the ship with the acting troupe, which suddenly appears when the top deck crashes in on the two. When the Player asks them why they are on board, the men let him read Hamlet's letter, which spells out not Hamlet's death but their own.

Tired of the confusion and uncertainty that has engulfed them and tired of the Player's obscure references to death and illusion, Guildenstern grabs a dagger from the Player and stabs him. The Player miraculously rises up, however, with the dagger still in his stomach, and demonstrates to Guildenstern that it is a trick knife with a retracting blade. More confused than ever, the two minor players wonder if they could have avoided becoming involved in all of this confounding madness. The film's final scene takes place back in Denmark, with heaps of dead bodies on the floor near the dead king's throne. It is the final bloody scene of *Hamlet*, played out to its preordained conclusion. After a quick image of two hangman's ropes dangling in the wind and the announcement that Rosencrantz and Guildenstern are dead, the film ends.

As a film, *Rosencrantz and Guildenstern Are Dead* is a visual delight that remains faithful to the play. Director Stoppard has added several visual touches to the film that, for the most part, accentuate the play's theme of incomprehensible forces at work in the universe. For example, throughout the film, Rosencrantz fashions various mechanical objects out of random pieces of paper. He creates boats, pinwheels, paper airplanes, and even a small biplane, all of which he eagerly shows to Guildenstern, who ignores him. In one of the cleverest scenes of the film, Rosencrantz launches one of his paper airplanes and the camera follows its flight path as it glides past Hamlet and Ophelia as they speak dramatic lines from Shakespeare's play. These comedic contraptions point out how certain known laws of nature can be hit on accidentally and then misinterpreted, enhancing the play's message that words, actions, and life itself can all easily be misconstrued.

In another very playfully striking visual scene, Rosencrantz and Guildenstern play a word game involving each man asking the other questions and then answering the questions with still more questions. When one of them answers with a statement, the other shouts, "One-love!" or "Game point!" as if they were engaged in a game of tennis. The scene is appropriately filmed on a tennis court and the camera bounces back and forth, shifting between the points of view of each man as he shouts out another question. In the most outrageous visual gag, Rosencrantz dons a face mask and stuffs his ears with rags while trying to take a nap on board the ship. When the ship is attacked by pirates, the figurehead of the pirate ship crashes into the two men's quarters. Rosencrantz sleeps on, however, until the figurehead, which is in the shape of a beautiful woman, looms directly over his head. When he finally removes his sleeping mask, he spots the figure of the woman and, thinking she is part of a pleasurable dream, rises up and kisses it. All these extra visual flourishes are delightful to watch and are played by the superb cast with a benign offhandedness. Because many of the gags are so clever, however, they tend to overshadow the dialogue. Stoppard goes almost too far, overcompensating in his efforts to make his play a more cinematic experience.

It is interesting to note that most of Stoppard's visual gags are in the style of old slapstick routines that are worthy of such comic performers as Stan Laurel and Oliver Hardy, W. C. Fields, and Buster Keaton. In fact, Stoppard has admitted that, while he was planning the film, he wanted Rosencrantz and Guildenstern to act as if they were an Elizabethan Laurel and Hardy, which is actually very much in line with Shakespeare's concept of these two confused, minor characters whose identities are continually being confused by all the other characters in the original tragedy. Stoppard also admitted that only he could properly treat his own play with the correct amount of disrespect, which is the reason that he insisted on directing the filmed version himself.

By treating his own play with gleeful disrespect, while at the same time playing up the comical, convoluted qualities of Shakespeare's classic tragedy, Stoppard has achieved something very special. He has managed to avoid directing a static "filmed stage version" of a play that many considered a thoroughly theatrical and very uncinematic absurdist comedy. Stoppard, who has written many successful screenplays during his career, proves in his first outing as a film director that he possesses a very irreverent cinematic style. This style is one that enhances his subject matter and brings out the comic potentials in a story about the overwhelming, incomprehensible, and ultimately insane forces of nature that lord over every human being's life, whether the person is a minor bit player or a featured actor.

Jim Kline

Reviews
American Film: Magazine of the Film and Television Arts. XVI, February, 1991, p. 48.
Boxoffice. December, 1990, p. R-94.
Chicago Tribune. March 17, 1991, V, p. 6.
The Hollywood Reporter. February 8, 1991, p. 9.
Los Angeles. February, 1991, p. 123.

Los Angeles Times. February 20, 1991, p. F1.
The New Republic. CCIV, February 4, 1991, p. 28.
The New York Times. February 8, 1991, p. B5.
The New Yorker. LXVII, February 25, 1991, p. 87.
People Weekly. February 18, 1991, p. 18.
Rolling Stone. November 29, 1990, p. 121.
Sight and Sound. I, June, 1991, p. 58.
The Times Literary Supplement. May 24, 1991, p. 19.
Variety. CCCXL, September 24, 1991, p. 83.
Vogue. February, 1991, p. 214.
The Washington Post. March 15, 1991, p. C7.

RUSH

Production: Richard D. Zanuck; released by Metro-Goldwyn-Mayer
Direction: Lili Fini Zanuck
Screenplay: Pete Dexter; based on the book by Kim Wozencraft
Cinematography: Kenneth MacMillan
Editing: Mark Warner
Production design: Paul Sylbert
Set decoration: Phillip Leonard
Casting: Shari Rhodes
Sound: Hank Garfield
Costume design: Colleen Atwood
Music: Eric Clapton
Music supervision: Becky Mancuso and Tim Sexton
MPAA rating: R
Running time: 120 minutes

Principal characters:
Jim Raynor	Jason Patric
Kristen Cates	Jennifer Jason Leigh
Larry Dodd	Sam Elliott
Walker	Max Perlich
Will Gaines	Gregg Allman
Nettle	Tony Frank
Willie Red	Special K McCray

Director Lili Fini Zanuck says that, in her search for film material, an unusual story is what attracts her. *Rush* is a love story, primarily, but it is harrowing, tragic, and viscerally told. The story's unlikely backdrop for romance is the sleazy world of small-time drug dealers in the fictional town of Katterly, Texas. The dealers are stalked and then set up by two narcotics agents, Jim Raynor (Jason Patric) and Kristen Cates (Jennifer Jason Leigh). Jim and Kristen become lovers and then addicts, strung out on the drugs that they confiscate. The screenplay is taken from the best-selling book by Kim Wozencraft, loosely based on her experiences as a narcotics officer in Pasadena, Texas, in the 1970's. Even though the story has a fast pace and intense action, Director Zanuck insists she was not interested in a police story or action film. She calls her film "a character piece in dark surroundings."

The film begins in darkness. From the inside of a wall safe that he has just opened, the viewer sees the face of Will Gaines (Gregg Allman), a suspected big-time drug dealer and local duke of crime in the bar and brothel scene. In an innovative, four-minute, uncut sequence, the camera follows the well-dressed, long-haired Gaines past the gambling tables of a back room, out through the dance floor of the front barroom, past the habitués at the barrail, and outside into his car. The car radio furnishes more setting: It is the end of 1974, the year of the Patty Hearst kidnapping and Watergate.

Soon, Gaines must stop to eject a stowaway bum sleeping in the back of his Cadillac. The caustic humor of this scene and the opening establishes the power and cool demeanor of Will Gaines. He obviously owns the bar and, somehow, most of the people who greet him there. In the bar watching Gaines is Jim Raynor, an undercover narcotics officer who has been placed in the neighborhood to catch Gaines dealing drugs. Jim's lack of composure is contrasted with Gaines's cool. Arriving at police headquarters with drug purchases eventually used as evidence against the people from whom he buys, Jim seems uncertain and ill at ease.

Jim's supervisor, Larry Dodd (Sam Elliott), takes him to pick a partner in order to complete the Gaines assignment. Raynor is impressed with a new recruit, Kristen Cates, and asks Dodd to hire her. Dodd disapproves of involving a woman officer, especially a rookie, in the undercover network, but she turns out to be eager and tough. She is warned that undercover narcotics work is not what she might think it is: "It gets ugly and you get ugly with it," her streetwise partner warns her. "You'll hate yourself." Impressed with Kristen's shooting skill and her steely resolve, Jim gives her a crash course on the demands of undercover narcotics work, including how to take drugs convincingly. He tests her ability to roll a joint and smoke it, and using a harmless powder, he shows her how to shoot up. Dealers, he explains, will want proof that they are dealing with real customers. They will not be able to pretend they are two drug addicts unless they sometimes do the dope. Jim explains that they will be on their own, in dangerous surroundings, with only their cover to protect them.

Jim and Kristen immediately embark on a series of forays and encounters that expose them to drug use and dealers' laws. Kristen seems to have second thoughts, but she soon snorts cocaine bought from a boyishly naïve dealer and car thief named Walker (Max Perlich), who attempts to befriend the couple. She is also becoming emotionally tied to Jim. When they buy drugs from a dealer named Willie Red (Special K McCray), he suddenly insists with chilling hostility that she shoot up as Jim has just done. Thus, Kristen experiences her first rush as Willie Red looks on and gloats delightedly. The incident frightens her and chastens her enthusiasm. Yet she confesses to Jim the next morning that "I liked being there with you, and I liked being scared." "I like it too much," her partner responds.

In fact, Jim is already addicted and regularly holds back portions of the drugs that he has collected. Kristen disapproves but does not interfere. Together they begin a slow descent into the chaotic life of drug craving and confusion. One night, they are threatened by speed dealers that Walker brings to their home, and Kristen comes to the chilling realization that she has become addicted and disoriented. Meanwhile, Walker has been coerced into joining them in their attempt to obtain evidence against Gaines. Walker, like Kristen, is half-frightened all the time and begins to spend more and more time at her place, either strung out or high and paranoid.

When Kristen meets with Larry Dodd to drop off some envelopes of captured drugs, her supervisor notices her anxiety and the change in her nature. She is covering for her partner, as Jim is hopelessly addicted. His arm shows massive bruises and injured veins from injections. Kristen is not much better: She has foraged through the carpet to find dropped pills, and her life is spinning out of control. Dodd soon guesses that his agents have crossed the fine line between undercover work and voluntary drug use, and he confronts Raynor. The two narcotics agents are asked to meet with Dodd and Police Chief Nettle (Tony Frank), a fundamentalist crusader whose real interest in Gaines is piqued by an alleged ownership of sex shops and brothels in town. He tells the agents that they will "make the case" or else—even if they have to plant the drugs on him. (Gaines has never been seen selling narcotics and repeatedly refuses the agents' overtures.) When Jim and Kristen resist Nettle's demand, the police chief threatens to expose Jim's own drug use and have him arrested in the sweep operation. Kristen ministers to Jim through his ordeal of withdrawal.

On the day of the sweep, scores of dealers are herded by officers into holding cells. Gaines sits alone and threatens Jim and Kristen with a knowing look as they pass. The worst incident that day, however, is their discovery that Walker has hanged himself. Kristen had warned him to leave town, but he refused to do so, as he was ashamed of duping his friends in his cowardly attempt to save himself from prison. Sitting that night in the blinding light of a doughnut shop, Kristen and Jim mourn his death and, subconsciously, the death of their innocence as well. Kristen especially seems to have gotten old during the months of undercover work and drug use. Struggling with the underhanded method of their investigation, Kristen tries weakly to insist that the difference was that "our intentions were good." Yet, they compromised themselves by participating in the vice they were commissioned to fight.

Kristen later testifies in front of a grand jury that Gaines sold her and Officer Raynor cocaine, but she is sickened by the polite applause and congratulations they give her for her "courageous work." Jim and Kristen then go underground to avoid reprisals from those arrested. Their lives have been shattered by the operation, and they live in a trailer in fear. All each has left to cherish is the other's presence, and Jim must keep up a permanent armed watch. Finally, Kristen awakens on the couch one night to find a gun barrel pointed at her face. She pushes it away as it goes off, and in the ensuing exchange, Jim is mortally wounded. She never sees the attacker.

In the final scenes, one learns that Kristen has resigned from the police force, but she is called back to testify in the Gaines trial. Exposed to the intense gaze of Gaines, she confesses that the Gaines cocaine was a "stash"—that it was pinned on him. By this act, which shocks the court and her former supervisors, she seems to have regained a measure of her dignity and a clearer notion of what was right and wrong with her previous actions. She also knows, through Gaines's surreptitious signals, that he is Jim's assassin. Gaines goes free, but the final scenes imply that Kristen takes her revenge for Jim's death. Gaines leaves the bar one night and must stop again to eject some backseat stowaway. As he turns around angrily, he is met by a rifle blast. His killer is never shown.

Rush is a fictionalized account of the actions, dangers, and issues that undercover narcotics officers faced in the 1970's. It is also a thriller and a love story. Most reviewers applauded its surface authenticity and congratulated Zanuck for the verve and intensity of the film. The director clearly understood and tried to convey some idea of the drug politics of the times. Recreational use of drugs was widespread, and local efforts to capture drug dealers were vigorous, often overzealous, and dangerous for the investigators. Officers used drugs to be effective, and drug dealers became "snitches," as in the case of Walker, superbly played by Max Perlich. Lines of conduct became blurred and agents regularly planted evidence and committed perjury. Shot in and around Houston, the film carefully captures the aura of the South in that era. Eric Clapton's bluesy score and Colleen Atwood's perceptive costume design will also bring back ghosts from that decade for many viewers. Gregg Allman's brief but commanding scenes also help to evoke the atmosphere of the 1970's.

Nevertheless, the themes of the morality of undercover investigations, the violence of police work, and the desperation of drug addiction are all secondary to the theme of tragic love. Moreover, most critics reserved their unqualified praise for the acting skills of Jason Patric and Jennifer Jason Leigh, who were able to portray their characters' descents into drug addiction with a terror made almost palpable, while simultaneously exuding the warm rushes of affection that the partners felt growing for each other. Their performances are accomplished and seductive. A few critics, however, found that while their credibility as cops and lovers was excellent, the two characters never really became distinctive as individuals, with their own motives and backgrounds to define them clearly. Such reviewers had more praise for the slippery character Walker, who exemplifies the strange contingencies of the drug life. Perlich appeared in another drug-related film, *Drugstore Cowboy* (1989).

Lili Fini Zanuck's first Hollywood success was discovering and developing *Cocoon* (1985). She went on to coproduce *Driving Miss Daisy* (1989), and that film's extraordinary success encouraged her to take the risks of directing her first film, *Rush*. In it, she succeeds in her primary goal, which was to tell a good story. The film is powerful because of its momentum and the vivid depiction of the unpredictable world that surrounds her characters.

JoAnn Balingit

Reviews
Boxoffice. February, 1992, p. R-15.
Chicago Tribune. January 10, 1992, VII, p. 38.
The Christian Science Monitor. January 17, 1992, p. 12.
Film Comment. November/December, 1991, p. 64.
The Hollywood Reporter. December 5, 1991, p. 5.
Los Angeles Times. December 21, 1991, p. F1.
The New York Times. December 22, 1991, p. 20.
Newsweek. CXIX, January 13, 1992, p. 67.
Premiere. January, 1992, p. 74.
Rolling Stone. January 9, 1992, p. 55.
Variety. CCCXLV, December 9, 1991, p. 76.
The Washington Post. January 10, 1992, p. D1.

SCENES FROM A MALL

Production: Paul Mazursky for Touchstone Pictures and Silver Screen Partners IV;
  released by Buena Vista
Direction: Paul Mazursky
Screenplay: Roger L. Simon and Paul Mazursky
Cinematography: Fred Murphy
Editing: Stuart Pappé
Production design: Pato Guzman
Art direction: Steven J. Jordan
Set decoration: Les Bloom
Sound: Les Lezarowitz
Costume design: Albert Wolsky
Music: Marc Shaiman
MPAA rating: R
Running time: 87 minutes

> *Principal characters:*
> Deborah Fifer . . . . Bette Midler
> Nick Fifer . . . . Woody Allen
> Mime . . . . Bill Irwin
> Dr. Hans Clava . . . . Paul Mazursky

In *Scenes from a Mall*, Paul Mazursky's most highly flawed film to date, the director makes yet another attempt at satirizing life in Beverly Hills, the land of blatant, concentrated consumerism. The film focuses on marital bliss and agony by offering one day in the life of a quintessentially successful Jewish couple as they prepare to celebrate their sixteenth wedding anniversary. This cinematic exploration, however, reads more like an outsider's look at a therapy session rather than any kind of scathing social commentary. As Dyan Cannon proved in her self-indulgent, semi-autobiographical film *The End of Innocence* (1990), therapy does not necessarily make the most entertaining dramas.

Nick Fifer (Woody Allen), a high-powered sports attorney, and Deborah Fifer (Bette Midler), a pop psychologist whose marital self-help book is topping the bestseller list, plan to celebrate their sixteenth wedding anniversary by having several friends over for sushi. They schedule in a lovemaking session around their mutual paging beepers, then head off to the trendy Beverly Center shopping mall in Beverly Hills to retrieve their respective gifts. While there, Nick confesses his extramarital affairs and Deborah is shocked, then angered. Finally, she confesses to her own two-year relationship with a colleague, Dr. Hans Clava (Paul Mazursky). The couple takes turns at running the gamut of emotions before eventually reconciling.

Mired in his own need to act as some sort of social documentarist, Mazursky fails to imbue *Scenes from a Mall* with any real dramatic structure. He apparently is content to present his audience with low-grade farce that lacks any true social satire or wit. His latest film is more a series of vignettes than a dramatic tale in which characters move past the external conflict to effect some tangible internal change. Mazursky enjoys having his characters withhold information merely for the comedic payoff of the moment. There is no linear development to the story that stems from character motivation, but simply episodic gimmickry presented as disposable entertainment.

Mazursky never uses the setting of the mall as another form of visual social commentary, the way Allen uses New York City in some of his best work, such as *Annie Hall* (1977) or *Manhattan* (1979). When Allen presents shots of palm trees, garish architecture, and Los Angeles eateries, it is a reflection of the attitudes of the film's main protagonist, Alvy Singer, toward the Californian life-style that he finds so repulsive. Rarely is any location or setting in Allen's work used as merely a backdrop for the action. What Mazursky fails to accomplish in *Scenes from a Mall* is this visual articulation of the meaninglessness of what the main characters are experiencing, as evidenced by the writers' choice of the vapidness and superficiality of their physical surroundings. The mall represents a microcosm of Southern Californian, upwardly mobile society, manifesting the iconography of forced urbanism, the façade of an urban community in much the same way as Los Angeles itself is merely a shell of a city, a sprawling metropolis without a definite center, a symbolic pulse. Rather than generate a forced claustrophobia through the story line, Mazursky has chosen to externally impose it through the setting of the mall. Because no one in this film is truly struggling against the meaninglessness of it all, however, the result is merely prolonged meandering moments of emptiness that are devoid of any significant social commentary. Mazursky falls victim to the very thing that he seems to want to critique: He gives his audience all form and very little substance to sink its teeth into.

Furthermore, neither of the film's main characters reacts to or interacts with the mall. It would have been more compelling if the mall itself were treated almost as a third character in the story. As it is, however, the protagonists could have been placed anywhere; the mall is actually quite insignificant to the story. Without the mall to give this story its backbone, there is little left to support the narrative structure.

Critics were quick to note that the film's title was obviously intended as an educated satire on the Swedish film director Ingmar Bergman's intensely passionate and painfully honest examination of relationships, *Scener ur ett äktenskap* (1973; *Scenes from a Marriage*). Critics and filmmakers may talk about homages, but without a strong story line or characters for the audience to care about the film is merely an empty slate against which intertextual jokes and gags are played. For example, when Nick remarks that he is sick of his friend who is always promoting New York over Los Angeles, the joke is only amusing because it is being delivered by Woody Allen, the bard of New York whose anti-Los Angeles stance has fueled many of his own films. (It is reputed that Allen is such a West Coast phobic that he insisted on filming *Scenes from a Mall* in Connecticut despite its Los Angeles setting.)

Much of what Mazursky apparently finds amusing is already dated, for example his choosing sushi as the fare of the Yuppie set. This no longer seems trendy because

American culture changes so often, and one is hard-pressed to imagine any couple trying to impress their friends by picking up sushi at the mall. While it is acknowledged that Mazursky is trying to make a point regarding the mall as a microcosm of Los Angeles society, his methods of illustrating this view are not at all effective.

There have been a plethora of bombastic films about life in Los Angeles. Steve Martin's *L.A. Story* (1991; reviewed in this volume) is far more successful than Mazursky's film in creating entertaining snippets of social commentary. The problem with Mazursky's work is that his clever little scenes do nothing to further the narrative flow. They are entertaining in themselves but fail to intensify the drama, to add to the build and, as a result, they feel more like some comedian's stand-up routine: funny observations about life, but not a story, and certainly not enough to warrant a feature-length film.

One cannot help but wonder what would have drawn Allen to this project. An unparalleled filmmaker with an eye for social satire and the understanding that scenes cannot arbitrarily be included in a film without contributing to the narrative, Allen is a man who generally appreciates his own limitations, particularly as an actor. There are few moments in *Scenes from a Mall* in which Allen seems comfortable with his character. There obviously is little that he can relate to or bring to the role, and the chemistry between Allen and Midler, "The Divine Miss M," is stilted and unbelievable. The casting must have seemed perfect on paper, but Mazursky never allows his actors to cut loose with their emotions, to do their respective comedic routines. Midler is best when she is at her most outrageous and flamboyant, while Allen seems lost without his trademark neurotic whinings. Mazursky asks both actors to subvert the very things that enable them to bring characters to life and, as a result, evoke emotion from the viewing audience. Mazursky seems to be striving for art combined with insight, but with *Scenes from a Mall*, he presents low farce with minimal feeling.

Patricia Kowal

Reviews
Chicago Tribune. February 22, 1991, VII, p. 29.
The Christian Science Monitor. March 7, 1991, p. 11.
Films in Review. XLII, May, 1991, p. 186.
The Hollywood Reporter. February 21, 1991, p. 10.
Los Angeles Times. February 22, 1991, CX, p. F1.
The New York Times. February 22, 1991, p. B3.
Rolling Stone. February 21, 1991, p. 84.
Time. CXXXVII, February 25, 1991, p. 77.
Variety. February 21, 1991, p. 2.
The Village Voice. February 26, 1991, XXXVI, p. 53.
The Wall Street Journal. February 21, 1991, p. A11.
The Washington Post. February 22, 1991, CXIV, p. B7.

THE SEARCH FOR SIGNS OF INTELLIGENT LIFE IN THE UNIVERSE

Production: Paula Mazur for Tomlin and Wagner Theatricalz, in association with Showtime; released by Orion Classics
Direction: John Bailey
Screenplay: Jane Wagner; based on her play
Cinematography: John Bailey
Editing: Carol Littleton
Art direction: Ed Richardson
Costume design: David Paredes
Music: Jerry Goodman
MPAA rating: PG-13
Running time: 106 minutes

> *Principal characters:*
> All characters .... Lily Tomlin

In a singular display of form in the service of content, the Orion Pictures logo meshes with lovely imagery of the Milky Way over the opening credits of *The Search for Signs of Intelligent Life in the Universe*. Lily Tomlin's disembodied voice asks for the envelope—so she can push it. Push it she does, bringing forth Jane Wagner's unlikely troop of compelling characters as they brush the fringe of one another's lives. Unfortunately, the filmmakers did not recognize that the cosmic glue holding the nebulous work together resides in Tomlin's instantaneous transformations. Each persona was first created by the actress on the barren stage with only the addition of some precise lighting and sound design. In attempting to overexploit the stylistic devices of the film medium, however, director John Bailey damages the effectiveness of Tomlin as a medium in and of herself.

The question of how to "open up" a play on film is as old as the narrative cinema. Sometimes the results are positive. Howard Hawks's *His Girl Friday* (1940) reworked the story line of the theater piece *The Front Page*, turning one of the newspapermen into a woman. It added the crackle of screwball-comedy romance by casting one of a new breed of wisecracking tough dames, Rosalind Russell, opposite the debonair Cary Grant. In 1965, Robert Wise shot Richard Rodgers and Oscar Hammerstein's *The Sound of Music* story on location in breathtaking Austria, where its epic scope played a foil to the larger-than-life musical and political melodrama. With *The Elephant Man* (1980), the imperialistic themes of the staged event were shifted by David Lynch, so that the film version plays to a postindustrial American audience. For these high points, however, there are many lows. In theatrical transposition, additional, inappropriate baggage is often grafted onto the existing elements. In the hopes of rendering the material more "cinematic," filmmakers try to take advantage of a freely roving camera or virtuoso editor's technical abilities. Although it is important to acknowledge the distinctive properties of the two different forms of expression, it is also necessary to isolate some essential spark at the core about which a focus can be maintained.

Yet, audience expectations are another major factor. Individuals who feel a strong emotional bond to an original version can be left disappointed with deviations of any kind. Viewers without a vested interest in reliving every faithful detail of the source, however, can soon lose patience if the material is ploddingly, dispassionately reproduced. Hence, it is difficult to create an adaptation of a recent success without disappointing someone. The major flaw in *The Search for Signs of Intelligent Life in the Universe* is that everything designed to open it up to the screen is more distracting than enhancing. The uniqueness of Tomlin is that she is able, in the most minimal of settings, to flit back and forth between her characterizations in the bat of an eye. The dynamic of this phenomenon clearly mesmerizes the live audiences inside the theater, upon which the film's opening sequence finally swoops down. Yet, the filmmakers did not have enough faith that theatrical techniques would hold the viewer beyond that proscenium.

Instead of allowing Tomlin to utilize the viewer's own imagination, the material fabrication of each character is made devastatingly concrete. Starting with Trudy, the bag lady who is the neighborhood extraterrestrial ambassador, the actress appears in full-bodied makeup and costume. This decision introduces a level of distance by which the spectator is drawn into analyzing and judging the craft of the makeup artist. At the introduction of each subsequent voice, the film jolts to a likewise fully made-up version then usually cuts back to the actress' performance at the theater. It is annoying because one begins to anticipate which moment these external stylized forces and special effects will arbitrarily intrude. Sometimes, a whole scene involving two or more characters is played out completely on another set piece. One episode depicts a crotchety grandfather sparring with a long-suffering grandmother on opposite sides of the room. It is obviously Tomlin appearing on-screen with herself, but the effect transpires on a flatly lit set and seems less like cinema than the splicing together of different kinds of theater.

The abrupt visuals not only keep the viewer from concentrating on and enjoying Tomlin, they interrupt the delicate balance of the play's internal rhythms. Angry, alienated teen Agnes wears more than a dozen zippers. Part of the fun of the play is in watching as Tomlin goes through them all, using her timing skills and our visualization capabilities. The charm is in the small surprises as they are pulled out of thin air. In the film, however, the form consistently undercuts such nuances.

Yet, despite the distractions, much of the play's thematic content shines through. The script is terribly intelligent and is so well structured that it is able to keep an astounding number of balls in the air. The humor of the piece stems from the sincerity with which the individuals present their points of view. Thankfully, as the narrative progresses toward the end, the material is occasionally allowed to soar with less intervention.

The premise is that the self-proclaimed crazy bag lady, Trudy, has been chosen as a channel for beings from another planet to learn if there is, in fact, anything to write home about. She provides a link to the differing scenarios unfolding in the outlying regions of her community near the corner of "Walk-and-Don't Walk." Trudy literally taps into the assorted psyches around her and channels the information to the extraterrestrials while the viewer participates vicariously. The humanity and the lack of condescension are what enables this multicharacter piece to fly. Each perspective is true and genuine in its owner's unique befuddlement. In the midst of their tangential, mostly unaware connections, these individuals are struggling with what has gone wrong and are somehow battling the realities of contemporary life.

There are some unlikely regrets and pearls of wisdom to share, as with the divorced athlete who wonders, "What's the point in being a hedonist if you're not having a good time?" Quotable lines are delivered in understated, heartbreaking verisimilitude that captures a complexity of fragmented human experience that cinema rarely achieves in its mainstream format. One young woman, in trying to shrug off the false hopes of a lifetime, admits that "I don't even think of the Kennedys anymore . . . well, in Novembers." It is this sense of backstory that makes the film resonate beyond its borders. Even Agnes, alienated from her cold scientific father and banished lesbian mother, provides a chilling portrait of what American society has foisted onto its youth by espousing the virtues of G. Gordon Liddy's "self-help book." The trick to surviving life in the United States today, she surmises, is analogous to sticking one's hand in the candle flame and learning "not to mind it."

The Search for Signs of Intelligent Life in the Universe is grounded in the concerns that have come to be connected with Tomlin. Politics, the feminist movement, and lesbian issues take on a historical scope that reaches further than the actress has been able to achieve in her television appearances and feature-film career. Credit must be given to Wagner for orchestrating such an ambitiously large concept. If anything, the tone strikes one as being strangely derivative of Robert Altman's twenty-four-character opus, *Nashville* (1975), in which Tomlin played a single role. The ways in which the characters overlap are deft and skillful, not overbearing.

Even the contrived linear progression provided by Trudy's study seems surprisingly gentle and thoughtful. Believability is maintained in choosing not to give each individual the same degree of progression in the course of the drama. One extended sequence traces a woman from the early zeal of the feminist movement to her current state of postmodern bewilderment and undoubtedly comes closest to many viewers' own experiences. Strategically placed, it acts as a very effective climax and leaves the strongest impression. Most reviewers were understandably more impressed by these themes than by the overall production.

Mary E. Belles

Reviews
Boxoffice. October, 1991, p. R-72.

Chicago Tribune. January 17, 1992, VII, p. 40.

The Christian Science Monitor. October 15, 1991, LXXXIII, p. 11.

Los Angeles Times. October 11, 1991, CX, p. F10.

Los Angeles Times. October 21, 1991, CX, p. F3.

The New Republic. October 7, 1991, CCV, p. 28.

The New York Times. September 27, 1991, CXLI, p. B2.

The New Yorker. LXVII, October 7, 1991, p. 100.

Newsweek. CXVIII, October 7, 1991, p. 65.

Time. CXXXVIII, September 30, 1991, p. 81.

Variety. May 16, 1991, p. 2.

The Village Voice. October 8, 1991, XXXVI, p. 64.

The Wall Street Journal. October 10, 1991, p. A12.

THE SILENCE OF THE LAMBS

Production: Edward Saxon (AA), Kenneth Utt (AA), and Ron Bozman (AA) for
   Strong Heart/Demme; released by Orion Pictures
Direction: Jonathan Demme (AA)
Screenplay: Ted Tally (AA); based on the novel by Thomas Harris
Cinematography: Tak Fujimoto
Editing: Craig McKay
Production design: Kristi Zea
Art direction: Tim Galvin
Set decoration: Karen O'Hara
Sound: Christopher Newman and Tom Fleishman
Special makeup effects: Carl Fullerton and Neal Martz
Costume design: Colleen Atwood
Music: Howard Shore
MPAA rating: R
Running time: 118 minutes

> *Principal characters:*
> Clarice Starling .... Jodie Foster (AA)
> Dr. Hannibal Lecter .... Anthony Hopkins (AA)
> Special Agent Jack Crawford .... Scott Glenn
> Jame Gumb .... Ted Levine
> Catherine Martin .... Brooke Smith

Jonathan Demme's *The Silence of the Lambs* spawned a spate of heated critical
debate regarding the artistic merit of bringing to the screen a tale of mass murderers
who mutilate their victims, particularly women. The film outraged several distinct
groups, including women and gay activists who claimed to be ill-represented by the
depiction of the women characters as weak and succumbing to patriarchal societal
structure and by the mass murderer Buffalo Bill as a mentally unstable transsexual.
The film is far more challenging if viewed from a political context rather than merely
as an examination of filmmaking technique.

Clarice Starling (Jodie Foster), a bright, ambitious trainee at Washington's Federal
Bureau of Investigation (FBI), is selected by the head of the behavioral science
department, Special Agent Jack Crawford (Scott Glenn), to interview Dr. Hannibal
Lecter (Anthony Hopkins), a sociopathic mass murderer with a penchant for devour-
ing anyone who is unfortunate enough to provoke his contempt. Crawford deceives
Starling into thinking that her mission is merely scientific observation. What he really
is hoping for is that Lecter will provide the Bureau with valuable information that will
help them track down the country's latest serial killer, Jame Gumb (Ted Levine),
known as "Buffalo Bill" because of his gruesome trademark of skinning his victims
and stuffing a rare moth chrysalis down their throats. Lecter, himself a brilliantly
insightful psychiatrist, is currently held at a hospital for the criminally insane. When

Starling sets out to confront the monster, she must descend the bowels of evil, both physically and metaphorically, in order to reach him.

When Starling finally confronts the infamous "Hannibal the Cannibal," what she finds is an extremely perceptive man who is capable of deducing her entire life with merely a glance at her "second-rate shoes." Lecter is contemptuous at first, insulted that his nemesis at the FBI would send a neophyte to do battle with him, but he is unable to unnerve Starling. She never averts her gaze and eventually piques the doctor's interest, who wants to know more about Crawford's protégée. He agrees to provide her with insights into the mind of the serial killer, but with one potentially dangerous stipulation: a game of *quid pro quo* in which Starling must provide him with revelations about her tormented inner self. Starling hesitantly agrees, despite Crawford's warning to "not let Lecter inside your head."

Starling and Lecter have only four scenes together, but the relationship that develops between the two is the most compelling part of *The Silence of the Lambs*. The film's pace falters whenever Foster leaves the frame; her characterization of the ambitious young recruit is so restrained, yet riveting. Hopkins' portrayal of Lecter captures viewers' attentions, but it is important to remember how much more difficult it is to play a real person, as opposed to a monster. Despite being burdened with several flashback scenes and a metaphor-laden monologue in which Starling explains her need to "save the lambs," the world's victims, Foster imbues her character with an inner strength that is fueled by a deep-seated vulnerability. It is this combination that both of the men in the story tap into, and while they do attempt to exploit her weaknesses, they also respect the young woman's intelligence and ambition enough to want to help her. In addition, Starling's relationships with the two men are based on respect and not merely blind faith in patriarchy.

The Silence of the Lambs offers a slightly different take on the conventional old cop/ young cop formula. By providing a strong female lead, the filmmakers are able to explore the arena of mentorship in a way that has seldom been done. Rather than rebelling against the patriarchal structure of society, Starling realizes that she must find a way to work within the confines of reality. Some critics objected to this woman-as-neophyte scenario, but in real life, women have few fairy godmothers to look up to as mentors. Starling is savvy enough to accept the reality of her situation and, in turn, exploit it to her own advantage. She is constantly confronted with the inevitability of seeking out the aid of male experts and is continually forced to push aside the recurring sexism, however innocuous it may appear.

Based on the 1988 novel of the same name, *The Silence of the Lambs* is the second of author Thomas Harris' serial killer thrillers to make it to the big screen. His 1981 *Red Dragon* became *Manhunter* (1986), directed by Michael Mann, the creator of the stylistic television show *Miami Vice*, and was the first to introduce audiences to the character of Dr. Hannibal (the Cannibal) Lecter, as interpreted by actor Brian Cox. For *The Silence of the Lambs*, however, Hopkins takes over the role of the brilliant sociopath, imbuing the character with a chilling stillness that is more unnerving than the most fiendish monsters of the horror genre. The role offers the accomplished stage actor one of his finest characterizations since the equally disconcerting ventriloquist and his alter ego, Fats, in writer William Goldman's *Magic* (1978).

Far more compelling, however, is the award-winning performance by Foster as the young FBI recruit. Foster garnered attention in Martin Scorsese's *Alice Doesn't Live Here Anymore* (1975), but it was her work as the young prostitute in Scorsese's ultimate depiction of urban alienation, *Taxi Driver* (1976), that thrust her into the public eye. The unfortunate incident with John Hinckley, Jr., who shot President Ronald Reagan in order to impress Foster, seemed to highlight Foster's choice of roles that on the surface seemed to accentuate the victim status of the characters: *The Hotel New Hampshire* (1984) and *Five Corners* (1987), as well as her Academy Award-winning performance as the gang-rape victim Sarah Tobias in *The Accused* (1988). Yet, lurking beneath each of these characters is an inner strength and resolve that ultimately help each of her characters to triumph over adversity. This victim element is still present in Foster's character in *The Silence of the Lambs*, much less obvious than in past roles, but nevertheless there. There is a sense of violation that occurs when Lecter plays his mind games with Starling, a kind of psychological penetration that is accompanied by a strange courting ritual. Once again, however, as Foster herself has proven in her own life, it is possible for the victim to become the victor.

It is difficult to resolve one's ambivalence about *The Silence of the Lambs*. The conception of the character of Starling is compelling (the clarity of vision with regard to the character's movement throughout the script is inspired): a female victim struggling with her own evolutionary process within the framework of a male-dominated society. Clarice is a positive role model for women viewers: a strong, intelligent female who must allow herself to be exploited, but never fully, in order to further her career—a refreshing change from the Cinderella rescue fairy tale of Julia Roberts in *Pretty Woman* (1990). Yet, one feels that the film's execution by director Jonathan Demme constantly undermines Clarice's strengths. The ending is particularly troublesome. By allowing the camera to move away from Clarice and to rest on Lecter, Demme parallels one of the central conflicts of the story: Clarice is not permitted to "own" the story. In the same way that Crawford will ultimately be rewarded for the capture of Buffalo Bill, Lecter is rewarded for his superior intelligence and criminal cunning; the men in the world will always loom larger, and equality of the sexes will remain elusive. While it is realistic that Clarice's moment of glory will quickly fade, it is disappointing that Demme has chosen to deprive Clarice of his audience's affections and admiration for her for even the briefest of moments.

The Silence of the Lambs is the first thriller to win Best Picture and is only the third film to capture all five of the major Academy Awards. Frank Capra's *It Happened One Night* (1934) and Michael Douglas' production of *One Flew Over the Cuckoo's Nest* (1975) are the only other films to win Best Picture, Director, Actress, Actor, and Screenplay. It is interesting to note that *The Silence of the Lambs* opened in most cities on Valentine's Day—the day reserved for celebrating relationships—because the film offers a bizarre twist on the old courting ritual.

Patricia Kowal

Reviews

American Film: Magazine of the Film and Television Arts. XVI, February, 1991, p. 49.
Boston Globe. February 14, 1991, CCXXXIX, p. 105.
Boxoffice. January, 1991, p. R-2.
Chicago Tribune. February 14, 1991, V, p. 6.
The Christian Science Monitor. March 1, 1991, p. 10.
Cinéfantastique. XXII, February, 1992, p. 16.
Entertainment Weekly. March 1, 1991, p. 38.
Films in Review. XLII, May, 1991, p. 185.
The Hollywood Reporter. CCCXVI, February 4, 1991, p. 9.
Los Angeles Times. February 13, 1991, CX, p. F1.
The New York Times. February 14, 1991, p. B1.
The New Yorker. LXVII, February 25, 1991, p. 87.
Newsweek. CXVII, February 18, 1991, p. 64.
Rolling Stone. March 7, 1991, p. 87.
Variety. CCXXX, February 4, 1991, p. 2.
The Village Voice. February 19, 1991, XXXVI, p. 61.
The Washington Post. February 14, 1991, CXIV, p. B1.

SLEEPING WITH THE ENEMY

Production: Leonard Goldberg; released by Twentieth Century-Fox
Direction: Joseph Ruben
Screenplay: Ronald Bass; based on the novel by Nancy Price
Cinematography: John W. Lindley
Editing: George Bowers
Production design: Doug Kraner
Art direction: Joseph P. Lucky
Set decoration: Lee Poll
Set design: Stan Tropp
Sound: Susumu Tokunow
Costume design: Richard Hornung
Music: Jerry Goldsmith
MPAA rating: R
Running time: 98 minutes

> *Principal characters:*
> Laura Burney (Sara Waters) . . . . Julia Roberts
> Martin Burney . . . . Patrick Bergin
> Ben Woodward . . . . Kevin Anderson
> Chloe . . . . Elizabeth Lawrence
> Fleishman . . . . Kyle Secor

What is frustrating about many contemporary suspense films is not that they are "merely thrillers," but that the hastily applied label is so often used to sidestep the groundwork of a proper story. The weakest of Hitchcockian melodrama seldom shirks in its responsibilities to probe character depth as it intrigues with a heightened plot.

At the entry point of *Sleeping with the Enemy*, sweet innocent Laura Burney (Julia Roberts) is miserably acting out a charade of marriage to psychotic Martin Burney (Patrick Bergin). In their cold, high-tech Cape Cod structure, he terrorizes her over such minuscule details as the arrangement of hand towels and the kitchen cupboards. Her fear is quite clearly palpable, as Martin savagely strikes her in an outburst of obsessive, paranoid jealousy. What is not made clear until much later is the fact that, during the last six months, she has taken practical steps toward implementing a fake drowning scenario for herself. This information comes through an after-the-fact voice-over device. In fact, most of the background of the story is held back and doled out as the later chase ensues. Consequently, rather than being in on the decision to leave and all that it represents to the character, the viewer is treated to much fawning but a basically vague presentation of the young wife's suffering.

For a touted feminist statement, Roberts' Laura is unusually objectified. Dwarfed within the frame's enormous dimensions, she stares blankly, giving away little clue as to what is churning behind the façade that she must maintain. It is a directorial choice that puts a premium on withholding, not developing or exploring. While this method of playing off surprise is not exactly unwatchable, the experience tends to wash over the viewer in a less memorable way than the potential of the situation promises.

A storm provides the opportunity for Laura to slip off a sailboat, exploit her swimming skills of which her husband was unaware, and dash back to retrieve prepacked belongings. While the crazed Martin searches for her body, she is donning a wig and catching a bus, on which a kindly lady offering an apple sparks the closest thing to an explanation of what has transpired before. In a stressful moment, she leaves behind the obligatory clue that will expose her entire hoax to Martin.

Calling herself "Sara Waters," she sets up housekeeping rather painlessly in a time-frozen Midwest town. With enough money to move right into a lovely homespun dwelling, Sara gleefully keeps messy cupboards and disarrayed hand towels. She has already moved her blind mother, Chloe (Elizabeth Lawrence), to a nursing home nearby, telling Martin that the ill woman had died. With the help of Ben Woodward (Kevin Anderson), a quirky but sensitive theater professor at the local college, Laura masquerades as yet another character in order to visit Chloe.

Martin is there waiting at the home ahead of Laura. He has been maniacally tracking his lost possession with all the means at his disposal. By cutting frequently to his vengeful quest for much of the latter portion of the film, tension is imposed onto the Laura/Sara scenes from without. Such editing is much more responsible for any suspense than the writing, which is depressingly limited in scope and believability.

Martin moves in for the kill as Laura is beginning to trust and respond to Ben's sincere intentions. At a carnival sequence, Martin trails the lovers quite like in Alfred Hitchcock's *Strangers on a Train* (1951). With exposition finally out of the way, the suspense builds respectably, considering the triteness that has gone before. The revisiting of the hand towel and cupboard motif fosters an effective pitch, and it is difficult not to respond to the manipulatively voyeuristic placement of the camera, which is accompanied by ominous music. These tricks, however, as well executed as they may be, could work easily as well aimed at a total stranger because there is not much basis for knowing the heroine intimately. Not that one does not like her or feel for her peril, but there is a lack of identification because her transition simply has not been dramatized in a satisfactory way. Information is relayed after the fact, often lacking any solid localization within the psyche of Laura.

Dramatization is paramount at those character-forming, defining moments that are the hardest on which to follow through. In her stylized speech on the bus, Laura refers almost surrealistically to her own painful ordeal in the third person. This is, unfortunately, how the audience is responding to her at the same point: someone who is distant, pitiable, yet not quite identifiable. The scene has a bizarre shaft of European sensibility, obviously unintentional because the next line is delivered by a homespun lady who looks as if she has stepped off of a Frank Capra set. The woman calls Laura a brave girl. The audience, however, is constantly being told things, and is rarely shown or invited to participate in Laura's predicament.

After this shift in the action, there could have been a real sense of understandable progression to show the young woman realizing and facing up to the implications of what she has undertaken. Such an approach might have even justified such a disengaged beginning. Instead, homey settings, no less lush and patrician for their rural quality, serve only as backdrop to predictable clichés. The middle is the most insipid portion of the film, as exemplified by a virtual music video interlude in the prop room of the theater. Although the details of suspense in the final sequences are well attended to, these earlier failings rob the resolution of a specifically personalized sense of triumph. Certainly, there is no questioning the heroine's final actions: The villainous husband is evil personified, neatly contained in one ominous shape. He is a generic, one-dimensional darkness in counterpoint to her sweetly bland, generic goodness. If the script had opted for more meaningful presentation of the obstacles for such a woman confronting the day-to-day reality of even the most cloistered of small-town Americana locales, the audience could have been privileged to a rare transformation.

The camera is more effective at putting the viewer into Martin's point of view in order to foster suspense. An important distinction that Hitchcock makes is that the audience must be made aware of the definitive threat that is ahead of the character in order to achieve suspense. Such a strategy builds toward a heightened emotional pitch, rather than merely opting to surprise the character and audience at the same time. Suspense does legitimately kick in for the last third of the film. Stylistic film gimmickry pulls the frame back from Laura to an uneasy distance at which Martin could be lurking. Yet, the climax seems hollow next to a masterpiece of richly unnerving psychological character exploration such as *Vertigo* (1958). Hitchcock would likewise never offer such a charmless, one-dimensional monster as Martin. Dialogue tells, secondhand, that Martin had once been charming to his wife, but the viewer never sees this personality and thus has a hard time believing it. One only need think of *Rebecca* (1940) or *Suspicion* (1941) for more engaging depictions of similar situations.

Sleeping with the Enemy also falls short of Joseph Ruben's earlier *The Stepfather* (1987), in which a low budget and a better script kept the story grounded in the real world. The filmmakers of *Sleeping with the Enemy* believe that they have made a disturbing, controversial thriller for mass consumption, but their high production-value star vehicle for Roberts pales in comparison to the hallmarks of the genre.

The reviews for the film were mildly disapproving, some indicting the showcase aspect of Roberts, who had starred in the Cinderella fantasy *Pretty Woman* (1990) the year before. Others took the social responsibility line and criticized the system for corrupting the meticulously crafted believability of Nancy Price's novel. By adding high gloss, the film sacrificed what could have been a memorable woman's story. Paying better attention to the dictates of dramatic construction and offering access to the character's development, *Sleeping with the Enemy* might have actually staved off some of the social realist's significant qualms at the same time.

Mary E. Belles

Reviews

Boston Globe. February 8, 1991, CCXXXIX, p. 39.
Chicago Tribune. February 8, 1991, VII, p. 19.
The Christian Science Monitor. March 1, 1991, p. 10.
Entertainment. March 1, 1991, p. 43.
Film Journal. XCIV, February 2, 1991, p. 12.
Films in Review. XLII, May, 1991, p. 186.
The Hollywood Reporter. CCCXVI, February 4, 1991, p. 9.
Los Angeles Times. February 8, 1991, CX, p. F1.
The New York Times. February 8, 1991, p. B10.
The New Yorker. LXVI, February 11, 1991, p. 73.
Newsweek. CXVIII, February 18, 1991, p. 64.
Rolling Stone. DXCIX, March 7, 1991, p. 90.
San Francisco Chronicle. February 8, 1991, CXXVII, p. C1.
Time. CXXXVII, February 11, 1991, p. 79.
Variety. CCXXX, February 4, 1991, p. 2.
The Village Voice. XXXVI, February 12, 1991, p. 55.
The Village Voice. XXXVI, February 19, 1991, p. 70.
The Washington Post. February 8, 1991, p. B1.

SOAPDISH

Production: Aaron Spelling and Alan Greisman; released by Paramount Pictures
Direction: Michael Hoffman
Screenplay: Robert Harling and Andrew Bergman; based on a story by Harling
Cinematography: Ueli Steiger
Editing: Garth Craven
Production design: Eugenio Zanetti
Art direction: Jim Dultz
Set decoration: Lee Poll
Casting: Lora Kennedy
Sound: Petur Hliddal, Tom Johnson, Jack Leahy, and David Slusser
Costume design: Nolan Miller
Music: Alan Silvestri
MPAA rating: PG-13
Running time: 96 minutes

> *Principal characters:*
> Celeste Talbert .... Sally Field
> Jeffrey Anderson .... Kevin Kline
> David Barnes .... Robert Downey, Jr.
> Montana Moorehead .... Cathy Moriarty
> Rose Schwartz .... Whoopi Goldberg
> Lori Craven .... Elisabeth Shue
> Betsy Faye Sharon .... Carrie Fisher
> Edmund Edwards .... Garry Marshall
> Ariel Maloney .... Teri Hatcher
> Blair Brennan .... Paul Johansson

Soapdish is a witty, well-acted, and visually striking look at the world of daytime television drama. It satirizes those who spend absurd amounts of time staking out slender bits of turf. It suggests that the lives that daytime shows present reflect not the everyday experience of audiences but that of the self-obsessed, emotionally pretentious people who work in them. In addition, *Soapdish* warns that the interplay of acting and real-life may be a truly curious process, one that is at once comical, erratic, and dangerous.

To lay out *Soapdish*'s convoluted plot is no easy task. Yet, its improbable baroqueness is precisely what this film is about. The audience meets several key characters as they arrive for a daytime television awards banquet: David Barnes (Robert Downey, Jr.), the manipulative, obsequious, and libidinal producer of the series *The Sun Also Sets*; Montana Moorehead (Cathy Moriarty), a husky-voiced, conniving actress for whom Barnes has an eye; and Celeste Talbert (Sally Field), the long-standing star of *The Sun Also Sets* who is billed as "America's sweetheart" but whom others call a "bad news buffet" and the "queen of misery."

These opening scenes also introduce the film's style, one that is as self-conscious as the actors it portrays. Director Michael Hoffman, cinematographer Ueli Steiger, and production designer Eugenio Zanetti fill the frame with lush sets, huge close-ups, and sweeping camera moves to parallel the melodramatic manner of soap operas. They also seem to wish—for purposes that are not always clear—to reproduce the style of 1950's and 1960's cinema: abstract graphics behind the titles, Cuban big band music, split-frame compositions, and visual wipes as a transition from one sequence to another. Most striking is the use of saturated, vibrant, and technicolor-like hues (especially red and orange) throughout the film. Zanetti claimed that it was the filmmakers' intention to play with the idea of daytime television as an actor's hell, to offer it as "a playful rendering of Dante's Inferno." There was also a second purpose, according to Zanetti: "We chose colors that are neurotic—orange and reds. With the women of *Soapdish* there is this crescendo of craziness."

Celeste's own mood plunges from elation (when she wins an award at the film's opening) to misery, insecurity, and bluster as she discovers that her man has left her. She finds solace in two people: Rose Schwartz (Whoopi Goldberg), her series writer and personal confidante, and Lori Craven (Elisabeth Shue), an acting ingenue who is Celeste's niece.

Celeste's life and career, however, will become even more soap-operalike if Barnes and Moorehead have their way. Moorehead covets the lead in *The Sun Also Sets*; she entices Barnes with promises of sex if he will conspire with her to tarnish Talbert's image and force her off the series. Their first suggestion is that Talbert's character kill a mute homeless character, Angelique (or vice versa—it does not seem to matter). This plan backfires, however, because the actress portraying the homeless person turns out to be Talbert's niece—Talbert wants to work with her, not take a break from the series.

Moorehead and Barnes then decide to bring back a character who was decapitated long ago in the series. This suggestion creates one of the film's most amusing moments: In response to this inane plot idea, Rose retorts "How am I supposed to write for a guy who doesn't have a head?!" Of course, the plot becomes twisted to permit the character's return and this allows the return of the actor who played him. Jeffrey Anderson (Kevin Kline) has been performing in awful dinner-theater engagements and has long held a grudge against Talbert, with whom he once had an affair and who, he believes, banished him from the series. When Talbert sees that Anderson has returned to reprise the role, she faints on the set. When she discovers that her niece is about to begin an affair with him, she becomes doubly upset; she clearly harbors a love-hate relationship with the man.

Soapdish's plot becomes truly convoluted, however, when Jeffrey Anderson and Lori Craven must kiss on the set as part of the soap's evolving intrigue. Talbert jumps in to break it up, revealing that Lori is not her niece but her daughter and that Anderson is the father. This real-life drama is captured by the cameras of a national entertainment program and rebroadcast to millions. Will this lead to the jettisoning of Talbert from the series, as Moorehead wishes? Hardly. The head of network daytime programming wants to keep her because the incident has generated invaluable publicity for the show.

Talbert, Anderson, and Craven try to sort things out. Says Craven, in a bit of dialogue that describes the film on several levels: "This place is crawling with subplots." Adds Anderson: "One more date and we would have had a Greek tragedy on our hands." For Moorehead—so far incapable of dethroning Talbert—it is still not enough of a tragedy. She lies to the press that she is pregnant by Anderson. All this has become too much for the show's producers and the actors involved. At least one character must be "killed off" in what will be probably the series' most highly rated episode. Not even the actors will know in advance who it will be: They will find out as they read the teleprompters.

The film's final act provides an extraordinary climax, filled with absurdities, plot twists, and emotional resolutions. Anderson—who refuses to wear his glasses— misreads the teleprompter at every turn ("Angelique," he declares authoritatively, "has a rare case of brake fluid!"). Moorehead shows up unexpectedly on the set—she was not written into the script—and suggests a brain transplant for the mute Angelique. Lori suddenly begins to speak and, departing from character, declares that she finally accepts her parents. Rose appears on the set and announces that Moorehead could not be pregnant in real life because she is a transsexual. (Needless to say, this news throws producer David Barnes a bit offstride.) The outcome is that Talbert, Anderson, and Craven find emotional satisfaction, freeing themselves—at least for now—from narcissism; the series becomes an even bigger hit, garnering a bouquet of daytime television awards; and Moorehead is exiled to the dinner-theater circuit.

Actor Kevin Kline has argued that *Soapdish* is about "art imitating life imitating art imitating life." As glib and impenetrable as that quote may be, it does explain both the film's underlying structure and its message. Faking and confusing reality is what this film is about. Talbert and Anderson both transpose lines from old performances to "real-life." A dinner-theater employee keeps calling Anderson by his stage name. Talbert "recasts" her daughter as her niece, for convenience. Barnes, who has a marionette theater in his office, pretends not to manipulate his actors. Talbert, to shore up her self-confidence, visits a shopping mall, where Rose pretends to "recognize" the star in order to generate fan attention. Barnes acts out a headache to get his way. Talbert orders Anderson to use his "real voice" when talking to their daughter. Anderson refuses to admit to poor eyesight. Moorehead is not of the gender that she appears to be.

"I don't want any more lying, any deception of any kind," announces Lori in an attempt to set up the ground rules for her family's future happiness. With these words, *Soapdish* ultimately becomes a gentle appeal for generosity, humility, and emotional honesty.

Marc Mancini

Reviews

America. CLXIV, June 22, 1991, p. 683.
Boxoffice. August, 1991, p. R-51.
Chicago Tribune. May 31, 1991, VII, p. 35.
The Connoisseur. CCXXI, June, 1991, p. 38.
Films in Review. XLII, July, 1991, p. 255.
The Hollywood Reporter. May 28, 1991, p. 6.
Los Angeles Times. May 31, 1991, p. F1.
New Statesman and Society. IV, August 23, 1991, p. 30.
The New York Times. May 31, 1991, p. B1.
Newsweek. June 24, 1991, p. 61.
Sight and Sound. I, September, 1991, p. 48.
Variety. May 28, 1991, p. 2.
The Washington Post. May 31, 1991, p. C1.

STAR TREK VI
The Undiscovered Country

Production: Ralph Winter and Steven-Charles Jaffe for Leonard Nimoy; released by
  Paramount Pictures
Direction: Nicholas Meyer
Screenplay: Nicholas Meyer and Denny Martin Flinn; based on a story by Leonard
  Nimoy, Lawrence Konner, and Mark Rosenthal and upon the television series *Star
  Trek*, created by Gene Roddenberry
Cinematography: Hiro Narita
Editing: Ronald Roose
Production design: Herman Zimmerman
Art direction: Nilo Rodis-Jamero
Set decoration: Mickey S. Michaels
Casting: Mary Jo Slater
Visual effects supervision: Scott Farrar
Special visual effects: Industrial Light and Magic
Sound: Gene S. Cantamessa
Makeup supervision: Michael J. Mills
Special alien makeup creation: Edward French
Costume design: Dodie Shepard
Music: Cliff Eidelman
MPAA rating: PG
Running time: 109 minutes

Principal characters:

Captain James T. Kirk	William Shatner
Mr. Spock	Leonard Nimoy
Dr. Leonard "Bones" McCoy	DeForest Kelley
Montgomery "Scotty" Scott	James Doohan
Pavel Chekov	Walter Koenig
Commander Uhura	Nichelle Nichols
Captain Hikaru Sulu	George Takei
Lieutenant Valeris	Kim Cattrall
Chancellor Gorkon	David Warner
General Chang	Christopher Plummer
Sarek	Mark Lenard
Martia	Iman
Admiral Cartwright	Brock Peters
Federation president	Kurtwood Smith
Azetbur	Rosana DeSoto
Klingon ambassador	John Schuck
Klingon defense attorney Worf	Michael Dorn

"Once again, we have saved civilization as we know it," says Captain James T. Kirk (William Shatner) at the end of *Star Trek VI: The Undiscovered Country*. "Fortunately, they won't prosecute," quips Dr. Leonard "Bones" McCoy (DeForest Kelley). This exchange, as well as many others like it, demonstrates what the *Star Trek* filmmakers have discovered in six films based on the 1960's television series: *Star Trek* is at its best when it serves as a parody of itself and of the science-fiction genre, and most especially when the seven original crew members—Kirk, Mr. Spock (Leonard Nimoy), McCoy, Pavel Chekov (Walter Koenig), Uhura (Nichelle Nichols), Montgomery Scott (James Doohan), and Sulu (George Takei)—take center stage and play off one another. Through the years, their verbal bantering and countless sacrifices have underscored their heartfelt loyalty and mutual friendship. These qualities combined with their sense of adventure are what maintain the devotion of *Star Trek*'s fans. This combination was best demonstrated in *Star Trek IV: The Voyage Home* (1986), which was also the highest-grossing *Star Trek* film as of the release of *Star Trek VI*. Unfortunately, *Star Trek VI* veers slightly from this model by splitting the triumvirate Kirk-Spock-McCoy and by leaving little screen time to the other four.

At the release of *Star Trek VI*, twenty-five years had passed since the television series' inception in 1966, and the principal players showed their age. Production notes stated that this was the final voyage of the *Enterprise* as captained by Kirk, although this statement was rendered suspect by previous sequels that sported far more apocalyptic denouements than this one. In *Star Trek II: The Wrath of Khan* (1982), Spock died, and in *Star Trek III: The Search for Spock* (1984), the *Enterprise* was destroyed. Be that as it may, *Star Trek VI* certainly has an air of finality about it that is reinforced by the characters themselves. Kirk records in his log that this will be his last voyage as captain of the *Enterprise*; Spock says that he plans to be replaced by his Vulcan protégé, Lieutenant Valeris (Kim Cattrall); and McCoy mentions his upcoming retirement. The death of *Star Trek*'s creator, Gene Roddenberry, before the film's release in December, 1991, contributed to the overall feeling of finality. When Kirk queries "have we grown so old that we have outlived our usefulness?" the phrase is double-edged. Are Kirk and crew too old to serve Starfleet any longer? Are William Shatner and the others now too old for these roles? Time, and box office, will tell.

Created in the 1960's, when the Cold War between the United States and the Soviet Union was peaking, the original television series highlighted the outerspace confrontations between the two great "universal" powers of the future—the Klingon Empire and the Federation—that were engaged in their own cold war. The mission of the starship *Enterprise* has always been "to seek out and explore strange new worlds . . . to boldly go where no man"—or "no one," as Kirk adds in this film (a reference to the 1980's and 1990's *Star Trek: The Next Generation* television series)—"has gone before." True to its premise, the series was indeed innovative. It used an alien (Spock) as second in command. A black woman, a Japanese American, and a Russian were in key positions at a time when there were few minorities on American television. The series examined environmentalism, racial prejudice, politics, sexism, and many other contemporary themes—serving as a mirror for society at that time.

The sixth *Star Trek* film adheres to this principle, with the breakup of the Klingon Empire and the proposed end to the cold war. *Star Trek*'s release in December, 1991, coincided with the breakup of the Soviet Union. Events in the film concerning the once-great Klingon Empire neatly paralleled this real-life event. In *Star Trek VI*, the Klingons suffer a mining disaster, causing a moon to explode above their planet (paralleling the Soviet Union's Chernobyl accident in 1986). Realizing that they have spent all of their money and resources on the military, they are unable to handle the environmental repercussions of the explosion; the end of their empire is imminent.

The Klingons wish to talk peace, and Spock has volunteered Kirk and the *Enterprise* to meet a Klingon ship and escort Klingon Chancellor Gorkon (David Warner) safely to peace talks on Earth. When Kirk, who hates Klingons because he blames them for the death of his son, asks Spock why he volunteered him for such a mission, Spock sagely replies: "Only Nixon could go to China." Thus begins a tale of epic proportions, involving heads of state, treachery, betrayal, exile, intrigue, and murder. It is appropriate that William Shakespeare is repeatedly quoted, most often by Klingon General Chang (Christopher Plummer)—the actor himself having been a member of the Royal Shakespeare Company. "To be or not to be," quotes Chang at the state dinner hosted by Kirk on board the *Enterprise*. "Of course, you can't really appreciate Shakespeare until you have read him in the original Klingon," adds Chang. Another British icon, the fictional detective Sherlock Holmes, is called upon, however, when a mysterious series of events are perpetrated following the dinner.

Two photon torpedoes that appear to have originated from the *Enterprise* are fired at the Klingon vessel. As a result, the Klingon ship's gravity system is disabled. Two people in Federation uniforms and magnetic boots beam aboard and kill several Klingons, including the chancellor. When the Klingons threaten to retaliate, Kirk surrenders, and he and Dr. McCoy beam aboard the Klingon vessel to try to help. They are arrested and taken to Klingon court, where they are found guilty and sentenced to a penal colony on the remote and icy planet of Rura Penthe. The Klingons force the Federation's compliance by threatening to cancel the proposed peace talks.

Meanwhile, Spock and Valeris work to solve the mystery of what has occurred, in true Holmesian fashion. "When we eliminate the impossible, whatever remains, no matter how improbable, is the truth," quotes Spock. He believes that another ship is involved, one with an advanced cloaking device that fired on the Klingon ship. As Spock pieces together the evidence aboard the *Enterprise*, Kirk and McCoy befriend a fellow prisoner, Martia, a shape shifter who is first seen as a beautiful, alluring woman (played by fashion model Iman)—one of the better costume and makeup jobs of the film. Although defying laws of mass conservation, the special effects of her shape-shifting are state of the art. Martia helps Kirk and McCoy to escape to the planet's surface, a freezing wasteland, so that the *Enterprise* will be able to track and rescue them. Kirk realizes that they have been set up, however, just as prison officials trap them. Meanwhile, Spock discovers a conspiracy that involves both Federation officers and Klingons—those who fear the end of the hostilities between the two great nations. Among them are Valeris and Chang. Spock rescues Kirk and McCoy, they destroy

Chang's Bird of Prey ship, and the *Enterprise* rushes to the site of the peace talks in time to prevent the assassination of the Federation president (Kurtwood Smith).

In *Star Trek VI*, production values remain high, a result in part of the return of Industrial Light and Magic, the special effects team that also worked on the excellent *Star Trek IV*. The overall color of the film, however, seems washed out and murky, and some scenes, particularly those of the interior of the ice planet Rura Penthe, are bleak and uninspired. Although the costuming is quite good, there is little that is new. The casting of Christopher Plummer as Chang was a coup, maintaining the fine tradition of formidable adversaries who have confronted Captain Kirk through the years.

Frustrating for fans of the old series is when a character fails to act "in character," such as when McCoy struggles to save the life of Chancellor Gorkon and the viewer waits, in vain, to hear McCoy's clichéd, "He's dead, Jim." Disappointing also are numerous moments in which the filmmakers do not remain true to premises established during the television series. Spock's sudden, violent use of the Vulcan mind meld to extract information from conspirator Valeris jars the viewer familiar with the principle: The mind meld is supposedly a very personal, involved linking of two minds and souls, to the betterment of both. Nevertheless, Leonard Nimoy as Spock remains the quintessential Vulcan: Whether because of his own physical characteristics or his mannerisms, Nimoy has defined the Vulcan appearance and spirit, and all the other "Vulcans" never appear to be more than actors wearing elaborate prostheses.

Despite numerous references throughout the film to this, their "final" voyage, in the last moments of the film, Spock, when confronted by a Starfleet directive to report back to space dock to be decommissioned, replies—with one of his infrequent and well-timed expletives—that if he were human he would tell them to "go to Hell." In an unusually literary response, Kirk voices the fanciful words of J. M. Barrie's Peter Pan, "second star to the right and straight on till morning," likening the *Enterprise* and its crew to the young boy who refused to grow up.

Cynthia K. Breckenridge

Reviews

Boxoffice. January, 1992, p. R-1.
Chicago Tribune. December 6, 1991, VII, p. 31.
The Christian Science Monitor. December 12, 1991, p. 14.
Cinéfantastique. XXII, February, 1992, p. 44.
Cinefex. February, 1992, p. 40.
The Hollywood Reporter. December 6, 1991, p. 9.
Los Angeles Times. December 6, 1991, p. F1.
The New York Times. December 6, 1991, p. B1.
Omni. XIV, December, 1991, p. 48.
Variety. December 6, 1991, p. 2.
The Wall Street Journal. December 11, 1991, p. A14.
The Washington Post. December 6, 1991, p. D1.

STRAIGHT OUT OF BROOKLYN

Production: Matty Rich for American Playhouse Theatrical Films and Blacks 'N
  Progress; released by the Samuel Goldwyn Company
Direction: Matty Rich
Screenplay: Matty Rich
Cinematography: John Rosnell
Editing: Jack Haigis
Art direction: no listing
Casting: Dorise Black and Shirley Matthews
Sound: Donna Farnum and William Kozy
Music: Harold Wheeler
MPAA rating: R
Running time: 91 minutes

> *Principal characters:*
> Ray Brown .... George T. Odom
> Frankie Brown .... Ann D. Sanders
> Dennis Brown .... Lawrence Gilliard, Jr.
> Carolyn Brown .... Barbara Sanon
> Shirley .... Reana E. Drummond
> Larry .... Matty Rich
> Kevin .... Mark Malone

Hollywood has traditionally liked to surround its filmmakers with Cinderella
biographies, ones that are often fabricated. In the case of Matty Rich, the African-
American creator of *Straight Out of Brooklyn*, the Cinderella image is valid. Writing
the film at the age of nineteen, he also acted in, produced, and directed the feature
color film with full Hollywood backing. Even more amazing, he is largely self-taught
and comes from humble social origins with no theatrical connections.

Straight Out of Brooklyn takes place in the Red Hook housing project in Brooklyn
where Rich lived until he was ten years old. His major protagonists are the Browns,
who are prime examples of the working poor in the United States. Ray Brown (George
T. Odom), the father, is a gas station attendant and his wife, Frankie (Ann D. Sanders),
is a part-time housemaid. Daughter Carolyn (Barbara Sanon) is distraught that her
drunken father beats her mother, and teenage son Dennis (Lawrence Gilliard, Jr.)
burns with the need to find a better life for himself, his family, and his girlfriend.

The film opens with a long shot of the housing project, which is neither the best nor
the worst in Brooklyn. Off to one side one can see the Statue of Liberty far away in the
river and on the other side one sees cars zipping along the Brooklyn Queens
Expressway, completely indifferent to the housing project below. Rich returns to such
shots from time to time in the film, which is very interesting visually. At night, the
project lighting makes the buildings appear menacing. There is always the sound of

voices shouting or guns shooting, becoming a hidden ghetto Greek chorus revealing the terror behind the bland brick exteriors.

The story also unfolds with the predictability and air of a Greek tragedy. When sober, Ray is likable enough. He gives gifts to his children, wants his family to eat supper together, and is proud that he has sustained a family unit. Once he begins to drink, however, he breaks glass and furniture, goes into verbal rages, and beats his wife. Each of these outbursts is worse than the preceding one. In long soliloquies spoken into a mirror or merely into the air, Ray blames his problems on white people. While there is truth in some of what he says, Ray refuses to take responsibility for his own drinking and how he is destroying his family.

Frankie is so aware of the hardships that her husband has endured that she accepts her own oppression. When her daughter begs her to go away, she responds by insisting that the daughter forgive her father's misdeeds. Frankie tries to hide her wounds when going out to work, but the bruises and scars become so severe that the woman who finds work for her says she can no longer place a woman in her condition and that Frankie must seek help. Frankie refuses, loyal to her husband whatever the consequences. She will make no complaints to the police or seek counseling.

Dennis views his family with increasing rage. He wants to restrain his father physically, but his younger sister and mother hold him back. He finally concludes that the only way out is to secure a large amount of money quickly. Dennis takes his girlfriend, Shirley (Reana E. Drummond), to the Brooklyn Heights Promenade, where they gaze across the East River and look at Wall Street landmarks. Dennis says that people on Wall Street got there by being ruthless and that he too will be ruthless. Shirley urges him to think of going to college or taking other long-term steps to alter his life. He replies that there is no time for such dreams and that college is for saps or white people.

Ignoring Shirley's commonsense advice, Dennis begins to plot a robbery with his two closest friends, Larry (Rich) and Kevin (Mark Malone). Larry repeatedly, but not very energetically, suggests that they might all be better off if they found jobs. Mostly, however, he and Kevin hang out, eyeballing women and making wisecracks. They are constantly on the brink of physical confrontations with other African-American men, but mainly they fast-talk their way out of confrontations or run away. Meanwhile, Dennis determinedly continues to think about the robbery scheme.

Like his notions about Wall Street, Dennis' plan is simplistic, characterized more by its boldness than any chance of success. His idea is to rob a local hoodlum who collects money for a drug dealer. He convinces himself that he is doing no wrong because money will not be taken from innocent people. One enormous weakness in the film's credibility is that the group never anticipates that the drug dealer will seek them out. Compounding this implausibility is that the young men secure the loan of a car from a relative living in the area, obtain a rifle from a local gun dealer, and never think of using masks to hide their faces.

A sense of doom fills the cinematic air as the day of the robbery approaches. When Shirley is told about the plan, she tells Dennis that he must choose between her and the robbery. Challenged that she is not backing up her man, she replies that she will not support stupidity and will not allow her life to be destroyed because he insists on unreasonable behavior. The contrast between Shirley's attitude and Frankie's is pointed, if obvious.

The armed robbery goes off smoothly, but the robbed collector gets a full-face view of the unmasked Dennis and the escape car is so slow that he would have time to take down a license number. Any thoughtful viewer would assume that, as soon as the robbery is completed, there is a provision for a quick exit from Red Hook. Instead, the young men count their money in a hallway only to find the sum is much larger than they had thought. Kevin and Larry want to give the money back in order to escape punishment. Dennis laughs at them and takes responsibility for keeping the loot.

Before he can take whatever next step was planned, Dennis is confronted with a family crisis. Ray has again beaten Frankie and, a day later, Frankie passes out from the effects of internal injuries. She is rushed to the hospital, where Carolyn and Dennis watch her die. In the interim, the drug dealers have come to the housing project looking for Dennis and his friends. After a long day in which the robbers cannot be found, the drug dealers spot Ray. They shoot him in the courtyard of one of the buildings. Thus, the film ends with both parents dead and both children still in jeopardy. Like a nineteenth century novel, the film is given a written epigram for its final image. The epigram pleads for the community to change the behavior and attitudes that have resulted in the tragedy just rendered.

While Rich shares many of the themes and techniques of other young African-American filmmakers who made Hollywood films in the early 1990's, he is particularly interested in the plight of the African-American family and he avoids cheap sensationalism. His female characters are well drawn and far more complex than in the work of such contemporaries as Spike Lee. Shirley is unique for her clear view of what the world is about and what her best path might be. Carolyn, the youngest of the Browns, seems to be the only person in the family who has the potential to escape its pathology. If Frankie is too accepting of her fate, she is certainly credible and represents the plight of many battered women.

Despite its strong narrative, *Straight Out of Brooklyn* will appear somewhat amateurish to most viewers. It has the feel of a student film or what used to be termed an "underground" film. The sound quality is far from state of the art, the camera work is pedestrian, and the editing is sluggish. Moreover, with the strong exception of Odom as Ray, the cast of unknowns, almost all of whom are making film debuts, cannot carry the emotional loads that the roles demand. Larry and Kevin have amusing raps, but these resemble television skits and do not fit comfortably into the pace of a full-length film. Although they are drawn from the life experiences of Rich, they seem contrived and cutely imposed on the action.

Many of the film's weaknesses stem from the script. While it is true that many robberies by young men are ineptly planned, the specifics of this robbery are absurd. Other sequences, such as Ray being surly on his job or the hoodlums threatening one another, are stiffly written and clichéd. When characters offer strange excuses for their actions, one is never sure whether the screenwriter believes that they are deluding themselves or that they are making valid observations in a crude manner. The one consistency, and saving grace, in the script is that Rich never glamorizes poverty or crime. Unfortunately for the film, his authorial voice, like the voice of his fictional Larry, is not resolute enough for the forces with which he must contend.

Despite these drawbacks, Rich's achievement is considerable. With only one month's study at New York University's film school, he has trained himself mainly by reading books and watching films. While only seventeen years old, he used $5000 in credit card loans to capture the film's original scenes on celluloid. He then went on an African-American radio station to ask potential investors to see what he had already accomplished. This appeal eventually brought in $70,000. All the new backers were African-American, giving the film a solid vote of confidence from the community that it sought to examine. With this new money, Rich got enough of the film together to interest American Playhouse Theatrical Films, a Public Broadcasting System (PBS) subsidiary dedicated to aiding new American filmmakers, particularly those whose cultures have been discriminated against for one reason or another. Rich was then able to complete his film in time for the 1991 Sundance Film Festival, another event dedicated to emerging independent filmmakers of diverse cultures. At Sundance, *Straight Out of Brooklyn* was given a Special Jury Award.

If *Straight Out of Brooklyn* is not a masterpiece, it is nevertheless an impressive film debut. Unlike better-known young African-American filmmakers, Rich has chosen to focus on the family unit and to hold his characters accountable for self-destructive behavior. More experience and better financing will improve the technical quality of subsequent films. Stronger scripts and acting are also likely. Matty Rich is a filmmaker to keep one's eye on.

Dan Georgakas

Reviews
The Hollywood Reporter. April 29, 1991, p. 6.
Los Angeles Times. May 31, 1991, p. F8.
The New Republic. CCV, August 5, 1991, p. 26.
The New York Times. May 22, 1991, p. B3.
Newsweek. CXVII, May 27, 1991, p. 58.
Premiere. IV, August, 1991, p. 104.
Rolling Stone. June 13, 1991, p. 108.
Variety. January 23, 1991, p. 13.
Video. XV, January, 1992, p. 68.
The Wall Street Journal. June 20, 1991, p. A12.
The Washington Post. June 28, 1991, p. D1.

STRANGERS IN GOOD COMPANY

Origin: Canada
Released: 1990
Released in U.S.: 1991
Production: David Wilson for National Film Board of Canada; released by First Run
  Features and Castle Hill, in association with Bedford Entertainment
Direction: Cynthia Scott
Screenplay: Gloria Demers with Cynthia Scott, David Wilson, and Sally Bochner
Cinematography: David de Volpi
Editing: David Wilson
Scenic artist: Christiane Gagnon
Sound: Jacques Drouin
Costume design: Elaine Langlais
Music: Marie Bernard
MPAA rating: PG
Running time: 105 minutes
Also known as: The Company of Strangers

> *Principal characters:*
> Alice .... Alice Diabo
> Constance .... Constance Garneau
> Winifred .... Winifred Holden
> Cissy .... Cissy Meddings
> Mary .... Mary Meigs
> Catherine .... Catherine Roche
> Michelle .... Michelle Sweeney
> Beth .... Beth Webber

Cynthia Scott first came up with the idea of a film about "people who are old," an expression that she prefers to "old people," when she visited a seniors' club in Montreal. While she admits to being swept away by their energy and spirit, it was something much more subtle that made *Strangers in Good Company* inescapable for her: "Although they suffer from the physical problems of old age, they're the same people they always were." After an extensive casting search, which at one point left Scott scouting hair salons frequented by the elderly, shooting began with a largely biographical script, tailored to fit the actresses' lives. They were never actually shown the script; instead, the women embellished as they went along. Soon into the filming process, however, even the skeletal support provided by the script was discarded, and what appears on the screen is solely the women, virtually without any amelioration or adulteration. As Scott says, "They're not 'acting.' They're themselves."

Every film begins with a premise, a reason for the characters to meet, to interact, to resolve their conflicts, and as initially improbable as the premise behind this film may seem, the characters move quickly from staged to real life. The film begins with a misadventure: Mechanical failure derails their sight-seeing expedition, which is at that point approximately twenty miles outside Quebec in the Mont Tremblant region. Pragmatically, the youngest of the passengers Catherine (Catherine Roche), who is a sixty-eight-year-old mechanically inclined nun, uses what is at hand to work on the bus (including a fingernail file), while the others make their way to an abandoned house to set up camp. Finally, failing to repair the bus, Roche leaves to hike for help. The film itself is the story of the three nights that the women spend alone in the wilderness, with "action" highlights including the gathering of provisions (frogs and mushrooms that they find and fish that they catch with a pantyhose net), the entertainment (bird songs, sketches, belly dances), and the conversations that reveal their memories and chart their stories.

Finally, the women are rescued, but by that point it is clear that any such outside help is superfluous: They are perfectly capable of rescuing themselves in a more interesting and a less material way. While it has been good naturedly referred to as "Outward Bound on Golden Pond," the film is finally very simple: no agenda, little action, but a good bit of talk. Probably the best way to understand the film is through its structure and its characters.

Structurally, the film is a cinematic string of pearls, a series of closely connected episodes in which the women, either alone or in small groups, reveal and explore their successes and failures. In a key scene, Beth (Beth Webber), eighty-three, one of the women for whom the wilderness trek and the aging process are quite painful, sits with Michelle (Michelle Sweeney), thirty-one, the young bus driver, while Webber recounts her passage from beauty and youth through loss to loneliness. At the climax of the scene and with Sweeney's urging, Webber removes her wig, transforming herself from prim and nervous to disheveled but clearly human. In another scene, Cissy (Cissy Meddings), seventy-six, a chirpy, oddly disconnected but endearing widow, is bird-watching with Mary (Mary Meigs), seventy-one, a handsome, elegant artist. Meigs explains to Meddings that she has no man in her life because she is a lesbian. Replies Meddings without a pause, "Oh, that's good." Additionally, a group of women discuss what they remember best about being young and in love, recounting the frustration of currently having similar feelings of equal intensity whose expression is made impossible by the physical, not mental or emotional, process of growing older. Alice (Alice Diabo), seventy-four, a Mohawk Indian, remembers walking from the reservation to town to dance with the young man who became her husband. Her vivid recollection of his physical perfection countered by that of the subsequent decline of their marriage is one of the many difficult realities in the film.

Critics have disagreed about the effectiveness of one of the film's techniques that forms a bridge between structure and character. Interspersed throughout the film are still photographs of the women when young, in some cases pictured with family members, most of whom have died. It has been argued that the photographs are disruptive, and it is true that they shock, providing strident contrast to the aging and honestly aged faces that fill the screen more regularly. While startling, however, the photographs, in their simplest understanding, have true value as reminders of the inescapability of time. They also anchor these women and their stories in a world that is real enough to make their pain and their successes palpable.

The episodic nature of the film and the interspersing of still and action sequences create a pattern reflected further in the characterization of the women and by the counterpoint of smooth cinematography. The characters enter the film in a brightly colored bus which not only navigates the country roads as the credits roll but also serves as a symbol of the women themselves. The vehicle is oddly out of place, a motorized visitor from a busier, more purposeful world, buzzing and tipping through the stillness and verdant fields through which it passes—an intruder, soon to be more threatened than threatening. The bus is a minivan; the women are its equivalent in their world. It is no wonder that the bus falters; it is poorly equipped for the realities of this world. It is also no wonder that the women emerge frightened, uncertain of and unprepared for the frontier experience that awaits them. This is not the world that they understand and in which they function daily, if unhappily.

When the women emerge from the waylaid bus, there is no introduction or background given. Instead, the camera shows them picking their way gingerly across the fields, complaining, worrying, waist-high in weeds, with panicked looks on their faces. They are out of place, uncomfortable, negative, so that even their discovery of the ruined house at this point seems to suggest more problems than possibilities. It is important that the audience understand the fear and discomfort that the women experience as they work to survive, because that initial discomfort sets the tone for the sure-footedness that follows. Not much time passes before the women have constructed sleeping pallets out of straw, found the lake and gazebo farther into the woods, divided up the duties, and set about their new lives. The same surprise that the photographs work on the audience is foreshadowed by the decrepit way in which they enter the wilds, only to spring to action shortly after.

Even once the women spring to new life, the audience only learns bits and pieces of their pasts, slowly understanding them in the context of both the present and the past. Each of the characters has multiple layers to her life that the episodes reveal. Meddings, for example, has survived the London Blitz of World War II, a stroke that left her almost dead, and the death of her beloved husband. To counter these losses, however, she is also shown to be of infinite patience and accepting of people, the world, and her lot in it all. More broadly, the women suffer great collective sadness through the process of recollecting their lives, but they also grow strong as they rebuild lives for themselves in the wild.

The long shots and close-ups of David de Volpi's cinematography function as part of the system, too, such as when he pulls back to let the audience see a string of exceptionally elderly women picking their way across the field. Yet, when the travelers tell their stories, the camera moves in and with great clarity focuses on wrinkles, gray hair, various blemishes. It is one of the great powers of the film that the audience is drawn to the beauty of the women's faces, and certainly part of the pleasure of viewing the film exists in the invitation to look at them with great clarity and honesty. De Volpi captures the scenes of nature with dew and awe intact, enhancing the audience's understanding of how the nervous old people on the flailing bus become the lively confident women swimming in the lake, dancing, and laughing.

The film's beauty highlights nature's healing powers and the women's resiliency yet never renders them clichés. Scott and her crew avoid taking the process and the film beyond an acceptable reality; the women still rise and take a rainbow-colored assortment of medications. Yet, each woman achieves her own brand of success. Constance (Constance Garneau), ninety-two, the oldest pioneer, finally decides to discard her various pills, opting to live a different life for the time that is left for her— but it is important that her passage to that point is hard won.

Even with the artfully handled cinematography and the editing, the characters remain the essence of the film, and any of the small action episodes of sketching, creating beds, telling jokes, and cooking should not be confused with the film's true progress: the women's calm yet pressing explorations and acceptance of themselves and one another. Also, to see the women as types—as Mohawk grandmother, nonagenarian bird caller, polyester-clad belly dancer (seventy-seven-year-old Wini-fred Holden), Walkman-toting nun, or young hipster—is only to caricature them, to try to capture them in a space which they quickly outgrow. While this film is small in scope and roar, it is huge in its range and heart. They "become their own best selves, . . . drawing strength from each other's weaknesses." At film's end, a plane arrives to take them skyward, and the rambling bus that once held them is discarded.

Critics have found the film "an upside, antipodal *Lord of the Flies*," and Scott herself places it among the new "big thing" of films about elderly people. Neverthe-less, the film offers "an epiphany for the price of a movie ticket" and an affirmation of life and death that avoids being saccharine or overly simplified. It is the story of genuine, valuable struggles, not all of which are finally won. As one character says, "It's all guesswork," and the remarkable unremarkableness of their lives is a power that liberates.

Roberta F. Green

Reviews

Boston Globe. October 10, 1991, p. 94.
Chicago Tribune. July 12, 1991, VII, p. 42.
The Hollywood Reporter. May 10, 1991, p. 26.
The Hollywood Reporter. September 16, 1991, p. 5.
Los Angeles Times. September 13, 1991, p. F9.
Maclean's. September 24, 1990, p. 57.
New Woman. XXI, June, 1991, p. 24.
The New York Times. May 10, 1991, p. B10.
New York Woman. April, 1991, p. 35.
San Francisco Chronicle. October 11, 1991, p. D5.
Variety. CCCXL, September 10, 1990, p. 57.
The Washington Post. July 13, 1991, p. C1.

THE SUPER

Production: Charles Gordon for Largo Entertainment, in association with JVC
    Entertainment; released by Twentieth Century-Fox
Direction: Rod Daniel
Screenplay: Sam Simon
Cinematography: Bruce Surtees
Editing: Jack Hofstra
Production design: Kristi Zea
Art direction: Jeremy Conway
Set decoration: Leslie Pope
Casting: Avy Kaufman
Sound: Tom Brandau
Costume design: Aude Bronson-Howard
Stunt coordination: Jery Hewitt
Music: Miles Goodman
MPAA rating: R
Running time: 86 minutes

> *Principal characters:*
> Louie Kritski .... Joe Pesci
> Big Lou Kritski .... Vincent Gardenia
> Naomi Bensinger .... Madolyn Smith Osborne
> Marlon .... Rubén Blades
> Heather .... Stacey Travis
> Irene Kritski .... Carole Shelley
> Tito .... Kenny Blank
> Gilliam .... Paul Benjamin
> Leotha .... Beatrice Winde

Louie Kritski (Joe Pesci) grew up under the dubious tutelage of his New York
slumlord father, Big Lou (Vincent Gardenia), and is now dutifully following in his
father's footsteps when he is given his own first slum building in the East Village as a
birthday present. Big Lou, who owns twenty-seven such tenements of his own, has
successfully drummed his theory of landlording into his son: "When a Kritski gets a
building, what does he do with it? Nothing!"

One day, however, this lack of care catches up with Louie. Naomi Bensinger
(Madolyn Smith Osborne), a housing authority attorney, successfully prosecutes
Louie. His sentence is to spend 120 days under house arrest in his own building—or
until his building is up to code. He takes apartment 5C, which he advertised as a
"furnished, fifth-floor charmer, close to shopping." The apartment is possibly the
worst in the slum building, where commodes overflow, rats roam, boilers fail to
function, and electricity is nonexistent.

Fixing the building would not seem like such a problem for the wealthy Louie, but there is a hitch: His father plans on leaving Louie his other twenty-seven buildings, but only if Louie refuses to make repairs in his own building. Trying to settle into his distasteful situation until his father and his lawyer can appeal the conviction, Louie meets many of his neighbors. Among them is a young boy who is wise beyond his years, Tito (Kenny Blank). Tito lives with his grandmother because his father is a drug dealer and his mother has disappeared. Another new neighbor is Marlon (Rubén Blades), a crafty street hustler who finds several innovative ways to scam Louie out of his money.

Little by little, Louie begins to fix his building, but only as things affect his own life. At first, he tries to fix only his own apartment, but under Naomi's watchful eye he does more while trying, crassly and unsuccessfully, to woo her. While he is in control of a very basic part of his tenants' lives and seems to loathe them, his loneliness soon makes him want to make friends with them, although grudgingly.

When Tito's grandmother refuses to let Tito keep a bicycle bought for him with his father's drug money, Louie explains that his father makes his money from other people's misery. As Tito observantly points out, he is not unlike Louie's father. This hits home with Louie, and while his father is on vacation in Bermuda, he buys heaters for everyone. Eventually, he begins the building's much-needed overhauling.

The Super is an awkward film to watch. It is difficult, in hard economic times, to make light of such a despicable situation, but director Rod Daniel and screenwriter Sam Simon try—and without much success. This is Simon's first produced feature-film script, and Daniel's previous directorial efforts include *Teen Wolf* (1985), *Like Father Like Son* (1987), and *K-9* (1989). This relative lack of experience has given birth to a choppy film in what one critic called the "white-man-gets-a-conscience" genre that became popular in the early 1990's.

The Super was shot on location in New York City's East Village. More than seventy-five members of the neighborhood were hired to help with locations, security, and traffic control; to assist in the set dressing and art departments; and to work as extras. This may be the best thing the film does for the plight of the poor, because the story itself contains nothing new. Feeling sympathy for these people seems to be one of the film's goals, but it is a clumsily handled one. What does help carry audiences through the film's running time is the performance by Joe Pesci. Cast in the title role, Pesci succeeds in portraying a character who is basically an unlikable jerk with a small degree of lovability. A trait seen in his previous films, especially 1990's *Home Alone* and *GoodFellas*, this inexplicable ability of Pesci's is invaluable in films where major characters seem to be totally unredeemable.

As Louie Kritski, Pesci is comical as well as callused. Although cowed by his father, Pesci's Louie seems fearless of those whom most affluent whites would fear. What he lacks in physical stature, he makes up for in bravado. Yet, the Louie on the basketball court and on the dance floor is an agonizing stereotype of the awkward white guy with no sense of rhythm or grace. Just as punishing is Louie's unabashed sexual overtures to attorney Naomi Bensinger. (Even more unjustifiable in the script is her apparent premature warm-up to his obnoxious ways.)

These concerns are only some of the script's faults. The worst is that there are no surprises in it. Everyone knows that Louie will eventually have a change of heart, and, although it is presented in a fairly plausible manner, his transformation is couched in flat comedy and overdone slapstick. Only occasionally does the banter between characters reach above the level of the trite. Another problem arises with the character of Tito. As written, he is too precocious and unbelievable. His incredible wisdom, the audience is led to believe, comes from his being forced to grow up too soon because of his environment. Instead he appears to be merely a facile tool used by the writer as an easy way to make his point and move the plot along.

Technically, many of the film's sound effects are overdone, and there are so many unnecessary point-of-view camera angles that viewers might be inclined to vertigo— especially when they are combined with one of the many, many close-ups. *The Super* is barely saved by Pesci's enigmatic lovableness.

Beverley Bare Buehrer

Reviews
Boxoffice. December, 1991, p. R-92.
Chicago Tribune. October 4, 1991, VII, p. 33.
Hispanic. May, 1991, p. 60.
The Hollywood Reporter. October 4, 1991, p. 7.
The Houston Post. October 5, 1991, p. F9.
Los Angeles Times. October 4, 1991, p. F6.
The New York Times. October 4, 1991, p. B8.
People Weekly. October 14, 1991, p. 17.
Premiere. IV, August, 1991, p. 12.
USA Today. October 4, 1991, p. 6D.
Variety. October 4, 1991, p. 3.
The Village Voice. XXXVI, October 29, 1991, p. 70.
The Wall Street Journal. October 10, 1991, p. A13.
The Washington Post. October 4, 1991, p. B7.

SWITCH

Production: Tony Adams for HBO, in association with Cinema Plus, L.P.; released by
    Warner Bros.
Direction: Blake Edwards
Screenplay: Blake Edwards
Cinematography: Dick Bush
Editing: Robert Pergament
Production design: Rodger Maus
Art direction: Sandy Getzler
Set decoration: John Franco, Jr.
Sound: Jerry Jost
Costume design: Ellen Mirojnick
Music: Henry Mancini
MPAA rating: R
Running time: 103 minutes

Principal characters:
Amanda Brooks	Ellen Barkin
Walter Stone	Jimmy Smits
Margo Brofman	JoBeth Williams
Sheila Faxton	Lorraine Bracco
Arnold Friedkin	Tony Roberts
Steve Brooks	Perry King
Satan	Bruce Martyn Payne
Liz	Lysette Anthony
Felicia	Victoria Mahoney
Higgins	Basil Hoffman
Steve's secretary	Catherine Keener
Dan Jones	Kevin Kilner

It is always interesting to confront a Blake Edwards motion picture because the
viewer never quite knows what to expect. At his best, Edwards can be brilliantly
comic. He has an uncanny talent for orchestrating farcical situations, and comedy has
been his forte since he made *The Pink Panther* (1964), its sequel, *A Shot in the Dark*
(1964), and three additional sequels during the 1970's. His first film as writer,
producer, and actor was *Panhandle* in 1948. The first film he directed was *Bring Your
Smile Along* in 1955. After 1947, he wrote the popular radio series *Richard Diamond,
Private Detective*, and after 1958, he created two popular television series, *Peter Gunn*
and *Mr. Lucky*. His earliest triumph as a director was *Breakfast at Tiffany's* (1961),
which earned an Oscar nomination for Audrey Hepburn. His best film, perhaps, was
Victor/Victoria (1982), which, like *Switch*, is a farce arising out of gender confusion.
On the downside are comedies that are sexist and crude, including his hit film *10*

with Dudley Moore and Bo Derek scoring perfectly in 1979 and *Skin Deep*, with its glowing crudities, starring John Ritter as a hopeless womanizer in 1989. Then there are films that are downright nasty and vindictive, such as *S.O.B.* (1981), in which Edwards seemed to be working too hard to repay old debts, creating a picture that was sometimes ill-tempered and mean-spirited. *Switch* has its moments of nastiness, but overall, Edwards is in good form here, even though some reviewers were repulsed by the film's homophobic bluntness. In the era of political correctness, Edwards refuses to compromise his notions of comedy and gender. That is integrity.

Switch gets off to a heavenly start but quickly turns diabolical and devilish. It is about the hereafter and a restless spirit given a second chance at life, but it is not a ghostly gossamer romantic fantasy. Instead, it is a satire with an edge about a selfish churl named Steve Brooks (Perry King) who is murdered by three women whom he has treated badly. The three women first attempt to drown him in a hot tub. When that fails, Margo (JoBeth Williams) shoots him point-blank. They dump his body in the East River. Steve's spirit arrives naked in purgatory (this is, after all, a Blake Edwards comedy), but an all-forgiving God sends him back. If Steve can find one woman who likes him, then he will be permitted to enter heaven. If not, there will be hell to pay.

Enter the devil in the form of a sleazy little guy who makes a wicked suggestion that complicates the situation. Brooks is sent back, but not as a man. Instead, Steve becomes a woman played by Ellen Barkin, whose performance is the best in the film. At that point, the comedy really comes to life, so to speak. The challenge for Barkin is an interesting one filled with comedic potential—to think and act like a man trapped in a woman's body. She meets the challenge, and then some. She walks like a man, talks like a man, thinks like a man, but looks like an attractive woman.

Thus, Steve Brooks becomes Amanda Brooks. ("A-MAN-da, get it?" one small-town reviewer wrote proudly.) The first thing that she does is to pose as the victim's half sister and maneuver her way into his job as an advertising copywriter. Then she blackmails Margo, the smartest and wealthiest of the three conspirators, into setting her up with a $41,000 wardrobe. She dazzles the head of a cosmetics corporation (Lorraine Bracco), who is a lesbian, into shifting advertising accounts to her firm. She knows how to use sex appeal to her advantage, but she cannot find a woman who liked her when she was a man. Walter (Jimmy Smits), her buddy from the old days, attempts to adjust to the "switch," but ends up falling in love with her, though she has trouble "relating" to him. The plot has many twists, turns, and surprises to offer in this generally good-natured satire. It takes Barkin rather too long to learn to walk in high heels, and this trivial dilemma is overstressed. Even so, Barkin is terrific.

The latter part of the film, however, is a bit maudlin. After a night of barhopping, Walter becomes impossibly drunk and Amanda allows him to stay the night in her apartment. She wakes up the next morning to discover that she has lost her virginity and later on discovers that she is pregnant. On the morning after, while Amanda is accusing Walter of date-rape, Margo comes calling and hides the murder weapon in Amanda's apartment because Margo knows that Steve's body has been found in the river. The police search the apartment and find the revolver. Amanda is brought to trial on murder charges, and naturally, no one will believe her story; she is incarcerated. There are further complications. Amanda develops diabetes and a heart murmur. Carrying the child to term may kill her, but she will not hear of an abortion. A baby girl is born and innocently loves her mother. Amanda then dies, her mission fulfilled, and presumably goes straight to heaven. Walter is left to look after his child. Demanding viewers may choke over this sentimental conclusion.

Switch was inspired by (if not adapted from) *Goodbye Charlie* (1964), a Vincente Minnelli film starring Debbie Reynolds and Tony Curtis, adapted from the play by George Axelrod. Among East Coast newspaper reviewers, only Rita Kempley of *The Washington Post* made this connection, though in his magazine review for *Movieline*, Stephen Farber made much the same point. The studio listed Blake Edwards as director and writer, apparently not wanting to advertise the source or the inspiration. Attitudes toward women have changed much since 1964, however, so a new treatment was probably justifiable.

Edwards almost always has his detractors, yet the central portion of *Switch* is charged with a high level of effective comic energy. The reviews were mixed. *The Washington Post* review was headlined "Blake Edwards Goes Bust," and Kempley criticized the director's shots at homosexuals. Stephen Hunter of the *Baltimore Sun* thought the film was idiotic but also conceded that it was "quite funny." Vincent Canby of *The New York Times* called it "the longest comedy ever made," but conceded that the lines can be punchy. At one point, Margo is chastised on the street by an animal-rights advocate who says of her mink "Do you know how many poor animals they had to kill to get that coat?" In reply, Margo snarls, "Do you know how many rich animals I had to sleep with to get that coat?" (The diction is politely paraphrased in the interest of taste.)

There are good performances to be found from Williams, Bracco, Smits, and Tony Roberts, as Steve's dishonest boss at the advertising agency, in addition to Barkin. The humor is farcical and crude, but effective. The film was no doubt intended to exploit the success of *Ghost* (1990), giving it a tweak and a cynical twist. Jack Kroll of *Newsweek* praised the film for offending "every faction in this splintered culture of gender." Kroll conceded that the film's solution to its cosmic dilemma was not perfect, but added that "nobody since Preston Sturges could have come closer than Edwards." This could be the best undervalued comedy of 1991.

James M. Welsh

Reviews
Baltimore Sun. May 10, 1991, Maryland Live, p. 18.
Chicago Tribune. May 10, 1991, VII, p. 43.
Films in Review. XLII, July, 1991, p. 257.
The Hispanic. July, 1991, p. 56.
The Hollywood Reporter. April 3, 1991, p. 9.

Los Angeles Times. May 10, 1991, p. F4.
Movieline. XI, June, 1991, p. 26.
The New York Times. May 10, 1991, p. B8.
Newsweek. CXVII, May 20, 1991, p. 56.
Premiere. IV, April, 1991, p. 24.
Rolling Stone. May 2, 1991, p. 47.
Variety. April 3, 1991, p. 2.
Video Review. XII, December, 1991, p. 96.
The Washington Post. May 10, 1991, p. C6.
The Washington Post. May 10, 1991, Weekend, p. 61.

TATIE DANIELLE

Origin: France
Released: 1991
Released in U.S.: 1991
Production: Charles Gassot for TELEMA/FR3 Films and Champ Poirier, in association with Sofica Investimage, Sofimage, Sofica Creations, and Images Investissements; released by Prestige
Direction: Étienne Chatiliez
Screenplay: Florence Quentin
Cinematography: Philippe Welt
Editing: Catherine Renault
Production design: Geoffroy Larcher
Sound: Guillaume Sciama and Dominique Dalmasso
Costume design: Elisabeth Tavernier
Music: Gabriel Yared
MPAA rating: no listing
Running time: 110 minutes

Principal characters:
Tatie Danielle	Tsilla Chelton
Catherine Billard	Catherine Jacob
Sandrine	Isabelle Nanty
Odile	Neige Dolsky
Jean-Pierre Billard	Eric Prat
Jeanne Billard	Laurence Février
Madame Lafosse	Virginie Pradal
Jean-Marie Billard	Mathieu Foulon
Totoff	Gary Ledoux
Doctor Wilms	André Wilms

On the tail of a long and highly prestigious career in advertising, Étienne Chatiliez burst on the filmmaking scene with the smashing critical and commercial success *La Vie est un long fleuve tranquille* (1988; *Life is a Long Quiet River*). Reuniting with the producer and cowriter of that film, Chatiliez once again shocked and delighted French and American audiences with his second film, *Tatie Danielle*.

Debunking the myth that little old ladies are sweet, docile, and eager to love and be loved, eighty-two-year-old Danielle Billard (Tsilla Chelton) is a caricature of the meanest, nastiest, most malicious, and gleefully spiteful old woman that ever drew breath with which to complain. Her prized pet is a ferocious but loyal Doberman pinscher, aptly named "Onyourmark" because Danielle misses no opportunity to sic Onyourmark on any unsuspecting human or canine passerby. Danielle lives in a charming house in a small town, where she delights daily in trampling the border of flowers planted by her faithful servant, Odile (Neige Dolsky). Danielle is a merciless slave driver who is never satisfied and demands ever more and quicker service from Odile. Danielle routinely wakes Odile in the middle of the night by pounding on the wall with a cane. Danielle demands sugar water from Odile, who futilely reminds her that the doctor has limited her sugar intake. Even after Odile fulfills the request, Danielle calls her a hussy out of sheer determination to have the last word.

The last word often comes in the form of monologues delivered to a portrait of Danielle's deceased husband. Since her beloved, cross-eyed Edouard died fifty years ago, Danielle has apparently been conducting animated mock conversations with the comical portrait above her bureau. She pitifully prays for death so that she may join Edouard, begging him to come for her because she is so unhappy. Danielle cannot even keep from lying to her dead husband's portrait: If she is unhappy, it is because misery is what most pleases her. It is from Danielle's confidences with Edouard that her treachery is repeatedly revealed.

In addition to playing little tricks on Odile—trying to convince her that she is losing her mind, stealing Odile's pocket money while accusing Odile of stealing hers, and telling her relatives who visit from Paris that Odile beats her—Danielle may be plotting Odile's death. For weeks, Danielle has been nagging the frail old woman to clean a chandelier. When the fall from the ladder kills Odile, Danielle gazes at the body of the poor woman and smiles, "Paris, here we come!"

Danielle's grandnephew, Jean-Pierre (Eric Prat), and his wife, Catherine (Catherine Jacob), are only too thrilled to have their Tatie (Auntie) Danielle move in with them. Both orphans themselves, along with Jean-Pierre's sister, Jeanne (Laurence Février), Tatie Danielle is the only extended family that they have and the closest thing to a grandparent for their children, Jean-Marie (Mathieu Foulon) and little Totoff (Gary Ledoux). They make room in their modest apartment and turn their lives upside down in an effort to please Tatie Danielle, not knowing that Tatie Danielle sees their welcome as a challenge to test how much they will endure.

The little family is as much a caricature as Tatie Danielle. Jean-Pierre is the loving head of the household who affectionately notices and praises his wife's every effort to please. Catherine is the hardworking yet always cheerful beautician and mother whose dearest wish is to please Tatie Danielle. As parents, they are so idyllic and proud of their children that they do not even notice that their elder son, Jean-Marie, is flamboyantly effeminate and merely praise him for what they call his creative sense of color and style. Most adorable is the youngest Billard, Totoff. Unlike most children who must be coerced into kissing elderly relatives, Totoff dotes on his Tatie Danielle and is hurt when she brushes off his hugs and kisses with impatience and irritation. When Totoff proudly escorts Tatie Danielle to the park, Tatie Danielle leaves a trail of flower petals by which to find her way home and strands Totoff in the park to guiltily, tearfully, and needlessly search for his lost Tatie.

Disbelieving that Tatie Danielle could actually be mean, the Billards continually blame themselves for causing Tatie Danielle whatever discomfort provokes her slights. She refuses to eat the meals that Catherine struggles to prepare, then raids the refrigerator at midnight. When the Billards take her for a tour of Paris, Tatie yawns, dozes off, and finally states that she would not wish such an afternoon on anyone. Even this picture-perfect family's demeanor is tested, however, when Tatie Danielle embarrasses them in front of guests by feigning incontinence during a dinner party.

Scheduled for a month's vacation in Greece, the Billards plan to leave Tatie Danielle in the care of Jean-Pierre's sister, Jeanne. Jeanne kindly claims to be looking forward to spending time with her aunt, despite Tatie Danielle's constant criticism of everything from Jeanne's choice of flower arrangements to her relationship with a younger man. When Jeanne becomes pregnant and her lover leaves her, however, her protective brother and his loving wife decide that, in her delicate emotional and physical condition, Jeanne must not be exposed to the slings and arrows of outrageous Tatie Danielle. An advertisement is placed in search of a paid companion. Tatie prays to Edouard's portrait to help her get even.

What she gets is a big surprise in the form of a young woman named Sandrine (Isabelle Nanty). The only woman to respond to the Billards' advertisement, Sandrine proves more than competent in taking care of Tatie Danielle. Though initially willing to please, Sandrine soon sees through the old woman's shenanigans and will have none of them. When Tatie Danielle declines dinner and then later asks for a snack, Sandrine tells her that she can just wait until the next meal. When Tatie Danielle demands sugar water in the middle of the night, Sandrine refuses and advises that, if she drinks less, she might be less likely to wet the bed. When Tatie Danielle throws a temper tantrum, Sandrine goes so far as to slap her. Once the tears dry and the shock wears off, Tatie Danielle realizes that she may have met her match. She is more correct than she knows.

Tatie Danielle attempts to befriend Sandrine and eventually to obligate her with gifts of money and precious jewelry. Sandrine cannot be bought, however, further confounding the somewhat tamed, but still tenacious, Tatie Danielle. When the two women come to blows over Sandrine's determination to spend time with her American boyfriend, Sandrine storms out, leaving Danielle to ransack the apartment in revenge. Whether genuinely or melodramatically half out of her mind, Tatie Danielle sets fire to the apartment, resulting in a full-scale media event in which the Billards are charged with neglect and Tatie Danielle becomes the darling of Paris. Yet, this incident is not the end.

Surviving legal turmoil and near emotional breakdown, the Billards put their lives back together and amazingly remain devoted to, if finally a little wary of, Tatie Danielle. Having had enough of status quo, Tatie Danielle escapes the nursing home where she has lived and dominated since the fire and runs away with Sandrine, the one person who challenges and truly likes her, leaving the Billards bewildered but undoubtedly better for it.

Together, Chatiliez and writer Florence Quentin create an atmosphere torn between comedy and drama, slapstick and abuse. Every time the laughs begin to amass, the filmmakers throw something very sobering at the audience. Tatie Danielle's disdain for her relatives' old cocker spaniel is comic until she actually kicks the dog and eventually abandons it at the side of the highway. Sandrine's resistance to Tatie Danielle's machinations is commendable until she strikes the old woman so hard that she is knocked off her feet. The effect is a rollercoaster of emotions, rendering the audience unsure of how to react.

Though Tatie Danielle is her first major film role, Tsilla Chelton has had a long and exciting career in entertainment. A member of Marcel Marceau's original mime troupe and a drama coach herself, Chelton has appeared in more than fifty stage productions, often having created lead roles in the plays of French theater's most admired playwrights and directors. Ten years younger than the character she plays, Chelton ceased to color her hair to its usual red and even shaved her forehead and eyebrows to assume the near-death quality of the character. Proving that her golden rule is to submit totally to a role, Chelton remained in character throughout the four months of shooting. Eventually, even the camera crew forgot that she was not really a mean, cantankerous old woman.

Eleah Horwitz

Reviews

American Film: Magazine of the Film and Television Arts. XVI, March, 1991, p. 60.
The American Spectator. XXIV, August, 1991, p. 35.
Boxoffice. February, 1991, p. R-16.
Chicago Tribune. June 14, 1991, VII, p. 34.
The Christian Science Monitor. August 9, 1991, p. 14.
The Hollywood Reporter. May 24, 1991, CCCXVII, p. 5.
Los Angeles Times. CC, May 24, 1991, p. F10.
The Nation. CCLII, June 24, 1991, p. 862.
The New York Times. CXL, May 17, 1991, p. B6.
Punch. CCC, April 10, 1991, p. 45.
Rolling Stone. May 2, 1991, p. 47.
Variety. CCCXXXIX, April 25, 1990, p. 28.
Village View. May 24-30, 1991, p. 15.

TEENAGE MUTANT NINJA TURTLES II
The Secret of the Ooze

Production: Thomas K. Gray, Kim Dawson, and David Chan for Golden Harvest, in association with Gary Propper; released by New Line Cinema
Direction: Michael Pressman
Screenplay: Todd W. Langen; based on characters created by Kevin Eastman and Peter Laird
Cinematography: Shelly Johnson
Editing: John Wright and Steve Mirkovich
Production design: Roy Forge Smith
Art direction: Mayne Schuyler Berke and Geoffrey S. Grimsman
Set decoration: Brendan Smith and Kosmo Houlton-Vinyl
Casting: Lynn Stalmaster
Sound: David Kirschner, Gregg Landaker, Steve Maslow, and Rick Kline
Sound editing: Michael Hilkene
Costume design: Dodie Shepard
Animatronic characters: Jim Henson's Creature Shop
Creature creative supervision: John Stephenson
Creature visual supervision: Jane Gootnick
Creature design: Ray Scott, Nigel Booth, Vin Burnham, Pete Brooke, Jamie Courtier, Verner Gresty, and Neal Scanlon
Chief puppeteer: Mak Wilson
Animatric puppeteers: David Greenaway, Mak Wilson, Robert Tygner, Robert Mills, Kevin Clash, Susan Dacre, Richard Boyd, Gordon Robertson, and Rick Lyon
Dance choreography: Myrna Gawryn
Stunt coordination and martial arts choreography: Pat Johnson
Music supervision: Murray Deutch and Stu Cantor
Music: John Du Prez
Song: Vanilla Ice and Earthquake, "Ninja Rap"
MPAA rating: PG
Running time: 88 minutes

> *Principal characters:*
> April O'Neil .... Paige Turco
> Michelangelo .... Michelan Sisti
> (voice of Robbie Rist)
> Donatello .... Leif Tilden
> (voice of Adam Carl)
> Raphael .... Kenn Troum
> (voice of Laurie Faso)
> Leonardo .... Mark Caso
> (voice of Brian Tochi)

```
Professor Jordan Perry  ................ David Warner
Splinter ...................... (voice of Kevin Clash)
Keno ............................ Ernie Reyes, Jr.
Shredder .......................... Francois Chau
                          (voice of David McCharen)
Tatsu .............................. Toshiro Obata
                          (voice of Michael McConnohie)
Chief Sterns ...................... Raymond Serra
Rahzar ............................ Mark Ginther
                          (voice of Frank Welker)
Tokka ............................. Kurt Bryant
                          (voice of Frank Welker)
News manager ................... Michael Pressman
Vanilla Ice .............................. Himself
```

Teenage Mutant Ninja Turtles was originally a cartoon series and enjoyed a certain notoriety among comic book-reading schoolchildren. Just as the adventures of Dick Tracy, Batman, and Superman before them, it was only a matter of time before these karate-chopping characters would work their ninja magic on film. Before the first ninja turtles film in 1990, there was skepticism within the film industry as to the likely success of adapting this particular comic strip to the screen. Those bandanna-wearing turtles, however, ranked in the top ten grossing films for the season. Such unqualified success encouraged the filmmakers to make this sequel.

For their comeback, New York City is again the backdrop to the turtles' exploits, perhaps because it boasts the largest sewer system in the world. During a routine pizza delivery to the apartment of news anchorwoman April O'Neil (Paige Turco), Keno (Ernie Reyes, Jr.) notices a delivery van parked outside a mall. Keno is suspicious and decides to take a look. Unfortunately, he stumbles into a burglary in progress. When the masked thieves come toward him, Keno unleashes karate strokes on the bewildered robbers. Despite the fact that the young karate expert seems to be winning against all odds, more and more masked men appear, which seems to signal the arrival of the ninja turtles. Within minutes, the four ninja turtles—Michelangelo (Michelan Sisti), Donatello (Leif Tilden), Raphael (Kenn Troum), and Leonardo (Mark Caso)—have the situation under control, with all the burglars unconscious and piled neatly one on top of another.

April returns to her apartment to find it in a complete shambles. On the table is a stack of pizza boxes, which indicates that April has houseguests. Moments later, the four ninja turtles come into the apartment through the open window. April explains that she is in the middle of investigating a case of pollution by the corporation TGRI. Professor Jordan Perry (David Warner) heads the department that is actively clearing up the toxic waste. Apparently, TGRI deceived the public into thinking that the chemical waste was no longer a problem and that all the toxic canisters had been accounted for by the company. This proved not to be the case. In fact, Shredder

(Francois Chau) has both stolen the toxic waste and kidnapped the professor in order to create mutant monsters. Through a series of experiments, the professor creates two prehistoric monsters known as Rahzar (Mark Ginther)—a mutant wolf—and Tokka (Kurt Bryant)—a snapping turtle mutation. These creatures are let loose in New York to find and kill the ninja turtles. Realizing the danger to their own lives and April's, the intrepid turtles once again take refuge in the cavernous environs of the New York sewer system.

Shredder challenges the mutant turtles to come and meet him in a disused warehouse where they can do battle. The two monsters are unleashed on the turtles, and an enormous fight begins. An adjoining wall to the warehouse is broken during the fight and the turtles, along with Shredder and the mutant monsters, then continue their battle in a disco. From the disco, the turtles crash through another wall and land on a wharf. The final showdown comes when Shredder, who has already ingested some of the toxic green ooze, becomes twice as tall and personally attacks the turtles. In his fury, Shredder begins to tear down the pylons that support the wharf. In doing so, he is crushed under the falling beams. In order to escape, the teenage ninjas jump into the harbor and use their turtle abilities for the first time.

Sequels of successful films (*Teenage Mutant Ninja Turtles* grossed more than $100 million) inevitably create viewer interest. Because of the success of the first film, it was inevitable that a sequel would be made. Furthermore, because the mutant turtles were so successful in their first showing, the story and plot did not seem to be as important the second time around. In fact, the entire story is about nondescript green ooze which has genetic-changing potential. What is actually being offered in this sequel is another opportunity to watch and enjoy the antics of these unique comic strip characters.

While *Teenage Mutant Ninja Turtles II: The Secret of the Ooze* may be entertaining, some have raised questions as to its standards and whether it constitutes acceptable filmmaking for children. Perhaps the most disturbing feature of the film may be that the ninja turtles mix violence with humor. To karate chop and leave unconscious numerous criminals is all in a day's work, because they are a law unto themselves and not accountable to authority. Their mentor, Splinter (voice of Kevin Clash), may be construed as a guardian or authority figure except for the fact that this mutant rat talks gibberish. The rat figure speaks in flowery, meaningless language, such as, "there is a Master who is a Master," and "a light [that] illuminates the shadows." Such artificial wisdom is typical of the general theme of the film, as the story exists so that the ninja turtles can show how wonderful they are at karate chopping their enemies.

While the martial arts and the ninja tradition have a basis in history, glorifying violence in this manner by turtles, which are traditionally seen as docile creatures, is questionable. The idea that the only way to entertain children is to show violence because it is popular has become a worrying trend for some people. The unprecedented success of motion pictures such as *E.T.: The Extra-Terrestrial* (1982) and *Home Alone* (1990), however, attests that children can enjoy good stories with morals, even if those morals are simple.

Since the mutant turtles are basically puppets, their actual creation is mainly the result of the fine workmanship of Jim Henson's Creature Shop. The craft of animatronics was certainly advanced by the work necessary to produce such life-size creatures as these turtles. Unfortunately, the teenage mutant ninja turtles are not as endearing or as interesting as those creatures that make the television series *Sesame Street* (Public Broadcasting System) so appealing. Perhaps one of the reasons that this sequel has such little aesthetic value is because the filming and editing happened simultaneously. Filming was completed only a year after the release of the original because the producers were not certain whether "Turtlemania" would last, and they wanted to use the interest in these characters for its obvious commercial possibilities.

Richard G. Cormack

Reviews
Boxoffice. May, 1991, p. R-28.
Chicago Tribune. March 22, 1991, VII, p. 35.
Cinéfantastique. XXI, April, 1991, p. 4.
The Hollywood Reporter. March 22, 1991, p. 9.
Los Angeles Times. March 22, 1991, p. F1.
The New York Times. March 22, 1991, p. C1.
Premiere. IV, March, 1991, p. 12.
Rolling Stone. April 18, 1991, p. 99.
Sight and Sound. I, August, 1991, p. 56.
Variety. March 22, 1991, p. 2.
Video. XV, October, 1991, p. 61.
Video Review. XII, September, 1991, p. 69.
The Washington Post. March 22, 1991, p. F7.

TERMINATOR II
Judgment Day

Production: James Cameron for Carolco, Mario Kassar, and Pacific Western, in association with Lightstorm Entertainment; released by TriStar Pictures
Direction: James Cameron
Screenplay: James Cameron and William Wisher
Cinematography: Adam Greenberg
Editing: Conrad Buff, Mark Goldblatt, and Richard A. Harris
Production design: Joseph Nemec III
Art direction: Joseph P. Lucky
Set decoration: John M. Dwyer
Set design: Walter Martishius and Carole L. Cole
Casting: Mali Finn
Visual effects: Dennis Muren (AA), Stan Winston (AA), Gene Warren, Jr. (AA), and Robert Skotak (AA)
Sound: Tom Johnson (AA), Gary Rydstrom (AA), Gary Summers (AA), and Lee Orloff (AA)
Sound effects editing: Gary Rydstrom (AA) and Gloria S. Borders (AA)
Special makeup effects: Stan Winston (AA) and Jeff Dawn (AA)
Costume design: Marlene Stewart
Stunt coordination: Joel Cramer and Gary Davis
Music: Brad Fiedel
MPAA rating: R
Running time: 135 minutes

Principal characters:
The Terminator	Arnold Schwarzenegger
Sarah Connor	Linda Hamilton
John Connor	Edward Furlong
T-1000	Robert Patrick
Dr. Silberman	Earl Boen
Miles Dyson	Joe Morton
Tarissa Dyson	S. Epatha Merkerson
Enrique Salceda	Castulo Guerra
Tim	Danny Cooksey
Janelle Voight	Jenette Goldstein
Todd Voight	Zander Berkeley

"I'll be back." This statement, intoned by a cyborg in *The Terminator* (1984), became one of the most remembered lines of 1980's cinema. In that film, a relentless, virtually unstoppable machine which resembles a human being (and is played by Arnold Schwarzenegger) is sent back from the future. Its mission is to kill Sara Connor

(Linda Hamilton), a waitress whose unborn son will, in the year 2029, lead a war against Skynet, an all-powerful computer whose legion of killer machines has unleashed a nuclear apocalypse and which seeks to wipe out all humankind. "I'll be back" also describes the inevitable sequel to the earlier cult classic. *Terminator II: Judgment Day* reunites director James Cameron, stars Schwarzenegger and Hamilton, and much of the first film's creative team. The result is a huge, ambitious, and clever work, one that, in general, satisfies the expectations that such a sequel necessarily creates.

Terminator II's pretitle sequence paints a gritty, gruesome picture. Postnuclear infernos and stalking robots have wiped three billion people from the face of the earth. The camera often lingers on the charred skeletons of toys, swings, and slides. Such child-related objects will remain one of the film's key leitmotifs. A T-800 "Schwarzenegger" version Terminator once again arrives via a time machine, presumably to mop up the job that its predecessor failed to finish. In an amusing bit of action, the Terminator walks naked into a motorcycle bar, seizes the clothing and motorcycle of a swaggering patron, and easily fights off a squadron of bikers. This mixture of mayhem and humor will mark much of the film's action, thus lightening, somewhat, the potential oversolemnity of *Terminator II*. As in the original film, a second, less intimidating character from the future materializes, presumably to protect the young future messiah, John Connor (Edward Furlong). The child is in a foster home; his mother has apparently gone mad—she is in an asylum.

Up to this point, the film has been merely a flashier reprieve of its source work. Yet, *Terminator II*'s ingenious story structure soon begins to reveal itself: The menacing Terminator is not the villain—it has been reprogrammed by the adult future Connor to protect his juvenile self—and the James Dean look-alike "human" (Robert Patrick), garbed in a police uniform, turns out to be an advanced T-1000 terminator out to kill Connor. In addition, Sarah, cynical with the knowledge of the holocaust to come, has transformed herself into a female fighting machine. She has become a terminator. The rest of the film will be built on these ironies and reversals. The child will help to humanize the Terminator and his mother, and both will unite to defeat the even more dangerous, yet far more humanlike, T-1000.

The T-1000's capabilities lift both the narrative and the visuals to a rarefied level. Cameron has harnessed fully the computerized special effects that he first toyed with in the *The Abyss* (1989). The T-1000 is made of liquid metal. It oozes through jail bars, easily reconsolidates its body parts even when split, elongates its arms into deadly hooks or spikes, and disguises itself as other characters or even as the floor. These startling and spectacular images mark a major leap forward in special effects (for which the film won an Academy Award), putting *Terminator II* in a select group of visual milestones that includes *Forbidden Planet* (1956), *2001: A Space Odyssey* (1968), and *Star Wars* (1977).

From here on, *Terminator II*'s plot becomes one great seek-and-destroy chase, with five major action sequences. The first is the most kinetic (and perhaps overextended) of the five: The T-1000, who eventually commandeers a truck, chases the boy through concrete-lined flood control basins, with the Terminator working mightily to protect him. The second action sequence portrays Sarah's asylum breakout. A significant pause occurs for character exposition when the trio flee to a dusty, desertlike refuge. It is here that Sarah, in a dream, sees the apocalypse to come: The opening sequence is reprised with full-blown horror, with Los Angeles landmarks pulverized and children stripped of their skins.

These awful visions, and the reunion with her son, recharge Sarah with purpose and renew her wish to protect future generations. (This motivation is not unlike what mobilizes the central female character in Cameron's 1986 *Aliens*.) Sarah sets out to kill Miles Dyson (Joe Morton), the computer scientist who has studied the remains of the first terminator and, with insights gained from this futuristic technology, will someday fashion Skynet. (These ironic, sometimes bewildering cause-and-effect circles are typical of the film.) This third action sequence is aborted when Sarah cannot bring herself to terminate Miles. He, in turn, becomes their ally in a mission to destroy the dooming artifacts from the future.

The fourth action set piece takes place at the laboratory, with the Terminator holding off hundreds of police officers without killing a single one. The situation is a bit preposterous, but it does follow the film's narrative logic—the boy has ordered the Terminator to stop killing people—and supports Cameron's thematic wish to create a violent film which preaches nonviolence or, as the director put it, "the first action movie advocating world peace."

The final action sequence takes place at a steel foundry and is linked to the previous one by a truck-helicopter chase. The Terminator and the T-1000 square off in a final duel, which includes several narrative reversals, false climaxes, and a crescendo of effects. The Terminator prevails, but it must terminate itself by plunging into a vat of molten ore. If found, its technology could set the awful future back into motion. This sacrificial act by a machine to save humankind brings a fully counterbalancing conclusion to the two-film tale.

Terminator II is full of such dualities. At its best, Cameron's use of colliding ironies serves the film's message: Humans are both sensitive and beastlike; machines can create both wonders and madness; fate dictates destiny, yet purpose shapes the future; inconsequential acts and individuals can produce significant and overwhelming results. At its worst, however, the dependency on such dualities serves to contradict or confuse, muddling the film's message and undercutting the director's ambitious intent. Were Cameron's thematic ambitions for the Terminator saga even greater than at first glance? Critic Richard Corliss has proposed this argument. He has pointed out that the story parallels that of the New Testament, with a soldier from another world (the archangel Gabriel) visiting a woman (the Virgin Mary) to announce that she is to be mother to a messiah (John Connor has the same initials as Jesus Christ). She flees with him into the desert, where an angel of death becomes a protector/father. Here, this hypothetical allegory begins to take on strange permutations, as it is the Terminator who redeems humankind through its death after a resurrection.

That Cameron's ambitions are fully apparent on a cinematic level, however, is incontrovertible. The white and blue imagery, interrupted only occasionally by reds, yellows, and oranges, conveys the film's cold fury. The frenetic editing brings powerful momentum to the narrative, although at 135 minutes, *Terminator II* is bloated and could use tighter editing. Brad Fiedel's music is appropriately epic yet never intrudes, and both the special effects and the stunts are truly astonishing. For $88 million, the film's official budget, all this should be so. Moreover, with so much invested, the ultimate proof is at the box office. That proof came quickly: *Terminator II* earned $53 million in its first five days of release.

Marc Mancini

Reviews
Boxoffice. August, 1991, p. R-48.
Chicago Tribune. July 3, 1991, V, p. 1.
The Christian Science Monitor. July 5, 1991, p. 10.
Cinéfantastique. XXI, June, 1991, p. 11.
Films in Review. XLII, September, 1991, p. 336.
The Hollywood Reporter. July 1, 1991, p. 8.
Los Angeles Times. July 3, 1991, p. F1.
The New York Times. July 3, 1991, p. B1.
The New Yorker. LXVII, July 29, 1991, p. 60.
Rolling Stone. August 8, 1991, p. 78.
Sight and Sound. I, September, 1991, p. 50.
Time. CXXXVIII, July 8, 1991, p. 55.
Variety. July 1, 1991, p. 2.

THELMA AND LOUISE

Production: Ridley Scott and Mimi Polk for Pathe Entertainment and Percy Main
  Productions; released by Metro-Goldwyn-Mayer/United Artists
Direction: Ridley Scott
Screenplay: Callie Khouri (AA)
Cinematography: Adrian Biddle
Editing: Thom Noble
Production design: Norris Spencer
Art direction: Lisa Dean
Set decoration: Anne Ahrens
Set design: Alan Kaye
Sound: Keith A. Wester
Costume design: Elizabeth McBride
Stunt coordination: Bobby Bass
Music: Hans Zimmer
MPAA rating: R
Running time: 129 minutes

Principal characters:
Louise .... Susan Sarandon
Thelma .... Geena Davis
Hal .... Harvey Keitel
Jimmy .... Michael Madsen
Darryl .... Christopher McDonald
J. D. .... Brad Pitt
Max .... Stephen Tobolowsky
Harlan .... Timothy Carhart

It is difficult to take *Thelma and Louise* seriously when a major decision regarding its ending was made because the filmmakers feared that the dummies used in the final car stunt might be seen by the audience. This fact seems to be an appropriate metaphor for the entire film because it is easy to be mesmerized by the novel idea of having two women on the road in a variation of the standard "male buddy picture." Upon critical examination of the film and its longer-range ramifications, however, the film's moments begin to slip through one's fingers like sand in an hourglass. Fair or not, had *Thelma and Louise* been the tale of two men, it is doubtful that many viewers would have given it more than a cursory viewing. Yet, because it involves women on the lam, it is subjected automatically to an entirely different set of criteria.

Louise (Susan Sarandon), a cynical, world-weary waitress, convinces her slightly ditzy friend, Thelma (Geena Davis), to leave her domineering husband, Darryl (Christopher McDonald), behind for a weekend trip. The vacation is also a chance for Louise to avoid waiting for her noncommittal musician boyfriend, Jimmy (Michael

Madsen), to return from yet another road trip.

Trouble quickly ensues, however, when a few drinks and a suggestive dance at a roadside bar convince a smooth-talking stranger, Harlan (Timothy Carhart), that he is entitled to a quick bout of sex with Thelma in the parking lot, despite her objections. Louise intervenes, yet the assailant refuses to display the appropriate amount of repentence for his actions. Louise shoots and kills him during this confrontation. Convinced that no one will believe that Thelma did not "ask for it," Louise refuses to contact the police, instead ordering her younger, more naïve friend back into the car. Louise deduces that her only option is to flee to Mexico, although she refuses to travel through Texas, where she herself was raped. The remaining two-thirds of the film becomes a flight from both the law and the constraints of a patriarchal society.

Thelma and Louise is deceiving. While, at first viewing, it is easy to get caught in its headiness, in the thrill of watching two of Hollywood's finest actresses take to the road, this film has difficulties surviving the polemics that it stirs among feminists and film craftspersons alike. In interviews, the first-time screenwriter, Callie Khouri, contradicted herself as to her motivations behind the writing of *Thelma and Louise*. Khouri noted her disgust with the typical cinematic portrayal of women as primarily prostitutes or showpieces on the arms of the leading men. Khouri said: "I wanted to put two women on the screen that you haven't seen before. I'd had it with going to the movies and seeing women I do not relate to. I don't know who they are." Yet, while *Thelma and Louise* does spare the audience the type of macho male-bonding that dominates such films as *Backdraft* (1991; reviewed in this volume), the two women are never afforded many moments of intimate relating. They merely blare the radio as they speed down the highway. Khouri, a former music-video producer, insisted that she was not influenced by any other films that preceded hers, leading one to wonder what formed the basis for her assessment. While the writer wanted to be congratulated for her novel idea, she refused to be held responsible for any informed accounting of cinema history.

Furthermore, Khouri objected strongly to criticism leveled at her work by others who were clearly offended by the categorizing of *Thelma and Louise*, with its recurring images of revenge, retribution, and sadistic behavior, as a "feminist" work. Khouri insisted that *Thelma and Louise* was simply a film about women outlaws and that "it's not fair to judge it in terms of feminism," despite the fact that the writer describes herself as a feminist and admits that the film reflects her point of view implicitly.

Thelma and Louise is imbued with stunning cinematography and breathtaking scenery, all designed to emphasize the film's big-screen importance while providing some of the most compelling shots of a vintage turquoise Thunderbird convertible flying down the open roads ever to have graced the screen. (Furthermore, actress Susan Sarandon should put an end to any further debate over women's driving abilities.) Yet the high-gloss, high-tech look of *Thelma and Louise* is actually one of the film's weaknesses. Ridley Scott, renowned for his visual stamp on such films as *Alien* (1979) and *Blade Runner* (1982), was a poor choice as director because he has never been known for character studies or for the ability to elicit strong performances from his actors. Fortunately for Scott, the two actresses chosen for *Thelma and Louise*—Geena Davis and, more important, Sarandon—are strong women with very definite ideas and convictions. It was Sarandon, in fact, who suggested several significant changes in the script, particularly in the farewell scene between her character and Jimmy. Although both actresses transcend the material (and both earned Academy Award nominations), it is Sarandon who gives the stronger, although less flamboyant, performance as the world-weary Louise. As the characters commit themselves deeper to a life on the run, the condition of their clothing, makeup, and hair loses its importance.

While Mexico seems the logical retreat for the protagonists of all Westerns, it remains a problematic choice for *Thelma and Louise* as an update of the old genre. If these heroines are escaping male domination and stereotypical sexism, why would a woman such as Louise insist on going to what may be one of the most chauvinistic places? Granted, the film is intended as a new twist on an old genre, but perhaps it would have been more successful if the decisions and actions of the two women were more logical and more in keeping with their respective characters. Louise's refusal to journey through Texas becomes one of the film's running gags and reads like a cheap variation of the line, "Who are those guys?" uttered by the title characters in screenwriter William Goldman's classic neo-Western, *Butch Cassidy and the Sundance Kid* (1969).

Khouri was quoted as saying: "It's really troubling to me how acceptable the idea of murdering and raping women is as a dramatic device. . . . I loved *The Silence of the Lambs* but it's also just some more goddamn dead women." That film, however, had a more thoughtfully conceived, more fully realized script. *The Silence of the Lambs* (1991; reviewed in this volume) presents a compelling examination of one woman's calculated manipulation of the constraints of a patriarchal society. Unlike Khouri's characters, Clarice Starling (Jodie Foster) never surrenders to the fatalism that women will never be free in "a man's world." Clarice is used repeatedly as bait and, in a sense, is mentally raped by both her mentor and the vile Dr. Lecter, but this view of the passivity of some women represents merely a starting point. *The Silence of the Lambs* offers a movement beyond the defeatist acceptance displayed by Khouri's characters that women must pay for a few days of freedom. The film also demonstrates the more mature ability of Clarice to manipulate the system rather than to rebel futilely, as do Thelma and Louise whose actions result in little more than a hollow victory. Unlike *The Silence of the Lambs*, which starts with dead women, *Thelma and Louise* ends with not merely dead women but glorified dead women. Thelma and Louise's freedom is just such a hollow victory. Nothing is gained but a few days on the road with no makeup and several bottles of Wild Turkey. In the end, Thelma's "self-realization" is nothing but self-destructive and criminal, while Louise's decision to end her life on a high note appears as little more than a woman pushed to the edge.

Thelma and Louise should have been a great film and a box-office success, given the caliber of the actresses and the potential of the material (the film won an Academy

Award for Best Original Screenplay). By choosing simply to place two female characters in a male-oriented action-adventure, however, the filmmakers created a motion picture which merely worships that which is viewed traditionally as male and denigrates all that is powerful in being female.

Patricia Kowal

Reviews

American Film: Magazine of the Film and Television Arts. XVI, May, 1991, p. 22.
Boston Globe. May 24, 1991, CCXXIX, p. 45.
Boxoffice. May, 1991, p. R-26.
Chicago Tribune. May 24, 1991, VII, p. 38.
The Christian Science Monitor. June 17, 1991, p. 11.
Entertainment Weekly. I, May 24, 1991, p. 44.
Film Comment. XXVII, July, 1991, p. 26.
Films in Review. XLII, July, 1991, p. 256.
The Hollywood Reporter. May 6, 1991, CCCXVII, p. 5.
Los Angeles Times. May 24, 1991, CX, p. F1.
Maclean's. CIV, May 27, 1991, p. 64.
New York Magazine. XXIV, June 10, 1991, p. 55.
The New York Times. May 24, 1991, p. B1.
The New Yorker. LXVII, June 3, 1991, p. 86.
Newsweek. CXVII, May 27, 1991, p. 59.
Rolling Stone. April 18, 1991, p. 97.
San Francisco Chronicle. May 24, 1991, CXXVII, p. E1.
Time. CXXXVII, May 27, 1991, p. 64.
Variety. May 6, 1991, CCXXXI, p. 2.
The Village Voice. May 28, 1991, XXXVI, p. 51.
The Wall Street Journal. May 30, 1991, CXXIV, p. A12.
The Washington Post. May 24, 1991, CXIV, p. B1.

TRUTH OR DARE

Production: Jay Roewe and Tim Clawson for Propaganda Films; released by Miramax
Direction: Alek Keshishian
Cinematography: Robert Leacock, Doug Nichol, Christophe Lanzenberg, Marc Reshovsky, Daniel Pearl, and Toby Phillips
Editing: Barry Alexander Brown
Sound: Lon E. Bender
Music: Madonna
Musical sequences editing: John Murray
MPAA rating: R
Running time: 118 minutes

Principal characters:
Madonna	Herself
Warren Beatty	Himself
Donna Delory	Herself
Niki Harris	Herself
Luis Camacho	Himself
Oliver Crumes	Himself
Salim Gauwloos	Himself
Jose Guitierez	Himself
Kevin Stea	Himself
Gabriel Trupin	Himself
Carlton Wilborn	Himself

Madonna's voice is heard over the opening credits as she contemplates her state of shock the morning after the final show of her lengthy and strenuous "Blond Ambition" concert tour. It is an interesting notion: How does a superstar performer feel when the show is over? Viewers of *Truth or Dare* will never know, however, because with Madonna, the performance never ends.

Only her erstwhile companion Warren Beatty, himself notoriously publicity shy and protective of his privacy, comments on the inanity of exposing every aspect of one's personal life, from the intimate to the mundane, to public scrutiny. When a doctor examining Madonna's overworked throat asks if she would like to stop the examination long enough to ask the camera crew to leave the room, Beatty jumps in with a sarcastic, "Why?!" Why, he wonders aloud, would she want to live if it is off-camera? What is there to say if it is off-camera? With a patronizing smile and a wave of her hand, Madonna dismisses both her lover and what may be the most honest revelation in the film.

Apparently, Madonna considers herself to be above such customs as privacy. She also behaves as though she is superior to the conventions of kindness to fans, respect to her coworkers, and common courtesy in general. Madonna treats everyone around her like bothersome pets. During a complicated stadium set-up, she taps her foot and rolls her eyes, as if the dozens of people rushing around with checklists and electrical equipment were demanding something unreasonable of her instead of trying to make her look and sound her best on stage that night. She freely admits that she has consciously chosen coperformers who are emotionally crippled in some way and need her to be a mother figure in their lives. Madonna observes that working with her must be the thrill of their lives, which it probably is. Yet, while it may be the most thrilling and lucrative work that any of her associates will ever do, Madonna's employees must sacrifice their identities in exchange.

An example of this loss of identity is the sequence showing one of Madonna's dancers, Ollie Crumes, awaiting a visit from his father, whom he has not seen in five years. Ollie lies on a bed and tells the camera that he forgives his father for abandoning him, his brother, and their mother. He peers anxiously out the window of his hotel room and phones the front desk to make sure his father will be properly greeted. When the father finally arrives, the two men share an uncomfortable moment together before Madonna appears to shake hands with and receive compliments from Ollie's father, who lights up with the same excited anticipation that his son had showed for him. Ollie fades into the background. Clearly, the father would never have considered the reunion had he not been lured by the promise of meeting the celebrity.

From there, the filmmaker cuts to Madonna in concert performing one of many songs whose lyrics deal with family, specifically the father-daughter relationship. Her own relationship with her father is hinted at but not really explored in phone calls and in a scene in which Madonna greets her father before a performance and drags him on stage at the end of a concert, inviting the audience to join her in singing "Happy Birthday" to him. She confides to her crew that knowing her father was watching made her self-conscious during the more sexually explicit portions of her act, then later defensively lectures her father on the concept of artistic expression when he diplomatically calls the performance "arty." Throughout the film, Madonna uses those around her as "straight men" off of whom to bounce her opinions, jokes, and philosophies.

Surrounded by fellow celebrities in her dressing room after a concert, Madonna is introduced to actor Kevin Costner, who includes in his compliments on the concert the word "neat." Madonna thanks him weakly, then upon his departure, makes a show of feigned gagging at his schoolboy phraseology. Costner's status as a fellow performer of at least equal respect and recognition in the entertainment industry and the seeming embarrassment of the other celebrities and noncelebrities who witnessed the scene do not seem to matter to Madonna. Costner, it seems, had the last word when he told *People* magazine that Madonna herself had invited him to the concert that night.

In Beatty's case, the last word was "goodbye." After numerous scenes of Madonna criticizing and ridiculing her lover, it is no surprise that Beatty disappears from the film. Beatty then sought to have all of his scenes cut, especially in light of their break-up. But the lack of explanation about his mid-film departure suggests that no event or emotion unapproved by or unflattering to Madonna is allowed to be shown. The irony is in what Madonna considers flattering. The words and rituals that she repeats day after day often portray her as bored and superior, lonely but unable to relate to anyone as an equal. Before each performance, she joins hands with her dancers and prays for the ability to perform well that night. Halfway through her long and rambling appeal, however, Madonna switches from entreating and professing faith in God to entreating and professing faith in herself.

When the tour comes to Madonna's hometown of Detroit, she is visited by a childhood friend named Moira. Looking much older than Madonna, Moira is clearly a woman who has had a hard life and is in awe of the powerful and pampered star for whom she once baby-sat. Madonna proudly recalls a lesbian encounter with Moira, which the embarrassed Moira denies taking place. Moira asks if Madonna ever received a letter that asked her to be the godparent of Moira's child. Madonna recalls the letter but never responded to it. When Madonna tires of the conversation, she excuses herself with clichés about having to get dressed and promising to call soon. Moira sums up the superstar she has known since childhood with an unprintable but astute epithet. Although Madonna seems to retreat when threatened by closeness, she later talks about Moira and admires a painting Moira gave her. In another room, Moira cries remembering how her heart went out to Madonna when, as a small child, Madonna lost her mother.

Suddenly, Madonna is at the cemetery where her mother is buried. She has not been there since she was a child and has to ask where the grave is. She brings flowers and assumes a number of dramatic poses at the grave, even lying down next to it and suggesting that she be buried there herself one day. If this scene is intended to be touching, then it fails: The visit seems to be staged for the benefit of the documentary.

Also seemingly staged is the scene from which the film gets its title. Madonna and her dancers sit around the breakfast table playing "truth or dare." Madonna dares her colleagues to do a multitude of embarrassing things. When Madonna herself is dared to simulate oral sex with a bottle of mineral water, she is delighted to comply.

Besides Madonna, whose self-conscious, self-congratulating vision of herself is the driving force of the film, the other creative element was director Alek Keshishian. Madonna is credited with entrusting her public image and more than four million dollars of her own money to the young director, whose only credits were a few music videos. She was impressed with his own background as a singer and dancer, as well as his senior thesis project at Harvard University: a pop opera adaptation of Emily Brontë's classic novel *Wuthering Heights*, which was the first of its kind permitted at Harvard and for which he earned a summa cum laude degree. Keshishian jumped at the opportunity to follow Madonna around the world with a camera, but only after exacting from her the promise of total access. Madonna turned the tables, however, and attempted to direct the director, who had to leave the room and entrust the shots to his crew. He eventually had to instruct the crew to dress all in black and not to respond to Madonna when she attempted to direct them. Keshishian's choice of color film for the concert sequences and black and white for the backstage scenes may be the most telling symbol of the film. The approach renders the concert performances as accessible as the music videos on television and Madonna's personal life as a staged and stylized portrait, manipulated to the artist's satisfaction.

Whatever a viewer may think of *Truth or Dare*'s celebrated center of attention, she is undeniably intriguing—one moment beautiful and the next vulgar, one moment barking orders and the next laughing with a friend. Where Madonna intended to garner praise for baring her soul, however, she invites criticism for thinking that the audience would mistake her practiced ponderings and gestures for insight. This film might have succeeded if only Madonna had dared to tell the truth.

Eleah Horwitz

Reviews

Boxoffice. July, 1991, p. R-42.
Chicago Tribune. May 17, 1991, VII, p. 33.
The Christian Science Monitor. May 21, 1991, p. 15.
Films in Review. XLII, July, 1991, p. 261.
GQ. LXI, May, 1991, p. 65.
The Hollywood Reporter. May 3, 1991, p. 9.
L.A. Weekly. XIII, May 10-16, 1991, p. 35.
Los Angeles Times. May 10, 1991, p. F1.
The New Republic. June 10, 1991, p. 26.
The New York Times. May 10, 1991, p. B1.
Newsweek. May 13, 1991, p. 66.
Rolling Stone. May 30, 1991, p. 75.
Sight and Sound. I, July, 1991, p. 5.
Time. CXXXVII, May 6, 1991, p. 62.
Variety. May 3, 1991, p. 2.
Village View. May 10-16, 1991, p. 13.
The Village Voice. May 14, 1991, p. 51.
The Wall Street Journal. May 23, 1991, p. A12.
The Washington Post. May 17, 1991, p. B1.

UNTIL THE END OF THE WORLD

Origin: Australia, Germany, and France
Released: 1991
Released in U.S.: 1991
Production: Anatole Dauman and Jonathan Taplin for Road Movies Filmproduktion, Argos Films, and Village Roadshow Pictures; released by Warner Bros.
Direction: Wim Wenders
Screenplay: Peter Carey and Wim Wenders; based on an original idea by Wenders and Solveig Dommartin
Cinematography: Robby Müller
Editing: Peter Przygodda
Production design: Thierry Flamand
Sound editing: Barbara Von Weiterhausen
Costume design: Montserrat Casanova
High-definition video design: Sean Naughton
Music: Graeme Revell
Songs: CAN, Nick Cave and the Bad Seeds, Neneh Cherry, Crime and the City Solution, Depeche Mode, Peter Gabriel, Gondwanaland, Daniel Lanois, Lou Reed, R.E.M., Robbie Robertson, Jane Siberry with k.d. lang, Patti Smith and Fred Smith, Talking Heads, T-Bone Burnett, U2, and Elvis Costello
MPAA rating: R
Running time: 178 minutes

Principal characters:
Sam Farber	William Hurt
Claire Tourneur	Solveig Dommartin
Eugene Fitzpatrick	Sam Neill
Henry Farber	Max von Sydow
Philip Winter	Rüdiger Vogler
Burt	Ernie Dingo
Edith Farber	Jeanne Moreau
Chico	Chick Ortega
Krasikova	Elena Smirnova
Raymond	Eddy Mitchell
Mr. Mori	Ryu Chishu
Bernie	Allen Garfield
Elsa Farber	Lois Chiles

At the beginning of the 1990's, looking into the future took filmmaking by storm. Beginning with *Total Recall* (1990) and *Freejack* (1992), the trend was continued with *Until the End of the World*, which explored what present-day civilization might look like eight years into the future.

The year is 1999, and Claire Tourneur (Solveig Dommartin) is spending a weekend in Venice with some friends. On her return journey home to France, the satellite that controls the movement of cars throughout Europe malfunctions. Frustrated with the long delays, Claire takes off cross-country. A car overtakes her and the occupant throws a bottle out of the window, causing Claire's car to hit the other automobile and spin out of control. A nearby inn acts as an overnight stop for Claire and the two male occupants of the car, Chico (Chick Ortega) and Raymond (Eddy Mitchell). Claire is approached by one of the men to take money back to Paris from a bank that they have just robbed. Claire agrees to their request in exchange for a sizeable part of the money.

While making a call to her boyfriend, novelist Eugene Fitzpatrick (Sam Neill), Claire meets Trevor McFee (John Hurt), the alias of Sam Farber, to whom she gives a lift back to Paris. Farber steals Claire's cut of the stolen money while she is asleep. Intent on retrieving her money, Claire hires private detective Philip Winter (Rüdiger Vogler), who tracks Farber down by using a machine that shows where he had last used his credit card. Unfortunately for Claire, no sooner do they find Farber than he manages to slip away unnoticed. This cat-and-mouse journey takes them to Russia, China, Portugal, and Germany. Finally, in Japan, Farber agrees that Claire can help him to take photographs of his family and friends. These photographs are taken on a special machine developed by Sam's father, Henry (Max von Sydow), in order that his mother, Edith (Jeanne Moreau), who is blind, can see them. The camera can take photographs of the mind.

From Japan, Claire and Sam travel to the United States. While in San Francisco, Claire photographs some of the images of family members. Because of the intense concentration required and the great strain put upon the eyes by the machine, Sam is beginning to experience headaches and extremely sore eyes. Once all the images have been gathered, Sam and Claire return to Australia so that the rest of the experiment can be carried out. While they cross the Australian Outback by small plane, a nuclear explosion in space destroys the main communications satellite, which disables the plane and forces them to crash land. After a few days of walking in the desert, they finally arrive at the aboriginal village where Sam's family is living.

Henry Farber's laboratory is located underground and is full of advanced technology. The images gathered by Sam are successfully transmitted to his mother, who is able to see for the first time since her childhood. Another application of the invention is that the machine can record dreams, and soon Sam and Claire become addicted to watching their own dreams. Claire is placed in a large fenced area because she will do nothing more than watch her dreams from morning to dusk. Finally, Claire's estranged boyfriend, Eugene Fitzpatrick, manages to cure her of this addiction and takes her back to Paris. Dissatisfied with her life, Claire becomes an astronaut.

Much of the first part of the story of *Until the End of the World* is designed to confuse. Sam is portrayed in the beginning as a double agent who has stolen some important government secret. In reality, he is on a humanitarian mission to help his mother see again. This seeming deception is not convincing, however, because the character never seems like a criminal in the first place. In fact, the clumsiest part of the entire film and the one designed for the greatest dramatic impact is the death of Sam's mother. After the success of the imagining process, Edith Farber dies and her friends go into deep mourning. Yet, because this character is only introduced near the end of the film, her death makes absolutely no impact.

Until the End of the World is a film that begins with great promise and bravura but falls into the fatal flaw of making the secondary story and its characters the main story. Action and pacing are provided by the numerous locations that Sam Farber visits, but the reason for his travels does not become evident until halfway into the film. Trying to hide Sam's real identity and the facts about his actions seems a rather weak ploy. Knowing that he is collecting images so that a dying blind woman might see is intriguing, yet it is an aspect of the story that is never fully developed.

In fact, there are many subplots that are introduced and simply left unexplained. Claire's relationship with her boyfriend is the only constant theme that runs the entire length of the motion picture. Claire's involvement with the two bankrobbers never reaches any plausible conclusion, nor does the fact that a bounty hunter named Burt (Ernie Dingo) is also following Sam around the world. Characters who were introduced earlier in the film are used later simply to keep the story moving. The detective Philip Winter, after his initial activity in tracking Sam, then takes on a secondary role, as does the novelist Eugene Fitzpatrick.

This is a film with many moods, none of which complements one of the others. The continual shifting of focus becomes confusing and distracting, and the message is never quite clear. At one stage, the story is definitely about the dangers of nuclear explosions in outer space, but this theme becomes important only at certain junctions and never makes a definite statement. Another story element that propels the story from the beginning of the film is that of Claire and Sam's romance. Claire realizes that she truly loves and cares for Sam, but because of his obsession with the project of gaining images, the romance comes to nothing. By the time that they reach Australia, the two are quite estranged. With no obvious direction, the final scenes of the film deal with the obsessions that Claire and Sam have with their own dreams. The research that was meant as an aid to humankind becomes destructive in the hands of Claire and Sam. Claire becomes neurotic and must be placed in a cage for her own well-being.

Even though the film has a general direction, the combination of the various segments does not become a whole. Yet many elements of this film are worth noting. For example, the film creates a definite sense of taking place in the future, as the set design and futuristic ideas are quite unique. There are such inventions as the videofax, televised conferences, and a machine that can track people anywhere in the world. Even the subterranean laboratory that houses the massive video screens of Dr. Farber is impressive. Nevertheless, these images and concepts do not pull the film into any cohesive whole with a single unified message.

Director Wim Wenders is best known for the part that he played in the New German Cinema of the 1970's. During that period, he released *Alice in den Städten* (1974; *Alice in the Cities*), *Im Lauf der Zeit* (1976; *Kings of the Road*), and *Der amerikanische Freund* (1977; *The American Friend*). These three films established the basis of

Wenders' philosophy of life and, ultimately, the reason that he films what he does in the way that he does. Wenders is best known for exploring the themes of isolation, rootlessness, and the effects of new technology on humanity's understanding of itself. A comparison of Wenders' films shows these ever-recurring themes, and those early German films of the 1970's find their full expression in *Until the End of the World*. Wenders continues to make his existential statements on film with a special emphasis on the destructive nature of technology, particularly that which is associated with the transferring of video images. Wenders imagines a machine that can suck the very thoughts from people's unconsciouses. This fixation on images and the unconscious is also seen in *Alice in the Cities*, when the same Philip Winter (Rüdiger Vogler) holds onto Polaroid images as a way of remembering the past. When Sam and Claire become completely engrossed with the imaging machine, Wenders once more emphasizes the dehumanizing effect of technology.

Until the End of the World allows Wenders to express his views on a much grander scale and uses many more countries than in his previous road pictures. This film tends to border on the excessive, however, and Wenders' message is lost in the overly complicated plot. Wenders' world is a figment of his imagination—a figment that somehow was made into a motion picture.

Richard G. Cormack

Reviews
American Film: Magazine of the Film and Television Arts. XVII, January, 1992, p. 51.
Boxoffice. February, 1992, p. R-15.
Chicago Tribune. January 17, 1992, VII, p. 32.
The Christian Science Monitor. January 6, 1992, p. 13.
Esquire. CXVI, December, 1991, p. 53.
The Hollywood Reporter. September 11, 1991, p. 5.
Los Angeles Times. December 25, 1991, p. F4.
The New Republic. CCVI, February 3, 1992, p. 28.
The New York Times. December 25, 1991, p. 12.
Rolling Stone. January 23, 1992, p. 50.
Variety. September 11, 1991, p. 3.
The Washington Post. January 17, 1992, p. C1.

WHAT ABOUT BOB?

Production: Laura Ziskin for Touchstone Pictures, in association with Touchwood
   Pacific Partners I; released by Buena Vista
Direction: Frank Oz
Screenplay: Tom Schulman; based on a story by Alvin Sargent and Laura Ziskin
Cinematography: Michael Ballhaus
Editing: Anne V. Coates
Production design: Leslie Dilley
Art direction: Jack Blackman
Set decoration: Anne Kuljian
Casting: Glenn Daniels
Sound: Ed White
Costume design: Bernie Pollack
Music: Miles Goodman
MPAA rating: PG
Running time: 99 minutes

Principal characters:
Bob Wiley .... Bill Murray
Dr. Leo Marvin .... Richard Dreyfuss
Fay Marvin .... Julie Hagerty
Siggy Marvin .... Charlie Korsmo
Anna Marvin .... Kathryn Erbe
Mr. Guttman .... Tom Aldredge
Mrs. Guttman .... Susan Willis
Phil .... Roger Bowen
Lily .... Fran Brill
Dr. Tomsky .... Doris Belack
Joan Lunden .... Herself

What are psychiatrists afraid of? What could possibly be psychologically threatening to professionals trained in the art and science of managing minds, analyzing
anxieties, and quelling qualms? Smug psychiatrist Dr. Leo Marvin (Richard Dreyfuss)
discovers his nightmare the day he meets Bob Wiley (Bill Murray).
   Dr. Marvin is a selective and expensive therapist who has written a best-selling
guide entitled *Baby Steps* in which he advises his readers that any problem or fear can
be handled if it is taken one "baby-step" at a time. To Dr. Marvin's extreme pride, *Baby
Steps* has caught the attention of the national news program *Good Morning America*,
whose crew plans to meet the doctor and his family at their New Hampshire lakeside
retreat. Dr. Marvin's wife, Fay (Julie Hagerty), daughter, Anna (Kathryn Erbe), and
son, Siggy (Charlie Korsmo), are less than thrilled at the prospect of yet another
vacation being turned into a rung on Leo's professional ladder. Both the doctor and his

family will find their vacation far from what they expect.

While Dr. Marvin is lost in a self-congratulatory fog, he receives a call from another therapist, one who is less successful and bitter about it. The therapist asks Dr. Marvin to help him by taking a former client of his, a nice fellow simply in need of reassurance. Dr. Marvin magnanimously fulfills the request, foreseeing yet another cured patient easily added to his list. On the other end, the therapist hangs up the phone and raises his hands to heaven in thanks for freedom from Bob Wiley. Before Dr. Marvin can alert his secretary to expect the new patient's call or advise her to schedule him for after the Marvins' vacation, Bob has already called and arranged an appointment for that very afternoon.

Bob arrives panting, having run up the more than forty flights of stairs to Dr. Marvin's office because elevators are one of Bob's phobias. As Bob explains to Dr. Marvin in a confidential whisper, he has problems. When something frightens Bob (and everything does), he experiences symptoms such as hot flashes, cold sweats, numbness in his lips, hands, and feet, headaches, stomachaches, and confusion. The list would go on if not cut short by Dr. Marvin, whose sessions last less than an hour. Dr. Marvin thinks nothing of Bob's sense of urgency or his dramatic symptoms, and he merely sells Bob a copy of *Baby Steps* to read for "homework" while the doctor is away. Bob is grateful and tries out the *Baby Steps* concept at once, much to the gratification of Dr. Marvin and to the terror of the occupants of the elevator that Bob forces himself to board, screaming all the way down to the lobby.

As Bob, his former therapist, the audience, and everyone but Dr. Marvin may have guessed, it will not be that easy to cure Bob. Driven by extreme panic, Bob brilliantly manipulates the doctor's answering service into giving him the doctor's phone number and the name of the town in which he and his family are vacationing. When Dr. Marvin is unsympathetic to Bob's pleas by telephone, Bob finds the courage to buy a bus ticket and, despite the other passengers' irritation over his constant whimpering and requests to knock him unconscious, tracks the doctor down. With his pet goldfish, Gil, in a bottle on a string around his neck, Bob stands in the middle of the tiny New England town and screams the doctor's name in the hopes that Dr. Marvin or someone who knows him will respond. As luck would have it, Dr. Marvin and his family are in town shopping. Dr. Marvin is astonished to see that the patient he so easily dismissed is not so easily dismissable. The more Dr. Marvin scolds and rejects Bob's pursuit as inappropriate, the more Bob grows attached to the doctor and what he perceives to be Dr. Marvin's insight and attention to his woes.

Despite Bob's pleading, Dr. Marvin refuses to spend time with Bob. He writes Bob a clever prescription instructing him to take a vacation from his problems, which works for about two minutes until Bob is so overcome with the doctor's brilliance that he cannot bear to be without him for a minute more. Bob is aided by two townspeople who are very resentful of Dr. Marvin. Mr. and Mrs. Guttman (Tom Aldredge and Susan Willis) saved up for years to buy the house that Dr. Marvin and his new money stole from them. If directing Bob to Dr. Marvin's home could be irritating to the doctor, then they will be glad to take Bob there themselves.

Though Dr. Marvin warns his family not to speak to Bob, the doctor is far too occupied with his impending interview to see that they obey. In addition, being used to his distractedness, they clearly are accustomed to making decisions for themselves. To Dr. Marvin's disbelief, when Bob appears at the Marvins' summer home, he is invited in, fed, warmed, and defended by Dr. Marvin's wife and children. The dysfunctional Bob has much in common with the Marvin family. They too are burdened with fears and anxieties, and they receive precious little attention from the doctor. In time, Bob does more to help the Marvins to overcome their problems, and they to overcome his, than the egocentric Dr. Marvin has done for any of them.

The final straw in the psychiatrist's psyche is broken when Bob steals the limelight from Dr. Marvin in his *Good Morning America* interview. Bob so charms the crew that he becomes the focus of the piece and elicits a promise from the reporter to come back in a few months and follow up on Bob's progress. Dr. Marvin plans to see to it that this will never happen. Under the pretense of taking Bob for a nice ride, Dr. Marvin delivers Bob to a nearby sanitarium, where he assumes that a colleague will examine Bob, recognize his obvious deviance, and commit him. It is Dr. Marvin who will soon have to be committed, however, when Bob entertains the hospital's staff with jokes and anecdotes, convincing them that he is as sane as the next man, unless the next man is Dr. Marvin.

As the doctor's schemes to rid himself of this "human Krazy-Glue" escalate, so does Bob's recovery. Unfortunately for Dr. Marvin, Bob makes the most insightful progress out of the doctor's most murderous prescription yet. Thinking himself rid of Bob, Dr. Marvin drags himself home to find that Bob has carved a permanent place in the family. Even the dynamite-induced explosion of the Marvin's lakeside villa, which has Mr. and Mrs. Guttman cheering cosmic justice, does not shake Bob's or the Marvin family's newfound security and happiness. As for Dr. Marvin, well, with any luck, Bob will find him a good psychiatrist.

Both Dreyfuss and Murray have reputations for playing brash, crude, difficult, fundamentally unlikable characters. They are repeatedly cast in these roles because they themselves are so irresistibly lovable that they make those difficult characters appeal to even the most indifferent audience. Bill Murray's comic career started in the renowned Second City Theater. Murray became more widely known when he joined the "Not-Ready-For-Prime-Time Players" on *Saturday Night Live*, for which he won an Emmy Award for writing. He has since appeared in many films, the most successful of which may be *Caddyshack* (1980), *Tootsie* (1982), and *Ghostbusters* (1984) and its sequel (1989). Murray also wrote, produced, directed, and starred in *Quick Change* (1990).

Richard Dreyfuss' credits are extensive. He has starred in such delightful comedy-dramas as *Always* (1989), *Once Around* (1991; reviewed in this volume), and *Rosencrantz and Guildenstern Are Dead* (1991; reviewed in this volume). Dreyfuss' films have included such hits as *Jaws* (1975), *Close Encounters of the Third Kind* (1977), *Down and Out in Beverly Hills* (1986), *Tin Men* (1987), and Neil Simon's *The Goodbye Girl* (1977), for which he won an Academy Award for Best Actor.

Director Frank Oz first became known to the public as the voice of many of Jim Henson's Muppets, including Cookie Monster, Fozzie Bear, and the irrepressible Miss Piggy. As an actor, he appeared in *The Blues Brothers* (1980) and *An American Werewolf in London* (1981), and he also performed the character of Yoda in two films in the *Star Wars* trilogy—*The Empire Strikes Back* (1980) and *Return of the Jedi* (1983). Oz made his directing debut with *The Muppets Take Manhattan* (1984), and he also directed *Little Shop of Horrors* (1986) and *Dirty Rotten Scoundrels* (1988), both of which influenced producer Laura Ziskin in her choice of Oz to direct *What About Bob?*

Ziskin was the executive producer of Touchstone Pictures' high-grossing hit *Pretty Woman* (1990). *What About Bob?*'s additional screenwriters are both Academy Award winners—Tom Schulman for his original screenplay *Dead Poets Society* (1989), and Alvin Sargent for *Julia* (1977) and *Ordinary People* (1980). *What About Bob?* is unlikely to produce similar honors for its creators, but it is nevertheless a delight to watch.

Eleah Horwitz

Reviews
Chicago Tribune. May 17, 1991, VII, p. 32.
Film Review. November, 1991, p. 35.
The Hollywood Reporter. May 17, 1991, CCCXVII, p. 10.
Los Angeles Times. CC, May 17, 1991, p. F1.
New York. May 27, 1991, p. 62.
The New York Times. CXL, May 17, 1991, p. B6.
Premiere. IV, June, 1991, p. 59.
Sight and Sound. I, November, 1991, p. 55.
Time. May 27, 1991, CXXXVII, p. 64.
Variety. May 17, 1991, CCXXXI, p. 2.
Video. XV, December, 1991, p. 80.
Village View. May 17-23, 1991, p. 29.
The Washington Post. May 17, 1991, p. B1.

WHITE FANG

Production: Marykay Powell for Walt Disney Pictures and Silver Screen Partners IV; released by Buena Vista
Direction: Randal Kleiser
Screenplay: Jeanne Rosenberg, Nick Thiel, and David Fallon; based on the novel by Jack London
Cinematography: Tony Pierce-Roberts
Editing: Lisa Day
Production design: Michael Bolton
Art direction: Sandy Cochrane
Set decoration: Brian Kasch
Sound: David Kelson
Costume design: Jenny Beavan and John Bright
Stunt coordination: Rich Barker
Music: Basil Poledouris
MPAA rating: PG
Running time: 104 minutes

Principal characters:

Alex Larson	Klaus Maria Brandauer
Jack Conroy	Ethan Hawke
Skunker	Seymour Cassel
Beauty Smith	James Remar
Belinda	Susan Hogan
Luke	Bill Moseley
Tinker	Clint B. Youngreen
Grey Beaver	Pius Savage
Heather	Suzanne Kent
White Fang	Jed
Bear	Bart the bear

Jack London's novel *White Fang* (1906) is difficult to adapt to the screen because, like London's better-known Yukon novel, *The Call of the Wild* (1903), it is told mainly from the point of view of an animal. As in the earlier film version of *White Fang* (1936), starring Michael Whalen and Jean Muir, the adapters have had to invent human characters and a new plot, retaining only bits and pieces of the original story.

In this Walt Disney version of *White Fang*, the hero is a nineteen-year-old youth named Jack Conroy (Ethan Hawke) who comes to snowbound Alaska during the Klondike Gold Rush to find his deceased father's lost mine. Jack is what the old-timers call a *chechaquo*—a newcomer who expects to find gold nuggets under every bush and has no conception of the perils awaiting him. On the day of his arrival, he is robbed of most of his savings by a wicked trio headed by Beauty Smith (James Remar).

Jack is able to persuade an experienced miner, Alex Larson (Klaus Maria Brandauer), to guide him to the mine and help him get started digging for gold.

In casting young Hawke with veteran Brandauer, the Disney filmmakers have followed the tried-and-true Hollywood formula of teaming a young newcomer with a mature actor who serves as mentor and model and lends the production an air of greater dignity. This was done, for example, with the young Tom Cruise, who was teamed with Paul Newman in *The Color of Money* (1986) and with Dustin Hoffman in *Rain Man* (1988) before Cruise had developed the strength to fly alone. Hawke, who looks like a very young Nick Nolte, is a competent actor but does not possess the superstar appeal of Cruise. In fact, Hawke seems to have been selected for the lead in *White Fang* because he looks like the boy next door. Brandauer, an Austrian, is the only familiar face in the film. He is best known to American filmgoers for his role opposite Meryl Streep and Robert Redford in *Out of Africa* (1985), for which he received an Academy Award nomination as Best Supporting Actor.

Jack's quest for gold begins with a spectacular long shot of the "Golden Staircase," a flight of steps hacked out of the impacted snow on the side of an enormous mountain. Hundreds of prospectors are toiling up this staircase under the weight of tent rolls, food, cooking utensils, weapons, and mining gear, all of them driven by the lust for gold. The scene immediately establishes the central theme of man's smallness versus nature's grandeur and is faithful in this regard to London's original story.

Everything goes badly for Jack and Larson right from the beginning. They lose most of their ammunition when Jack falls through the ice and nearly drowns. Then, the temperature drops to record lows and they find they are being pursued by a pack of wolves. Their companion Skunker (Seymour Cassel) is eaten by the wolves, along with most of the sled dogs. They finally realize that their dogs are being lured away from the safety of the camp by a female wolf who must be part-dog because of her uncanny understanding of human ways. She is wounded by one of their last remaining bullets and crawls back to die at the entrance to her den, where her sole surviving cub is waiting. This little ball of fur, three-quarters wolf and one-quarter dog, is White Fang, the animal hero of the story.

The most harrowing episode in the film is true to the original novel. Without ammunition, Jack and Larson must keep a circle of bonfires burning for protection. They cannot allow themselves to fall asleep, and it is only with difficulty and peril that they can obtain wood to replenish their fires. Periodically, they must fight off the ravenous wolves with burning brands and hot coals. At the last moment, they are saved from death by the arrival of a group of armed prospectors.

In the meantime, little White Fang is forced to leave his mother's body and fend for himself in the wilderness. He is found by an Indian who trains him to be a working dog. White Fang grows to be a fearsome fighter because he has a dog's intelligence and a wolf's ferocity. Eventually, his Indian master is tricked into selling him to the treacherous Beauty Smith, who intends to make a fortune by matching White Fang against other dogs in fights to the death. Smith systematically tortures and starves the wolf-dog in order to bring out the worst in his nature. Sadistic men come from all over the region to pit their dogs against Smith's champion fighter, and Smith continues to become richer from the betting. One day, a stranger appears with a kind of dog that no one has ever seen before: a pit bull. White Fang is baffled by the dog's fighting tactics, and soon the creature's powerful jaws are clamped on his throat.

The film's credits include a disclaimer that reads: "All animal action was monitored by the American Humane Association, which commends the filmmakers for the responsible and sensitive treatment given to animals throughout the production." At times, however, it is a little too obvious that White Fang's opponents in the dog ring are the handiwork of a taxidermist. A second disclaimer, authorized by an organization called Defenders of Wildlife, reads in part: "Jack London's *White Fang* is a work of fiction. There has never been a documented case of a healthy wolf or pack of wolves attacking a human in North America." This calls to mind the thesis of the motion picture *Never Cry Wolf* (1983)—that wolves do not deserve the bad reputation that has caused them to be nearly exterminated in North America and that they are essential to the ecological balance of the wilderness.

Jack and Larson happen to be in town on the day of the fight with the pit bull. Jack takes pity on White Fang and rescues him from his opponent's deadly jaws. Larson backs Jack up with his rifle when Jack says that he is taking White Fang as compensation for the money that Smith stole from him on the day of Jack's arrival. Jack and Larson have come to town to have some ore samples assayed. They learn they have found a valuable vein in Jack's father's mine. Unfortunately, Smith and his henchmen also learn about their rich diggings and plan to kill Jack and Larson and jump their claim.

Because of his long period of mistreatment, White Fang is mistrustful of all humans. Jack is kind and patient with the animal and eventually has him eating out of his hand. White Fang becomes devoted to Jack and proves his loyalty by defending him against Smith and his henchmen when they appear. Jack and Larson are rich. They plan to go to San Francisco and open a hotel. Jack realizes, however, that he has not had enough of the wilderness and that he cannot bear to leave White Fang behind. At the last moment, he refuses to board the ship and waves goodbye to Larson as the ship leaves the harbor. The final shots show Jack and his White Fang romping together in the virgin forest.

The Walt Disney version of London's *White Fang* is a simple story and reminiscent of all the other films that have been made about the Yukon, including Charlie Chaplin's classic *The Gold Rush* (1925). The main attraction of the Disney film is its rich color photography. The endless stretches of untracked snow and rugged mountains have never been more beautifully presented on film.

Bill Delaney

Reviews
Boxoffice. March, 1991, p. R-13.

Chicago Tribune. January 18, 1991, VII, p. 39.
The Hollywood Reporter. January 18, 1991, p. 13.
Los Angeles. March, 1991, p. 129.
Los Angeles Times. January 18, 1991, p. F4.
The New York Times. January 18, 1991, p. B6.
Premiere. IV, January, 1991, p. 12.
Sight and Sound. I, June, 1991, p. 65.
Variety. January 18, 1991, p. 2.
Video. XV, August, 1991, p. 44.
Video Review. XII, July, 1991, p. 68.
The Washington Post. January 19, 1991, p. C13.

MORE FILMS OF 1991

Abbreviations: *Pro.* = Production *Dir.* = Direction *Scr.* = Screenplay *Cine.* = Cinematography *Ed.* = Editing *P.d.* = Production design *A.d.* = Art direction *S.d.* = Set decoration *Mu.* = Music *MPAA* = MPAA rating *R.t.* = Running time

---

ACROSS THE TRACKS

Pro. Dale Rosenbloom; Rosenbloom Entertainment *Dir.* Sandy Tung *Scr.* Sandy Tung *Cine.* Michael Delahoussaye *Ed.* Farrel Levy *P.d.* Thomas Meleck *S.d.* Andrew Shourd *Mu.* Joel Goldsmith *MPAA* R *R.t.* 100 min. *Cast:* Rick Schroder, Brad Pitt, David Anthony Marshall, Carrie Snodgress.

The relationship between two teenage brothers is examined in this film: Joe (Brad Pitt) is determined to escape his trailer-park existence with his widowed mother (Carrie Snodgress) by winning a track scholarship, and Billy (Rick Schroder) returns home from reform school and attends a different high school on the other side of town. At first leery of Billy's return, Joe eventually suggests he join his school's track team—which pits the two brothers against each other.

ALL I WANT FOR CHRISTMAS

Pro. Marykay Powell; Paramount Pictures *Dir.* Robert Lieberman *Scr.* Thom Eberhardt and Richard Kramer *Cine.* Robbie Greenberg *Ed.* Peter E. Berger and Dean Goodhill *P.d.* Herman Zimmerman *A.d.* Randall McIlvain *S.d.* Masako Masuda, Ron Yates, and John M. Dwyer *Mu.* Bruce Broughton *MPAA* G *R.t.* 92 min. *Cast:* Ethan Randall, Thora Birch, Harley Jane Kozak, Jamey Sheridan, Amy Oberer, Lauren Bacall, Leslie Nielsen, Kevin Nealon, Andrea Martin, Patrick LaBrecque.

All that seven-year-old Hallie (Thora Birch) wants for Christmas is for her divorced parents (Harley Jane Kozak and Jamey Sheridan) to remarry so that they can be a family again, a wish that she entrusts to a department store Santa Claus (Leslie Nielsen). Her thirteen-year-old brother, Ethan (Ethan Randall), not believing in Santa, decides to take matters in his own hands and develops an elaborate plan in order to help things along.

AMBITION

Pro. Richard E. Johnson for Spirit; Miramax *Dir.* Scott D. Goldstein *Scr.* Lou Diamond Phillips *Cine.* Jeffrey Jur *Ed.* Scott D. Goldstein *P.d.* Marek Dobrowolski *Mu.* Leonard Rosenman *MPAA* R *R.t.* 100 min. *Cast:* Lou Diamond Phillips, Clancy Brown, Cecilia Peck, Richard Bradford, Willard Pugh, Grace Zabriskie, Katherine Armstrong, J. D. Cullum, Haing S. Ngor, Maria Rangel, Teresa Bowman, Karen Landry, Chris Mulkey, David Burton Morris, Celeste Yarnall.

Lou Diamond Phillips stars in, as well as wrote the screenplay for, this thriller about an ambitious, as-yet-unpublished novelist, Mitchell Osgood, who wants to write about a mass murderer, Albert Merrick (Clancy Brown). When he finds that another writer has the assignment, Osgood hires Merrick, now on parole, to work in his bookstore and wages psychological warfare on him in order to encourage Merrick to resume his former, criminal activities—even setting up his own father (Haing S. Ngor) to be Merrick's next victim.

AMERICAN BLUE NOTE

Pro. Ralph Toporoff for Vested Interests; Panorama Entertainment *Dir.* Ralph Toporoff *Scr.* Gilbert Girion; based on a story by Ralph Toporoff and Girion *Cine.* Joey Forsyte *Ed.* Jack

Haigis *P.d.* Charles Lagola *A.d.* Katharine Frederick *Mu.* Larry Schanker *MPAA* PG-13 *R.t.* 96 min. *Cast:* Peter MacNicol, Tim Guinee, Jonathan Walker, Carl Capotorto, Charlotte d'Amboise, Bill Christopher-Myers, Louis Guss, Sam Behrens, Trini Alvarado.

This comedy set in the 1960's centers on the Jack Solow Quintet, a group of professional jazz musicians led by Jack Solow (Peter MacNicol). Although Jack has great dreams, the band manages only to play gigs at weddings and bars, and it is up to him to keep them from giving up altogether.

AMERICAN NINJA IV: THE ANNIHILATION

Pro. Christopher Pearce; Cannon International *Dir.* Cedric Sundstrom *Scr.* David Geeves; based on characters created by Avi Kleinberger and Gideon Amir *Cine.* Joseph Wein *Ed.* Claudio Ytruc *P.d.* Ruth Stripling *Mu.* Nicolaas Tenbroek *MPAA* R *R.t.* 100 min. *Cast:* Michael Dudikoff, David Bradley, James Booth, Dwayne Alexandre, Robin Stille, Ken Gampu.

In this weak sequel to *American Ninja III: Blood Hunt* (1989), grade-school teacher and ninja warrior Joe Armstrong (Michael Dudikoff) must save the world from an Arab sheik who is developing a portable nuclear weapon, by battling his evil henchman (James Booth) and ninja army.

AN AMERICAN SUMMER

Pro. James Slocum; released by Boss Entertainment Group *Dir.* James Slocum *Scr.* James Slocum *Cine.* Bruce Dorfman and Steven Soderberg *Ed.* Ron Rosen *P.d.* Damon Fortier *A.d.* Edward L. Conley III and Barrett Sherwood *S.d.* Miki Berman *Mu.* Roger Neill *MPAA* PG-13 *R.t.* 99 min. *Cast:* Michael Landes, Brian Austin Green, Joanna Kerns, Amber Susa, Sherrie Krenn, Wayne Pere, Tony Crane, Brian Krause.

While his parents undergo a divorce back home in Chicago, fourteen-year-old Tom (Michael Landes) spends the summer of 1978 with his bohemian Aunt Sunny (Joanna Kerns) in California. At first reluctant to go, Tom soon meets Fin (Brian Austin Green), with whom he learns to surf and have fun, meets girls, and even experiences some adventure.

AMERICAN TABOO

Pro. Steve Lustgarten, Sali Borchman, and Ron Schmidt; Lustgarten Entertainment Organization *Dir.* Steve Lustgarten *Scr.* Steve Lustgarten *Cine.* Lee Nesbit, Steve Lustgarten, and Eric Edwards *Ed.* Steve Lustgarten and Ron Schmidt *Mu.* Dana Libonati and Dan Brandt *R.t.* 94 min. *Cast:* Jay Horenstein, Nicole Harrison, Mark Rabiner.

A shy, withdrawn photographer's assistant, Paul (Jay Horenstein), becomes obsessed by the beautiful, teenage girl next door, Lisa (Nicole Harrison). Apparently more outgoing and forward than he, yet only half his age, Lisa helps Paul shed his inhibitions by becoming his lover.

AND YOU THOUGHT YOUR PARENTS WERE WEIRD

Pro. Just Betzer for Panorama Film International; Trimark Pictures *Dir.* Tony Cookson *Scr.* Tony Cookson *Cine.* Paul Elliott *Ed.* Michael Ornstein *P.d.* Alexander Kicenki *S.d.* Nancy Booth *Mu.* Randy Miller *MPAA* PG *R.t.* 92 min. *Cast:* Joshua Miller, Edan Gross, Marcia Strassman, Alan Thicke (voice), Susan Gibney, John Quade, Sam Behrens.

When two brothers (Edan Gross and Joshua Miller) work to perfect their robot in order to support their mother (Marcia Strassman) after their father's death, they discover that the spirit of Dad (voice of Alan Thicke) has returned to inhabit the robot.

AN ANGEL AT MY TABLE (New Zealand, 1991)

Pro. Bridget Ikin for Hibiscus Films, in association with the New Zealand Film Commission; Fine Line Features *Dir.* Jane Campion *Scr.* Laura Jones; based on the autobiographies by Janet Frame *Cine.* Stuart Dryburgh *Ed.* Veronika Haussler *P.d.* Grant Major *Mu.* Don McGlashan *MPAA* R *R.t.* 158 min. *Cast:* Kerry Fox, Alexia Keogh, Karen Fergusson, Iris

Churn, K. J. Wilson, Andrew Binns, William Brandt.

Divided into three sections—"To the Is-Land," "An Angel at My Table," and "The Envoy from Mirror City"—this film is based on the autobiographical writings of New Zealand novelist Janet Frame. Misdiagnosed as mentally ill, Frame (Kerry Fox) endures eight years of hospitalization and shock treatments and eventually becomes a celebrated author.

ANOTHER YOU

Pro. Ziggy Steinberg; TriStar Pictures *Dir.* Maurice Phillips *Scr.* Ziggy Steinberg *Cine.* Victor J. Kemper *Ed.* Dennis M. Hill *P.d.* Dennis Washington *A.d.* John P. Bruce *S.d.* Richard McKenzie and Robert R. Benton *Mu.* Charles Gross *MPAA* R *R.t.* 98 min. *Cast:* Richard Pryor, Gene Wilder, Mercedes Ruehl, Stephen Lang, Vanessa Williams, Phil Rubenstein.

Richard Pryor and Gene Wilder star as Eddie, a paroled con man, and George, a pathological liar recently released from a sanitarium. Teamed up as a condition of Eddie's parole, the two become embroiled in a scheme in Beverly Hills, whereby George impersonates a missing billionaire.

ANTIGONE/RITES OF PASSION

Pro. Amy Greenfield for Eclipse *Dir.* Amy Greenfield *Scr.* Amy Greenfield; based on *Oedipus at Colonus* and *Antigone*, by Sophocles *Cine.* Hilary Harris and Judy Irola *Ed.* Peter Friedman (words and music) and Amy Greenfield (images and music) *Mu.* Glenn Branca, Diamanda Galas, Paul Lemos, Elliott Sharp, and David Van Tieghem *R.t.* 85 min. *Cast:* Amy Greenfield, Bertram Ross, Janet Eilber, Henry Montes, Silvio Facchin, Sean McElroy.

A reworking in dance of the classic tale by Sophocles, this interpretation centers on Antigone (Amy Greenfield), who martyrs herself by her loyalty to her dead brother, Polynices (Henry Montes), accused of being a traitor to the state.

ANTONIA AND JANE (Great Britain, 1991)

Pro. George Faber for BBC Films; Miramax Films *Dir.* Beeban Kidron *Scr.* Marcy Kahan *Cine.* Rex Maidment *Ed.* Kate Evans *P.d.* John Asbridge *Mu.* Rachel Portman *R.t.* 77 min. *Cast:* Imelda Staunton, Saskia Reeves, Bill Nighy, Brenda Bruce, Joe Absolom, Allan Corduner, Lila Kaye, Richard Hope, Iain Cuthbertson, Sheila Allen, Ian Redford, Alfred Marks.

Antonia and Jane is a comic exploration of two women's longtime friendship—and its inherent jealousy, resentment, and envy. Antonia (Saskia Reeves) and Jane (Imelda Staunton), who have been friends since childhood, prepare for their once-a-year lunch.

THE BALLAD OF THE SAD CAFE

Pro. Ismail Merchant for Merchant Ivory Productions; Angelika Films *Dir.* Simon Callow *Scr.* Michael Hirst; based on the novella by Carson McCullers, and on the play by Edward Albee *Cine.* Walter Lassally *Ed.* Andrew Marcus *P.d.* Bruno Santini *A.d.* Michael T. Roberts *S.d.* Scott Hale *Mu.* Richard Robbins *R.t.* 100 min. *Cast:* Vanessa Redgrave, Keith Carradine, Cork Hubbert, Rod Steiger.

Set in a small town in the South during the Great Depression, this adaptation of a Carson McCullers' novella stars Vanessa Redgrave as Miss Amelia, a café owner and moonshiner. Her life is disrupted when a hunchback dwarf (Cork Hubbert), who claims to be her cousin Lymon, and her former husband (Keith Carradine), fresh out of prison, arrive in town.

BEASTMASTER II: THROUGH THE PORTAL OF TIME

Pro. Sylvio Tabet for Republic Pictures and Films 21; New Line Cinema *Dir.* Sylvio Tabet *Scr.* R. J. Robertson, Jim Wynorski, Sylvio Tabet, Ken Hauser, and Doug Miles; based on a story by

Wynorski and Robertson and on characters created by Paul Pepperman and Don Coscarelli, adapted from the novel *The Beastmaster*, by Andre Norton   *Cine.* Ronn Schmidt   *Ed.* Adam Bernardi   *P.d.* Allen Jones   *A.d.* Patrick Tatopoulos   *S.d.* Ritch Kremer   *Mu.* Robert Folk   *MPAA* PG-13   *R.t.* 107 min.   *Cast:* Marc Singer, Kari Wuhrer, Wings Hauser, Sarah Douglas, Charles Young, Charles Hyman, Eric Waterhouse, Robert Z'Dar, John Fifer, James Avery, Robert Fieldsteel.

Marc Singer stars as Dar, muscular hero of the mythical land of Arok, who is called to battle his evil brother Arklon (Wings Hauser), in this fantasy adventure. Arklon time-travels to 1990's Los Angeles to steal a powerful nuclear weapon, and when Dar follows him, Dar meets a modern-day woman (Kari Wuhrer) who joins him in his heroic effort to save the world.

BEAUTIFUL DREAMERS (Canada, 1990)

Pro. Michael Maclear and Martin Walters, in association with the National Film Board; Cinexus/Famous Players and C/FP Distribution, Inc.   *Dir.* John Kent Harrison   *Scr.* John Kent Harrison   *Cine.* Francois Protat   *Ed.* Ron Wisman   *P.d.* Seamus Flannery   *Mu.* Lawrence Shragge   *R.t.* 105 min.   *Cast:* Colm Feore, Rip Torn, Wendel Meldrum, Sheila McCarthy, Colin Fox, David Gardner, Barbara Gordon, Marsha Moreau, Albert Schultz.

Based on real-life events, this drama set in 1880 centers on American poet Walt Whitman (Rip Torn) and his visit to London in Ontario, Canada. While there, he befriends the city's mental asylum superintendent, Dr. Bucke (Colm Feore), and encourages the doctor's humane, untraditional approach to treating the patients.

BILL AND TED'S BOGUS JOURNEY

Pro. Scott Kroopf for Interscope Communications and Nelson Entertainment; Orion Pictures   *Dir.* Pete Hewitt   *Scr.* Ed Solomon and Chris Matheson   *Cine.* Oliver Wood   *Ed.* David Finfer   *P.d.* David L. Snyder   *A.d.* Gregory Pickrell   *S.d.* Gerald Sigmon, Mark Poll, and Carol Bentley   *Mu.* David Newman   *MPAA* PG   *R.t.* 98 min.   *Cast:* Keanu Reeves, Alex Winter, William Sadler, Joss Ackland, George Carlin, Hal Landon, Jr., Pam Grier, Amy Stock-Poynton, Sarah Trigger, Annette Azcuy, William Throne, Brendan Ryan, Taj Mahal.

A terrorist from the future sends two robots back in time to kill Bill (Alex Winter) and Ted (Keanu Reeves). The two teenagers must fight their way back from the afterlife and eventually, with the aid of aliens and the Grim Reaper (William Sadler), save their girlfriends and win the Battle of the Bands, which assures their place in the future.

BINGO

Pro. Thomas Baer; TriStar Pictures   *Dir.* Matthew Robbins   *Scr.* Jim Strain   *Cine.* John McPherson   *Ed.* Maryann Brandon   *P.d.* Mark Freeborn   *A.d.* David Willson   *S.d.* Rose Marie McSherry and Annmarie Corbett   *Mu.* Richard Gibbs   *MPAA* PG   *R.t.* 87 min.   *Cast:* Cindy Williams, David Rasche, Robert J. Steinmiller, Jr., David French, Kurt Fuller, Joe Guzaldo, Glenn Shadix, Bingo, Maui, Max.

In this comedy, a former circus dog, Bingo, finds a new home with a young boy, Chuckie (Robert J. Steinmiller, Jr.), and his family, only to lose it when they move and leave him behind. Bingo endures many trials and tribulations as he travels alone cross-country to re-join Chuckie.

BLESS THEIR LITTLE HEARTS

Pro. Billy Woodberry   *Dir.* Billy Woodberry   *Scr.* Charles Burnett   *Cine.* Charles Burnett and Patrick Melly   *Ed.* Billy Woodberry   *R.t.* 80 min.   *Cast:* Nate Hardman, Kaycee Moore, Angela Burnett, Ronald Burnett, Kimberly Burnett.

Centering on an out-of-work black family man, Charlie Banks (Nate Hardman), this film portrays Charlie's growing frustration and isolation in modern society where a man without a job is considered worthless.

BLOOD AND CONCRETE

Pro. Richard LaBrie for Copeland/Colichman; I.R.S. Media, Inc. *Dir.* Jeffrey Reiner *Scr.* Richard LaBrie and Jeffrey Reiner *Cine.* Declan Quinn *Ed.* Richard LaBrie and Jeffrey Reiner *P.d.* Pamela Woodbridge *A.d.* Wendy Guidery *S.d.* Robert Stover *Mu.* Vinny Golia *MPAA* R *R.t.* 97 min. *Cast:* Billy Zane, Jennifer Beals, James Le Gros, Darren McGavin, Nicholas Worth, Mark Pellegrino, Harry Shearer, William Bastiani.

When car thief Joey Turks (Billy Zane) hides in a cemetery after being stabbed, he meets singer/drug addict Mona (Jennifer Beals), who is about to commit suicide. The two join forces and must elude gangsters and the police, all of whom seek a hidden stash of drugs.

BLUE DESERT

Pro. David Andrew Peters for Neo Motion Pictures, in association with First Look Pictures *Dir.* Bradley Battersby *Scr.* Arthur Collis and Bradley Battersby *Cine.* Paul Murphy *Ed.* Debra Bard *P.d.* Michael T. Perry *A.d.* David Cannon and Dara L. Waxman *Mu.* Joel Goldsmith *R.t.* 98 min. *Cast:* Courteney Cox, D. B. Sweeney, Craig Sheffer, Sandy Ward, Philip Baker Hall.

When a young cartoonist, Lisa (Courteney Cox), is raped in New York City, she flees to a small desert town. There she meets a drifter, Randall (Craig Sheffer), whose unwanted advances drive her into the deceptively protective arms of a police officer, Steve (D. B. Sweeney).

BODY PARTS

Pro. Frank Mancuso, Jr.; Paramount Pictures *Dir.* Eric Red *Scr.* Eric Red and Norman Snider; based on a story by Patricia Herskovic and Joyce Taylor, and on the novel *Choice Cuts*, by Boileau-Narcejac *Cine.* Theo Van de Sande *Ed.* Anthony Redman *P.d.* Bill Brodie *A.d.* Alicia Keywan *S.d.* Steve Shewchuk *Mu.* Loek Dikker *MPAA* R *R.t.* 88 min. *Cast:* Jeff Fahey, Lindsay Duncan, Kim Delaney, Brad Dourif, Zakes Mokae, Peter Murnik, Paul Benvictor, John Walsh, Nathaniel Moreau, Sarah Campbell.

When a criminal psychologist, Bill Crushank (Jeff Fahey), is injured in a near-fatal car accident, his right arm is amputated and replaced by a new one received from a recently executed psychopathic murderer. As the new arm develops a murderous mind of its own, Bill investigates its origin and tracks down two other body-part recipients from the same donor.

BOOK OF LOVE

Pro. Rachel Talalay; New Line Cinema *Dir.* Robert Shaye *Scr.* William Kotzwinkle; based on his novel *Jack in the Box* *Cine.* Peter Deming *Ed.* Terry Stokes *P.d.* C. J. Strawn *A.d.* Timothy Gray *S.d.* James R. Barrows *Mu.* Stanley Clarke *MPAA* PG-13 *R.t.* 87 min. *Cast:* Chris Young, Keith Coogan, Josie Bissett, Jill Jaress, Aeryk Egan, Tricia Leigh Fisher, John Cameron Mitchell, Danny Nucci, John Achorn, Michael McKean, Beau Dremann.

Recently divorced Jack Twiller (Michael McKean) reminisces about his senior year in high school in the 1950's—when adolescent Jack (Chris Young) is infatuated with the beautiful, blonde Lily (Josie Bissett). From his situation in the future, Jack now examines why he favored Lily over the one girl who appreciated him, Gina (Tricia Leigh Fisher).

THE BOY WHO CRIED BITCH

Pro. Louis Tancredi; Pilgrims 3 Corporation *Dir.* Juan José Campanella *Scr.* Catherine May Levin *Cine.* Daniel Shulman *Ed.* Darren Kloomok *P.d.* Nancy Deren *Mu.* Wendy Blackstone *R.t.* 105 min. *Cast:* Harley Cross, Karen Young, Jesse Bradford, J. D. Daniels, Gene Canfield, Moira Kelly, Adrien Brody, Dennis Boutsikaris, John Rothman, Samuel Wright, Kario Salem.

This drama centers on a child psychopath, Dan (Harley Cross), who is sent to an institution by his mother (Karen Young) because she is unable to handle his growing vicious tendencies.

BRIDE OF RE-ANIMATOR
Pro. Brian Yuzna for Wildstreet Pictures, Keith Walley/Paul White, and 50th St. Films; Troma, Inc. *Dir.* Brian Yuzna *Scr.* Woody Keith and Rick Fry; based on a story by Brian Yuzna, Keith, and Fry and on *Herbert West: Re-Animator*, by H. P. Lovecraft *Cine.* Rick Fichter *Ed.* Peter Teschner *P.d.* Philip J. C. Duffin *Mu.* Richard Band *MPAA* R *R.t.* 97 min. *Cast:* Jeffrey Combs, Bruce Abbott, Claude Earl Jones, Fabiana Udenio, David Gale, Kathleen Kinmont, Mel Stewart, Irene Forrest.

A sequel to *Re-Animator* (1985), this grisly horror film features two doctors, Herbert West (Jeffrey Combs) and Dan Cain (Bruce Abbott), who return to a Massachusetts hospital from doing penance in Peru for crimes committed in the previous film. West has since made a new discovery: He can now re-animate severed body parts, and proceeds to do so, creating, among other things, the woman of the title.

BRIGHT ANGEL
Pro. Paige Simpson and Robert MacLean for Northwood/Bright Angel; Hemdale *Dir.* Michael Fields *Scr.* Richard Ford *Cine.* Elliot Davis *Ed.* Melody London and Clement Barclay *P.d.* Marcia Hinds-Johnson *A.d.* Bo Johnson *S.d.* Jan Bergstrom *Mu.* Christopher Young *MPAA* R *R.t.* 94 min. *Cast:* Dermot Mulroney, Lili Taylor, Sam Shepard, Valerie Perrine, Burt Young, Bill Pullman, Benjamin Bratt, Mary Kay Place, Delroy Lindo, Sheila McCarthy, Kevin Tighe.

Two troubled adolescents, George (Dermot Mulroney) and Lucy (Lili Taylor), travel from Montana to Wyoming: Lucy hopes to get her brother out of jail, and George is looking for his mother (Valerie Perrine), who has recently left his father (Sam Shepard). Along the way, they encounter two dangerous criminals (Burt Young and Bill Pullman).

CADENCE
Pro. Richard Davis for Republic Pictures Corp. and International Movie Group, in association with Northern Lights Entertainment; New Line Cinema *Dir.* Martin Sheen *Scr.* Dennis Shryack and Martin Sheen; based on the novel *Count a Lonely Cadence*, by Gordon Weaver *Cine.* Richard Leiterman *Ed.* Martin Hunter *P.d.* Ian Thomas *Mu.* Georges Delerue *MPAA* PG-13 *R.t.* 90 min. *Cast:* Charlie Sheen, Martin Sheen, F. Murray Abraham, Larry Fishburne, Blu Mankuma, Michael Beach, Harry Stewart, John Toles-Bey, James Marshall, Ramon Estevez.

Martin Sheen makes his directorial debut in this film about a private, Franklin Bean (Charlie Sheen), who is thrown into the stockade when he gets drunk following the death of his father. Bean learns about racial prejudice as he befriends his five fellow prisoners, all black, and confronts the bigoted and bullying sergeant, Otis McKinney (Martin Sheen).

CAREER OPPORTUNITIES
Pro. John Hughes and A. Hunt Lowry for Hughes Entertainment; Universal Pictures *Dir.* Bryan Gordon *Scr.* John Hughes *Cine.* Don McAlpine *Ed.* Glenn Farr and Peck Prior *P.d.* Paul Sylbert *A.d.* Guy Barnes *S.d.* Kathe Klopp *Mu.* Thomas Newman *MPAA* PG-13 *R.t.* 85 min. *Cast:* Frank Whaley, Jennifer Connelly, Dermot Mulroney, Kieran Mulroney, John M. Jackson, Jenny O'Hara, Noble Willingham, Barry Corbin, John Candy, William Forsythe, Danny Nelson.

In this John Hughes comedy, freeloading twenty-one-year-old Jim Dodge (Frank Whaley) finds himself as a night janitor in a large department store and is locked in on his first night with a beautiful rich girl (Jennifer Connelly). They talk over their miserable high school years and get to know each other better, until burglars (Dermot Mulroney and Kieran Mulroney) arrive determined to clean out the store.

CHAMELEON STREET

Pro. Dan Lawton; Northern Arts Entertainment *Dir.* Wendell B. Harris, Jr. *Scr.* Wendell B. Harris, Jr. *Cine.* Daniel S. Noga *Ed.* Wendell B. Harris, Jr. *A.d.* Tim Alvaro *Mu.* Peter Moore *MPAA* R *R.t.* 98 min. *Cast:* Wendell B. Harris, Jr., Angela Leslie, Amina Fakir, Paula McGee, Daven Kiley, Alfred Bruce Bradley, Gary Irwin, Colette Haywood.

First-time writer/director/actor Wendell B. Harris, Jr., fictionalizes the true story of William Douglas Street, a brilliant, African-American, lower-class Detroit man who, during a fifteen-year span, passed himself off as a doctor, a lawyer, a *Time* magazine reporter, and a French exchange student at Yale University.

CHEAP SHOTS

Pro. William Coppard, Jerry Stoeffhaas, and Jeff Ureles for Twin Swans Film Associates; Hemdale Films *Dir.* Jeff Ureles and Jerry Stoeffhaas *Scr.* Jeff Ureles and Jerry Stoeffhaas *Cine.* Thom Marini *Ed.* Ken McIlwaine *P.d.* Carl Zollo *A.d.* Anne La Lopa *Mu.* Jeff Beal *MPAA* PG-13 *R.t.* 87 min. *Cast:* Louis Zorich, David Patrick Kelly, Mary Louise Wilson, Michael Twaine, Clarke Gordon, Patience Moore.

A proprietor (Louis Zorich) of an isolated motel and his friend (David Patrick Kelly) relieve their boredom by videotaping the sexual escapades of a couple in one of the cabins. When they inadvertently photograph the couple's murder, the killers want the tape.

CHILD'S PLAY III

Pro. Robert Latham Brown for David Kirschner; Universal Pictures *Dir.* Jack Bender *Scr.* Don Mancini; based on characters created by Mancini *Cine.* John R. Leonetti *Ed.* Edward A. Warschilka, Jr., and Scott Wallace *P.d.* Richard Sawyer *S.d.* Ethel Robins Richards, Sean Haworth, Carole Cole, and James Truesdale *Mu.* Cory Lerios and John D'Andrea *MPAA* R *R.t.* 89 min. *Cast:* Justin Whalin, Perrey Reeves, Jeremy Sylvers, Travis Fine, Dean Jacobson, Brad Dourif (voice), Peter Haskell, Dakin Matthews, Andrew Robinson, Burke Byrnes.

Chucky's back, the doll inhabited by the soul of a pathological murderer, and returns to harass Andy (Justin Whalin), now sixteen years old and attending a military school. When Chucky (voice of Brad Dourif) decides to try to enter the body of an eight-year-old boy (Jeremy Sylvers), the horror begins.

A CHINESE GHOST STORY III (China, 1991)

Pro. Tsui Hark; Film Workshop Co. Ltd. *Dir.* Ching Siu Tung *Scr.* Tsui Hark, Roy Szeto, and Tom Lau *Mu.* Romeo Diaz and James Wong *R.t.* 104 min. *Cast:* Tony Leung, Wang Hsu Hsien, Jacky Cheung, Lau Shun, Lau Siu Ming, Nina Li.

In this action-packed adventure, filled with martial arts and elaborate swordplay, a monk (Lau Shun) from ancient China and his acolyte Fong (Tony Leung) find the Orchid Temple, home of an evil Tree Demon (Lau Siu Ming). There, Fong falls in love with a beautiful ghost, Lotus (Wang Hsu Hsien), who has been sent to ruin him.

CHOPPER CHICKS IN ZOMBIE TOWN

Pro. Maria Snyder; Troma *Dir.* Dan Hoskins *Scr.* Dan Hoskins *Cine.* Tom Fraser *Ed.* W. O. Garrett *A.d.* Rodney McDonald *Mu.* Daniel Day *MPAA* R *R.t.* 84 min. *Cast:* Jamie Rose, Catherine Carlen, Lycia Naff, Vicki Frederick, Kristina Loggia, Gretchen Palmer, Nina Peterson, Whitney Reis, Ed Gale, Don Calfa.

A group of women bikers looking for a good time try to save a small town from its murderous mortician (Don Calfa), who is killing its citizens and turning them into zombies.

CLASS OF NUKE 'EM HIGH PART II: SUBHUMANOID MELTDOWN

Pro. Lloyd Kaufman and Michael Herz; Troma Team *Dir.* Eric Louzil *Scr.* Lloyd Kaufman,

Eric Louzil, Carl Morano, Marcus Roling, Jeffrey W. Sass, Matt Unger, and Andrew Osborne; based on an original story by Kaufman, Morano, and Unger *Cine.* Ron Chapman *Ed.* Gordon Grinberg *P.d.* Cheryl Pitkin *Mu.* Bob Mithoff *MPAA* R *R.t.* 95 min. *Cast:* Brick Bronsky, Lisa Gaye, Leesa Rowland, Michael Kurtz, Scot Resnick, Shelby Shepard, Jacquelyn Rene Moen.

In this low-budget science-fiction spoof, a mad scientist (Lisa Gaye) at Tromaville Institute of Technology has created a race of subhumanoids to work as slaves. The school's ace reporter, Roger Smith (Brick Bronsky), investigates the evil corporation behind this, while a giant mutant squirrel crushes the environs.

CLOSE MY EYES (Great Britain, 1991)
Pro. Therese Pickard for Castle Hill *Dir.* Stephen Poliakoff *Scr.* Stephen Poliakoff *Cine.* Witold Stok *Ed.* Michael Parkinson *P.d.* Luciana Arrighi *A.d.* John Ralph *S.d.* Robyn Hamilton-Doney *Mu.* Michael Gibbs *MPAA* R *R.t.* 109 min. *Cast:* Alan Rickman, Clive Owen, Saskia Reeves, Karl Johnson, Lesley Sharp, Kate Gartside, Karen Knight.

This drama details the incestuous love affair between a woman (Saskia Reeves) and her younger brother (Clive Owen)—as well as the reactions of the woman's husband (Alan Rickman)—as a means of exploring modern sexual mores.

CLOSET LAND
Pro. Janet Meyers for Imagine Entertainment; Universal *Dir.* Radha Bharadwaj *Scr.* Radha Bharadwaj *Cine.* Bill Pope *Ed.* Lisa Churgin *P.d.* Eiko Ishioka *A.d.* Kenneth A. Hardy *S.d.* Gary Matteson *Mu.* Richard Einhorn *MPAA* R *R.t.* 90 min. *Cast:* Madeleine Stowe, Alan Rickman.

In this grim portrayal of political oppression, Madeleine Stowe stars as a writer of children's books accused by the state of promoting subversive ideas through her stories. She is taken and tortured by a man (Alan Rickman) in an interrogation room, but turns the tables with her moral courage and ability to escape mentally into her fantasy world.

COMPANY BUSINESS
Pro. Steven-Charles Jaffe; Metro-Goldwyn-Mayer *Dir.* Nicholas Meyer *Scr.* Nicholas Meyer *Cine.* Gerry Fisher *Ed.* Ronald Roose *P.d.* Ken Adam *A.d.* Albrecht Konrad *Mu.* Michael Kamen *MPAA* PG-13 *R.t.* 98 min. *Cast:* Gene Hackman, Mikhail Baryshnikov, Kurtwood Smith, Terry O'Quinn, Daniel Von Bargen, Oleg Rudnick, Geraldine Danon, Nadim Sawalha.

Gene Hackman stars as a former CIA agent who is recalled by the CIA to exchange $2 million and a KGB mole (Mikhail Baryshnikov) for another CIA agent in Berlin. When the exchange goes wrong, the two find themselves pursued across Europe by their respective agencies.

CONVICTS
Pro. Jonathan D. Krane and Sterling Van Wagenen, in association with Sterling Entertainment Co.; MCEG *Dir.* Peter Masterson *Scr.* Horton Foote; based on his play *Cine.* Toyomichi Kurita *Ed.* Jill Savitt *P.d.* Dan Bishop *A.d.* Dianna Freas *S.d.* Michael Martin *Mu.* Peter Melnick *R.t.* 92 min. *Cast:* Robert Duvall, Lukas Haas, James Earl Jones, Starletta DuPois, Mel Winkler, Calvin Levels, Carlin Glynn, Gary Swanson.

Set in Texas on Christmas Eve, 1902, this screen adaptation of Horton Foote's play stars Robert Duvall as crusty, old Soll Gautier, an aging and forgetful plantation owner who uses black convicts as cheap labor. Told through the narrative point of view of thirteen-year-old Horace Robedaux (Lukas Haas), the story centers on Soll's struggle with the concept of his own mortality.

COOL AS ICE
Pro. Carolyn Pfeiffer and Lionel Wigram for Koppelman/Bandier-Carnegie Pictures, in

association with Alive Films; Universal Pictures *Dir.* David Kellogg *Scr.* David Stenn *Cine.* Janusz Kaminski *Ed.* Debra Goldfield *P.d.* Nina Ruscio *A.d.* Carey Meyer *S.d.* Sally Nicolaou *Mu.* Stanley Clarke *MPAA* PG *R.t.* 90 min. *Cast:* Vanilla Ice, Kristin Minter, Michael Gross, Sydney Lassick, Dody Goodman, Naomi Campbell, Candy Clark, John Haymes Newton.

Rap musician Vanilla Ice makes his lukewarm acting debut as Johnny, a young man who rides into a small town with his motorcycle friends. When he falls in love with a young local woman (Kristin Minter) whose parents are in a witness protection program, he must help them when old enemies appear.

CROOKED HEARTS

Pro. Rick Stevenson, Dale Pollock, and Gil Friesen for A&M Films; Metro-Goldwyn-Mayer *Dir.* Michael Bortman *Scr.* Michael Bortman; based on the novel by Robert Boswell *Cine.* Tak Fujimoto *Ed.* Richard Francis-Bruce *P.d.* David Brisbin *Mu.* Mark Isham *MPAA* R *R.t.* 105 min. *Cast:* Vincent D'Onofrio, Jennifer Jason Leigh, Peter Berg, Peter Coyote, Noah Wyle, Cindy Pickett, Juliette Lewis, Marg Helgenberger.

Outwardly a normal, middle-class family, the Warrens soon prove to be dysfunctional: The philandering father (Peter Coyote) argues constantly with his oldest son (Vincent D'Onofrio), and the middle son (Peter Berg) has quit college. Despite numerous crises, the family eventually works to reconcile their differences.

CURLY SUE

Pro. John Hughes; Warner Bros. *Dir.* John Hughes *Scr.* John Hughes *Cine.* Jeffrey L. Kimball *Ed.* Peck Prior and Harvey Rosenstock *P.d.* Doug Kraner *A.d.* Steven Schwartz *S.d.* Sam Schaffer and Marjorie Fritz-Birch *Mu.* Georges Delerue *MPAA* PG *R.t.* 101 min. *Cast:* James Belushi, Kelly Lynch, Alisan Porter, John Getz, Fred Dalton Thompson, Cameron Thor, Viveka Davis.

Filmed on location in Chicago, *Curly Sue* follows the adventures of nine-year-old Curly Sue (Alisan Porter), an orphan reared from infancy by her penniless guardian, Bill Dancer (James Belushi). The pair meets a cynical, worldly, and wealthy lawyer, Grey Allison (Kelly Lynch), who reluctantly befriends them. The result is unexpected—the three together become a loving, although unconventional, family.

THE DARK BACKWARD

Pro. Brad Wyman and Cassian Elwes for William Talmadge/L.A. Dreams, Backward Films, and Adam Rifkin; Greycat Films *Dir.* Adam Rifkin *Scr.* Adam Rifkin *Cine.* Joey Forsyte *Ed.* Peter Schink *P.d.* Sherman Williams *A.d.* Wendy Guidery *Mu.* Marc David Decker *MPAA* R *R.t.* 97 min. *Cast:* Judd Nelson, Bill Paxton, Wayne Newton, Lara Flynn Boyle, James Caan, Rob Lowe, King Moody.

A shy garbageman (Judd Nelson) who aspires to be a stand-up comic gets his big break when he grows a third arm and is booked as a novelty act. This premise provides the backdrop for a weird, quirky black comedy.

DARK OBSESSION (also known as *Diamond Skulls*. Great Britain, 1991)

Pro. Tim Bevan for Film Four International, British Screen, and Working Title; Circle Releasing *Dir.* Nicholas Broomfield *Scr.* Tim Rose Price *Cine.* Michael Coulter *Ed.* Rodney Holland *P.d.* Jocelyn James *Mu.* Stanley Myers, Richard Harvey, and Hans Zimmer *MPAA* NC-17 *R.t.* 86 min. *Cast:* Gabriel Byrne, Amanda Donohoe, Michael Hordern, Judy Parfitt, Struan Rodger, Douglas Hodge, Peter Sands, David Delve, Ralph Brown, Sadie Frost.

In this British suspense-thriller, a wealthy nobleman, Sir Hugo Buckton (Gabriel Byrne), is obsessed with the idea that his beautiful wife (Amanda Donohoe) is having an affair with her

Argentinian business partner. When he is out with friends and is very drunk, he runs down and kills a woman whom he momentarily mistook to be his wife. Although he feels no guilt for what he did, he attempts to keep his crime a secret, at the urging of his business associate (Struan Rodger).

DEAD SPACE
Pro. Mike Elliott; Concorde *Dir.* Fred Gallo *Scr.* Catherine Cyran *Cine.* Mark Perry *Ed.* Lawrence Jordon *P.d.* Gary Randall *S.d.* Colin de Rouin *Mu.* Daniel May *MPAA* R *R.t.* 78 min. *Cast:* Marc Singer, Laura Tate, Bryan Cranston, Judith Chapman, Lori Lively, Frank Roman, Randy Reinholz, Rodger Hall, Greg Blanchard, Liz Rogers.

In this science-fiction thriller, spaceman Steve Krieger (Marc Singer) investigates a distress signal from a planetary research laboratory, only to discover that scientists have accidentally created a malevolent virus that now threatens them all.

DEAD WOMEN IN LINGERIE
Pro. Erica Fox for Seagate Films *Dir.* Erica Fox *Scr.* Erica Fox and John Romo *Cine.* John C. Newby *Ed.* Mark Stratton and Stacia Thompson *P.d.* Adam Leventhal *Mu.* Ciro Hurtado *R.t.* 87 min. *Cast:* John Romo, Maura Tierney, June Lockhart, Lyle Waggoner, Dennis Christopher, Jerry Orbach.

In this mystery set in the 1990's in the Los Angeles garment district, Detective Nick Marnes (John Romo) investigates the murders of several Hispanic lingerie models.

DECEIVED
Pro. Michael Finnell, Wendy Dozoretz, and Ellen Collett, in association with Silver Screen Partners IV; Touchstone Pictures *Dir.* Damian Harris *Scr.* Mary Agnes Donoghue and Derek Saunders; based on a story by Donoghue *Cine.* Jack N. Green *Ed.* Neil Travis *P.d.* Andrew McAlpine *A.d.* Gregory P. Keen *S.d.* Gordon Sim *Mu.* Thomas Newman *MPAA* PG-13 *R.t.* 103 min. *Cast:* Goldie Hawn, John Heard, Robin Bartlett, Ashley Peldon, Tom Irwin.

In this mystery thriller, Goldie Hawn stars as an art restorer, Adrienne, whose husband of six years, Jack Saunders (John Heard), is suspected in a forgery. When he is supposedly killed in a car accident, Adrienne discovers that the real Jack Saunders died years ago, and she turns detective to uncover the truth.

DECEMBER
Pro. Richard C. Berman and Donald Paul Pemrick for Copeland/Colichman; I.R.S. Media *Dir.* Gabe Torres *Scr.* Gabe Torres *Cine.* James Glennon *Ed.* Rick Hinson and Carole Kravetz *P.d.* Garreth Stover *A.d.* Kenneth A. Hardy *S.d.* Margaret Goldsmith *Mu.* Deborah Holland *MPAA* PG *R.t.* 91 min. *Cast:* Balthazar Getty, Jason London, Brian Krause, Wil Wheaton, Chris Young, Robert Miller, Ann Hartfield, Soren Bailey.

Five senior boys at a New England prep school debate the morality of war and patriotism on the eve of the United States' entrance into World War II. A theatrical film based on dialogue, the limited action takes place over two days and primarily in the boys' dormatory room.

DEFENSELESS
Pro. Renee Missel and David Bombyk for New Visions Pictures; Seven Arts through New Line Cinema *Dir.* Martin Campbell *Scr.* James Hicks; based on a story by Hicks and Jeff Burkhart *Cine.* Phil Meheux *Ed.* Lou Lombardo and Chris Wimble *P.d.* Curtis A. Schnell *A.d.* Colin D. Irwin *S.d.* Douglas A. Mowat *Mu.* Curt Sobel *MPAA* R *R.t.* 104 min. *Cast:* Barbara Hershey, Sam Shepard, Mary Beth Hurt, J. T. Walsh, Kellie Overbey, Jay O. Sanders, John Kapelos, Sheree North, Randy Brooks.

Barbara Hershey stars as T. K. Katwuller, an attorney who is having an affair with shady businessman Steven Seldes (J. T. Walsh), who she discovers is married to her former college

roommate and friend (Mary Beth Hurt). Trouble ensues when Seldes is found murdered shortly
after T. K. had a violent argument with him, and she goes to court to defend his wife who is
arrested for the murder.

DELUSION

Pro. Daniel Hassid for Seth M. Willenson and Cineville, Inc.; I.R.S.   *Dir.* Carl Colpaert   *Scr.*
Carl Colpaert and Kurt Voss   *Cine.* Geza Sinkovics   *Ed.* Mark Allan Kaplan   *P.d.* Ildiko Toth
Mu. Barry Adamson   *MPAA* R   *R.t.* 100 min.   *Cast:* Jim Metzler, Jennifer Rubin, Kyle Secor,
Jerry Orbach, Robert Costanzo.

A businessman, George (Jim Metzler), driving across the Nevada desert with money he has
stolen from his company, finds himself in much more trouble when he picks up two stranded
travelers—a psychotic hit man, Chevy (Kyle Secor), and his kooky girlfriend, Patty (Jennifer
Rubin).

DICE RULES: THE ANDREW DICE CLAY CONCERT MOVIE

Pro. Fred Silverstein for Fleebin Dabble; Seven Arts   *Dir.* Jay Dubin   *Scr.* Concert material by
Andrew Dice Clay; "A Day in the Life" screenplay by Lenny Shulman, based on a story by Clay
Cine. Michael Negrin and Charlie Lieberman   *Ed.* Mitchell Sinoway and John K. Currin   *P.d.*
Jane Musky   *A.d.* Scott A. Ault   *S.d.* Francesca Root   *MPAA* NC-17   *R.t.* 87 min.   *Cast:*
Andrew Dice Clay, Maria Parkinson, Eddie Griffin, "Noodles" Levenstein, Michael "Wheels"
Parise, "Hot Tub" Johnny West, Sylvia Harman, Lee Lawrence, Sumont, Fred Silverstein.

In this "concert movie," comedian Andrew Dice Clay unleashes his sexist, racist persona to
ridicule minorities, women, the elderly, and so on. Composed predominantly of material from
his Madison Square Garden concert, this film opens with a short film called "A Day in the Life,"
narrated by Clay, which shows how buying a leather jacket changed his life.

DOGFIGHT

Pro. Peter Newman and Richard Guay; Warner Bros.   *Dir.* Nancy Savoca   *Scr.* Bob Comfort
Cine. Bobby Bukowski   *Ed.* John Tintori   *P.d.* Lester W. Cohen   *A.d.* Daniel Talpers   *S.d.*
Sarah Stollman and Jessica Lanier   *Mu.* Mason Daring   *MPAA* R   *R.t.* 92 min.   *Cast:* River
Phoenix, Lili Taylor, Richard Panebianco, Anthony Clark, Mitchell Whitfield, Holly Near,
E. G. Daily.

In this drama set in 1963, several Marines hold a contest, on their last night before shipping
out, to see who can find the ugliest date. Eddie Birdlace (River Phoenix) chooses Rose (Lili
Taylor), who is at first thrilled to be asked. When she discovers the reason why, her anger and
humiliation prompt Eddie to try and make amends.

DON JUAN, MY LOVE (Spain, 1991)

Pro. BMG Films Production in collaboration with RTVE and Productora Andaluza de
Programas; International Film Exchange   *Dir.* Antonio Mercero   *Scr.* Joaquin Oristrell and
Antonio Mercero   *Cine.* Carlos Suárez   *Ed.* Rosa Graceli-Salgado   *P.d.* Rafael Palmero   *Mu.*
Bernardo Bonezzi   *R.t.* 96 min.   *Cast:* Juan Luis Galiardo, María Barranco, Loles León, Rossy
de Palma, Jose Sazatornil, Vicente Diez, Pedro Reyes, Verónica Forque.

In this farce, the ghost of the legendary Don Juan (Juan Luis Galiardo) rises from the grave in
late twentieth century Spain in order to perform a good deed and escape purgatory. Comic
mishaps arise when the former womanizer is mistaken for an actor (also played by Galiardo)
who not only is portraying the don onstage but also embodies Don Juan's former arrogant and
lascivious manner.

DON'T TELL MOM THE BABYSITTER'S DEAD

Pro. Robert Newmyer, Brian Reilly, and Jeffrey Silver for HBO, in association with Cinema Plus
L.P. and Mercury/Douglas Films, and Outlaw; Warner Bros.   *Dir.* Stephen Herek   *Scr.* Neil

Landau and Tara Ison   *Cine.* Tim Suhrstedt   *Ed.* Larry Bock   *P.d.* Stephen Marsh   *A.d.* Patricia Klawonn   *S.d.* Kara Lindstrom   *Mu.* David Newman   *MPAA* PG-13   *R.t.* 105 min. *Cast:* Christina Applegate, Joanna Cassidy, John Getz, Josh Charles, Keith Coogan, Concetta Tomei, David Duchovny, Kimmy Robertson, Jayne Brook, Eda Reiss Merin, Robert Hy Gorman, Danielle Harris, Christopher Pettiet.

Five children are left on their own when the elderly babysitter (Eda Reiss Merin), hired by their vacationing Mom (Concetta Tomei), dies. Without money, the eldest (Christina Applegate) snares a job as an assistant in the fashion industry to help support the family until Mom returns.

DOUBLE IMPACT

Pro. Ashok Amritraj and Jean-Claude Van Damme for Stone Group Pictures; Columbia Pictures   *Dir.* Sheldon Lettich   *Scr.* Sheldon Lettich and Jean-Claude Van Damme; based on a story by Lettich, Van Damme, Steve Meerson, and Peter Krikes   *Cine.* Richard Kline   *Ed.* Mark Conte   *P.d.* John Jay Moore   *A.d.* Okowita and Rosa Pang Shiu Cheung   *S.d.* Shelley Lynn Warner, Gregory Hunt Van Horn, Suzette Sheets, and Eric Lam Yau Sang   *Mu.* Arthur Kempel   *MPAA* R   *R.t.* 118 min.   *Cast:* Jean-Claude Van Damme, Geoffrey Lewis, Alan Scarfe, Alonna Shaw, Philip Chan Yan Kin, Cory Everson, Bolo Yeung, Sarah-Jane Varley, Andy Armstrong.

Jean-Claude Van Damme plays twins separated as babies when their parents are murdered in Hong Kong by their father's business partner (Alan Scarfe). When Chad (Van Damme)—reared by a family friend (Geoffrey Lewis) in California—and his brother, Alex (also played by Van Damme)—reared in a Hong Kong orphanage—are reunited in Hong Kong as adults, the two seek revenge on their parents' killer.

DROP DEAD FRED

Pro. Paul Webster for Polygram and Working Title Films; New Line Cinema   *Dir.* Ate De Jong   *Scr.* Carlos Davis and Anthony Fingleton; based on a story by Elizabeth Livingston   *Cine.* Peter Deming   *Ed.* Marshall Harvey   *P.d.* Joseph T. Garrity   *A.d.* Randall Schmook   *S.d.* Colin Tugwell   *Mu.* Randy Edelman   *MPAA* PG-13   *R.t.* 98 min.   *Cast:* Phoebe Cates, Rik Mayall, Marsha Mason, Tim Matheson, Carrie Fisher, Keith Charles, Ashley Peldon, Daniel Gerroll, Ron Eldard.

When a young woman, Elizabeth (Phoebe Cates), loses both her husband and her job, she goes to live with her mother (Marsha Mason), where she rediscovers her imaginary childhood friend, Drop Dead Fred (Rik Mayall). Together, the two re-create some of the mischief they made when Elizabeth was a child.

DUTCH

Pro. John Hughes and Richard Vane for Hughes Entertainment; Twentieth Century-Fox   *Dir.* Peter Faiman   *Scr.* John Hughes   *Cine.* Charles Minsky   *Ed.* Paul Hirsch and Adam Bernardi   *P.d.* Stan Jolley   *A.d.* Tracy Bousman and Chris Burian-Mohr   *S.d.* Jackie Carr   *Mu.* Alan Silvestri   *MPAA* PG-13   *R.t.* 105 min.   *Cast:* Ed O'Neill, Ethan Randall, JoBeth Williams, Christopher McDonald, Ari Meyers, E. G. Daily, L. Scott Caldwell.

In this comedy, good-natured working-class Dutch (Ed O'Neill) agrees to pick up the snobbish, ill-mannered son, Doyle (Ethan Randall), of his girlfriend (JoBeth Williams) from an expensive boarding school and drive him home for Thanksgiving. Angry over his parents' divorce, Doyle makes the trip as difficult for Dutch as he can—leading to multiple amusing mishaps.

EMINENT DOMAIN

Pro. Shimon Arama for Alan Neuman/SVS Inc./Arama Entertainment/Harlech Films; Triumph Releasing Corp.   *Dir.* John Irvin   *Scr.* Andrzej Krakowski and Richard Gregson   *Cine.* Witold

Adamek   *Ed.* Peter Tanner   *P.d.* Allan Starski   *Mu.* Zbigniew Preisner   *MPAA* PG-13   *R.t.* 102 min.   *Cast:* Donald Sutherland, Anne Archer, Jodhi May, Paul Freeman, Bernard Hepton.

Donald Sutherland stars as Jozef Burski, a highly placed Polish bureaucrat, who suddenly finds himself a victim of persecution by the state when his job is taken from him, his daughter, Eva (Jodhi May), is kidnapped, and his wife, Mira (Anne Archer), is driven to a nervous breakdown.

ERNEST SCARED STUPID

Pro. Stacy Williams for Touchstone Pictures, in association with Touchwood Pacific Partners I; Buena Vista Pictures   *Dir.* John Cherry   *Scr.* Charlie Gale and Coke Sams; based on a story by John Cherry and Sams   *Cine.* Hanania Baer   *Ed.* Craig Bassett   *P.d.* Chris August   *A.d.* Mark Ragland   *S.d.* Linda J. Vipond   *Mu.* Bruce Arntson and Kirby Shelstad   *MPAA* PG   *R.t.* 91 min.   *Cast:* Jim Varney, Eartha Kitt, Austin Nagler, Shay Astar, Jonas Moscartolo, Ernst Fosselius (voice).

Jim Varney reprises his role of dim-witted, but good-natured, Ernest P. Worrell of the small town of Briarwood. When Ernest lets loose an evil troll (Jonas Moscartolo) that threatens the local children, he needs the help of a witch (Eartha Kitt) to vanquish it.

EVE OF DESTRUCTION

Pro. David Madden for Nelson Entertainment and Interscope Communications; Orion Pictures   *Dir.* Duncan Gibbins   *Scr.* Duncan Gibbins and Yale Udoff   *Cine.* Alan Hume   *Ed.* Caroline Biggerstaff   *P.d.* Peter Lamont   *A.d.* Matthew Jacobs   *S.d.* David Koneff   *Mu.* Philippe Sarde   *MPAA* R   *R.t.* 98 min.   *Cast:* Gregory Hines, Renée Soutendijk, Michael Greene, Kurt Fuller, John M. Jackson, Loren Haynes, Ross Malinger, Nelson Mashita, Alan Haufrect, Kevin McCarthy, Jeff McCarthy, Nancy Locke, Bethany Richards.

In this science fiction thriller, Gregory Hines plays Jim McQuade, a government agent sent to track down a nuclear weapon that has gone astray, the EVE VIII (Renée Soutendijk). This robot, assembled in the exact image of its creator, Dr. Eve Simmons (Soutendijk), down to her own thoughts and memories, has gone haywire and is now obsessed with carrying out a sort of warped feminist revenge.

EVERYBODY'S FINE (*Stanno tutti bene*. Italy, 1990)

Pro. Angelo Rizzoli for Erre Produzioni, Films Ariane, TFI Films, Sovereign Pictures, and Silvio Berlusconi Communications; Miramax   *Dir.* Giuseppe Tornatore   *Scr.* Giuseppe Tornatore, Tonino Guerra, and Massimo de Rita   *Cine.* Blasco Giurato   *Ed.* Mario Morra   *A.d.* Andrea Crisanti   *S.d.* Nello Giorgetti   *Mu.* Ennio Morricone   *R.t.* 112 min.   *Cast:* Marcello Mastroianni, Michèle Morgan, Marino Cenna, Roberto Nobile, Valeria Cavali, Norma Martelli, Salvatore Cascio, Fabio Iellini.

Elderly Matteo (Marcello Mastroianni) leaves his native Sicily to tour Italy and pay surprise visits to each of his five grown children. Matteo is the one who is surprised, however, as he slowly comes to realize that his "successful" children are not as well-off as he had thought.

FINAL APPROACH

Pro. Eric Steven Stahl for Filmquest Pictures Production; Trimark Pictures   *Dir.* Eric Steven Stahl   *Scr.* Eric Steven Stahl and Gerald Laurence   *Cine.* Eric Goldstein   *Ed.* Stefan Kut   *P.d.* Ralph E. Stevic   *S.d.* Arnoldo Frabitz   *Mu.* Kirk Hunter   *MPAA* R   *R.t.* 100 min.   *Cast:* James B. Sikking, Hector Elizondo, Madolyn Smith, Kevin McCarthy.

A psychiatrist (Hector Elizondo) tries to help an Air Force test pilot, Colonel Jason Halsey (James B. Sikking), recover his memory following his bailing out of his aircraft and its subsequent crash. The psychiatrist administers various tests that prompt flashbacks to Halsey's youth, marriages, and professional career—yet his recovery is jeopardized by the top-secret nature of his mission. The film is more notable for its soundtrack, which marks the first fully digitized feature film, than for its plot or characters.

FIREHEAD

Pro. Peter Yuval for A.I.P. Studios and Winters Group, in association with Sovereign Investment Corp.; Pyramid   *Dir.* Peter Yuval   *Scr.* Peter Yuval and Jeff Mandell   *Cine.* Paul Maibaum   *Ed.* Steve Nielson   *A.d.* Buz Crump   *Mu.* Vladimir Horunzhy   *MPAA* R   *R.t.* 88 min.   *Cast:* Chris Lemmon, Gretchen Becker, Christopher Plummer, Brett Porter, Martin Landau.

When a Russian defector (Brett Porter) with telekinetic powers starts destroying American weapons factories, a research scientist (Chris Lemmon) and a beautiful CIA agent (Gretchen Becker) are sent to stop him, while an evil government agent (Christopher Plummer) tries to take advantage of the situation.

FLIGHT OF THE INTRUDER

Pro. Mace Neufeld; Paramount Pictures   *Dir.* John Milius   *Scr.* Robert Dillon and David Shaber; based on the novel by Stephen Coonts   *Cine.* Fred J. Koenekamp   *Ed.* C. Timothy O'Meara and Steve Mirkovich   *P.d.* Jack T. Collis   *A.d.* E. Albert Heschong   *S.d.* Nick S. Navarro, Richard Franklin Mays, Joseph E. Hubbard, and Mickey S. Michaels   *Mu.* Basil Poledouris   *MPAA* PG-13   *R.t.* 115 min.   *Cast:* Danny Glover, Willem Dafoe, Brad Johnson, Rosanna Arquette, Tom Sizemore, Dann Florek, Jared Chandler, Justin Williams, J. Kenneth Campbell, Fred Dalton Thompson.

Vietnam War squadron leader Camparelli (Danny Glover) has his hands full in 1972, the seventh year of the war, trying to keep his men in line, with pilots and bombardiers risking their lives to hit seemingly useless targets during the Paris peace talks. Conflict arises when pilot Jake Grafton (Brad Johnson), whose bombardier companion has just been killed, teams up with newcomer Virgil Cole (Willem Dafoe), who is on his third tour of duty, to undertake an unauthorized bombing of a missile depot in Hanoi.

FOREVER MARY (Italy, 1991)

Pro. Claudio Bonivento for Numero Uno International Sri; Cinevista   *Dir.* Marco Risi   *Scr.* Sandro Petraglia and Stefano Rulli; based on a story by Aurelio Grimaldi and on his novel *Meri per sempre*   *Mu.* Giancarlo Bigazzi   *R.t.* 100 min.   *Cast:* Michele Placido, Alessandro di Sanzo, Claudio Amendola, Francesco Benigno.

In this Italian drama, a teacher (Michele Placido) volunteers to work at a notorious boys' reformatory school. Compassionate and self-controlled, he endures the boys' hatred and cruelty, while attempting to befriend them.

FREDDY'S DEAD: THE FINAL NIGHTMARE

Pro. Robert Shaye and Aron Warner; New Line Cinema   *Dir.* Rachel Talalay   *Scr.* Michael DeLuca; based on a story by Rachel Talalay and on characters created by Wes Craven   *Cine.* Declan Quinn   *Ed.* Janice Hampton   *P.d.* C. J. Strawn   *A.d.* James R. Barrows   *S.d.* Rebecca Carriaga   *Mu.* Brian May   *MPAA* R   *R.t.* 90 min.   *Cast:* Robert Englund, Lisa Zane, Shon Greenblatt, Lezlie Deane, Ricky Dean Logan, Breckin Meyer, Yaphet Kotto, Roseanne Arnold, Tom Arnold, Alice Cooper.

In this fifth sequel to *A Nightmare on Elm Street* (1984), set ten years later, supernatural murderer Freddy Krueger (Robert Englund) has apparently killed all the children in town and goes looking for more victims. In his search, he encounters his own estranged child, and they meet in a final confrontation, presented in 3-D.

F/X II: THE DEADLY ART OF ILLUSION

Pro. Jack Wiener and Dodi Fayed; Orion Pictures   *Dir.* Richard Franklin   *Scr.* Bill Condon;

based on characters created by Robert T. Megginson and Gregory Fleeman *Cine.* Victor J. Kemper *Ed.* Andrew London *P.d.* John Jay Moore *A.d.* Gregory P. Keen *S.d.* Gordon Sim *Mu.* Lalo Schifrin *MPAA* PG-13 *R.t.* 109 min. *Cast:* Bryan Brown, Brian Dennehy, Rachel Ticotin, Joanna Gleason, Philip Bosco, Kevin J. O'Connor, Tom Mason, Josie DeGuzman, John Walsh.

In this sequel to *F/X* (1986), set five years later, Bryan Brown and Brian Dennehy reprise the roles of Rollie Tyler, a special-effects expert, and Leo McCarthy, a police detective, respectively. When a police officer (Tom Mason), who is also the former husband of Rollie's girlfriend (Rachel Ticotin), persuades Rollie to use his expertise on a case, Rollie turns to old friend Leo for help.

GEORGE'S ISLAND (Canada, 1991)

Pro. Maura O'Connell for J&M Entertainment, Salter Street Films, and the National Film Board of Canada; New Line Cinema *Dir.* Paul Donovan *Scr.* Maura O'Connell and Paul Donovan *Cine.* Les Krizsan *Ed.* Stephen Fanfara *P.d.* Bill Fleming *S.d.* Judy Arsenault *Mu.* Marty Simon *MPAA* PG *R.t.* 89 min. *Cast:* Ian Bannen, Sheila McCarthy, Maury Chaykin, Nathaniel Moreau, Vicki Ridler, Brian Downcy, Irene Hogan, Gary Reineke.

In this fantasy/adventure, Miss Birdwood (Sheila McCarthy), the odd teacher of a young orphan boy, George (Nathaniel Moreau), takes him from his grandfather (Ian Bannen) and places him in a cruel foster home. George and his grandfather then escape to an island haunted by the ghosts of Captain Kidd and his pirates.

GET BACK

Pro. Henry Thomas and Philip Knatchbull for Allied Filmmakers, in association with M.P.L. and Front Page Films; Seven Arts/Carolco *Dir.* Richard Lester *Cine.* Robert Paynter and Jordan Cronenweth *Ed.* John Victor Smith *Mu.* John Lennon and Paul McCartney *MPAA* PG *R.t.* 89 min. *Cast:* Paul McCartney, Linda McCartney, Hamish Stuart, Robbie McIntosh, Paul (Wix) Wickens, Chris Whitten.

This film is composed of footage filmed during former Beatle Paul McCartney's 1989-1990 world concert tour, intercut by newsreel footage of 1960's-era events and popular figures.

GOIN' TO CHICAGO

Pro. Paul Leder; Poor Robert *Dir.* Paul Leder *Scr.* Paul Leder *Cine.* Francis Grumman *Ed.* Paul Leder *Mu.* Bob Summers *R.t.* 95 min. *Cast:* Cleavon Little, Viveca Lindfors, Gary Kroeger, Eileen Seeley, Guy Killum, Dick Sargent.

Set in 1968, a year of political and social turmoil, this film centers on two young college graduates and lovers, Aaron (Gary Kroeger) and Elinor (Eileen Seeley), who take off a year to work on Eugene McCarthy's presidential election campaign. Aaron, however, soon tires of this and heads to Europe to travel, leaving Elinor to continue her work.

HANGFIRE

Pro. Brad Krevoy and Steve Stabler; Motion Picture Corp. of America *Dir.* Peter Maris *Scr.* Brian D. Jeffries *Cine.* Mark Norris *Ed.* Peter Maris *P.d.* Stephen Greenberg *Mu.* Jim Price *MPAA* R *R.t.* 89 min. *Cast:* Brad Davis, Kim Delaney, Jan-Michael Vincent, Ken Foree, Lee de Broux, George Kennedy, James Tolkan, Yaphet Kotto, Blake Conway, Lyle Alzado, Lou Ferrigno, Robert Miano, Collin Bernsen, Peter Lupus, Nancy Schuster, Lawrence Rothschild, Myron Dubow.

In this tepid action/adventure, a serial killer (Lee de Broux) leads an escape during a prison evacuation following a toxic spill. When the convicts invade a small town and hold the townspeople hostage, the National Guard, led by Lieutenant Colonel Johnson (Jan-Michael Vincent), and a local sheriff (Brad Davis) vie for their release.

HANGIN' WITH THE HOMEBOYS

Pro. Richard Brick; New Line Cinema   *Dir.* Joseph B. Vasquez   *Scr.* Joseph B. Vasquez   *Cine.* Anghel Decca   *Ed.* Michael Schweitzer   *A.d.* Isabel Bau Madden   *S.d.* Anne Czerwatuik   *Mu.* Joel Sill and David Chackler   *MPAA* R   *R.t.* 88 min.   *Cast:* Doug E. Doug, Mario Joyner, John Leguizamo, Nestor Serrano, Kimberly Russell, Mary B. Ward, Reggie Montgomery, Christine Claravall.

This drama set in the south Bronx centers on four young men: Willie (Doug E. Doug) and Tom (Mario Joyner)—who are African American—and Johnny (John Leguizamo) and Vinny (Nestor Serrano)—who are Puerto Rican. The four fight, party, meet women, and philosophize about life during the course of one Friday night that they spend together.

THE HARD WAY

Pro. William Sackheim and Rob Cohen; Universal Pictures   *Dir.* John Badham   *Scr.* Daniel Pyne and Lem Dobbs; based on a story by Dobbs and Michael Kozoll   *Cine.* Don McAlpine and Robert Primes   *Ed.* Frank Morriss and Tony Lombardo   *P.d.* Philip Harrison   *A.d.* John Kasarda   *S.d.* Susan Bode   *Mu.* Arthur B. Rubinstein   *MPAA* R   *R.t.* 111 min.   *Cast:* Michael J. Fox, James Woods, Stephen Lang, Annabella Sciorra, John Capodice, Luis Guzman, L. L. Cool J, Mary Mara, Delroy Lindo, Conrad Roberts, Christina Ricci, Penny Marshall.

Michael J. Fox stars as egotistical Hollywood actor Nick Lang, who has starred in action/ adventure fare and who now desires to break away from his stereotype and play a serious role. Sparks fly when, in order to learn the trade, Lang is paired with a hard-core New York police officer, John Moss (James Woods), who is on the trail of a serial killer (Stephen Lang) called the Party Crasher.

HARLEY DAVIDSON AND THE MARLBORO MAN

Pro. Jere Henshaw for Krisjair/Laredo; Metro-Goldwyn-Mayer   *Dir.* Simon Wincer   *Scr.* Don Michael Paul   *Cine.* David Eggby   *Ed.* Corky Ehlers   *P.d.* Paul Peters   *A.d.* Lisette Thomas   *S.d.* Lynn Wolverton Parker   *Mu.* Basil Poledouris   *MPAA* R   *R.t.* 98 min.   *Cast:* Mickey Rourke, Don Johnson, Chelsea Field, Daniel Baldwin, Giancarlo Esposito, Tom Sizemore, Vanessa Williams, Robert Ginty, Tia Carrere.

Mickey Rourke and Don Johnson star as the title characters, respectively, in this action/ adventure set in Burbank, California, in 1996. When the two band together to save their favorite hangout by robbing the bank that is going to foreclose on its owner, they discover that the armored truck they rob is not carrying cash but drugs.

HEAR MY SONG (Great Britain, 1991)

Pro. Alison Owen-Allen for Film Four International, British Screen, Windmill Lane, and Limelight; Miramax Films   *Dir.* Peter Chelsom   *Scr.* Peter Chelsom and Adrian Dunbar; based on a story by Chelsom   *Cine.* Sue Gibson   *Ed.* Martin Walsh   *P.d.* Caroline Hanania   *A.d.* Katharine Naylor   *Mu.* John Altman   *MPAA* R   *R.t.* 113 min.   *Cast:* Ned Beatty, Adrian Dunbar, David McCallum, Tara Fitzgerald, Shirley Anne Field, William Hootkins, James Nesbitt.

Based on real-life Irish tenor Josef Locke, who fled England in the 1950's in the wake of tax evasion charges, this romantic comedy centers on Mickey O'Neill (Adrian Dunbar), a wily nightclub owner who books a certain Mr. X (William Hootkins) as a Locke look-alike. When this act results in Mickey's losing his club, reputation, and girlfriend (Tara Fitzgerald), he embarks on a comic journey to Ireland to find the real Locke (Ned Beatty).

HEARING VOICES

Pro. Sharon Greytak, sponsored by the New York Foundation for the Arts; Phoenix International   *Dir.* Sharon Greytak   *Scr.* Sharon Greytak   *Cine.* Doron Schlair   *A.d.* Chere

Ledwith *Mu.* Wes York *R.t.* 87 min. *Cast:* Erika Nagy, Stephen Gatta, Tim Ahern, Michael Davenport.

After undergoing a surgical procedure that permanently alters her life-style, a New York City model (Erika Nagy) must come to terms with the physical and emotional scars as well as with her romantic feelings for a homosexual man (Stephen Gatta).

HEAVEN AND EARTH (Japan, 1991)

Pro. Yutaka Okada; Triton Pictures *Dir.* Haruki Kadokawa *Scr.* Toshio Kamata, Isao Yoshihara, and Haruki Kadokawa; based on the novel by Chogorǫ Kaionji *Cine.* Yonezo Maeda *Ed.* Akira Suzuki and Robert C. Jones *P.d.* Hiroshi Tokuda *Mu.* Tetsuya Komuro *MPAA* PG-13 *R.t.* 106 min. *Cast:* Takaaki Enoki, Masahiko Tsugawa, Atsuko Asano, Tsunehiko Watase, Naomi Zaizen, Binpachi Ito, Isao Natsuyagi, Stuart Whitman.

Set in sixteenth century Japan, this film centers on the famous battle of Kawanakajima, between two warlords who wish to reunite Japan, Kagetora (Takaaki Enoki) and Takeda (Masahiko Tsugawa). Although light on plot, the film contains epic battle scenes to rival those of Akira Kurosawa's *Kagemusha* (1980) or *Ran* (1985).

HENNA (India, 1991)

Pro. India Impact and R. K. Film *Dir.* Randhir Kapoor *Scr.* Jainendra Jain; based on a story by K. A. Abbas and J. Sathe *Cine.* Radhu Karmarkan *Ed.* Suesh Bhatt *Mu.* Ravindra Jain *R.t.* 200 min. *Cast:* Rishi Kapoor, Zeba Bhaktiar, Ashvini Bhave, Saeed Jaffrey.

In this Indian drama, a Kashmiri playboy (Rishi Kapoor) falls in love with a Pakistani woman, Henna (Zeba Bhaktiar), when he finds himself stranded in a small village following an automobile accident.

HIGHLANDER II: THE QUICKENING

Pro. Peter S. Davis and William Panzer for Ziad El Khoury and Jean-Luc Defait, in association with Lamb Bear Entertainment; InterStar *Dir.* Russell Mulcahy *Scr.* Peter Bellwood; based on a story by Brian Clemens and William Panzer and on characters created by Gregory Widen *Cine.* Peter Meheux *Ed.* Hubert C. de la Bouillerie and Anthony Redman *P.d.* Roger Hall *A.d.* John King *Mu.* Stewart Copeland *MPAA* R *R.t.* 88 min. *Cast:* Christopher Lambert, Virginia Madsen, Sean Connery, Michael Ironside, John C. McGinley, Allan Rich.

In this sequel to *Highlander* (1986), Christopher Lambert returns as the immortal MacLeod, now an old man on a dying Earth in the year 2024. It is revealed that he and his friend Ramirez (Sean Connery) were actually aliens exiled to Earth by their home planet's evil dictator (Michael Ironside), who is once again pursuing MacLeod. MacLeod must elude the hired killers while working with a radical environmentalist (Virginia Madsen) who is trying to save the planet.

THE HITMAN

Pro. Don Carmody; Cannon Pictures *Dir.* Aaron Norris *Scr.* Robert Geoffrion and Don Carmody *Cine.* João Fernandes *Ed.* Jacqueline Carmody *P.d.* Douglas Higgins *A.d.* Eric Fraser *S.d.* Barry Brolly *Mu.* Joel Derouin *MPAA* R *R.t.* 95 min. *Cast:* Chuck Norris, Michael Parks, Al Waxman, Alberta Watson, Salim Grant, Ken Pogue, Marcel Sabourin, Bruno Gerussi, Frank Ferrucci.

Chuck Norris returns in this action/adventure as a New York police officer, Cliff Garret, who is betrayed and left for dead by his longtime partner, Ronny Delaney (Michael Parks). When Garret emerges several years later with a new identity, he goes undercover for the Drug Enforcement Agency as a hitman for a gang leader (Al Waxman) in Seattle.

HOUSE PARTY II

Pro. Doug McHenry and George Jackson; New Line Cinema *Dir.* Doug McHenry and George Jackson *Scr.* Rusty Cundieff and Daryl G. Nickens; based on characters created by Reginald

Hudlin   *Cine.* Francis Kenny   *Ed.* Joel Goodman   *P.d.* Michelle Minch   *A.d.* Karen A. Steward   *S.d.* Philip Madison and Rosalyn Myles   *Mu.* Vassal Benford   *MPAA* R   *R.t.* 94 min. *Cast:* Christopher Reid, Christopher Martin, Tisha Campbell, Iman, Louie Louie, Martin Lawrence, D. Christopher Judge, Georg Stanford Brown, Queen Latifah, Kamron, Tony Burton, William Schallert, Brian George, Lucien George, Paul Anthony George, Helen Martin, Randy Harris.

Rap musicians Kid 'N Play (Christopher Reid and Christopher Martin) return in this sequel to *House Party* (1990). When Kid enrolls in college, Play takes the tuition money to pay a conniving record promoter (Iman), who subsequently disappears. The duo then stage a pajama party on campus to raise the necessary funds.

HUDSON HAWK

Pro. Joel Silver for Silver Pictures/Ace Bone; TriStar Pictures   *Dir.* Michael Lehmann   *Scr.* Steven E. de Souza and Daniel Waters; based on a story by Bruce Willis and Robert Kraft   *Cine.* Dante Spinotti   *Ed.* Chris Lebenzon and Michael Tronick   *P.d.* Jack DeGovia   *A.d.* John R. Jensen   *Mu.* Michael Kamen and Robert Kraft   *MPAA* R   *R.t.* 95 min.   *Cast:* Bruce Willis, Danny Aiello, Andie MacDowell, James Coburn, Richard E. Grant, Sandra Bernhard, Donald Burton, Don Harvey, David Caruso, Andrew Bryniarski, Lorraine Toussaint, Frank Stallone, Stephano Molinari.

Recently released from prison, ace burglar Hudson Hawk (Bruce Willis) is recruited to steal several Leonardo da Vinci works. He sets about this task with his partner, Tommy Five-Tone (Danny Aiello), only to discover that the CIA and the Vatican are involved.

IF LOOKS COULD KILL

Pro. Craig Zadan and Neil Meron; Warner Bros.   *Dir.* William Dear   *Scr.* Darren Star; based on a story by Fred Dekker   *Cine.* Doug Milsome   *Ed.* John F. Link   *P.d.* Guy J. Comtois   *A.d.* Real Proulx   *S.d.* Gilles Ard and Jean Kazemirchuk   *Mu.* David Foster   *MPAA* PG-13   *R.t.* 88 min.   *Cast:* Richard Grieco, Linda Hunt, Roger Rees, Robin Bartlett, Gabrielle Anwar, Geraldine James, Michael Siberry, Carole Davis, Frederick Coffin, Tom Rack, Roger Daltrey, Oliver Dear, Cyndy Preston.

In this weak spoof of a James Bond-like action/adventure, a high school student, Michael Corben (Richard Grieco), on a trip to France with his classmates, is mistaken for CIA agent Michael Corben—and finds himself caught in a web of intrigue and romance.

THE IMPORTED BRIDEGROOM

Pro. Pamela Berger for Lara Classics; ASA Communications   *Dir.* Pamela Berger   *Scr.* Pamela Berger; based on a story by Abraham Cahan   *Cine.* Brian Heffron   *Ed.* Amy Sumner and Michael Levine   *P.d.* Martha Seely   *Mu.* Bevan Manson and Rosalie Gerut   *R.t.* 91 min. *Cast:* Eugene Troobnick, Avi Hoffman, Greta Cowan, Annette Miller, Miriam Varon.

A Jewish immigrant (Eugene Troobnick), living in turn-of-the-century Boston, returns to his native Poland in order to find a suitable husband for his daughter (Greta Cowan). When he returns with a timid scholar (Avi Hoffman), his daughter objects, voicing instead her preference for an American-born husband.

IMPROMPTU

Pro. Stuart Oken and Daniel A. Sherkow for Sovereign Pictures, in association with Governor Prods. and Les Films Ariane; Hemdale Films   *Dir.* James Lapine   *Scr.* Sarah Kernochan   *Cine.* Bruno De Keyzer   *Ed.* Michael Ellis   *A.d.* Gerard Daoudal   *Mu.* John Strauss   *MPAA* PG-13 *R.t.* 109 min.   *Cast:* Judy Davis, Hugh Grant, Mandy Patinkin, Bernadette Peters, Julian Sands, Ralph Brown, Georges Corrace, Anton Rodgers, Emma Thompson, Anna Massey, John Savident, Elizabeth Spriggs.

This romantic comedy set in nineteenth century Europe is based on the real-life affair between George Sand (Judy Davis) and Frederic Chopin (Hugh Grant), who meet during a weekend stay at the country home of royalty. Romantic intrigue develops among the many visiting "artistes," who also include Alfred de Musset (Mandy Patinkin), Franz Liszt (Julian Sands), his lady friend (Bernadette Peters), and Eugene Delacroix (Ralph Brown).

THE INDIAN RUNNER
Pro. Don Phillips for Mount Film Group, in association with MICO/NHK Enterprises; Metro-Goldwyn-Mayer/United Artists *Dir.* Sean Penn *Scr.* Sean Penn *Cine.* Anthony B. Richmond *Ed.* Jay Cassidy *P.d.* Michael Haller *A.d.* Bill Groom *S.d.* Derek Hill *Mu.* Jack Nitzsche *MPAA* R *R.t.* 126 min. *Cast:* David Morse, Viggo Mortensen, Valeria Golino, Patricia Arquette, Charles Bronson, Sandy Dennis, Dennis Hopper, Jordan Rhodes, Enzo Rossi, Kathy Jensen, Annie Pearson.

In this drama, which marks actor Sean Penn's directorial debut, two brothers—Joe (David Morse), a police officer, and Frank (Viggo Mortensen), a Vietnam veteran recently released from prison—clash in the small Nebraska town where they grew up.

INFINITY
Pro. A. J. Brato; Alternative Distribution System *Dir.* Alex Gelman *Scr.* A. J. Brato *Cine.* Eric Goldstein *Ed.* A. Lori Tucci *Mu.* Michael Linn and Robert J. Walsh *MPAA* PG *R.t.* 90 min. *Cast:* Megan Blake, Moises Bertran, Newell Tarrant, Fred E. Baker, Patricia Place.

When a former pilot (Newell Tarrant) returns with his wife (Patricia Place) and teenage daughter (Megan Blake) to a South Pacific island where he survived a crash, the family meets a young man (Moises Bertran) with telepathic ability.

THE INNER CIRCLE
Pro. Claudio Bonivento; Columbia Pictures *Dir.* Andrei Konchalovsky *Scr.* Andrei Konchalovsky and Anatoli Usov *Cine.* Ennio Guarnieri *Ed.* Henry Richardson *P.d.* Ezio Frigerio *A.d.* Gianni Giovagnoni and Vladimir Murzin *Mu.* Eduard Artemyev *MPAA* PG-13 *R.t.* 134 min. *Cast:* Tom Hulce, Lolita Davidovich, Bob Hoskins, Alexandre Zbruev, Feodor Chaliapin, Jr., Bess Meyer, Marla Baranova, Irina Kuptchenko.

This drama set in Moscow in 1939 centers on Soviet leader Joseph Stalin's film projectionist, Ivan (Tom Hulce)—an ordinary man who develops an overwhelmingly strong allegiance to his boss. Existing in a perpetual state of terror, Ivan still remains devoted to Stalin and is willing to sacrifice everything to maintain his status.

IRON MAZE (USA and Japan, 1991)
Pro. Ilona Herzberg and Hidenori Ueki for Edward R. Pressman, Oliver Stone, and Trans-Tokyo Corporation; Castle Hill *Dir.* Hiroaki Yoshida *Scr.* Tim Metcalfe; based on a story by Hiroaki Yoshida and Metcalfe and on the short story "In the Grove," by Ryunosuke Akutagawa *Cine.* Morio Saegusa *Ed.* Bonnie Koehler *P.d.* Toby Corbett *A.d.* Gary Kosko *S.d.* Diana Stoughton *Mu.* Stanley Myers *MPAA* R *R.t.* 104 min. *Cast:* Jeff Fahey, Bridget Fonda, Hiroaki Murakami, J. T. Walsh, Gabriel Damon, John Randolph, Peter Allas.

When the son—Sugita (Hiroaki Murakami)—of a Japanese billionaire is found beaten in an abandoned steel mill that he owns in a small town in Pennsylvania, a local man—Barry (Jeff Fahey)—confesses to the crime. Multiple versions of the events leading to their fight are given by Sugita, Barry, and Sugita's American wife (Bridget Fonda), and it is the responsibility of the local police chief (J. T. Walsh) to discover the truth.

JOEY TAKES A CAB
Pro. Albert Band; Bandwagon Productions, Inc. *Dir.* Albert Band *Scr.* Frank Ray Perilli *Cine.* Jim Stewart *Ed.* Peter Teschner *Mu.* Fritz Heede *R.t.* 82 min. *Cast:* Lionel Stander,

Kathleen Freeman, Jackie Gayle, Michael J. Pollard, Royal Dano, Eileen Brennan, Kaye Ballard, Frank Ray Perilli.

When elderly stand-up comedian Joey Ray (Lionel Stander) dies, a motley crew of show-business folk gather at the funeral home to share humorous and raunchy memories of their old friend.

JOURNEY OF HOPE (Switzerland, 1990)

Pro. Alfi Sinniger for Catpics and Peter Fueter for Condor Productions; Miramax Films   *Dir.* Xavier Koller   *Scr.* Xavier Koller   *Cine.* Elemer Ragalyi   *Ed.* Galip Iyitanir   *Mu.* Manfred Eicher   *R.t.* 110 min.   *Cast:* Necmettin Cobanoglu, Nur Surer, Emin Sivas, Yaman Okay, Mathias Gnaedinger, Dietmar Schoenherr.

Based on a true story and winning a 1990 Academy Award for Best Foreign-Language Film, this motion picture recounts the journey of a Kurdish farmer (Necmettin Cobanoglu), his wife (Nur Surer), and their seven-year-old son (Emin Sivas) from Turkey to a better life in Switzerland. It proves to be an apparently futile journey of sacrifice, as these three must sell their land, leave family behind, and endure much hardship.

JULIA HAS TWO LOVERS

Pro. Bashar Shbib for Oneira Pictures International; South Gate Entertainment   *Dir.* Bashar Shbib   *Scr.* Daphna Kastner and Bashar Shbib; based on a story by Kastner   *Cine.* Stephen Reizes   *Ed.* Bashar Shbib and Dan Foegelle   *Mu.* Emilio Kauderer   *MPAA* R   *R.t.* 91 min. *Cast:* Daphna Kastner, David Duchovny, David Charles, Tim Ray, Clare Bancroft, Martin Donovan, Anita Olanick.

While a children's book writer, Julia (Daphna Kastner), contemplates her live-in lover's marriage proposal, a man calls on the telephone—a wrong number. Thus begins a revealing, and lengthy, conversation with a charming stranger in which the two pour out their hearts to each other and fall in love. In the end, however, Julia finds it was too good to be true.

KICKBOXER II

Pro. Tom Karnowski for Kings Road Entertainment; Trimark Pictures   *Dir.* Albert Pyun   *Scr.* David S. Goyer   *Cine.* George Mooradian   *Ed.* Alan E. Baumgarten   *P.d.* Nicholas T. Preovolos   *Mu.* Tony Riparetti and James Saad   *MPAA* R   *R.t.* 90 min.   *Cast:* Sasha Mitchell, Peter Boyle, Cary-Hiroyuki Tagawa, Dennis Chan, Michel Qissi, John Diehl, Mattias Hues, Heather McComb.

Kickboxer and teacher David Sloan (Sasha Mitchell) is drawn back into the ring to battle evil competitor Tong Po (Michel Qissi) in order to avenge the murder of his two brothers.

KING RALPH

Pro. Jack Brodsky for Mirage/JBRO; Universal Pictures   *Dir.* David S. Ward   *Scr.* David S. Ward; based on the novel *Headlong*, by Emlyn Williams   *Cine.* Kenneth MacMillan   *Ed.* John Jympson   *P.d.* Simon Holland   *A.d.* Clinton Cavers   *S.d.* Peter Walpole   *Mu.* James Newton Howard   *MPAA* PG   *R.t.* 97 min.   *Cast:* John Goodman, Peter O'Toole, John Hurt, Camille Coduri, Richard Griffiths, Leslie Phillips, James Villiers, Joely Richardson, Niall O'Brien, Julian Glover.

When the entire royal family of Great Britain suddenly dies, a Las Vegas lounge singer, Ralph (John Goodman), becomes king because his grandmother had an affair with a prince. Aided by his very proper secretary, Willingham (Peter O'Toole), King Ralph undertakes the role, but finds his position threatened by a conniving British lord (John Hurt).

A KISS BEFORE DYING

Pro. Robert Lawrence for Initial Film; Universal Pictures   *Dir.* James Dearden   *Scr.* James Dearden; based on the novel by Ira Levin   *Cine.* Mike Southon   *Ed.* Michael Bradsell   *P.d.* Jim

Clay *A.d.* Rod McClean and Chris Seagers *Mu.* Howard Shore *MPAA* R *R.t.* 95 min. *Cast:* Matt Dillon, Sean Young, Max Von Sydow, Diane Ladd, James Russo, Adam Horovitz, Martha Gehman, Ben Browder.

Ellen Carlsson (Sean Young) seeks the truth about the death of her twin sister, Dorothy (also played by Young), suspecting murder. Unfortunately, she learns that her sister's murderer is her own husband, Jonathan Corliss (Matt Dillon), an unscrupulous opportunist determined to let nothing and no one stand in his way to the top of the empire of Ellen's copper magnate father (Max Von Sydow).

KISS ME A KILLER
Pro. Catherine Cyran; Califilm *Dir.* Marcus DeLeon *Scr.* Christopher Wooden and Marcus DeLeon *Cine.* Nancy Schreiber *Ed.* Glenn Garland and Richard Gentner *P.d.* James R. Shumaker *A.d.* Amy B. Ancona *Mu.* Nigel Holton *MPAA* R *R.t.* 92 min. *Cast:* Julie Carmen, Robert Beltran, Guy Boyd, Ramon Franco, Charles Boswell, Sam Vlahos, Brad Blaisell, A. C. Santos, Pancho Sanchez.

Two lovers—a singer, Tony (Robert Beltran), and the wife of a nightclub owner, Teresa (Julie Carmen)—plot the murder of Teresa's husband (Guy Boyd) in order to take over his club and be together.

KORCZAK (Poland, 1991)
Pro. Regina Ziegler, Janusz Morgenstern, and Daniel Toscan du Plantier; New Yorker Films *Dir.* Andrzej Wajda *Scr.* Agnieszka Holland *Cine.* Robby Müller *Ed.* Ewa Smal *P.d.* Allan Starski *S.d.* Anna Kowarska and Magdalena Dipont *Mu.* Wojciech Kilar *R.t.* 113 min. *Cast:* Wojtek Pszoniak, Ewa Dalkowska, Piotr Kozlowski, Marzena Trybala, Wojcieh Klata, Adam Siemion, Karolina Czernicka.

This film portrays the life of a Polish hero, doctor, and educator, Janusz Korczak (played by Wojtek Pszoniak), who protected Jewish orphans in a Warsaw ghetto during the Nazi Holocaust. When given the chance to escape, Korczak courageously chooses to remain with his children, eventually dying at Treblinka.

THE LAST BOY SCOUT
Pro. Joel Silver and Michael Levy for Silver Pictures and Geffen Pictures; Warner Bros. *Dir.* Tony Scott *Scr.* Shane Black *Cine.* Ward Russell *Ed.* Stuart Baird, Mark Goldblatt, and Mark Helfrich *P.d.* Brian Morris *A.d.* Christiaan Wagener *S.d.* Eric Orbom and John Anderson *Mu.* Michael Kamen *MPAA* R *R.t.* 105 min. *Cast:* Bruce Willis, Damon Wayans, Chelsea Field, Noble Willingham, Taylor Negron, Danielle Harris, Halle Berry, Bruce McGill, Chelcie Ross, Joe Santos, Clarence Felder.

Down-and-out private detective Joe Hallenbeck (Bruce Willis) teams up with suspended football quarterback Jimmy Dix (Damon Wayans) to hunt down the killers of Dix's girlfriend (Halle Barry), who was Hallenbeck's client. Their quest uncovers a conspiracy among professional sports leaders and politicians to legalize sports gambling.

LATE FOR DINNER
Pro. Dan Lupovitz and W. D. Richter for Castle Rock Entertainment, in association with New Line Cinema and Granite Pictures; Columbia *Dir.* W. D. Richter *Scr.* Mark Andrus *Cine.* Peter Sova *Ed.* Richard Chew and Robert Leighton *P.d.* Lilly Kilvert *A.d.* Scott Harris and John Warnke *S.d.* Rosemary Brandenburg *Mu.* David Mansfield *MPAA* PG *R.t.* 92 min. *Cast:* Brian Wimmer, Peter Berg, Marcia Gay Harden, Colleen Flynn, Kyle Secor, Michael Beach, Peter Gallagher, Cassy Friel, Ross Malinger, Steven Schwartz-Hartley, John Prosky, Bo Brundin, Donald Hotton.

In this fantasy that begins in 1962, Willie (Brian Wimmer) and his brother-in-law, Frank

(Peter Berg), unwittingly become part of a cryonics experiment and are frozen for almost three decades. When they return home twenty-nine years later, many surprises await them.

LET HIM HAVE IT (Great Britain, 1991)
Pro. Luc Roeg and Robert Warr for Le Studio Canal Plus Film Trustees, Vivid, and Vermilion, in association with British Screen; Fine Line Features *Dir.* Peter Medak *Scr.* Neal Purvis and Robert Wade *Cine.* Oliver Stapleton *Ed.* Ray Lovejoy *P.d.* Michael Pickwoad *A.d.* Henry Harris *Mu.* Michael Kamen *MPAA* R *R.t.* 115 min. *Cast:* Chris Eccleston, Paul Reynolds, Tom Bell, Tom Courtenay, Eileen Atkins, Clare Holman, Mark McGann, Michael Gough, Michael Elphick, Murray Melvin, Ronald Fraser, Clive Revill, James Villiers.

Based on a real-life story, this drama reenacts the events and social and political climate leading to the murder of a London police officer and the ensuing trial. Although mentally retarded nineteen-year-old Derek Bentley (Chris Eccleston) had not pulled the trigger during the warehouse robbery and subsequent shootout with police, he was hanged on the evidence that he told gun-toting sixteen-year-old Chris Craig (Paul Reynolds) to "Let him have it"—an ambiguous phrase that Bentley's defense counsel insisted was meant to tell Craig to relinquish the weapon.

LIEBESTRAUM
Pro. Eric Fellner; Metro-Goldwyn-Mayer and Pathe Entertainment *Dir.* Mike Figgis *Scr.* Mike Figgis *Cine.* Juan Ruiz Anchia *Ed.* Martin Hunter *P.d.* Waldemar Kalinowski *A.d.* Michael T. Perry *S.d.* David Lubin *Mu.* Mike Figgis *MPAA* R *R.t.* 105 min. *Cast:* Kevin Anderson, Pamela Gidley, Bill Pullman, Kim Novak, Graham Beckel.

In this mystery, a man (Kevin Anderson) has an affair with the wife (Pamela Gidley) of a college friend (Bill Pullman) when he returns to a small town to visit his estranged mother (Kim Novak). At the same time, he finds himself mysteriously drawn to a rundown building that is about to be torn down, which was the site of a murder of a man and woman by the woman's jealous husband several decades earlier.

LIFE STINKS
Pro. Mel Brooks for Brooksfilms; Metro-Goldwyn-Mayer *Dir.* Mel Brooks *Scr.* Mel Brooks, Rudy De Luca, and Steve Haberman; based on a story by Brooks, Ron Clark, De Luca, and Haberman *Cine.* Steven Poster *Ed.* David Rawlins *P.d.* Peter Larkin *A.d.* Josan Russo *S.d.* Carroll Johnston and Marvin March *Mu.* John Morris *MPAA* PG-13 *R.t.* 90 min. *Cast:* Mel Brooks, Lesley Ann Warren, Jeffrey Tambor, Stuart Pankin, Howard Morris, Rudy De Luca, Teddy Wilson, Michael Ensign, Matthew Faison, Billy Barty.

Mel Brooks portrays a ruthless billionaire, Goddard Bolt, who plans to renovate a Los Angeles slum—and in the process, oust its poverty-stricken residents. Bolt makes a bet with a jealous colleague, Vance Crasswell (Jeffrey Tambor), in order to gain control of the entire property: He must survive one month as a homeless person in that neighborhood, with no money or resources.

LIONHEART
Pro. Ash R. Shah and Eric Karson for Sunil R. Shah/Imperial Entertainment; Universal *Dir.* Sheldon Lettich *Scr.* Sheldon Lettich and Jean-Claude Van Damme; based on a story by Van Damme and on a screenplay by S. N. Warren *Cine.* Robert C. New *Ed.* Mark Conte *P.d.* Gregory Pickrell *A.d.* Brian Densmore *S.d.* Woodward Romine, Jr., and Kerry Longacre *Mu.* John Scott *MPAA* R *R.t.* 105 min. *Cast:* Jean-Claude Van Damme, Harrison Page, Deborah Rennard, Lisa Pelikan, Ashley Johnson, Voyo, Michel Qissi, Brian Thompson.

Jean-Claude Van Damme returns as Lyon, a French Foreign Legionnaire who deserts in order to make his way to Los Angeles to help his brother who has been injured in a drug deal. After his brother dies, Lyon competes in illegal, underground fights run by the beautiful Cynthia (Deborah Rennard) to support his sister-in-law and niece.

LIVIN' LARGE

Pro. David V. Picker for WMG Pictures; the Samuel Goldwyn Company   *Dir*. Michael Schultz   *Scr*. William Mosley-Payne   *Cine*. Peter Collister   *Ed*. Christopher Holmes   *A.d*. Angie Riserbato   *S.d*. Penny Barrett   *Mu*. Herbie Hancock   *MPAA* R   *R.t*. 96 min.   *Cast:* Terrence (T. C.) Carson, Lisa Arrindell, Blanche Baker, Nathaniel (Afrika) Hall, Julia Campbell, Bernie McInerney, Loretta Devine.

When an ambitious, young African American, Dexter Jackson (Terrence "T. C." Carson), grabs the microphone from a dead reporter during a hostage scene and completes the broadcast, he finds himself catapulted into a successful career in broadcast journalism. In this comic satire, Dexter then finds himself forced to betray his friends and his race in order to improve the ratings.

LONELY IN AMERICA

Pro. Tirlok Malik and Phil Katzman for Apple Productions; Arista Classics   *Dir*. Barry Alexander Brown   *Scr*. Satyajit Joy Palit and Barry Alexander Brown; based on a story by Tirlok Malik   *Cine*. Phil Katzman   *Ed*. Tula Goenka   *A.d*. Eduardo Capilla   *S.d*. Irina Bilic   *Mu*. Gregory Arnold   *MPAA* PG-13   *R.t*. 94 min.   *Cast:* Ranjit Chowdry, Adelaide Miller, Tirlok Malik, Robert Kessler.

A young man (Ranjit Chowdry) emigrates from his native India to New York City, where, although isolated and lonely, he completes a night-school course in computers, finds a job, and meets a beautiful woman (Adelaide Miller).

THE LONG WEEKEND (O' DESPAIR)

Pro. Gregg Araki for Desperate Pictures   *Dir*. Gregg Araki   *Scr*. Gregg Araki   *Cine*. Gregg Araki   *Ed*. Gregg Araki   *Mu*. Steven Fields (Iron Curtain), Fred's Crashop, Steve Burr, and Dirt Production Co.   *R.t*. 87 min.   *Cast:* Bretton Vail, Maureen Dondanville, Andrea Beane, Nicole Dillenberg, Marcus d'Amico, Lance Woods.

This independent, experimental feature-length film centers on one weekend in the lives of three couples, all recent college graduates, when they attempt to figure out what to do with their lives and examine their own sexual orientation.

LOST IN SIBERIA (Great Britain, 1991)

Pro. Gagik Gasparyan and Alexander Mood; Spectator International Film   *Dir*. Alexander Mitta   *Scr*. Alexander Mitta, Valery Fried, Yuri Korotkov, and James Brabazon   *Cine*. Vladimir Shevtsik   *P.d*. Valeri Yurkevitch and Vitali Klimenkov   *R.t*. 107 min.   *Cast:* Anthony Andrews, Yelena Mayorova, Ira Mikhalyova, Vladimir Ilyin.

When a British archaeologist (Anthony Andrews) is captured by the KGB in the Middle East and sent to Siberia as a spy, he must endure many hardships—including the cruelty of Stalin's bureaucracy when prison officials continue to hold him after it has been proved that he is not guilty.

LOVE AND MURDER (Canada, 1988)

Pro. Steven Hilliard Stern for Sharmhill Productions, Inc.; Southpaw   *Dir*. Steven Hilliard Stern   *Scr*. Steven Hilliard Stern   *Cine*. David Herrington   *Ed*. Ron Wisman   *P.d*. Tony Hall   *Mu*. Matthew McCauley   *MPAA* R   *R.t*. 88 min.   *Cast:* Todd Waring, Kathleen Lasky, Ron White.

When a struggling Toronto photographer (Todd Waring) investigates the suicide of a woman in the building across the street, he has the help of his girlfriend (Kathleen Lasky) and an over-eager police officer (Ron White).

LOVE WITHOUT PITY (France, 1989)
Pro. Alain Rocca; Orion Classics   *Dir.* Eric Rochant   *Scr.* Eric Rochant   *Cine.* Pierre Novion
Ed. Michele Darmon   *S.d.* Thierry François   *Mu.* Gérard Torikian   *MPAA* R   *R.t.* 94 min.
Cast: Hippolyte Girardot, Mireille Perrier, Yvan Attal, Jean Marie Rollin, Cécile Mazan, Aline
Still, Paul Pavel.

A charming and unambitious waster and womanizer, Hippo (Hippolyte Girardot), falls in love
with beautiful, intellectual, and ambitious Nathalie (Mireille Perrier). Their tale of mismatched
love takes place against the dynamic backdrop of contemporary Paris.

MCBAIN
Pro. J. Boyce Harman, Jr.; Shapiro Glickenhaus Entertainment   *Dir.* James Glickenhaus   *Scr.*
James Glickenhaus   *Cine.* Robert M. Baldwin, Jr.   *Ed.* Jeffrey Wolf   *P.d.* Charles C. Bennett
Mu. Christopher Franke   *MPAA* R   *R.t.* 102 min.   *Cast:* Christopher Walken, Maria Conchita
Alonso, Michael Ironside, Steve James, Jay Patterson, T. G. Waites, Victor Argo, Hechter
Ubarry, Russell Dennis Baker, Chick Vennera, Luis Guzman, Forrest Compton, Dick Boccelli,
Nigel Redding.

In this action/adventure, Christopher Walken stars as the title character, a Vietnam veteran recalled to action in a Colombian revolution in order to avenge the death of the man who saved his
life in Vietnam (Chick Vennera).

MANNEQUIN TWO: ON THE MOVE
Pro. Edward Rugoff for Gladden Entertainment; Twentieth Century-Fox   *Dir.* Stewart Raffill
Scr. Edward Rugoff, David Isaacs, Ken Levine, and Betsy Israel; based on characters created by
Rugoff and Michael Gottlieb   *Cine.* Larry Pizer   *Ed.* John Rosenberg and Joan Chapman
P.d. William J. Creber   *A.d.* Norman B. Dodge, Jr.   *S.d.* Scot Jacobson   *Mu.* David McHugh
MPAA PG   *R.t.* 95 min.   *Cast:* Kristy Swanson, William Ragsdale, Meshach Taylor, Terry
Kiser, Stuart Pankin, Cynthia Harris, Andrew Hill Newman, John Edmondson, Phil Latella,
Mark Gray, Julie Foreman.

In this sequel to *Mannequin* (1987), a store-window mannequin once more comes to life. This
time, it is Jessie (Kristy Swanson), a beautiful medieval peasant girl who was put under the spell
of a wicked magician (Terry Kiser) for a thousand years to prevent her marrying a handsome
prince (William Ragsdale). When modern-day window dresser Jason (also played by Ragsdale)
removes her necklace, she comes to life—only to find herself pursued by the descendant of the
magician (also played by Kiser).

THE MARRYING MAN
Pro. David Permut for Hollywood Pictures, in association with Silver Screen Partners IV; Buena
Vista   *Dir.* Jerry Rees   *Scr.* Neil Simon   *Cine.* Donald E. Thorin   *Ed.* Michael Jablow   *P.d.*
William F. Matthews   *A.d.* Mark Mansbridge   *S.d.* Jim Duffy   *Mu.* David Newman   *MPAA* R
R.t. 105 min.   *Cast:* Kim Basinger, Alec Baldwin, Robert Loggia, Elisabeth Shue, Armand
Assante, Paul Reiser, Fisher Stevens, Peter Dobson, Steve Hytner, Jeremy Roberts, Big John
Studd, Tony Longo, Tom Milanovich, Tim Hauser, Carey Eidel.

In this Neil Simon comedy, wealthy toothpaste heir and playboy Charley Pearl (Alec Baldwin)
travels to Las Vegas to enjoy a bachelor-party weekend with his friends before his marriage to a
Hollywood studio mogul's daughter (Elisabeth Shue). There, he falls in love with a beautiful
lounge singer, Vicki Anderson (Kim Basinger), the girlfriend of gangster Bugsy Siegel (Armand
Assante). The film follows Charley and Vicki's stormy eight-year love life as they marry,
divorce, and remarry several times.

MEET THE APPLEGATES
Pro. Denise Di Novi for New World Pictures; Triton Pictures   *Dir.* Michael Lehmann   *Scr.*

Redbeard Simmons and Michael Lehmann *Cine.* Mitchell Dubin *Ed.* Norman Hollyn *P.d.*
Jon Hutman *A.d.* Kara Lindstrom and Adam Lustig *S.d.* Nancy Nye *Mu.* David Newman
MPAA R *R.t.* 90 min. *Cast:* Ed Begley, Jr., Stockard Channing, Dabney Coleman, Bobby
Jacoby, Cami Cooper, Glenn Shadix, Susan Barnes, Adam Biesk, Savannah Smith Boucher,
Phillip Arthur Ross, Steven Robert Ross.

When a breed of enormous Brazilian insects begins to suffer from the destruction of the rain
forests, it sends one of its families (who can metamorphose into human form) to the suburbs.
Their assignment is to blow up a nuclear power plant, thus eliminating destructive human life
from the planet. The plan backfires when the family adapts all too well to being human.

MEN OF RESPECT
Pro. Ephraim Horowitz for Central City Films and Arthur Goldblatt Productions; Columbia
Pictures *Dir.* William Reilly *Scr.* William Reilly *Cine.* Bobby Bukowski *Ed.* Elizabeth
Kling *P.d.* William Barclay *A.d.* Caty Maxey *Mu.* Misha Segal *MPAA* R *R.t.* 113 min.
Cast: John Turturro, Katherine Borowitz, Dennis Farina, Peter Boyle, Lilia Skala, Steven
Wright, Rod Steiger, Stanley Tucci, Carl Capotorto.

In this modern-day *Macbeth*, set in the New York underworld, ruthless Mike Battaglia (John
Turturro) kills mafia boss Charlie D'Amico (Rod Steiger) at the urging of his ambitious wife,
Ruthie (Katherine Borowitz), in order to usurp his place. Trouble and guilt quickly escalate, to
the predictably tragic finale.

MINDWALK (Austria, 1990)
Pro. Adrianna Aj Cohen for Atlas Production Company, in association with Mindwalk
Productions; Triton Pictures *Dir.* Bernt Capra *Scr.* Floyd Byars and Fritjof Capra; based on a
story by Bernt Capra and on the book *The Turning Point*, by Fritjof Capra *Cine.* Karl Kases
Ed. Jean Claude Piroue *Mu.* Philip Glass *MPAA* PG *R.t.* 112 min. *Cast:* Liv Ullmann, Sam
Waterston, John Heard, Ione Skye, Emmanuel Montes.

A physicist (Liv Ullman), a politician (Sam Waterston), and a poet (John Heard) meet on the
island of Mont-Saint-Michel and discuss their philosophies and worldviews.

THE MIRACLE (Ireland, 1991)
Pro. Stephen Woolley and Redmond Morris for Palace/Promenade; Miramax *Dir.* Neil Jordan
Scr. Neil Jordan *Cine.* Philippe Rousselot *Ed.* Joke Van Wijk *P.d.* Gemma Jackson *A.d.*
David Wilson *Mu.* Anne Dudley *MPAA* R *R.t.* 97 min. *Cast:* Beverly D'Angelo, Donal
McCann, Niall Byrne, Lorraine Pilkington, J. G. Devlin, Cathleen Delaney, Tom Hickey, Shane
Connaughton, Ruth McCabe.

Set in a small Irish seacoast town, this drama centers on a teenage boy, Jimmy (Niall Byrne),
and his friend, Rose (Lorraine Pilkington). Unhappy with their lives at home, they spend their
time together making up stories about the people who pass by. One, a beautiful American
woman, Renée (Beverly D'Angelo), so captures Jimmy's imagination that he falls in love with
her—only to discover that she is his mother who he thought died years ago.

MORTAL THOUGHTS
Pro. John Fiedler and Mark Tarlov for New Visions Entertainment and Polar Entertainment
Corporation, in association with Rufglen Films; Columbia Pictures *Dir.* Alan Rudolph *Scr.*
William Reilly and Claude Kerven *Cine.* Elliot Davis *Ed.* Tom Walls *P.d.* Howard
Cummings *A.d.* Robert K. Shaw, Jr. *S.d.* Beth Kushnick *Mu.* Mark Isham *MPAA* R *R.t.*
104 min. *Cast:* Demi Moore, Glenne Headly, Bruce Willis, John Pankow, Harvey Keitel, Billie
Neal, Frank Vincent, Kelly Cinnante.

Cynthia Kellogg (Demi Moore) relates to the police the events that led to the murder of the
abusive husband (Bruce Willis) of her best friend, Joyce Urbanski (Glenne Headly). Cynthia

tries to account for her role in the tragedy, but the police remain unsatisfied. By taking advantage of certain camera techniques, director Alan Rudolph has fashioned a clever mystery tale which also serves as an experiment in viewer identification.

MY HEROES HAVE ALWAYS BEEN COWBOYS
Pro. Martin Poll and E. K. Gaylord II; the Samuel Goldwyn Company   *Dir*. Stuart Rosenberg *Scr*. Joel Don Humphreys   *Cine*. Bernd Heinl   *Ed*. Dennis M. Hill   *Mu*. James Horner   *MPAA* PG   *R.t*. 106 min.   *Cast:* Scott Glenn, Kate Capshaw, Ben Johnson, Balthazar Getty, Tess Harper, Gary Busey, Mickey Rooney, Clarence Williams III, Dub Taylor, Clu Gulager, Dennis Fimple, Megan Parlen.

Rodeo cowboy H. D. Dalton (Scott Glenn) returns home to Oklahoma after suffering serious injuries, only to find that his father (Ben Johnson) has been committed to an old-age home by his sister (Tess Harper) and her husband (Gary Busey), and that his former girlfriend, Jolie (Kate Capshaw), has been widowed with two children. For the first time, H. D. is forced to take on responsibility when he brings his father home, renews his relationship with Jolie, and tries to save the homestead.

MYSTERY DATE
Pro. Cathleen Summers; Orion Pictures   *Dir*. Jonathan Wacks   *Scr*. Parker Bennett and Terry Runte   *Cine*. Oliver Wood   *Ed*. Tina Hirsch   *P.d*. John Willett   *A.d*. Willie Heslup   *S.d*. Kim MacKenzie   *Mu*. John Du Prez   *MPAA* PG-13   *R.t*. 99 min.   *Cast:* Ethan Hawke, Teri Polo, Brian McNamara, Fisher Stevens, B. D. Wong, Tony Rosato, Don Davis.

When a shy college student, Tom McHugh (Ethan Hawke), returns home for the summer and is smitten by a beautiful neighbor, Geena Matthews (Teri Polo), his brash older brother, Craig (Brian McNamara), sets him up on a date. The mystery date turns into a dangerous adventure when Craig loans Tom his car and credit cards, and Tom becomes embroiled in a case of mistaken identity involving his brother's shady business dealings and murder.

NECESSARY ROUGHNESS
Pro. Mace Neufeld and Robert Rehme; Paramount Pictures   *Dir*. Stan Dragoti   *Scr*. Rick Natkin and David Fuller   *Cine*. Peter Stein   *Ed*. John Wright and Steve Mirkovich   *P.d*. Paul Peters *S.d*. Lynn Wolverton Parker   *Mu*. Bill Conti   *MPAA* PG-13   *R.t*. 108 min.   *Cast:* Scott Bakula, Hector Elizondo, Robert Loggia, Harley Jane Kozak, Larry Miller, Sinbad, Fred Dalton Thompson, Rob Schneider, Jason Bateman, Andrew Bryniarski, Duane Davis, Michael Dolan, Marcus Giamatti, Kathy Ireland.

Newly hired football coach Gennero (Hector Elizondo) of Texas State University has the seemingly impossible task of forming a winning team from "real" students when the school's former coach and athletes are disqualified because of numerous playing violations. Scott Bakula also stars as Paul Blake, the team's new thirty-four-year-old quarterback, who is trying to make a comeback from his high school days.

THE NEVERENDING STORY II: THE NEXT CHAPTER (Germany, 1990)
Pro. Dieter Geissler for Time-Warner Co.; Warner Bros.   *Dir*. George Miller   *Scr*. Karin Howard; based on the novel *The Neverending Story*, by Michael Ende   *Cine*. Dave Connell *Ed*. Peter Hollywood and Chris Blunden   *P.d*. Bob Laing and Gotz Weidner   *Mu*. Robert Folk *MPAA* PG   *R.t*. 89 min.   *Cast:* Jonathan Brandis, Kenny Morrison, Clarissa Burt, Alexandra Johnes, Martin Umbach, John Wesley Shipp, Helena Michell, Chris Burton, Thomas Hill.

In this sequel to *The Neverending Story* (1984), an all-new cast plays the familiar characters of Bastian (Jonathan Brandis), Atreyu (Kenny Morrison), and the Empress (Alexandra Johnes). This time, Bastian himself enters the magic land of Fantasia to team up with Atreyu against a wicked sorceress, Xayide (Clarissa Burt), who threatens the realm of dreams and stories.

NIGHTSONGS
Pro. Thomas A. Fucci; FN Films *Dir.* Marva Nabili *Scr.* Marva Nabili *Cine.* Marva Nabili *Ed.* Fritz Liepe *A.d.* Mark Johnson *Mu.* R. I. P. Hayman *R.t.* 113 min. *Cast:* Mabel Kwong, David Lee, Victor Wong, Ida F. O. Chung.

Writer-director-cinematographer Marva Nabili examines the illusion of the American Dream as she portrays the life of an immigrant Asian family living in Manhattan. She focuses on a young immigrant Chinese Vietnamese woman (Mabel Kwong) who has recently come to live with her relatives, and on the family's teenage son (David Lee) and his difficulties adjusting to their new life.

NO SECRETS
Pro. Morgan Mason, John Hardy, and Shauna Shapiro Jackson for Curb Communications, in association with Mike Curb and Lester Korn; I.R.S. Releasing Corp. *Dir.* Dezso Magyar *Scr.* William Scheuer and Dezso Magyar *Cine.* Sandi Sissel *Ed.* Suzanne Fenn *P.d.* Clare Scarpulla *Mu.* Vinny Golia *MPAA* R *R.t.* 92 min. *Cast:* Adam Coleman Howard, Amy Locane, Heather Fairfield, Traci Lind.

Three teenage girls, Jennifer (Amy Locane), Claire (Heather Fairfield), and Sam (Traci Lind), are sent to a remote California ranch by their parents, where they meet a mysterious stranger, Manny (Adam Coleman Howard). They allow him to stay at the ranch, although it turns out he is an Army deserter suspected of murder, and each girl vies for his attention. Yet, all three girls promise there will be no secrets among them.

NOTHING BUT TROUBLE
Pro. Robert K. Weiss for Applied Action; Warner Bros. *Dir.* Dan Aykroyd *Scr.* Dan Aykroyd; based on a story by Peter Aykroyd *Cine.* Dean Cundey *Ed.* Malcolm Campbell and James Symons *P.d.* William Sandell *S.d.* Michael Taylor and James Tocci *Mu.* Michael Kamen *MPAA* PG-13 *R.t.* 94 min. *Cast:* Chevy Chase, Dan Aykroyd, John Candy, Demi Moore, Valri Bromfield, Taylor Negron, Bertila Damas, John Daveikis.

Yuppies Chris Thorne (Chevy Chase) and Diane Lightson (Demi Moore) end up with "nothing but trouble" when they drive through a small town called Valkenvania with two Brazilian billionaires and commit a minor traffic violation. When decrepit "hanging" judge Alvin Valkenheiser (Dan Aykroyd) pronounces a death sentence, Chris and Diane try to escape from the dungeons of the judge's Gothic mansion, with the judge's love-sick granddaughter (John Candy) in hot pursuit.

OLD EXPLORERS
Pro. David Herbert, William Pohlad, and Tom Jenz for River Road; Taurus *Dir.* William Pohlad *Scr.* William Pohlad; based on the play by James Cada and Mark Keller *Cine.* Jeffrey Laszlo *Ed.* Miroslav Janek *P.d.* Peter Stolz *Mu.* Billy Barber *MPAA* PG *R.t.* 100 min. *Cast:* José Ferrer, James Whitmore, Jeff Gadbois, Caroline Kaiser, William Warfield.

Two elderly widowers (José Ferrer and James Whitmore) engage in fantasy role-playing, imagining themselves on Indiana Jones-like quests in search of the Fountain of Youth, Atlantis, and the like, in order to escape the loneliness and tedium of old age.

ONE GOOD COP
Pro. Laurence Mark, in association with Silver Screen Partners IV; Hollywood Pictures *Dir.* Heywood Gould *Scr.* Heywood Gould *Cine.* Ralf Bode *Ed.* Richard Marks *P.d.* Sandy Veneziano *A.d.* Daniel E. Maltese and Rick Butler *S.d.* John Anderson and Justin Scoppa, Jr. *Mu.* David Foster and William Ross *MPAA* R *R.t.* 105 min. *Cast:* Michael Keaton, Rene Russo, Anthony LaPaglia, Kevin Conway, Rachel Ticotin, Tony Plana, Benjamin Bratt, Grace Johnston, Rhea Silver-Smith, Blair Swanson.

A principled New York City police officer, Artie Lewis (Michael Keaton), and his wife (Rene Russo) inherit a family—three little girls—from Artie's widowed partner when he is killed in the line of duty. When the authorities try to take the girls away from him because he and his wife do not earn enough money, Artie finds himself forced to break the law he has for so long worked to uphold.

OSCAR

Pro. Leslie Belzberg for Touchstone Pictures, in association with Silver Screen Partners IV; Buena Vista *Dir.* John Landis *Scr.* Michael Barrie and Jim Mulholland; based on the play by Claude Magnier *Cine.* Mac Ahlberg *Ed.* Dale Beldin *P.d.* Bill Kenney *A.d.* Wm. Ladd Skinner *S.d.* Rick T. Gentz, Nick Navarro, Sally Thornton, Richard F. Mays, Lawrence Hubbs, and Steven Wolff *Mu.* Elmer Bernstein *MPAA* PG *R.t.* 109 min. *Cast:* Sylvester Stallone, Chazz Palminteri, Peter Riegert, Don Ameche, Kirk Douglas, Vincent Spano, Ornella Muti, Joycelyn O'Brien, Marisa Tomei, Tim Curry, Elizabeth Barondes, Eddie Bracken, Linda Gray, Kurtwood Smith, Yvonne DeCarlo, Ken Howard, William Atherton, Martin Ferrero, Harry Shearer, Richard Romanus, Joey Travolta, Jim Mulholland.

This farce centers on one hectic morning in the life of gangster Angelo "Snaps" Provolone (Sylvester Stallone), who has made a deathbed promise to his father to quit his illegitimate business. He endures the myriad visits of minor characters ringing at the front door, mixed-up pieces of luggage, and other ever-mounting obstacles as he awaits a meeting with a group of bankers whom he hopes to join in order to "go straight."

OUT FOR JUSTICE

Pro. Steven Seagal and Arnold Kopelson; Warner Bros. *Dir.* John Flynn *Scr.* David Lee Henry *Cine.* Ric Waite *Ed.* Robert A. Ferretti *P.d.* Gene Rudolf *A.d.* Stephen M. Berger *S.d.* Gary Moreno and Ronald R. Reiss *Mu.* David Michael Frank *MPAA* R *R.t.* 91 min. *Cast:* Steven Seagal, William Forsythe, Jerry Orbach, Jo Champa, Shareen Mitchell, Sal Richards, Gina Gershon, Jay Acovone.

Martial-arts expert Steven Seagal returns to the screen, this time as Brooklyn police detective Gino Felino, who is seeking revenge on the savage killer (William Forsythe) who murdered Gino's partner. Although formulaic and light on plot, the film is replete with action sequences and propagates Seagal's image as a sensitive-but-deadly action hero.

OVERSEAS (France, 1991)

Pro. Serge Cohan-Solal for Paradise Productions; Aries Films *Dir.* Brigitte Roüan *Scr.* Brigitte Roüan, Philippe Le Guay, Christian Rullier, and Cedric Kahn; based on a story by Roüan *Cine.* Dominique Chapuis *Ed.* Yann Dedet and Laurent Roüan *A.d.* Roland Deville *Mu.* Pierre Foldes and Mathieu Foldes *R.t.* 96 min. *Cast:* Nicole Garcia, Brigitte Roüan, Marianne Basler, Philippe Galland, Yann Dedet, Bruno Todeschini.

Set in Algiers in the 1950's, this drama centers on the Franco-Algerian war and the lives of three sisters—Zon (Nicole Garcia), Malene (Brigitte Roüan), and Gritte (Marianne Basler). The same set of circumstances is seen through the eyes of each sister.

PAPER MASK (Great Britain, 1991)

Pro. Christopher Morahan for Film Four International, Granada, and British Screen; Castle Hill Productions, Inc. *Dir.* Christopher Morahan *Scr.* John Collee; based on his novel *Cine.* Nat Crosby *Ed.* Peter Coulson *P.d.* Caroline Hanania *A.d.* Andrew Rothschild *Mu.* Richard Harvey *MPAA* R *R.t.* 105 min. *Cast:* Paul McGann, Amanda Donahoe, Frederick Treves, Tom Wilkinson.

When a hospital employee (Paul McGann) grows dissatisfied with his work, he assumes the identity and responsibilities of a doctor who was killed in a car accident. His scheme succeeds—

partly due to the help of a kind nurse (Amanda Donohoe), who eventually falls in love with him—to the point that he risks becoming corrupted by his newly-acquired power.

A PAPER WEDDING (Canada, 1991)

Pro. Aimee Danis; Capitol Entertainment *Dir.* Michel Brault *Scr.* Jefferson Lewis and Andrée Pelletier *Cine.* Sylvain Brault *Ed.* Jacques Gagne *Mu.* Martin Fournier *R.t.* 90 min. *Cast:* Genevieve Bujold, Manuel Aranguiz, Dorothée Berryman, Teo Spychalski, Monique Lepage, Gilbert Sicotte.

Genevieve Bujold stars as a thirty-nine-year-old college professor who marries Pablo (Manuel Aranguiz), a Chilean political refugee, in order to prevent his being deported by the government. When they are forced to live together for three days to fool an immigration official (Gilbert Sicotte), they fall in love.

PARADISE

Pro. Scott Kroopf and Patrick Palmer for Touchstone Pictures, in association with Touchwood Pacific Partners I, Jean François Lepetit/Interscope Communications; Buena Vista Pictures *Dir.* Mary Agnes Donoghue *Scr.* Mary Agnes Donoghue; based on the film *Le Grand Chemin*, by Jean-Loup Hubert *Cine.* Jerzy Zielinski *Ed.* Eva Gardos and Debra McDermott *P.d.* Evelyn Sakash and Marcia Hinds *S.d.* Donna J. Hattin *Mu.* David Newman *MPAA* PG-13 *R.t.* 110 min. *Cast:* Melanie Griffith, Don Johnson, Elijah Wood, Thora Birch, Sheila McCarthy, Eve Gordon, Louise Latham, Greg Travis, Sarah Trigger, Timothy Erskine, Richard K. Olsen.

Ben and Lily Reed (Don Johnson and Melanie Griffith) have been unable to sustain their relationship after the death of their son—both have retreated into their own private worlds because neither can bear the guilt and pain. The arrival of Willard (Elijah Wood), the son of Lily's childhood friend, forces them to confront and accept their loss.

THE PASSION OF MARTIN

Pro. Evelyn Nussbaum and Alexander Payne *Dir.* Alexander Payne *Scr.* Alexander Payne *Cine.* David Rudd *Ed.* Alexander Payne *Mu.* John O'Kennedy *R.t.* 60 min. *Cast:* Charley Hayward, Lisa Zane.

Love evolves into obsession when a lonely photographer, Martin (Charley Hayward), begins a romance with a beautiful young woman, Rebecca (Lisa Zane), and his absurd fantasies lead to comic confrontations.

PASTIME

Pro. Eric Tynan Young and Robin B. Armstrong; Miramax Films *Dir.* Robin B. Armstrong *Scr.* D. M. Eyre, Jr. *Cine.* Tom Richmond *Ed.* Mark S. Westmore *P.d.* David W. Ford *S.d.* Ellen Totleben *Mu.* Lee Holdridge *MPAA* PG *R.t.* 94 min. *Cast:* William Russ, Glenn Plummer, Jeffrey Tambor, Dierdre O'Connel, Noble Willingham, Scott Plank.

This drama centers on a losing 1957 baseball team in California and two of its players: Roy Dean Bream (William Russ) is a forty-one-year-old relief pitcher fighting a heart problem, and Tyrone Debray (Glenn Plummer) is a seventeen-year-old up-and-coming black pitcher, both of whom are ostracized by their teammates.

THE PEOPLE UNDER THE STAIRS

Pro. Marianne Maddalena and Stuart M. Besser for Alive Films; Universal Pictures *Dir.* Wes Craven *Scr.* Wes Craven *Cine.* Sandi Sissel *Ed.* James Coblentz *P.d.* Bryan Jones *A.d.* Steven Lloyd Shroyer *S.d.* Molly Flanegin *Mu.* Don Peake *MPAA* R *R.t.* 102 min. *Cast:* Brandon Adams, Everett McGill, Wendy Robie, A. J. Langer, Ving Rhames, Sean Whalen, Bill Cobbs, Kelly Jo Minter, Conni Marie Brazelton.

In this horror story, a teenage boy, Fool (Brandon Adams), and two friends break into the house of his family's landlords (Everett McGill and Wendy Robie), intending to rob them. He instead discovers multiple horrors: "the people under the stairs," the couple's tortured daughter, and the house itself and its endless threats.

THE PERFECT WEAPON

Pro. Mark DiSalle and Pierre David; Paramount Pictures   *Dir*. Mark DiSalle   *Scr*. David Campbell Wilson   *Cine*. Russell Carpenter   *Ed*. Wayne Wahrman   *P.d*. Curtis Schnell   *A.d*. Colin D. Irwin   *S.d*. Archie D'Amico   *Mu*. Gary Chang   *MPAA* R   *R.t*. 112 min.   *Cast:* Jeff Speakman, John Dye, Mako, James Hong, Mariska Hargitay, Dante Basco, Seth Sakai, Toru Tanaka.

Martial-arts expert Jeff Sanders (Jeff Speakman) returns to Los Angeles to revenge the death of his friend and mentor, Kim (Mako), at the hands of an Asian crimelord (James Hong). The film has a thin plot but excellent martial-arts sequences.

PERFECTLY NORMAL (Canada, 1991)

Pro. Michael Burns; Four Seasons Entertainment   *Dir*. Yves Simoneau   *Scr*. Eugene Lipinski and Paul Quarrington; based on a story by Lipinski   *Cine*. Alain Dostie   *Ed*. Ronald Sanders   *P.d*. Anne Pritchard   *Mu*. Richard Gregoire   *MPAA* R   *R.t*. 104 min.   *Cast:* Robbie Coltrane, Michael Riley, Deborah Duchene, Eugene Lipinski, Kenneth Welsh, Jack Nichols.

A shy brewery worker, Renzo Parachi (Michael Riley), who plays hockey and loves the opera, picks up a gregarious hitchhiker, Alonzo Turner (Robbie Coltrane). Alonzo subsequently moves into Renzo's apartment and takes over his life—he encourages Renzo to date a waitress at the hockey rink, and he convinces Renzo to finance an Italian restaurant with opera singing, with Alonzo at the helm.

PINK NIGHTS

Pro. Phillip Koch and Sally Marschall; New World Films   *Dir*. Phillip Koch   *Scr*. Phillip Koch   *Cine*. Charlie Leiberman   *Ed*. Phillip Koch and Sally Marschall   *S.d*. Gail Specht   *Mu*. Jim Tullio and Jeffrey Vanston   *MPAA* PG   *R.t*. 87 min.   *Cast:* Kevin Anderson, Larry King, Peri Kaczmarek, Shaun Allen, Jessica Vitkus, Jonathan Michaels.

A lonely teenage boy, Danny (Kevin Anderson), suddenly finds himself with three girlfriends (Shaun Allen, Peri Kaczmarek, and Jessica Vitkus), to the surprise of not only himself but also his play-the-field best friend, Jeff (Larry King).

THE PIT AND THE PENDULUM

Pro. Albert Band for Full Moon Entertainment; Paramount Pictures   *Dir*. Stuart Gordon   *Scr*. Dennis Paoli; based on the short story by Edgar Allan Poe   *Cine*. Adolfo Bartoli   *Ed*. Andy Horvitch and Bert Glatstein   *A.d*. Giovanni Natalucci   *Mu*. Richard Band   *MPAA* R   *R.t*. 95 min.   *Cast:* Lance Henriksen, Rona De Ricci, Jonathan Fuller, Jeffrey Combs, Tom Towles, Stephen Lee, Frances Bay, Oliver Reed.

In this violent and bloody adaptation of an Edgar Allan Poe story, Torquemada (Lance Henriksen), an obsessed priest, tortures and kills suspected witches. When he falls in love with a beautiful woman, Maria (Rona De Ricci), he has her arrested as a suspected witch in order to trap her and her husband in his castle dungeon.

PIZZA MAN

Pro. Gary W. Goldstein for Megalomania   *Dir*. J. D. Athens   *Scr*. J. D. Athens   *Cine*. Fred Samia   *Ed*. J. D. Athens   *P.d*. Theodore Charles Smudde   *A.d*. Francisco Gutierrez   *S.d*. Jane van Tamelen   *Mu*. Daniel May   *R.t*. 90 min.   *Cast:* Bill Maher, Annabelle Gurwitch, David McKnight, Andy Romano, Sam Pancake, Bob DeLegall, Bryan Clark, Cathy Shambley, Ron Darian.

In this satiric comedy, a pizza delivery man, Elmo Bunn (Bill Maher), is determined to collect

$15.23 owed on a pizza that he delivered to a warehouse in East Hollywood. During his quest, he discovers an elaborate political conspiracy involving such public figures of the 1980's as Ronald Reagan (Bryan Clark), Michael Dukakis (Ron Darian), and Geraldine Ferraro (Cathy Shambley).

POINT BREAK

Pro. Peter Abrams and Robert L. Levy for Largo Entertainment and Abrams/Levy/Guerin; Twentieth Century-Fox *Dir.* Kathryn Bigelow *Scr.* W. Peter Iliff; based on the story by Rick King and Iliff *Cine.* Donald Peterman *Ed.* Howard Smith *P.d.* Peter Jamison *A.d.* Pamela Marcotte *S.d.* Ann Harris and Linda Spheeris *Mu.* Mark Isham *MPAA* R *R.t.* 122 min. *Cast:* Patrick Swayze, Keanu Reeves, Gary Busey, Lori Petty, John McGinley, James Le Gros, John Philbin, Bojesse Christopher, Julian Reyes, Daniel Beer.

Johnny Utah (Keanu Reeves), a cocky, young FBI agent assigned to solve a rash of bank robberies in Southern California, goes undercover among a group of maverick surfers. He meets Bodhi (Patrick Swayze), a master surfer and guru who has created a cult of outlaw adventurers who seek the ultimate thrill in the most dangerous pursuits, including crime. The men become locked in a duel in which their physical and mental powers are pushed to the edge.

POPCORN (USA and Jamaica, 1991)

Pro. Torben Johnke, Gary Goch, and Ashok Amritraj for Movie Partners, in association with Century Films; Studio Three Film Corp. *Dir.* Mark Herrier *Scr.* Tod Hackett; based on a story by Mitchell Smith *Cine.* Ronnie Taylor *Ed.* Stan Cole *P.d.* Peter Murton *A.d.* John Myhre *S.d.* Hugh Scaife *Mu.* Paul J. Zaza *MPAA* R *R.t.* 91 min. *Cast:* Jill Schoelen, Tom Villard, Dee Wallace Stone, Derek Rydall, Malcolm Danare, Elliott Hurst, Freddie Marie Simpson, Kelly Jo Minter, Yvette Solar, Tony Roberts, Ray Walston, Karen Witter, Bruce Glover.

In this take-off on 1950's horror films, a group of university film students and their professor (Tony Roberts) host an all-night horror marathon to raise money for their school. Amusement turns to mayhem as a mad killer runs rampant through the theater, and the nightmares of a student, Maggie (Jill Schoelen), become all too real.

THE POPE MUST DIE (Great Britain, 1991)

Pro. Stephen Woolley for Palace and British Screen, in association with Film Four International, Miramax Film Corporation, and Michael White; Miramax Films *Dir.* Peter Richardson *Scr.* Peter Richardson and Pete Richens *Cine.* Frank Gell *Ed.* Katherine Wenning *P.d.* John Ebden *MPAA* R *R.t.* 90 min. *Cast:* Robbie Coltrane, Beverly D'Angelo, Herbert Lom, Alex Rocco, Paul Bartel, Balthazar Getty, William Hootkins.

A corrupt cardinal (Alex Rocco) arranges to replace the dying Pope with a priest he can manipulate, but through a "clerical" error, goodnatured, guitar-playing Father Albinizi (Robbie Coltrane) gets the job and upsets the cardinal's plans for the Vatican.

PRAYER OF THE ROLLERBOYS

Pro. Robert Mickelson for Gaga Communications, Fox/Lorber, and Academy Entertainment, in association with JVC, TV Tokyo, and Mickelson-King- Iliff; Castle Hill *Dir.* Rick King *Scr.* W. Peter Iliff *Cine.* Phedon Papamichael *Ed.* Daniel Loewenthal *P.d.* Thomas A. Walsh *A.d.* Jay Klein *S.d.* Natalie K. Pope *Mu.* Stacy Widelitz *MPAA* R *R.t.* 94 min. *Cast:* Corey Haim, Patricia Arquette, Christopher Collet, J. C. Quinn, Julius Harris, Devin Clark, Mark Pellegrino.

Set in a devastated Los Angeles of the future, this film centers on a gang called the Rollerboys, led by Gary Lee (Christopher Collet), who preaches about a new world order while peddling drugs and fascism. Griffin (Corey Haim), a terrific skater, is recruited by police to infiltrate the gang and discover its headquarters.

PRISONERS OF THE SUN (Australia, 1991)
Pro. Charles Waterstreet, Denis Whitburn, and Brian A. Williams for Village Roadshow Pictures and Siege; Skouras Pictures *Dir.* Stephen Wallace *Scr.* Denis Whitburn and Brian A. Williams *Cine.* Russell Boyd *Ed.* Nicholas Beauman *P.d.* Bernard Hides *Mu.* David McHugh *MPAA* R *R.t.* 109 min. *Cast:* Bryan Brown, George Takei, Terry O'Quinn, John Bach, Toshi Shioya, Tetsu Watanabe, John Polson, Deborah Unger, John Clarke.

Based on a true story, this drama centers on the trial of Japanese officers, following World War II, charged with the mass murder of Australian prisoners of war at a camp on a South Seas island. Bryan Brown stars as the prosecutor who suspects Vice Admiral Baron Takahashi (George Takei) to be the culprit, but who is defeated in his quest to convict him by the Allies themselves for political reasons.

PROBLEM CHILD II
Pro. Robert Simonds for Imagine Films Entertainment; Universal Pictures *Dir.* Brian Levant *Scr.* Scott Alexander and Larry Karaszewski; based on characters created by Alexander and Karaszewski *Cine.* Peter Smokler *Ed.* Lois Freeman-Fox *P.d.* Maria Caso *A.d.* Allen Terry *S.d.* Damon Medlen *Mu.* David Kitay *MPAA* PG-13 *R.t.* 91 min. *Cast:* John Ritter, Michael Oliver, Jack Warden, Laraine Newman, Amy Yasbeck, Ivyann Schwan, Gilbert Gottfried, Paul Willson, Charlene Tilton.

In this sequel to *Problem Child* (1990), Junior (Michael Oliver) and his father, Ben (John Ritter), move to a new town, where Ben meets lonely divorcées of whom Junior does not approve, among them LaWanda Dumore (Laraine Newman). Junior, a "problem child," teams with an even worse problem, Trixie (Ivyann Schwan), in an effort to bring Ben and Trixie's mother (Amy Yasbeck) together.

PURE LUCK
Pro. Lance Hool and Sean Daniel; Universal Pictures *Dir.* Nadia Tass *Scr.* Herschel Weingrod and Timothy Harris *Cine.* David Parker *Ed.* Billy Weber *P.d.* Peter Wooley *A.d.* Hector Romero, Jr. *S.d.* Arturo Brito *Mu.* Jonathan Sheffer *MPAA* PG *R.t.* 96 min. *Cast:* Martin Short, Danny Glover, Sheila Kelley, Sam Wanamaker, Scott Wilson, Harry Shearer.

An accident-prone accountant, Eugene Proctor (Martin Short), is hired to track down a lost, similarly accident-prone heiress (Sheila Kelley) because her father (Sam Wanamaker) is convinced by his company's psychologist (Harry Shearer) that such a person is most likely to stumble onto her trail. Detective Raymond Campanella (Danny Glover) agrees to accompany Proctor, allowing him to believe that he is in charge of the investigation.

THE REFLECTING SKIN (Great Britain, 1990)
Pro. Dominic Anciano and Ray Burdis for British Screen, BBC Films, Zenith Productions, and Fugitive Films; Prestige, a division of Miramax Films *Dir.* Philip Ridley *Scr.* Philip Ridley *Cine.* Dick Pope *Ed.* Scott Thomas *A.d.* Rick Roberts *S.d.* Andrea French *Mu.* Nick Bicat *R.t.* 106 min. *Cast:* Viggo Mortensen, Lindsay Duncan, Jeremy Cooper, Sheila Moore, Duncan Fraser, David Longworth.

Told from the viewpoint of eight-year-old Seth (Jeremy Cooper), this film, set in the 1950's, depicts a nightmarish summer in the life of the young boy. A series of events—the kidnapping and murder of his friends, his father's suicide, and his brother's illness from radiation poisoning—cause Seth to believe that their odd neighbor, a widow (Lindsay Duncan), is a vampire responsible for these tragedies.

REQUIEM FOR DOMINIC (Austria, 1991)
Pro. Norbert Blecha for Terra Film; Hemdale *Dir.* Robert Dornhelm *Scr.* Michael Kohlmeier and Felix Mitterer *Cine.* Hans Selikovsky *Ed.* Ingrid Koller and Barbara Heraut *Mu.* Harald

Kloser *MPAA* R *R.t.* 89 min. *Cast:* Felix Mitterer, Viktoria Schubert, August Schmolzer, Angelica Schutz, Antonia Rados, Nikolas Vogel.

Based on a true story and using actual documentary footage taken during the revolution in Romania by director Robert Dornhelm, this film centers on Paul Weiss (Felix Mitterer), who returns to his native Romania during the 1989 revolution to see his old friend Dominic (August Schmolzer). When Paul learns that Dominic has been taken prisoner, has been accused of being a mass murderer, and is dying of gunshot wounds, he mounts an investigation to prove his friend's innocence—an investigation that puts his own life in danger.

RETURN TO THE BLUE LAGOON

Pro. William A. Graham for Price Entertainment/Randal Kleiser; Columbia Pictures *Dir.* William A. Graham *Scr.* Leslie Stevens; based on the novel *The Garden of God*, by Henry De Vere Stacpoole *Cine.* Robert Steadman *Ed.* Ronald J. Fagan *P.d.* Jon Dowding *A.d.* Paul Ammitzboll *Mu.* Basil Poledouris *MPAA* PG-13 *R.t.* 100 min. *Cast:* Milla Jovovich, Brian Krause, Lisa Pelikan, Courtney Phillips, Garette Patrick Ratliff, Emma James, Jackson Barton, Nana Coburn, Brian Blain, Peter Hehir.

In this weak sequel/remake of the adolescent coming-of-age film *The Blue Lagoon* (1980), the son, Richard (Brian Krause), of the original island couple (Brooke Shields and Christopher Atkins), ends up on the same island with a young girl, Lilli (Milla Jovovich), where the two grow into adolescence and fall in love.

RICH GIRL

Pro. Michael B. London for Film West; Studio Three Film Corporation *Dir.* Joel Bender *Scr.* Robert Elliot *Cine.* Levie Isaacks *Ed.* Mark Helfrich and Richard Candib *P.d.* Richard McGuire *S.d.* Charlie Doane *Mu.* Jay Chattaway *MPAA* R *R.t.* 96 min. *Cast:* Jill Schoelen, Don Michael Paul, Ron Karabatsos, Sean Kanan, Paul Gleason, Melanie Tomlin, Cherie Currie, Bentley Mitchum, Willie Dixon, Trudi Forestal.

Rich girl Courtney (Jill Schoelen) leaves her home, father (Paul Gleason), and fiancé (Sean Kanan) to work as a waitress in a nightclub. When she falls in love with the singer (Don Michael Paul) of the club's band, her privileged background and former fiancé threaten the relationship.

ROLLING STONES AT THE MAX

Pro. Michael Cohl, Andre Picard, and Martin Walters for BCL Group and IMAX Corp., in association with Promotour U.S., Inc. *Dir.* Julien Temple, Roman Kroitor, David Douglas, Noel Archambault, and Christine Strand *Cine.* David Douglas, Andrew Kitzanuk, and Haskell Wexler *Ed.* Daniel W. Blevins, Toni Myers, Jim Gable, and Lisa Regnier *Mu.* Rolling Stones *MPAA* R *R.t.* 89 min. *Cast:* Mick Jagger, Keith Richards, Charlie Watts, Ron Wood, Bill Wyman.

This feature-length film documents the 1990 Rolling Stones' "Steel Wheels/Urban Jungle" concert tour. Filmed with the innovative IMAX ("maximum image") technology, this picture allows the viewer a bird's-eye view of the concert, projected onto a five-story-high screen, and boasts an equally sophisticated sound system.

ROVER DANGERFIELD

Pro. Willard Carroll and Thomas L. Wilhite for Rodney Dangerfield, in association with Hyperion Pictures; Warner Bros. *Dir.* Jim George and Bob Seeley *Scr.* Rodney Dangerfield; based on a story by Dangerfield and Harold Ramis *Ed.* Tony Mizgalski *P.d.* Fred Cline *Mu.* David Newman *MPAA* G *R.t.* 74 min. *Voices:* Rodney Dangerfield, Susan Boyd, Ronnie Schell, Ned Luke, Shawn Southwick, Dana Hill, Sal Landi, Tom Williams, Chris Collins, Robert Bergen, Paxton Whitehead, Ron Taylor, Bert Kramer, Eddie Barth, Ralph Monaco, Tress MacNeille, Michael Sheehan, Lara Cody.

When a Las Vegas comedian/dog, Rover (voice of Rodney Dangerfield), is thrown over Hoover Dam by his owner's jealous boyfriend, he takes shelter on a farm. Although Rover finds that farm life is hard work, his newfound love for the collie next door (voice of Susan Boyd) sees him through. Dangerfield was the primary creative force behind this animated feature.

RUN

Pro. Raymond Wagner for Hollywood Pictures, in association with Silver Screen Partners IV; Buena Vista   *Dir.* Geoff Burrowes   *Scr.* Dennis Shryack and Michael Blodgett   *Cine.* Bruce Surtees   *Ed.* Jack Hofstra and Stephen E. Rivkin   *P.d.* John Willett   *A.d.* Willie Heslup   *S.d.* Elizabeth Wilcox   *Mu.* Phil Marshall   *MPAA* R   *R.t.* 91 min.   *Cast:* Patrick Dempsey, Kelly Preston, Ken Pogue, Alan C. Peterson, Christopher Lawford, Marc Strange.

Law school student Charlie Farrow (Patrick Dempsey) finds himself in big trouble when he winds up in a small town playing cards and winning big. One of the locals (Alan C. Peterson), becoming infuriated, attacks Charlie and gets killed—he was the son of the local crime boss, Halloran (Ken Pogue). Charlie now finds himself on the run and on his own against an entire town that is on Halloran's payroll.

SAM AND SARAH

Pro. Wanda Rohm and Robert Rothman; Full Circle Films   *Dir.* John Strysik   *Scr.* Robert Rothman and John Strysik   *Cine.* Michael Goi   *Ed.* John Strysik and Michael Goi   *P.d.* Thomas B. Mitchell   *Mu.* Craig Snider and Elliott Delman   *R.t.* 90 min.   *Cast:* Robert Rothman, Kathleen Sykora, Michael Bacarella, Carolyn Kodes.

In this drama, two homeless people become friends when Sam (Robert Rothman) saves Sarah (Kathleen Sykora) from a gang attack and she brings the injured Sam to her shelter in an abandoned building.

SCISSORS

Pro. Mel Pearl, Don Levin, and Hal Polaire for DDM Film Corp.; Vidmark   *Dir.* Frank De Felitta   *Scr.* Frank De Felitta; based on a story by Joyce Selznick   *Cine.* Anthony B. Richmond   *Ed.* John Schreyer   *P.d.* Craig Stearns   *A.d.* Randy Moore   *S.d.* Kara Lindstrom   *Mu.* Alfi Kabiljo   *R.t.* 105 min.   *Cast:* Sharon Stone, Steve Railsback, Ronny Cox, Michelle Phillips, Vicki Frederick.

An antique doll collector, Angie (Sharon Stone), fends off a red-bearded attacker in an elevator with a pair of scissors—then later finds herself hermetically sealed in an apartment with a dead, red-bearded man with scissors in his back, slowly being driven mad by some mysterious aggressor.

SEX, DRUGS, ROCK AND ROLL

Pro. Frederick Zollo; Avenue Pictures   *Dir.* John McNaughton   *Scr.* Eric Bogosian   *Cine.* Ernest Dickerson   *Ed.* Elena Maganini   *P.d.* John Arnone   *MPAA* R   *R.t.* 96 min.   *Cast:* Eric Bogosian.

Eric Bogosian brings to life ten vivid characters in John McNaughton's screen version of Bogosian's stage play *Sex, Drugs, Rock and Roll*.

SHATTERED

Pro. Wolfgang Petersen, John Davis, and David Korda, for Bodo Scriba/Willi Baer/Capella Films, in association with Davis Entertainment Company; Metro-Goldwyn-Mayer   *Dir.* Wolfgang Petersen   *Scr.* Wolfgang Petersen; based on the novel *The Plastic Nightmare*, by Richard Neely   *Cine.* Laszlo Kovacs   *Ed.* Hannes Nikel and Glenn Farr   *P.d.* Gregg Fonseca   *A.d.* Bruce Miller   *S.d.* Dorree Cooper   *Mu.* Alan Silvestri   *MPAA* R   *R.t.* 97 min.   *Cast:* Tom Berenger, Bob Hoskins, Greta Scacchi, Joanne Whalley-Kilmer, Corbin Bernsen, Theodore Bikel, Scott Getlin.

After a devastating car crash, Dan Merrick (Tom Berenger) struggles to overcome his amnesia and to resume his life. His suspicions about the behavior of his wife, Judith (Greta Scacchi), both before and after the accident, however, lead him to Gus Klein (Bob Hoskins), a private detective who assists Dan in discovering the shocking truth about his past.

SHIPWRECKED (Norway, 1991)

Pro. John M. Jacobsen for Walt Disney Pictures; Buena Vista *Dir.* Nils Gaup *Scr.* Nils Gaup, Bob Foss, Greg Dinner, and Nick Thiel; based on the novel *Haakon Haakonsen*, by O. V. Falck-Ytter *Cine.* Erling Thurmann-Andersen *Ed.* Niels Pagh-Andersen *P.d.* Harald Egede-Nissen and Roger Cain *A.d.* Per Mörk and John Miles *S.d.* Dagfinn Kleppan, Jon Arvesen, Paul Delieu, and Hroar Hesselberg *Mu.* Patrick Doyle *MPAA* PG *R.t.* 90 min. *Cast:* Stian Smestad, Gabriel Byrne, Louisa Haigh, Trond Peter Stamsö Munch, Kjell Stormoen, Björn Sundquist, Eva Von Hanno.

A fourteen-year-old boy named Hakon (Stian Smestad) is forced to sign on a cargo ship in order to save his family's farm. Once at sea, he harbors a stowaway girl, Mary (Louisa Haigh), and incurs the wrath of the ship's first mate, Merrick (Gabriel Byrne), who is actually a dangerous pirate in disguise. Eventually, after being stranded alone on a deserted South Sea island, the boy vanquishes the pirate, captures his treasure, and returns home a wealthy and self-possessed young man.

SHOUT

Pro. Robert Simonds; Universal Pictures *Dir.* Jeffrey Hornaday *Scr.* Joe Gayton *Cine.* Robert Brinkmann *Ed.* Seth Flaum *P.d.* William F. Matthews *A.d.* P. Michael Johnston *S.d.* Jim Duffy *Mu.* Randy Edelman *MPAA* PG-13 *R.t.* 89 min. *Cast:* John Travolta, James Walters, Heather Graham, Richard Jordan, Linda Fiorentino, Scott Coffey, Glenn Quinn, Frank von Zerneck, Michael Bacall.

Set in a small Texas town in the 1950's, this drama centers on a teenage boy, Jesse Tucker (James Walters), who lives in an orphanage run by a petty tyrant (Richard Jordan). Music teacher Jack Cabe (John Travolta) wins the boys' friendship when he introduces them to rock-and-roll music, but then he must flee when an outstanding warrant for his arrest is discovered by the sheriff.

SHOWDOWN IN LITTLE TOKYO

Pro. Mark L. Lester and Martin E. Caan; Warner Bros. *Dir.* Mark L. Lester *Scr.* Stephen Glantz and Caliope Brattlestreet *Cine.* Mark Irwin *Ed.* Steven Kemper and Robert A. Ferretti *P.d.* Craig Stearns *A.d.* Bill Rae *S.d.* Ellen Totleben *Mu.* David Michael Frank *MPAA* R *R.t.* 76 min. *Cast:* Dolph Lundgren, Brandon Lee, Cary-Hiroyuki Tagawa, Tia Carrere, Toshiro Obata.

Two police officers—one a Caucasian reared in Japan, Detective Kenner (Dolph Lundgren), and the other an Asian American reared in California, Johnny Murata (Brandon Lee)—team up to fight a major Japanese criminal organization and its leader (Cary-Hiroyuki Tagawa), who murdered Kenner's parents.

SLACKER

Pro. Richard Linklater for Detour Filmproduction; Orion Classics *Dir.* Richard Linklater *Scr.* Richard Linklater *Cine.* Lee Daniel *Ed.* Scott Rhodes *A.d.* Debbie Pastor *MPAA* R *R.t.* 97 min. *Cast:* Richard Linklater, Rudy Basquez, Jean Caffeine, Jan Hockey, Stephan Hockey, Mark James, Samuel Dietert, Bob Boyd, Jennifer Schaudies.

Employing a cast of nearly one hundred, most of whom are not professional actors, this independent film by twenty-nine-year-old producer/director/writer Richard Linklater examines the lives of "slackers" in Austin, Texas. These people are mostly in their twenties and find themselves between school and a career, pondering the meaning of life and generally avoiding responsibility.

THE SLEAZY UNCLE (Italy, 1989)
Pro. Leo Pescarolo and Guido De Laurentiis for Castle Hill; Quartet Films *Dir.* Franco Brusati *Scr.* Leo Benvenuti, Piero De Bernardi, and Franco Brusati; based on a story by Brusati *Cine.* Romano Albani *Ed.* Gianfranco Amicucci *P.d.* Dante Ferretti *S.d.* Francesca Lo Schiavo *Mu.* Stefano Marcucci *R.t.* 105 min. *Cast:* Vittorio Gassman, Giancarlo Giannini, Andrea Ferreol, Kim Rossi Stuart, Beatrice Palme, Simona Cavallari, Stefania Sandrelli.

The life of a staid businessman, Riccardo (Giancarlo Giannini), is turned upside down when a long-lost uncle (Vittorio Gassman) appears. Conniving and lecherous Uncle Luca takes Riccardo's money as well as his woman—yet earns his respect as Riccardo discovers his uncle not only has an engaging personality but also is an internationally respected poet.

THE SPIRIT OF '76
Pro. Susie Landau and Simon Edery for Castle Rock, Black Diamond, and Commercial Pictures; Columbia *Dir.* Lucas Reiner *Scr.* Lucas Reiner; based on a story by Roman Coppola and Reiner *Cine.* Stephen Lighthill *Ed.* Glen Scantlebury *P.d.* Daniel Talpers *A.d.* Isabella Kirkland *Mu.* David Nichtern *MPAA* PG-13 *R.t.* 82 min. *Cast:* David Cassidy, Olivia d'Abo, Geoff Hoyle, Leif Garrett.

Three time travelers (David Cassidy, Olivia d'Abo, and Geoff Hoyle) journey from the year 2176 to 1976 in order to get a copy of the U.S. Constitution.

SPLIT
Pro. Barbara Horscraft for Starker Films; AIP *Dir.* Chris Shaw *Scr.* Chris Shaw *Cine.* Chris Shaw *Ed.* Chris Shaw *P.d.* Chris Shaw *Mu.* Chris Shaw, Robert Shaw, and Ugi Tojo *R.t.* 84 min. *Cast:* Timothy Dwight, Chris Shaw, Joan Bechtel, John Flynn.

In this grim futuristic parable set in San Francisco, evil humanoids have taken control of Earth. One man, Starker (Timothy Dwight), eludes them, and with him carries humanity's hope for salvation.

STEPPING OUT
Pro. Lewis Gilbert; Paramount Pictures *Dir.* Lewis Gilbert *Scr.* Richard Harris; based on his play *Cine.* Alan Hume *Ed.* Humphrey Dixon *P.d.* Peter Mullins *A.d.* Alicia Keywan *S.d.* Steve Shewchuk *Mu.* Peter Matz *MPAA* PG *R.t.* 105 min. *Cast:* Liza Minnelli, Shelley Winters, Bill Irwin, Ellen Greene, Julie Walters, Robyn Stevan, Jane Krakowski, Sheila McCarthy, Andrea Martin, Carol Woods, Luke Reilly, Nora Dunn.

Liza Minnelli stars as Mavis Turner, a former professional dancer who sings in bars with her boyfriend and teaches an amateur tap-dance class on the side. When she is asked to have the class perform in a charity show, she rises to the occasion and molds them into a cohesive and competent group.

STONE COLD
Pro. Yoram Ben Ami for Stone Group Pictures and Mace Neufeld/Yoram Ben Ami/Walter Doniger; Columbia Pictures *Dir.* Craig R. Baxley *Scr.* Walter Doniger *Cine.* Alexander Gruszynski *Ed.* Mark Helfrich *P.d.* John Mansbridge and Richard Johnson *S.d.* Phil Shirey *Mu.* Sylvester Levay *MPAA* R *R.t.* 93 min. *Cast:* Brian Bosworth, Lance Henriksen, William Forsythe, Arabella Holzbog, Sam McMurray, Richard Gant, Paulo Tocha, David Tress.

In this action/adventure film, former football linebacker Brian Bosworth stars as a maverick police officer persuaded by FBI agents to go undercover and infiltrate the Brotherhood, an evil motorcycle gang led by Chains (Lance Henriksen). Although light on plot, the film is replete with action sequences.

STRICTLY BUSINESS
Pro. Andre Harrell and Pam Gibson, in association with Island World; Warner Bros. *Dir*. Kevin Hooks *Scr*. Pam Gibson and Nelson George *Cine*. Zoltan David *Ed*. Richard Nord *P.d*. Ruth Ammon *A.d*. Rowena Rowling *S.d*. Sonja Roth *Mu*. Michel Colombier *MPAA* PG-13 *R.t*. 84 min. *Cast:* Tommy Davidson, Joseph C. Phillips, Anne-Marie Johnson, Halle Berry, David Marshall Grant, Jon Cypher, Sam Jackson, Kim Coles, Paul Butler, James McDaniel, Paul Provenza, Annie Golden, Sam Rockwell, Ira Wheeler, Sarah Stavrou.

When Waymon (Joseph C. Phillips), an uptight, ambitious young African-American corporate executive, falls for a luscious nightclub dancer (Halle Berry), he loses his grip on business and nearly loses his job. His streetwise buddy, Bobby (Tommy Davidson), saves the day, however, by teaching Waymon that he does not need to sacrifice joy to win success.

SUBURBAN COMMANDO
Pro. Howard Gottfried; New Line Cinema *Dir*. Burt Kennedy *Scr*. Frank Cappello *Cine*. Bernd Heinl *Ed*. Terry Stokes *P.d*. Ivo Cristante *Mu*. David Michael Frank *MPAA* PG *R.t*. 90 min. *Cast:* Hulk Hogan, Christopher Lloyd, Shelley Duvall, Larry Miller, William Ball, JoAnn Dearing, Jack Elam, Michael Faustino, Tony Longo, Mark Calaway, Laura Mooney, Dennis Burkley, Luis Contreras, Christopher Neame, Jennifer Delora.

This science fiction/fantasy centers on an alien renegade warrior, Shep Ramsey (Hulk Hogan), who lands on Earth and rents an apartment from a suburban couple, Charlie (Christopher Lloyd) and Jenny (Shelley Duvall) Wilcox. When Charlie discovers the truth about their new tenant, the two join forces against the bounty hunters sent to find Ramsey, and become friends.

SUPERSTAR: THE LIFE AND TIMES OF ANDY WARHOL
Pro. Chuck Workman for Marilyn Lewis Entertainment Ltd.; Aries Film *Dir*. Chuck Workman *Scr*. Chuck Workman *Cine*. Burleigh Wartes *Ed*. Chuck Workman *R.t*. 85 min. *Cast:* Andy Warhol, Holly Woodlawn, Dennis Hopper, Ultra Violet, Tom Wolfe, Sylvia Miles, Irving Blum, Paul Warhola, Fran Lebowitz.

This documentary features the enigmatic life of commercial artist Andy Warhol. Incorporating views of his art with interviews of Warhol himself and contemporary footage of friends and associates, writer-director-producer Chuck Workman examines Warhol's contributions to the art world and his era.

SWAN LAKE: THE ZONE (*Lebedyne ozero: Zona*. Ukraine and USSR, 1990)
Pro. Virko Baley and Yuri Illienko for Video Ukraine and Kobza International, in association with Swea Sov Consult (Sweden) and Dovzhenko Film Studio (Ukraine); Zeitgeist Films *Dir*. Yuri Illienko *Scr*. Sergei Paradjanov and Yuri Illienko; based on short stories by Paradjanov *Cine*. Yuri Illienko *Ed*. Eleanora Summovska *P.d*. Oleksandr Danylenko *Mu*. Virko Baley and Yuri Illienko *R.t*. 96 min. *Cast:* Victor Solovyov, Liudmyla Yefymenko, Pylyp Illienko, Maya Bulhakova, Victor Demertasch, M. Tzuzura, V. Tzybenko, O. Danylenko, S. Povarov, V. Kotko, A. Kuzmenko, O. Nikel-Shyskin, I. Demianov, A. Nykyforov, S. Kharun.

In this Soviet drama, a man (Victor Solovyov) escapes from prison and is helped by a woman (Liudmyla Yefymenko) until her jealous young son (Pylyp Illienko) turns him in to the authorities. Boasting little dialogue, the film mixes fantasy with reality to make a grim statement on Soviet prison life.

SWEET TALKER (Australia, 1991)
Pro. Ben Gannon for New Visions Pictures and New Town; Seven Arts through New Line Cinema *Dir*. Michael Jenkins *Scr*. Tony Morphett; based on a story by Bryan Brown and Morphett *Cine*. Russell Boyd *Ed*. Neil Thumpston and Sheldon Kahn *P.d*. John Stod-

dart *A.d.* John Wingrove *Mu.* Richard Thompson and Peter Filleul *MPAA* PG *R.t.* 88 min. *Cast:* Bryan Brown, Karen Allen, Justin Rosniak, Chris Haywood, Bill Kerr, Bruce Spence.

Harry Reynolds (Bryan Brown), a con artist recently released from prison, tries to sell a phony investment scheme to the residents of a small coastal town. Harry's sense of decency rises to the surface, however, when he falls in love with his landlady (Karen Allen), a single mother with a young son (Justin Rosniak).

THE TAKING OF BEVERLY HILLS
Pro. Graham Henderson for Nelson Entertainment; Columbia Pictures *Dir.* Sidney J. Furie *Scr.* Rick Natkin, David Fuller, and David J. Burke; based on a story by Sidney J. Furie, Natkin, and Fuller *Cine.* Frank Johnson *Ed.* Anthony Gibbs *P.d.* Peter Lamont *Mu.* Jan Hammer *MPAA* R *R.t.* 95 min. *Cast:* Ken Wahl, Matt Frewer, Harley Jane Kozak, Robert Davi, Lee Ving James, Branscombe Richmond, Lyman Ward, William Prince, George Wyner.

In this weak action/adventure, several disgruntled former police officers fake a toxic spill in Beverly Hills in order to evacuate the residents and loot and pillage the area. Quarterback Boomer Hayes (Ken Wahl), ignorant of the evacuation and, thus, the only resident left, joins forces with one of the conspirators (Matt Frewer) to foil the bad guys.

TALKIN' DIRTY AFTER DARK
Pro. Patricia A. Stallone; New Line Cinema *Dir.* Topper Carew *Scr.* Topper Carew *Cine.* Misha Suslov *Ed.* Claudia Finkle *P.d.* Naomi Shohan *A.d.* Daniel Whifler and Bruton Jones *S.d.* Larry Dias *MPAA* R *R.t.* 86 min. *Cast:* Martin Lawrence, John Witherspoon, Jedda Jones, "Tiny" Lister, Jr., Phyllis Yvonne Stickney, Darryl Sivad.

Set in a comedy club in a black Los Angeles neighborhood, this film centers on Terry (Martin Lawrence), an aspiring stand-up comic. Featuring real-life stand-up comics, the picture follows their on- as well as off-stage antics.

TAXI BLUES (USSR and France, 1990)
Pro. Marin Karmitz and Aleksandr Golutva for Lenfilm, ASK Eurofilm, MK2 Prods., and La Sept; MK2 Productions *Dir.* Pavel Lounguine *Scr.* Pavel Lounguine *Cine.* Denis Evstigneyev *Ed.* Elizabeth Guido *A.d.* Valeri Yurkevitch *Mu.* Vladimir Chekassine *R.t.* 110 min. *Cast:* Piotr Mamonov, Piotr Zaitchenko, Vladimir Kachpur, Natalia Koliakanova, Hal Singer, Elena Safonova, Sergei Gazarov.

This statement on modern Soviet society depicts the lives of two men: one a drunken Jewish musician, Liocha (Piotr Mamonov); the other a macho cab driver, Shlikov (Piotr Zaitchenko). They meet when Liocha neglects to pay his taxi fare and Shlikov finds him and takes his saxophone as payment. Thus follows a love-hate relationship between the two as Shlikov sobers up Liocha and puts him to work, and Liocha turns around and becomes a famous musician virtually overnight.

TED AND VENUS
Pro. Randolf Turrow and William Talmadge for Krishna Shah, Gondola Films, and L.A. Dreams; Double Helix *Dir.* Bud Cort *Scr.* Paul Ciotti and Bud Cort; based on a story by Ciotti *Cine.* Dietrich Lohmann *Ed.* Katina Zinner and Peter Zinner *P.d.* Lynn Christopher *A.d.* Robert Stover *S.d.* Gene Serdena *Mu.* David Robbins *MPAA* R *R.t.* 100 min. *Cast:* Bud Cort, Jim Brolin, Kim Adams, Carol Kane, Pamella D'Pella, Brian Thompson, Bettye Ackerman, Woody Harrelson, Timothy Leary, Andrea Martin, Martin Mull, Tracy Reiner, Vincent Schiavelli, Arleen Sorkin, Rhea Perlman, Gena Rowlands.

When a weird poet/beach bum, Ted (Bud Cort), becomes obsessed with a beautiful social worker, Linda (Kim Adams), his bizarre antics force Linda to take legal action.

TERMINI STATION (Canada, 1991)

Pro. Allan King for Saturday Plays; Northern Arts Entertainment *Dir.* Allan King *Scr.* Colleen Murphy *Cine.* Bryan R. R. Hebb *Ed.* Gordon McClellan *P.d.* Lillian Sarafinchan *Mu.* Mychael Danna *R.t.* 105 min. *Cast:* Colleen Dewhurst, Megan Follows, Gordon Clapp, Debra McGrath, Elliott Smith, Leon Pownall.

Set in Canada, this drama centers on a dysfunctional family that is haunted by its dark past. Aging alcoholic mother Molly Dushane (Colleen Dewhurst) makes life miserable for her son Harvey (Gordon Clapp)—with whom she lives and who threatens to put her in a hospital—and his brow-beaten wife, Liz (Debra McGrath). Meanwhile, angry daughter Micheline (Megan Follows), who works part-time as a prostitute, opens old wounds with her mother that provoke the film's climax.

THOUSAND PIECES OF GOLD

Pro. Kenji Yamamoto and Nancy Kelly for American Playhouse Theatrical Films and Maverick Films International Ltd., in association with Film Four International; Greycat Films *Dir.* Nancy Kelly *Scr.* Anne Makepeace *Cine.* Bobby Bukowski *Ed.* Kenji Yamamoto *P.d.* Dan Bishop *S.d.* Dianna Treas *Mu.* Gary Remal Malkin *R.t.* 105 min. *Cast:* Rosalind Chao, Chris Cooper, Michael Paul Chan, Dennis Dun.

In this Western, a young Chinese woman, Lalu (Rosalind Chao)— renamed Polly—is sold by her father to a gambler and bar manager, Hong King (Michael Paul Chan), and goes to live in an Idaho mining town. Forced to work as a prostitute, Polly shows her courage and strength in this story of survival in the American West.

A TIME TO DIE

Pro. Joseph Merhi, Richard Pepin, and Charla Driver; PM Entertainment Group, Inc. *Dir.* Charles T. Kanganis *Scr.* Charles T. Kanganis *Cine.* Ken Blakey *Ed.* Paul Volk *P.d.* Greg Martin *Mu.* Louis Febre *MPAA* R *R.t.* 95 min. *Cast:* Traci Lords, Jeff Conaway, Robert Miano, Jesse Thomas, Nitchie Barrett, Richard Roundtree, Bradford Bancroft, Gino Dente, Daphne Cheung, Victor Vadales, Manuel Cabral, Nicole Picard, Jan Flame, Jeannie Martinez.

Traci Lords stars as a photographer who was falsely convicted on drug charges and who is now working for the police department as part of her parole. When she witnesses the murder of a pimp by the corrupt police officer (Robert Miano) who arrested her, she fears for her life.

TOO MUCH SUN

Pro. Lisa M. Hansen for CineTel Films, Inc.; New Line Cinema *Dir.* Robert Downey *Scr.* Robert Downey, Laura Ernst, and Al Schwartz; based on a story by Schwartz *Cine.* Robert Yeoman *Ed.* Joe D'Augustine *P.d.* Shawn Hausman *Mu.* David Robbins *MPAA* R *R.t.* 110 min. *Cast:* Robert Downey, Jr., Eric Idle, Andrea Martin, Jim Haynie, Laura Ernst, Leo Rossi, Ralph Macchio, Howard Duff, Jennifer Rubin, Lara Harris, James Hong, Melissa Jenkins.

A conniving priest (Jim Haynie) convinces a dying man (Howard Duff) to leave his money to the church if his children do not produce a grandchild within a year. The clincher is that both son (Eric Idle) and daughter (Andrea Martin) are homosexual—but that does not keep them from trying.

TOY SOLDIERS

Pro. Jack E. Freedman, Wayne S. Williams, and Patricia Herskovic, in association with Island World; TriStar Pictures *Dir.* Daniel Petrie, Jr. *Scr.* Daniel Petrie, Jr., and David Koepp; based on the novel by William P. Kennedy *Cine.* Thomas Burstyn *Ed.* Michael Kahn *P.d.* Chester Kaczenski *Mu.* Robert Folk *MPAA* R *R.t.* 112 min. *Cast:* Sean Astin, Wil Wheaton, Keith Coogan, Andrew Divoff, Louis Gossett, Jr., Denholm Elliott, T. E. Russell, George Perez, Mason Adams, Michael Champion, R. Lee Ermey, Jerry Orbach.

Spoiled, rich boys at a Virginia prep school, led by ringleader Billy Tepper (Sean Astin), play pranks and indulge in other inane activities, under the nose of the headmaster (Louis Gossett, Jr.). When a terrorist band takes over the school and holds its students hostage—led by the son (Andrew Divoff) of an imprisoned drug lord, demanding his father's release—the boys must work together to outsmart their captors and save their lives.

TRUE COLORS

Pro. Herbert Ross and Laurence Mark; Paramount Pictures   *Dir.* Herbert Ross   *Scr.* Kevin Wade   *Cine.* Dante Spinotti   *Ed.* Robert Reitano and Stephen A. Rotter   *P.d.* Edward Pisoni *A.d.* William Barclay   *S.d.* Robert J. Franco   *Mu.* Trevor Jones   *MPAA* R   *R.t.* 111 min.   *Cast:* John Cusack, James Spader, Imogen Stubbs, Mandy Patinkin, Richard Widmark, Dina Merrill, Philip Bosco, Paul Guilfoyle.

Ambition and greed are the driving forces behind the actions of Peter Burton (John Cusack): He drops out of law school to work for a U.S. senator in Washington; he steals the blue-blooded girlfriend (Imogen Stubbs) of his former college buddy, Tim (James Spader), and then betrays him; and he blackmails the senator to further his own political ambitions.

TRUE IDENTITY

Pro. Carol Baum and Teri Schwartz for Touchstone Pictures, in association with Silver Screen Partners IV; Buena Vista   *Dir.* Charles Lane   *Scr.* Andy Breckman   *Cine.* Tom Ackerman   *Ed.* Kent Beyda   *P.d.* John DeCuir, Jr.   *A.d.* Geoff Hubbard   *S.d.* Karen A. O'Hara and Leslie Bloom   *Mu.* Marc Marder   *MPAA* R   *R.t.* 92 min.   *Cast:* Lenny Henry, Frank Langella, Charles Lane, J. T. Walsh, Anne-Marie Johnson, Andreas Katsulas, Michael McKean, Peggy Lipton, Bill Raymond, James Earl Jones, Darnell Williams, Christopher Collins, Melvin Van Peebles.

Lenny Henry stars as Miles Pope, an African-American New York actor, who, with the help of his friend Duane (director Charles Lane), disguises himself as a white man in order to escape a gangster (Frank Langella).

TRULY, MADLY, DEEPLY (Great Britain, 1991)

Pro. Robert Cooper; the Samuel Goldwyn Company   *Dir.* Anthony Minghella   *Scr.* Anthony Minghella   *Cine.* Remi Adefarasin   *Ed.* John Stothart   *P.d.* Barbara Gasnold   *Mu.* Barrington Pheloung   *R.t.* 107 min.   *Cast:* Juliet Stevenson, Alan Rickman, Bill Paterson, Michael Maloney, Jenny Howe.

Suffering severe depression following the death of her live-in lover, Jamie (Alan Rickman), Nina (Juliet Stevenson) retreats increasingly into the house she is having renovated. When her extreme mourning actually brings Jamie back from the dead, at first rejoicing at her good fortune, Nina finds him to be more a burden than an asset, and in the end, she is forced to choose between the living and the dead.

TRUST

Pro. Bruce Weiss for Zenith, in association with True Fiction Pictures; Fine Line Features   *Dir.* Hal Hartley   *Scr.* Hal Hartley   *Cine.* Michael Spiller   *Ed.* Nick Gomez   *P.d.* Daniel Ouellette *A.d.* Julie Fabian   *Mu.* Phil Reed   *MPAA* R   *R.t.* 90 min.   *Cast:* Adrienne Shelly, Martin Donovan, Merritt Nelson, John MacKay, Edie Falco.

Two young people, a pregnant teenager—Maria (Adrienne Shelly)—and an electronics expert—Matthew (Martin Donovan)—both kicked out of their homes by their parents, meet and fall in love.

TWENTY-NINTH STREET

Pro. David Permut; Twentieth Century-Fox   *Dir.* George Gallo   *Scr.* George Gallo; based on a story by Frank Pesce and James Franciscus   *Cine.* Steven Fierberg   *Ed.* Kaja Fehr   *P.d.* Robert

Ziembicki *A.d.* Dayna Lee *S.d.* Jerry Hall and Hugh Scaife *Mu.* William Olvis *MPAA* R
R.t. 101 min. *Cast:* Danny Aiello, Anthony LaPaglia, Lainie Kazan, Frank Pesce, Robert
Forster, Ron Karabatsos, Rick Aiello, Vic Manni, Pete Antico, Donna Magnani, Richard Olsen,
Philip Ciccone, Paul Lazar, Leonard Termo, Karen Duffy, Tony Monte.

Screenwriter George Gallo's directorial debut is based on the real-life story of Frank Pesce,
Jr., who appears in the film as his own elder brother. Anthony LaPaglia plays Pesce, a young man
cursed with good luck, ever irritating his father (Danny Aiello), who seems to bear the opposite
curse.

TWENTY-ONE

Pro. Morgan Mason and John Hardy for Curb Communications and Anglo International Films
Limited; Triton Pictures *Dir.* Don Boyd *Scr.* Zoe Heller and Don Boyd; based on a story by
Boyd *Cine.* Keith Goddard *Ed.* David Spiers *P.d.* Roger Murray-Leach *A.d.* Terrie Wixon
Mu. Phil Sawyer *MPAA* R *R.t.* 101 min. *Cast:* Patsy Kensit, Jack Shepherd, Patrick Ryecart,
Rufus Sewell, Sophie Thompson, Maynard Eziashi.

Patsy Kensit stars as a promiscuous, young Englishwoman who indulges in several love
affairs and settles in New York City.

TWO EVIL EYES

Pro. Achille Manzotti and Dario Argento for Heron Communications and Gruppo Bema/ADC;
Taurus Entertainment *Dir.* George Romero ("The Curious Facts in the Case of Mr. Valdemar")
and Dario Argento ("The Black Cat") *Scr.* George Romero, Dario Argento, and Franco Ferrini
Cine. Peter Reniers and Beppe Maccari *Ed.* Pasquale Buba *P.d.* Cletus Anderson *S.d.* Diana
Stoughton *Mu.* Pino Donaggio *MPAA* R *R.t.* 120 min. *Cast:* Adrienne Barbeau, Ramy
Zada, Harvey Keitel, Madeleine Potter, Sally Kirkland, Bingo O'Malley, Martin Balsam, Kim
Hunter.

This film features adaptations of two Edgar Alan Poe stories: "The Curious Facts in the Case
of Mr. Valdemar" and "The Black Cat." In the former, a rich, elderly man, Valdemar (Bingo
O'Malley), dies while hypnotized by his doctor (Ramy Zada), who is conspiring with
Valdemar's wife (Adrienne Barbeau) to gain control of Valdemar's money. In the second, a
photographer (Harvey Keitel) of crime scenes is driven mad by an evil cat.

THE UNBORN

Pro. Rodman Flender; Califilm *Dir.* Rodman Flender *Scr.* Henry Dominic *Cine.* Wally
Pfister *Ed.* Patrick Rand *P.d.* Gary Randall *Mu.* Gary Numan and Michael R. Smith *MPAA*
R *R.t.* 87 min. *Cast:* Brooke Adams, Jeff Hayenga, James Karen, K Callan, Jane Cameron,
Rick Dean, Kathy Griffin, Wendy Kamenoff, Laura Stockton, Jonathan Emerson, Janice Kent,
Matt Roe, Jessica Zingali, Daryl Haney.

When a woman (Brooke Adams) becomes pregnant through in vitro fertilization administered by a mysterious doctor (James Karen), doubts cause her to abort the long-desired baby—
unfortunately, the fetus does not die.

URANUS (France, 1991)

Pro. Renn Productions, Films A2, and D.D. Productions, with the participation of Soficas Sofi-
Arp and Sofica Investimage 2 and 3; Prestige and Miramax Films *Dir.* Claude Berri *Scr.*
Claude Berri and Arlette Langmann; based on the novel by Marcel Ayme *Cine.* Renata Berta
Ed. Hervé de Luze *P.d.* Patrick Bordier *S.d.* Bernard Vezat *R.t.* 100 min. *Cast:* Philippe
Noiret, Gérard Depardieu, Jean-Pierre Marielle, Michel Blanc, Florence Darel, Danielle
Lebrun, Gérard Desarthe, Michel Galabru.

Set in 1945 in a small village in France, this film centers on a number of villagers—Watrin
(Philippe Noiret), a schoolteacher; Léopold, (Gérard Depardieu), a café owner; Archambaud

(Jean-Pierre Marielle), a family man; and Gaigneux (Michel Blanc), the local communist leader; among others—and the post-war search for Nazi collaborators.

V. I. WARSHAWSKI

Pro. Jeffrey Lurie for Hollywood Pictures, in association with Silver Screen Partners IV; Buena Vista *Dir.* Jeff Kanew *Scr.* Edward Taylor, David Aaron Cohen, and Nick Thiel; based on a story by Taylor and on the novels by Sara Paretsky *Cine.* Jan Kiesser *Ed.* C. Timothy O'Meara *P.d.* Barbara Ling *A.d.* Larry Fulton and William Arnold *S.d.* Lauren Polizzi, Anne H. Ahrens, and Kathe Klopp *Mu.* Randy Edelman *MPAA* R *R.t.* 89 min. *Cast:* Kathleen Turner, Jay O. Sanders, Charles Durning, Angela Goethals, Nancy Paul, Frederick Coffin, Charles McCaughan, Stephen Meadows, Wayne Knight, Lynnie Godfrey, Anne Pitoniak, Stephen Root, Robert Clotworthy, Tom Allard, Michael G. Hagerty.

When a boyfriend (Stephen Meadows) of private investigator V. I. Warshawski (Kathleen Turner) is murdered, his thirteen-year-old daughter, Kat (Angela Goethals), whom she was babysitting, teams with Warshawski to solve the crime.

VIA APPIA (Germany, 1991)

Pro. Norbert Friedlander; Strand Releasing International *Dir.* Jochen Hick *Scr.* Jochen Hick *Cine.* Peter Christian Neumann *Ed.* Claudia Vogeler *Mu.* Charly Schoppner *R.t.* 94 min. *Cast:* Peter Senner, Guilherme de Padua, Yves Jansen, Margaret Schmidt.

A young German flight attendant (Peter Senner) travels to Rio de Janeiro in order to find the man who intentionally exposed him to AIDS (acquired immune deficiency syndrome) during a sexual encounter. His quest is not driven by revenge, however, but by a desire to face honestly his impending death.

WARLOCK

Pro. Steve Miner for Arnold Kopelson; Trimark Pictures *Dir.* Steve Miner *Scr.* D. T. Twohy *Cine.* David Eggby *Ed.* David Finfer *P.d.* Roy Forge Smith *A.d.* Gary Steele *S.d.* Jennifer Williams *Mu.* Jerry Goldsmith *MPAA* R *R.t.* 102 min. *Cast:* Julian Sands, Richard E. Grant, Lori Singer, Mary Woronov, Kevin O'Brien, Richard Kuss.

In this tale of good versus evil, a Warlock (Julian Sands) and a witch-hunter named Redferne (Richard E. Grant) travel through magic from seventeenth century Boston to late twentieth century Los Angeles. As the Warlock continues his evil work for his master, Redferne is joined by a waitress (Lori Singer), a victim of one of Warlock's spells, and they try to track him down.

WHORE

Pro. Dan Ireland and Ronaldo Vasconcellos; Trimark Pictures *Dir.* Ken Russell *Scr.* Ken Russell and Deborah Dalton; based on the play *Bondage*, by David Hines *Cine.* Amir Mokri *Ed.* Brian Tagg *P.d.* Richard Lewis *A.d.* Naomi Shohan *S.d.* Amy Wells *Mu.* Michael Gibbs *MPAA* NC-17 *R.t.* 85 min. *Cast:* Theresa Russell, Benjamin Mouton, Antonio Fargas, Sanjay, Elizabeth Morehead, Michael Crabtree, John Deihl, Robert O'Reilly, Charles McCaulay, Jason Kristofer, Jack Nance, Frank Smith, Jason Saucier.

This drama centers on a day in the life of a prostitute, Liz (Theresa Russell). As Liz plies her dangerous trade, she complains about her life and her customers, while flashbacks dramatize her early days in the profession, her failed marriage, and her feelings toward her estranged son.

WILD HEARTS CAN'T BE BROKEN

Pro. Matt Williams for Walt Disney Pictures, in association with Silver Screen Partners IV; Buena Vista *Dir.* Steve Miner *Scr.* Matt Williams and Oley Sassone *Cine.* Daryn Okada *Ed.* Jon Poll *P.d.* Randy Ser *A.d.* Thomas Fichter *S.d.* Tony Fanning, James A. Kinney, and Jean Alan *Mu.* Mason Daring *MPAA* G *R.t.* 88 min. *Cast:* Gabrielle Anwar, Michael Schoeffling, Cliff Robertson, Dylan Kussman, Kathleen York, Frank Renzulli, Nancy Moore

Atchison, Lisa Norman, Shelley Peterson Boyle, Cherri Reiber.

In this inspirational film based on a true story, a fifteen-year-old orphan girl, Sonora Webster (Gabrielle Anwar), runs away from her aunt's farm during the Depression to join the carnival. Achieving celebrity status high-diving astride a horse, her career is threatened when she becomes blind following a bad dive.

A WOMAN'S TALE

Pro. Paul Cox and Santhana Naidu for Illumination Films, in association with Beyond Films Limited; Orion Classics *Dir.* Paul Cox *Scr.* Paul Cox and Barry Dickins *Cine.* Nino Martinetti *Ed.* Russell Hurley *P.d.* Neil Angwin *Mu.* Paul Grabowsky *MPAA* PG-13 *R.t.* 94 min. *Cast:* Sheila Florance, Gosia Dobrowolska, Norman Kaye, Chris Haywood, Myrtle Woods.

This moving drama centers on an elderly woman, Martha (Sheila Florance), who is sick with cancer. An ebullient, rebellious soul, Martha clings to life as she fights death. This courageous character is based on the actress who plays her.

YEAR OF THE GUN

Pro. Edward R. Pressman, in association with Initial Films; Triumph *Dir.* John Frankenheimer *Scr.* David Ambrose; based on the novel by Michael Mewshaw *Cine.* Blasco Giurato *Ed.* Lee Percy *P.d.* Aurelio Crugnola *A.d.* Luigi Quintili *S.d.* Franco Fumagalli *Mu.* Bill Conti *MPAA* R *R.t.* 111 min. *Cast:* Andrew McCarthy, Valeria Golino, Sharon Stone, John Pankow, Mattia Sbragia, George Murcell, Lou Castel.

When an American journalist (Andrew McCarthy), who is based in Rome in 1978, writes a fictional account of the activities of the Red Brigade, a radical political group, his narrative is so close to the truth that he is suspected of being a spy.

YOUNG SOUL REBELS (Great Britain, 1991)

Pro. Nadine Marsh-Edwards for British Film Institute and Film Four International, in association with Sankofa Film & Video, La Sept, and Kinowelt & Iberoamericana; Prestige *Dir.* Isaac Julien *Scr.* Paul Hallam, Derrick Saldaan McClintock, and Isaac Julien *Cine.* Nina Kellgren *Ed.* John Wilson *P.d.* Derek Brown *A.d.* Debra Overton *Mu.* Simon Boswell *R.t.* 103 min. *Cast:* Valentine Nonyela, Mo Sesay, Dorian Healy, Frances Barber, Sophie Okonedo, Jason Durr, Gary McDonald, Debra Gillett, Danielle Scillitoe.

Set in London in 1977, against the backdrop of Queen Elizabeth's Silver Jubilee, this suspense-thriller centers on two young men—Chris (Valentine Nonyela) and Caz (Mo Sesay)—who operate a pirate black radio station that plays funk. When their homosexual friend is murdered, Chris discovers a cassette tape with the murderer's voice and is subsequently arrested for the crime.

OBITUARIES

Henry Wilson Allen (1912-October 26, 1991). Allen was a writer at MGM's cartoon unit from 1937 to 1955. Known for his surrealistic humor, he wrote many of Tex Avery's animated classics in the 1940's and early 1950's. Later in his career, Allen began writing Western novels under the pen names of Will Henry and Clay Fisher; seven of these books were made into films, including *The Tall Men* (1955) and *Yellowstone Kelly* (1959).

Irwin Allen (June 12, 1916-November 2, 1991). Allen was a writer, director, and producer who was best known for his disaster films of the early 1970's, including the memorable *The Poseidon Adventure* (1972) and *The Towering Inferno* (1974). He won an Academy Award for his documentary feature *The Sea Around Us* (1952). Allen also produced a number of television series, most of which were in the adventure genre. His additional film credits include *The Lost World* (1960), *Voyage to the Bottom of the Sea* (1961), *The Swarm* (1978), and *Beyond the Poseidon Adventure* (1979).

Jean Arthur (October 17, 1905-June 19, 1991). Born Gladys Greene, Arthur was a popular actress of the 1930's and early 1940's. She was known for playing wisecracking women whose tough exterior covered a warm heart. Arthur's unconventional looks kept her from leading roles early in her career, which began with John Ford's *Cameo Kirby* (1923), and after a series of popular but unchallenging roles, she left Hollywood for a two-year stint on Broadway in 1932. When she returned, she found her breakthrough role in Ford's gangster comedy *The Whole Town's Talking* (1935) opposite Edward G. Robinson. She appeared in three classic Frank Capra social comedies—*Mr. Deeds Goes to Town* (1936), *You Can't Take It with You* (1938), and *Mr. Smith Goes to Washington* (1939)—and Capra later called her his favorite actress. Her role in *The More the Merrier* (1943) earned for her an Academy Award nomination. Ironically, this film turned out to be one of her last. Long known as a recluse, Arthur grew weary of the demands on her privacy that went with being a Hollywood star. When her contract with Columbia expired in 1944, she left Hollywood, returning only twice, for *A Foreign Affair* (1948) and *Shane* (1953). Her additional film credits include *Drug Store Cowboy* (1925), *The Canary Murder Case* (1929), *The Plainsman* (1937), *History Is Made at Night* (1937), *Easy Living* (1937), *Only Angels Have Wings* (1939), *The Devil and Miss Jones* (1941), *The Talk of the Town* (1942), *A Lady Takes a Chance* (1943), and *The Impatient Years* (1944).

Peggy Ashcroft (December 22, 1907-June 14, 1991). Dame Peggy Ashcroft was a distinguished British actress best known for her work on the stage, where she starred in numerous productions opposite such leading men as Laurence Olivier, Michael Redgrave, Ralph Richardson, and John Gielgud. Her most notable film role was in *A Passage to India* (1984), for which she won an Academy Award as Best Supporting Actress. Her additional screen credits include *The Wandering Jew* (1933), *The Thirty-nine Steps* (1935), and *Sunday, Bloody Sunday* (1971).

Howard Ashman (1952-March 14, 1991). Ashman was a lyricist who, with collaborator Alan Menken, wrote songs for the stage play and film *Little Shop of Horrors* (1986). He and Menken won an Academy Award for their song "Under the Sea" from the Disney animated feature *The Little Mermaid* (1989). He won a posthumous Academy Award for the title song from Disney's *Beauty and the Beast* (1991; reviewed in this volume), cowritten with Menken.

Jacques Aubuchon (1924-December 28, 1991). Aubuchon was a character actor who appeared extensively on stage, television, and film. His screen career peaked in the 1950's, when he appeared in such films as *So Big* (1953), *Beneath the Twelve Mile Reef* (1953), *Thunder Road* (1958), and *The Shaggy Dog* (1959).

Joy Batchelor (May 12, 1914-May 14, 1991). Batchelor was a British animator and producer who formed a partnership with John Halas (whom she later married) in 1940. Many of their productions were propaganda efforts for the British government; *Animal Farm* (1954) remains the only British feature-length animated production. Their *Automania 2000* (1963) was nominated for an Academy Award as Best Short Film. Batchelor's additional film credits include *Handling Ships* (1945), *The Owl and the Pussycat* (1953), *Dam the Delta* (1960), and *What Is a Computer?* (1970).

Ralph Bellamy (June 17, 1904-November 29, 1991). Bellamy was an actor who played lead roles in B-films and supporting roles in several important screwball comedies during a career that spanned nearly half a century. He starred as detective Ellery Queen in a series of films for Columbia; his Queen was portrayed as a bumbling incompetent. He is best known, however, for his roles alongside Cary Grant in *The Awful Truth* (1937), for which he was nominated for an Academy Award as Best Supporting Actor, and *His Girl Friday* (1940). In both films, he played the man who lost the girl to Grant. Bellamy began to be typecast in dull, stolid roles; by the mid-1940's, he decided to concentrate primarily on the stage to get the roles he preferred, although he continued to appear in films occasionally. He won a Tony Award in 1958 for his portrayal of Franklin Roosevelt in the play *Sunrise at Campobello* and reprised the role in the 1960 film of the same name. His last film was *Trading Places* (1983). In 1987, he was given an honorary Academy Award for "unique artistry and his distinguished service to the profession of acting." Bellamy's additional screen credits include *Rebecca of Sunnybrook Farm* (1932), *Carefree* (1938), *Ellery Queen, Master Detective* (1940), *Ellery Queen and the Perfect Crime* (1941), *The Ghost of Frankenstein* (1942), *Rosemary's Baby* (1968), and *Oh, God!* (1977).

Edward A. Blatt (1905-February 12, 1991). Born in Russia, Blatt was a playwright who worked in film in a variety of roles, directing several films in the 1940's. His directing credits include *Between Two Worlds* (1944), *Escape in the Desert* (1945), and *Smart Woman* (1948).

Eleanor Boardman (August 19, 1898-December 12, 1991). Boardman was an actress whose career spanned the silent and sound eras. She first gained fame as a model and then broke into film with *The Stranger's Banquet* (1922). In 1926, she married director King Vidor and starred in his *The Crowd* (1928), among others. Boardman and Vidor were divorced in 1931. She made only a few films after the advent of sound, including Cecil B. De Mille's remake of *The Squaw Man* (1931). Her additional film credits include *Three Wise Fools* (1923), *The Wife of the Centaur* (1924), *Mamba* (1930), and *The Big Chance* (1933).

Lillian Bond (January 18, 1910-January 18, 1991). Born in England, Bond acted on the British stage before coming to the United States. She was a leading lady in several films in the 1930's, often playing the "other woman." Her screen credits include *The Squaw Man* (1931), *Hot Saturday* (1932), *The Old Dark House* (1932), *China Seas* (1935), *The Westerner* (1940), and *The Picture of Dorian Gray* (1945).

Edwina Booth (September 13, 1909-May 18, 1991). Born Edwina Woodruff, Booth was an actress best known for her role opposite Harry Carey in *Trader Horn* (1931), which began as a silent film and was converted to sound after filming had begun. The rigors of filming on location in Africa left Booth bedridden for five years, ending her film career. Her additional film credits include *Manhattan Cocktail* (1928), *The Vanishing Legion* (1931), and *The Midnight Patrol* (1932).

Steve Broidy (1906-April 29, 1991). Broidy was president of Monogram Pictures-Allied Artists from 1945 to 1965. Monogram was known for its low-budget Westerns and serials, featuring such cowboy stars as John Wayne and Tex Ritter. The studio used the name Allied Artists for its more prestigious films, such as *The Babe Ruth Story* (1948). In 1953, Broidy dropped the name Monogram entirely, and the studio continued on as Allied Artists, producing such films as *Friendly Persuasion* (1956), *Love in the Afternoon* (1957), *El Cid* (1961), and *Fifty-five Days at Peking* (1963). In 1965, Broidy became an independent producer, founding Motion Pictures International.

Coral Browne (July 23, 1913-May 29, 1991). Born in Australia, Browne was an actress who specialized in character roles in films such as *Let George Do It* (1940), *Auntie Mame* (1958), and *The Drowning Pool* (1975). She met her husband, Vincent Price, when the two were filming *Theatre of Blood* (1973). Her additional screen credits include *The Roman Spring of Mrs. Stone* (1961), *The Killing of Sister George* (1968), and *The Ruling Class* (1972).

Bernard Burton (1898-February 26, 1991). Burton was an editor and producer who began working in film in 1918. He edited a number of films for Universal in the 1920's and 1930's, including *Show Boat* (1936) and *One Hundred Men and a Girl* (1937). As a producer, he specialized in B-musicals, including the Andrews Sisters vehicle *Give Out Sisters* (1942), *Get Hep to Love* (1944), and *This Is the Life* (1944).

Niven Busch (April 26, 1903-August 25, 1991). Busch was a novelist and screenwriter who was best known for his pioneering introduction of psychological elements into the Western genre. His 1944 novel *Duel in the Sun* was made into a film by King Vidor in 1946. He also wrote the script for Raoul Walsh's *Pursued* (1947), starring Robert Mitchum. His original story for *In Old Chicago* (1938) earned for him an Academy Award nomination. His additional screenwriting credits include *The Crowd Roars* (1932), *Babbitt* (1934), *The Westerner* (1940), *The Postman Always Rings Twice* (1946), and *Distant Drums* (1951).

Gene Callahan (1909-December 25, 1991). Callahan was a production designer whose work earned for him two Academy Awards: for set decoration on *The Hustler* (1961) and for art direction on *America America* (1963). He was nominated for two additional Academy Awards, for *The Cardinal* (1963) and *The Last Tycoon* (1976), the latter with Jack Collins. His additional film credits include *Butterfield 8* (1960), *Julia* (1977), *The World According to Garp* (1982), and *Annie* (1982).

Frank Capra (May 18, 1897-September 3, 1991). Capra was an American director whose work in the 1930's and 1940's earned for him a place among the finest American filmmakers of all time. A determined populist, Capra made films in which the average man fought the system and won. Born in Sicily, his family immigrated to California in 1903; after serving in the Army during World War I, he learned the film business on the job while making amateur films in San Francisco. In Hollywood, he wound up with Mack Sennett, who assigned him to work with comedian Harry Langdon, for whom Capra directed two films: *Tramp Tramp Tramp* (1926) and *The Strong Man* (1926). After falling out with Langdon, he signed with Columbia Pictures in 1928 and made sixteen films for the studio in the next three years. It was in 1931 that he first began to make the socially conscious films upon which his reputation is based. Two of his early efforts were sufficiently controversial as to be banned in some areas: *The Miracle Woman* (1931), which was based on the life of evangelist Aimee Semple McPherson, and *The Bitter Tea of General Yen* (1933), which dealt with interracial love. Nevertheless, he also made popular comedies such as *Platinum Blonde* (1931) and *Lady for a Day* (1933), which earned for Capra his first Academy Award nomination.

His breakthrough came the next year with the seminal screwball comedy *It Happened One Night* (1934), which won an unprecedented five major Academy Awards for Best Picture, Director, Screenplay (by Robert Riskin), Actor (Clark Gable), and Actress (Claudette Colbert). He followed up that triumph with *Mr. Deeds Goes to Town* (1936), which featured Gary Cooper as a millionaire fighting for the poor and for which Capra won his second Academy Award. It was also the first film to list its director's name above the title. His next film, *Lost Horizon* (1937), was an expensive failure, but Capra rebounded with *You Can't Take It with You* (1938), a comedy starring Jean Arthur and James Stewart which won two Academy Awards: Best Picture and Capra's third award for Best Direction. Stewart also starred as a naïve senator in corrupt Washington, D.C., in *Mr. Smith Goes to Washington* (1939), for which both star and director were nominated for Academy Awards. Capra's final film before the war was *Meet John Doe* (1941), a seriocomic look at the potential for fascism in the United States.

During World War II, Capra directed several documentary films in the Academy Award-winning "Why We Fight" series, including *Prelude to War* (1942) and *War Comes to America* (1944). After the war, his powers seemed to wane; the only truly outstanding film he made in the last fifteen years of his career was *It's a Wonderful Life* (1946), the James Stewart Christmas classic that Capra named as his favorite film. He made only five more films, the last of which, *A Pocketful of Miracles* (1961), was a remake of *Lady for a Day*. In 1971, he published his autobiography, *Frank Capra: The Name Above the Title*. His additional film credits include *So This Is Love* (1928), *Rain or Shine* (1930), *The Negro Soldier* (1944), *Arsenic and Old Lace* (1944), *State of the Union* (1948), *Here Comes the Groom* (1951), and *A Hole in the Head* (1959).

James Carreras (1909-June 9, 1991). Carreras was a British studio executive. Along with Will Hammer, he founded Hammer Films in 1948; the studio became the most successful production company in the history of British film. The studio specialized in low-budget horror and gothic films, often made by director Terence Fisher and starring Peter Cushing (who often played Baron Frankenstein) and Christopher Lee (who was frequently seen as Count Dracula). Carreras was knighted in 1970.

Joan Caulfield (June 1, 1922-June 18, 1991). Caulfield was an actress who worked extensively in film and television in the 1940's and 1950's. She was one of Paramount's top female stars, appearing in such films as *Duffy's Tavern* (1945), *Blue Skies* (1946), and *Monsieur Beaucaire* (1946). Beginning in the 1950's, she began to concentrate on television work, although she continued to appear in such films as *The Rains of Ranchipur* (1955), *Cattle King* (1963), and *Red Tomahawk* (1967).

Bert Convy (1935-July 15, 1991). Convy was an actor, singer (as a member of the 1950's pop group the Cheers), and television performer who is best known for his stints as a game-show host in the 1970's. His film credits include *Semi-Tough* (1977) and *Hero at Large* (1980).

Carmine Coppola (1910-April 26, 1991). Coppola was a composer who began working in film at the suggestion of his son, director Francis Ford Coppola, for whom he worked extensively. His first major score was for *Finian's Rainbow* (1968), and he and collaborator Nino Rota won an Academy Award for their score of *The Godfather, Part II* (1974). He was nominated for an Academy Award for his song "Promise Me You'll Remember," in *The Godfather, Part III* (1990). His additional film credits include *Apocalypse Now* (1979) and *The Black Stallion* (1979).

Ken Curtis (July 12, 1916-April 27, 1991). Born Curtis Gates, Curtis was an actor who specialized in Westerns. He broke into show business as a singer, performing with the Tommy Dorsey Orchestra as Frank Sinatra's replacement and later with the cowboy singing group the Sons of the Pioneers. In the mid-1940's, he made a series of singing-cowboy films for Columbia, including *Rhythm Roundup* (1945) and *Cowboy Blues* (1946). In 1952, he married director John Ford's daughter and subsequently appeared in a number of Ford's films, including *Mister Roberts* (1955) and *The Searchers* (1956). He was perhaps best known for his role as Festus in the long-running television Western *Gunsmoke*. His additional screen credits include *Singing on the Trail* (1946), *The Last Hurrah* (1958), *The Alamo* (1960), and *Cheyenne Autumn* (1964).

Brad Davis (1950-August 8, 1991). Davis was an actor best known for his starring role in

Midnight Express (1978), in which he played a man imprisoned in a Turkish jail for smuggling drugs. His additional film credits include *A Small Circle of Friends* (1980), *Querelle* (1982), *Heart* (1987), and *Cold Steel* (1987).

Jerome Davis (1917-April 10, 1991). Davis was a screenwriter in the 1940's and 1950's who later became a television producer in a career that spanned more than thirty years. His screenwriting credits include *Pagan Love Song* (1950), *Apache War Smoke* (1952), *Cult of the Cobra* (1955), *The Girl Rush* (1955), and the Dean Martin-Jerry Lewis vehicle *Pardners* (1956).

Carol Dempster (1902-February 1, 1991). Dempster was an actress during the silent era. She began her career as a dancer, and was given a small role in D. W. Griffith's *The Greatest Thing in Life* (1918). Griffith was smitten by her, and Dempster appeared in several more of his films, including *True Heart Susie* (1919) and *The Love Flower* (1920). Evidently his affection was not reciprocated; in 1926, Dempster married a stockbroker and retired from the screen. Her additional film credits include *Scarlet Days* (1919), *Dream Street* (1921), *Sherlock Holmes* (1922), *Sally of the Sawdust* (1925), and *The Sorrows of Satan* (1926).

Colleen Dewhurst (June 23, 1926-August 22, 1991). Dewhurst was an actress best known for her work on the stage, where she won Tony Awards for her performances in *All the Way Home* and *A Moon for the Misbegotten* in addition to numerous other honors. Dewhurst twice married and divorced actor George C. Scott, and their son, Campbell Scott, is an actor. Dewhurst and Campbell Scott were featured in the Julia Roberts vehicle *Dying Young* (1991; reviewed in this volume). Her additional film credits include *The Nun's Story* (1959), *A Fine Madness* (1966), *The Cowboys* (1972), *Annie Hall* (1977), and *Ice Castles* (1979).

Mel Dinelli (1912-November 28, 1991). Dinelli was a screenwriter and playwright who specialized in thrillers. His screenwriting credits include *The Spiral Staircase* (1946), *The Window* (1949), *The Reckless Moment* (1949), *Beware, My Lovely* (1952), *Jeopardy* (1953), and *Step down to Terror* (1958).

Oliver Drake (1903-August 5, 1991). Drake was a writer and director of B-Westerns. He wrote such Gene Autry vehicles as *The Sagebrush Troubador* (1935) and *Boots and Saddles* (1937). He directed *The Texas Tornado* (1934), *Today I Hang* (1942), and *Song of the Sierras* (1947). His additional screenwriting credits include *When a Man Rides Alone* (1933), *Racketeers of the Range* (1939), and *The Boss of Hangtown Mesa* (1942).

Dixie Dunbar (January 19, 1919-August 29, 1991). Born Christina Dunbar, Dunbar was a dancer and actress who appeared in a number of musicals and light comedies in the 1930's. She retired from films after her marriage in 1938, although she worked on stage and television into the 1950's. Her film credits include *George White's Scandals* (1934), *Sing Baby Sing* (1936), *Pigskin Parade* (1936), *Rebecca of Sunnybrook Farm* (1938), and *Alexander's Ragtime Band* (1938).

Jack Dunning (1916-February 25, 1991). Dunning was a film editor who worked at MGM for four decades. Along with collaborator Ralph E. Winters, Dunning earned an Academy Award for his work on *Ben-Hur* (1959). His additional film credits include *Cass Timberlane* (1947), *Across the Wide Missouri* (1951), *The Last Time I Saw Paris* (1954), *The Tender Trap* (1955), and *The Brothers Karamazov* (1958).

Mildred Dunnock (January 25, 1906-July 5, 1991). Dunnock was a stage and film actress who is best known for her portrayal of Linda Loman, the wife in *Death of a Salesman* (1951). She first performed the role on Broadway and later earned an Academy Award nomination for reprising the role on film. She specialized in character parts and was also nominated for an Academy Award for her work in *Baby Doll* (1956). Her additional film credits include *The Corn Is Green* (1945), *Viva Zapata!* (1952), *Love Me Tender* (1956), *Peyton Place* (1957), *Butterfield 8*

(1960), and *Sweet Bird of Youth* (1962).

Morton Fine (1916-March 7, 1991). Fine was a producer and screenwriter who worked in partnership with director David Friedkin. They are best known for their work on the innovative television series *I Spy*, but they also worked in film. Fine produced and cowrote *Hot Summer Night* (1957) and *Handle with Care* (1958). He also cowrote the screenplay to Sidney Lumet's *The Pawnbroker* (1965). His additional screenwriting credits include *The Fool Killer* (1965), *The Greek Tycoon* (1978), and *Caboblanco* (1980).

Redd Foxx (1922-October 11, 1991). Born John Elroy Sanford, Foxx was an African-American stage comedian and actor. He first earned notoriety in the 1950's by performing risqué material in nightclubs and on records. In 1972, he found stardom in the highly successful television series *Sanford and Son*. He appeared occasionally in films, including *Cotton Comes to Harlem* (1970), *Norman . . . Is That You?* (1976), and *Harlem Nights* (1989).

James Franciscus (January 31, 1934-July 8, 1991). Franciscus was a handsome leading man best known for his television roles in such series as *Naked City* and *Mr. Novak*. He also made numerous films between his debut in *Four Boys and a Gun* (1957) and *Butterfly* (1981). His additional screen credits include *I Passed for White* (1960), *Youngblood Hawke* (1964), *Beneath the Planet of the Apes* (1970), *Jonathan Livingston Seagull* (1973), *The Greek Tycoon* (1978), and *Nightkill* (1980).

Everett Freeman (February 2, 1911-January 24, 1991). Freeman was a producer and screenwriter whose film career spanned more than three decades. He was nominated for an Academy Award for his work on *It Happened on Fifth Avenue* (1947). His additional screen credits include *Married Before Breakfast* (1937), *The Secret Life of Walter Mitty* (1947), *Jim Thorpe—All American* (1951, which he also produced), *My Man Godfrey* (1957), *The Glass Bottom Boat* (1966, which he coproduced), and *The Maltese Bippy* (1979).

Anton Furst (1944-November 24, 1991). Furst was a special effects designer who contributed to many of the top moneymaking films of the 1970's and 1980's. His special effects company, Holoco, worked on *Star Wars* (1977) and *Superman* (1978), and as a production designer, Furst worked on *Batman* (1989), for which he and collaborator Peter Young won an Academy Award for set decoration. His additional film credits include *Alien* (1979), *Moonraker* (1979), *Outland* (1981), and *Full Metal Jacket* (1987).

George Gobel (1919-February 24, 1991). Gobel was a comic actor who was a prominent figure in the early days of television, where his hangdog style earned him great popularity. He was featured in two films: *The Birds and the Bees* (1956) and *I Married a Woman* (1958).

Bill Graham (1931-October 26, 1991). Born Wolfgang Grajonca in Berlin, Graham was a major figure in 1960's and 1970's popular music. He owned the Fillmore East and Fillmore West auditoriums, managed several San Francisco rock groups, and promoted numerous concert tours. He had a role in Francis Ford Coppola's *Apocalypse Now* (1979) and helped produce Oliver Stone's *The Doors* (1991; reviewed in this volume).

Mauri Grashin (1900-February 8, 1991). Grashin was a writer who specialized in comedy. Entering show business via vaudeville and burlesque, he moved to Hollywood in 1929, where he wrote the screenplay for Laurel and Hardy's first sound film *Unaccustomed as We Are* (1929). He contributed scripts for numerous Our Gang and Three Stooges shorts, and his work on the Mickey Rooney vehicle *Hide-Out* (1934) earned for him an Academy Award nomination. His additional film credits include *Sons of the Pioneers* (1942), *Pardon My Stripes* (1942), and *Arthur Takes Over* (1948).

Graham Greene (October 2, 1904-April 3, 1991). Greene was one of the major British novelists of the twentieth century. He also wrote screenplays on occasion, including versions of his own novels or plays. In addition to those adapted by Greene himself, many of his other works were filmed. Greene's screenplays include *Twenty-one Days Together* (1940), *Brighton Rock* (1947), *The Third Man* (1949), *Saint Joan* (1957), *Our Man in Havana* (1959), and *The Comedians* (1967).

Milton Gunzburg (1909-April 6, 1991). Gunzburg was a screenwriter who later pioneered three-dimensional filmmaking techniques. His best-known screenplay was *Tennessee Johnson* (1942). After taking up photography, Gunzburg helped form Natural Vision Corp., a group of technicians who developed 3-D in the early 1950's. He also worked on *Bwana Devil* (1952), *House of Wax* (1953), and *The Charge at Feather River* (1953).

A. B. Guthrie (1900-April 26, 1991). Guthrie was a Pulitzer Prize-winning novelist who chronicled the taming of the West in such works as *The Big Sky* and *The Way West*, both of which were made into films starring Kirk Douglas (in 1952 and 1967, respectively). His one foray into filmmaking came when he wrote the screenplay for George Stevens' *Shane* (1953), for which he won an Academy Award.

Harry-Krimer (March 10, 1896-January 4, 1991). Born Felix Rosenthal, Harry-Krimer was a French actor of the silent era. He is best known for his role of Rouget de Lisle in Abel Gance's *Napoleon* (1927). His additional film credits include *La Course du flambeau* (1925), *Atlantic* (1929), and *Deux fois vingt ans* (1930).

Gloria Holden (September 5, 1908-March 22, 1991). Holden was a British actress who appeared in many Hollywood films in the 1930's and 1940's, often in femme fatale roles. Her screen credits include *Dracula's Daughter* (1936), *The Life of Emile Zola* (1937), *Miss Annie Rooney* (1942), *A Kiss for Corliss* (1949), and *The Eddy Duchin Story* (1956).

Donald Houston (November 6, 1923-October 13, 1991). Houston was a burly blond Welsh actor who played leads and second leads in numerous British films from the early 1940's to the early 1980's. His screen credits include *The Blue Lagoon* (1949), *A Run for Your Money* (1949), *The Red Beret* (1953), *Room at the Top* (1958), *The Longest Day* (1962), *Where Eagles Dare* (1969), and *Voyage of the Damned* (1976).

John Hoyt (1904-September 15, 1991). Born John Hoysradt, Hoyt was a character actor who appeared in eighty feature films and had numerous television roles. His screen credits include *My Favorite Brunette* (1947), *When Worlds Collide* (1951), *Androcles and the Lion* (1952), *Julius Caesar* (1953), *The Blackboard Jungle* (1955), and *The Time Travelers* (1964).

Floyd Huddleston (1918-September 27, 1991). Huddleston was a songwriter who, along with collaborator George Brunes, was nominated for an Academy Award for the song "Love," from the Disney animated feature *Robin Hood* (1973). His additional film credits include *The Ballad of Josie* (1967), *Midnight Cowboy* (1969), and *The Aristocats* (1970).

Ian McLellan Hunter (1915-March 5, 1991). Hunter was a screenwriter who was blacklisted in the 1950's for his political views. Ironically, his contributions to the last film on which he worked under his own name during that era, *Roman Holiday* (1953), earned for him an Academy Award. He worked under a variety of pseudonyms for the next fifteen years; he was credited under his own name for *A Dream of Kings* (1969), after which time he concentrated on writing for television. His additional film credits include *Meet Dr. Christian* (1939), *Second Chorus* (1940), and *A Woman of Distinction* (1950).

Wilfrid Hyde-White (May 12, 1903-May 6, 1991). Hyde-White was a British character actor who specialized in comedy. He is best remembered for his role as Colonel Pickering in *My Fair Lady* (1964). His additional screen credits include *Elephant Boy* (1937), *The Third Man* (1949), *Carry On Nurse* (1960), *Ten Little Indians* (1966), *The Magic Christian* (1970), and *Oh, God! Book II* (1980).

Dean Jagger (November 7, 1903-February 5, 1991). Jagger was an actor whose film career lasted for more than half a century. His first film was the silent *The Woman from Hell* (1929), and he appeared primarily in B-films throughout the 1930's. His roles improved in the 1940's, culminating in *Twelve O'Clock High* (1949), for which he won an Academy Award as Best Supporting Actor. Jagger specialized in Westerns, including *Western Union* (1941) and *Rawhide* (1951). By the 1960's, he was appearing extensively in television, most prominently in the series *Mr. Novak*. His additional film credits include *Brigham Young—Frontiersman* (1940), *The Robe* (1953), *White Christmas* (1954), *Bernadine* (1957), *King Creole* (1958), *Elmer Gantry* (1960), and *Vanishing Point* (1971).

Leo Katcher (1911-February 27, 1991). Katcher was an author who wrote occasionally for film. His screenplay of *The Eddy Duchin Story* (1956) earned for him an Academy Award nomination. His additional screenwriting credits include Joseph Losey's remake of *M* (1951) and Nicholas Ray's *Party Girl* (1958).

Charles A. Kaufman (1904-May 2, 1991). Kaufman was a screenwriter best known for his work with director John Huston. He wrote Huston's controversial World War II documentary *Let There Be Light* (1946), which depicted shell-shocked survivors of combat. He also produced the screenplay for the director's feature film *Freud* (1962). His additional film credits include *Breakfast for Two* (1937), *The Saint in New York* (1938), and *Model Wife* (1941).

Robert Kaufman (1931-November 21, 1991). Kaufman was a screenwriter who specialized in comedy. He wrote extensively for television. His best-known film was *Divorce American Style* (1967), for which he and collaborator Norman Lear were nominated for an Academy Award. His additional film credits include *Ski Party* (1965), *Getting Straight* (1970), *Love at First Bite* (1979), and *How to Beat the High Cost of Living* (1980).

Sylvia Fine Kaye (1913-October 28, 1991). Kaye was a composer and producer who is best known for her work with her husband, Danny Kaye. She wrote the music for such Kaye films as *Up in Arms* (1944), *The Kid from Brooklyn* (1946), and *The Secret Life of Walter Mitty* (1947). As a producer, two of her films were nominated for Academy Awards: *The Moon Is Blue* (1953) and *The Five Pennies* (1959). Her additional film credits include *Wonder Man* (1945), *The Inspector General* (1949), and *The Court Jester* (1956).

Klaus Kinski (1926-November 23, 1991). Born Claus Nakszynski in Danzig, Poland, Kinski was an actor who appeared in nearly two hundred films. Because he was an international star who was willing to work in inferior films if better roles were unavailable, Kinski's career is a mixed bag. Some of his best work was done for German director Werner Herzog, who directed Kinski in *Aguirre the Wrath of God* (1973) and *Nosferatu* (1979). The film that brought him to the attention of American audiences was *Doctor Zhivago* (1965). His daughter is actress Nastassia Kinski. His additional film credits include *Ludwig II* (1955), *For a Few Dollars More* (1966), *Woyzeck* (1978), *Fitzcarraldo* (1982), and *Android* (1982).

Jerzy Kosinski (June 14, 1933-May 3, 1991). Born in Poland, Kosinski was an acclaimed author who wrote the screenplay for the film version of his satiric 1971 novel *Being There* (1979). Two years later, he received good reviews for his portrayal of Communist Grigory Zinoviev in Warren Beatty's *Reds* (1981).

Ronald Lacey (1935-May 15, 1991). Lacey was a character actor who specialized in playing villains. He is best remembered for his portrayal of Nazis in two Steven Spielberg films, *Raiders of the Lost Ark* (1981) and *Indiana Jones and the Last Crusade* (1989). His additional screen credits include *Zulu Dawn* (1979), *Nijinsky* (1980), and *Valmont* (1989).

Michael Landon (October 31, 1936-July 1, 1991). Born Eugene Maurice Orowitz, Landon was an actor and producer best known for his television roles in such popular series as *Bonanza*,

Little House on the Prairie, and *Highway to Heaven*. He had little time left to devote to film, and most of his screen credits came early in his career; these include *I Was a Teen-age Werewolf* (1957), *God's Little Acre* (1958), *Maracaibo* (1958), *High School Confidential!* (1958), *The Legend of Tom Dooley* (1959), and *The Errand Boy* (1961).

David Lean (March 25, 1908-April 16, 1991). Lean was a British director best known for his epic films of the 1950's and 1960's, when he won two Academy Awards for his direction of *The Bridge on the River Kwai* (1957) and *Lawrence of Arabia* (1962). He first made his mark in film as an editor and was hired by writer-director Noel Coward to work on *In Which We Serve* (1942); his contributions to this film were so extensive that he demanded and received credit as codirector. His partnership with Coward continued, with Lean directing Coward's *Blithe Spirit* (1945) and *Brief Encounter* (1945); he earned the first of his nine Academy Award nominations for the latter film. A second nomination followed a year later with the first of Lean's two Charles Dickens adaptations, *Great Expectations* (1946). By the mid-1950's, he had proven himself to be an important international filmmaker; 1957's World War II epic *The Bridge on the River Kwai* took him to new heights of popularity. Starring Alec Guinness as a British officer in a Japanese prison camp, the film won seven Academy Awards, including Best Picture. It was five years before Lean released another film, but the result proved worth the wait. *Lawrence of Arabia*, with Peter O'Toole as the charismatic T. E. Lawrence, was a popular and critical success, earning eight Academy Awards, including Best Picture. His next film was even more popular: His sweeping adaptation of Boris Pasternak's epic of the Russian Revolution, *Doctor Zhivago* (1965), won five Academy Awards and was a huge box-office success. Ironically, Lean was to make only two more films during his entire career. Though the film won two Academy Awards, Lean admitted that the critical and commercial failure of *Ryan's Daughter* (1970) disheartened him. His only other new film was *A Passage to India* (1984), a critical success that was ignored by most viewers. Lean's last project was to supervise the 1989 re-release of *Lawrence of Arabia*, with several deleted scenes restored. His additional films were *This Happy Breed* (1944), *Oliver Twist* (1948), *The Passionate Friends* (1949), *The Sound Barrier* (1952), *Hobson's Choice* (1954), and *Summer Madness* (1955).

Eugène Lourié (1905-May 26, 1991). Born in Russia, Lourié moved to France as a teenager, where he worked in ballet before becoming the leading French art director in the early days of sound film. He worked extensively with director Jean Renoir on films such as *La Grande Illusion* (1937; *Grand Illusion*, 1937) and *La Règle du jeu* (1939; *Rules of the Game*, 1939). When Renoir moved to Hollywood in 1941, Lourié followed. Later in his career, he became known for his ability to integrate special effects into his designs; he earned an Academy Award nomination for his work on *Krakatoa, East of Java* (1969). He also directed a handful of science fiction films, including *The Beast from Twenty Thousand Fathoms* (1953) and *Gorgo* (1961). His additional film credits include *Madame Bovary* (1934), *La Bête humaine* (1938; *The Human Beast*, 1938), *The River* (1951), *Limelight* (1952), *Shock Corridor* (1963), *The Royal Hunt of the Sun* (1969), and *An Enemy of the People* (1978).

Keye Luke (1904-January 12, 1991). Born in China, Luke was perhaps the most successful Asian-American actor in Hollywood, working extensively in films and television for more than half a century. Early in his career, he played the famous "Number One Son" in nine of the popular Charlie Chan films of the 1930's, including *Charlie Chan in Paris* (1935) and *Charlie Chan at the Opera* (1936). He also had a recurring role as Dr. Kildare's rival in such films as *Dr. Gillespie's New Assistant* (1942). He continued to make films throughout his life, enjoying a resurgence of popularity in the 1980's in a series of comedies such as *Gremlins* (1984) and *A Fine Mess* (1986). His additional film credits include *Oil for the Lamps of China* (1935), *The Good*

Earth (1937), *Love Is a Many-Splendored Thing* (1955), *The Hawaiians* (1970), *The Mighty Quinn* (1989), and *Alice* (1990).

James McCallion (1919-July 11, 1991). McCallion was a character actor best known for his role as Pappy McMahon, the sailor rescued by John F. Kennedy in *PT 109* (1963). He also worked extensively in television. His additional screen credits include *Code of the Streets* (1939), *Pride of the Bluegrass* (1939), *Vera Cruz* (1954), and *North by Northwest* (1959).

James MacDonald (1906-February 1, 1991). MacDonald worked for the Disney studio's sound effects department for four decades, providing voices and other noises for Disney's animated shorts and features. He was the voice of Mickey Mouse in countless cartoons from 1946 to 1976. His feature film credits include *Snow White and the Seven Dwarfs* (1937), *Cinderella* (1950), and *Alice in Wonderland* (1951).

John McIntire (June 27, 1907-January 30, 1991). McIntire was a character actor who appeared in many Westerns and action films. In addition to his film work, he is remembered as the man who replaced Ward Bond on the television series *Wagon Train*. He was married to actress Jeanette Nolan. His screen credits include *Call Northside 777* (1948), *The Asphalt Jungle* (1950), *Psycho* (1960), *Flaming Star* (1960), *Elmer Gantry* (1960), and *Rooster Cogburn* (1975).

Aline MacMahon (May 3, 1899-October 12, 1991). MacMahon was an actress who specialized in playing serious women in both leading and supporting roles. She was nominated for an Academy Award for Best Supporting Actress for her work in *Dragon Seed* (1944). Her additional film credits include *Five Star Final* (1931), *Babbitt* (1934), *Ah, Wilderness!* (1935), *The Mighty McGurk* (1947), *The Eddie Cantor Story* (1953), and *The Young Doctors* (1961).

Fred MacMurray (August 30, 1908-November 5, 1991). MacMurray was a popular actor who specialized in playing light comedy in films and television. He was a musician and bandleader as a teenager, and his acting roles grew out of his appearances in Broadway musicals. His feature film debut came in *Friends of Mr. Sweeney* (1934), and the following year his performance opposite Claudette Colbert in *The Gilded Lily* (1935) led to leading roles in a career that would last for decades. He worked prolifically throughout the 1930's, appearing in several films each year. Perhaps because he was cast against type, his role in Billy Wilder's *film noir Double Indemnity* (1944), with Barbara Stanwyck, earned numerous accolades. He continued to appear in a variety of films over the next fifteen years, including *Father Was a Fullback* (1949), *The Caine Mutiny* (1954), and *The Rains of Ranchipur* (1955). In 1959, his career received a significant boost when he appeared in the first of his five Disney features, *The Shaggy Dog* (1959). His last significant dramatic role came from Billy Wilder again, in *The Apartment* (1960). Shortly thereafter, he began appearing in the popular television series *My Three Sons*, which ran from 1960 through 1972 and solidified his appeal as an avuncular comic actor. He was married to actress June Haver. MacMurray's additional film credits include *Alice Adams* (1935), *Cocoanut Grove* (1938), *And the Angels Sing* (1944), *The Egg and I* (1947), *The Far Horizons* (1955), *The Absent-Minded Professor* (1961), *Son of Flubber* (1963), *Follow Me, Boys!* (1966), and *Charley and the Angel* (1973).

Richard Maibaum (May 26, 1909-January 1, 1991). Maibaum was a screenwriter best known for his work on the James Bond films. He was the sole author or coauthor of the scripts for *Dr. No* (1962), *From Russia with Love* (1963), *Goldfinger* (1964), *Thunderball* (1965), *On Her Majesty's Secret Service* (1969), *Diamonds Are Forever* (1971), *The Man with the Golden Gun* (1974), *The Spy Who Loved Me* (1977), *For Your Eyes Only* (1981), *Octopussy* (1983), *The Living Daylights* (1987), and *License to Kill* (1989). His additional film credits include *We Went to College* (1936), *I Wanted Wings* (1941), *The Great Gatsby* (1949), and *Killers of Kilamanjaro* (1959).

Daniel Mann (August 8, 1912-November 21, 1991). Mann was a director who was known for his ability to bring out the best in actresses. Shirley Booth, in *Come Back, Little Sheba* (1952), Anna Magnani, in *The Rose Tattoo* (1955), and Elizabeth Taylor, in *Butterfield 8* (1960), won Academy Awards in films directed by Mann. His additional film credits include *Teahouse of the August Moon* (1956), *The Last Angry Man* (1959), *Our Man Flint* (1966), *For Love of Ivy* (1968), *Willard* (1971), and *Lost in the Stars* (1974).

Bernard Miles (September 27, 1907-June 14, 1991). Miles was a British character actor known for playing rustic roles. He worked extensively on stage and in film in a career that lasted more than fifty years. His film credits include *Channel Crossing* (1933), *Great Expectations* (1946), *Nicholas Nickleby* (1947), *The Man Who Knew Too Much* (1956), *Moby Dick* (1956), and *Run Wild, Run Free* (1969).

Gene Milford (1902-December 23, 1991). Milford was an editor who worked on many notable films. He was nominated for an Academy Award for *One Night of Love* (1934) and won Academy Awards for his work on Frank Capra's *Lost Horizon* (1937) and Elia Kazan's *On the Waterfront* (1954). His additional film credits include *Platinum Blonde* (1931), *Baby Doll* (1956), *A Face in the Crowd* (1957), *Splendor in the Grass* (1961), *The Chase* (1966), *Wait Until Dark* (1967), and *There Was a Crooked Man . . .* (1970).

Yves Montand (October 13, 1921-November 9, 1991). Born Ivo Livi in Italy, Montand was a French singer and actor who made films in Europe and the United States. He was discovered by singer Edith Piaf; the two became lovers, and she helped him get his first film role in *Étoile sans lumière* (1946; *Star Without Light*, 1946); his next film, *Les Portes de la nuit* (1946; *Gates of the Night*, 1946), in which he introduced the song "Autumn Leaves," made him a star, though he continued to be better known as a singer than as an actor until he made the suspense thriller *Le Salaire de la peur* (1953; *The Wages of Fear*, 1953). His screen reputation as the classic Gallic lover was solidified in his first American film, *Let's Make Love* (1960), in which he starred opposite Marilyn Monroe (with whom he had a well-publicized love affair). Politically, he was an outspoken leftist, and his films often reflected his political views. He frequently worked with director Constantin Costa-Gavras, such as in *Z* (1969), *L'Aveu* (1970; *The Confession*, 1970), and *État de siège* (1973; *State of Siege*, 1973). His last significant roles were in *Jean de Florette* (1986) and *Manon des sources* (1986; *Manon of the Spring*, 1987). He was married to actress Simone Signoret. His additional film credits include *L'Idole* (1948), *Les Sorcières de Salem* (1957; *The Crucible*, 1957), *My Geisha* (1962), *Paris brûle-t-il?* (1966; *Is Paris Burning?* 1966), *Vivre pour vivre* (1967; *Live for Life*, 1967), *On a Clear Day You Can See Forever* (1970), and *Clair de femme* (1979).

Judy Moorcroft (1935-December 13, 1991). Moorcroft was a costume designer who was nominated for Academy Awards for her work on *The Europeans* (1977) and *A Passage to India* (1984). Her additional screen credits include *Yentl* (1983), *The Killing Fields* (1984), *Shanghai Surprise* (1986), *A Month in the Country* (1987), and *Fools of Fortune* (1990).

Ruth Morley (1925-February 12, 1991). Morley was a costume designer who was nominated for an Academy Award for her work on *The Miracle Worker* (1962). Her offbeat costumes for Diane Keaton in *Annie Hall* (1977) were widely copied by fashionable women. Her additional film credits include *Taxi Driver* (1976), *Kramer vs. Kramer* (1979), *Tootsie* (1982), *Ghost* (1990), and *The Prince of Tides* (1991; reviewed in this volume).

Reggie Nalder (1911-November 19, 1991). Born in Australia, Nalder was a character actor who specialized in playing mysterious characters. His film credits include *Adventures of Captain Fabian* (1951), *Betrayed* (1954), *The Man Who Knew Too Much* (1956), *The Manchurian Candidate* (1962), *Fellini's Casanova* (1976), and *Salem's Lot* (1979).

Alex North (December 4, 1910-September 8, 1991). North was a prolific and much-honored composer who contributed scores to many successful films. In 1985, he was given an honorary Academy Award "in recognition of his brilliant artistry in the creation of memorable music for a host of distinguished motion pictures." Among the fifteen films for which his scores were nominated for Academy Awards were *Viva Zapata!* (1952), *Unchained* (1955, for the music to the song "Unchained Melody"), *Spartacus* (1960), *Cleopatra* (1963), *The Agony and the Ecstasy* (1965), *Who's Afraid of Virginia Woolf?* (1966), *The Shoes of the Fisherman* (1968), and *Under the Volcano* (1984).

Joe Pasternak (September 19, 1901-September 13, 1991). Born in Hungary, Pasternak was a producer who was credited with saving Universal Studios in the 1930's. He immigrated to the United States as a teenager and broke into film with Paramount Pictures by 1923. In 1926, he was appointed manager of Universal's Berlin operations, where he began making the popular musicals for which he became known. In 1935, he returned to the United States, bringing with him director Henry Koster; he and Koster made a series of successful films with Deanna Durban, beginning with *One Hundred Men and a Girl* (1937). He helped revive Marlene Dietrich's career with the Western comedy *Destry Rides Again* (1939). Pasternak moved to MGM in 1941, where he remained until his retirement in 1968. Throughout his career, he specialized in light, entertaining films, many of which had a significant musical component. He worked with singing actors as diverse as Judy Garland, with whom he made *Presenting Lily Mars* (1943) and *Summer Stock* (1950); Mario Lanza, with whom he made *The Toast of New Orleans* (1950) and *The Great Caruso* (1951); and Elvis Presley, with whom he made two of his last films, *Girl Happy* (1965) and *Spinout* (1966). His additional film credits include *Three Smart Girls* (1936), *It Started with Eve* (1941), *Thousands Cheer* (1943), *Song of Russia* (1944), *A Date with Judy* (1948), *The Merry Widow* (1952), *Please Don't Eat the Daisies* (1960), *Where the Boys Are* (1960), and *The Courtship of Eddie's Father* (1963).

Ben Piazza (1933-September 7, 1991). Piazza was an actor who appeared regularly in film and television from his screen debut in *A Dangerous Age* (1957) through *Guilty by Suspicion* (1991). His additional film credits include *The Hanging Tree* (1959), *The Bad News Bears* (1976), *Apocalypse Now* (1979), *Mask* (1985), and *Rocky V* (1990).

Eddie Quillan (March 31, 1907-July 19, 1991). Quillan was an actor who played leading as well as supporting roles in a career that began in vaudeville and silent films. He appeared in Mack Sennett shorts before making his first feature, *Show Folks* (1928). His additional film credits include *The Godless Girl* (1929), *Girl Crazy* (1932), *Mutiny on the Bounty* (1935), *Young Mr. Lincoln* (1939), *The Grapes of Wrath* (1940), *Song of the Sarong* (1945), *Brigadoon* (1954), *Promises! Promises!* (1963), and *The Ghost and Mr. Chicken* (1966).

Aldo Ray (September 25, 1926-March 27, 1991). Born Aldo DaRe, Ray was an actor; as a former football player and Navy frogman, his athletic frame and raspy voice made him a natural for the action films in which he specialized in the 1950's. He is best remembered for his military roles in such films as *Battle Cry* (1955), *Men in War* (1957), and *The Naked and the Dead* (1958). His career began to decline in the 1960's, although he continued to appear in such films as *Riot on Sunset Strip* (1967) and *The Green Berets* (1968). By the end of his career, he was reduced to playing in low-budget horror films such as *Terror on Alcatraz* (1986) and *Shock 'Em Dead* (1990). His additional film credits include *Saturday's Hero* (1951), *The Marrying Kind* (1952), *Miss Sadie Thompson* (1953), *We're No Angels* (1955), *What Did You Do in the War, Daddy?* (1966), *The Bad Bunch* (1976), and *The Sicilian* (1987).

Lee Remick (December 14, 1933-July 2, 1991). Remick was an actress known for bringing quality to a wide variety of roles. She began acting as a child and performed on Broadway as a teenager. Her first film role was one of the leads in *A Face in the Crowd* (1957), which she followed with a sultry performance in *The Long Hot Summer* (1958). At this point in her career, she was being touted as an American Brigitte Bardot, but she quickly proved to be more than simply a sex symbol. She gave a powerful performance in *Anatomy of a Murder* (1959) and was nominated for an Academy Award for her protrayal of an alcoholic wife opposite Jack Lemmon in *Days of Wine and Roses* (1962). While making *Hard Contract* (1969), she met and later married British filmmaker William Gowans, which led to her living in England until 1982. During that time, she worked primarily on British films, returning to Hollywood occasionally for such films as *Sometimes a Great Notion* (1971) and *A Delicate Balance* (1973). In the latter stages of her career, she worked primarily in television and on stage. Her additional film credits include *Sanctuary* (1961), *Baby, the Rain Must Fall* (1965), *No Way to Treat a Lady* (1968), *The Detective* (1968), *The Omen* (1976), *Telefon* (1977), and *The Europeans* (1979).

Tony Richardson (June 5, 1928-November 14, 1991). Richardson was a British director best known for his cinematic adaptation of *Tom Jones* (1963), which won four Academy Awards, including Best Picture as well as the award for Best Director for Richardson. He first gained notice in the 1950's as one of England's "Angry Young Men"—writers and other artists who rebelled against the placid postwar ethos. After directing the stage play, he filmed John Osborne's *Look Back in Anger* (1959) with Richard Burton. Similar efforts followed, all in stark black and white: *The Entertainer* (1960), *A Taste of Honey* (1961), and *The Loneliness of the Long Distance Runner* (1962). Thus the colorful, lusty *Tom Jones* (based on a novel by Henry Fielding) was quite a change of pace for Richardson, and it was a commercial as well as a critical success. His first American film, *Sanctuary* (1961), was a disappointment, but he returned to Hollywood for the satiric classic *The Loved One* (1965), which found an audience and has become a cult favorite. He worked in a variety of styles thereafter, though his output slowed and none of his later work added significantly to his reputation. Perhaps the best of these films were *The Charge of the Light Brigade* (1968), *A Delicate Balance* (1973), and another film based on a Henry Fielding novel, *Joseph Andrews* (1977). He was married for a time to actress Vanessa Redgrave, and their daughter, Natasha Richardson, is also an actress. Richardson's additional film credits include *Hamlet* (1969), *Ned Kelly* (1970), *Dead Cert* (1973), *The Border* (1982), and *The Hotel New Hampshire* (1984).

Laura Kerr Rivkin (1902-May 5, 1991). Born Laura Hornickel, Rivkin was a screenwriter who often collaborated with her husband, Allen Rivkin. Together, they wrote *The Farmer's Daughter* (1947), *My Dream Is Yours* (1949), *Grounds for Marriage* (1950), and *Battle Circus* (1953).

Gene Roddenberry (August 19, 1921-October 24, 1991). Roddenberry was a television writer and producer who created the popular *Star Trek* series. A modest success at best as a network series, the show has made more than a billion dollars in syndication, by Roddenberry's estimate. In the aftermath of the science-fiction boom of the late 1970's, Roddenberry brought his cast to the big screen with *Star Trek: The Motion Picture* (1979), which he produced and which Robert Wise directed. Roddenberry had no direct involvement with the film's sequels, although he did consult on the scripts.

Jean Rogers (March 25, 1916-February 24, 1991). Born Eleanor Lovegren, Rogers was an actress who had leading roles in many B-pictures and serials during the 1930's and 1940's. She is best remembered for her role as Dale Arden, the heroine of the Flash Gordon serials in which she starred opposite Buster Crabbe. Her film credits include *Flash Gordon* (1936), *Ace Drummond* (1936), *Mysterious Crossing* (1936), *Flash Gordon's Trip to Mars* (1938), *Charlie Chan in Panama* (1940), *Dr. Kildare's Victory* (1942), *Gay Blades* (1946), and *The Second Woman* (1951).

Natalie Schafer (1912-April 10, 1991). Schafer was a character actress who is best remembered for her role as Lovey Howell, the wealthy wife of Jim Backus' character, Thurston Howell, on the television series *Gilligan's Island*. Her screen credits include *Marriage Is a Private Affair* (1944), *Dishonored Lady* (1947), *The Snake Pit* (1948), *The Girl Next Door* (1953), *Anastasia* (1956), *Bernadine* (1957), *Susan Slade* (1961), and *The Day of the Locust* (1975).

Roy Seawright (1905-April 30, 1991). Seawright was a pioneering special effects expert who began his screen career in 1925 in Hal Roach comedies. After working on Our Gang and Laurel and Hardy films, he developed the "ectoplasm" techniques that were used extensively to permit the ghosts in the Topper films to appear and disappear. He was nominated for Academy Awards for his work on *Topper Takes a Trip* (1939), *One Million B.C.* (1940), and *Topper Returns* (1941).

Eileen Sedgwick (1895-March 15, 1991). Sedgwick was an actress who starred in serials and action films of the silent era. In 1928, she used the name Greta Yoltz in a handful of films; the next year, she married and then retired from films. Her screen credits include *Eagle's Nest* (1915), *Lure of the Circus* (1918), *The Great Radium Mystery* (1919), *Terror Trail* (1921), *Wolf Pack* (1922), *Girl of the West* (1925), *The Vanishing West* (1928), *A Girl in Every Port* (1928), and *Beautiful but Dumb* (1928).

George Sherman (July 14, 1908-March 15, 1991). Sherman was a prolific director of B-films in the 1930's and 1940's. Working at Republic Pictures, he made eight films with John Wayne, including *Pals of the Saddle* (1938) and *Three Texas Steers* (1939). He also worked with Gene Autry in *Rhythm of the Saddle* (1938), *Mexicali Rose* (1939), and *South of the Border* (1939). He moved to Columbia in 1944 and then to Universal in 1948, where he was able to work on films with somewhat larger budgets. He maintained his association with Wayne, producing the star's *The Comancheros* (1961); Sherman's last directorial effort was Wayne's *Big Jake* (1971). Sherman also worked extensively in television. His additional screen credits include *The Purple Vigilantes* (1938), *Jesse James Jr.* (1942), *Feudin' Fussin' and a-Fightin'* (1948), *The Golden Horde* (1951), *Comanche* (1956), *Hell Bent for Leather* (1960), and *Smoky* (1966).

Don Siegel (October 26, 1912-April 20, 1991). Siegel was a director known for his taut suspense and action films. After failing as an actor, he joined Warner Bros. as a technician in 1933, where he wound up directing short subjects. Two of these films, *Star in the Night* (1945) and *Hitler Lives?* (1945), won Academy Awards (for two-reel and documentary short subjects, respectively). His first feature film was *The Verdict* (1946). His work on low-budget films such as *Riot in Cell Block 11* (1954), *Invasion of the Body Snatchers* (1956), and *Baby Face Nelson* (1957) won audiences in the United States and also earned for him praise from French critics-turned-filmmakers Jean-Luc Godard and François Truffaut. He extracted from Elvis Presley the singer/actor's best dramatic performance in the Western *Flaming Star* (1960); perhaps because there was no singing in the film, it was a box-office disappointment. In the late 1960's, Siegel was given bigger budgets for films such as *Madigan* (1968) and *Coogan's Bluff* (1968). The latter film was the first of several Siegel films to star Clint Eastwood; it was also one of Eastwood's first American films after his ascent to stardom in Sergio Leone's "spaghetti Westerns." The most popular (and most controversial) of these Siegel-Eastwood collaborations was *Dirty Harry* (1971), in which Eastwood portrayed a violent and utterly ruthless police officer. Siegel was not involved in any of the film's sequels, although he and Eastwood teamed up for several more films, most notably *Escape from Alcatraz* (1979). His last major successes were John Wayne's last film, *The Shootist* (1976), and the thriller *Telefon* (1977). Siegel appeared in cameo roles in Eastwood's self-directed *Play Misty for Me* (1971) and his own *Charley Varrick* (1973). He was married for a time to actress Viveca Lindfors; their son, Kristoffer Tabori, is an actor. His additional film credits include *The Big Steal* (1949), *Private Hell 36* (1954), *The Lineup* (1958),

Hound Dog Man (1959), *Two Mules for Sister Sara* (1970), *The Beguiled* (1971), *Rough Cut* (1980), and *Jinxed!* (1982).

Milton Subotsky (1920-June 27, 1991). Subotsky was a producer who began his career in feature films by capitalizing on the teenage fascination with rock and roll. He wrote and produced *Rock, Pretty Baby* (1956), including nine of the film's songs; *Jamboree* (1957); and Richard Lester's directorial debut *It's Trad, Dad!* (1962), also known as *Ring-a-Ding Rhythm*. Each of these films featured a skimpy plot and a large amount of singing by the pop stars of the day. Later in his career, Subotsky produced a lucrative series of horror and science-fiction films, of which the biggest hit was *Tales from the Crypt* (1972). His additional screen credits include *Dr. Who and the Daleks* (1965), *Scream and Scream Again* (1970), *I, Monster* (1972), and *The Land That Time Forgot* (1975).

Margaret Tallichet (1913-May 3, 1991). Tallichet was an actress who appeared in supporting roles in a number of films in the 1930's and early 1940's. She married director William Wyler in 1938, and thereafter her acting career diminished in scope. Her film credits include *The Prisoner of Zenda* (1937), *A Star Is Born* (1937), *The Stranger on the Third Floor* (1940), and *It Started with Eve* (1941).

Danny Thomas (January 6, 1914-February 6, 1991). Born Amos Muzyad Jacobs, Thomas was an actor and television producer. His television series *Make Room for Daddy* enjoyed immense popular success in the 1950's. He is the father of actress Marlo Thomas. Though best remembered for his work in television, Thomas did act in films, including *The Unfinished Dance* (1947), *Big City* (1948), *I'll See You in My Dreams* (1951), and *The Jazz Singer* (1953).

Richard Thorpe (February 24, 1896-May 1, 1991). Thorpe was a director who worked in a variety of genres for more than four decades, principally for MGM. He broke into film as an actor in *Burn 'Em up Barnes* (1921). By 1923, he was directing; over the next seven years, he made nearly one hundred films, including *Three O'Clock in the Morning* (1924, in which he also starred), *Speedy Spurs* (1926), and *King of the Kongo* (1929). In 1935, he signed with MGM, where he remained until his retirement in 1967. His versatility and even temperament made him an ideal director in an era in which the studio system reigned supreme, although these same attributes probably prevented him from developing a personal style that would have made him stand out among his peers. Among his more than seventy sound-era films are *Tarzan Escapes* (1936), *The Adventures of Huckleberry Finn* (1939), *Cry Havoc* (1943), *Two Girls and a Sailor* (1944), *What Next, Corporal Hargrove?* (1945), *A Date with Judy* (1948), *Three Little Words* (1950), *The Great Caruso* (1951), *Ivanhoe* (1952), *Jailhouse Rock* (1957), *Fun in Acapulco* (1963), and *The Last Challenge* (1967).

Gene Tierney (November 20, 1920-November 6, 1991). Tierney was an actress who was a major star for Twentieth Century-Fox in the 1940's. She had important roles in *Tobacco Road* (1941) and *Belle Star* (1941), as well as the title role in the classic mystery *Laura* (1944). She was nominated for an Academy Award for her portrayal of a pathologically possessive woman in *Leave Her to Heaven* (1945); ironically, her own personal life was in the process of unraveling as well. She was subject to bouts of manic depression, which were exacerbated when her daughter was born severely handicapped. She continued to perform capably in films, including *Dragonwyck* (1946) and *The Ghost and Mrs. Muir* (1947). By the early 1950's, however, her personal life was again causing her anguish; in the aftermath of her divorce from husband Oleg Cassini and failed romances with then-Navy officer John F. Kennedy and Aly Khan, she suffered a nervous breakdown and was institutionalized for nearly two years. Although she occasionally made films thereafter, her career never really recovered. Her final screen appearance was in *The Pleasure Seekers* (1964). Tierney's additional film credits include *The Return of Jesse James*

(1940), *Heaven Can Wait* (1943), *A Bell for Adano* (1945), *The Razor's Edge* (1946), *Night and the City* (1950), *Plymouth Adventure* (1952), *The Egyptian* (1954), *Advise and Consent* (1962), and *Toys in the Attic* (1963).

Regis Toomey (August 13, 1902-October 12, 1991). Toomey was a character actor whose career spanned nearly fifty years and two hundred films. He also worked extensively in television. His film credits include *Alibi* (1929), *State Trooper* (1933), *Union Pacific* (1939), *His Girl Friday* (1940), *Northwest Passage* (1940), *Spellbound* (1945), *The Big Sleep* (1947), *The Boy with Green Hair* (1948), *The High and the Mighty* (1954), *Guys and Dolls* (1955), *Voyage to the Bottom of the Sea* (1961), and *Change of Habit* (1969).

Tom Tryon (January 14, 1926-September 4, 1991). Tryon was an actor who abandoned films to become a best-selling novelist. As an actor, he is best known for his lead role in Otto Preminger's *The Cardinal* (1963). After filming *Color Me Dead* (1969), he decided to try his hand at fiction. He was an immediate success, writing both gothic horror and historical fiction. His additional acting credits include *The Scarlet Hour* (1956), *The Story of Ruth* (1960), *The Longest Day* (1962), *In Harm's Way* (1965), and *The Glory Guys* (1965).

Thorley Walters (1913-July 6, 1991). Walters was a British actor who specialized in comedy. He began making films in the mid-1930's with *Love Test* (1934), but his greatest success came in the 1950's, in such classic British comedies as *Who Done It?* (1956), *Blue Murder at St. Trinian's* (1958), and *Man in a Cocked Hat* (1959). In the 1960's, he began appearing in such horror films as *The Phantom of the Opera* (1962) and *Dracula—Prince of Darkness* (1966). His additional film credits include *Private's Progress* (1956), *The Truth About Women* (1958), *Rotten to the Core* (1965), *The Wrong Box* (1966), *There's a Girl in My Soup* (1970), *The Adventure of Sherlock Holmes' Smarter Brother* (1975), and *The Little Drummer Girl* (1984).

Marjorie Warfield (1902-April 15, 1991). Born Marjorie Warfield Chase, Warfield was an actress during the silent era. She made one sound film, *Some Night* (1929), before retiring from the screen to concentrate on stage and radio work. Her film credits include *The Girl from God's Country* (1921), *Grub Stake* (1923), *The Courtship of Miles Standish* (1923), *Bag and Baggage* (1924), and *Laddie* (1929).

Sunday Wilshin (1904-March 19, 1991). Wilshin was a British stage and film actress known for her beauty. She appeared in Alfred Hitchcock's *Champagne* (1928), one of his last silent films. Her additional film credits include *Pages of Life* (1922), *The Chance of a Night-Time* (1931), *Michael and Mary* (1931), *The Love Contract* (1932), and *Marry Me* (1932).

Richard Wilson (December 25, 1915-August 21, 1991). Wilson was an actor, screenwriter, director, and producer who is best known for his association with Orson Welles. He was a member of Welles's Mercury Theater and was the director's executive assistant on *Citizen Kane* (1941, in which he also acted), *The Magnificent Ambersons* (1942), and *Journey into Fear* (1943). He was Welles's associate producer on *The Lady from Shanghai* (1948, in which he also performed) and *Macbeth* (1948). As a director, he was known for making realistic gangster films and Westerns, such as *Al Capone* (1959) and *Invitation to a Gunfighter* (1964). His additional film credits include *Man with the Gun* (1955, which he also cowrote), *The Big Boodle* (1957), *Raw Wind in Eden* (1958, which he also cowrote), *Pay or Die* (1960, which he also produced), *Wall of Noise* (1963), and *Three in the Attic* (1968, which he also produced).

Dick Winslow (1915-February 7, 1991). Winslow was an actor who appeared in character roles in numerous films and television programs. His film credits include *Tom Sawyer* (1930), *Mutiny on the Bounty* (1935), *The Benny Goodman Story* (1955), *Airport* (1970), and *The Shootist* (1976).

Luigi Zampa (January 2, 1905-August 15, 1991). Zampa was an Italian director who was an important part of the neorealism movement in the aftermath of World War II. His early films, including *Vivere in pace* (1946; *To Live in Peace*, 1946), *L' onorevole Angelina* (1947; *Angelina*, 1947), *Anni difficili* (1948; *Difficult Years*, 1948), *Processo alla città* (1952; *City on Trial*, 1952), and *Anni facili* (1953; *Easy Years*, 1953), were trenchant analyses of postwar Italian society. Zampa's reputation declined after the mid-1950's, as his artistic vision seemed to stagnate. His additional film credits include *Fra Diavolo* (1941), *Campane a martello* (1949; *Children of Change*, 1949), *La romana* (1954; *Woman of Rome*, 1954), *Il vigile* (1960), and *Bello onesto emigrato australia sposerebbe compaesana illibata* (1971; *A Girl in Australia*, 1971).

LIST OF AWARDS

Academy Awards
Best Picture: The Silence of the Lambs
Direction: Jonathan Demme (*The Silence of the Lambs*)
Actor: Anthony Hopkins (*The Silence of the Lambs*)
Actress: Jodie Foster (*The Silence of the Lambs*)
Supporting Actor: Jack Palance (*City Slickers*)
Supporting Actress: Mercedes Ruehl (*The Fisher King*)
Original Screenplay: Callie Khouri (*Thelma and Louise*)
Adapted Screenplay: Ted Tally (*The Silence of the Lambs*)
Cinematography: Robert Richardson (*JFK*)
Editing: Joe Hutshing and Pietro Scalia (*JFK*)
Art Direction: Dennis Gassner and Nancy Haigh (*Bugsy*)
Visual Effects: Dennis Muren, Stan Winston, Gene Warren, Jr., and Robert Skotak
    (*Terminator II*)
Sound Effects Editing: Gary Rydstrom and Gloria S. Borders (*Terminator II*)
Sound: Tom Johnson, Gary Rydstrom, Gary Summers, and Lee Orloff
    (*Terminator II*)
Makeup: Stan Winston and Jeff Dawn (*Terminator II*)
Costume Design: Albert Wolsky (*Bugsy*)
Original Score: Alan Menken (*Beauty and the Beast*)
Original Song: "Beauty and the Beast" (*Beauty and the Beast*: music, Alan
    Menken; lyrics, Howard Ashman)
Foreign-Language Film: Mediterraneo (Italy)
Short Film, Animated: Manipulation (Daniel Greaves)
Short Film, Live Action: Session Man (Seth Winston and Rob Fried)
Documentary, Feature: In the Shadow of the Stars (Allie Light and Irving Saraf)
Documentary, Short Subject: Deadly Deception (Debra Chasnoff)
Honorary Oscar: Satyajit Ray
Gordon E. Sawyer Award: Ray Harryhausen
Irving G. Thalberg Memorial Award: George Lucas

Directors Guild of America Award
Director: Jonathan Demme (*The Silence of the Lambs*)

Writers Guild Awards
Original Screenplay: Callie Khouri (*Thelma and Louise*)
Adapted Screenplay: Ted Tally (*The Silence of the Lambs*)

New York Film Critics Awards
Best Picture: The Silence of the Lambs
Direction: Jonathan Demme (*The Silence of the Lambs*)

Actor: Anthony Hopkins (*The Silence of the Lambs*)
Actress: Jodie Foster (*The Silence of the Lambs*)
Supporting Actor: Samuel L. Jackson (*Jungle Fever*)
Supporting Actress: Judy Davis (*Barton Fink* and *Naked Lunch*)
Screenplay: David Cronenberg (*Naked Lunch*)
Cinematography: Roger Deakins (*Barton Fink*)
Foreign-Language Film: Europa, Europa (France and Germany)
New Director: John Singleton (*Boyz 'n the Hood*)

Los Angeles Film Critics Awards
Best Picture: Bugsy
Best Animated Film: Beauty and the Beast
Direction: Barry Levinson (*Bugsy*)
Actor: Nick Nolte (*The Prince of Tides*)
Actress: Mercedes Ruehl (*The Fisher King*)
Supporting Actor: Michael Lerner (*Barton Fink*)
Supporting Actress: Jane Horrocks (*Life Is Sweet*)
Screenplay: James Toback (*Bugsy*)
Cinematography: Roger Deakins (*Barton Fink* and *Homicide*)
Original Score: Zbigniew Preisner (*At Play in the Fields of the Lord*; *The Double Life of Véronique*; and *Europa, Europa*)
Foreign-Language Film: La Belle Noiseuse (France)

National Society of Film Critics Awards
Best Picture: Life Is Sweet
Direction: David Cronenberg (*Naked Lunch*)
Actor: River Phoenix (*My Own Private Idaho*)
Actress: Alison Steadman (*Life Is Sweet*)
Supporting Actor: Harvey Keitel (*Bugsy, Mortal Thoughts*, and *Thelma and Louise*)
Supporting Actress: Jane Horrocks (*Life Is Sweet*)
Screenplay: David Cronenberg (*Naked Lunch*)
Cinematography: Roger Deakins (*Barton Fink*)
Documentary: Paris Is Burning (Jennie Livingston and Barry Swimar)
Foreign-Language Film: The Double Life of Véronique (France and Poland)

National Board of Review Awards
Best English-Language Film: The Silence of the Lambs
Direction: Jonathan Demme (*The Silence of the Lambs*)
Actor: Warren Beatty (*Bugsy*)
Actress: Susan Sarandon (*Thelma and Louise*) and Geena Davis (*Thelma and Louise*), tie
Supporting Actor: Anthony Hopkins (*The Silence of the Lambs*)
Supporting Actress: Kate Nelligan (*Frankie and Johnny*)

Foreign-Language Film: Europa, Europa (France and Germany)
Documentary: Hearts of Darkness (Fax Bahr and George Hickenlooper)
The D. W. Griffith Career Achievement Award: Robert Mitchum
Special Award for Animation: Beauty and the Beast

Golden Globe Awards
Best Picture, Drama: Bugsy
Best Picture, Comedy or Musical: Beauty and the Beast
Direction: Oliver Stone (*JFK*)
Actor, Drama: Nick Nolte (*The Prince of Tides*)
Actress, Drama: Jodie Foster (*The Silence of the Lambs*)
Actor, Comedy or Musical: Robin Williams (*The Fisher King*)
Actress, Comedy or Musical: Bette Midler (*For the Boys*)
Supporting Actor: Jack Palance (*City Slickers*)
Supporting Actress: Mercedes Ruehl (*The Fisher King*)
Screenplay: Callie Khouri (*Thelma and Louise*)
Original Score: Alan Menken (*Beauty and the Beast*)
Original Song: "Beauty and the Beast" (*Beauty and the Beast*: music, Alan
   Menken; lyrics, Howard Ashman)
Foreign-Language Film: Europa, Europa (France and Germany)
Cecil B. De Mille Award: Robert Mitchum

Golden Palm Awards (Forty-fourth Cannes International Film Festival)
Golden Palm: Barton Fink (Joel Coen and Ethan Coen)
Grand Prix: La Belle Noiseuse (Jacques Rivette)
Actor: John Turturro (*Barton Fink*)
Actress: Irène Jacob (*The Double Life of Véronique*)
Supporting Performance: Samuel L. Jackson (*Jungle Fever*)
Direction: Joel Coen (*Barton Fink*)
Jury Prize: Europa, Europa (Lars von Trier) and *Outside of Life* (Maroun
   Bagdadi), tie
Grand Technical Prize: Lars von Trier (*Europa, Europa*)
Camera d'Or: Jaco van Dormael (*Toto the Hero*)

British Academy Awards
Best Picture: The Commitments
Direction: Alan Parker (*The Commitments*)
Actor: Anthony Hopkins (*The Silence of the Lambs*)
Actress: Jodie Foster (*The Silence of the Lambs*)
Supporting Actor: Alan Rickman (*Robin Hood*)
Supporting Actress: Kate Nelligan (*Frankie and Johnny*)
Original Screenplay: Anthony Minghella (*Truly, Madly, Deeply*)

Adapted Screenplay: Dick Clement, Ian La Frenais, and Roddy Doyle (*The Commitments*)
Original Score: Jean-Claude Petit (*Cyrano de Bergerac*)
Best Foreign-Language Film: The Nasty Girl (Germany)
Flaherty Documentary Award: Thirty-Five Up (Michael Apted)

MAGILL'S
CINEMA
ANNUAL

TITLE INDEX

DIRECTOR INDEX

DIRECTOR INDEX

489

SCREENWRITER INDEX

SCREENWRITER INDEX

494

SCREENWRITER INDEX

CINEMATOGRAPHER INDEX

EDITOR INDEX

ALLEN, DEDE
  Addams Family, The   19
AMICUCCI, GIANFRANCO
  Sleazy Uncle, The [1989]   454
ANDERSON, WILLIAM
  At Play in the Fields of the
  Lord   27
ARAKI, GREGG
  Long Weekend (O' Despair),
  The   441
ATHENS, J. D.
  Pizza Man   448

BAIRD, STUART
  Last Boy Scout, The   439
BARCLAY, CLEMENT
  Bright Angel   424
BARD, DEBRA
  Blue Desert   423
BASSETT, CRAIG
  Ernest Scared Stupid   431
BAUMGARTEN, ALAN E.
  Kickboxer II   438
BEAUMAN, NICHOLAS
  Prisoners of the Sun   450
BELDIN, DALE
  Oscar   446
BERGER, PETER E.
  All I Want for Christmas   419
  Dead Again   97
BERNARDI, ADAM
  Beastmaster II   421
  Dutch   430
BEYDA, KENT
  True Identity   458
BHATT, SUESH
  Henna   435
BIGGERSTAFF, CAROLINE
  Eve of Destruction   431
BLEVINS, DANIEL W.
  Rolling Stones at the Max   451
BLUNDEN, CHRIS
  Neverending Story II, The
  [1990]   444
BOCK, LARRY
  Don't Tell Mom the Babysitter's
  Dead   429
BODBIJL, MARINA
  Prospero's Books   299
BOEGLIN, ARIANE
  Daddy Nostalgia [1990]   93
BOWERS, GEORGE
  Sleeping with the Enemy   360
BOYLE, PETER
  Robin Hood   332
BRADSELL, MICHAEL
  Kiss Before Dying, A   438
BRANDON, MARYANN
  Bingo   422
BRENNER, DAVID
  Doors, The   115

BRICMONT, WENDY GREENE
  My Girl   239
BROWN, BARRY ALEXANDER
  Truth or Dare   403
BROWN, O. NICHOLAS
  City Slickers   77
BROWN, ROBERT
  Dying Young   124
BUBA, PASQUALE
  Two Evil Eyes   459
BUFF, CONRAD
  Terminator II   395
BURTON, BERNARD
  Obituaries   464

CAMBAS, JACQUELINE
  Frankie and Johnny   150
CAMBERN, DONN
  Butcher's Wife, The   64
CAMPBELL, MALCOLM
  Nothing but Trouble   445
CANDIB, RICHARD
  Rich Girl   451
CANNON, BRUCE
  Boyz 'n the Hood   55
CARMODY, JACQUELINE
  Hitman, The   435
CARNOCHAN, JOHN
  Beauty and the Beast   39
CARTER, JOHN
  Five Heartbeats, The   142
CASSIDY, JAY
  Indian Runner, The   437
CHAPMAN, JOAN
  Mannequin Two   442
CHEW, RICHARD
  Late for Dinner   439
CHURGIN, LISA
  Closet Land   426
CLARK, JIM
  Meeting Venus   224
CLAYTON, CURTISS
  My Own Private Idaho   247
  Rage in Harlem, A   307
COATES, ANNE V.
  What About Bob?   411
COBLENTZ, JAMES
  People Under the Stairs,
  The   447
COHEN, STEVEN
  Rambling Rose   311
COLE, STAN
  Popcorn   449
CONTE, MARK
  Double Impact   430
  Lionheart   440
COULSON, PETER
  Paper Mask   446
CRAFFORD, IAN
  Class Action   81

CRAVEN, GARTH
  Soapdish   364
CURRIN, JOHN K.
  Dice Rules   429

DARMON, MICHELE
  Love Without Pity [1989]   442
D'AUGUSTINE, JOE
  Mobsters   231
  Too Much Sun   457
DAVIS, BATTLE
  Frankie and Johnny   150
DAY, LISA
  White Fang   415
DEDET, YANN
  Overseas   446
DE LA BOUILLERIE, HUBERT
  Highlander II   435
  Other People's Money   283
DE LUZE, HERVÉ
  Uranus   459
DIXON, HUMPHREY
  Mister Johnson   228
  Stepping Out   454
DU YUAN
  Ju Dou [1990]   191
DUNNING, JACK
  Obituaries   466

EHLERS, CORKY
  Harley Davidson and the Marlboro
  Man   434
ELLIS, MICHAEL
  Impromptu   436
EVANS, KATE
  Antonia and Jane   421

FAGAN, RONALD J.
  Return to the Blue Lagoon   451
FANFARA, STEPHEN
  George's Island   433
FARDOULIS, MONIQUE
  Madame Bovary   216
FARR, GLENN
  Career Opportunities   424
  Shattered   452
FEHR, KAJA
  Twenty-ninth Street   458
FENN, SUZANNE
  No Secrets   445
  Rapture, The   315
FERRETTI, ROBERT A.
  Out for Justice   446
  Showdown in Little Tokyo   453
FINFER, DAVID
  Bill and Ted's Bogus
  Journey   422
  Defending Your Life   101
  Warlock   460
FINKLE, CLAUDIA
  Talkin' Dirty After Dark   456

501

EDITOR INDEX

ART DIRECTOR INDEX

505

BUTLER, RICK
One Good Cop 445

CAIN, ROGER
Shipwrecked 453

CALLAHAN, GENE
Man in the Moon, The 221
Obituaries 464

CAMBERO, CARLOS G.
High Heels 170

CANNON, DAVID
Blue Desert 423

CAO JIU-PING
Ju Dou [1990] 191

CAPILLA, EDUARDO
Lonely in America 441

CARASIK, CHERYL
Grand Canyon 158

CARR, CINDY
Fisher King, The 139
Regarding Henry 319

CARR, JACKIE
Dutch 430

CARRIAGA, REBECCA
Freddy's Dead 432

CARTER, FRED
Robin Hood 332

CARTWRIGHT, CAROLYN
City of Hope 72

CASO, MARIA
Problem Child II 450

CAVERS, CLINTON
King Ralph 438

CHITTY, ALISON
Life Is Sweet 208

CHRISTOPHER, LYNN
Ted and Venus 456

CLAY, JIM
Kiss Before Dying, A 438

CLINE, FRED
Rover Dangerfield 451

COCHRANE, SANDY
White Fang 415

COHEN, LESTER W.
Dogfight 429

COLE, CAROLE
Child's Play III 425
Terminator II 395

COLLIS, JACK T.
Flight of the Intruder 432

COMTOIS, GUY J.
Dying Young 124
If Looks Could Kill 436

CONLEY, EDWARD L., III
American Summer, An 420

CONWAY, JEREMY
Super, The 380

COOPER, DORREE
Shattered 452

CORBETT, ANNMARIE
Bingo 422

CORBETT, TOBY
Iron Maze 437

CORENBLITH, MICHAEL
He Said, She Said 166

CREBER, WILLIAM J.
Mannequin Two 442

CRISANTI, ANDREA
Everybody's Fine [1990] 431

CRISTANTE, IVO
Suburban Commando 455

CROWE, DESMOND
Not Without My Daughter 263

CRUGNOLA, AURELIO
Year of the Gun 461

CRUMP, BUZ
Firehead 432

CUMMINGS, HOWARD
Mortal Thoughts 443

CUMMINS, ERIN
Father of the Bride 132

CZERWATUIK, ANNE
Hangin' with the Homeboys 434

DALE, MARCIE
Queens Logic 303

D'AMBROSIO, LORENZO
Open Doors [1989] 279

D'AMICO, ARCHIE
Perfect Weapon, The 448

DANYLENKO, OLEKSANDR
Swan Lake [1990] 455

DAOUDAL, GERARD
Impromptu 436

DAVIS, DAN
Once Around 271
Regarding Henry 319

DEAN, LISA
Thelma and Louise 399

DE CHAUVIGNY, MANU
Belle Noiseuse, La [1990] 43

DECUIR, JOHN, JR.
True Identity 458

DEGOVIA, JACK
Hudson Hawk 436

DELIEU, PAUL
Shipwrecked 453

DENSMORE, BRIAN
Lionheart 440

DEREN, NANCY
Boy Who Cried Bitch, The 423

DE ROUIN, COLIN
Dead Space 428

DESCENNA, LINDA
Defending Your Life 101
Rocketeer, The 336

DETITTA, GEORGE, SR.
Billy Bathgate 47

DEVILLE, ROLAND
Overseas 446

DIAS, LARRY
Talkin' Dirty After Dark 456

DIERS, DON
Five Heartbeats, The 142

DILLEY, LESLIE
Guilty by Suspicion 163
What About Bob? 411

DIPONT, MAGDALENA
Korczak 439

DOANE, CHARLIE
Rich Girl 451

DOBROWOLSKI, MAREK
Ambition 419

DODD, DEREK
Object of Beauty, The 267

DODGE, NORMAN B., JR.
Mannequin Two 442

DOLAN, KATHLEEN
Frankie and Johnny 150

DOWDING, JON
Return to the Blue Lagoon 451

DUFFIELD, TOM
Grand Canyon 158

DUFFIN, PHILIP J. C.
Bride of Re-Animator 424

DUFFY, JIM
Marrying Man, The 442
Shout 453

DUGIED, JACQUES
My Father's Glory [1990] 235
My Mother's Castle [1990] 243

DULTZ, JIM
Soapdish 364

DURRELL, WILLIAM J., JR.
Doctor, The 111

DWYER, JOHN M.
All I Want for Christmas 419
Terminator II 395

EBDEN, JOHN
Pope Must Die, The 449

EDWARDS, VAUGHAN
Rosencrantz and Guildenstern Are
Dead 340

EGEDE-NISSEN, HARALD
Shipwrecked 453

ELLIOTT, WILLIAM
Hot Shots! 182
Regarding Henry 319

ELTON, PHILIP
Kafka 200

FABIAN, JULIE
Trust 458

FAGO, AMEDEO
Open Doors [1989] 279

FANNING, TONY
Wild Hearts Can't Be
Broken 460

FERNANDEZ, RICHARD
Delirious 104

FERRETTI, DANTE
Sleazy Uncle, The [1989] 454

FETTIS, GARY
Doctor, The 111

FICHTER, THOMAS
Wild Hearts Can't Be
Broken 460

ART DIRECTOR INDEX

ORBOM, ERIC
Last Boy Scout, The 439
Ricochet 327
OUELLETTE, DANIEL
Trust 458
OVERBERG, RICK
Prospero's Books 299
OVERTON, DEBRA
Young Soul Rebels 461

PACELLI, JOSEPH G., JR.
Hook 178
PALMERO, RAFAEL
Don Juan, My Love 429
PALTRINIERI, STEFANO
Comfort of Strangers, The [1990] 85
PANG SHIU CHEUNG, ROSA
Double Impact 430
PARKER, LYNN WOLVERTON
Harley Davidson and the Marlboro Man 434
Necessary Roughness 444
PASTOR, DEBBIE
Slacker 453
PAULL, LAWRENCE G.
City Slickers 77
PELTON, DALE ALLEN
Doc Hollywood 107
PERRY, MICHAEL T.
Blue Desert 423
Liebestraum 440
PETERS, KATHRYN
Boyz 'n the Hood 55
PETERS, PAUL
Harley Davidson and the Marlboro Man 434
Necessary Roughness 444
PICKRELL, GREGORY
Bill and Ted's Bogus Journey 422
Lionheart 440
PICKWOAD, MICHAEL
Let Him Have It 440
PINTER, HERBERT
Black Robe 51
Mister Johnson 228
PISONI, EDWARD
Queens Logic 303
True Colors 458
PITKIN, CHERYL
Class of Nuke 'em High Part II 425
PLUMMER, CHAS. B.
City of Hope 72
Poison 290
POLIZZI, LAUREN
Delirious 104
V. I. Warshawski 460
POLL, LEE
Sleeping with the Enemy 360
Soapdish 364
POLL, MARK
Bill and Ted's Bogus Journey 422

POPE, LESLIE ANN
Prince of Tides, The 294
Super, The 380
POPE, NATALIE K.
Prayer of the Rollerboys 449
POVEDA, JEAN-LOUIS
Daddy Nostalgia [1990] 93
PRATT, ANTHONY
Not Without My Daughter 263
PRECHT, ANDREW
Hook 178
PREOVOLOS, NICHOLAS T.
Kickboxer II 438
PRITCHARD, ANNE
Perfectly Normal 448
PROULX, REAL
If Looks Could Kill 436

QUARANTA, GIANNI
Comfort of Strangers, The [1990] 85
QUINTILI, LUIGI
Year of the Gun 461

RAE, BILL
Showdown in Little Tokyo 453
RAGLAND, MARK
Ernest Scared Stupid 431
RALPH, JOHN
Close My Eyes 426
Robin Hood 332
RANDALL, GARY
Dead Space 428
Unborn, The 459
RANDOM, IDA
Defending Your Life 101
REBAR, CLOUDIA
Doc Hollywood 107
REISS, RONALD R.
Out for Justice 446
REMACLE, DONALD J.
Butcher's Wife, The 64
REYNOLDS, RICHARD
Defending Your Life 101
RICHARDS, ETHEL ROBINS
Child's Play III 425
RICHARDSON, ED
Search for Signs of Intelligent Life in the Universe, The 352
RISERBATO, ANGIE
Livin' Large 441
ROBERTS, MICHAEL T.
Ballad of the Sad Cafe, The 421
ROBERTS, RICK
Reflecting Skin, The [1990] 450
RODIS-JAMERO, NILO
Star Trek VI 368
ROELFS, JAN
Prospero's Books 299
ROMERO, HECTOR, JR.
Pure Luck 450
ROMINE, WOODWARD, JR.
Lionheart 440

ROOME, SIOBHAN C.
He Said, She Said 166
ROOT, FRANCESCA
Dice Rules 429
ROSEMARIN, HILTON
Billy Bathgate 47
ROSEN, CHARLES
Butcher's Wife, The 64
ROSENBERG, PHILIP
Other People's Money 283
ROSS, NEIL
American Tail: Fievel Goes West, An 23
ROTH, SONJA
Strictly Business 455
ROTHSCHILD, ANDREW
Paper Mask 446
ROWLAND, CRICKET
Doors, The 115
Dying Young 124
ROWLING, ROWENA
Strictly Business 455
ROYSDEN, TOM
Other People's Money 283
RUDOLF, GENE
Out for Justice 446
RUSCIO, NINA
Cool as Ice 426
RUSSO, JOSAN
Life Stinks 440

SAKASH, EVELYN
Paradise 447
SALLIS, CRISPIAN
JFK 186
SANDELL, WILLIAM
Nothing but Trouble 445
SANDERS, THOMAS E.
Hook 178
SANTINI, BRUNO
Ballad of the Sad Cafe, The 421
SARAFINCHAN, LILLIAN
Termini Station 457
SAWYER, RICHARD
Child's Play III 425
SCAIFE, HUGH
Popcorn 449
Twenty-ninth Street 458
SCARPULLA, CLARE
No Secrets 445
SCHAFFER, SAMARA (SAM)
Curly Sue 427
Five Heartbeats, The 142
Little Man Tate 212
SCHMOOK, RANDALL
Drop Dead Fred 430
SCHNELL, CURTIS
Defenseless 428
Perfect Weapon, The 448
SCHUTT, DEBORAH
Fried Green Tomatoes 154
SCHWARTZ, STEVEN
Curly Sue 427

ART DIRECTOR INDEX

511

MUSIC INDEX

MUSIC INDEX

PERFORMER INDEX

ABBOTT, BRUCE
  Bride of Re-Animator   424
ABEL, CASSI
  My Girl   239
ABRAHAM, F. MURRAY
  Cadence   424
  Mobsters   231
ABRAMOWSKY, KLAUS
  Europa, Europa [1990]   128
ABRIL, VICTORIA
  High Heels   170
ABSOLOM, JOE
  Antonia and Jane   421
ACHORN, JOHN
  Book of Love   423
ACKERMAN, BETTYE
  Ted and Venus   456
ACKLAND, JOSS
  Bill and Ted's Bogus
    Journey   422
  Object of Beauty, The   267
ACOVONE, JAY
  Out for Justice   446
ADAMS, BRANDON
  People Under the Stairs,
    The   447
ADAMS, BROOKE
  Unborn, The   459
ADAMS, KIM
  Ted and Venus   456
ADAMS, MASON
  Toy Soldiers   457
AHERN, TIM
  Hearing Voices   434
AHERNE, MICHAEL
  Commitments, The   89
AIELLO, DANNY
  Hudson Hawk   436
  Once Around   271
  Twenty-ninth Street   458
AIELLO, RICK
  Twenty-ninth Street   458
ALCALAY, MOSCU
  Meeting Venus   224
ALDREDGE, TOM
  Other People's Money   283
  What About Bob?   411
ALEXANDER, JACE
  City of Hope   72
ALEXANDRE, DWAYNE
  American Ninja IV   420
ALLARD, TOM
  V. I. Warshawski   460
ALLAS, PETER
  Iron Maze   437
ALLEN, KAREN
  Sweet Talker   455
ALLEN, KEITH
  Kafka   200
ALLEN, MIKKI
  Regarding Henry   319

ALLEN, SHAUN
  Pink Nights   448
ALLEN, SHEILA
  Antonia and Jane   421
ALLEN, WOODY
  Scenes from a Mall   349
ALLMAN, GREGG
  Rush   345
ALONSO, MARIA CONCHITA
  McBain   442
ALTMAN, BRUCE
  Regarding Henry   319
ALVARADO, TRINI
  American Blue Note   419
ALZADO, LYLE
  Hangfire   433
AMECHE, DON
  Oscar   446
AMENDOLA, CLAUDIO
  Forever Mary   432
ANDERSEN, BIBI
  High Heels   170
ANDERSON, DION
  Dying Young   124
ANDERSON, KEVIN
  Liebestraum   440
  Pink Nights   448
  Sleeping with the Enemy   360
ANDERSON, STANLEY
  He Said, She Said   166
ANDREWS, ANTHONY
  Lost in Siberia   441
ANGLADE, JEAN-HUGUES
  Femme Nikita, La [1990]   135
ANTHONY, LYSETTE
  Switch   383
ANTICO, PETE
  Twenty-ninth Street   458
ANWAR, GABRIELLE
  If Looks Could Kill   436
  Wild Hearts Can't Be
    Broken   460
APPLEGATE, CHRISTINA
  Don't Tell Mom the Babysitter's
    Dead   429
ARANGUIZ, MANUEL
  Paper Wedding, A   447
ARANHA, RAY
  City of Hope   72
ARBONA, GILLES
  Belle Noiseuse, La [1990]   43
ARCHER, ANNE
  Eminent Domain   430
ARESTRUP, NIELS
  Meeting Venus   224
ARGO, VICTOR
  McBain   442
ARKIN, ADAM
  Doctor, The   111

ARKIN, ALAN
  Rocketeer, The   336
ARKINS, ROBERT
  Commitments, The   89
ARMSTRONG, ANDY
  Double Impact   430
ARMSTRONG, KATHERINE
  Ambition   419
ARNOLD, ROSEANNE
  Freddy's Dead   432
ARNOLD, TOM
  Freddy's Dead   432
ARQUETTE, PATRICIA
  Indian Runner, The   437
  Prayer of the Rollerboys   449
ARQUETTE, ROSANNA
  Flight of the Intruder   432
ARRINDELL, LISA
  Livin' Large   441
ARTHUR, JEAN
  Obituaries   462
ASANO, ATSUKO
  Heaven and Earth   435
ASHCROFT, PEGGY
  Obituaries   462
ASNER, ED
  JFK   186
ASSANTE, ARMAND
  Marrying Man, The   442
ASTAR, SHAY
  Ernest Scared Stupid   431
ASTIN, SEAN
  Toy Soldiers   457
ATCHISON, NANCY MOORE
  Wild Hearts Can't Be
    Broken   460
ATHERTON, WILLIAM
  Oscar   446
ATKINE, FEODOR
  High Heels   170
ATKINS, EILEEN
  Let Him Have It   440
ATTAL, YVAN
  Love Without Pity [1989]   442
AUBUCHON, JACQUES
  Obituaries   462
AVERY, JAMES
  Beastmaster II   421
AYKROYD, DAN
  My Girl   239
  Nothing but Trouble   445
AZCUY, ANNETTE
  Bill and Ted's Bogus
    Journey   422

BACALL, LAUREN
  All I Want for Christmas   419
BACALL, MICHAEL
  Shout   453

517

518

PERFORMER INDEX

BERRY, HALLE
Last Boy Scout, The   439
Strictly Business   455
BERRYMAN, DOROTHÉE
Paper Wedding, A   447
BERTRAN, MOISES
Infinity   437
BHAKTIAR, ZEBA
Henna   435
BHAVE, ASHVINI
Henna   435
BIESK, ADAM
Meet the Applegates   442
BIKEL, THEODORE
Shattered   452
BINGO
Bingo   422
BINNS, ANDREW
Angel at My Table, An   420
BIRCH, THORA
All I Want for Christmas   419
Paradise   447
BIRK, RAYE
Doc Hollywood   107
BIRKIN, JANE
Belle Noiseuse, La [1990]   43
Daddy Nostalgia [1990]   93
BISHOP, KELLY
Queens Logic   303
BISSETT, JOSIE
Book of Love   423
BLADES, RUBÉN
Super, The   380
BLAIN, BRIAN
Return to the Blue Lagoon   451
BLAISELL, BRAD
Kiss Me a Killer   439
BLAKE, MEGAN
Infinity   437
BLANC, MICHEL
Prospero's Books   299
Uranus   459
BLANCHARD, GREG
Dead Space   428
BLANCHE, ROLAND
Femme Nikita, La [1990]   135
BLANK, KENNY
Super, The   380
BLASI, SILVERIO
Open Doors [1989]   279
BLESSED, BRIAN
Robin Hood   332
BLOSSOM, ROBERTS
Doc Hollywood   107
BLUM, IRVING
Superstar   455
BLUTEAU, LOTHAIRE
Black Robe   51
BOARDMAN, ELEANOR
Obituaries   463
BOCCELLI, DICK
McBain   442

BOCHNER, LLOYD
Naked Gun 2½, The   252
BOEN, EARL
Terminator II   395
BOGARDE, DIRK
Daddy Nostalgia [1990]   93
BOGOSIAN, ERIC
Sex, Drugs, Rock and Roll   452
BOKMA, PIERRE
Prospero's Books   299
BOND, LILLIAN
Obituaries   463
BOONE, MARK, JR.
Delirious   104
BOOTH, EDWINA
Obituaries   463
BOOTH, JAMES
American Ninja IV   420
BOROWITZ, KATHERINE
Men of Respect   443
BOSCO, PHILIP
F/X II   432
True Colors   458
BOSÉ, MIGUEL
High Heels   170
BOSWELL, CHARLES
Kiss Me a Killer   439
BOSWORTH, BRIAN
Stone Cold   454
BOUCHER, SAVANNAH SMITH
Meet the Applegates   442
BOUDET, JACQUES
Femme Nikita, La [1990]   135
BOUISE, JEAN
Femme Nikita, La [1990]   135
BOUTSIKARIS, DENNIS
Boy Who Cried Bitch, The   423
BOWEN, ROGER
What About Bob?   411
BOWMAN, TERESA
Ambition   419
BOYD, BOB
Slacker   453
BOYD, GUY
Kiss Me a Killer   439
BOYD, SUSAN
Rover Dangerfield   451
BOYLE, LARA FLYNN
Dark Backward, The   427
Mobsters   231
BOYLE, PETER
Kickboxer II   438
Men of Respect   443
BOYLE, SHELLEY PETERSON
Wild Hearts Can't Be
Broken   460
BRACCO, LORRAINE
Switch   383
BRACKEN, EDDIE
Oscar   446
BRADFORD, JESSE
Boy Who Cried Bitch, The   423

BRADFORD, RICHARD
Ambition   419
BRADLEY, ALFRED BRUCE
Chameleon Street   425
BRADLEY, DAVID
American Ninja IV   420
BRANAGH, KENNETH
Dead Again   97
BRANDAUER, KLAUS MARIA
White Fang   415
BRANDIS, JONATHAN
Neverending Story II, The
[1990]   444
BRANDT, WILLIAM
Angel at My Table, An   420
BRATT, BENJAMIN
Bright Angel   424
One Good Cop   445
BRAZELTON, CONNI MARIE
People Under the Stairs,
The   447
BRENNAN, EILEEN
Joey Takes a Cab   437
BRIDGES, JEFF
Fisher King, The   139
BRIDGES, LLOYD
Hot Shots!   182
BRILL, FRAN
What About Bob?   411
BRIMBLE, NICK
Robin Hood   332
BROADBENT, JIM
Life Is Sweet   208
BRODY, ADRIEN
Boy Who Cried Bitch, The   423
BROLIN, JIM
Ted and Venus   456
BROMFIELD, VALRI
Nothing but Trouble   445
BRONSKY, BRICK
Class of Nuke 'em High Part
II   425
BRONSON, CHARLES
Indian Runner, The   437
BROOK, JAYNE
Don't Tell Mom the Babysitter's
Dead   429
BROOKES, JACQUELINE
Naked Gun 2½, The   252
BROOKS, ALBERT
Defending Your Life   101
BROOKS, MEL
Life Stinks   440
BROOKS, RANDY
Defenseless   428
BROSNAN, PIERCE
Mister Johnson   228
BROWDER, BEN
Kiss Before Dying, A   438
BROWN, BRYAN
F/X II   432
Prisoners of the Sun   450
Sweet Talker   455

519

PERFORMER INDEX

PERFORMER INDEX

PERFORMER INDEX

PERFORMER INDEX

531

536

SUBJECT INDEX

The selection of subject headings combines standard Library of Congress Subject Headings and common usage in order to aid the film researcher. Cross references, listed as *See* and *See also*, are provided when appropriate. While all major themes, locales, and time periods have been indexed, some minor subjects covered in a particular film have not been included.

SUBJECT INDEX